Economic Complexity and Evolution

More information about this series at
http://www.springer.com/series/11583

Andreas Pyka • John Foster
Editors

The Evolution of Economic and Innovation Systems

Springer

Editors
Andreas Pyka
Chair for Economics of Innovation
University of Hohenheim
Stuttgart
Germany

John Foster
School of Economics
University of Queensland
Brisbane, Queensland
Australia

Some of the contributions have been published in the Journal of Evolutionary Economics, Volume 24 (2), 2014

ISSN 2199-3173 ISSN 2199-3181 (electronic)
ISBN 978-3-319-13298-3 ISBN 978-3-319-13299-0 (eBook)
DOI 10.1007/978-3-319-13299-0

Library of Congress Control Number: 2015934229

Springer Cham Heidelberg New York Dordrecht London

Printed on acid-free paper

Springer International Publishing AG Switzerland is a part of Springer Science+Business Media (www.springer.com)

Contents

Introduction: The Evolution of Economic and Innovation Systems

John Foster and Andreas Pyka

Abstract The theme of the 14th International Joseph A. Schumpeter Conference 2012 held in Brisbane, was "the evolution of economic systems, through innovation, entrepreneurship and competitive processes." This was intended to be broad enough to encompass a wide range of submitted papers in evolutionary economics and related areas. This book is the outcome of a strong competition among the papers submitted after the conference. The contributions selected show the scope of analysis in evolutionary economics as well as the explanatory power with respect to economic dynamics and long term economic development.

The theme of the 14th International Joseph A. Schumpeter Conference, held from July 2nd to 5th 2012, was "the evolution of economic systems, through innovation, entrepreneurship and competitive processes." This was intended to be broad enough to encompass a wide range of submitted papers in evolutionary economics and related areas. However, perhaps more than in previous conferences, there was a focus upon viewing economic evolution from the perspective of complex systems science, suitably defined for application in economic contexts. This reflected the ongoing interest in complex economic systems that had existed at the University of Queensland for two decades. Some will remember the first 'Brisbane Club' international workshop on this perspective on evolutionary economics at UQ in 1999 and the resultant volume edited by Foster and Metcalfe in 2001. Although having the Schumpeter Conference in Brisbane was viewed by many of us as a fitting conclusion to the Brisbane Club series of meetings, the Club met once again in Vienna in 2013 thanks to excellent efforts of Kurt Dopfer. However, the 2012 Schumpeter Conference was much more than just an extension of this tradition. As with previous conferences, a very diverse range of research questions were

J. Foster (✉)
University of Queensland, Brisbane, QLD, Australia
e-mail: j.foster@uq.edu.au

A. Pyka
University of Hohenheim, Stuttgart, Germany

A. Pyka, J. Foster (eds.), *The Evolution of Economic and Innovation Systems*, Economic Complexity and Evolution, DOI 10.1007/978-3-319-13299-0_1
Modified and extended version from Journal of Evolutionary Economics 24(2), Springer 2014.

addressed and they stimulated robust discussion and debate. The vibrancy and relevance of modern research in evolutionary economics was there for all to see and this was in no small measure due to the high proportion of early career researchers presenting at the Conference.

The five plenary sessions dealt with: Asian emergence—causes and consequences; innovation policy—evolutionary economic perspectives; knowledge, entrepreneurship and the evolution of markets; modelling macroeconomic behaviour when economic systems are recognized as complex; neo-Schumpeterian evolutionary economics—where has it been going and what is its future? We were very privileged to be able to listen to the following invited speakers: Peter Allen, Ping Chen, Terry Cutler, Giovanni Dosi; Alan Hughes, David Lane, Keun Lee, Deirdre McCloskey, Stan Metcalfe, Jason Potts and Ulrich Witt.

There were 61 parallel sessions including: finance and innovation; economic growth; energy and economic evolution; the evolution of the firm; managing innovation; education and innovation; technological paradigms and evolution; Schumpeter revisited; industry linkages; patents; energy innovation—corporate strategy; demand and consumption; evolutionary perspectives on 'knowledge'; productivity growth; energy innovation—policy; innovation networks; spillovers; innovation case studies; advances in evolutionary economic theory; long waves, finance and global crisis; behavioral perspectives on economic evolution; Chinese economic development; climate change policy; patents, startups and disruption; complex systems; catch up; overcoming socio-cultural obstacles to innovation; new ventures; evolution of the 'green economy'; East Asian growth; spin-offs; innovation policy; emergence in complex economic systems; spatial perspectives on economic evolution; innovation and firm performance; entrepreneurship; energy and green innovation; political economy, law and innovation; history-friendly modeling; the labor market; competition and selection; advances in evolutionary modeling; university-industry collaboration; persistence, inertia and path dependence; complex evolving networks; research collaboration and the emergence of capabilities; human capital; absorptive capacity; development-industrialization; international collaboration on innovation; health; technological spillovers.

This book is both the outcome of a strong competition among the papers submitted after the conference and the result of a thematic focus of the editors on a core issue of evolutionary economics. Some contributions already appeared in Volume 24 (2), a Special Issue of the Journal of Evolutionary Economics. Some of these reprints are additionally extended for this book to provide information that is more detailed and additional backgrounds. Both variants are clearly marked for the reader of this volume. The contributions selected show the scope of analysis in evolutionary economics as well as the explanatory power with respect to economic dynamics and long term economic development. The book is structured in three major sections dealing with the conference topic: The *evolution of economic systems*, the *evolution of innovation systems* and *entrepreneurship and innovation competition*.

In the first section, *evolution of economic systems*, we start with John Foster's Presidential Address entitled "Energy, Knowledge and Economic Growth." He views economic growth as a self-organized process with energy use and new knowledge associated with energy use as major co-evolutionary drivers. Ping Chen's chapter "Metabolic Growth Theory: Market-Share Competition, Learning Uncertainty, and Technology Wavelets" focuses on the trade-off between stability and complexity of an ecological-industrial system. His growth and technological development theory allows for non-linear economic development in waves combining the thinking of Adam Smith, Thomas Robert Malthus and Joseph Alois Schumpeter. To address issues of economic welfare is one of the major difficulties in evolutionary economics because it is hard if not impossible to find a yardstick because of the open development and the uncertainty inherent to all innovation. In his chapter entitled, "Towards a General Model of the Innovation—Subjective Well-Being Nexus" Hans-Jürgen Engelbrecht introduces the concept of procedural utility to overcome the difficulties in addressing welfare issues stemming from uncertainty and dynamics inherent to innovation processes. Esben Sloth Andersen and Jakob Rubaek Holm focus on the varieties of selection processes responsible for economic evolution. In their chapter "The Signs of Change in Economic Evolution", they differ between three selection mechanisms they label intentional, stabilizing and diversifying selection and explain the meaning of each selection mechanism for economic evolution. The last chapter in this section by Zheng Lu and Xiang Deng deals with an application of evolutionary reasoning and regional policy to analyze the impact of policy reforms on the economic system in China since 1999.

The second section of this book also places emphasis on the systemic character of economic evolution and focuses on the important concept of innovation systems. Peter Allen's chapter "Evolution, Complexity, Uncertainty and Innovation" introduces to the varieties of complex systems, the required assumptions and limitations and most important to their explanatory power for economic reasoning. Felix Munoz and Maria-Isabel Encinar highlight the interaction of agents' intentions for emergent phenomena in economic evolution. Their chapter "Intentionality and the Emergence of Complexity: an Analytical Approach" complements Andersen's and Holm's reflections on selection mechanisms by proposing an analytical approach based on agents' action plans to explain emerging patterns in economic behavior. Peter Hall's and Robert Wylie's chapter entitled "Isolation and Technological Innovation" analyze conditions for disruptive change in technological evolution stemming from isolation and introduce to two cases of military innovations to illustrate their reasoning. The following chapter "The Emergence of Technological Paradigms: The Evolutionary Process of Science and Technology in Economic Development" by Keiichiro Suenaga focuses on complex transition processes. He offers an analytical perspective to get a grip on the imponderability of uncertainty in processes of science and knowledge driven paradigmatic changes. Hans-Peter Brunner and Kislaya Prasad apply agent-based models to analyze structural change in South-Asian regions and introduce to policy experiments using this model. Their chapter "Policy Exploration with Agent-Based, Economic Geography Methods of Regional Economic Integration in South-Asia" also offers a link to Peter Allen's varieties of complex systems. Lykke Margot Ricard finally is concerned with a European case of technology diffusion. In her chapter "Coping with System

Failure: Why Connectivity Matters to Innovation Policy" she applies social network analysis to find out how technology platforms emerge and change in the current European energy system.

Section three of this book is entitled *entrepreneurship and innovation competition* and the chapters there focus on the sectorial, firm and individual perspective of innovation processes. Compared to the previous sections the following 11 chapters also choose more applied questions or address central issues in an evolutionary innovation-driven economic development. The first chapter authored by Harold Paredes-Frigolett and Andreas Pyka addresses innovation networks and firm entry strategies to knowledge pools organized in networks. "A Generic Innovation Network Formation Strategy" for firms embedded in geographic environments endowed with only poor knowledge and business opportunities can be a re-location into prolific networks which also can be part of a policy strategy. In the chapter "Property Rights as a Complex Adaptive System: How Entrepreneurship Transforms Intellectual Property Structures" David Harper treats intellectual property rights as a complex adaptive system which offers entrepreneurs opportunities and which is changed by entrepreneurial actions. These feedback effects determine meso-levels as structures within the macro intellectual property rights. Gunnar Eliasson and Pontus Braunerhjelm apply their competence bloc theory on economic development in the Baltic Sea region. They show that "Entrepreneurial Catch-up and New Industrial Competence Bloc Formation in the Baltic Sea Region" is possible and require a strong policy orientation on the improvement of the conditions for entrepreneurs. Abiodun Egbetokun and Ivan Savin pick up an old question in innovation economics: why do firms cooperate in innovation if they run into danger to lose knowledge to potential competitors? Their contribution "Absorptive Capacity and Innovation: When is it Better to Cooperate?" introduces to a new model which focuses on knowledge distances, voluntary and involuntary spillovers as well as the required investments to integrate external knowledge. The next chapter of this contributed volume "Innovation and Finance: A Stock Flow Consistent-Analysis of Great Surges of Development" by Alessandro Caiani and Antoine Godin links Neo-Schumpeterian and Post-Keynesian approaches to analyze the finance-innovation nexus which allows to explain the co-evolutionary relationship between technological change, demand and finance acknowledging for structural changes. The chapter "Restless Knowledge, Capabilities and the Nature of the Mega-Firm" by Harry Bloch and Stan Metcalfe adds to the competence-based approach of the theory of the firm important insights from evolutionary economics. In a similar vein Giovanni Cerulli and Bianca Poti address in their contribution "The Role of Management Capacity in the Innovation Process for Firm Profitability". Stefan Hitzschke again introduces a geographic dimension in his chapter "Industrial Growth and Productivity Change in German Cities: A Multilevel Investigation". Despite converging of urban industrial value creation, he founds diverging growth rates in employment for German cities. Bernado Maggi and Daniel Muro also focus on joint and interdependent growth dynamics, this time for European countries. Their chapter entitled "A Dynamical Model of Technology Diffusion and Business Services for the Study of the European Countries Growth and Stability" provides with a detailed description of their statistical approach and with policy conclusions, which can be derived from their analysis. Marcelo de Carvalho Pereira and David Dequech introduce to “A History-Friendly Model of the Internet Access Market: the Case of Brazil”. With the help of an agent-based simulation model, they reproduce important dynamics and interactions empirically measured in Brazil. The last chapter “Micro, Macro, and Meso Determinants of Productivity Growth in Argentinian Firms” authored by Verónica Robert, Mariano Pereira, Gabriel Yoguel and Florencia Barletta is an application of the evolutionary feedback story between the different levels in an economy and deals with firm productivity growth in Argentina.

All chapters of this contributed volume of the International Joseph A. Schumpeter Society Conference from 2012 in Brisbane, Australia join the focus on complex adaptive systems as an adequate framework for evolutionary economic analysis. The contributions make clear how far the evolutionary complex methodology is developed and how rich the explanatory power of economic analysis can be with the right instruments: Changes of the system like innovation-driven economic development or economic crisis become endogenous phenomena, which are analyzed immediately without exogenous shocks and/or the application of restrictive assumptions. Interactions among heterogeneous actors and the emergence and diffusion of new knowledge triggers the interesting dynamics and structural transitions which are only analytically accessible with the methodologies and frameworks provided by evolutionary Schumpeterian economics.

Part I
The Evolution of Economic Systems

Energy, Knowledge and Economic Growth

John Foster

Abstract It is argued that the explosive growth experienced in much of the World since the middle of the 19th Century is due to the exploitation and use of fossil fuels which, in turn, was made possible by capital good innovations that enabled this source of energy to be used effectively. Economic growth is viewed as the outcome autocatalytic co-evolution of energy use and the application of new knowledge associated with energy use. It is argued that models of economic growth should be built from innovation diffusion processes, unfolding in history, rather than from a timeless aggregate production function. A simple 'evolutionary macroeconomic' model of economic growth is developed and tested using almost two centuries of British data. The empirical findings strongly support the hypothesis that growth has been due to the presence of a 'super-radical innovation diffusion process' following the industrial deployment of fossil fuels on a large scale in the 19th Century. Also, the evidence suggests that large and sustained movements in energy prices have had a very significant long term role to play.

1 Introduction

"As long as supplies of both mechanical and heat energy were conditioned by the annual quantum of insolation and the efficiency of plant photosynthesis in capturing incoming solar radiation, it was idle to expect a radical improvement in the material conditions of the bulk of mankind" (Wrigley 2010, p. 17).

This paper was presented in preliminary form as the Presidential Address at the International J.A. Schumpeter Society Conference, July2–5th 2012, University of Queensland, Brisbane, Australia. I would like to thank Maxine Darnell for providing advice concerning the treatment of energy in the British economic history literature. Roger Fouquet and Jakob Madsen kindly provided me with their historical data. Thanks are also due to Stan Metcalfe, Jakob Madsen and David Stern for their extensive comments and criticisms of a previous version of this paper. However, all errors and omissions remain the responsibility of the author.

J. Foster (✉)
School of Economics, University of Queensland, Brisbane, Queensland 4072, Australia
e-mail: j.foster@uq.edu.au

A. Pyka, J. Foster (eds.), *The Evolution of Economic and Innovation Systems*, Economic Complexity and Evolution, DOI 10.1007/978-3-319-13299-0_2
Reprinted from Journal of Evolutionary Economics, 24(2), Springer 2014.

It is well accepted in the conventional literature on economic growth that, as time passes, we have upward movements in what is viewed as an aggregate production function, as the substitution of new capital for old raises productivity. The problem with this perspective on growth is that shifts of, and movements along, aggregate production functions are very difficult to disentangle using historical data. So what is quite a useful analytical construct for application in short periods at the microeconomic level of inquiry, is not an appropriate vehicle for understanding aggregate economic growth over long periods despite its wide adoption in the literature on economic growth. Solow (1957) famously found, using neoclassical economic theory and a Cobb-Douglas production function, that about 80 % of economic growth was unexplained by the growth of capital and labour when he modelled US time series data. In other words, the upward shift of the aggregate production function was massively more important than shifts along it. This upward shift, by force of logic, was the most important factor in explaining economic growth, yet it was deemed by Solow to be outside economic theory and vaguely referred to as due to 'technical progress'.

In the 1980s, endogenous growth theorists noted the inadequacy of the Solow model and began to explore what the technical progress 'black box' might contain and how its contents might be expressed theoretically. But, in doing so, they started from the same neoclassical micro-analytical perspective on economic behaviour as had Solow, with all its attendant problems (Fine 2000). By making a range of clever, but very restrictive, assumptions, this kind of conventional economic theorizing came to be employed with little cognizance of the kinds of behavioural motivations that actually drive the entrepreneurship and innovation that lie at the core of the evolutionary process that generates economic growth.[1] Because of this, the conclusions contained in the endogenous growth literature turn out to be somewhat pedestrian: we need more 'ideas', more R&D, more education, more training. This is a rather obvious list and, as Solow (2007) recently pointed out, the importance of these drivers was well understood back in the 1960s, if not before (see in particular Denison (1974) for a backward look and update).

Because this kind of theorizing is ahistorical at its core, it cannot tell us much about the actual historical processes that result in economic growth and, thus, it provides little guidance as to where we are likely to end up in the future. This is a serious problem because, as population growth surges, as output per capita rises rapidly and as environmental degeneration accelerates, we really need to know how the economic processes that result in growth actually work and where they are likely to drive us in the future. Even a cursory glance at the remarkable exponential growth path that the World has been on since the mid-19th Century raises a fundamental question: when will such growth come to an end? We know that continual exponential growth is an arithmetical and logical impossibility. Indeed, it

[1]Galor and Michalopoulos (2012) claimed that it is possible to capture entrepreneurship in a neoclassical model. Typically, their highly mathematical model contains many very abstract assumptions that invalidate its relevance to the history that they discuss.

is almost universally true that populations of species in organic-based systems that exploit a free energy source follow a sigmoid growth path to a capacity limit. Only the early growth phase is approximated by exponential growth. And we know that there have already been human civilizations in the past 10,000 years that have hit growth limits with some even collapsing (see, Diamond (2005), Landes (1998) and Tainter (1988) for examples).

Looking at economic growth as an outcome of a historical process draws us towards theoretical approaches that connect directly with history. We require what Dopfer (1986) called a 'histonomic' approach. A historical process is, necessarily, a non-equilibrium one, characterized by a degree of time irreversibility and continual structural change, sometimes slow sometimes fast. Historians tell us that such change is not random, and evolutionary economists see it as the outcome of an evolutionary economic process that involves economic self-organization, which generates a vast variety of economic processes, goods and services, and competitive selection, that resolves this variety and, in so doing, raises productivity, raises quality, lowers costs and, ultimately, leads to organizational concentrations that have economic power (Dopfer 2006). This is a truly 'endogenous' perspective on economic growth (Foster 2011a).

The purpose here is to apply this 'evolutionary macroeconomic' perspective to understand the astonishing and unparalleled economic growth explosion that has occurred over the past two centuries. This perspective centres upon the co-evolutionary relationship between the growth in energy use and the expansion of knowledge to facilitate such growth. This was discussed in Foster (2011b) which, in turn, was inspired by the theoretical approach to growth in all 'dissipative structures' by Schneider and Kay (1994), popularized in Schneider and Sagan (2005), and Smil (2008). The empirical work on economic growth by Robert Ayres and Benjamin Warr, reported in a series of articles and consolidated in Ayres and Warr (2009), also motivated the research reported here. The modelling methodology used is econometric, as developed in Foster and Wild (1999a).

The evolutionary macroeconomic methodology, which replaces the production function with the innovation diffusion curve at the core of growth modelling, is designed to discover simple aggregate representations of the behaviour of complex economic systems that are not based upon 'simplistic' neoclassical micro-foundations (Foster 2005), as is the case in the Solow model and variants built upon it, but on historical tendencies that are observed when knowledge cumulates and there is a source of energy available to allow growth in economic activity to occur. Here it is shown that it is possible to find empirical support for a very simple evolutionary macroeconomic explanation of economic growth using almost two centuries of data. These findings can be compared to those in two recent articles by Madsen et al. (2010) and Stern and Kander (2012) where economic growth is also modelled using very long samples of time series data. However, the methodology adopted in both studies is in sharp contrast to that adopted here. In both, the modelling is constructed on Solow's theoretical foundations.

2 The evolutionary macroeconomic perspective on growth

Foster (1987) proposed an 'evolutionary macroeconomic' approach to analysing the determinants of economic growth. This was operationalized as an empirical methodology in Foster and Wild (1999a, b) and is summarized in Foster (2011a). Economic growth, as measured by GDP growth, is looked on, not as an aggregated behavioural entity, but as a statistical aggregation of the measurable economic value that arises out of a complex and irreducible process of economic evolution that unfolds in historical time. Instead of thinking of economic growth simply as an aggregation of the behaviour of a 'representative agent' engaged in constrained optimization in a timeless setting, it is viewed as being initiated through entrepreneurship, innovation and the adoption of new skills (Baumol 2002).[2] Since this involves a great deal of uncertainty, constrained optimization is impossible over long periods (Foster and Metcalfe 2012).

From radical innovations there follow diffusion processes that involve increases in the organized complexity of an economic system. The outcome of much learning-by-doing, incremental innovation and competitive selection, all processes taking place in historical time, is a range of viable economic activities that yield productive processes and products that grow in number, at falling cost. These economic activities are consolidated in effective organizational structures that are dominated by sets of routines which, inevitably, introduce a degree of time irreversibility or 'lock-in' (Arthur 1994). In such processes, there is little doubt that constrained optimization is applied when it is feasible but, given the sheer complexity of any networked productive organization, this is very difficult to do in any general way. To establish order and a productive capability, the operation of rules and routines has to dominate, as Nelson and Winter (1982) explained so vividly. So it is essential that any theory of economic growth, and associated empirical methodology, should be built with this historically-based evolutionary economic process at its core, not upon an idealized representation of constrained optimization and a timeless production function.

Conventional economists try to answer questions about economic growth starting with an aggregate production function that contains stocks of 'physical capital' and 'human capital.' But there are serious problems with such an approach once we acknowledge that we are dealing with continual structural change and the formation of productive structures with irreversible features in historical time. The capital stock clearly has a very important role to play in economic growth but it not just another 'factor of production.' It is a magnitude that is the end product of acts of inventiveness, entrepreneurship and innovative creativity and, as such, it is a complex network of 'structured knowledge' that has cumulated over time in physical capital (Arrow 1962). It is the physical core upon which other kinds of new

[2]It is instructive that Aghion and Howitt (1998), who hijacked the term 'Schumpeterian' for their endogenous growth theorizing, do not even have 'entrepreneur' or 'entrepreneurship' in the index of their 190 page book.

knowledge can be developed and applied, for example, in organisational innovations and the development of new skills.

The existence of a capital stock makes it possible to apply a flow of non-human energy to generate economic value, as measured by GDP, in excess of that possible by application human effort alone. The capital stock is a durable and multi-use structure which offers the opportunity for many other kinds of new knowledge to be generated that can produce economic value and, thus, it creates a 'niche' into which GDP can grow in the future. Economic growth is not just about 'more of the same' it is about ongoing qualitative change in the economic system. Thus, although we can think of any productive process in terms of its inputs and outputs, there can be no meaningful 'equilibrium' association between them over long periods when structural change is significant.

Indeed, over the past two decades, it has become well understood that many macroeconomic time series do not have simple deterministic trends which they regress to. The hypothesis that such series have 'unit roots' often cannot be rejected, i.e., there is no support for the hypothesis of a deterministic trend and, therefore, such a series cannot be viewed as oscillating around a long run equilibrium path. Such a series is wholly dependent upon its past history. Undeterred, proponents of economic theories that predict input-output equilibrium solutions search for 'co-integration' between such time series. This, it is argued, provides evidence in support of a 'long run equilibrium' relationship between the chosen variables. Often, but not always, an 'equilibrium correction model,' is estimated using stationary first-differenced data, plus an equilibrium correction term (commonly the residual error in an estimated co-integrating equation). Interestingly, when a Solow style equilibrium growth equation is estimated with a significant constant term, the latter is usually deemed to represent 'technical progress'. But, from an equilibrium correction methodological perspective, such an equation has no long run equilibrium solution yet, theoretically, it is still viewed as an 'equilibrium growth model'. This is precisely the disconnection between modelling and conventional economic theory that Davidson et al. (1978) pointed to in developing their equilibrium correction methodology over thirty years ago. The correct interpretation of the Solow evidence is that economic growth is the outcome of a non-equilibrium, historical process and it must be treated as such.

The evolutionary macroeconomic approach to modelling economic growth starts with complex systems theory which immediately tells us two things. Firstly, all economic systems are, necessarily, dissipative structures, importing free energy and exporting entropy, and, as such, they will grow in the presence of useable energy and the flow of energy is something that we can measure (Brown et al. 2011). Secondly, we also know that an economic system can only become more complex, and, thus, be able to grow, if new knowledge can cumulate and be applied in useful ways. This is much harder to measure. Although various proxies for the 'stock' of knowledge have been used in the endogenous growth literature, such as patents and education, it is not possible to measure the actual flow of entrepreneurial activities associated with new knowledge. Knowledge is not a stock but, rather, a virtual structure that can be drawn upon by the innovative and the entrepreneurial to generate economic value.

We know from innumerable studies of innovation that 'radical' applications of new knowledge result in growth until a limit is approached where the innovative niche is filled. Such growth is widely observed to follow a sigmoid 'innovation diffusion curve' with respect to historical time. As output expands, productivity rises and unit costs fall. At the macroeconomic level of inquiry, a multitude of these curves can average into a smooth macro growth curve which, itself, as famously suggested by Joseph Schumpeter, can follow a sigmoid path in the wake of a radical innovation of fundamental importance (Perez 2002; Freeman and Louca 2002).

We have to acknowledge the thermodynamic character of all economic systems: there must exist an 'energy gradient' which can be drawn upon to allow a system to do work. All dissipative structures attempt to reduce such gradients (Schneider and Sagan 2005). For a long time in human history, a large proportion of the population did mainly physical work, fuelled by a food energy gradient. However, humans in modern times have devised capital goods to do physical work using flows of non-human energy. Work now is only minimally physical in nature: the 'machine operator' and the 'knowledge worker' are now the norm.

Unlike in physio-chemical dissipative structures, the energy gradient available to living organisms is not always exogenous. Following the terminology of Foster (2005), at the 3rd Order of Complexity, humans, almost uniquely, apply non-genetically transmitted creative knowledge to generate economic value and run down energy gradients that have been deliberately accessed. But to get beyond the application of hand tools and capital goods related to animal power, humans have had to operate at a 4th Order of Complexity whereby they are able to cooperate in economic organizations using 'understandings' to enable the creation and use of very complex capital goods that enhance their capacity to generate greater amounts of economic value. Starting with the deliberate exploitation of wood, charcoal, wind and water power, humans developed a capacity to overcome the thermodynamic limit of a finite 'organic' energy gradient. But this did not have a dramatic effect on economic growth until fossil fuels, which had been known about and used for a long time, became applied at large scale using efficient and versatile steam engines in the 19th Century.

It follows that, for humans, growth has become heavily dependent upon the creation of what we can label as a 'knowledge gradient' that is specifically 'economic'. For example, there was always coal and oil available in the ground, it was only when knowledge of how to extract and use such energy became available that it could enable economic growth (Georgescu-Roegen 1971). The relative cheapness of such energy per joule, compared to the organic and solar sourced energy relied upon previously, offered unrivalled opportunities to accumulate and use new knowledge that could generate economic value. This relied almost entirely on the human ability to create capital goods to mine fossil energy more effectively and to create and use others to generate economic value. Thus, the 'core knowledge' that has created opportunities for rapid growth using fossil fuels has been that embodied in energy-using capital goods.

The creation and use of new capital goods has shifted physical work away from human effort to a greater reliance on non-human energy flow. This has involved the construction of a knowledge gradient that could be reduced by historical processes such as: learning-by-doing, in the context of the production and use of new capital goods; incremental technical innovations that made capital goods more productive and diverse in their application; and organizational, institutional and product innovations. A knowledge gradient differs in nature from an energy one because, as endogenous growth theorists have stressed, using knowledge does not diminish it in a literal sense. However, knowledge does get 'used up' as the potential applications of it become exhausted. Also, the capital goods in which it is embedded can become obsolete as time passes. For example, there is no point in using the very best knowledge concerning the production of steam locomotives in a world of electric trains.

In reality, it is not easy to discover and reduce a knowledge gradient that has the potential to generate economic value. Only entrepreneurial individuals and groups can do this by combining ideas and skills in imaginative new ways with the goal of making money. Only a minority of them is successful. The knowledge gradient that makes GDP growth possible begins with the embodiment of technical knowledge in capital goods but its full extent is dependent on a complex interaction of cultural, social, political and economic understandings that is specific to different countries, regions and cities (Acemoglu and Robinson 2012). It is this which determines whether a new capital good sparks off multiple applications in future economic interactions or just sits unused to rust. Indeed, interacting cultural, social and political factors can even prevent the innovative development and/or use of capital goods, utilizing non-human energy, because of the threat posed to vested interests.

3 The super-radical innovation diffusion hypothesis

The hypothesis that is offered here is that the industrial deployment of fossil fuels at scale in the early 19th Century gave rise to a 'super-radical innovation diffusion process' that resulted in explosive economic growth. However, the importance of fossil fuels in the industrial revolution is not a new idea – a debate in economic history has been raging for decades on this topic and, indeed, claims that energy was the sole driver of explosive economic growth are unconvincing even amongst those historians who attribute a vital role to fossil fuels in the industrial revolution (see, for example, Allen (2009) and Wrigley (2010)). The application of new knowledge is essential for economic growth but the application of a very powerful energy source opened up possibilities in the application of knowledge that were never previously attainable. The work of historians such as Mokyr (2002) and McCloskey (2010), claiming that a revolution in the composition of knowledge and related cultural change that commenced as early as the 17th century, was of primary importance, is not denied here. It is not likely that the scientific and engineering advances using fossil fuels in the 19th Century would have happened without the radical shifts in the knowledge base that governed economic activities in the 18th Century (see Chapman (1970)). For example, without the 'Scottish Enlightenment' cultural development in the 18th Century, it is unlikely that James Watt would have developed his superior steam engine. The Watt steam engine was a very radical innovation because it both provided an increase in mining productivity and a powerful device to use fossil fuels in a range of applications.

From the 17th Century, on in the United Kingdom, which will be our main focus here, economic growth increased because of changes in the nature of knowledge which also increased agricultural productivity (particularly the growing of potatoes which yielded about three times the food energy per acre compared to other foodstuffs (Nunn and Qian 2011). Early industrialization involved the creative design and construction of capital goods, as did agriculture, but growth in what some historians label 'the first industrial revolution' was ultimately curtailed by limits on knowledge of how to deploy more powerful capital goods economically.[3] Wood and charcoal became scarce, useful sites for water driven mills became harder to find and the horsepower required began to limit the amount of agricultural land available for food growing. In contrast, coal mining did not take up large amounts of land and a miner could produce about 100 times more energy than an agricultural worker. However, the novel capital investments necessary to make mining more productive, to transport coal and to build the capital goods to use it effectively were massive challenges.

In 19th Century Britain it was remarkable how these challenges were met. It was a century of radical creative destruction: horses, water mills, windmills, wood burning and charcoal production and all the trades associated with them began to be swept away in favour of Watt's improved steam engine to pump water out of mines, re-circulate water in mill races, drive trains, generate electricity, etc.[4] This 'creative destruction,' that enabled the effective and economic use of fossil fuel energy, was intensified in the early 20th Century with expansion of the use of gas in heating and the shift to oil for transportation, electricity generation, etc. The combustion engine and the electric motor took over from the steam engine as the key power drivers in capital goods.

But such a transition involved socio-political traumas and Europe became a continent that suffered all of the political pressures that came with a radical structural transformation that involved a sustained shift away from labour and horse power to fossil fuel driven machine power. The occupational churning and rapid increase in capital investment and mining capacity, stimulated by the First World War, ultimately resulted in large amounts of excess capacity and structural unemployment in the 1920s and 1930s. The coal driven economy experienced serious problems. Coal consumption in the UK peaked in 1914 and mining over-expanded in the War. Afterwards, British coal prices were held up to maintain

[3]See, for example, Deane (1969), Harley (1982), Crafts (2005) and Wrigley (2010) for extended discussion concerning the existence, or otherwise, of the first industrial revolution.

[4]Harris (1967) pointed out that steam engines were used extensively in the 18th Century to pump water out of coal mines, even though they were relatively inefficient, because they used 'waste' coal fragments that had little commercial value.

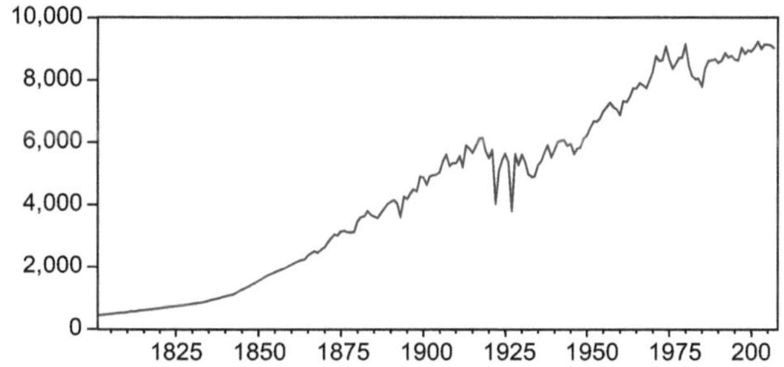

Fig. 1 UK energy consumption 1800–2010 (in Petajoules)

miners' wages but this only exacerbated an excess supply situation resulting in the bankruptcy of many privately owned mines. Business investment in new capital stock was cut back because of the relatively high real price of both energy and labour and associated uncertainty. This generated an effective demand problem, as identified by John Maynard Keynes in 1936. This transitional problem was not fully eliminated until the stimulative effect of the Second World War operated.

Coal production had peaked in 1913 at around 300 million tons but by 2010 it had fallen to just over 20 million tons. The UK became more and more dependent on imported coal, particularly after the Second World War, but the price of coal remained fairly stable – it was still at around its 1880 real price in 1967 (Fouquet 2008). After the 2nd World War, oil consumption grew rapidly and coal became mainly dedicated to the generation of electricity with tar, coke and gas as by products. Dependence on imported oil also increased although this was moderated with the emergence of North Sea supplies in the 1970s. In what looks like a sigmoid curve for energy (Fig. 1), there was an oil-related 'sub-sigmoid' diffusion curve after the 2nd World War. By the early 21st Century, total energy consumption had plateaued.

Despite the interwar slowdown, the longer term tendency for economic growth to occur at a high and sustained rate was relatively unaffected (Fig. 2). The interwar period was not one where energy was in short supply but, rather, there was a lack of new knowledge as to how to extract energy more economically and to deploy it effectively and in new ways.[5]

Stanley Jevons (1866) had worried about the implications of the heavy British dependence on coal but he seriously underestimated the durability of the growth of knowledge process that had started. Institutional innovations are generally slow in agrarian societies, but not so in 19th Century industrial communities in the UK where the gains from investing heavily in new capital goods and reorganizing society to take advantage of fossil fuel power were so attractive.

[5]Field (2011) has provided convincing evidence that, in the US case, this resulted in a sharp rise in inventive and innovative behaviour in the 1930s.

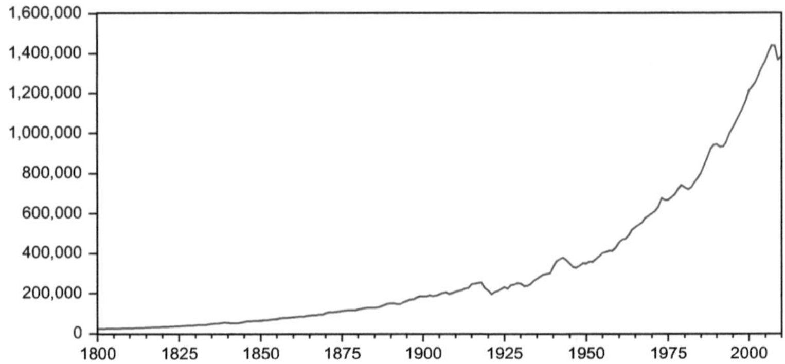

Fig. 2 British real GDP: 1830–2010 (US$ million, 1990 prices)

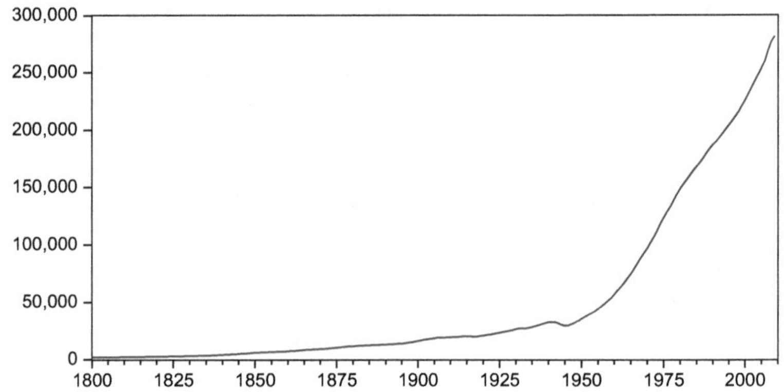

Fig. 3 British net capital stock: 1800–2010 (£Million, 1990 prices)

Capital goods have been identified as the primary vehicle for catalysing economically valuable knowledge in the presence of a fossil fuel energy gradient. In Fig. 3, the upsurge in the net capital stock in Britain is very clear. The massive release of unskilled labour that this implied allowed a shift in employment towards service activities which provided the specialized expertise required to design and construct new capital goods, as well as the productive and industrial systems that they operate in and the provision of a large range of services for mass consumption. This shift was most marked after the Second World War when growth in the capital stock was significantly higher than previously.[6] So, the knowledge gradient, built

[6]It has been commonly assumed in a number of neoclassically-based studies of economic growth that the capital-output and/or the capital-labour ratio have been approximately constant. In the British case, the former in 2010 was about 2.5 times greater that it was in 1900 and the latter about 12 times greater.

upon knowledge embedded in capital goods, has not been static but has been continually growing. Thus, the 'niche' that GDP could grow into has continually increased.

4 The United Kingdom: a suitable case for treatment

The idea that global economic growth has been on a long sigmoid diffusion curve is not new. Recently Miranda and Lima (2011) and, before them, Boretos (2009) explored this possibility using global data. However, the problem with global studies is the paucity of long time series and it is not clear that the relatively small segment of time series data available to these researchers is actually on a sigmoid growth path. Also, since each country's growth experience is unique, we can only understand global growth by looking at each of them separately and understanding the interactions between them. The global economy is a network structure connected by production and trade. But it is a very incomplete network which has become more connected and, thus, more complex and organized over time. Only careful historical study of every country can track how this global process has unfolded and how related cultural, social, institutional and economic circumstances have shifted over long periods of time (Acemoglu and Robinson 2012). Here we report the results of tests of the super radical innovation diffusion hypothesis for only one, very important country. The United Kingdom was selected for study for two reasons: firstly, it was first into the 'industrial revolution' and is now a stable, advanced 'post-industrial' country. It has exhibited the longest 'explosive' growth path of any country and, over the past two centuries, it has not been disturbed by serious internal political crises or invasions. Secondly, there are available long data sets that stretch well back into the 19th century that can shed light on our hypothesis.

The industrial revolution was, in large measure, due to technical, organizational and institutional innovations that had their roots back in the 16th Century. In the early 18th Century about 80 % of global output of coal was produced in the UK (Wrigley 2010). At that time, coal was used largely for domestic heating. Steam engines, although they existed, remained relatively inefficient. But the British developed a lead in coal mining technology and a key driver of the development of Watt's much more efficient steam engine was the need to pump water quickly and effectively out of coal mines. By the 19th Century, although many factories were still powered by water because costs had been sunk and marginal cost was very low, new industrial sites began to be powered by steam engines, fuelled by coal. By the early 20th Century, coal energy began to be used in all sectors via electrical power generation. The availability of combustion engines using distillates also began to transform economic production in radical ways in the early 20th Century because of revolutionary new transportation capabilities. Innovators could profit from designing machines that used powerful fossil fuels, directly or indirectly, and, in an autocatalytic way, the increasing demand for fossil fuels lowered their cost

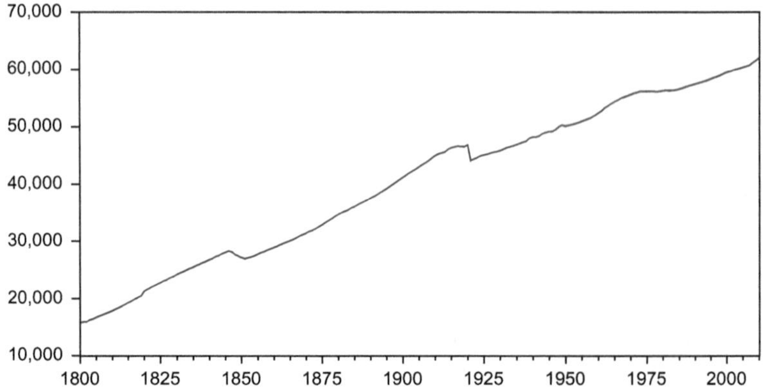

Fig. 4 UK population: 1820–2010 (Thousands)

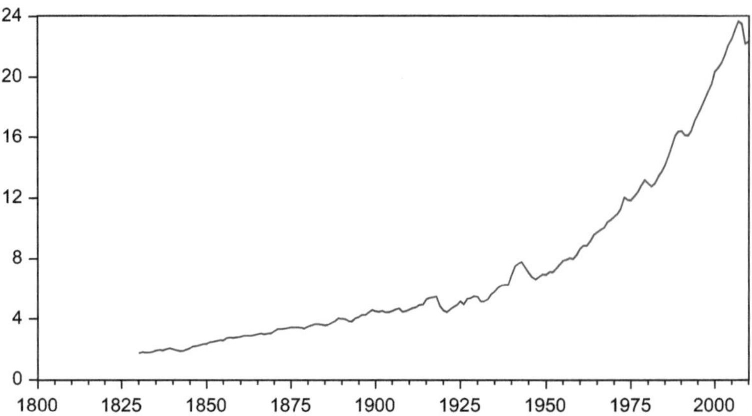

Fig. 5 British real GDP per capita 1830–2010 (US$ thousand, 1990 prices)

as scale economies, learning by doing and incremental innovations, in exploration, mining and delivery, did their work.

Although real GDP has followed a long period trajectory which is close to exponential, despite the traumatic experiences of a depression and two world wars, population growth has been approximately linear (Fig. 4).[7] So population has grown ever more slowly than GDP per capita (Fig. 5) which is a very 'un-Malthusian' finding.[8]

---

[7]The two negative blips are caused by the potato famine (1845-1852) and Irish independence (1922).

[8]Interestingly, despite its reputation as a 'mature' economy, the UK continued, up to the recession of 2009, to record a labour productivity growth rate that was not only consistently positive but on a continual rising trend, despite the massive shift towards service sector activities.

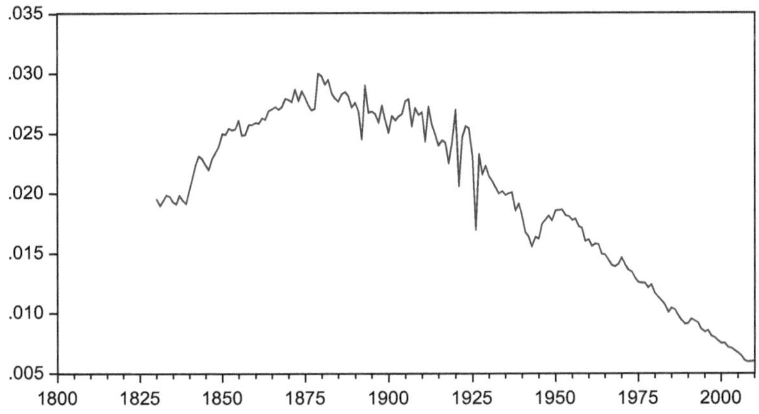

Fig. 6 British energy to GDP ratio: 1830–2010

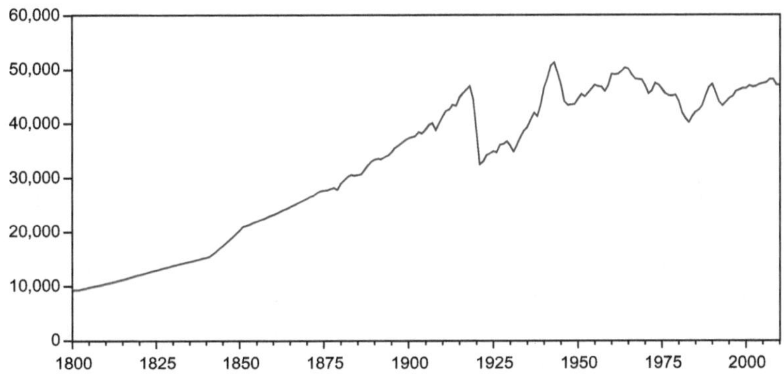

Fig. 7 British total hours worked 1800–2010

The energy to GDP ratio, since about 1880, has been falling consistently, reflecting steady increases in the efficiency of the extraction, transportation and use of fossil fuels (Fig. 6). The ratio rose prior to 1880, because of the significant investments in new mines, steam driven machinery and associated infrastructure which took time to fully utilize.

Labour effort is clearly fundamental in any economy, whether it is devoted to physical work or to mental activities. It is very striking in Fig. 7 that, labour hours trended upwards until 1919 after which they oscillated around a fairly static level up to the present. In 2010, total labour hours were only marginally above their 1919 level. Over the same period, the UK population grew by 33 %. Thus, we can see that The First World War was pivotal in the shift from a mainly labour to a more capital intensive economy in relation to the provision of physical energy. Before the War, there was still a significant role for horse and human physical labour. We saw in Fig. 3 that the fast surge in the capital stock, releasing labour into the growing

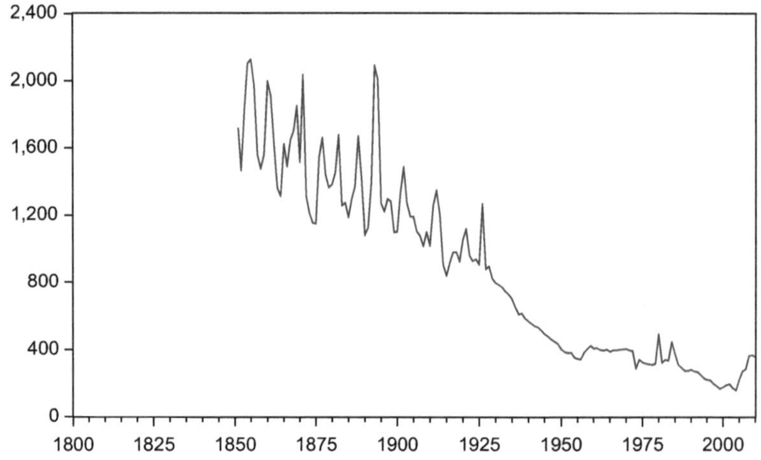

Fig. 8 British average real energy price: 1851–2010 (£in 2000 prices)

service sector did not occur until after World War Two. The interwar years involved a difficult transition with the capital stock hardly rising and labour hours dropping significantly.

So do these charts suggest that a super-radical innovation diffusion process may have been in operation? As has been pointed out, in the presence of a diffusion process with a growing K-limit, we need not observe a sigmoid curve in the case of GDP until the K-limit stops increasing. However, a sigmoid curve is in evidence in the case of energy consumption. This has been paralleled by a steady fall in the price of energy (see Fig. 8, in Fouquet (2011)). By 2007, energy was about one sixth of its real price in the early 19th Century. This is a typical finding in the presence of an innovation diffusion process, with price falling as scale rises and increases in efficiency, both in production and use, occur.

On innovation diffusion curves, unit costs usually stop falling and begin to rise after the point of inflexion, as cost economies become harder to achieve and dominant organizations begin to rent seek. We can see that the real price of energy has now stopped falling and is increasing. It is notable that, up to 1930, the price of energy fluctuated because fossil energy was in short supply and, thus, sensitive to movements in demand. From the Great Depression on, supplies of coal and oil tended to exceed demand and price became stable and determined by supply side costs. In the 1970s, suppliers, again, had some market power because of the strong global demand that had built up in the post-war boom. Since the global financial crisis in 2008, real energy prices have attained their 1970s peak range again although they still remain low by historical standards. However, this has not yet held back GDP growth.

5 An innovation diffusion model of long-term UK growth

Because economic growth is the outcome of a co-evolutionary process, where the application of new knowledge and increased energy use are complementary, we have a methodological choice. We can choose, as in endogenous growth theory, to focus upon the role of knowledge in a general way, or we can focus specifically on the impact of new knowledge on the growth in energy consumption and increases in the efficiency of its use, as in Ayres and Warr (2009) and Stern and Kander (2012).[9] Both approaches lay claim to explaining most of the 'Solow residual.' For Ayres and Warr (2009), it is energy flow that is important, with the key role of new knowledge being to get energy sources do more work.[10] Importantly, in both approaches, it is new knowledge embodied in capital goods that is the key. In Ayres and Warr (2009), it is about the development of more and better capital goods to turn energy into work. In endogenous growth models it is the capacity of people in the R&D sector to produce new capital goods that embody new ideas that drives growth.

Here, it is also fully accepted that the capital stock, as a structure containing embodied knowledge specifically designed to use energy to do work, is important. However, the capital stock is not viewed as a direct determinant of economic growth, as it is in the aggregate production function approach, but it is, instead, viewed as a core determinant of the niche that GDP can enter through innovation diffusion. Now, it is commonplace in growth theory to see capital investment (or growth of the net capital stock) as the prime mover but here it is the cumulative level of the net capital stock that determines the energy-related economic potential of a country. It is the conduit through which cheap fossil fuels, directly and indirectly, have facilitated the transformation of materials and human effort into a vast range of goods and services of measurable economic value.[11]

The capital stock is the energy-driven building block that enables technical, organizational, institutional and product innovations to happen. It is the tip of the knowledge gradient iceberg. Think of Henry Ford's re-organization of factory production, the new laws of contract that emerged in the late 19th Century in Britain or the laws that facilitated the formation of joint stock companies. It is because of all of these innovations that a given capital stock can sustain growth into the

[9]Stern and Kander (2012) stepped back from the endogenous growth framework, instead, employing a variant of the Solow growth model using a CES production function with time varying elasticities of substitution. They reported that, for Sweden, energy seems to have played an important role in the determination of economic growth over two centuries. Ayres and Warr (2009) also viewed the Cobb-Douglas specification as too restrictive, preferring a more realistic Linex production function to which they add 'useful work' to capture energy flow and energy efficiency effects.

[10]There is no particular focus on energy in most endogenous growth models although it does figure in some studies (see Pittel and Rübbelke (2010) for a review).

[11]Howitt and Aghion (1998) also, saw the capital stock as the main conduit for innovation. However, the neoclassically-based theory that they offer is very different, analytically, to the evolutionary macroeconomic one proposed here and it is not operationalisable econometrically.

future that is not necessarily delimited only by the supply of energy. For example, investments in computers in the 1970s and 1980s made possible large increases in GDP because of innovations in mobile computing power, software development and electronic communications. The massive increase in the proportion of GDP in services has been due to the provision of capital goods which have facilitated the economic delivery of increasingly diverse services and the release of labour to do so.

So what we have is the reverse of the Solow growth model: the primary source of growth is the innovation diffusion process that Solow consigned to his 'residual.' Innovation diffusion cannot be just an add-on to a production function – in reality, shifts in production functions and movements along them cannot be separated. It is innovation, due to acts of entrepreneurship, which gives rise to new demands for inputs. So the core of our growth model must be innovation diffusion, not a production function. Foster and Wild (1999a) developed an augmented logistic diffusion model (ALDM) to represent diffusion in the specific context of financial sector development. However, following Metcalfe (2003), industrial development more broadly is better represented by a Gompertz growth model.[12] For the purposes of econometric estimation, the Mansfield sigmoid specification was selected, as in Foster and Wild (1999a), but with a Gompertz representation of innovation diffusion:

$$\boldsymbol{Y_t = Y_{t-1} + aY_{t-1}\left[1 - lnY_{t-1}/lnK\right]} \qquad (1)$$

Where **Y** is GDP, ***a*** is the logistic diffusion coefficient and ***lnK*** is the zero growth limit.

equivalently:

$$\boldsymbol{(Y_t - Y_{t-1})\,/Y_{t-1} = a - a\left[\ln Y_{t-1}/\ln K\right]} \qquad (2)$$

Approximating logarithmically:

$$\boldsymbol{\ln Y_t - \ln Y_{t-1} = a - a\left[\ln Y_{t-1}/\ln K\right]} \qquad (3)$$

However, Eq. 3 is incomplete because we know that, in parallel with this innovation diffusion process, there must be increases in physical work driven by human effort, the application of energy and/or increases in the efficiency of both. This is a thermodynamic necessity. Physical work done comes from two sources: labour time and energy consumption.

Let ***e*** be the proportional change in total energy consumption ($\boldsymbol{lnE_t}$ - $\boldsymbol{lnE_{t-1}}$) and ***h*** the proportional change in labour hours ($\boldsymbol{lnH_t}$ - $\boldsymbol{lnH_{t-1}}$).[13] Let ***C*** be the net

[12]The results reported using the logistic specification are very similar but the Gompertz results offer a much more plausible representation of the diffusion process at that has been at work.

[13]Since all product innovations are the outcome of the efforts of labour and there are also continual increases in the efficiency of energy use, making it cheaper per joule, ***a*** can be viewed as the sum

capital stock and let us assume that there is a log-linear relationship between it and K. Thus, we have an augmented Gompertz diffusion model (AGDM), including a quasi-random shock term, u:[14]

$$\begin{aligned}\ln Y_t - \ln Y_{t-1} = a - (a/n)\left[\ln Y_{t-1}/\ln C_{t-1}\right] + b\,(e_t, e_{t-1}\ldots e_{t-n}) \\ +g\,(h_t, h_{t-1}\ldots h_{t-n}) + u\end{aligned} \tag{4}$$

When the available niche is dictated by the size of a capital stock designed to take advantage of cheap energy, there must be a shift of physical work done, away from labour time towards energy consumption. Released labour shifts into non-physical work activities, raising GDP. This is what we observe in the historical data. In addition to these shifts, induced by innovation diffusion, there are also short term fluctuations in energy use and labour time. For example, in recessionary conditions, production is curtailed and GDP growth falls, resulting in excess capacity and unemployment. In booms and wartime conditions a given productive structure may be used more intensively and, consequently, its net capital stock may run down at an accelerated rate.

The 'gross' innovation diffusion effect is a and 'net' effect is $[a - (a/n)[lnY_{t-1}/lnC_{t-1}]$. As lnY approaches its lnK limit, the net innovation diffusion effect tends to zero. So what is a 'qualitative' knowledge diffusion effect disappears, leaving only the 'quantitative' impacts of changes in energy consumption and labour hours worked. These can push lnY above the lnK limit, but this is corrected as lnY/lnK rises above unity. In this sense, lnK is a 'soft ceiling.'

Our hypothesis is that explosive growth, from the early 19th century on, was due to the creation and use of a capital stock explicitly designed to extract and use fossil fuel. In addition, we saw in Fig. 8 that the price of energy fell sharply up to the end of the 1950s. Falling energy prices should make marginal investment projects profitable, which suggests that we should observe a negative relationship between energy price and the size of the capital stock. However, the capital stock is mostly inherited from the past at any point in time so we can expect it to only slowly adjust to a changing energy price. We can use a simple 'partial adjustment' model to capture this slow adjustment:[15]

$$\mathrm{In}C_t^{*}w + f\,(\mathrm{In}P_t, \mathrm{In}P_{t-1\ldots}\mathrm{In}P_{t-n}) + u \tag{5}$$

Where C_t^{*} is the capital stock in a stationary state.

of two connected diffusion coefficients. Thus, it is possible for GDP to grow at a faster rate than these inputs.

[14]Foster and Wild (1999b) provide evidence suggesting that the errors in an innovation diffusion growth model should not be strictly random.

[15]This formulation is similar to the 'capital stock adjustment principle' (Matthews 1959), not in a cyclical context where GDP is the main independent variable, but operative over the much longer time scale relevant to economic growth.

If there is partial adjustment and we add an undefined sequence of lagged dependent variables to capture the unstable behaviour of capital investment in the short term, we get:

$$\begin{aligned}\ln C_t - \ln C_{t-1} = z\left(\ln C_t^* - \ln C_{t-1}\right) + f\left(\left[\ln C_{t-1} - \ln C_{t-2}\right]\ldots\ldots\right.\\ \left.\left[\ln C_{t-n-1} - \ln C_{t-n}\right]\right) + u\end{aligned} \tag{6}$$

Where: z is between 0 and 1.

Substituting for C_t^* in Eq. 6, we get

$$\begin{aligned}\ln C_t - \ln C_{t-1} = zw + zf\left(\ln P_t, \ln P_{t-1\ldots\ldots} \ln P_{t-n}\right) - z\ln C_{t-1}\\ + f\left(\left[\ln C_{t-1} - \ln C_{t-2}\right]\ldots\ldots\left[\ln C_{t-n-1} - \ln C_{t-n}\right]\right) + u\end{aligned} \tag{7}$$

If the lagged dependent variables are short term in their impact, we would expect their estimated coefficients to sum to less than unity.

Equation 7 is a very sparse explanation of the capital stock. The only explanatory variable is the price of energy. Without it, there is no partial adjustment and the capital stock follows an oscillating path (with drift if there is a significant constant term). Up until the early 19th Century it is likely that the capital stock did, indeed, follow such a path. It was an economy dominated by labour and animal power, fuelled by food. The dramatic game shifter was fossil fuel deployment and the tendency for energy price to fall significantly.

Partial adjustment specifications commonly include the contemporaneous value of the driving variable. In Eq. 6, an unspecified set of lagged prices is included. This implies a double lagging effect. It may take a long time for an energy price to begin to affect the capital stock and a further period before the full effect is felt. Thus, a fall in energy price initiates plans to expand the capital stock, with the current capital stock only being used more intensively at the lower input price. In the face of uncertainty, such planning can last a long time before significant changes in the aggregate capital stock occur, as discussed by Dixit and Pindyck (1994). Furthermore, these commencements are not uniform, they can occur over a lengthy period. We can have no *a priori* view concerning such lags in a complex economic system, it is an empirical matter. However, if our co-evolutionary hypothesis is correct we should find that these price impacts have been large.

The speed at which energy price effects impact on the capital stock depends on the capacity of an economy to transition towards a different energy mix. In the 19th and early 20th century, it took a long time to transition away from all the physical capital associated with human and animal power, fuelled by food, towards physical capital driven by fossil fuels. All those horse drawn vehicles, ploughs, blacksmith's shops using wood and charcoal, water driven mills, etc., had sunk cost characteristics that kept them viable while fossil fuel prices were still high. Add to this habitual behaviour, legal arrangements tailored to old technologies and the action of vested interests and the outcome was a slow transition.

Accepting that ***K*** has not been fixed has important implications for how we interpret our AGDM modelling. If the capital stock grows faster than GDP, then Eq. 4 tells us that this will *raise* the rate of economic growth – so we should observe no tendency for GDP to go towards a limit. If they both grow at the same rate (at a constant ***lnY/nlnC*** ratio that is less than one) then we shall observe the net diffusion effect following an exponential growth path, reminiscent of the Solow (1957) 'residual growth' finding. If GDP grows faster than the capital stock, the ***lnY/nlnC*** ratio will rise and, when it is unity, the net diffusion effect will be zero. Growth can still occur but it will be 'quantitative' growth driven by growth in energy and/or labour inputs and likely to be temporary in a state of structural transition.

6 Results

The UK is a very good source of historical data for modelling economic growth. It is possible to obtain data from 1800 to 2010. However, even though it did not make much difference to the results, Eq. 4 was estimated over the period 1831–2010 for two reasons. First, the best and most consistent estimates of GDP, by Maddison (2008a), commence annually in 1830 – data before that year involves annual interpolations of estimated decadal data and, as such, they lack realistic annual variation.[16] Generally, historical economic data before 1830 tends to be very unreliable, interpolated from very fragmentary observations.[17] Second, historical investigation suggests that around 1830 is close to the take-off of the large scale commercial use of fossil fuels. The first public railway for steam locomotives commenced in 1825, from Stockton to Darlington. This signalled the beginning of the wide use of Trevithick's high pressure steam engine at commercial scale.

It is not possible to have a prior view of the lags involved in our model since we are dealing with a complex economic system so a simple 'general to specific' elimination method was used to obtain a parsimonious representation of the lag structures for each variable. Also, given that there is a significant literature on the direction of causation between energy and GDP, Granger causality tests were conducted.

The results are reported in Table 1. The hypothesis that causation runs from energy growth to GDP growth is strongly supported, in line with the literature reviewed by Stern (2011).[18]

---

[16]Irish independence shifted population and GDP time series for the UK in the Maddison data. The impact of this was checked in the modelling and found not to be a problem.

[17]There has been considerable controversy concerning the reliability of data used by 'cliometricians' prior to 1830. See, For example, Allen (2008).

[18]Note that the total energy consumption data used in the modeling was for England and Wales, rather than the UK. So there is an implicit assumption that there is a fixed ratio between the two.

Table 1 Granger causality tests

Sample: 1800–2010, Lags 6			
Null Hypothesis:	Obs.	F-Statistic	Probability
$lnE_t - lnE_{t-1}$ does not Granger Cause $lnY_t - lnY_{t-1}$	204	1.06611	0.38437
$lnY_t - lnY_{t-1}$ does not Granger Cause $lnE_t - lnE_{t-1}$		4.06387	0.00074

Table 2 OLS estimates of Eq. 4: 1831–2010

Dependent Variable:	$[\ln Y_t - \ln Y_{t-1}]$	
Variable	Coefficient	t-Statistic
Constant	0.16	4.66
e_t	0.15	4.94
e_{t-1}	0.14	4.20
e_{t-2}	0.06	2.05
e_{t-4}	−0.04	−1.57
h_t	0.67	9.07
h_{t-1}	−0.17	−2.22
$[lnY/lnC]_{t-1}$	−0.12	−4.27
R-squared	0.56	
Adj. R-squared	0.54	
Durbin-Watson	1.85	

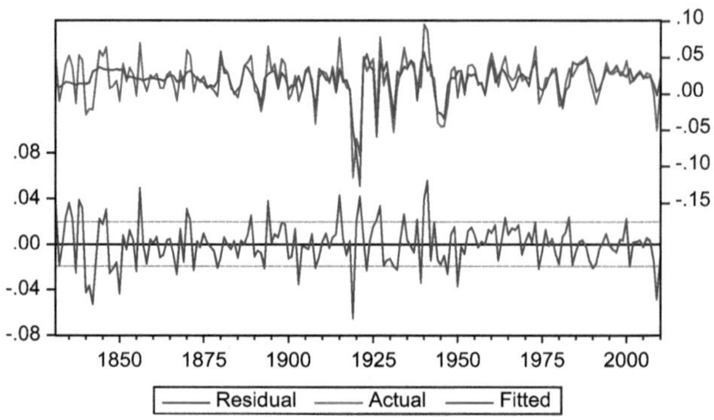

Fig. 9 Actual to predicted chart OLS Estimates of Eq. 4: 1831–2010

The general to specific result for Eq. 4 is reported in Table 2. It is a very strong result for a time series specification using first differenced data. Recursive least squares estimation reveals a strong tendency for the parameter estimates to be very stable as the sample size is increased. As early as 1925, all of the parameters become very stable. However, the actual-to-predicted graph in Fig. 9 shows that

Examination of Scottish and UK population statistics suggested that England and Wales, indeed, is a good proxy, especially when it is the rate of growth of total energy consumption that is the explanatory variable used in the modeling.

Table 3 OLS estimates of Eq. 4: 1831–2010 with historical impulse dummy variables

Dependent Variable:	$[lnY_t–lnY_{t-1}]$	
Variable	Coefficient	t-Statistic
Constant	0.13	4.34
e_t	0.14	5.31
e_{t-1}	0.11	3.86
e_{t-2}	0.04	1.68
e_{t-4}	−0.04	−2.12
h_t	0.61	9.45
h_{t-1}	−0.14	−2.10
$[lnY/lnC]_{t-1}$	−0.10	−3.84
DUM184042	−0.05	−4.51
DUM1856	0.05	2.95
DUM1919	−0.08	−4.33
DUM1941	0.05	3.14
DUM2009	−0.05	−2.90
R-squared	0.70	
Adjusted R-squared	0.66	
Durbin-Watson	1.91	

there were some significant outlier years. Historical investigation indicated that impulse dummies for 1840-42, 1856, 1919, 1941 and 2009 were all warranted.

The results reported in Table 3, using ‘history compatible’ impulse dummy variables, are quite similar to those without. The Recursive Least Squares modelling again reveals strong parameter stability.

Because of the interdependent nature of GDP and energy, the specification was re-estimated using Two Stage Least Squares (TSLS). The instrumental variables were chosen on the basis of a well-determined estimated logistic model of the growth in energy consumption which was found to be heavily dependent on the rate of population growth (***gpop***), as well as GDP growth. All significant lags, identified using ‘general to specific’ elimination of variables, were included, plus the level of energy consumption lagged one year, which was significant and negatively signed, supporting the hypothesis that a logistic limit on energy consumption growth was present.[19] As can be seen in Table 4, accounting for the potential endogeneity of the growth in energy consumption does not change the result very much. The cumulative elasticity estimate on energy consumption growth falls from about 0.25 to 0.23.

It is noticeable in the actual-to-predicted plots in Fig. 9 that the fit becomes tighter around 1880, which is about the time when the energy to GDP ratio stopped rising and began its secular fall (see Fig. 6). So it seemed sensible to re-estimate to model

[19]Instrument List: e_{t-1}, e_{t-2}, e_{t-4}, h_{t-1}, h_{t-1}, ***DUM*** **184042**, ***DUM*** **1856**, ***DUM*** **1919**, ***DUM*** **1941**, ***DUM*** **2009**, $gpop_t$, $gpop_{t-1}$, $gpop_{t-2}$, $gpop_{t-5}$, $gpop_{t-6}$, $gpop_{t-7}$, E_{t-1}

Table 4 TSLS estimates of Eq. 4: 1831–2010[20] with historical impulse dummy variables

Dependent Variable:	$[lnY_t - lnY_{t-1}]$	
Variable	Coefficient	t-Statistic
Constant	0.13	4.21
e_t	0.13	3.44
e_{t-1}	0.11	3.33
e_{t-2}	0.04	1.57
e_{t-4}	−0.05	−2.14
h_t	0.62	8.96
h_{t-1}	−0.14	−2.05
$[lnY/lnC]_{t-1}$	−0.09	−3.70
*DUM*1840–42	−0.05	−4.50
*DUM*1856	0.05	2.96
*DUM*1919	−0.8	−4.33
*DUM*1941	0.05	3.12
*DUM*2009	−0.05	−2.91
R-squared	0.69	
Adjusted R-squared	0.66	
Durbin-Watson stat	1.91	

from 1880 on to check its stability. The results in Table 5 are similar to those using the full sample. Again, the Recursive Least Squares results indicate strong parameter stability.

The final test conducted was to estimate the model over the more recent post World War Two period, when GDP growth was at its highest. Being a much smaller sample, the expectation was that the previously estimated lag structure would be less well-defined and that is what was found.

Once again, the results in Table 6 using this recent sample are remarkably similar to those using the full sample. Parameter stability remains very strong and the fit is excellent (Fig. 10).

So, overall, very strong support has been found for the super-radical innovation diffusion hypothesis concerning economic growth in the UK, as specified in Eq. 4. Coefficient estimates were obtained by summing the coefficients on the contemporaneous and each significant lagged variable in all three sample periods.

It is clear from Table 7 that we are dealing with a highly stable model in which the estimated coefficients are all very significant and correctly signed.[20] The average coefficient on energy consumption growth is 0.26 and that on labour hours growth 0.49. Although the former estimated coefficient is smaller, it contributed more to

[20]It should be borne in mind that the presence of measurement error in explanatory variables biases estimated coefficients downwards. This is likely to be the case when using long series of annual data. However, it is not possible to assess the magnitude of such bias except to note that the observed stability of estimated coefficients in different sample periods suggest that such bias is likely to be small.

Table 5 OLS estimates of Eq. 4: 1880–2010 with historical impulse dummy variables

Dependent Variable:	$[lnY_t - lnY_{t-1}]$	
Variable	Coefficient	t-Statistic
Constant	0.16	4.50
e_t	0.13	5.25
e_{t-1}	0.11	3.73
e_{t-2}	0.03	1.50
e_{t-4}	−0.04	−2.07
h_t	0.61	10.00
h_{t-1}	−0.13	−1.98
$[lnY/lnC]_{t-1}$	−0.12	−4.05
*DUM*1919	−0.09	−4.56
*DUM*1941	0.05	3.34
*DUM*2009	−0.05	−3.22
R-squared	0.76	
Adjusted R-squared	0.74	
Durbin Watson	1.94	

Table 6 OLS estimates of Eq. 4: 1947–2010

Dependent Variable:	$[lnY_t - lnY_{t-1}]$	
Variable	Coefficient	t-Statistic
Constant	0.16	2.55
e_t	0.20	3.08
e_{t-1}	0.11	1.77
h_t	0.63	6.01
h_{t-1}	−0.20	−2.07
$[lnY/lnC]_{t-1}$	−0.12	−2.23
*DUM*2009	−0.05	−3.51
R-squared	0.6	
Adj. R-squared	0.58	
Durbin-Watson	1.88	

GDP growth than the latter which was related more to fluctuations in GDP growth. The sum of the two estimated coefficients is 0.73 so no support has been provided for the existence of a Cobb Douglas production function. There are returns to scale, or more accurately in this context, returns to increasing work input, but they are diminishing. The existence of an innovation diffusion process is supported with a strongly significant negative sign on the $[lnY/lnC]_{t-1}$ estimated coefficient (a/n). When n was derived, using the estimate of a in Table 7, it was also found to be very stable at an average of 1.34 across the samples.

Although there is strong support for the existence of a Gompertz diffusion process, we do not observe a sigmoid curve for GDP. In Fig. 11, the ratio of GDP to K, i.e., ln $Y/nlnC$, is plotted over the 1800–2010 period for $n = 1.34$. It is clear that K rose only modestly relative to GDP up to the 2nd World War but it has risen faster

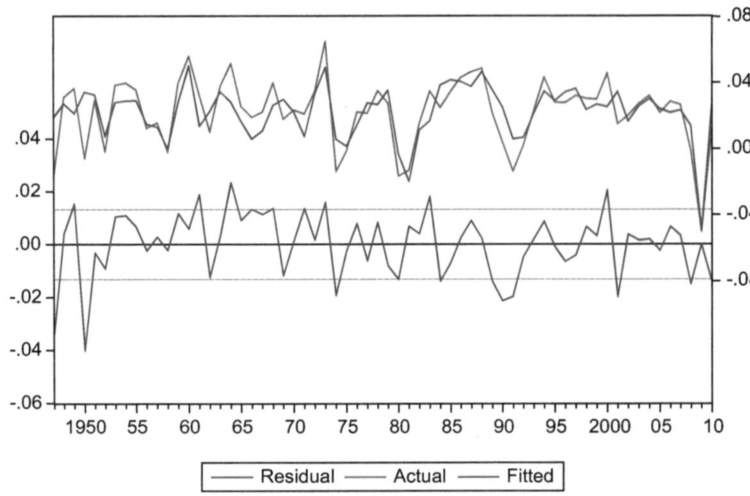

Fig. 10 Actual to predicted chart OLS Eq. 4: 1947–2008

Table 7 Cumulated coefficient estimates in three samples

Coefficient	1831–2010	1880–2010	1947–2010
a	0.13	0.16	0.16
b	0.25	0.23	0.31
g	0.47	0.49	0.51
a/n	−0.10	−0.12	−0.12
n	1.37	1.33	1.32

since then in an era dominated by oil and the specialization of coal in electricity generation.

We can see that, prior to 1840, the ***lnY*** to ***lnK*** ratio was unity which indicates that the previous innovation diffusion process, sometimes referred to as the 'first industrial revolution,' associated with a capital stock largely driven by solar and organic sources of energy, had come to an end. From 1840 on, the dramatic transition to the fossil fuel driven economy had commenced and we observe the ratio falling along an oscillating path, providing a boost to economic growth with the largest temporary reversals occurring during the two world wars. The sharp reduction in the post-World War Two era came to an end after the energy shocks of the 1970s, but the ratio, being about 14 % below unity, still made a significant positive contribution to economic growth via the net diffusion effect in 2010. A steady ratio, at any level less than unity, however, implies that the net diffusion effect is approximately exponential and that was the case in the UK for the three decades up to 2010.

Prior to the World War Two, the ***K*** limit was only about 7 % above the prevailing level of GDP, on average. This is the niche made available for GDP growth by the prevailing capital stock when used in all manner of innovative

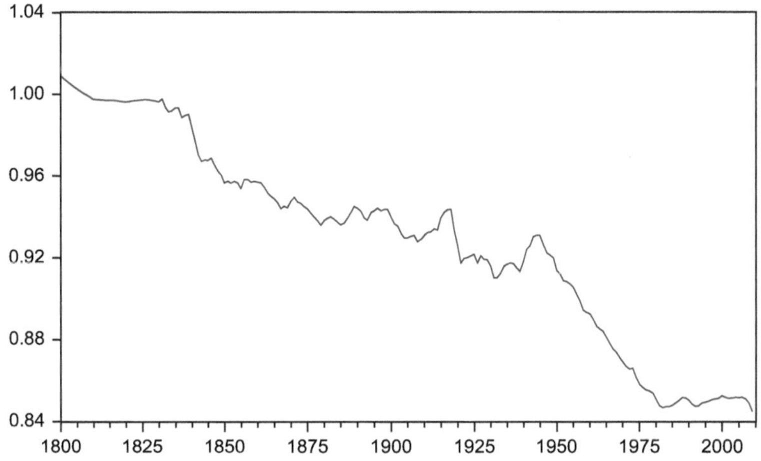

Fig. 11 The estimated ratio ***of lnY*** to ***lnK***

projects. With a ***K*** limit at 14 % higher than the prevailing level of GDP in 2010, the UK, a mature, post-industrial economy, thus, still seemed to have significant growth potential based upon its past history, even without a further increase in the size of its net capital stock. The massive shift to service sector activity has allowed ***K*** to run well ahead of GDP. This has been particularly marked in the era of computers and associated innovations in data storage and communication. From a longer term perspective, the UK economy seems to be increasing knowledge at a fast enough rate to not require further increases in energy consumption. This is what happened with the other core flow in the productive process, labour time, in the early 20th Century. This, of course, means that economic growth is much more strongly dependent on growth in the application of knowledge than it was a century ago. Whether this situation can be sustained depends on future movements in the net capital stock which is still largely driven by electricity and distillates produced from fossil fuels.

It has been argued that economic growth has been a result of the large scale exploitation of fossil fuels and that this was due to the availability of energy that was much cheaper per joule than in the past, making previously uneconomic capital good projects viable. This hypothesis, captured in Eq. 7, was tested using 135 years of data.[21] The results reported in Table 8 confirm the hypothesis that there is strong inertia in the capital stock, but that it is not a random walk, and that there is a strong negative impact of energy prices. As expected, this impact operates with a

[21]Energy prices are sourced from Fouquet (2011). It is inadvisable to go further back in history than 1850 because earlier estimates of energy prices, based upon very fragmentary, infrequent and localized data, are notoriously unreliable.

Table 8 OLS Results for Eq. 7: 1875–2009

Dependent Variable:	$lnC_t - lnC_{t-1}$	
Variable	Coefficient	t-Statistic
Constant	0.436	5.30
lnC_{t-1}	−0.019	−5.20
lnP_{t-15}	−0.009	−2.57
lnP_{t-19}	−0.014	−3.56
lnP_{t-22}	−0.011	−2.73
$lnC_{t-1}lnC_{t-2}$	1.07	13.45
$lnC_{t-2} - lnC_{t-3}$	−0.30	−3.75
$lnC_{t-5} - lnC_{t-6}$	−0.27	−3.31
$lnC_{t-6} - lnC_{t-7}$	0.21	2.73
R-squared	0.87	
Adjusted R-squared	0.87	
Durbin-Watson	1.84	
Breusch-Godfrey Serial Correlation LM Test:		
F-statistic 1.83	Prob. F(2,126)	0.16
Obs*R-squared 3.87	Prob. Chi-Square(2)	0.14

very long lag. Only after 15 years is there a statistically significant effect on the capital stock and this effect continues for another 7 years. The cumulative long term price elasticity is found to be high, at -1.8. So these findings suggest that movements in energy prices have been of key importance in determining long term economic growth possibilities in the UK over the past one and a half centuries. What are the future implications of this evidence concerning the impact of energy prices? The International Energy Agency has predicted that the real price of electricity globally is likely to rise by about 15 % over the next decade. It is likely that petrol and diesel will rise by more. If we take 15 % as a conservative estimate of the overall energy price rise to industrial consumers, and this rise is sustained, our model predicts that the capital stock, at the prevailing state of technology, would eventually decline by over 25 % in the UK case. This decline would not be sudden, taking 15 years to have a significant effect which would be spread over another 7 years. However, the ultimate impact of the lower ***K***-limit on GDP growth would be large. Offsetting this would require a major transition to cheaper energy sources and/or radical breakthroughs in the efficiency of energy use, i.e., raising ***K*** for any given energy-using net capital stock. We know that this has already been happening but it would have to accelerate if energy prices rise significantly and permanently. In many ways, this is a race against time because it can take decades to develop technologies that can be used to drive radical innovation in capital goods and associated methods of using them.

7 Conclusion

In this article, a hypothesis has been offered and tested, namely, that the explosive growth that has been experienced since the early/mid-19th Century was due to the large scale exploitation and use of fossil fuels via the growth of knowledge embedded in a capital stock designed for this purpose. Thus, the energy-driven capital stock is viewed as the key repository of embedded knowledge that made high economic growth possible. Strong empirical support for this co-evolutionary hypothesis has been found in a very well-determined and stable innovation diffusion explanation of economic growth in the case of the UK. The results show that the use of new knowledge has led to very significant economies in the use of labour time and, in recent decades, the same has been occurring with energy consumption. GDP in the UK continues to have a long term growth rate that is approximately exponential, but inputs of labour time, and now energy, have stabilized. Evidence was also found that movements in energy prices have a large impact upon the size of the capital stock, operative with a long delay.

These findings pose a serious dilemma for the UK and, by implication, for the World as a whole. First of all, future GDP growth possibilities for the UK seem to be available. But these findings may be misleading. In the modelling, no account has been taken of the negative externalities associated with economic growth – pollution, congestion, environmental destruction, etc. These are all visibly impacting on the UK, as well as other countries. So it may well be that, even though GDP grows strongly, a rapidly increasing proportion of this growth, and the capital stock utilized, will be devoted to measures that combat such negative externalities. Thus, 'externality corrected' GDP per capita could fall, even when GDP is rising. Dyke (1990) referred to this as a state where an 'entropy debt' is being paid in order for an economic system to survive. Secondly, if real energy prices are, indeed, shifting up to a higher level, because of the higher costs of delivering more difficult to access fossil fuels, combined with higher costs to access alternative energy sources that are in the early stage of development, then, with a lag of over a decade, there will be a slowly rising but strongly negative impact upon the size of the capital stock. If the capital stock ceases to grow, or even falls, then growth will tend towards a zero limit, in line with our super-radical innovation diffusion curve findings.

Already, a different kind of economy is taking shape, as happened in the early 20th Century, but it is not clear what the exact nature of this transition is and what its consequences will be. When the knowledge gradient rises so fast that it overwhelms the natural tendency for the growth of a system to tend to a fixed capacity limit, there is a tendency for such a system to 'stall' just as an aeroplane does when it climbs too steeply after take-off. We see this in, for example, the cumulative growth of interdependent, optimistic beliefs in a stock market bubble. Such bubbles don't burst at a diffusion limit but do so when price growth is very high and the realization suddenly dawns that the cumulated 'knowledge' embedded in stock prices is inconsistent with the state of the real economy. In the case of economic growth, the potential inconsistency is with the capacity of the natural environment to endure ever higher levels of GDP using a larger and larger stock of capital goods. In the past, some environmental disasters have occurred because, environmental exploitation, such as agriculture, was not managed in a way that allowed it to grow steadily to a sustainable limit. Instead, growth was too rapid and, thus, the system became unable to cope with exogenous shocks when they came along. The 'Dustbowl' experience in the US in the interwar years is a good example, as are some of the cases discussed in Tainter (1988).

So the picture that has been provided of British economic growth is one of spectacular past success, continuing growth prospects, but with transitional dangers looming on the horizon. To what extent can we see parallels in the global economy? As was noted, this is not easy to assess because all countries are in different cultural, social, political and institutional circumstances.[22] However, based upon Angus Maddison's data, Global GDP seems to have taken off about half a century after the UK with the same explosive tendency (Maddison 2008b). Undoubtedly, the co-evolutionary process of fossil fuel exploitation and the growth of embedded knowledge in the capital stock has also been the key driver of global growth. But there are early indications that cheaply available sources of oil and coal globally are beginning to run out.

Nonetheless, the super-radical innovation diffusion process may not have run its full course yet. Globally, the discovery and exploitation of large stores of unconventional natural gas in shale and coal seams is beginning to compensate for diminishing stocks of cheap oil and may mitigate the tendency for energy prices to rise. So the total energy consumption trajectory may well have a third sub-logistic fossil segment that keeps economic growth going at a brisk pace. However, the exploitation of these new fossil fuel reserves will do little to diminish the threat that cumulating negative externalities pose in a World that seems to be heading towards nine billion people by 2040. Indeed, the provision of new supplies of unconventional gas may well delay an orderly transition to renewable energy at low cost with possibly severe socio-political and environmental consequences. From a thermodynamic perspective, the problem lies, not with accessing new sources of energy, but with the availability of entropy sinks. However, since all this lies in the domain of radical uncertainty and, thus, beyond the compass of simple modelling exercises using historical data, we can only speculate about such possibilities and the responses that different countries might make to the large structural changes that lie ahead.

[22]See Gordon (2012) for discussion, using a different perspective, of the prospects of future growth in what is currently the World's leading economy, the United States.

8 Sources

C Total UK capital stock (million at 1990 prices), from Madsen et al. (2010) with updates.

E Total UK energy index of consumption in petajoules, not including food. From Warde, P., *Energy consumption in England and Wales, 1560-2000*, CNR, (2007) with updates from the UK National Statistical Office

H Total hours worked in UK (millions). From Madsen et al. (2010) with updates

P Average UK price of energy (£(in 2000 prices) per toe. From Fouquet (2008, 2011) with updates

POP UK Population ('000) From Maddison (2008a) with updates

Y UK Real GDP (million 1990 International Geary-Khamis dollars). From Maddison (2008a), with updates.

References

Acemoglu D, Robinson J (2012) Why nations fail: the origins of power, prosperity, and poverty. Crown Publishers, New York

Aghion P, Howitt P (1998) Endogenous growth theory. Mass, MIT Press, Cambridge

Allen RC (2008) A review of Gregory Clark's a farewell to alms: a brief economic history of the world. J Econ Lit 46(4):946–973

Allen RC (2009) The british industrial revolution in global perspective. Cambridge University Press, Cambridge

Arrow KJ (1962) The economic implications of learning by doing. Rev Econ Stud 29(3):155–173

Arthur WB (1994) Increasing returns and path dependence in the economy. University of Michigan Press, Ann Arbor

Ayres RU, Warr B (2009) The economic growth engine: how energy and work drive material prosperity. Edward Elgar, Cheltenham

Baumol WJ (2002) The free market innovation machine: analyzing the growth miracle of capitalism. Princeton University Press, Princeton

Boretos GP (2009) The future of the global economy. Technol Forecast Soc Chang 76(2009):316–326

Brown JH, Burnside WR, Davidson AD, DeLong JP, Dunn WC et al. (2011) Energetic limits to economic growth. BioScience 61:19–26

Chapman SD (1970) Fixed capital formation in the british cotton industry, 1770–1815. Econ Hist Rev 23(2):235–266

Crafts N (2005) The first industrial revolution: resolving the slow growth/rapid industrialization paradox. J Eur Econ Assoc 3(2–3):525–534

Davidson JEH, Hendry DF, Srba F, Yeo S (1978) Econometric modelling of the aggregate time series relationship between consumers' expenditure and income in the UK. Econ J 88:661–92

Deane P (1969) The first industrial revolution. Cambridge University Press, Cambridge

Denison EF (1974) Accounting for United States economic growth 1929-1969. The Brookings Institution, Washington D.C

Diamond J (2005) Collapse: how societies choose to fail or succeed. Viking Books, New York

Dixit AK, Pindyck RS (1994) Investment under uncertainty. Princeton University Press, Princeton

Dopfer K (1986) The histonomic approach to economics: beyond pure theory and pure experience. J Econ Issues XX(4):989–1010
Dopfer K (2006) The evolutionary foundations of economics. Cambridge University Press, Cambridge
Dyke C (1990) Cities as dissipative structures. In: Weber B, Depew DJ, Smith JD (eds) Entropy, information, and evolution: new perspectives on physical and biological evolution. Mass.: MIT Press, Cambridge, pp 162–185
Field AJ (2011) A great leap forward: 1930s depression and U.S. economic growth. Yale University Press, New Haven
Fine B (2000) Endogenous growth theory: a critical assessment. Camb J Econ 24(2):245–265
Foster J (1987) Evolutionary macroeconomics. Unwin Hyman, London (Reproduced in the Routledge Revivals Series, 2011)
Foster J (2005) From simplistic to complex adaptive systems in economics. Camb J Econ 29: 873–892
Foster J (2011a) Evolutionary macroeconomics: a research agenda. J Evol Econ Springer 21(1): 5–28
Foster J (2011b) Energy, aesthetics and knowledge in complex economic systems. J Econ Behav Organ 80(1):88–100
Foster J, Metcalfe JS (2012) Economic emergence: an evolutionary economic perspective. J Econ Behav Organ Elsevier 82(2):420–432
Foster J, Wild P (1999a) Econometric modelling in the presence of evolutionary change. Camb J Econ 23:749–770
Foster J, Wild P (1999b) Detecting self-organisational change in economic processes exhibiting logistic growth. J Evol Econ 9:109–133
Fouquet R (2008) Heat power and light. Edward Elgar, Cheltenham
Fouquet R (2011) Divergences in long run trends in the prices of energy and energy services. Rev Environ Econ Policy 5(2):196–218
Freeman C, Louca F (2002) As time goes by: from the industrial revolutions to the information revolution. Oxford University Press, Oxford
Galor O, Michalopoulos S (2012) Evolution and the growth process: natural selection of entrepreneurial traits. J Econ Theory 147(2):756–777
Georgescu-Roegen N (1971) The entropy law and the economic process. Harvard University Press, Boston
Gordon RJ (2012) Is US growth over? Faltering innovation confronts the six headwinds. NBER Working Paper No. 18315, http://www.nber.org/papers/w18315
Harley CK (1982) British industrialization before 1841: evidence of slower growth during the industrial revolution. J Econ Hist 42(2):267–289
Harris JR (1967) The employment of steam power in the Eigtheenth Century. History 52(175):133–148
Howitt P, Aghion P (1998) Capital accumulation and innovation as complementary factors in long-run growth. J Econ Growth 3:111–130
Jevons WS (1866) The coal question. Macmillan, London
Landes DS (1998) The wealth and poverty of nations: why are some so rich and others so poor? W.W. Norton, New York
Maddison A (2008a) Statistics on world population, GDP and per capita GDP, 1–2006 AD. http://www.ggdc.net/maddison/
Maddison A (2008b) The west and the rest in the world economy: 1000–2030, Maddisonian and Malthusian interpretations. World Econ 9(4)
Madsen JB, Ang JB, Banerjee R (2010) Four centuries of British economic growth: the roles of technology and population. J Econ Growth 15:263–290
Matthews RCO (1959) The trade cycle. James Nisbet Ltd at, Cambridge University Press, Cambridge
Metcalfe JS (2003) Industrial growth and the theory of retardation. precursors of an adaptive evolutionary theory of economic change. Revue économique, Presses de Sciences-Po 54(2):407–431

McCloskey D (2010) Bourgeois dignity: why economics can't explain the modern world. University of Chicago Press
Miranda LCM, Lima CAS (2011) On the forecasting of the challenging world future scenarios. Technol Forecast Soc Chang 78:1445–1470
Mokyr J (2002) The gifts of athena: historical origins of the knowledge economy. Princeton University press, Princeton
Nelson R, Winter S (1982) An evolutionary theory of economic change. Mass.: Belknap Press of Harvard University Press, Cambridge
Nunn N, Qian N (2011) The Potato's contribution to population and urbanization: evidence from a historical experiment. Q J Econ 126:593–650
Perez (2002) Technological revolutions and financial capital. Edward Elgar, Cheltenham
Pittel K, Rübbelke D (2010) Energy supply and the sustainability of endogenous growth BC3 Working Paper Series (No.10, July) Basque Centre for Climate Change
Schneider ED, Kay JJ (1994) Life as a manifestation of the second law of thermodynamics. Math Comput Model 19:25–48
Schneider ED, Sagan D (2005) Into the cool: energy flow, thermodynamics and life. University of Chicago press, Chicago
Smil V (2008) Energy in nature and society: general energetics of complex systems. MIT Press
Solow RM (1957) Technical change and the aggregate production function. Rev Econ Stat 39(3):312–320
Solow RM (2007) The last 50 years in growth theory and the next 10. Oxford review of economic policy, vol 23(1) Oxford University Press, pp 3–14, Spring
Stern DI (2011) The role of energy in economic growth in ecological economic reviews. Robert Costanza, Karin Limburg & Ida Kubiszewski, Eds. Ann. N.Y. Acad. Sci. 1219:26–51
Stern DI, Kander A (2012) The role of energy in the industrial revolution and modern economic growth. Energy J 33(3):125–152
Tainter JA (1988) The collapse of complex societies. Cambridge University Press, Cambridge
Wrigley EA (2010) Energy and the english industrial revolution. Cambridge University Press, Cambridge, UK

Metabolic Growth Theory: Market-Share Competition, Learning Uncertainty, and Technology Wavelets

Ping Chen

Abstract Both exogenous and endogenous growth theories in neoclassical economics ignore the resource constraints and wavelike patterns in technology development. The logistic growth and species competition model in population dynamics provides an evolutionary framework of economic growth driven by technology wavelets in market-share competition. Learning by doing and knowledge accumulation ignores the interruptive nature of technology advancement. Creative destruction can be understood by using knowledge metabolism. Policies and institutions co-evolve during different stages of technology life cycles. Division of labor is limited by the market extent, numbers of resources, and environment fluctuations. There is a trade-off between the stability and complexity of an ecological-industrial system. Diversified patterns in development strategy are shaped by culture and environment when facing learning uncertainty. The Western mode of division of labor is characterized by labor-saving and resource-intensive technology, while the Asian and Chinese modes feature resource-saving and labor-intensive technology. Nonlinear population dynamics provides a unified evolutionary theory from Smith, Malthus, to Schumpeter in economic growth and technology development.

1 Introduction

There are two conflicting views of technology development. Neoclassical growth theories consider technology progress as a smooth trajectory with perfect foresight, which can be described by log-linear models in the form of Cobb-Douglas function (Solow 1957; Romer 1986; Aghion and Howitt 1998; Dasgupta 2010; Kurz 2012). Economic historians recognize wavelike patterns and revolutionary changes in

P. Chen (✉)
Center for New Political Economy, Fudan University, Shanghai, China

National School of Development, Peking University, Beijing, China
e-mail: pchen@nsd.pku.edu.cn

A. Pyka, J. Foster (eds.), *The Evolution of Economic and Innovation Systems*, Economic Complexity and Evolution, DOI 10.1007/978-3-319-13299-0_3
Modified and extended version from Journal of Evolutionary Economics 24(2), Springer 2014.

industrial economies (Schumpeter 1939; Toffler 1980; Ayres 1989; Rostow 1990; Piketty 2014). We will develop the second approach in this article by introducing nonlinear population dynamics into market-share competition.

The equilibrium perspective prescribes a uni-directional causality to convergence (exogenous growth theory in capital accumulation) or divergence (endogenous growth theory in knowledge accumulation) in economic growth. However, biological evolution and industrial revolution reveals a clear pattern of dynamic metabolism and complex patterns in a two-way evolution towards convergence and/or divergence in different periods and regions.

Historically, it was Malthus, an economist, whose theory of resource constrain for population growth inspired Darwin's theory of biological evolution (Malthus 1798, 2008; Darwin 1859). The logistic model and the prey–predator model were introduced in modeling business cycles (Goodwin 1967; Samuelson 1971; Day 1982). We will consider a new factor of culture strategy when facing learning uncertainty, which is useful in understanding different modes of division of labor in historical development (Chen 1987).

In this article, we will raise two basic issues in growth theory.

First, what is the nature of knowledge? Endogenous growth theory offers a static picture of knowledge accumulation through learning by doing (Arrow 1962). This theory implies an increasing polarization between rich (early-movers) and poor (late-comers). This picture is not compatible with world history, with the rise and fall of nations and civilizations.

Second, how can one understand the roots of global warming and the ecological crisis? The neoclassical Cobb-Douglas production function in AK model implies unlimited resources. This framework cannot address the contemporary issues of the ecological crisis and global warming.

It is known that industrial economies are driven by sequences of new technologies, such as coal, petroleum, electricity and nuclear energy, which exploit new resources. Wavelike technology development can be described by population dynamics with resource constraints, notably the S-shaped logistic curve and the Lotka-Volterra model for species competition (Pianka 1983; Nicolis and Prigogine 1977). Schumpeter's long waves and creative destruction can be described by metabolic movements of logistic wavelets. Culture plays a strategic role when facing learning uncertainty. The Western mode of the division of labor is characterized by labor-saving and resource-intensive technology, while the Chinese mode is mainly driven by resource-saving but labor-intensive technology.

This article is organized by the following: Section 2 discusses some basic facts on resource disparity and uneven growth in world history that raises challenges to growth theory. Section 3 develops the logistic model of growth and technology competition under resource constraints (Chen 1987). The implications of nonlinear solutions, including the S-shaped curve and the logistic wavelet, are discussed from the perspective of evolutionary dynamics. Section 4 introduces the cultural factor in learning strategy when facing a new but uncertain resource or market.

The division of labor is limited by the market extent, number of resources, and environmental fluctuations. There is a trade-off between stability and diversity. Section 4.2 discusses historical puzzles in civilization bifurcation that can be explained by our approach (Chen 2008, 2010). Section 5 addresses basic issues in economic methodology. Section 6 concludes with a comparison between the equilibrium and evolutionary perspectives in growth theory.

2 Uneven Economic Growth and Limits of Neoclassical Growth Theories

The Solow model of exogenous growth predicted a convergence trend in economic growth based on the assumption of constant returns to scale (1957) while the Romer model of endogenous growth claimed a divergence trend based on increasing returns to scale in knowledge accumulation (Romer 1986; Arrow 1962; Lucas 1988). However, observed patterns in the world economy are more complex than the predictions of neoclassical growth models (see Tables 1 and 2).

We can see that the U.S. had the highest growth rate between 1913 and 1950, Japan from 1950 to 1970, and China from 1970 to 2010. We did not see a rigid

Table 1 Historical statistics (1913–2001)

Annual average compound rate of GDP growth							
	WEuro	EEuro	Asia	US	Japan	fUSSR	China
1913–1950	1.19	0.86	0.82	*2.84*	**2.21**	2.15	−0.02
1950–1973	4.79	4.86	**5.17**	3.93	*9.29*	4.84	5.02
1973–2001	2.21	1.01	**5.41**	2.94	2.71	−0.42	*6.72*

Data source: Maddison (2007). WEuro means western Europe; EEuro as eastern Europe, fUSSR as the former Soviet Union. Here, Asia data excluded Japan
Bold numbers indicate the largest figure in the row

Table 2 Uneven growth in globalization (Annual average growth rate of Real GDP per decade)

Period	1970s	1980s	1990s	2000s
China	*6.2*	*9.3*	*10.4*	*10.5*
Japan	3.8	4.6	1.2	0.7
US	3.2	3.2	3.4	1.6
Germany	2.9	2.3	1.9	0.9
East Asia	4.4	**5.5**	3.3	4.0
L. America	**6.1**	1.5	3.2	3.1
E. Europe	4.4	2.3	−2.0	**4.3**
W. Europe	3.1	2.3	2.1	1.1
Australia & New Zealand	2.8	2.9	**3.6**	3.0
World	3.8	3.1	2.8	2.5

Data source: United Nations Statistics
Bold numbers indicate the largest figure in the row

Table 3 Cross country comparison in 1993 (Maddison 1998)

Region	Arable Land (%)	Population (millions)	Arable land per capita (ha)
China	10	1,178	**0.08**
Europa	28	507	0.26
US	19	239	0.73
fUSSR	10	203	0.79
Japan	12	125	**0.04**
India	52	899	0.19
Brazil	6	159	0.31
Australia	6	18	*2.62*
Canada	5	28	1.58

Here, arable land is measured by percentage of the total area

convergent or divergent trend for each region or from a cross-country comparison. Instead, we see changing trends with the rise and fall of nations.

It is known that the rise of the West was driven by resource expansion under colonialism (Pomeranz 2000). In terms of per capita arable land, East Asia including Japan and China has much less arable land compared to Western countries (Table 3).

There is a striking difference between Asia's small grain farms and large western farms in corn and cattle agri-business. Obviously, an individualist culture is deeply rooted in a resource-intensive and labor-saving technology, while a collectivist culture is associated with resource-scarce and a population-dense environment. The role of culture and resource in the modernization catch-up game will be discussed in Sect. 4.2. Our observation on patterns in resource and population started from a cross-country comparison, which can be extended to any industrial analysis if relevant data are available.

3 Logistic Model of Limited Growth and Species Competition

The Cobb-Douglas production function in neoclassical economics can be transformed into a log-linear function, which means unlimited growth without resource limits or market extents. The studies of resource limits need the development of nonlinear dynamics.

3.1 Limited and Unlimited Growth in Economic Dynamics

Adam Smith clearly stated in his third chapter of the Wealth of Nations that the division of labor is limited by the market extent (Smith 1776). This statement was called the Smith Theorem by George Stigler (1951). Malthus further pointed out that population growth is limited by natural resources (Malthus 1798, 2008).

The Smith concept of "market extent" and the Malthus idea of "resource constraint" can be described by carrying capacity N* in the nonlinear logistic model of population growth. When applying the ecological model to economic growth, we need to change the name of corresponding variables. In the following discussion, we will put the original name in theoretical ecology into brackets after the economic variable, so that readers can clearly understand the original meaning and its economic meaning.

From the demand-side perspective, n is the number of buyers (population) and N* the market extent (population size), which is a function of income distribution. Here, the market extent is associated to population size with affordable income.

From the supply-side perspective, n is the output and N* the resource constraint, which is a function of existing technology and cost structure. For example, grain yield can be increased by the application of irrigation and fertilizer or new products like corn and potatoes historically.

The simplest model of limited growth is the logistic model with a quadratic function in evolutionary ecology (Pianka 1983):

$$\frac{dn}{dt} = f(n) = kn\left(N^* - n\right) \tag{1}$$

Here n is output (population), N^* is the resource limit (population size), k is output (population) growth rate.

The logistic model has a varying dynamic economy of scale:

$$\text{dynamic increasing return for } f' > 0 \textit{ when } 0 < n < \frac{N^*}{2} \tag{2a}$$

$$\text{dynamic diminishing return for } f' < 0 \textit{ when } \frac{N^*}{2} < n < N^* \tag{2b}$$

The logistic model is the simplest form of nonlinear dynamics. The reflection point may shift from the middle point, when *f(n)* is not a quadratic function.

In comparison, the AK model in neoclassical growth theory has fixed returns to scale without resource limits. Therefore, neoclassical firm theory is not capable of understanding changing economies of scale (Daly and Farley 2010).

The logistic model is also called the Verhulst equation in theoretical ecology (Pianka 1983). Its discrete-time version may produce the simplest chaos regime with only one variable. Deterministic chaos in discrete-time can be called "white chaos", since its frequency spectrum looks like white noise (May 1974; Day 1982; Chen 2010). Its continuous-time solution is a S-curve. The graphic patterns of unlimited (exponential) growth and limited (logistic) growth are shown in Fig. 1.

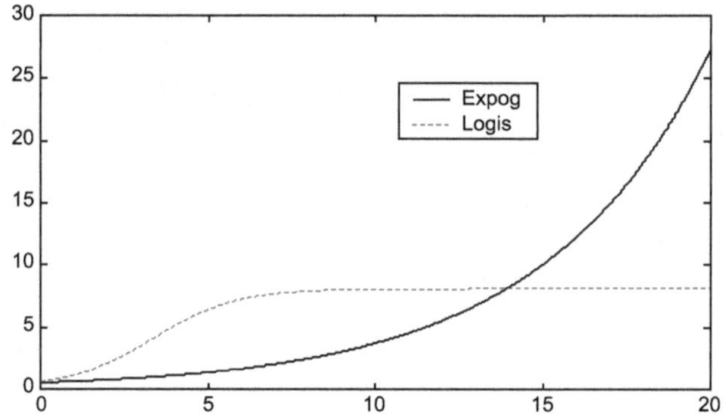

Fig. 1 Unlimited (*exponential*) vs. limited (*logistic*) growth

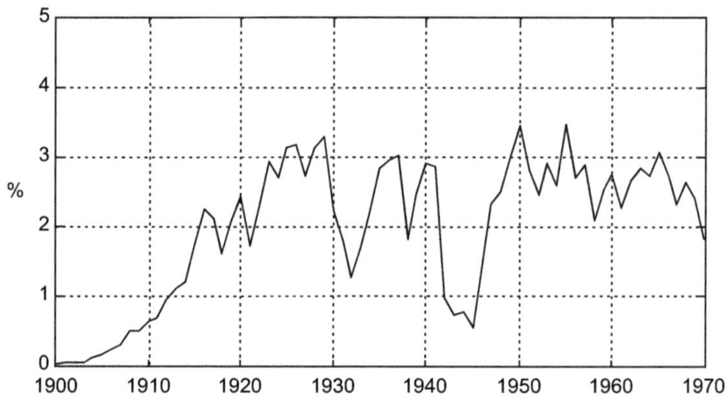

Fig. 2 The output percentage ratio to GDP in the U.S. automobile industry

When we adopt the logistic model in economic theory, our analytic unit is technology or industry. If the resource limit is arable land, our analytic unit can be a region or a state. In empirical analysis, the meaning of market extent or resource capacity depends on available data.

The logistic growth pattern can be clearly observed from sector industrial data, such as the output percentage ratio to GDP in the U.S. automobile industry in Fig. 2 (Chen 2010).

We can see that the U.S. auto industry took off between the 1900s and the 1920s, and reached the saturation stage before the 1930s. The S-shaped growth curve can be observed in firm and industrial growth in sector analysis.

3.2 Market-Share Competition Model in Open Economy

Now, we move from one technology to more technologies in a market-share competition. The simplest resource competition model is a two-species competition model or the Lotka-Volterra equation in theoretical biology (Pianka 1983).

$$\frac{dn_1}{dt} = k_1 n_1 (N_1 - n_1 - \beta\, n_2) - R_1 n_1 \tag{3a}$$

$$\frac{dn_2}{dt} = k_2 n_2 (N_2 - n_2 - \beta\, n_2) - R_2 n_2 \tag{3b}$$

Where n_1, n_2 are output (population) of technology or product (species) 1 and technology (species) 2; N_1 and N_2 their resource limit (carrying capacity); k_1 and k_2 their learning (population growth) rate; R_1 and R_2 their exit (death) rate; β is the competition (overlapping) coefficient in market-share (resource) competition $(0 \leq \beta \leq 1)$.

The equations can be simplified by introducing effective resource limits (carrying capacities)

$$C_i = N_i - \frac{R_i}{k_i} \tag{3c}$$

Here, we should emphasize the different perspective of technology development between neoclassical economics and evolutionary economics. General equilibrium models only consider features in a closed economy, such as the static model having fixed number of products with infinite life (Arrow and Debreu 1954), or dynamic model with random innovations (Aghion and Howitt 1992). In contrast, population dynamics mainly concerns an open economy, where new technology introduces new resource and new market. Therefore, nonlinear population dynamics is more realistic for industrial economy with interruptive technologies.

Our population dynamics describes a learning competition in facing a new (uncertain) resource. Here, population indicates the number of users of a specific technology. The entry and exit speed of the new technology is described by the learning and exit rates in the learning process. For mathematical simplicity, we put the learning rate at the quadratic term and the exit rate at the linear term. Therefore, the learning mechanism has a stronger impact than the exit mechanism in technology competition.

The meaning of the exit rate can be seen in Eq. (3c). Consider a case of agricultural development. If grain is the only food available for a population, then the exit rate for grain is $R_1 = 0$, and $C_1 = N_1$. However, if a new food, say, potatoes, are introduced, some portion of the population would switch from grain to potatoes, so that the exit rate $R_1 > 0$, and $C_1 < N_1$. The effective resource limit may be lower than the original land without competition.

The competition coefficient β measures the degree of competition. When $\beta = 0$, there is no competition between the two species. Both technologies may fully grow to reach their resource limits independently.

In neoclassical economics, relative price plays a central role in resource allocation. In an industrial economy, market-share plays a major role in shaping industrial structure. The competition coefficient can be estimated if market-share data is available in marketing research and industrial analysis.

Technology metabolism means the birth of new technology and the death of old technology. Technology competition may have two consequences: (1) old technology is replaced by new technology under condition (4a); or (2) old and new technologies co-exists under condition (4b).

$$\beta\left(N_2 - \frac{R_2}{k_2}\right) = \beta C_2 > C_1 = \left(N_1 - \frac{R_1}{k_1}\right) \tag{4a}$$

$$\beta < \frac{C_2}{C_1} < \frac{1}{\beta} \text{ Here } 0 < \beta < 1 \tag{4b}$$

Therefore, the new technology will wipe out the old technology if its resource limit is much higher than the old technology.

When two technologies co-exist, both the new and old technologies cannot fully utilize their resource potentials, since their equilibrium output is smaller than their resource limits (5a, 5b, 5c). The cost of creative destruction is the unrealized (excess) capacity.

$$n_1^* = \frac{C_1 - \beta C_2}{1 - \beta^2} < C_1 \tag{5a}$$

$$n_2^* = \frac{C_2 - \beta C_1}{1 - \beta^2} < C_2 \tag{5b}$$

$$\frac{1}{2}(C_1 + C_2) \le \left(n_1^* + n_2^*\right) = \frac{(C_1 + C_2)}{1 + \beta} \le (C_1 + C_2) \tag{5c}$$

For example, technology n_1 would reach full capacity of C_1 in absence of technology 2. After technology n_2 entered the market share competition, there are two possible outcomes for technology n_1: (1) Technology 1 is wiped out by technology 2, so that $n_1 = 0$ and $n_2 = C_2$. The cost of "creative destruction" is the total loss of old capacity C_1. This was the case when the handcraft textile industry was destroyed by machine industry in the early development stage. (2) Old and new technology coexist, so that both technologies have excess capacity: $(C_1 - n_1{}^*) > 0$ and $(C_2 - n_2{}^*) > 0$.

Here, species competition model sheds light on market-share competition. For example, if we have market-share data for major firms in computer industry, we may apply our model to marketing competition. If we have relevant data, we may also study arm race among nations.

Frank Knight made the distinction between predictable risk and unpredictable uncertainty (Knight 1921). Risk is often measured by variance in neoclassical econometrics. Here, we have two types of uncertainty: the arrival time of a new technology and the initial condition of a new technology. Therefore, there is no possibility for optimization or rational expectations in technology competition because of unpredictable uncertainty. Path dependence is the essential feature of technology development (David 1985; Arthur 1994).

Keynesian economics has no structural theory for "insufficient aggregate demand". Micro-foundations theory attributes macro fluctuations to household fluctuations in working hours, which is rejected by the Principle of Large Numbers (Lucas 1981; Chen 2002). Now we have a meso-foundation for macro growth cycles: the existence of excess capacity at the industrial level under technology metabolism. The observed costs in terms of excess capacity and related large unemployment are typical forms of dissipative energy or economic entropy (Georgescu-Roegen 1971).

3.3 Technology Life Cycle, Logistic Wavelets and Metabolic Growth

The concept of a product life cycle is widely used in economics and management literature (Vernon 1966; Modigliani 1976). We apply this concept to a technology life cycle. Traditionally, the life-cycle phenomenon can be described by a multi-period model in econometrics. Linear dynamical models, such as a harmonic wave with infinite life and a white noise model with a short life (Kydland 1995), are not proper for a life-cycle model, since a life cycle is a nonlinear phenomenon. The logistic wavelet with a finite life is a simple nonlinear representation for technology life cycles. Schumpeter's long waves and creative destruction can be described by a sequence of logistic wavelets in a technology competition model (Schumpeter 1934, 1939, 1950).

A numerical solution of Eq. (3) is shown in Fig. 3. Without competition, the growth path of technology (species) 1 would be a S-shaped logistic curve. However, the realized output of technology 1 resulting from competition with technology (species) 2 looks like an asymmetric bell curve. We call it the logistic wavelet, which is a result from the competition of new technology. The envelope of the aggregate output shows an uneven growth path that mimics the observed pattern of a time series from macroeconomic indexes. This scenario was first proposed by Peter Allen in Prigogine et al. (1977).

The wavelet representation can be applied in analyzing the lifecycle of products, firms, technologies, and nations (Eliasson 2005). The traditional life-cycle model in econometrics takes the form of discrete-time with linear dynamics (Browning and Crossley 2001), while the wavelet model is a continuous-time model in nonlinear

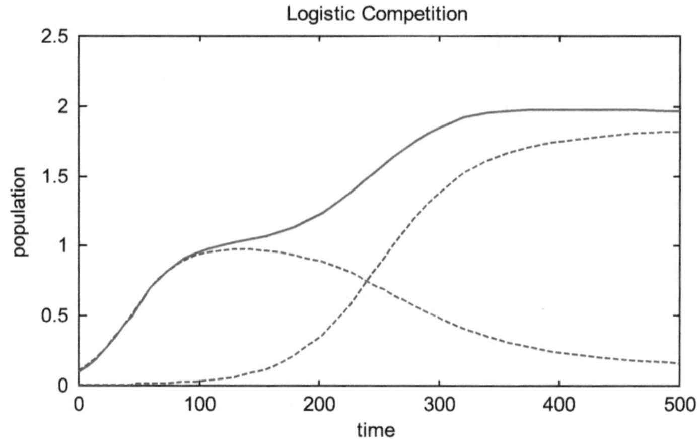

Fig. 3 Metabolic growth characterized by technology competition in Eq. (3). The old technology (*blue dashed line*) declines when new technology (*green dot and dash line*) emerges. The output envelope (*red solid line*) is the sum of their output of all technologies. Here, $\beta = 0.4$, $C_2/C_1 = 2$. The units here are arbitrary in computational simulation (colour figure online)

dynamics. The time scale of the logistic wavelet varies between product life cycles from several months to Kondratieff long waves over several decades.

The wavelet model of metabolic growth provides clear answer why capital accumulation has no infinite trend, since recurrent capital destruction along with obsolete industries (Piketty 2014).

In the real world, rise and fall of great nations not entirely depends on technology competition. For example, German took the lead in the second industrial revolution led by electric and chemical industry. However, British-American allies won the two world wars because of their dominance in navy power and resource share. This observation further supports our theory of market-share competition not only for economic competition, but also for military competition. In contrast, optimization approach in neoclassical economics produces a utopian market of self-centered optimization without competitors.

3.4 Capital and Institution Co-evolution During the Four Stages of Logistic Wavelet in Mixed Economies

The metabolic growth model provides a theoretical framework for capital movement and institutional co-evolution with the rise and fall of technology wavelets. We may divide the logistic wavelet into four stages: I. Infancy, II. Growth, III. Maturation, IV. Decline.

Neo-classical theory treats capital as a smooth growing stock that fails to explain the endogenous causes of business cycles and recurrent crisis.

The wavelet model of technology provides an endogenous mechanism of capital movement and policy changes.

At the first stage of infant technology, some survival threshold may exist. Before reaching this threshold, it is hard for an infant technology to survive. Some protection in intellectual property and foreign trade may be helpful for infant industries. Private investors are reluctant to invest in a new technology due to great uncertainty. R&D of new technology is mainly sponsored by the public sector and non-profit universities. For example, the Internet and GPS systems were first developed in universities and national labs for military research, and then transferred to commercial businesses.

At the second growth stage, the new technology shows its market potential, private capital jumps in; market-share expands rapidly, newly issued stock prices soars. At this stage, market competition is the driving force of market expansion. However, safety and environmental standards, as well as financial regulations, are necessary for constructive competition. Herd behavior may appear in generating market instability, such as the case of the dot-com bubble in 2000.

At the third stage of market saturation, corporate profits fall and industrial concentration increases. Monopolistic competition may stiffen new innovations. Anti-trust laws are useful for preventing market concentration and market manipulation. We saw the industry concentration trends in the 2000s after liberalization in the 1980s in the U.S., including telecommunication, computer, software, airline, banking, and retail markets. The 2008 financial crisis was rooted in the American disease where financial oligarchs crowded out the real economy (Johnson 2009; Chen 2010).

The big challenge occurs at the fourth decline stage. Some sunset industries struggle for survival or end up in bankruptcy. Past investment turns into big loss. Stock prices drop and financing costs goes up. Decisions on a life-saving investment or a cut-loss strategy are life-or-death issues for old industries. Large-scale unemployment demands government assistance. Transition from a sunset industry to a sunrise industry needs coordinated efforts between the private and public sector. A typical example is the coal industry in Britain, which was the driving force of industrial revolution in the eighteenth century but declined in the 1980s. Industrial policy for encouraging new radical technology (still in an infant stage) and retraining displaced workers from obsolete technology may be useful. Conventional monetary policy and Keynesian fiscal policy are not enough for structural adjustment at this stage. Conflicts or wars between sunset and sunrise industry groups more likely occur at this stage.

Similarly, institutional arrangements must adapt to different stages of technology life cycles. Clearly, the market force alone cannot insure a healthy economy since technology metabolism may generate substantial social instability and a strong impact to biodiversity. The transaction cost argument against regulation is misleading, since sustainability of an ecological system cannot be solely judged by minimizing entropy (waste heat or transaction costs) during industrialization (Chen 2007). The issue is not big vs. small government, but effective vs. incompetent government in dealing with complexity and stability of mixed economies. A selection mechanism in market regulation plays a central role in institutional evolution (Chen 2007).

3.5 Non-equilibrium Pricing Mechanism Evolving with Technology Wavelets

Here, non-equilibrium mechanism implies multiple pricing strategies evolving with changing technology wavelets. There is no unique optimal pricing in open competition that is prescribed by neoclassic price theory. Our perspective provides a sector foundation of uneven growth cycles (Rostow 1990).

At the first infancy stage, great uncertainty rules out equilibrium pricing in R&D. The competition among rival universities and institutes mainly about research conditions and research reputation. Researcher salaries are paid according to their rank and time that is common practice for public and non-profit organizations. It is hard to estimate the expected rate of return to capital in this stage. That is why that science and industrial policy is essential for national progress in higher education and research.

At the second growth stage, investors could see the light of potential application with considerable uncertainty. There is an intensive race to be the technology leader or market leader. However, equilibrium pricing mechanism rarely exists in a rapidly growing market, such as the Internet market. Many Internet products and services are offered for free usage in order to expand market share. Asset bubble may develop in stock market when investors seek high growth rate rather than stable dividends. In this stage, profit opportunity was associated with unpredictable uncertainty (Knight 1921). The role of capital is decisive in the battle for market-share. It is capital, not labor that dominates the distribution of wealth in a capitalist society (Piketty 2014). Extremely high income for top managers and dealmakers comes from percentage gain rather than timely pay in the market-share competition. Therefore, equal opportunity before the law cannot assure fair distribution of wealth.

In the third saturation stage, market slowing-down is visible in industry growth. Diminishing returns to capital are associated with industrial concentration. For small and medium firms, their surviving strategy is cost plus pricing. The profit margin varies with different entry barrier and cost structure. Market leaders would use strategic pricing to drive out competitors, or deter potential challengers from entering the market. Neoclassical asset pricing theory seems relevant mainly at this stage. However, there is little empirical evidence of marginal cost pricing in marketing practice.

In the fourth decline stage, the strategic issue for corporate management is staying-business or taking timely exit for minimizing potential loss. Again, unpredictable uncertainty rules the asset market. Stock price could be volatile and sensitive to any information even rumors. Government help is needed when the decline industry involves large unemployment and national interest.

In short, the pricing mechanism in an open competition market is dominated by strategic pricing in market-share competition. There is little room for "invisible hand", or equilibrium pricing in an open economy with rapidly changing technology. A fully developed complex price theory is needed in future studies.

4 Risk Attitude and Culture Diversity in Learning Strategy

From Table 3, the resource-population ratio varies greatly between Asian and Western countries. We may characterize Western civilization as a labor-saving but a resource-consuming culture, while Asian and Chinese civilizations are resource-saving but labor-consuming cultures (Chen 1990, 2010). Technologically speaking, China had the capability to discover America before Columbus (Menzies 2002). Needham asked the question why did science and capitalism originate in the West, not in China (Needham 1954). The answer can be traced from the interaction between environment and culture in history (Chen 1990).

There is an intensive debate on altruism in economics (Simon 1993). It is difficult to distinguish altruistic from selfish behavior from empirical observation. However, we can easily measure the risk attitude between different cultures, such as risk aversion versus risk taking in facing an unknown market or opportunity.

In neoclassical economics, economic risk is characterized by a static probability such as in the case of gambling; there is no uncertainty associated with a new market and a new technology in a strategic decision. In our dynamic competition model, we introduce a new kind of risk attitude in open economies: the risk of facing an unknown market or technology uncertainty. Both Knight (1921) and Keynes (1936) emphasized the role of uncertainty, which is different from risk in the sense of static statistics. Schumpeter's concept of the entrepreneurial spirit is critical in facing evolutionary uncertainty rather than static risk.

4.1 Learning by Imitating and Learning by Trying: Risk-Aversion and Risk-Taking Culture

The cultural factor plays an important role in decision-making and corporate strategy. There is a great variety in the degree of "individualism" between western and oriental cultures. Risk-aversion and risk-taking strategies differ when facing an emerging market or new technology. Clearly, the strategy of learning by doing is not applicable for an open economy, since the accumulation process is only relevant for existing technology (Arrow 1962). In a new market, knowledge comes from learning by trying, which is a trial and error process from an evolutionary perspective (Chen 1987). The alternative strategy is learning by imitating or following the crowd.

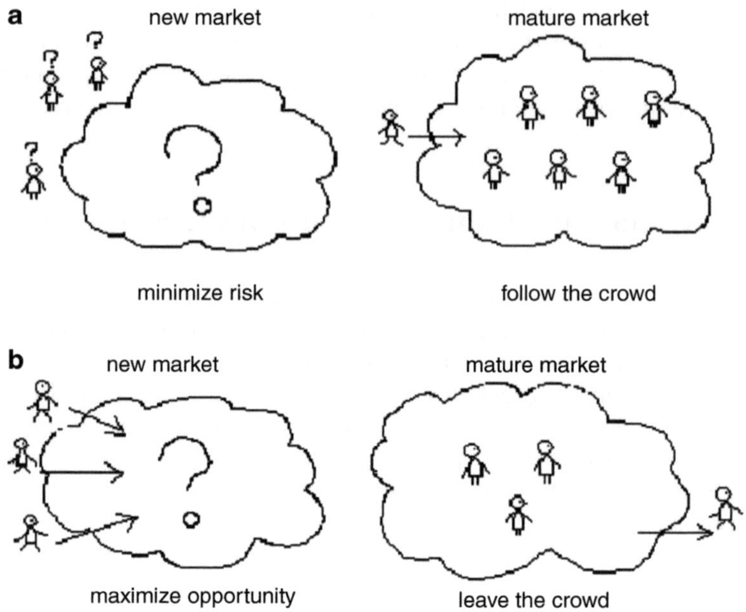

Fig. 4 **(a)** Risk-aversion behavior and **(b)** risk-taking behavior in competition for market share and technology advancement

The risk-taking and risk-aversion attitudes in facing a new market or technology can be visualized in Fig. 4.

From Fig. 4, different cultures have different rationales behind their risk attitudes. When facing an unknown market or unproved technology, risk-taking investors often take the lead and venture to maximize their opportunities, while risk-averting investors prefer to wait and follow the crowd to minimize their risk. A critical question is: Which corporate culture or market strategy can win or survive in a rapidly changing market? To answer this question, we need to integrate the culture factor into competition dynamics in Eq. (3).

In industrial economies, resource competition essentially is a learning competition in adopting new technology. For understanding the link between cultural diversity and resource variability, we may introduce a culture factor into species competition. The original logistic equation describes a risk-neutral behavior by assuming a constant exit rate. We introduce the behavioral parameter a by introducing a nonlinear exit rate as a function of the learner's population ratio (Chen 1987):

$$R\left(r, a, \frac{n}{N}\right) = r\left(1 - a\frac{n}{N}\right) \quad \text{Where} -1 < a < 1. \tag{6}$$

Here, n is the number of users of this new technology.

We may consider the constant r as a measure of the learning difficulty when adopting a new technology, which means that the harder to learn, the faster the exit. We put the behavioral factor at the exit rate for mathematical simplicity, since the original exit rate is a linear term. The modified exit rate becomes a quadratic term, so that we still have an analytic solution for this nonlinear dynamical model. Otherwise, we can only do numerical simulations using mathematical modeling.

The factor a is a measure of risk orientation. If $a > 0$, it is a measure of risk-aversion or collectivism. If $a < 0$, it is a measure of risk-taking or individualism. At the initial stage, few people dare to try a new market; the exit rate is the same for all people. However, when more and more people accept the new technology, business strategy becomes increasingly diversified. For risk aversion investors, their exit rate declines, since they feel deceasing risk. But risk-taking entrepreneurs are more likely to exit, since they feel decreasing opportunity. When varying a from minus one to plus one, we have a full spectrum of varying behavior, from the extreme risk-aversion conservatism to the extreme risk-taking adventurism. There are different meanings of conservatism between the West and the East. To avoid a conceptual misunderstanding, we will define risk-aversion behavior as a collectivist culture while risk-taking behavior as an individualist culture in learning strategy. Our inspiration comes from the perspective of cultural anthropology. Many observers attribute high innovation in the U.S. to American individualism, while rapid copying technology in Japan may relate to their collectivist culture (Kikuchi 1981).

4.2 Resource-Saving and Resource-Consuming Culture

The equilibrium rate of resource utilization is:

$$\frac{n^*}{N} = \frac{\left(1 - \frac{r}{Nk}\right)}{\left(1 - \frac{ra}{Nk}\right)} \tag{7a}$$

$$n^*_{a<0} < n^*_{a=0} < n^*_{a>0} \tag{7b}$$

From Eq. (7b), the resource utilization rate of the collectivist species ($n^*_{a>0}$) is higher than that of the individualist species ($n^*_{a<0}$). The individualist species needs a larger subsistence space than a collectivist one in order to maintain the same equilibrium size n^*. Therefore, individualism is a resource-consuming culture while collectivism is a resource-saving culture (Chen 1990). This difference is visible between Western individualism and Eastern collectivism. Cultural differences are rooted in economic structures and ecological constraints. Resource expansion is a key to understanding the origin of a capitalist economy and the industrial revolution (Pomeranz 2000).

Wallerstein once observed a historical puzzle that history looked to be irrational (1974): In the Middle Ages, China's population was near twice that of Western Europe while China's arable land was much less than Western Europe. According to the rational choice theory, China should have expanded its space while Europe should have increased in population. But the historical behavior was opposite!

> The European wastes space. Even at the demographic low-point of the beginning of the 15th century, Europe lacked space. . . . But if Europe lacks space, China lacks men. . .

This historical puzzle can be solved when we consider the link between a culture strategy and an agriculture structure. China's staple food is rice, which is a labor-intensive but land-saving technology. Diary food plays an important role in European culture. Dairy agriculture is a land-intensive and labor-saving technology. In response to increasing population pressures, China is used to increasing labor input for increasing grain yield, while Europeans are used to seeking new land for improving their living standard. That is why Chinese philosophy used to emphasize the harmony between men and nature, while Western strategy used to conquer nature. This is a cultural perspective to Needham's question. By the same reason, we can understand why Asian country's saving rates are much higher than in the West. Preparing for an uncertain future rather than seeking current happiness is deeply rooted in Chinese culture and history.

In this regard, the former Soviet Union was close to western individualism, since they had a strong motivation in expansionism.

When we study civilization history, we find that famers are more collectivist than nomads and sailors. Japanese culture is highly collectivism even it's city residents. However, Japanese foreign policy is more closely compared to the British Empire because it is an island country with a strong naval tradition. New technology in shipbuilding and navigation opened new resources in foreign trade and colonialism in addition to limited arable land.

4.3 Market Extent, Resource Variety, and Economy of Scale and Scope

We can easily extend our model from two technologies (species) to many technologies (species). In an ecological system with L technology (species), their resource limits (carrying capacities) are $N_1, N_2, \ldots, N_L$. The economy of scope and scale can be integrated into a complex system of coupling logistic-type competition equations. A scale economy is related to the market extent or resource limit N_i, while a scope economy can be described by the number of technologies (species) L. The degree of the division of labor can be characterized by the biodiversity, i.e. the coexistence of competing technologies.

Let's start with the simplest case of only two species with competing technologies and cultures (Chen 1987):

$$\frac{dn_1}{dt} = k_1 n_1 (N_1 - n_1 - \beta\, n_2) - r_1 n_1 \left(1 - \frac{a_1 n_1}{N_1}\right) \tag{8a}$$

$$\frac{dn_2}{dt} = k_2 n_2 (N_2 - n_2 - \beta\, n_1) - r_2 n_2 \left(1 - \frac{a_2 n_2}{N_2}\right) \tag{8b}$$

Here n_1, n_2 is the number of adopters in technology (species) one and two respectively. For simplicity, we only discuss the simplest case when $\beta = 1$ under complete competition.

We may solve Eq. (8) in the similar way in solving Eq. (2). The replacement condition and the co-existence condition are (9a) and (9b) respectively:

$$C_2 > \frac{\left(1 - \frac{a_2 r_2}{k_2 N_2}\right)}{\beta} C_1 \quad \text{for species 2 replace species 1} \tag{9a}$$

$$\frac{\beta}{\left(1 - \frac{a_1 r_1}{k_1 N_1}\right)} < \frac{N_2 - \frac{r_2}{k_2}}{N_1 - \frac{r_1}{k_1}} < \frac{1}{\beta}\left(1 - \frac{a_2 r_2}{k_2 N_2}\right) \tag{9b}$$

4.4 *The Impact of Environmental Fluctuations*

The next task is studying the impact of environmental fluctuations to system stability. The problem of a nonlinear dynamical system under random shocks can be solved by the Langevin equation and Fokker-Planck equation (May 1974; Chen 1987, 2010). Here, we only consider a simple case where a stream of random shocks adds to the resource limit of one technology N. The realized equilibrium size X_m would be reduced by a fluctuating environment with the variance of σ^2:

$$X_m = N \frac{\left(1 - \frac{r}{kN} - \frac{k\sigma^2}{2N}\right)}{\left(1 - \frac{ra}{kN}\right)} \quad \text{when } \sigma < \sigma_c = \sqrt{\frac{2N}{k}\left(1 - \frac{r}{kN}\right)} \tag{10a}$$

$$X_m = 0 \quad \text{when } \sigma > \sigma_c = \sqrt{\frac{2N}{k}\left(1 - \frac{r}{kN}\right)} \tag{10b}$$

If there exists some survival threshold in population size, then the collectivism has a better chance of surviving under external shocks because it has a larger population size.

Environmental fluctuations will reduce the resource limit of the equilibrium state, as seen from Eq. (10a). When fluctuations are larger than the threshold, the technology would die as in Eq. (10b). That is why some ancient civilizations disappeared due to a natural disaster or war. Economic development needs social stability.

When we consider environmental fluctuations to many species, we may realize the importance of biodiversity. Regional specialization effectively increases concentration of risk. Mass production in agriculture also intensifies the application of chemical fertilizer and pesticide. In another words, economy of scope is helpful for maintaining biodiversity.

4.5 Trade-Off Between Stability and Diversity and the Generalized Smith Theorem

For a more general case with many technologies, increasing the number of technologies will reduce system stability (May 1974). There is a trade-off between diversity and stability. Smith did not realize the importance of science and technology that introduces new resources and new markets, since the Industrial Revolution was still in its infancy during his time. We propose a generalized Smith Theorem (Chen 2005, 2010) as the following:

The division of labor is limited by the market extent (resource limit), biodiversity (number of resources), and environmental fluctuations (social stability).

Neoclassical growth models have an one-way evolution to convergence or divergence under linear stochastic dynamics. There may be a two-way evolution (or co-evolution) process towards complexity or simplicity in division of labor under nonlinear evolutionary dynamics. When social stability is high and new resources keep coming, the system may develop into a complex system, like the Industrial Revolution in the past. However, when social turmoil is high or resources are used up due to over population, a complex system may break down into a simple system, such as the collapse of the Roman Empire in the Middle Ages. Even in the modern era, industrial society coexists with traditional society and even primitive tribes. The basic mechanism is the interactions among population, environment, and technology.

4.6 Competition Scenario Between Individualism and Collectivism and Dynamical Picture of Schumpeter's Creative Destruction

There is a popular belief that individualism would beat collectivism, since individualism is more innovative in technology competition. However, there are three possibilities under different competition scenarios:

(i) Both species are individualists. From Eq. (9b), two individualist species may coexist. Competition between individualists would increase system diversity. The city-states in ancient Greece and Renaissance Italy are examples.
(ii) Both species are collectivists. Based on Eq. (9b), two collectivist species cannot coexist, the only result is one replaces the other. This is the story of peasant wars and dynastic cycles in Chinese history. Therefore, division of labor is hard to emerge in a purely collectivist society.
(iii) One individualist and one collectivist. This is the general case when competition is a game of uncertainty. This is a mixed economy with one collectivist and one individualist species. One interesting feature is that the stability of a mixed system is higher than the liberal system with two individualists. We may extend this result to a case with more than two species. This scenario is perceivable when we compare the two-party political system in the Anglo-Saxon countries and the multi-party political system in continental Europe.

What would happen in case (iii) when an individualist species competes with a collectivist one? They may coexist, or one replaces another, depending on their resource limits, learning ability, and cultural factors. We may add a few discussions to this case.

If two species have equal resources ($N_1 = N_2$), then, the collectivist species will replace the individualist one. If we compare (8a) with (3a), the late-comer in a collectivist culture may beat the individualistic leader even if $C_2 \leq C_1$ when $\beta \approx 1$ and $0 < a_2 \approx 1$. This is the story of how Japan and China caught up with the West in the 1970s and 2010s respectively. A collectivist culture can concentrate its resources on a "catching-up" game. The success or failure of the industrial policy depends on the government's ability for mobilizing strategic resources on emerging technologies, a typical feature of learning by imitating in the catching-up game.

The survival strategy for an individualist is to explore a larger resource, or learn faster. If we consider entrepreneurship as a risk-taking culture, then we may reach a similar conclusion to Schumpeter's (1939) that creative destruction is vital for capitalism in the competition between socialism (collectivism) and capitalism (individualism). Once innovations fail to discover new and larger resources, the individualist species will lose the game to the collectivist in the existing markets. This picture of changing economic powers is different from the permanent division between early-movers and late-comers in endogenous growth theory. Our model of learning strategy can be applied to an arm race or corporate strategy if the relevant data are available.

5 Issues in Methodology and Philosophy

There are several issues in methodology and philosophy. Keynes once remarked (1936):

> The classical theorists resemble Euclidean geometers in a non-Euclidean world who, discovering that in experience straight lines apparently parallel often meet, rebuke the

> lines for not keeping straight—as the only remedy for the unfortunate collisions which are occurring. Yet, in truth, there is no remedy except to throw over the axiom of parallels and to work a non-Euclidean geometry. Something similar is required today in economics.

Our population dynamics is an alternative framework to an optimization approach in neoclassical economics. This paradigm change induces fundamental shifts in the following issues.

5.1 Real Versus Monetary Economy

Neoclassical growth theory is a monetary system, where capital and population are driving forces in economic growth. Our population dynamics is a real system, where resource and population play key roles in economic growth. The theoretical issue is the relation between the real and virtual (monetary) economies. We are different with RBC school on the nature of technology changes. RBC school treats technology advances as random shocks without resource limit (Kydland and Prescott 1982), while we characterize technology advancement as logistic wavelets under resource constraints.

Historically, the core concepts in classical economics started from land, population, and capital. In neoclassical economics, there is an increasing trend of virtualization in economic theory. One important lesson from the 2008 financial crisis is the danger of over-expansion of the virtual economy in developed countries (Johnson 2009; Chen 2010).

According to BIS (Bank of International Settlement) data, the size of the global derivative market in Dec. 2012 was 632.6 trillion U.S. dollars, which is nearly 9 times the world total production or 40 times the U.S. GDP. There may be a dangerous link between virtualization in economic theory and virtualization in the U.S. economy.

5.2 Equilibrium Versus Non-equilibrium Mechanism

The optimization approach can only apply to an equilibrium system in a closed economy. There is a fundamental problem for general equilibrium models in the endogenous growth theory. In neoclassical economics, price plays a central role in creating equilibrium in the market exchange. The profit for a representative firm should be zero in the general equilibrium model. It means that capital cannot grow in a closed economy under general equilibrium. Clearly, microfoundations theory of endogenous growth fails to provide a consistent theory in capital accumulation and technology progress (Chen 2002).

In our metabolic growth theory, we did not introduce price factors into population dynamics, since there is no unique (linear) price in a non-equilibrium system in a market-share competition. In Sect. 3.4, profit opportunity mainly exists at the second growth stage. However, there is a trade-off between short-term profit and long-term market-share. You cannot calculate its optimal value when future market shares and competitor's strategies are unknown. That is why vision and strategy matters in technology competition. Capital loss mainly occurs at the fourth decline stage. The cost of the 2008 financial crisis was about 13 trillion U.S. dollars. The smooth picture of capital growth in neoclassical theory abstracts out the uncertainty in technology advancement from the linear-equilibrium perspective. Our scenario is more realistic than the neoclassical model in understanding firm behavior. In another words, there is no empirical evidence of marginal cost pricing. But there are abundant cases of strategic pricing in marketing practice (Shaw 2012).

Another example is the equilibrium trap of the so-called rebalancing policy promoted by Federal Reserve Chairman Ben Bernanke. China was more successful in dealing with the 2008 financial crisis in a non-equilibrium approach, which was characterized by large investments in infrastructure, such as high-speed trains, and new technology, including new energy and new materials. The U.S. Congress refused any structural reform and single-mindedly relied on the Federal Reserve policy of QE, another form of printing money. The European Union and Japan are dealing with the debt crisis by implementing limited fiscal and monetary policies.

Both neoclassical economics and Keynesian economics pay little attention to economic structure. The down-sloped IS curve theory is wrong in an open economy under non-equilibrium conditions. If you lower the interest rate, there are three, not just one, possibilities in the globalization era; In a healthy economy with growth prospects, lower interest rates will increase investment and production; In an uncertain economy, investors prefer to hold cash or reduce existing debts; In a sick economy, lower interest rates may cause large capital flight to foreign economies promising better returns. We found solid evidence of color chaos from macro and financial indexes (Chen 1996, 2005, 2008). The linear causality in the IS-LM scheme is simply an equilibrium illusion in a non-equilibrium world with economic complexity (Chen 2010).

5.3 Linear Versus Nonlinear Thinking

Linear thinking is the common feature of neoclassical growth models. Robert Solow was clearly aware of not only the symptom, but also the cause in neoclassical growth theory (Solow 1994). For example, increasing returns to scale would lead to an explosive economy, while diminishing returns to scale would generate a convergence trend that is not shown in historical data. Each innovation kills its predecessors in the Aghion and Howitt model of "creative destruction" (1992). In reality, many innovations are complementary with predecessors. The model of learning by doing simply ignores the important role of R&D for exploring new resources.

From our perspective, the shortcoming of neoclassical economics is linear thinking. Once we adopt the nonlinear perspective, even with the simplest logistic model, all troubles in neoclassical growth theory can be easily solved. For example, Schumpeter's creative destruction does not mean non-coexistence between old and new technology. Complementary technologies can emerge if their competition coefficients are small.

Any technology or industry has a life cycle, or more precisely, a wavelet. Let us consider the textile industry at a mature stage in developed countries. Certainly you have diminishing returns in capital if you continue to invest in the U.S., but you may still have increasing returns if you invest in Asia. There was a convergence trend when low technology moved from advanced to backward economies in the 1970s and 1980s. However, when the computer and Internet industries emerged in the West, foreign investment moved back to developed countries in order to catch the new opportunity of increasing returns to capital for new technology at the growth stage. You may have seen a temporary diverging trend between rich and poor countries in the 1990s. Why did China rapidly catch up to Asian tigers in the manufacturing industry in the 1990s and 2000s? Simply because China's economic scale and market extent was much larger than in Asian tigers and East European countries.

The policy implications of neoclassical growth theory for economic growth are dubious. The exogenous growth theory emphasizes the roles of population growth and capital accumulation. A recent study of increasing inequality since 1970s shows little evidence of "balanced growth path" (Solow 1957; Piketty 2014). The endogenous growth theory further enhances the accumulation role of knowledge capital. They do not understand that these factors can be double-edged swords.

During a visit to Egypt last summer, it was observed that the current turmoil in the Mid-East is deeply rooted in high population growth, limited food supply, and high unemployment rate among young educated people. Egypt's population growth rate is four times that of China, but the GDP growth rate is about one fourth that of China. Historically, Egypt was a main exporter of grain to Europe and now is a big importer of grain from the U.S. Egypt did not make major investments in family planning and farmland reconstruction like China in the past. Both the military regime and elected governments have little means to solve the resource-population problem on a short-term. The U.S. economy faces another problem. According to CIA data, the school life expectancy is 17 years in the U.S., UK, and Spain, 16 years in Germany, and 12 years in China and Egypt. According to endogenous growth theory, you may expect U.S. manufacturing should better compete with Germany and China. However, Steven Jobs, the late CEO of Apple Inc., bluntly told President Obama in 2012 that the U.S. stopped to train middle-level engineers on a large scale (Barboza et al. 2012). China once faced the shortage of skilled workers and industrial technicians. They solved the problem by introducing the German system of technical schools, not just the American system of higher education. Again, knowledge structure matters more than aggregate stock in economics. By introducing nonlinear interaction into growth theory, we have a more proper policy for economic growth and development.

5.4 *Theory Versus Simulation*

There is a big difference between theoretical models and computational simulations. Theory is aimed to catch general features from a wide range of observations at the cost of abstracting out many details, while simulation seeks to describe many details from a specific object at the cost of generalizing to other objects. In this regard, our market-share competition model is a theory, while system dynamics, as well as econometrics, are different approaches in economic simulation (Forrester 1961; Meadows et al. 2004). Competing simulation models are tested by empirical data. Competing theories in science are tested by controlled experiments. In economics, controlled experiments are limited in scale and scope. Economic schools of thought are mainly tested by historical trends and events. For example, the Great Depression shook the faith in the self-stabilizing market, so that Keynesian economics rose to replace classical economics in mainstream economics in the UK and the U.S. The Lucas theory of microfoundations and rational expectations became popular in the West during the stagnation era in the 1970s, and are now facing serious challenges from the 2008 financial crisis.

The exogenous theory of growth won a great deal of attention in the 1950s, which was the golden era for the U.S. after the WWII. The endogenous growth theory attracted a lot of attention during the hype of the dot.com boom and the so-called knowledge economy. After the failure of the Iraq war and the 2008 financial crisis, people started to doubt the convergence theory when so many countries were still in a poverty trap, and the sustainability of a developed economy. Our theory of metabolic growth is a mathematical way of new thinking in economics and world history. We share a similar view of anthropologists and historians that changes in climate and environment shaped by the history of civilizations (Morris 2010).

6 Conclusions

Technology advancement and resource exploitation is the driving force of an industrial economy. How to understand the dynamic interaction between technology, resources, and population is a fundamental issue in economics and history. Both exogenous and endogenous growth theory puts abstract capital as the driving force of economic growth but takes out the critical role of resources. In this regard, neoclassical growth theory is a big retreat from classical economists such as Smith and Malthus. Therefore, using neoclassical growth theory, it is hard to understand development mechanisms, environmental crisis, and recurrent cycles.

During the 2008 Financial Crisis, both monetary policy and fiscal policy had limited effects in developed countries without structural changes. The rise of China and emerging economies is mainly driven by technology advancement and structural reform (Chen 2010). The primary cause of business cycles and changing world order is technology wavelets. Market psychology and monetary movements only play secondary role in feedback dynamics. This is our lesson from the Great Recession in 2008, which is greatly different from the Great Depression in 1930s. The common limits among Keynes, Hayek, and Friedman were their ignorance of global competition and shifting power balance under technology revolution.

Our work based on population dynamics brings back the central idea of Adam Smith and Thomas Malthus that the division of labor is limited by the market extent and resource capacity. Nonlinear population dynamics is an alternative framework for economic dynamics. We made several contributions that are beyond the scope of neoclassical growth theory.

First, industrialization is characterized by a sequence of discoveries of new resources and new markets (Pomeranz 2000). Material wealth is associated with both scale (resource capacity) and scope (number of resources) economy. Therefore, material wealth in human society is closely linked to biodiversity. Division of labor may increase efficiency in utilizing existing resources, but not necessarily create new resources. Exchange economy is mainly about distribution of existing resources, not creating new resources. The nature of modernization is driven by advancement of science that opening new resources by new technology, not driven by accumulation of capital, knowledge or population if their growth has no link with proper development of science and technology.

Second, Schumpeter's "long waves" and "creative destruction" can be described by the rise and fall of technology wavelets that are derived from population dynamics (Schumpeter 1934, 1939, 1950). The observed growth cycles with nonlinear trends and irregular cycles from macro indexes can be interpreted as the envelopment of aggregated logistic wavelets (Prigogine et al. 1977), which build a link between technology wavelets at the industry level and business cycles at the macro level. Disaggregate approach by sector analysis is more useful than aggregate approach in understanding growth dynamics and industrial policy (Rostow 1990), since capital investment in obsolete technology or monetary game generate more harm than gain in economic growth.

Third, the sources of insufficient demand and job crisis in Keynesian economics can be understood from life cycles of technology wavelets. Structural unemployment is rooted from excess-capacity under technology competition. Unlike the microfoundations model in business cycle theory, this is the meso foundation of macro unemployment and recurrent cycles, since industrial economy is not consisted from free individual atoms at the household level, but organized into large clusters as technology organizations and industrial groups (Lucas 1981; Chen 1996, 2002).

Fourth, we have a better understanding of the nature of knowledge and the nonlinear patterns in economic growth. Exogenous growth theory treats technology advancement as a series of random shocks. Endogenous growth theory asserts that knowledge is an accumulation process. We uncover the metabolic nature in knowledge development. Modern technologies are shaped by scientific revolution. Paradigm changes and interruptive technologies indicate wavelike movements in science and technology development, which is radically different from the random walk in neoclassical models (Kuhn 1962). From the nonlinear perspective, we can see changing dynamic returns and co-evolution of organization and institution during the technology life cycle. Mixed economy is the very foundation for science and education. Invisible hand may play some role in technology diffusion. However, science research is highly organized activities guided by theory, institution and policy (Bernal 1969). Random events only have minor impact in history of science.

Fifth, culture plays a critical role in "great divergence" of civilization bifurcation (Clark 2007). The culture factor is introduced into learning competition. Risk-taking individualism and risk-aversion collectivism are different strategies for survival under a market-share competition. Different modes of division of labor are shaped by resource constraints and culture in history.

Sixth, we developed the generalized Smith Theorem that the division of labor is limited by the market extent, number of resources, and environmental fluctuations. There is a trade-off between system stability and system complexity. Economic evolution is a nonlinear two-way dynamic towards diversity and non-equilibrium. From ecological perspective, biodiversity imposes fundamental constraints to technology development and human evolution (Georgescu-Roegen 1971). Not all products of modern technology are compatible with eco-system. Destruction of biodiversity will lead to destruction of national and global wealth, since any accumulation of material wealth on earth is rooted in transformed energy flows from the solar system. Ecological constraints require regulated economy to protect biodiversity. Laissez fair policy is harmful to our earth village.

Seventh, our analytical unit is species or technologies. Microeconomics should pay more attention to competing sectors and industries, rather than representative agent model of households and firms. This implies that competition among technologies is more important than competition among individuals in economic growth. From biological perspective, human nature is a social animal, which cannot be unbounded greedy. Animal evolution is subjects to ecological constraints. Living organism only exists in finite time and space. Nonlinear demand and supply mechanism is closely linked to existence threshold and saturation limit in biology. Therefore, human behaviour must be competitive and cooperative at the same time for existence struggle. Neoclassical models with unbounded utility and production function simply violate basic laws in physics and biology. That is why econometrics based on linear regression can only be considered as "alchemy" but not science (Hendry 2001). We have solid evidence that real economies are living systems, that are nonlinear, non-stationary, and non-integrable systems (Chen 1996, 2010). We need a new economic framework, which is compatible with ecological constraints.

Finally, we pave the way for a unified theory in economics including micro, macro, finance, and institutional economics based on evolutionary complex dynamics. We pointed out that a neoclassical framework is not proper for an industrial economy, since the Hamiltonian system is a closed system in nature. Neoclassical concepts such as perfect information, rational expectations, noise-driven cycles, zero-transaction costs, infinite life, IS curves, long-run equilibrium, and unlimited growth, are utopian ideas that go against basic laws in physics and are non-observable in reality (Chen 2005, 2007, 2008, 2010). People are social individuals with life cycles and interactions. We developed a nonlinear oscillator model for color chaos (Chen 1996), the birth-death process for macro and financial fluctuations (Chen 2002), and a logistic competition model for metabolic growth (Chen 1987, 2008). We show that population dynamics is a useful model for a dissipative economic system in an open economy. The wavelets representation and these nonlinear models are building blocks for a unified theory of complex evolutionary dynamics in micro, meso, macro and institutional economics (Chen 2010). The new science of complexity develops new tools in nonlinear dynamics and non-equilibrium mechanisms (Nicolis and Prigogine 1977; Prigogine 1980, 1984), which are essential for understanding economic development and social evolution. In this sense, Keynes was quite right that we need a non-Euclidean geometry to develop a general theory of economics, since we live in a non-Euclidean world (Keynes 1936; Chen 2010).

Economists used to think that economic evolution is hard to formulate by mathematical language (Mirowski 1989). This is not true in the era of complexity science. Historical development can be well described by nonlinear and non-equilibrium dynamics. The key is finding the proper link between theory and observations.

Acknowledgements The author thanks Peter Allen, Wolfgang Weidlich, Edmond Phelps, Joseph Stiglitz, James Galbraith, Ulrich Witt, Justin Lin, Wolfram Elsner, Andreas Pyka, Laura Tyson, Zhengfu Shi, Weisen Li, Yinan Tang, Huajun Li, and Vivian Chen for their stimulating discussions. We also thank two anonymous reviewers for their stimulating comments.

References

Aghion P, Howitt P (1992) A model of growth through creative destruction. Econometrica 60(2):323–351

Aghion P, Howitt P (1998) Endogenous growth theory. MIT Press, Cambridge

Arthur WB (1994) Increasing returns and path dependence in the economy. University of Michigan Press, Ann Arbor, MI

Arrow KJ (1962) The economic implications of learning by doing. Rev Econ Stud 39:155

Arrow KJ, Debreu G (1954) Existence of an equilibrium for a competitive economy. Econometrica 22(3):265–290

Ayres RU (1989) Technological transformations and long waves. International Institute for Applied Systems Analysis, Laxenburg

Barboza D, Lattman P, Rampell C (2012) How the U.S. lost out on iphone work. New York Times. Jan 21, 24

Bernal JD (1969) Science in history, 3rd edn. Penguin, Harmondsworth

Browning M, Crossley TF (2001) The life-cycle model of consumption and saving. J Econ Perspect 15(3):3–22

Chen P (1987) Origin of the division of labor and a stochastic mechanism of differentiation. Eur J Oper Res 30:246–250

Chen P (1990) Needham's question and China's evolution—cases of non-equilibrium social transition. In: Scott G (ed) Time, rhythms and chaos in the new dialogue with nature, chapter 11. Iowa State University Press, Ames, IA, pp 177–198

Chen P (1996) A random walk or color chaos on the stock market?—time-frequency analysis of S&P indexes. Stud Nonlinear Dyn Econ 1(2):87–103

Chen P (2002) Microfoundations of macroeconomic fluctuations and the laws of probability theory: the principle of large numbers vs. rational expectations arbitrage. J Econ Behav Organ 49:327–344
Chen P (2005) Evolutionary economic dynamics: persistent business cycles, disruptive technology, and the trade-off between stability and complexity. In: Dopfer K (ed) The evolutionary foundations of economics, chapter 15. Cambridge University Press, Cambridge, pp 472–505
Chen P (2007) Complexity of transaction costs and evolution of corporate governance. Kyoto Econ Rev 76(2):139–153
Chen P (2008) Equilibrium illusion, economic complexity, and evolutionary foundation of economic analysis. Evol Inst Econ Rev 5(1):81–127
Chen P (2010) Economic complexity and equilibrium illusion: essays on market instability and macro vitality. Routledge, London
Clark G (2007) A farewell to alms: a brief economic history of the world. Princeton University Press, Princeton, NJ
Darwin C (1859) On the origin of species, by means of natural selection, or the preservation of favoured races in the struggle for life, vol 1. John Murray, London
Dasgupta D (2010) Modern growth theory. Oxford University Press, Oxford
Daly H, Farley J (2010) Ecological economics: principles and applications. Island Press, Washington, DC
David PA (1985) Clio and the economics of qwerty. Am Econ Rev Pap Proc 75:332–337
Day RH (1982) Irregular growth cycles. Am Econ Rev 72:404–414
Eliasson G (2005) The birth, the life and the death of firms. The Ratio Institute, Stockholm
Forrester JW (1961) Industrial dynamics. MIT Press, Cambridge, MA
Georgescu-Roegen N (1971) The entropy law and economic process. Harvard University Press, Cambridge, MA
Goodwin RM (1967) A growth cycle. In: Feinstein CH (ed) Socialism, capitalism and economic growth. Cambridge University Press, Cambridge, MA
Hendry DF (2001) Econometrics: alchemy or science? Essays in econometric methodology. Oxford University Press, Oxford
Johnson S (2009) The quiet coup. Atlantic 303(4):46–56
Keynes JM (1936) The general theory of employment, investment, and money. Macmillan, London
Kikuchi M (1981) Creativity and ways of thinking: the Japanese style. Phys Today 34:42–51
Knight FH (1921) Risk, uncertainty and profit. Sentry Press, New York
Kurz HD (2012) Innovation, knowledge, and growth: Adam Smith, Schumpeter, and moderns. Routledge, London
Kuhn T (1962) The structure of scientific revolutions. University of Chicago Press, Chicago
Kydland FE (1995) Business cycle theory. E. Edgar, Brookfield, VT
Kydland FE, Prescott EC (1982) Time to build and aggregate fluctuations. Econometrica 50(6):1345–1370
Lucas RE Jr (1981) Studies in business-cycle theory. MIT Press, Cambridge
Lucas RE Jr (1988) On the mechanics of economic development. J Monet Econ 22:3–42
Maddison A (1998) Chinese economic performance in the long run. OECD, Paris
Maddison A (2007) The world economy: a millennial perspective/historical statistics. OECD Development Center Studies, Paris
Malthus TR (1798, 2008) An essay on the principle of population. Oxford University Press, Oxford
May RM (1974) Stability and complexity in model ecosystems. Princeton University Press, Princeton, NJ
Meadows DH, Randers J, Meadows DL (2004) Limits to growth: the 30-year update. Chelsea Green, White River Junction, VT
Menzies G (2002/1421) The year China discovered the world. Morrow, New York
Mirowski P (1989) More heat than light. Cambridge University Press, Cambridge
Modigliani F (1976) Life-cycle, individual thrift, and the wealth of nations. Am Econ Rev 76(3):297–313
Morris I (2010) Why the west rules—for now. Farrar, New York

Needham J (1954) Science and civilization in China, vol I. Cambridge University Press, Cambridge
Nicolis G, Prigogine I (1977) Self-organization in nonequilibrium systems. Wiley, New York
Pianka ER (1983) Evolutionary ecology, 6th edn. Benjamin Cummings, San Francisco, CA
Piketty T (2014) Capital in the twenty-first century. Harvard University Press, Cambridge, MA
Pomeranz K (2000) The great divergence: China, Europe, and the making of the modern world economy. Princeton University Press, Princeton, NJ
Prigogine I (1980) From being to becoming: time and complexity in the physical sciences. Freeman, San Francisco, CA
Prigogine I (1984) Order out of Chaos. Bantam, New York
Prigogine I, Peter MA, Herman R (1977) Long term trends and the evolution of complexity. In: Laszlo E (ed) Goals in a global community: a report to the club of Rome. Pergamon Press, Oxford
Romer PM (1986) Increasing returns and long-run growth. J Polit Econ 94:1002–1038
Rostow WW (1990) The stages of economic growth, 3rd edn. Cambridge University Press, Cambridge
Samuelson PA (1971) Generalized predator–prey oscillations in ecological and economic equilibrium. Proc Natl Acad Sci USA 68(5):980–983
Schumpeter JA (1934) The theory of economic development. Harvard University Press, Cambridge
Schumpeter JA (1939) Business cycles, a theoretical, historical, and statistical analysis of the capitalist process. McGraw-Hill, New York
Schumpeter JA (1950) Capitalism, socialism and democracy, 3rd edn. Harper, New York
Shaw E (2012) Marketing strategy: from the origin of the concept to the development of a conceptual framework. J Hist Res Mark 4(1):30–55
Simon HA (1993) Altruism and economics. Am Econ Rev 83(2):156–161
Smith A (1776) The wealth of nations. Liberty Classics, Indianapolis
Solow RM (1957) Technical change and the aggregate production function. Rev Econ Stat 39(3):312–320
Solow RM (1994) Perspectives on growth theory. J Econ Perspect 8(1):45–54
Stigler GJ (1951) The division of labor is limited by the extent of the market. J Polit Econ 59:185–193
Toffler A (1980) The third wave. William Morrow, New York
Vernon R (1966) International investment and international trade in the product cycle. Q J Econ 80(2):190–207
Wallerstein I (1974) The modern world system I, capitalist agriculture and the origin of the European world-economy in the sixteenth century. Academic, New York

A General Model of the Innovation - Subjective Well-Being Nexus

Hans-Jürgen Engelbrecht

Abstract A model of the innovation – subjective well-being (SWB) nexus is needed to advance our understanding of the welfare implications of innovation. Building on an earlier contribution by Swann (G. M. Peter Swann, 2009, The Economics of Innovation, Edward Elgar, Cheltenham, UK), I first assemble the major building blocks of such a model and then discuss some of the many potential linkages between them. A central feature is the inclusion of multiple SWB impacts of processes as well as of outcomes. Some general issues that would have to be addressed in any empirical application are also discussed. SWB impacts are to be used as an additional indicator in the assessment of innovation, not as something to be maximised. By taking SWB into account, new insights might emerge that could result in either strengthening or modifying existing innovation policies, or in novel policies.

1 Introduction

What is the ultimate aim of innovation-driven economies? The standard answer given by many economists in the neoclassical tradition is 'to contribute to economic growth and the welfare of society'. Such an answer usually implicitly equates economic growth with increased welfare (in the form of increased output or consumption). Moreover, the success of innovation policies is also usually assessed

This is a revised version of a paper presented at the 14th International Schumpeter Society Conference (ISS), 2–5 July 2012, Brisbane, Australia. It was originally developed from a presentation the author gave at the workshop on 'Happiness, Innovation and Creativity' at the Fraunhofer Institute for Systems and Innovation Research (ISI) in Karlsruhe, Germany, 8–9 December 2011. The author thanks two reviewers of this journal, conference and workshop participants, and Peter Swann, for useful comments.

H.-J. Engelbrecht (✉)
School of Economics and Finance, Massey Business School, Massey University, Palmerston North, New Zealand
e-mail: H.Engelbrecht@massey.ac.nz

A. Pyka, J. Foster (eds.), *The Evolution of Economic and Innovation Systems*,
Economic Complexity and Evolution, DOI 10.1007/978-3-319-13299-0_4
Reprinted from Journal of Evolutionary Economics, 24(2), Springer 2014.

in terms of these outcomes (Stehnken et al. 2011). Schumpeterian economists, and evolutionary economists in general, seem to have contributed even less to answering the question, despite dismissing orthodox welfare economics as incompatible with evolutionary thinking. According to Schubert (2012a, 2013), they have often endorsed innovation itself as a welfare criterion, i.e. any policy that promotes innovation is seen as a good thing. This is, in some sense, surprising in light of Schumpeterian creative destruction suggesting positive as well as negative impacts of innovation, and a long list of other prominent economists and sociologists, past and present, commenting on this paradox of innovation and prosperity.[1] Some evolutionary economists are beginning to realise that an exploration of the links between innovation and well-being (however defined) is necessary, because without it policy advice has little or no foundation. As Schubert (2012a, p. 586) says in his introduction:[2]

> Innovation is a two-sided phenomenon: While it is generally beneficial in many senses of the word, it also tends to come with harmful side-effects for some of the individuals affected . . . in terms of increased uncertainty, anxiety, devaluation of human capital, dislocation, status loss, etc. . . . , rather than being unconditionally desirable, innovation and innovation-driven change have a complex normative dimension ... We cannot recommend policies to foster learning, change and innovation unless we can make a convincing case that this indeed enhances the actual *well-being* (or welfare) of the agents directly affected. (Italics in the original)

Schubert (2012a) proposes a well-being measure that focuses on 'effective preference learning', i.e. on a person's motivation and ability to learn new preferences in all domains of life. Innovation is worth promoting as long as it contributes to such learning. However, it is not made clear how this approach can be implemented in practice. In contrast, I suggest that much can potentially be learned about the well-being implications of innovation by employing Subjective Well-Being (SWB) measures, and that important opportunities for innovation research might be lost if we ignore them. In short, I suggest that Schumpeterian economics, as well as mainstream policy discourses for Knowledge-Based Economies (KBEs), could greatly benefit from taking into account insights from 'happiness research'.[3,4] While it has been argued by, e.g., Diener et al. (2009, chapter 4) that SWB measures can enhance economic analysis in a wide range of areas, a discussion specifically

---

[1]They include John Stuart Mill, Karl Marx, Ernst Friedrich Schumacher (see Swann 2009), as well as Richard Layard (2005), Diane Coyle (2011), among others.

[2]See Schubert (2012a, p. 586, footnote 2) for references to other evolutionary economists who have written on normative issues. Also see Dolfsma (2008, chapter 8), who aims to develop a dynamic Schumpeterian welfare perspective which focuses on long-term effects. However, he still equates social welfare with total output.

[3]The term happiness research is somewhat unfortunate because of its hedonistic connotations. In the economics literature it is synonymous with SWB research. I use it in that broad sense.

[4]Elsewhere I have highlighted the lack of links between the literature on policies for KBEs and that on policy implications of happiness research (see Engelbrecht 2007, 2012).

focussed on innovation seems to be almost entirely missing.[5] Yet, innovation researchers are beginning to ask questions like "shouldn't innovation policy-makers consider SWB more than in the past? Shouldn't policy-makers make SWB a precondition for the public support of innovation ...?" (Stehnken et al. 2011, p. 1). To begin to answer such questions, I argue we first need a general, and necessarily multi-faceted, model of the innovation-SWB nexus in order to highlight the potential complexities involved.

Some recent contributions seem to point in the same direction and support the view that exploration of the nexus is an idea that is 'in the air'. For example, this paper is in some important respects similar to Binder (2013), who also argues that SWB measures are well-suited as welfare indicators and benchmarks of societal progress in the context of innovative change, but he does not propose a general model of the nexus. Another example is Martin (2012), who reviews the main contributions of innovation studies since its inception approximately half a century ago and proposes 20 challenges for the coming decades. They are to jolt the reader "from taken-for-granted orthodoxies and cosy assumptions" (ibid., p.1). Arguably, many of the challenges are related to the building blocks (i.e. 'elements') and linkages associated with the general model introduced in this paper.[6] Empirical research on the relationship between innovation and SWB is also beginning to appear (e.g., Dolan and Metcalfe 2012).

There are a number of other, broader, developments that also suggest it might be opportune to link the literatures on innovation, KBEs and SWB: Innovation is increasingly asked to contribute to solving major societal challenges, like climate change, that are in various ways related to, but go beyond, the traditional contribution of innovation to economic growth (Stehnken et al. 2011; Rooney et al. 2012). Also, there is the issue of mental health, which is central to SWB. Mental illness is probably the largest single cause of misery in advanced KBEs (Layard 2005). The prevalence of mental illness in employed people, due to work-related stress and job strain, has reached high levels across the OECD and is now greatly affecting productivity in the workplace (OECD 2012). Moreover, it is likely that many 'disruptive technologies' will further transform business models, work, and the way we live in the near future (Manyika et al. 2013).

Last but not least, in recent years there have been an increasing number of proposals to develop SWB accounts, at many different levels of aggregation and for many different sub-groups of the population (Diener and Seligman 2004; Dolan and White 2007; Diener et al. 2009; Krueger et al. 2009; Stiglitz et al. 2009),

[5]Some of their examples of policy uses of SWB measures are relevant in the context of the innovation-SWB nexus, e.g. the discussion of unemployment and well-being in the workplace (Diener et al. 2009, chapter 10). The closest they come to commenting on innovation is a brief mention of the lack of knowledge of SWB impacts of technological change (ibid., p. 117).

[6]For example challenge 1 'from visible innovation to 'dark innovation'', challenge 6 'from innovation for economic productivity to innovation for sustainability ('green innovation')', challenge 7 'from risky innovation to socially responsible innovation' and challenge 8 'from innovation for wealth creation to innovation for well-being (or from 'more is better' to 'enough is enough')'.

and some national and international organisations and agencies have begun to use SWB measures as part of a larger overhaul of official statistics (Commission of the European Communities 2009; New Economics Foundation 2011; OECD 2011; Helliwell et al. 2012). How can we make sure that any official integrated system of SWB accounts will be of any use for knowledge policy making and, more specifically, innovation policy? What particular SWB measures should be adopted, given the large potential number of context-free as well as group, life domain and job facet specific measures that could be collected?

Again, to begin to answer such questions, we first need to develop a general model of the innovation-SWB nexus. This paper tries to contribute to this task by adapting and extending Swann's (2009, chapter 19) 'complex interactive model of innovation and wealth creation'. That model is based on a broad definition of wealth, i.e. Ruskinian wealth, which seems closer to quality of life, both in an objective and subjective sense, and how innovation might be linked to these different aspects of wealth.[7] I prefer to clearly distinguish between 'objective' and 'subjective' variables, thereby linking the model to the literature on SWB, as well as to a number of concepts of 'objective' wealth. However, Ruskinian aspects of wealth still play a large part in terms of linkages between different parts of the proposed model.

A central feature of the proposed model is the inclusion of multiple SWB impacts of *processes* as well as of *outcomes*. The former are a manifestation of what Frey et al. (2004) call procedural utility, i.e. the "noninstrumental pleasures and displeasures of processes" (ibid., p. 378). Procedural utility is neglected in orthodox economic welfare analysis that focuses on instrumental outcomes. However, it plays a large part in my conceptualisation of the innovation-SWB nexus.

It is important to emphasize that I do not endorse SWB as a social welfare criterion that is to be maximised. The issue is much too complex for that.[8] I simply argue that better and more comprehensive knowledge of the innovation-SWB nexus should be of interest to innovation researchers in its own right. I advocate measurement of SWB impacts as an *additional indicator* in the assessment of innovation and in innovation policy-making. It is hoped that by doing so, new insights might emerge which could, as the case may be, result either in strengthening or modifying already existing policy prescriptions, or in novel policies so far outside the scope of innovation policy. This view of the role of better SWB information for policy-making is therefore very similar, if not identical, to that of Diener et al. (2009) who advocate it in a much wider policy context. It is also similar, but not quite identical, to Binder's (2013) view, who argues that SWB measures "should ... be

[7]Ruskinian wealth is named after John Ruskin, the British philosopher and art historian.

[8]For example, the optimal level of SWB might be less than the highest level possible, it might vary between life domains and individuals, and there might be acceptable trade-offs between SWB and other objectives (Oishi et al. 2007). There is a large literature on the issue of whether policies should, or should not, maximise happiness. Hirata (2011) provides a good overview of the debate.

used to assess broadly the societal patterns of outcomes resulting from innovative activities" (ibid., p. 571).[9]

The next section first introduces the elements of the model before presenting the model itself. This is followed by a discussion of some of the many possible linkages between elements, and some further comments on major issues which would have to be addressed when implementing the model empirically. The last section provides a summary and concluding comments.

2 A general model

A convenient starting point for thinking about the innovation-SWB nexus is the question: 'Does innovation cause SWB or does SWB lead to innovation?'. The first part of the question is immediately recognisable as a normative issue for innovation policy, the second part hints at complex reverse causality and feedback effects.[10] A general model of the nexus should be able to accommodate both directions of causation, as well as a multitude of (direct and indirect) linkages between innovation, SWB and other relevant elements. In this section I first briefly introduce what I regard as the major elements that should be included in such a model. Each can be proxied by a number of alternative and/or complementary variables. The selection of elements and their proxy variables is a question of judgement and, therefore, contestable. I then introduce the general model and also discuss some reactions to this type of model.

2.1 *Assembling the pieces*

Innovation I use the generic definition of innovation as 'putting inventions to first commercial use'. In any application of the model, the specific nature of the innovation will be important. In principle, the model should be able to accommodate most types: Product, process, organisational and marketing innovations as defined in the *OSLO Manual* (OECD 2005), as well as other types of innovation,

[9]Binder (2013, p. 568) argues that this view can be termed the constitutional or institutional approach to happiness politics, whereas SWB maximisation can be termed the welfare economic approach. Although I broadly agree with the constitutional view, Binder's view of policy seems to be more hands-off then mine, aiming only at creating institutional frameworks that allow individuals to pursue SWB. I would argue that the model of the innovation-SWB nexus might also be used to identify discretionary policy interventions that aim at supporting SWB without trying to maximise it.

[10]It also hints at the issue of how to combine different SWB impacts, i.e. in this case overall SWB versus SWB in the workplace, an issue commented on further in Section 3.2.

e.g. radical versus incremental innovations, soft innovations etc. (Swann 2009, chapter 3, Stoneman 2010). The focus on commercial use seems to exclude many social innovations. They could be included in a slightly modified model. Moreover, many social innovations will impact on many parts of the model. It is probably fair to say that interdependences between commercial and social innovations are a so far under-researched topic.

Invention This element is meant to capture 'pre-commercial' idea generation. It can be proxied by its 'output' (i.e. invention) or its various potential 'inputs', e.g. research and development (R&D) expenditure, creativity, entrepreneurship, serendipity, luck. In any empirical application of the model, several of these are likely to be relevant and it might be appropriate to split them into separate elements. The inclusion of entrepreneurship is controversial from a Schumpeterian perspective.[11] Depending on the context, it could alternatively be included under innovation, or it could be included as a separate element.

Workplace and labour market For many people the work domain is an important, if not central, part of their life and identity. It potentially receives, as well as generates, many of the links associated with innovation in the model. With the development of KBEs over the last half century or so, there has been a shift in employment towards knowledge work, creating its own challenges and problems. For example, Drucker (1999) identified the need to increase knowledge worker productivity as the biggest management challenge of the 21st century. Human brains are the crucial resource in KBEs. They can be fragile and are prone to malfunction, especially when put under too much pressure. One is tempted to ask whether it is a coincidence that the rise of KBEs seems to have been accompanied by a rise in mental disorders and illnesses, like stress, anxiety and depression. However, focussing more specifically on the work domain and in particular on 'work as a process,' it is also known that a certain level of stress can help people succeed in challenging tasks, creating 'flow' experiences (Csikszentmihalyi 1990). Ng et al. (2009) suggest that research should explore how to maximise the benefits of stress without increasing its negative effects. In short, the workplace is intimately related to SWB in modern economies, and this needs to be acknowledged in innovation research. The major SWB impact of the labour market seems more straightforward, i.e. unemployment is known to usually have a very negative impact on SWB.

Product market Markets for goods and services are an essential part of the model, given the generic definition of innovation used here. It is well-known that relationships between innovations and markets are complex. Different market structures (perfect competition, oligopoly, monopoly) influence innovation in different ways, and innovation also influences market structure, e.g. by leading to higher firm

---

[11] Schumpeter firmly associated entrepreneurship with innovation. For a brief introduction to theories of creativity and entrepreneurship see, e.g., Swann (2009, chapters 9, 10).

concentration (or less, depending on the type of innovation).[12] Perfect competition is commonly regarded as least conducive to innovation, although Boldrin and Levine (2008) argue that a substantial amount of innovation does take place under this market form.

Material standard of living This element can be proxied by traditional economic performance variables like levels and growth rates of GDP and productivity, as well as alternative and newer variables which try to remedy shortcomings of the older established measures. In particular, comprehensive or total wealth (TW) has been developed as a stock measure compared to flow measures like GDP. TW is at the centre of the capital approach to development advocated by the World Bank (2011) and others, although measurement is still at a relatively early stage and controversial.[13]

Natural environment Living in the Anthropocene, i.e. in an age where humans impact the planet on a geological scale, but at a much faster than geological speed (The Economist 2011), any general model of the innovation-SWB nexus has to include as one of its elements the natural environment and its sustainability. The model needs to be able to capture not only the (positive and/or negative) environmental impacts of innovation, but also any feedback effects from the environment. Potential variables include pollution indicators, and many of the sustainability indicators put forward in the literature. However, by including SWB and the environment as separate elements, the model would have to be modified to accommodate composite sustainability indices that combine both.[14] Instead, I follow Stiglitz et al.'s (2009) advice that sustainability deserves separate measurement from current (objective and/or subjective) well-being. Another potentially relevant variable is the amenity value derived from natural capital (as noted earlier, natural capital itself is part of total wealth, i.e. it is an objective standard of living variable).

'Objective' well-being This element tries to capture all well-being and social welfare indicators other than SWB indicators and those specifically related to the natural environment and its sustainability. It includes consumption-based utility, i.e. mainstream economic welfare criteria, and also a multitude of 'objective'

[12]For a brief introduction to the issues, see Swann (2009, chapter 18).

[13]TW is conceptualised as the present value of (sustainable) consumption over a generation. Major TW subcategories are natural, produced and intangible capital. Measurement of natural capital is improving quickly, but it is still incomplete, excluding important resources like water and fisheries. Numerous assumptions have to be made when calculating natural and produced capital. They can and have been critisized (see, e.g., Perman et al. 2011). By far the largest component of TW is intangible capital. Due to lack of adequate data for many countries it is simply measured as a residual in World Bank (2011). The alternative approach of estimating *all* capital stocks *directly* and adding them up to obtain TW, plus correcting for a number of other issues associated with 'wealth accounting', has been advocated by Dasgupta (2010) and Arrow et al. (2010).

[14]Such as the Happy Planet Index (New Economics Foundation 2009) that combines happy life years (life satisfaction × life expectancy) and an adjusted ecological footprint; or Ng's (2008) environmentally responsible happy nation index.

quality-of-life indicators (e.g., health, education, and social indicators) and well-being indicators collected by many government and non-government organisations (see, e.g., Stiglitz et al. 2009; OECD 2011; New Economics Foundation 2011; Beaumont 2011).

Subjective well-being SWB is diverse, capturing different aspects of people's subjective experiences.[15] I advocate the use of life satisfaction (LSF) or evaluative well-being, in contrast to happiness or emotional (i.e. hedonic) well-being. The latter captures short-lived emotions. LSF captures longer-term considerations of the 'good life' and its ethical dimensions. Kahneman and Deaton (2010) and Deaton and Stone (2013) find that the two types of SWB have different correlates. They, therefore, emphasize the importance of distinguishing between the two.[16] In the context of trying to assess the SWB impacts of innovation, LSF seems, in general, to be the more appropriate SWB measure when the aim is to use SWB as an additional input into policy-making, and not as something to be maximised. Graham (2011), in her discussion of promises and dangers of using happiness indicators for policy purposes, calls this the choice between Aristotle and Bentham.

SWB can be measured for 'life as a whole', for specific life domains (e.g., work, family life), for particular groups of people in society, or even more specifically for particular job facets (Warr 2007). The different measures arguably convey different but complementary information about LSF of use to policy makers in the private and public sectors. In any particular implementation of the model, due consideration needs to be given to the appropriate choice of SWB measures.[17]

2.2 *Putting it all together*

Having introduced the elements, the general model is presented in Fig. 1. It tries to capture the multitude of potential links between innovation and SWB. Borrowing a phrase from Swann (2009, p. 236), one might call this the 'everything relates to everything else' model of the innovation-SWB nexus. Figure 1 is what in graph theory is called a complete graph. The model will become specific when implemented and adapted for particular innovations (this is beyond the scope of the current paper). In that process, some elements might get modified (e.g., splitting

[15]A detailed discussion of different SWB measures is beyond the scope of this paper. For further discussion see, e.g., Diener et al. (2009) and Helliwell et al. (2012).

[16]For example, happiness seems to satiate with high income, whereas LSF does not. Earlier, Inglehart et al. (2008) reported that a society's level of LSF is more closely related to economic conditions than is happiness.

[17]The multitude of potential SWB measures, even when the same general definition of SWB is used, indicates the need for some standardization, which will hopefully take the form of integrated national systems of SWB accounts.

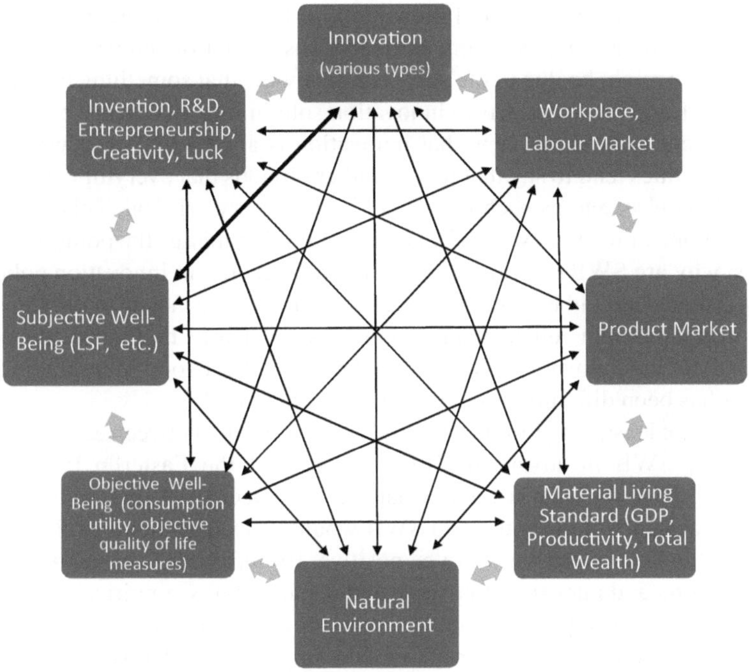

Fig. 1 A general model of the innovation – SWB nexus

'innovation' into several elements) and some links will become more important than others (and some might be found unimportant and dropped from the model).

Important features of the proposed model are similar to those mentioned in the literature on National Innovation Systems (NISs), and open to similar criticism. For example, Lundvall (1992, p. 8) argues that innovation is a ubiquitous phenomenon in the modern economy, that invention, innovation and diffusion are not separate stages, and that what to include in a National Innovation System (NIS) is context specific. Edquist (2005), in his assessment of the NISs approach, comments on what he perceives as its major weaknesses, i.e. conceptual diffuseness (no clear definition of NIS boundaries) and the lack of formal theory, suggesting it might be undertheorized. In Edquist's view, remedying the latter does not require that all elements and relations among them must be specified (he regards this as unrealistic, given the complexity of innovation systems). Instead, the NIS should be seen as a device to generate hypothesis about relations between specific variables in the system. An explanation of innovation processes will certainly be multicausal. All of these comments can also be made about the model of the innovation-SWB nexus.

Reactions to the type of model shown in Fig. 1 tend to be rather mixed. Swann[18] mentions that policy-makers seem to dislike his model of innovation and wealth creation. This might be due to the still prevalent view that something only counts as innovation if it is producer-driven innovation sold in markets. Many policy-makers also still seem to hold the view that innovation is always and everywhere a good thing. Academics tend to say that it is all rather obvious that everything is connected to everything else, and as such the model it is not very original. This was also the reaction of one of the reviewers of this paper. I think it misses the point. If it is all so obvious, why are SWB impacts rarely taken into account in innovation policy? The proposed model should be regarded as a simple *focussing device* to raise awareness of the many possible linkages and feedbacks. It clearly highlights the potential complexity of the innovation-SWB nexus, and provides a good snapshot impression of why it has been difficult to provide answers about it.[19]

Last but not least, Fig. 1 indicates why the relationship between economic growth and average SWB in advanced KBEs, i.e. part of the Easterlin Paradox, is so contested.[20] It is not clear a-priori what the net effect of all the links connecting the ‘material standard of living’ and SWB would be even if the direct impact of the former on the latter were known to be positive. By increasing our knowledge about the distribution and intensity of positive and negative links, empirical application of the model should also provide a new avenue for exploring the Paradox. If it turned out that there is one very strong negative link impacting on SWB, focussing policy on changing that link might have a strong effect on overall SWB.

3 Discussion of the proposed model

3.1 Linkages

The following discussion is not meant to be exhaustive. The potential number and complexity of relationships is simply too great. I leave it to the reader to try and think about possible additional linkages and feedbacks in the context of particular innovations of her/his choosing. I first locate the linear model of innovation in the model. Next, I focus on linkages emanating from the various elements,

[18]Personal communication, 30 April 2013.

[19]This resonates with Schumpeter’s view of the complexity of any normative analysis of creative destruction that led him to abandon any attempt at it (Schumpeter 1947, p. 155, footnote 12, reported in Schubert 2013, p. 228).

[20]For an introduction to the Easterlin Paradox controversy see Clark et al. (2008) and Easterlin et al. (2010). If it is accepted that economic growth in advanced KBEs is mostly due to productivity growth (which itself is mostly due to innovation), the literature on the Easterlin Paradox is highly relevant to the analysis of the innovation-SWB nexus.

concentrating on those associated with innovation, invention, the workplace and product markets. Some others will be mentioned only briefly.

3.1.1 The linear model of innovation as a special case (i.e. sub-set) of the model

As pointed out by Swann (2009), a complex model like that shown in Fig. 1 contains the old linear model of innovation, with causation running from invention, to innovation, to the workplace, resulting in new products or processes, enabling new, improved and/or cheaper products being sold in the market, thereby increasing GDP, consumption and utility/welfare. Swann discusses the severe limitations of such a simple model which neglects other linkages and feedback effects. In particular, it assumes that invention precedes innovation and that innovation only increases welfare/well-being if it increases GDP.

However, even if the linear model did apply and innovation increased conventionally measured welfare, it is easy to contemplate that the net impact of innovation on SWB might be weak or even negative. Procedural utility impacts might counteract outcome utility, e.g. if there are negative SWB impacts in the workplace or if consumption externalities exist. The latter might reduce any potentially positive SWB impacts of higher consumption due to negative effects on the environment (more garbage, lower amenity values, depleted resources) or due to status effects (keeping up with the Joneses, the hedonic treadmill). In any case, if, as suggested by behavioural economics, people's spending habits are less than perfectly rational and utility maximising, outcome utility becomes weaker and other SWB impacts become relatively stronger.

3.1.2 Some effects of innovation

The link between innovation and the workplace is very important for the overall SWB outcome of innovations. The issue of stress in the workplace, and its potentially negative as well as positive impacts on SWB, have already been mentioned. To expand on these themes, there are a number of related process innovations, like organisational and managerial innovations, re-engineering, changes in work practices, e.g. due to Information and Communication Technologies (Cohen 2003; Layard 2005; Bryson et al. 2013), that can create negative impacts. The literature on information overload, cognitive overload etc. also relates to this (Eppler and Mengis 2004). In contrast, policies aimed at increasing SWB of workers might increase productivity (Diener and Seligman 2004; Diener et al. 2009; Helliwell and Huang 2010). An important aspect is how to deal with risk and uncertainty, high levels of which go hand-in-hand with innovation.

A potentially very important direct link between innovation and SWB arises from the process of innovation itself (it similarly can apply to the process of invention). This deserves special mention because it has been argued by Phelps

(2009) that the distinctive merit of capitalism is not its power to create (material) wealth, but its ability to create engaging and rewarding work due to its emphasis on innovation, thereby enabling self-actualization and self-discovery. Phelps expressed similar views in his Nobel lecture (Phelps 2007), as well as in some earlier publications, calling such work attributes the essence of the good life. While these are statements about the very core of innovation-driven KBEs, their values and links to SWB, reality in the work domain for most people seems driven by the negative impacts mentioned earlier. However, Phelps views are an improvement over those of mainstream KBE analysts like, e.g., Foray (2006), who seem to have neglected any direct SWB impacts of the innovation process itself. So far there are few empirical studies exploring this issue.[21]

Some innovations bypass the workplace and create a direct link to the product market, i.e. those directly affecting the organisation of markets. Swann (2009) gives as examples the invention of the supermarket and e-business replacing smaller shops, increasing the need for travel by car and increasing the carbon footprint (thereby creating further links to environmental sustainability and SWB). There are also direct links from innovation to the natural environment. Positive links mentioned by Swann (ibid.) include the rejuvenation of inner cities, clean technologies and greater fuel efficiency, less noisy technologies. Negative environmental impacts include air and water pollution, and e-waste (due to rapid innovation in computers and software). There are also feedbacks from innovation to creativity and invention, e.g. a link going from innovators to inventors and researchers, in the sense that innovation often raises new research questions (Swann, ibid.).

It should also be acknowledged that not every innovation is acceptable to all consumers. For example, nuclear energy, genetically modified food, cloning, chlorination of drinking water etc. might reduce SWB for some, especially if consumers cannot circumvent adoption. Marketing might be used to make new goods and services acceptable (i.e. changing consumer preferences), as might be strategies that specifically focus on reducing the actual and perceived risks associated with adoption.[22] The direction of impact on SWB is less clear if consumers can refuse adoption, i.e. the SWB impact of ‘consumer resistance’ might be positive.

[21]One example is Dolan and Metcalfe (2012). Using a representative survey of the British population and new primary data, they find a strong link between innovation (proxied alternatively by being original and having imagination) and SWB (in the workplace and in life generally). They point out that more research is needed to determine causation. Their explanatory variables mostly capture personal attributes, some of which can be mapped into the model of the innovation-SWB nexus, but many potentially important factors are not included.

[22]For an introduction to the literature on consumer resistance to innovation adoption see Kleijnen et al. (2009).

3.1.3 Some effects of invention

The link from invention to innovation is that of the old linear model, i.e. some of the many inventions develop into commercially viable innovations, through varying combinations of creativity, R&D, entrepreneurship, serendipity and luck. However, Swann (2009) strongly suspects that much creativity contributes to wealth creation through different channels. He mentions direct links from creativity to the workplace: Companies might allow staff to spend half-a-day a week to pursue their own blue sky projects, which might, or might not, result in invention and/or innovation. If this increases work morale, it is likely to raise worker productivity (as well as SWB).

There are other direct links between creativity and SWB that bypass the workplace (and that are closer related to Ruskinian wealth or quality of life). For example, Swann mentions that hobbies pursued by people in their spare time, e.g. painting, writing, beautifying ones home, gardening etc., usually increase SWB. The latter two examples might also link to environmental sustainability. Swann further mentions the possibility of negative links between creativity and SWB, such as self-destructive lifestyles of highly creative people.

Another set of links connecting creativity, invention, as well as product market and consumption, is Von Hippel's (1988, 2005) user innovation by intermediate or final consumers. Commenting specifically on end user innovation Swann (2009, p. 239) goes so far to state that

> ..., we could say that the households use their own creativity to produce more from a given bundle of purchased goods and services. While I cannot quantify it, I suspect that this use of creativity may be just as important in wealth creation as that creativity which is channelled through innovation!

Last but not least, open source contributions, crowd sourcing and related voluntary peer production activities often link creativity, invention, innovation and SWB in KBEs, while also increasing productivity and TW. Note that depending on the characteristics of such activities and the degree of commercialisation of their outcomes, they could be classified as inventions or innovations. Benkler (2006) goes so far to argue that such activities are heralding the arrival of a new, although somewhat fragile, mode of production in the internet age which by-passes conventional work arrangements and markets.

3.1.4 Some effects of the workplace and labour market

There are many other links emanating from the workplace and labour market in addition to that going to the product market. The conditions one finds in the workplace can impact on creativity, invention and the many forms of employee-driven innovation (Høyrup et al. 2012), providing an important example of reverse causality neglected in the linear model of innovation (Swann 2009). As discussed earlier, conditions in the workplace *directly* impact on SWB. This is a key example of procedural utility (Frey et al. 2004), where procedures and institutions under which people live and work (e.g. hierarchies, labour laws) affect SWB.[23] Frey et al. (ibid.) find that procedural utility is of great importance in employment.

Swann (2009) also discusses workplace impacts on consumption. They can be positive or negative. An employer can promote healthy lifestyles (by providing healthy meals, time for exercises, gym memberships etc.) or unhealthy ones (e.g. work-related stress leading to alcoholism). These, then, again links to SWB. In extreme cases, workplace conditions can be so stressful that they increase the likelihood of employee suicide. The example of France Télécom comes to mind (Jolly and Saltmarsh 2009).

It is also possible that there are negative links between workplace conditions and the environment. Swann (2009) mentions environmental impacts of the early industrial revolution, but one can think of many current examples (e.g., processing of e-waste in Africa and the ship recycling yards near Chittagong in Bangladesh).

3.1.5 Some effects of product markets (the market place)

Purchasing final goods and services increases consumption. It is usually assumed that this also increases welfare and SWB. However, product markets might negatively impact on some people's SWB, e.g. when abundance of choice produces anxiety (Schwartz 2004) or when there are status effects. Moreover, Swann (2009) points out that the market place can have SWB impacts other then those associated with consumption. For example, some people derive great pleasure from browsing, be it in expensive high street shops, art auction houses, flea markets, bargain bins, garage sales, open homes, even if purchasing little or nothing. Markets might also provide ideas for innovators, both in terms of providing knowledge about what consumers want and by suggesting organisational changes (ibid.). There might also be SWB impacts because people judge market allocation processes as either fair or unfair. Frey et al. (2004) discuss at some length the literature associated with allocation procedures (of which the market mechanism is one) having procedural utility impacts.

3.1.6 Some other linkages

There are many other direct and indirect linkages that might be of importance when analysing the SWB impacts of a particular innovation. Some of the more obvious ones include: (a) The impacts of innovation-driven economic growth and consumption on environmental sustainability (linking 'standard of living' and 'natural environment'). Swann (2009) mentions that how and what we consume

[23]Frey et al. (2004, p. 385/6) argue, e.g., that "hierarchy constitutes a procedural disutility because it interferes with innate needs of self-determination".

affects the environment in different ways (house insulation, recycling, extent of car use etc.). This can further impact on SWB. There is also some research on the link between consumption of, specifically, digital products and SWB.[24] (b) The link from the natural environment, due to its amenity value, to SWB. (c) The direct and positive link from social capital, which is part of TW, to SWB (Helliwell and Putnam 2004; Helliwell and Wang 2009). (d) There might also be a direct link going from social capital to innovation (Akçomak and ter Weel 2009). (e) Swann (2009) mentions a number of links emanating from wealthy individuals: Creativity, invention and innovation might be supported by business angels or through philanthropy (e.g. large donations to universities). (f) There might be a link between entrepreneurship and SWB. However, the literature reports conflicting findings on this issue.[25]

3.2 Some other issues to consider

There are a number of other general issues that would be encountered in any empirical application of the model.

Subset of variables and links to be analysed The importance of each potential variable and link, as well as feedback effects and chains of causation, will differ by type of innovation, by which industries or sectors of the economy are involved, by who is affected (producers, consumers, other subgroups of the population). Choices and compromises will have to be made depending on the focus of the analysis and data availability. In short, only a subset of variables and links will be relevant and/or measurable.

To give but one example, should only one type of SWB be measured, e.g. LSF, or should impacts also be measured for other types of SWB? It is well established in the literature that for different SWB measures, e.g. hedonic versus eudaimonic, the direction of impact of an event can differ. Moreover, the type of SWB supportive of creativity might be different from the type of SWB impacts we want to measure in the population affected by an innovation. Even if we stick with one type of SWB measure, it is not clear whether, or if so how, different SWB impacts should be aggregated to achieve an overall impact measure. Analysts need to be aware of these issues and should explicitly justify their choices.[26]

---

[24]For example, Kavetsos and Koutroumpis (2011) find positive correlations for some products and argue this might have implications for public policy, e.g. for recognising internet access as a fundamental human right.

[25]See, e.g., Uhlaner and Thurik (2007) for findings derived from macro-level cross-country data, and Block and Koellinger (2009) and Carree and Verheul (2012) for findings obtained using micro-level data.

[26]Binder (2013) wants to impose more structure on the SWB analysis of innovations by restricting analysis to "life domains which impact on subjective well-being regardless of context and culture"

Level of aggregation There are likely to be different SWB impacts of an innovation, depending on whether the analysis is conducted at the micro-, meso- or macro level. Researchers should explore whether it is appropriate and feasible to conduct an analysis at different levels of aggregation, and whether they can be combined.[27] Also, the evaluation of SWB gains and losses is made more difficult when considering domain-specific SWB. Overall SWB might not change, despite losses and gains in specific domains. Whether this is acceptable or not is a normative question which should be addressed in any specific innovation study. It is also possible that there are (positive or negative) SWB spillovers from one life domain to another (e.g., there might be work-life balance issues, such as work stress negatively affecting a person's family life). Whether such issues can be explored depends on the available data. The development of consistent SWB accounts by statistical agencies might make this more feasible in future.

Time horizon There are usually trade-offs between short-term and long-term SWB impacts of innovation and, important from a Schumpeterian perspective, preferences evolve over time.[28] New products and/or product designs might increase SWB in the short run, but novelty usually wears off after a while. In general, features of human behaviour like cognitive fallacies, unanticipated adaptation, focusing illusion, memory bias etc.[29] add important time dimensions.[30] Moreover, it seems to be easier for people to adjust to unpleasant certainties than to uncertainty (Graham 2011). If possible, it should be explored how the degree of uncertainty associated with particular innovations varies over time, and how this affects SWB.[31] What time horizon(s) to use when implementing the model empirically is an important question that needs to be carefully considered. However, data availability etc. is likely to dictate pragmatic answers.

(ibid., p. 572). He calls this his 'life domain evaluation principle'. However, he is not very specific about what domains to include. There are potentially some similarities to several of the elements included in my general model, but his formulation seems overly restrictive.

[27] See Dopfer et al. (2004) on the importance of the meso in evolutionary economics. They argue meso change is central for understanding evolutionary dynamics.

[28] I do not assume preferences are unchanging over time. However, I do not explicitly comment on the issue of endogenous preferences in this paper, an issue which is central to Schubert's (2012a, b, 2013) work. The relationship between preference learning and SWB is a complex one that should be explored further.

[29] See, e.g., Hirata (2011, pp. 59–63).

[30] Binder (2013) proposes a second normative evaluation rule, i.e. the 'welfare dynamics principle', that is aimed at imposing structure on the SWB analyses of innovation over the medium and long run. It focuses exclusively on hedonic adaptation dynamics. While undoubtedly ambitious and challenging, it leaves out other dynamic relationships of the innovation-SWB nexus.

[31] While Schubert argues there needs to be novelty (and therefore uncertainty) so that people can learn new preferences, he does not highlight the potential impacts of uncertainty on SWB. Not only is it unclear how his approach can be implemented empirically, I would also argue that preference learning is not the same as welfare or well-being. It has its own SWB impacts, which are part of the dynamic relationships of the innovation-SWB nexus.

The issues become even more difficult when trying to take the (subjective and objective) well-being of future generations into account. This is another reason why measured SWB impacts cannot be used as the only criterion to judge the welfare implications of innovation. However, a more complete knowledge of SWB impacts of innovation should be important when addressing difficult normative issues and trade-offs associated with innovation.

Framework conditions So far I have not commented on broader societal factors or framework conditions, such as the nature of the innovation system, or 'culture' and 'values', that influence innovation, SWB, and the other elements of the model. It should be clear that they potentially affect all of them (one should think of further arrows connecting the elements to a surrounding frame). Determinants of the National and other Systems of Innovation include the Intellectual Property Rights regime, opportunities and incentives for talented individuals, and other institutional factors. Culture and values are contested areas of research that cover a broad literature in modern growth theory and in sociology. In the current context, a good starting point is the World Values Survey and research published by its founder and associates (Inglehart et al. 2004, 2008; Inglehart and Welzel 2005). They argue that high levels of SWB in advanced KBEs are associated with a specific set of values (self-expression or post-materialist values). However, it can be observed that even amongst what are often regarded as very similar advanced economies, people's beliefs and values about core KBE-elements differ, sometimes greatly so (Engelbrecht 2007). Moreover, Diener and Seligman (2004) report that negative effects of materialism in advanced economies may be one reason for the increase in mental illness. This seems to counterbalance Inglehart et al.'s more positive assessment, at least to a certain degree.

To summarize, a pragmatic approach will be required when implementing the model for specific innovations. Analysts should determine the most important variables and links between them, and also indicate what should but cannot be measured, both in the present and over time. Only the accumulation of such studies is likely to enable us to make progress in understanding the innovation-SWB nexus, and to address normative issues.

4 Summary and concluding comments

Building on Swann's (2009) contribution, I propose a complex, multifaceted general model of the many ways in which innovation and SWB may be connected, and advocate its implementation in empirical innovation studies. This would seem a natural progression of the economics of innovation, given the normative turn in innovation policy associated with today's big societal challenges and developments in SWB research, and increased efforts to collect SWB data on a more frequent, widespread and consistent basis. The model is general in the sense that its specification, i.e. in terms of variables used, their relative importance, the direction and relative importance of linkages, will depend on the innovation analysed, a task not undertaken in this paper. It would likely require a large multi-disciplinary effort.

Over time, accumulation of innovation studies that include a SWB perspective should provide evidence not only on overall SWB impacts of innovations, but also on issues such as the relative importance of procedural utility versus outcome utility, the impacts relative income and status effects have on both, any trade-offs involved, etc. The complexity of the innovation-SWB nexus should also be taken note of when trying to link SWB and innovation databases as suggested by, e.g., Diener et al. (2009). Although we are unlikely to ever be able to account for all of the SWB impacts of innovation, this should not be an excuse for giving up on efforts to take into account as many as possible.

One promising area for further research would seem to be a detailed exploration of the relationship between the general model of the innovation-SWB nexus and the literature on NISs.[32] One could envisage an approach best described as 'NIS + SWB'.[33] Whether SWB would be (more or less) an add-on to the NIS, or whether SWB impacts would more profoundly influence our understanding of the NIS, remains an interesting question to be explored. Also, given that learning (in all its forms) is central to NISs, an NIS+SWB approach might go some way toward enabling an empirical assessment of Schubert's evolutionary approach to well-being.

In any case, adoption of a SWB perspective in the economics of innovation should impact on the evaluation of innovations and on innovation policy. I agree with Swann's (2009, p. 271) concluding conjecture that a complex interactive view of innovation is likely to alter future government policy towards innovation. Such policy will take much wider societal considerations into account than the still dominant view that only assesses innovations in terms of their impacts on productivity, profitability, or similar economic performance measures. Increased awareness and knowledge of the innovation-SWB nexus should help governments and the public to realise trade-offs between innovation and SWB beyond what has been considered so far. Better knowledge about SWB impacts should provide an additional input into innovation and knowledge policy making, which might be quite subtle. Hirata also captures this sentiment when trying to answer the question what the 'happiness perspective' can contribute to good development:

> A society that looks towards happiness for orientation will probably not do everything differently. It will, however, strive to create conditions for a society in which production and consumption are subordinated to a good life rather than the other way around. It will not reduce citizens to consumers, and workers to production factors ...

[32] Lundvall (2011), e.g., acknowledges links between the quality of work, learning opportunities and innovation, and job satisfaction.

[33] This would also apply to other types of innovation systems, e.g. regional, sectoral, or technological.

> ... It can shake up conventional answers that suggest that the evident goal of development is economic growth and that technological progress will automatically bring well-being. (Hirata 2011, p. 153/4)

In short, while good development and the good life should not be reduced to SWB, the latter is surely an important part of the former. In a similar way, I have argued elsewhere (Engelbrecht 2007, 2012) that SWB research can and should contribute to the development of wisdom-based knowledge policies based on conceptions of the good life.[34] In a general sense, the model of the innovation-SWB nexus proposed in this paper is an attempt to contribute to the development of the analytical tools needed to advance the quest for wisdom-based knowledge policies.

References

Akçomak S, ter Weel B (2009) Social capital, innovation and growth: evidence from Europe. Eur Econ Rev 53(5):544–567

Arrow K, Dasgupta P, Goulder L, Mumford K, Oleson K (2010) Sustainability and the measurement of wealth. Working Paper 16599, National Bureau of Economic Research, Cambridge

Beaumont J (2011) Measuring national well-being–discussion paper on domains and measures. Office for National Statistics, UK

Benkler Y (2006) The wealth of networks: how social production transforms markets and freedom. Yale University Press, New Haven and London

Binder M (2013) Innovativeness and subjective well-being. Soc Indic Res 111:561–578

Block J, Koellinger P (2009) I can't get no satisfaction–necessity entrepreneurship and procedural utility. Kyklos 62(2):191–209

Boldrin M, Levine D (2008) Perfectly competitive innovation. J Monetary Econ 55:435–453

Bryson A, Dale-Olsen H, Barth E (2013) The effects of organizational change on worker well-being and the moderating role of trade unions. Ind Labor Relat Rev 66:989–1011

Carree M, Verheul I (2012) What makes entrepreneurs happy? Determinants of satisfaction amongst founders. J Happiness Stud 13(2):371–387

Clark A, Frijters P, Shields M (2008) Relative income, happiness, and utility: an explanation for the Easterlin Paradox and other puzzles. J Econ Lit 46(1):95–144

Cohen D (2003) Our modern times: the new nature of capitalism in the information age. MIT Press, Cambridge

Commission of the European Communities (2009) GDP and beyond: measuring progress in a changing world. Communication from the Commission to the Council and the European Parliament, COM (2009), 433 final, Brussels

Coyle D (2011) The economics of enough: how to run the economy as if the future matters. Princeton University Press, Princeton and Oxford

Csikszentmihalyi M (1990) Flow: the psychology of optimal experience. Harper & Row, New York

Daly H (1996) Beyond growth: the economics of sustainable development. Beacon Press, Boston

[34]On wisdom-based knowledge policies see, e.g., Rooney and McKenna (2005) and Rooney et al. (2010). The need to move from an information and KBE to a wisdom economy has also been pointed out by others, e.g. by Daly (1996), one of the founders of ecological economics.

Dasgupta P (2010) The place of nature in economic development. In: Rodrik D, Rosenzweig M (eds) Handbook of development economics, vol 5. North-Holland/Elsevier BV, Amsterdam, pp 4977–5046

Deaton A, Stone AA (2013) Two happiness puzzles. Am Econ Rev 103(3):591–597

Diener E, Seligman M (2004) Beyond money: toward an economy of well-being. Psychol Sci Public Interest 5(1):1–31

Diener E, Lucas R, Schimmack U, Helliwell J (2009) Well-being for public policy. Oxford University Press, Oxford and New York

Dolan P, Metcalfe R (2012) The relationship between innovation and subjective well-being. Res Pol 41:1489–1498

Dolan P, White M (2007) How can measures of subjective well-being be used to inform public policy?Perspect Psychol Sci 2(1):71–85

Dolfsma W (2008) Knowledge economies: organization, location and innovation. Routledge, London and New York

Dopfer K, Foster J, Potts J (2004) Micro-meso-macro. J Evol Econ 14:263–279

Drucker P (1999) Knowledge-worker productivity: the biggest challenge. Calif Manage Rev 41(2):79– 94

Easterlin R, Angelescu McVey L, Switek M, Sawangfa O, Smith Zweig J (2010) The happiness-income paradox revisited. PNAS 107(52):22463–22468

The Economist (2011) The geology of the planet: welcome to the Anthropocene. May 26th, p 14

Edquist C (2005) Systems of innovation: perspectives and challenges. In: Fagerberg J, Mowery DC, Nelson RR (eds) The Oxford handbook of innovation. Oxford University Press, Oxford and New York, pp 181–208

Engelbrecht HJ (2007) The (un)happiness of knowledge and the knowledge of (un)happiness: Happiness research and policies for knowledge-based economies. Prometheus 25(3):243–266

Engelbrecht HJ (2012) Knowledge-based economies and subjective well-being. In: David Rooney D, Hearn G, Kastelle T (eds) Handbook on the knowledge economy, volume 2. Edward Elgar, Cheltenham and Northampton, pp 54–67

Eppler M, Mengis J (2004) The concept of information overload: a review of literature from organization science, accounting, marketing, MIS, and related disciplines. Inf Soc 20(5):325–344

Foray D (2006) Optimizing the use of knowledge. In: Kahin B, Foray D (eds) Advancing knowledge and the knowledge economy. MIT Press, Cambridge, pp 9–15

Frey B, Benz M, Stutzer A (2004) Introducing procedural utility: not only what, but also how matters. J Institut Theor Econ 160:377–401

Graham C (2011) The pursuit of happiness: an economy of well-being. The Brookings Institution, Washington

Helliwell J, Huang H (2010) How's the job? Well-being and social capital in the workplace. Ind Labor Relat Rev 63(2):205–227

Helliwell J, Putnam R (2004) The social context of well-being. Phil Trans R Soc London B 359:1435–1446

Helliwell J, Wang S (2009) Trust and well-being. Paper presented at The 3rd OECD World Forum on Statistics, Knowledge and Policy: Charting Progress, Building Visions, Improving Life, Busan Korea, 27–30 October 2009. http://www.oecd.org/dataoecd/55/17/43964059.pdf. Accessed 5 May 2012

Helliwell J, Layard R, Sachs J (eds) (2012) World happiness report. The Earth Institute, Columbia University, New York

Hirata J (2011) Happiness, ethics and economics. Routledge, Taylor & Francis Group, London and New York

Høyrup S, Bonnafous-Boucher M, Hasse C, Lotz M, Møller K (eds) (2012) Employee-driven innovation: a new approach. Palgrave MacMillan, New York and Houndmills, Basingstoke

Inglehart R, Welzel C (2005) Modernization, cultural change, and democracy: the human development sequence. Cambridge University Press, New York

Inglehart R, Basanez M, Diez-Medrano J, Halman L, Luijkx R (2004) Human beliefs and values: a cross-cultural sourcebook based on the 1999–2002 values surveys. Siglo XXI Editores, Mexico
Inglehart R, Foa R, Peterson C, Welzel C (2008) Development, freedom, and rising happiness: a global perspective. Perspect Psychol Sci 3(4):264–285
Jolly D, Saltmarsh M (2009) Suicides in France put focus on workplace. The New York Times, September 29th. (accessed on-line January 9th, 2012)
Kahneman D, Deaton A (2010) High income improves evaluation of life but not emotional well-being. PNAS 107(38):16489–16493
Kavetsos G, Koutroumpis P (2011) Technological affluence and subjective well-being. J Econ Psychol 32:742–753
Kleijnen M, Lee N, Wetzels M (2009) An exploration of consumer resistance to innovation and its antecedents. J Econ Psychol 30(3):344–357
Krueger A, Kahneman D, Schkade D, Schwarz N, Stone A (2009) National time accounting: the currency of life. In: Krueger A (ed) Measuring the subjective well-being of nations: national accounts of time use and well-being. University of Chicago Press, Chicago and London, pp 9–86
Layard R (2005) Happiness: lessons from a new science. Penguin Press, New York
Lundvall BÅ (1992) Introduciton. In: Lundvall BÅ (ed) National systems of innovation: towards a theory of innovation and interactive learning. Pinter Publishers, London, pp 1–19
Lundvall BÅ (2011) Notes on innovation systems and economic development. Innov Dev 1(1):25–38
Manyika J, Chui M, Bughin J, Dobbs R, Bisson P, Marrs A (2013) Disruptive technologies: advances that will transform life, business, and the global economy. McKinsey Global Institute
Martin BR (2012) Innovation studies: Challenging the boundaries. In: Lundvall Symposium on the Future of Innovation Studies, 16–17 February 2012, Aalborg University. The submitted version, available at http://sro.sussex.ac.uk/38701/. Accessed 4 April 2013
New Economics Foundation (2009) The happy planet index 2.0. London. www.happyplanetindex.org., Accessed 5 May 2012
New Economics Foundation (2011) National accounts of well-being. http://www.nationalaccountsofwellbeing.org/learn/measuring/. Accessed 5 May 2012
Ng YK (2008) Environmentally responsible happy nation index: towards an internationally acceptable national success indicator. Soc Indic Res 85(3):425–446
Ng W, Diener E, Aurora R, Harter J (2009) Affluence, feelings of stress, and well-being. Soc Indic Res 94(2):257–271
OECD (2005) The measurement of scientific and technological activities - Oslo manual: guidelines for collecting and interpreting innovation data, 3rd edn. Commission Eurostat, Paris
OECD (2011) How's life? Measuring well-being. Paris
OECD (2012) Sick on the job? Myths and realities about mental health at work. Paris
Oishi S, Diener E, Lucas R (2007) The optimum level of well-being: can people be too happy?Perspect Psychol Sci 2(4):346–360
Perman R, Ma Y, Common M, Maddison D, McGilvray J (2011) Natural resource and environmental economics, 4th edn. Pearson Education Ltd, Harlow
Phelps E (2007) Macroeconomics for a modern economy. Am Econ Rev 97(3):543–561
Phelps E (2009) Refounding capitalism. Capital Soc 4(3):11, Article 2
Rooney D, McKenna B (2005) Should the knowledge-based economy be a savant or a sage? Wisdom and socially intelligent innovation. Prometheus 23(3):307–323
Rooney D, McKenna B, Liesch P (2010) Wisdom and management in the knowledge economy. Routledge, New York and Abingdon
Rooney D, Hearn G, Kastelle T (2012) Knowledge is people doing things, knowledge economies are people doing things with better outcomes for more people. In: Rooney D, Hearn G, Kastelle T (eds) Handbook on the knowledge economy, volume two. Edward Elgar, Cheltenham and Northampton, pp 1–14
Schubert C (2012a) Is novelty always a good thing? Towards an evolutionary welfare economics. J Evol Econ 22(3):585–619

Schubert C (2012b) Pursuing happiness. Kyklos 65(2):245–261
Schubert C (2013) How to evaluate creative destruction: reconstructing Schumpeter's approach. Cambr J Econ 37:227–250
Schumpeter JA (1947) The creative response in economic history. J Econ Hist 7(2):149–159
Schwartz B (2004) The paradox of choice: why more is less. HarperCollins Publishers, New York
Stehnken T, Muller E, Zenker A (2011) Happiness and innovation: avenues for further research, evoREG Research Note #18, November, 6 pages. http://www.evoreg.eu/docs/files/shno/Note_evoREG_18.pdf. Accessed 5 May2012
Stiglitz J, Sen A, Fitoussi J-P (2009) Report by the commission on the measurement of economic performance and social progress. www.stiglitz-sen-fitoussi.fr. Accessed 5 May 2012
Stoneman P (2010) Soft innovation: economics, product aesthetics, and the creative industries. Oxford University Press, Oxford
Swann GMP (2009) The economics of innovation: an introduction. Edward Elgar, Cheltenham and Northampton, MA
Uhlaner L, Thurik R (2007) Postmaterialism influencing total entrepreneurial activity across nations. J Evol Econ 17(2):161–185
Von Hippel E (1988) The sources of innovation. Oxford University Press, New York and Oxford. http://web.mit.edu/evhippel/www/sources.htm. Accessed 5 May 2012
Von Hippel E (2005) Democratizing innovation. MIT Press, Cambridge. http://web.mit.edu/evhippel/www/democ1.htm. Accessed 5 May 2012
Warr P (2007) Work, happiness, and unhappiness. Lawrence Erlbaum Associates, Mahwah
World Bank (2011) The changing wealth of nations: measuring sustainable development in the new millennium. Washington, D.C.

The Signs of Change in Economic Evolution

An analysis of directional, stabilizing and diversifying selection based on Price's equation

Esben Sloth Andersen and Jacob Rubæk Holm

Abstract Neo-Schumpeterian evolutionary economics has, since the early works of Nelson and Winter, defined evolution as the change of the mean of a characteristic of a population. This paper trancends the previous paradigm and explores novel aspects of evolution in economics. Within the traditional paradigm change is provided by directional selection (and directional innovation). However, the full definition of evolutionary processes has to include two important types of selection that change the variance without necessarily changing the mean. Stabilizing selection removes any outlier and diversifying selection promotes the coexistence of behavioural variants. This paper emphasizes the need for an integrated analysis of all three types of selection. It also demonstrates that the evolutionary algebra provided by Price's equation increases the intellectual coherence and power of thinking about selection and other aspects of evolutionary processes. Directional, stabilizing and diversifying selection are then related to fitness functions that can produce the different types of selection; and the functions are used for simple simulations of the change of the population distribution of a quantitative characteristic. Finally, the paper adds to evolutionary economics a novel way of using Price's equation to decompose the statistics of the changes of the frequency distributions. The changes of mean, variance, skewness and kurtosis are all decomposed as the sum of a selection effect and an intra-member effect. It is especially the signs of these effects that serve to define and characterize the different types of selection. Both this result and the general analysis of the types of selection are of relevance for applied evolutionary economics.

E.S. Andersen (✉) • J.R. Holm
Department of Business and Management, Aalborg University, Fibigerstraede 11, 9220 Aalborg, Denmark
e-mail: esa@business.aau.dk

A. Pyka, J. Foster (eds.), *The Evolution of Economic and Innovation Systems*,
Economic Complexity and Evolution, DOI 10.1007/978-3-319-13299-0_5
Reprinted from Journal of Evolutionary Economics, 24(2), Springer 2014.

1 Introduction

The analysis of directional selection is well-developed in evolutionary economics where it is often applied in empirical research and simulations in relation to productivity. This paper demonstrates that these analyses can be complemented by analyses of stabilizing selection and diversifying selection. It also demonstrates that the evolutionary algebra provided by Price's equation increases the intellectual coherence and power of thinking about selection and other aspects of evolutionary processes. The paper combines these aims by analysing the types of selection by means of the algebra of evolution provided by Price's equation.

Neo-Schumpeterian evolutionary economics has largely been based on the paradigm of directional evolution. From Nelson and Winter (1982) and onward, economic evolution has implicitly been defined as the change of the mean of an evolutionarily relevant characteristic of a population of firms. Evolution moves this mean in a particular direction; and when the mean does not change any more, evolution has come to a halt. This interpretation has been supported by the "Fisher principle" (Metcalfe 1994) of the distance from mean dynamics (or replicator dynamics) of a population of firms with different characteristics. Here positive directional selection can in principle always proceed, but the emergence of positive outliers is crucial. The movement of the mean characteristic is made by decreasing the variance. Thus evolution consumes variance as its fuel; and it comes to a halt unless new variance is supplied by innovation or mutation. Evolution can also fade out if the intensity of selection moves towards zero. Thus the paradigm of directional evolution is supported by a clear principle. Furthermore, it has been formalized by many well-developed models (Hanusch and Pyka 2007). Finally, the popularity of the paradigm is related to the (over)emphasis on productivity change within evolutionary economics. It is normally recognized that what evolves in a population of firms is ultimately a series of underlying characteristics rather than the firm-level productivities. But it is seldom recognized explicitly that these characteristics are not likely to progress in the same trend-like manner as the aggregative phenomenon of productivity. Even "evolutionary arms races" (Dawkins and Krebs 1979) cannot go on forever.

Although some concrete characteristics, during limited periods, will display a progressive evolutionary trend as depicted by the paradigm of directional evolution, we also observe two other types of evolution, as illustrated in Fig. 1. On the one hand, there is stabilizing evolution that tends to remove any change away from the favoured value of a characteristic. On the other hand, there are cases of diversifying evolution that promotes the coexistence of different types of behaviour within a population and may lead to the emergence of two separate populations. These two possibilities are well-established within evolutionary biology (Futuyma 2005, pp. 304–305, 345–350). Thus any biological analysis of natural selection would not be complete without considering the possibilities of directional, stabilizing and diversifying selection. Since the underlying genetics is normally unknown or complex, such analyses generally play the "phenotypic gambit" (Grafen 1984), that is, they study the change of directly observable characteristics. In the analysis of

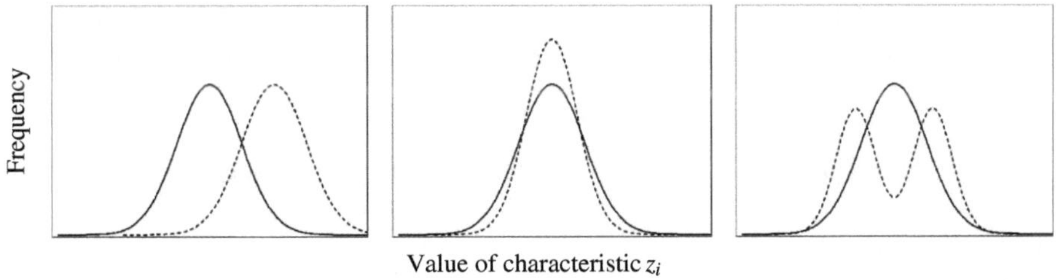

Fig. 1 Three types of pure selection. The *solid line* represent the pre-selection distribution of the characteristic and is identical across the three panels. The *dashed lines* represent the distribution of the characteristic after pure direction, pure stabilizing and pure diversifying selection respectively

economic evolution, it is easier to apply the methods of this phenotypic approach than the methods of the traditional genotypic approach. But there are still difficult-to-detect assumptions that are not useful in economic contexts – such as the normality of population distributions and the randomness of mutations. Even the fact that firms are diverse in a sustainable way is still not an established result within economics (Syverson 2011).

2 Price's equation and its usefulness

It is very helpful to analyze the different modes of selection within the totally general framework of Price's equation (Rice 2004, pp. 174–178). This seems the most obvious way of overcoming the one-sided paradigm of directional evolution within theoretical and applied evolutionary economics. However, Price's equation emerged from the statistical analysis of directional evolution. This analysis had already been developed when Schumpeter (2000, p. 184) in the 1930s called for "a quantitative theory of evolution". But he seems to have been unaware that it had already been provided by the great statistician and evolutionary biologist Fisher (1930). One reason for Schumpeter's neglect is that he emphasized the innovative part of the evolutionary process while Fisher emphasized directional selection. Another reason might have been that many biologists were also unaware of the path-breaking approach.

Since Fisher was in many respects forty years ahead of his time, the biological recognition and development of some of his major contributions took place in parallel with the emergence of modern evolutionary economics. Actually, Nelson and Winter (1982, p. 243n) remarked that their formal statistical analysis of pure selection processes "reminded us of Fisher's 'fundamental theorem of natural selection': 'The rate of increase in fitness of any organism at any time is equal to its genetic variance in fitness at that time' " (from Fisher 1930, p. 35). However, the result of Fisher as well as that of Nelson and Winter are most obviously relevant for the special case of pure selection processes. It was instead George Price who developed a general decomposition of evolutionary change that includes not only the effect of selection but also the effect of mutation or innovation (see Frank 1995, 1998). For the statistics of any adequately defined population of members, Price proved that

$$\text{Total evolutionary change} = \text{Selection effect} + \text{Intra-member effect} \quad (1)$$

This is the verbal version of Price's equation for directional evolution. The selection effect can be interpreted as the intensity of selection times the variance of the population. The intra-member effect is more difficult to interpret, but in economic evolution it includes the consequences of learning and innovation within the members of the population. Biological evolution is characterized by intra-member effects that are many times smaller than the selection effects (Frank 2012a). In contrast, applications of decomposition techniques that are mathematically identical to Price's equation on productivity data show selection effects that often amount to a relatively small share of total evolution (Foster et al. 1998, 2008; Disney et al. 2003; Bartelsman et al. 2004). This result is influenced by the problematic use of firms rather than individual routine activities as the units of selection. However, it probably also reflects that even the most narrowly defined intra-member effects in economic evolution are important. These effects seem to some extent to be the consequence of boundedly rational decisions that are influenced by higher-level selection pressures. Thus there seems to be both a direct and an indirect influence of selection. This suggests that the apparently discouraging result on the nature of economic evolution does not warrant an abandonment of Fisher's and Price's focus on the selection effect of Eq. 1.

The importance of Price's decomposition of directional evolutionary change has been difficult to understand, but during the last twenty years the situation has changed radically both in evolutionary biology (Frank 1998; Rice 2004) and in evolutionary economics. With respect to the latter, Metcalfe (2002, p. 90) pointed out that "[f]or some years now evolutionary economists have been using the Price equation without realising it." It may be added to Metcalfe's observation that formulations equivalent to Price's equation have also been used in productivity studies with few relations to evolutionary economics (e.g., Foster et al. 1998, 2002, 2008; Disney et al. 2003). In any case, we have arrived at a situation where the Fisher principle can be appreciated (Metcalfe 1994; Frank 1997) and where we can extend the application of Price's equation in many directions.

It should be noted that important extensions (Metcalfe 1997; Rice 2004, pp. 194–203; Metcalfe and Ramlogan 2006; Okasha 2006; Bowles and Gintis 2011, pp. 218–222) have emerged within the directional paradigm of economic evolution. The present paper develops a very different type of extension. The background is that Price's equation can be used to decompose *any* evolutionarily relevant characteristic. The relevant characteristic for stabilizing and diversifying evolution is the total change of the variance of the population distribution. For this case, we get the following version of Price's equation:

$$\text{Total change of variance} = \text{Selection effect} + \text{Intra-member effect} \quad (2)$$

If the selection effect of Eq. 2 is negative, we observe stabilizing selection. If it is positive, we have diversifying selection.

The paper has the aims of extending the concept of selection to include stabilizing and diversifying selection, and of demonstrating the power of Price's equation to this end. It starts by reviewing recent discussions in relation to Price's equation (Section 2). This review includes the presentation of a framework for analysing evolution that then is used for the definition and analysis of directional, stabilizing and diversifying selection (Section 3). These types of selection are then related to fitness functions that can produce the different types of selection; and the functions are used for simple simulations of the change of the population distribution of a quantitative characteristic (Section 4). Finally, Price's equation is used to decompose the statistics of the changes of the frequency distributions (Section 5). Section 6 discusses the implications of the results and venues for further research.

Although many presentations of Price's Eq. 1 are available (including Andersen 2004; Knudsen 2004), this section of the paper presents the equation, discusses its use and relates to recent discussions in the literature before we in the next section use Price's equation for the analysis of directional, stabilizing and diversifying evolution and selection. One reason is that the increased general use of the Price equation has led to misunderstandings and criticisms. Several criticisms have recently been summarized by van Veelen et al. (2012) and countered by Frank (2012b). We integrate a selective survey of this discussion in the following presentation of the equation. More importantly, our account for the equation may serve as an introduction to directional selection. In addition, we introduce core concepts and mathematical notation (see Table 1).

Two censuses Evolution is a population-level process in historical time. Price's equation allows an arbitrary specification of the population. Thus we are not restricted to analyse a population of firms. We can, for instance, analyse a population of regions, but the interpretation of the results becomes difficult unless we have a theory of the evolution of this type of population. Price's equation analyses the evolution of the population by means of data from two population censuses. We could have called them the pre-evolution census and the post-evolution census. However, we will not use these terms since Price's equation normally focuses on selection. The first census takes place at time t and can be called the pre-selection census of the pre-selection population P. The second census at time t' can be called the post-selection census of the post-selection population P'. There are no constraints on the choice of t and t', but a relatively short time span seems preferable because the environment of the population as well as the evolutionary mechanism are subject to change.

It was probably not least the assumption of having two censuses that led Price (1972, p. 485) to emphasize that his equation is "intended mainly for use in deriving general relations and constructing theories, and to clarify understanding of selection phenomena, rather than for numerical calculation". This is still true. Nevertheless, the conditions for making numerical calculations have radically improved since Price's equation was formulated. We now have census data of several biological populations and some economic systems.

Table 1 Core variables of Price's analytical framework

Variable	Definition	Interpretation
x_i		Size of member i in pre-selection census
s_i	$x_i / \sum_i x_i$	Population share of i in pre-selection census
x_i'		Size of member i in post-selection census
s_i'	$x_i' / \sum_i x_i'$	Population share of i in post-selection census
w_i	x_i'/x_i	Absolute fitness of i
$\overline{w}$	$\sum_i x_i' / \sum_i x_i$	Mean absolute fitness
ω_i	$w_i/\overline{w} \quad = s_i'/s_i$	Relative fitness of i
z_i		Characteristic of member i in pre-selection census
$\overline{z}$	$\sum_i s_i z_i$	Weighted mean of z in pre-selection census
$Var(z)$	$\sum_i s_i (z_i - \overline{z})^2$	Weighted variance of z in pre-selection census
z_i'		Characteristic of member i in post-selection census
Δz_i	$z_i' - z_i$	Change in characteristic of i
$\overline{z}'$	$\sum_i s_i' z_i'$	Weighted mean of z in post-selection census
$\Delta \overline{z}$	$\overline{z}' - \overline{z}$	Change in $\overline{z}$
$Cov(w, z)$	$\sum_i s_i (w_i - \overline{w})(z_i - \overline{z})$	Weighted covariance of w_i and z_i
$\beta_{w,z}$	$Cov(w, z)/Var(z)$	Slope of simple regression of w_i on z_i
$\beta_{z',z}$	$Cov(z', z)/Var(z)$	Slope of simple regression of z' on z_i
$E(w\Delta z)$	$\sum_i s_i w_i \Delta z_i$	Expectation of $w_i \Delta z_i$

Mapping between P and P' Price (1995) emphasized the necessity and difficulty of coupling the members of P and P'. If we consider a particular pre-selection population member indexed i, then all related members of P' should also be indexed by i. In the case of firm i of P, the i-indexed representatives in P' might be itself and its spin-offs. And a merged firm can be split in proportion to the initial sizes of firm i and firm j. Thus the evolutionary concept of a "member" of the post-selection population needed for the application of Price's equation is not always that of the same firm in the next period.

Firms that enter the population from the outside or are created from scratch cannot be included in the described mapping procedure – and thus need separate treatment. This treatment has been provided by Kerr and Godfrey-Smith (2009) for the case of the biological species of an ecosystem. But the solution is really quite straightforward. We simply add an entry effect in Price's Eq. 1. For reasons of symmetry we may also add the exit effect:

$$\begin{aligned}\text{Evolutionary change} &= \text{Entry effect} + \text{Exit effect}\\ &\quad + \text{Selection effect} + \text{Intra-member effect}\end{aligned}$$

Data and calculations We now come to the data that need to be collected for the pre-selection census at time t and the post-selection census at time t' – as well as the statistical variables that we calculate from these data (see Table 1). Let us briefly consider fitnesses and characteristics as well as the covariance between fitness and characteristic.

The data of the first census includes the size of each pre-population member x_i. From the data of the second census we calculate the size of each member of the post-population x_i'. Then we for all i-indexed members of the two populations calculate the population shares s_i and s_i' (in each population summing to unity). We also calculate the members' absolute fitness $w_i = x_i'/x_i$ and the population's mean fitness $\overline{w} = \sum s_i w_i$. The members' relative fitness (often called fitness) is obtained by dividing absolute fitness by the mean absolute fitness of the population: $\omega_i = w_i/\overline{w}$. Thus the mean of relative fitness $\overline{\omega} = 1$.

For each member i, the census data provide us with information on the quantitative characteristic whose evolution we want to analyse. We can study the evolution of *any* quantitative characteristic, including mathematical transformations of the data of the population. In any case, let these values of the characteristic be z_i and z_i'. The fact that members of economically relevant populations are often of very different sizes emphasizes the need of using the weighted mean characteristic $\overline{z}$ in the analysis. Price's equation decomposes the change of the weighted mean characteristic of the population $\Delta\overline{z}$. This change can come from the aggregate effect of intra-member change of characteristic Δz_i. But it can also be the result of the different fitnesses of members with different characteristics. Crucial for the latter effect is the pre-selection population variance of the characteristic $Var(z)$.

The core part of Price's partitioning of $\Delta\overline{z}$ is the statistical relationship between member fitnesses and their characteristics. Let us assume that we operate in terms of absolute fitnesses w_i. The data of the two censuses can be used to calculate $Cov(w, z)$, that is, the weighted covariance of w_i and z_i. This covariance can be interpreted as the part of evolutionary change that is caused by selection. The interpretation can be helped by the rewrite $Cov(w, z) = \beta_{w,z}\, Var(z)$. Here variance provides the fuel for selection while the regression coefficient is a measure of the intensity with which selection exploits this fuel. It has been argued van Veelen et al. (2012) that we are not facing a "real" covariance because of lacking explicit foundations in statistics and probability theory. But as can be seen from Table 1 the covariance element of Price's equation is not the sample covariance estimator of population covariance but rather the formula for population covariance. Thus when Price's equation is applied to population censuses rather than a sample the selection effect is population covariance divided by population fitness.

Price's equation with relative fitness We are now ready to consider the formally provable specification of Price's equation that was informally presented in Eq. 1. Since the proof of the equation is widely available (e.g., Frank 2012b), the problem is rather to identify the most useful version for evolutionary analysis. Price's equation in terms of relative fitness, ω_i, focuses squarely on the core issue of the analysis of evolutionary processes. The primary issue of evolutionary analysis is not the aggregate growth of the population but its structural change due to the differential growth of members with different values of the characteristic.

$$\underset{\text{Total change}}{\Delta\overline{z}} = \underset{\text{Selection effect}}{Cov(\boldsymbol{\omega}, z)} + \underset{\text{Intra-member effect}}{E(\boldsymbol{\omega}\Delta z)} = \beta_{\boldsymbol{\omega},z} Var(z) + E(\boldsymbol{\omega}\Delta z) \quad (3)$$

There are evolutionary problems in which population-level does matter and where it thus may be more instructive to use Price's equation in terms of absolute fitness rather than the elegant (3) but such problems are not considered in the current paper.

The left-hand side of Eq. 3 is the change of the mean characteristic of the population. The selection effect is basically expressed as the covariance between relative fitness and characteristic. This covariance can be rewritten as the product of the selection intensity $\beta_{\omega,z}$ and the variance $Var(z)$. There will be no selection effect if either $\beta_{\omega,z} = 0$ or $Var(z) = 0$. For a given $Var(z) > 0$, the size of the effect depends on the slope of the linear regression line. The intra-member effect is more difficult to interpret because the change of characteristic within each member is multiplied by its relative fitness. In any case, it disappears if $\Delta z_i = 0$ for all members of the population.

3 Three types of selection

When working with Price's equation it is tempting to define evolution solely as the change of the mean value of a directly observable characteristic of a population. This gives no problems as long as we work within the directional paradigm of evolutionary economics. But the consequence of the definition is that we exclude the pure forms of stabilizing and diversifying evolution that do not change the population mean. It is not useful to apply a concept of evolution that excludes the processes that keep a population near a local optimum or that bring forth the coexistence of population members with very different behaviours and characteristic values. To include these types of change we need to define evolution as *any* change of the frequency distribution of a characteristic of a population.

Evolution and pure selection The change of the frequency distribution is the outcome of the combined effects of selection and intra-member change. The primary reason why this combination is so important in economic evolution is that the two effects here often work in the same direction. The intra-member change is not the outcome of random mutations, but of the efforts of boundedly rational firms and individuals. The recognition of this fact might give the analysis of economic evolution a "Lamarckian" flavour (Nelson and Winter 1982, p. 11). In any case, the intra-member change effect can often be interpreted as reflecting reactions to the selection pressure. This is the reason why the two effects often work in the same direction. In other words, selection produces not only the selection effect on the characteristics of the initial population; it also produces parts of the reactions that lead to the intra-member effect between the two censuses. This important problem, however, is beyond the scope of the present paper. Here we will instead focus on the ordinary selection effect.

Directional selection The most obvious way of changing the frequency distribution is through directional selection. Two ways of approaching directional selection are illustrated by Fig. 2. In both panels, the pre-selection frequency distribution is to

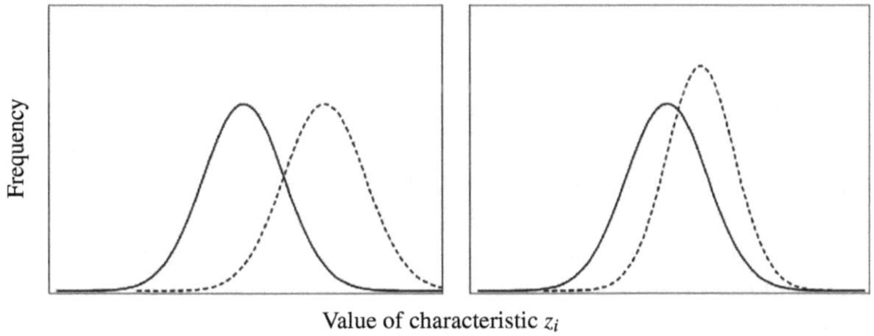

Fig. 2 Pure directional selection and the effect of a directional fitness function. The *left panel* depicts the concept of directional selection by leaving the variance unchanged. The *right panel* depicts the effect of a directional fitness function such as that of replicator dynamics, where $\Delta z_i = 0$

the left and the post-selection distribution is to the right. The left panel moves the frequency distribution such that the mean increases while the variance is left unchanged. Thereby it in the simplest possible way illustrates the definition of directional selection as the change of the mean characteristic (here in the positive direction). It is achieved through a combination of selection favouring higher values of the characteristic and intra-member processes adding novel, higher values of the characteristic to the population. In contrast, the right panel illustrates the effect of a directional fitness function that influences both the mean and the variance of the distribution and where no novel values of the characteristic are introduced. While the left panel illustrates directional selection in its pure form, the right panel depicts the stabilizing effect of a purely directional fitness function. The concept of directional selection represents an aspect of the evolutionary process that can be combined with stabilizing selection or other types of selection (Endler 1986; Rice 2004). This distance-from-mean dynamics implies that members with higher than mean value of the characteristic will have high relative fitness while those with low values will have lower fitness. The consequence is that the mean of the distribution increases while its variance decreases. (Endler 1986; Rice 2004). This possibility is left open if we define directional selection in terms of $\Delta \bar{z} = \bar{z}' - \bar{z}$. If $\Delta \bar{z} = 0$, there cannot be directional selection. If $\Delta \bar{z} \neq 0$, we use the covariance term in Eq. 3 to determine whether this is due to directional selection. If $Cov(\omega, z) > 0$ we observe positive directional selection. If $Cov(\omega, z) < 0$, we have negative directional selection.

The Chicago approach Although we have used Price's equation to define directional selection, this idea can be traced back to the Chicago school approach to phenotypic evolution (Lande and Arnold 1983; Conner and Hartl 2004, ch. 6). This approach can be expressed in relation to Price's equation (Rice 2004). Thus it emphasizes the variance of the characteristics of the population, covariance between characteristics and the reproduction of members, and the intertemporal inertia of the characteristics. By focusing on these requirements for phenotypic evolution rather than on the direct study of genetic evolution, this approach has been very successful for studying "natural selection in the wild" (Endler 1986; Brodie et al.

1995; Kingsolver et al. 2001; Conner and Hartl 2004, ch. 6; Kingsolver and Pfennig 2007).

Estimating the types of selection The Chicago approach provides a simple way of detecting the relative importance of directional selection and variance selection. This importance is estimated by multiple regressions for a large number of populations. The task is to estimate the relative fitness $Y_i = \omega_i = w_i/\overline{w}$ as the result of the additive effects of a linear term and a nonlinear term. The linear term is $X_1 = z_i$ and the nonlinear term is $X_2 = (z_i - \overline{z})^2$. Thus the multiple regression equation is

$$Y = a + b_1 X_1 + b_2 X_2 + \text{error} \tag{4}$$

where b_1 estimates the effect of directional selection and b_2 estimates the effect of variance selection. If b_1 is different from zero, there is directional selection. If b_2 is negative, we observe stabilizing selection. If b_2 is positive, we have diversifying selection. The two latter types of selection are often combined under the heading of variance selection (Endler 1986). We often see that variance selection coexists with directional selection. Although the formalism of Eq. 4 is simple, the production of studies that applies it is by no means easy. Nevertheless, the development of evolutionary economics would benefit significantly from a large number of such studies and their use for the evaluation of the relative importance of directional selection, stabilizing selection, and diversifying selection.

Defining the types of selection Although the Chicago approach is empirically oriented, its definitions of the types of selection are what matters in the present context (Rice 2004, p. 176). The definitions can be expressed on terms of covariances or of the regression coefficients of Eq. 4

- Directional selection involves a change of the mean of the frequency distribution that is explained by the covariance $Cov(\omega, z) = \beta_{\omega,z}\, Var(z)$. Directional selection is a nonzero linear regression of fitness on the characteristic. If $\beta_{\omega,z} > 0$, we have positive directional selection. If $\beta_{\omega,z} < 0$, we have negative directional selection.
- Stabilizing selection is a negative change of the variance of the frequency distribution produced by a negative $\beta_{\omega,(z-\overline{z})^2}$. This implies that $Cov(\omega, (z-\overline{z})^2) < 0$.
- Diversifying selection is a positive change of the variance of the frequency distribution produced by a positive $\beta_{\omega,(z-\overline{z})^2}$. This implies that $Cov(\omega, (z-\overline{z})^2) > 0$.

Directional selection is defined independently of the two other types of selection. This means that directional selection can coexist with stabilizing selection or diversifying selection.

Stabilizing selection and directional selection Fisher (1930) started his famous book by stating that "Natural Selection is not Evolution." Here he referred to the pure directional selection. His statement emphasized that biological selection can

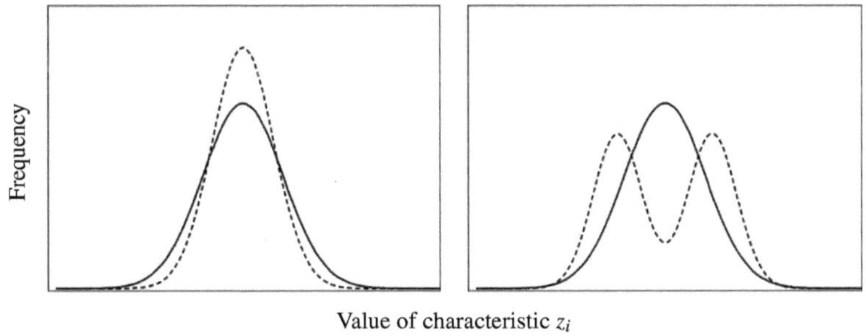

Fig. 3 The two pure types of variance selection. The *solid curve* depicts the initial frequency distribution while the *dashed curves* depict the results of different types of variance selection by presenting the post-selection distributions. *Left panel* pure stabilizing selection. *Right panel* pure diversifying selection

not only cause directional change but also bring this type of change to a halt at a fitness peak. Here stabilizing selection serves to weed out mutants that do not have the locally optimal value of the characteristic. If mutations tend to push the population in a particular direction, then stabilizing selection has to be sufficiently strong to keep $\Delta\bar{z} = 0$. In terms of Price's Eq. 3, the balancing condition is that $Cov(\omega, z) = -E(\omega\Delta z)$. However, this is not the only way stabilizing selection can keep the population near the characteristic with maximum fitness (Frank 2012a). Since biological mutations are random, they normally increase the variance of the characteristic around the fitness peak. To avoid evolutionary chaos, stabilizing selection has to be sufficiently strong to counter this increase of variance.

Comparing types of selection We have now defined directional selection in terms of the change of the mean of the frequency distribution. Similarly, we have defined stabilizing selection as the process that decreases the variance of the distribution and diversifying selection as the process that increases the variance. These definitions mean that directional selection can work together with one of the two types of variance selection. But the definitions also allow comparison between the pure types of selection. This comparison is provided by Figs. 2 and 3. The solid lines depict the frequency distribution of the pre-selection population. The dashed lines depict the post-selection distributions. As already mentioned, Fig. 2 depicts a selection process in which only the mean characteristic is changing. The two panels of Fig. 3 keep the mean unchanged while the variance changes. In the case of stabilizing selection the variance decreases. The variance increases with a process of diversifying selection.

Combining the types of selection We have already noted that the directional fitness function of replicator dynamics combines directional selection with stabilizing selection. More general issues of combination can be discussed concisely if we *assume* the existence of a nonlinear fitness function for the population (Endler 1986). The upward sloping part of the function of Fig. 4 represents predominantly positive directional selection. Furthermore, the part of the curve around the maximum

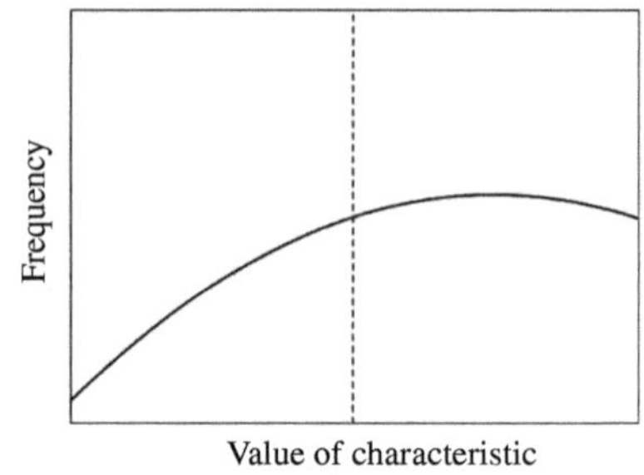

Fig. 4 The population composition and the type of selection. The *curve* depicts a non-linear fitness function. We have directional selection if the population is placed to the left of the *dashed line* and stabilizing selection to the right of the *dashed line*. If the population is distributed over the entire horizontal axis we have mixed selection pressures

represents stabilizing selection and the downward sloping part represents negative directional selection. The effect of this function depends on the composition of the pre-selection population. The population largely faces positive directional selection if the characteristics of its members are distributed to the left of the dashed line. We have stabilizing selection if the population is distributed to the right of the dashed line. However, the population faces a mix of directional and stabilizing selection if it is distributed over the entire range represented by the horizontal axis of the figure.

We encounter similar issues if the fitness function of Fig. 4 is changed to including a U-shape. However, polarization cannot go on forever. Therefore, the assumed function would have to include downward bends at each of the extreme values. Assuming that the fitness function is stable, the ultimate result of this diversifying selection will be two separate subpopulations that are both facing stabilizing selection.

Two-dimensional fitness function Although this paper concentrates on the evolution of a single characteristic, it is helpful to consider how we can represent a two-dimensional fitness function graphically. The result is a graph that will look familiar to students of microeconomics. We start by constructing a two-dimensional space of characteristics. Each point in this space represents a potential location of a member of the pre-selection population. This member has the value z_i^1 of characteristic 1 and z_i^2 of characteristic 2. Then we (perhaps based on estimates) assume the fitness level that corresponds to each point in the two-dimensional space of characteristics. The result is a fitness surface. Figure 5 depicts this surface as isofitness curves in the space of characteristics. These curves represent selection as working on the combined effect of the two characteristics; and the fitness maximum is marked by $+$. Fitness increases when we move from the origin toward the fitness maximum; but it decreases when we continue from the maximum towards the upper right corner.

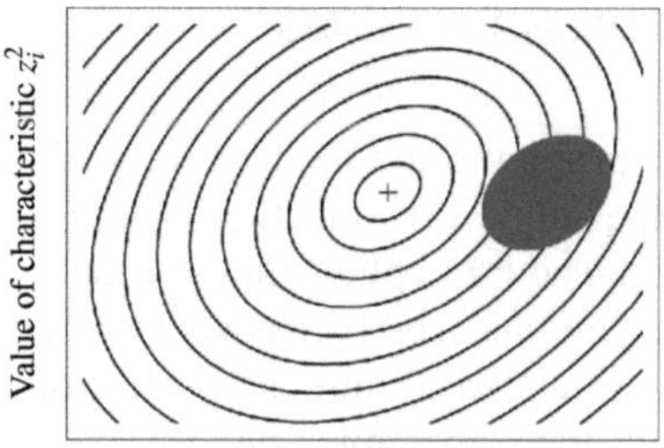

Fig. 5 Example of isofitness curves for two characteristics z_i^1 and z_i^2. The fitness peak is marked by +. At an earlier point of time, the isofitness curves had its peak in the middle of the *gray area*. This area represents a population that was relatively well adapted to a previous situation, but which has become maladapted because of the exogenous movement of the isofitness curves. With the depicted position of the curves, the population faces stabilizing selection with respect to characteristic z_i^2 and a mix of directional and stabilizing selection with respect to characteristic z_i^1

Figure 5 allows us to understand some of the complexities of selection in a two-dimensional space of characteristics. Let us assume that the fitness maximum originally was placed in the middle of the gray area. Furthermore, we assume that the population has moved to this area, where it has been subject to stabilizing selection with respect to both of its characteristics. However, fitness surfaces are generally not stable, though they may appear to be so, as they potentially move back and forth and from a longer-term perspective can appear to be fixed. Populations are thus facing the Sisyphus work of performing lagged adaptations to ever-changing selection pressures. The problem for the population in Fig. 5 is that the isofitness curves have moved so that the new maximum is the peak marked by + while the heterogeneous population is represented by the gray area. While this population was relatively well adapted to a previous situation, it has become maladapted because the isofitness curves have moved. The gray pre-selection population is still subject to stabilizing selection with respect the second characteristic. But in the new situation it confronts a combination of directional and stabilizing selection with respect to the first characteristic.

Further discussion of the topic of two-dimensional fitness surfaces is beyond the limits of this paper. But it should be noted that although we to some extent relate to Wright's (1932) famous formalization of selection in terms of "fitness landscapes", the two concepts are not exactly the same. While each point in Wright's landscapes in principle represents the analysed mean of a small and localized population, the fitness function surfaces of the Chicago school are based on data for a single population (Conner and Hartl 2004, pp. 210–211). However, both approaches serve to emphasize that we have to complement the well-known process of directional selection with an analysis of the processes of stabilizing selection and diversifying selection. Furthermore, we have to be very cautious when we are analyzing the evolution of a single characteristic of a population.

4 Three types of fitness functions

The understanding of the problems and methods related to the analysis of selection can be enhanced through examples of selection processes that have known properties because they are produced by explicit fitness functions. This approach has for evolutionary biology been emphasized by Endler (1986, pp. 260–271), and there is much need of producing simulated examples of selection processes in evolutionary economics. To be helpful, these examples have to be produced by simple fitness functions. In this section we define and simulate a directional fitness function, a stabilizing fitness function, and a diversifying fitness function.

Our fitness functions are all constructed so that they can produce such discrete-time simulations. To run these simulations we normally–apart from the initial population P – need the values of a couple of parameters. But the simulations are simplified by the fact that we do not provide any mechanism of intra-member change. Instead we assume $\Delta z_i = 0$. The consequence is that only the selection term of Price's Eq. 3 needs to be examined when we, in Section 5, turn to the analysis of the change of mean characteristic. However, both terms of the equation are needed for the analysis of the change of variance, skewness and kurtosis of the frequency distributions.

The initial population For the present purposes, we do not need to be realistic when defining the initial population P. On the contrary, what are needed are the simplest data data that provide the different types of fitness functions with lots of variance. We obtain such data by assuming a large population in which all values of the characteristic within a specified range are represented equally. Population P consists of 1000 members, and this number does not change during the simulations. Each member has a fixed value of its characteristic z_i. As the total size of the population is inconsequential to the simulations we specify each member to have an equal initial population share of $s_i = 1/1000$, and we can then refrain from considering member size, x_i, at all. The values of the characteristic are uniformly distributed over the interval $[\min(z), \max(z)]$. Thus the distance between members is $d = (\max - \min)/999$, and $z_1 = \min(z), z_2 = \min + d, z_3 = \min + 2d, \ldots, z_{1000} = \max(z)$. For the following simulations we specify the fitness function for absolute fitness, $w_i = w(z_i)$, and the population then evolves according to:

$$s_i' = s_i \frac{w_i}{\overline{w}} = s_i \omega_i \tag{5}$$

By using Eq. 5 we are assuming that the change in population share of member *i* is entirely determined by relative fitness but in empirical applications it is likely that population shares exhibit persistence. This could be explicitly modelled by allowing s_i' to be the weighted average of s_i and $s_i \omega_i$. However, as our simulations are meant to provide simple illustrations of the evolutionary processes the only consequence would be that we would have to run the simulations for additional rounds for the results to stand out clearly. Results can be seen after just 1 round of simulation with Eq. 5 and after 4 rounds they stand out very clearly.

Standardized presentation of results The simulation results can best be visualized as changes in the frequency distribution of the values of the characteristic. We employ a standardization of the range for z_i that has become widespread in the parts of evolutionary biology which are influenced by the above mentioned Chicago school approach to phenotypic evolution. This method has several advantages, including the increased ease of comparing different types of selection. Therefore, the initial uniform distribution of the characteristic has in our simulations been defined to have mean zero and standard deviation one. Since the variance of a uniform distribution is $\frac{1}{12}(\max - \min)^2$, z_i in our initial population P has a continuous uniform distribution $\mathrm{U}(\min = -\sqrt{3}, \max = \sqrt{3})$. In terms of standard deviations this implies that our population covers about 1.7 standard deviations on each side of the mean of zero.

Directional fitness function It is possible to define an unrealistic directional fitness function in which a particular value of the characteristic z_i under all circumstances gives the same absolute fitness w_i. However, we normally think of a process of positive directional selection in which the relative fitness ω_i of a member with characteristic z_i depends on its distance from a changing population mean $\overline{z}$. The logic of this fitness function is that $\omega_i = 1$ if $z_i - \overline{z} = 0$; but if $z_i - \overline{z} > 0$, then $\omega_i > 1$; and if $z_i - \overline{z} < 0$, then $\omega_i > 1$. Furthermore, ω_i should be proportional to the distance from the mean. What is called replicator dynamics or distance-from-mean dynamics has these properties. Thus we can use the following directional fitness function:

$$\omega_i = \frac{z_i + k}{E(z_i + k)} = \frac{z_i + k}{\overline{z_i} + k} = \frac{w_i}{\overline{w}} \tag{6}$$

The constant k is added to avoid negative fitness values and to avoid dividing by zero. The results of simulating the directional fitness function of Eq. 6 are depicted in the upper panel of Fig. 6, page 14. The dotted line represents the frequency distribution of the initial population (that was described above). The standardized mean is zero. This implies that the right half of the population has above mean fitness and the left half has below mean fitness. The result of the first round of selection is indicated by the dashed line. This round increases or shrinks the member shares in proportion to the distance from the mean of zero. The second round of selection is not depicted but it is based on $\overline{z} > 0$. The fourth round is based on an even higher $\overline{z}$. Its result is shown by the full line of the panel. However, it should be noted that a directional fitness function cannot on its own produce pure directional selection as selection necessarily consumes variance. Compared with the initial uniform distribution, the four rounds of applying the directional function have moved the mass of the distribution so that increasing mean and kurtosis is one consequence and decreasing variance and skewness is another consequence. As an example, assume that we are studying work organisation in a large factory

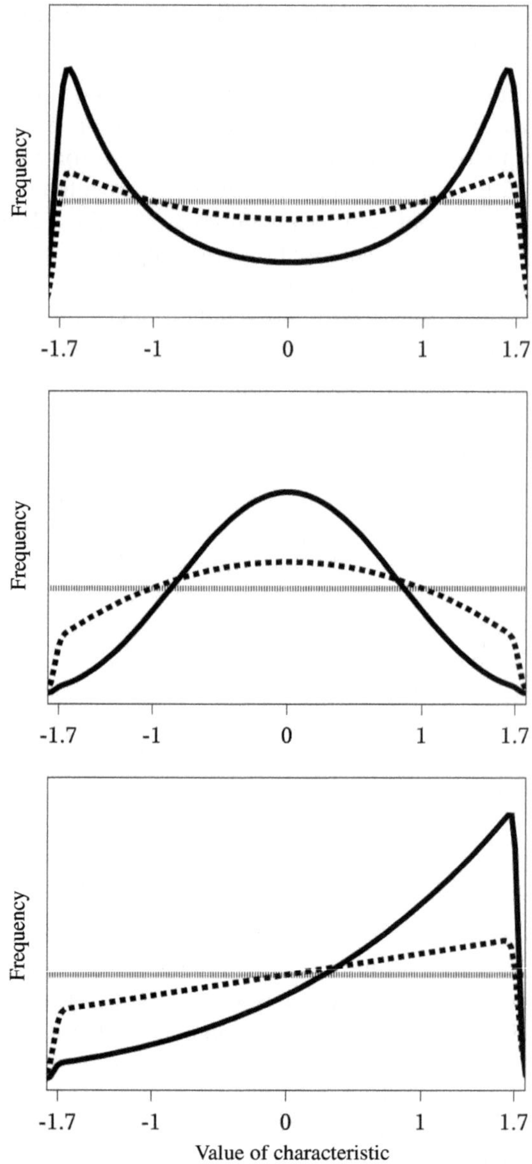

Fig. 6 Effects of one and four rounds of selection by different fitness functions. The *upper panel* is produced by the directional fitness function (6), the middle panel by the stabilizing function (7) with $z^* = 0$, and the *lower panel* by the diversifying function (8) with $\tilde{z} = 0$. Characteristics data are standardized to have a mean of zero and a standard deviation of unity initially. The *curves* are constructed as kernel density estimates over z_i in the simulated data and thus the distributions appear rounded near the minimum and maximum. From the viewpoint of evolutionary modelling this behaviour can be considered an artefact that should be ignored

paying a piece rate. Workers have complete discretion in organising their work so whatever practices result in a higher physical efficiency will spread to other workers (assuming that there is no collusion among workers). If workers can be more productive by stacking their goods higher then the average hight of the stack of goods next to each worker's station will evolve according to a directional fitness function. This process obviously cannot go on for ever but, as already mentioned, this is a typical element of directional selection.

Stabilizing fitness function Let us consider the properties of simple fitness functions that are able to produce stabilizing selection. The basic requirement is that there is maximum fitness related to a particular value of the characteristic, z^*. The logic of stabilizing fitness functions is that ω_i has its maximum if $z_i = z^*$. Furthermore, if $z_i < z^*$ or if $z_i > z^*$, then ω_i is smaller than its maximum. Finally, ω_i should be decreasing in some relation to the numerical distance $|z_i - z^*|$. These requirements for a stabilizing fitness function is fulfilled by a second degree polynomial with maximum at z^*; that is $w_i = -z_i^2 + 2z^*z_i + k$.

$$\omega_i = \frac{-z_i^2 + 2z^*z_i + k}{E(-z_i^2 + 2z^*z_i + k)} = \frac{w_i}{\overline{w}} \tag{7}$$

Again it is necessary to add k for computational reasons. This stabilizing fitness function resembles the directional fitness function of Eq. 6. But whereas (6) is linear, Eq. 7 has a maximum at $z_i = z^*$ and decreases symmetrically for higher and lower values of z_i.

The discussion in relation to Fig. 4 suggested that the outcome of applying a stabilizing fitness function depends on the localization of the characteristics of the population relative to the fitness maximum, z^*. We get pure stabilizing selection if the population is located symmetrically around the mean $\bar{z}$. The other possibility is that $z^* \neq \bar{z}$, and this possibility will be discussed below. Presently we consider the case in which $z^* = \bar{z}$. Given that $\Delta z_i = 0$ for all members, this implies that (7) does not change the mean of the frequency distribution.

The middle panel of Fig. 6 depicts the result of using Eq. 7 with $z^* = \bar{z}$ on the uniformly distributed pre-selection population specified above. This fitness function gradually brings the population closer to its fitness maximum by decreasing the variance and increasing the kurtosis of the frequency distribution. After many more rounds of simulation, the distribution will end up as being concentrated on the characteristic with maximum fitness, z^*. As an example consider again the large factory paying a piece rate and assume that a 5 minute break after an hour's work results in the highest physical efficiency. A shorter break means that the worker becomes tired and works slower towards the end of the day while a longer break entails squandering working time. So the mean break length per hour of work will converge on 5 minutes throughout the factory in a process of stabilizing selection.

Diversifying fitness function In principle, the specification of a diversifying fitness function assumes that there are two values of the characteristic that have maximum fitness, a lower value and a higher value. However, if these maxima are located outside the range of characteristic values that are represented in the population, then it is sufficient to know the location of the fitness minimum at $\bar{z}$. Wespecify our diversifying fitness function in a way that is closely related to the specification of Eq. 7. This diversifying function is

$$\omega_i = \frac{z_i^2 - 2\tilde{z}z_i + k}{E(z_i^2 - 2\tilde{z}z_i + k)} = \frac{w_i'}{\overline{w}} \tag{8}$$

Equation 8 produces a U-shaped parabola with minimum when $z_i = \tilde{z}$. Thus fitness increases on both sides of this fixed location of minimal fitness. To ensure comparability, we apply the positive constant k that was used in Eqs. 6 and 7.

The diversifying fitness function produces pure diversifying selection if the population is located symmetrically around the mean and this mean is equal to the minimum fitness $\tilde{z}$. This is the case for the above specified initial population. The results of one and four rounds of using Eq. 8 are shown in the lower panel of Fig. 6. In our standardized presentation of the data $\tilde{z} = \overline{z} = 0$. The shares of members near the mean steadily decrease while the fitness of those with extreme characteristics increase. Compared with the initial one, the distribution after four rounds is characterized by an increase of variance and a decrease of kurtosis. For an example of diversifying selection return once again to our factory. Workers have a choice of two different methods for fitting together two components. Some workers will initially be switching back and forth for a bit of variation but unless a worker uses the same method each time she misses out on the opportunity of specialisation. So over time the probability that any one methods is used across the factory will evolve in accordance with a diversifying fitness function.

Mixed selection The simulations of the quadratic fitness functions have served to illustrate pure forms of stabilizing selection and diversifying selection. A quick glance on these illustrations might give the impression that Eqs. 8 and 7 will always produce pure forms of selection. This impression is false for both equations, but we will emphasize the stabilizing fitness function. Figure 4 demonstrated that such a function can produce stabilizing selection, directional selection, and a mix between the two. In this figure the varying results depend on the composition of the population. But we can also (as in Fig. 5) move the fitness function. In the univariate case of Eq. 7, we obtain a similar result by changing from $z^* = 0$ to $z^* = 0.7$ (so that $\overline{z} < z^*$). The consequences are shown in Fig. 7 on page 16. Here the stabilizing fitness function has produced a mix of stabilizing selection and directional selection. More specifically, the function moves the frequency distribution closer to the maximum of 0.7 by increasing the mean, decreasing the variance, decreasing the skewness, and increasing the kurtosis.

5 Analyzing the fitness functions through Price's equation

After having discussed Price's equation and types of selection, the remaining task is to demonstrate and analyse the relationship between the types of selection and the fitness functions defined above by application of Price's equation. It is demonstrated

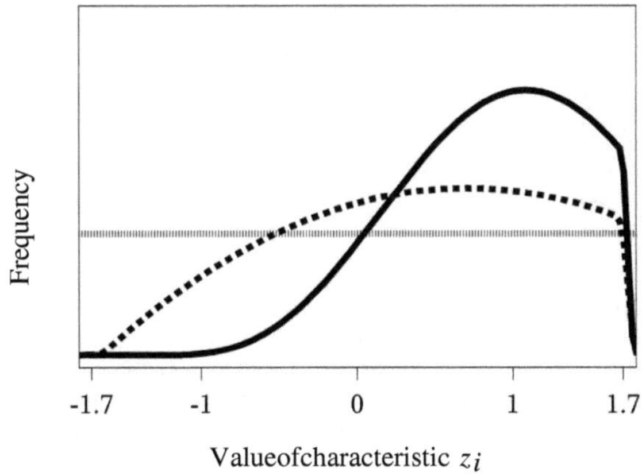

Fig. 7 Effects of one and four rounds of selection by the stabilizing fitness function with changed fitness maximum. The results are produced by Eq. 7 with $z^* = 0.7$. Characteristics data are standardized to have a mean of zero and a standard deviation of unity initially. The *curve* is constructed as a kernel density estimate over z_i in the simulated data and thus the distribution appears rounded near the minimum and maximum. From the viewpoint of evolutionary modelling this behaviour can be considered an artefact that should be ignored

in this section how Price's equation provides an exact and fruitful way of analysing the dynamics created by the fitness functions. We have in Section 2 seen how Price's Eq. 3 can be used to decompose the total change of the mean characteristic of the population. However, Price (1995, p. 391) pointed out that his equation can be used for the analysis of any "change produced by the selection process in a *population property* X related to property x of individual set members. (For example: X might be the arithmetic mean of the x_i or their variance, and correspondingly for X' and the x_i' values.)" This comprehensiveness of Price's equation is crucial for the analysis of the dynamics of the different fitness functions. This analysis is supported by the additional use of the equation to decompose the frequency distributions' change of variance, change of skewness, and change of kurtosis. As an introduction it is helpful to consider the descriptive statistics of the frequency distributions presented in Figs. 6 and 7.

Statistics of the distributions The figures of Section 4 visualize how the different types of selection can be represented by different changes in the initial population's frequency distribution of the characteristic z. Table 2 presents the statistics needed for comparing the distribution in P with the different distributions in P''''. The statistical characteristics of the initial distribution are given in the first data column of Table 2. The following columns present the statistics of the new distributions after four rounds of using the fitness functions.

By subtracting the first from the second data column of Table 2, we see that the directional fitness function has complex effects. In four rounds it has moved the mean in the positive direction by 0.69 standard deviations. At the same time it has

Table 2 Statistics of the standardized distributions of Figs. 6 and 7

	Initial	After four rounds of			
	distribution	Directional	Stabilizing	Diversifying	Mixed
Mean of z	0.00	0.69	0.00	0.00	0.59
Variance of z	1.00	0.68	0.45	1.56	0.39
Skewness of z	0.00	−0.85	0.00	0.00	−0.27
Kurtosis of z	1.80	2.93	2.48	1.37	2.40

The table presents statistics of the initial distribution and of the distributions produced by four rounds of the different types of fitness functions. Directional is the distribution produced by the directional fitness function (6). Diversifying is produced by the diversifying fitness function (8). Stabilizing and Mixed are produced by stabilizing fitness function (7) with two locations of maximum fitness, $z^* = 0$ and $z^* = 0.7$. It should be noted that the paper analyses the *changes* of these statistics. For instance, in the mixed case $\Delta\bar{z} = 0.59 - 0.00 = 0.59$ and $\Delta Var(z) = 0.39 - 1.00 = -0.61$

decreased the variance of the frequency distribution by nearly a third, provided a strong negative skewness, and increased the kurtosis of the distribution.

The third and fourth data column show the results of using the stabilizing fitness function (7) with $z^* = 0$ and the diversifying fitness function (8) with $\tilde{z} = 0$. By subtracting the first column from each of them we see that these fitness functions work only through the change of variance and kurtosis. The difference is that while stabilizing selection decreases variance and increases kurtosis, diversifying selection increases variance and decreases kurtosis. These results are based on the locations of the maximum fitness of the stabilizing function z^* and the minimum fitness of the diversifying function $\tilde{z}$. Both were placed at the mean of the distribution $\bar{z}$.

The last column of Table 2 shows the result of the stabilizing fitness function when the maximum fitness z^* is moved 0.7 standard deviations in the positive direction. Then four rounds of using Eq. 7 produce results that are rather similar to those produced by the directional function (6). The mean is moved by 0.59 standard deviations, variance is decreased, we see negative skewness, and kurtosis is increased. This similarity emphasizes that caution is needed when we try to characterize overall fitness functions as representing different types of selection.

Moments of the distributions The method of moments was introduced by the statistician and evolutionary biologist Karl Pearson (by a concept borrowed from physics). We consider the central moments of frequency distributions with characteristic z at the random variable. Then the mth central moment of the distribution is defined as

$$E\left[(z_i - \bar{z})^m\right] = \sum_i s_i (z_i - \bar{z})^m$$

The second central moment ($m = 2$) is the variance of the distribution. When the third central moment is divided by σ_z^3, we get the statistical concept of the skewness of the distribution. When the fourth central moment is divided by σ_z^4, we get one of the statistical concepts of kurtosis. The central moments characterize different aspects of the shape of the distribution. Odd moments ($m = 3{,}5, \ldots$) measure the asymmetry of the distribution while even moments ($m = 2{,}4, \ldots$) measure the symmetric spread around the mean. With increasing m the importance of outliers increases. Since outliers are crucial for evolutionary processes, the higher moments here have an importance that is not found in non-evolutionary uses of statistics (emphasized by Metcalfe 1994; and Rice 2004, p. 227).

Change of moments and Price's equation As already mentioned, Price's equation can be used for the partitioning of the change of the mean of any quantitative characteristic C. The only requirement is that we define the member values of the characteristic C_i such that $\overline{C}$ is the mean and $\Delta\overline{C}$ is the change we want to decompose. In the case of variance, the characteristic $(z_i - \overline{z})^2$ gives the expectation $\sum(z_i - \overline{z})^2 = Var(z)$. In the case of skewness, the characteristic is $(z_i - \overline{z})^3/\sigma_z^3$ since the expectation is the skewness of the distribution. In the case of kurtosis, the characteristic is $(z_i - \overline{z})^4/\sigma_z^4$ since the expectation is the kurtosis of the distribution. Thus we can use Price's Eq. 3 to decompose the change of the variance, skewness and kurtosis of the frequency distribution. The decompositions of the change in the distribution's variance, skewness and kurtosis are thus provided by

$$\begin{aligned} \Delta Var(z) &= Cov\left[\omega, (z-\overline{z})^2\right] + E\left[\omega\Delta(z-\overline{z})^2\right] \\ &= Cov(\omega, \upsilon) + E(\omega\Delta\upsilon) \end{aligned} \quad (9)$$

$$\begin{aligned} \Delta Skew(z) &= Cov\left[\omega, (z-\overline{z})^3/\sigma_z^3\right] + E\left[\omega\Delta((z-\overline{z})^3/\sigma_z^3)\right] \\ &= Cov(\omega, \gamma) + E(\omega\Delta\gamma) \end{aligned} \quad (10)$$

$$\begin{aligned} \Delta Kurt(z) &= Cov\left[\omega, (z-\overline{z})^4/\sigma_z^4\right] + E\left[\omega\Delta((z-\overline{z})^4/\sigma_z^4)\right] \\ &= Cov(\omega, \kappa) + E(\omega\Delta\kappa) \end{aligned} \quad (11)$$

By moving from decomposing the change of the mean in Price's Eq. 3 to decomposing the change of the variance in Eq. 9, we have started the analysis of the recursive process of selection. The original Price's equation deals only with the change from the pre-selection population to the post-selection population, but Eq. 9 provides us with a measure of the fuel that this change leaves for the movement of the mean between the post-selection population and the post-post-selection environment. If the amount of fuel is being gradually reduced the selection process will after many rounds of selection come to a halt–unless a change of the environment changes the fitness function or new fuel is provided by mutation or innovation.

There are three aspects of the selection process that are not adequately covered by the analysis of the change of the variance of the distribution. First, the outliers of the distribution of characteristics are crucial and they can be emphasized more than in the measure provided by the squared distances from the mean. We can also study higher central moments such as those dependent on $(z_i - \overline{z})^3$ and $(z_i - \overline{z})^4$. Second,

Table 3 Statistical components of the selection dynamics in Figs. 6 and 7

Statistical change that is decomposed	Term in Price's equation	After four rounds of Directional	Stabilizing	Diversifying	Mixed
Δ Mean	$Cov(\omega, z)$	0.69	0.00	0.00	0.59
	$E(\omega \Delta z)$	0.00	0.00	0.00	0.00
Δ Variance	$Cov(\omega, \upsilon)$	0.16	−0.55	0.56	−0.26
	$E(\omega \Delta \upsilon)$	−0.48	0.00	0.00	−0.35
Δ Skewness	$Cov(\omega, \gamma)$	1.26	0.00	0.00	0.83
	$E(\omega \Delta \gamma)$	−2.11	0.00	0.00	−1.11
Δ Kurtosis	$Cov(\omega, \kappa)$	0.40	−1.31	1.51	−0.65
	$E(\omega \Delta \kappa)$	0.72	1.98	−1.94	1.25

The total change of the different statistics can be found in Table 2. For instance, in the mixed case $\Delta Var(z) = -0.61$. This change is the sum of the covariance term and the expectation term: $-0.61 = -0.26 + (-0.35)$

the asymmetry of the distribution, as reflected by moments with odd powers, is also of importance for the selection process. Third, some types of selection can only be defined by reference to changes in the higher moments of the distribution. In general, we have to recognize that the statistics of the higher moments play a much larger role in evolution than in most other subjects. Therefore, it is important that we can use Price's equation to decompose the change of all these moments as demonstrated by Eq. 10 for skewness and Eq. 11 for kurtosis.

Analysing the change of the distributions The mean, variance, skewness and kurtosis of the initial distribution and the distributions produced by four rounds of applying the different fitness functions were shown in Table 2. The overall changes of these statistics have already been discussed. Now we turn to analysis of these changes by means of Price's equation: as the sums of covariance terms and expectation terms. The results are shown in Table 3. Let us start by the decomposition of the change of the mean. Since $\Delta z_i = 0$, the expectation term is zero and the whole change of 0.69 standard deviations produced by the directional fitness function is accounted for by the covariance term. The same is the case for the mixed type of selection produced by the stabilizing fitness function with maximum fitness different from the mean. In contrast, the pure types of stabilizing and diversifying selection do not change the mean.

The decompositions of the changes of variance are more interesting. From Table 2 we know that the directional fitness function produces an overall change of the variance of −0.32. However, the covariance term of Table 3 shows a positive selection effect of 0.16 while the expectation term shows a negative intra-member effect of −0.48. We have accounted for the overall change of variance since $-0.32 = 0.16 - 0.48$, but we now recognize the complexities of the process produced by the directional fitness function. We also recognize the difference between the directional function and the stabilizing function that has a maximum different from the mean. The latter also has an overall negative change of variance,

Table 4 Signs of the components of the analysed examples of selection dynamics

Statistical change that is decomposed	Term in Price's equation	Type of fitness function			
		Directional	Stabilizing	Diversifying	Mixed
Δ Mean	$Cov(\omega, z)$	POS	0	0	POS
	$E(\omega\Delta z)$	0	0	0	0
Δ Variance	$Cov(\omega, \upsilon)$	POS	NEG	POS	NEG
	$E(\omega\Delta\upsilon)$	NEG	0	0	NEG
Δ Skewness	$Cov(\omega, \gamma)$	POS	0	0	POS
	$E(\omega\Delta\gamma)$	NEG	0	0	NEG
Δ Kurtosis	$Cov(\omega, \kappa)$	POS	NEG	POS	NEG
	$E(\omega\Delta\kappa)$	POS	POS	NEG	POS

The signs are from Table 3

but this change is produced by two negative terms ($-0.61 = -0.26 - 0.35$). In contrast, the changes of variance by pure stabilizing and diversifying selection are solely produced by the covariance term.

The concepts of pure directional and pure stabilizing selection do not include the skewness of the frequency distribution. However, a change of skewness is found in the distributions produced by the directional fitness function (6) and the stabilizing fitness function (7) with maximum different from the mean. They both produces a negative change of skewness that is caused by a positive covariance term that is smaller than the negative expectation term.

The signs of change Although the details of the statistics of the decomposed overall changes of mean, variance, skewness and kurtosis are important, the different fitness functions can to a large extent be characterized by the signs of the covariance terms and the expectation terms. These signs are presented in Table 4. Let us start by comparing the results of applying the stabilizing function and the diversifying function with optima at $\bar{z}$. The pattern of signs is opposite. With respect to change of variance, the results of the stabilizing function have a negative covariance term while the diversifying function produces a positive covariance term. The same is the case for the covariance terms of the change of kurtosis. However, the change of overall kurtosis is also influenced by the positive expectation term of the stabilizing function and the negative expectation term of the diversifying function.

The comparison of the changes in the distribution produced by the directional function and the stabilizing function with a displaced maximum contains more elements. However, they have the same signs except in the case of the decomposition of the overall change of kurtosis. For the directional function the covariance term and the expectation term are both positive. However, for the mixed function of stabilization only the covariance term is positive while the expectation term is negative. We have not reported results for simulating negative directional selection but changes in the distribution of the characteristic induced by negative directional selection would not be identical to those induced by positive directional selection. In the case of negative rather than positive directional selection the mass of the distribution would shift towards the left tale rather than the right. The decompositions of the changes in mean and skewness would show the opposite signs when compared to positive directional selection. The decompositions of the changes in variance and kurtosis, however, would show the same signs.

The discussion of the current section highlights how quick recognition of the traces of the different fitness functions is facilitated by focusing on the pattern of signs of the two terms of Price's equation. However, further simulations are much needed for producing closer approximations to real evolutionary processes. First, different fitness functions might concurrently contribute to more realistic cases of selection. Second, real selection normally works concurrently on several characteristics of the members of the population. Third, we have to analyse the consequences of abandoning the assumption that $\Delta z_i = 0$.

6 Conclusion

The research underlying this paper had two closely connected aims. The first aim was to demonstrate how the well developed analysis of directional selection within evolutionary economics can be complemented by analyses of stabilizing selection and diversifying selection. The second aim was to demonstrate that the evolutionary algebra provided by Price's equation increases the intellectual coherence and power of thinking about selection and other aspects of evolutionary processes.

The first aim of the paper serves to counter the predominant directional paradigm within evolutionary economics that has led to a neglect of processes of evolution that are influenced by stabilizing selection and diversifying selection. Actually, these types of selection still lack generally acknowledged definitions. We suggested that – like in evolutionary biology–they should be defined by their influence on the variance of the population distribution of the values of a characteristic. Stabilizing selection is the negative change of this variance and diversifying selection is the positive change of variance. In contrast, directional selection is defined as the positive or negative change of the mean.

These definitions do not necessarily represent what is normally thought of as the different types of selection. This is one of the reasons why we complemented the basic concepts with the definitions of fitness functions that can produce the different types of selection. For instance, replicator dynamics provides a fitness function that is normally considered a core example of directional selection. It nevertheless not only influences the mean but also the variance. Similarly, the fitness functions that best represent stabilizing selection and diversifying selection only produces a change in variance without influencing the mean when we assume that it is very special characteristic values that produce maximum fitness and minimum fitness in these functions. Actually, the three fitness functions can produce so many patterns of change that there is a strong need of finding methods for detecting which processes have produced a particular pattern of change. We produced detectable patterns by using Price's equation to decompose the change produced by the different types of fitness functions with different parameters. Then the possible fingerprint is the set of eight signs of the two Price equation effects for the change of the mean, variance, skewness and kurtosis produced under different conditions by the different types of fitness functions.

The paper could not confront the more important issue of using the basic definitions of the types of selection to estimate the relative importance of directional selection, stabilizing selection and diversifying selection in economic evolution. The reason is that this estimation is an empirical problem beyond the scope of the current paper.

The second aim of this paper was to demonstrate the surprising analytical power of Price's equation, and a main contribution thus is the combination of discipline and flexibility that we got from thinking in terms of this equation. However, our review of recent controversies on Price's equation serves to emphasize the difficulties involved in its comprehension and application. We contributed to surmounting some of these by reviewing the different versions of Price's equation as well as specifying the analytical framework in which it can be used. This framework includes two censuses of a population, a mapping between the members of the pre-selection population and the post-selection population, the analysis of changes in the frequency distribution of a selected characteristic, the calculation of fitnesses, the decomposition of the changes of the distribution into the sum of selection effects and intra-member effects, and the analysis of these effects. The handling of these and other issues require the use of mathematical notation, and we largely used the standard notation that has developed in relation to Price's equation.

Although our exposition includes a number of novelties, we have basically been presenting the state of the art. The most concrete contribution to the literature is the analysis of the signs of the Price equation decomposition of the change of skewness and kurtosis. In any case, a main conclusion of this paper is that Price's algebra of evolution helps in improving the intellectual coherence and power of thinking about selection processes in economic life. Through multi-level analysis it can also help to disentangle parts of evolution that are not immediately revealed as being based on selection. The third condition for a long-term evolutionary process, besides from variance and replication, is novelty. In economics this generally means learning and innovation and it has here been confined to the intra-member effect but such processes also contain an element of selection among alternatives.

It remains to be seen whether the concepts of directional, stabilizing and diversifying evolution can also help the analysis of learning and innovation. If this is the case, there might be a chance of analyzing systematically broad ideas such as techno-economic paradigms, regimes and trajectories of evolution, and the distinction between radical and incremental innovation.

Acknowledgements Comments on an early version of this paper presented at the International Schumpeter Society Conference in Brisbane in July 2012, especially those of Michael Peneder and Stan Metcalfe, along with the comments of two anonymous reviewers are gratefully acknowledged. Any remaining errors or omissions are our own.

References

Andersen ES (2004) Population thinking, Price's equation and the analysis of economic evolution. Evol Inst Econ Rev 1:127–148

Bartelsman EJ, Bassanini A, Haltiwanger J, Jarmin RS, Schank T (2004) The spread of ICT and productivity growth: Is Europe lagging behind in the new economy? In: Cohen D, Garibaldi P, Scarpetta S (eds) The ICT revolution, productivity differences and the digital divide. Oxford University Press, Oxford and New York, pp 1–140

Bowles S, Gintis H (2011) A cooperative species: human reciprocity and its evolution. Princeton University Press, Princeton

Brodie ED, Moore AJ, Janzen FJ (1995) Visualizing and quantifying natural selection. Trends Ecol Evol 10:313–318

Conner JK, Hartl DL (2004) A primer of ecological genetics. Sinauer, Sunderland, Mass

Dawkins R, Krebs JR (1979) Arms races between and within species. Proc Royal Soc B Biol Sci 205:489–511

Disney R, Haskel J, Heden Y (2003) Restructuring and productivity growth in UK manufacturing. Econ J 113:666–694

Endler JA (1986) Natural selection in the wild. Princeton University Press, Princeton

Fisher RA (1930) The genetical theory of natural selection. Oxford University Press, Oxford

Foster L, Haltiwanger J, Krizan CJ (1998) Aggregate productivity growth: lessons from microeconomic evidence. National Bureau of Economic Research Working Paper Series, W6803

Foster L, Haltiwanger J, Krizan CJ (2002) The link between aggregate and micro productivity growth: evidence from retail trade. National Bureau of Economic Research Working Paper Series, 9120

Foster L, Haltiwanger J, Syverson C (2008) Reallocation, firm turnover, and efficiency: selection on productivity or profitability? Am Econ Rev 98:394–425

Frank SA (1995) George Price's contributions to evolutionary genetics. J Theor Biol 175:373–388

Frank SA (1997) The Price equation, Fisher's fundamental theorem, kin selection, and causal analysis. Evol 51(6):1712–1729

Frank SA (1998) Foundations of social evolution. Princeton University Press, Princeton

Frank SA (2012a) Natural selection. III. Selection versus transmission and the levels of selection. J Evol Biol 25:227–243

Frank SA (2012b) Natural selection. IV. The Price equation. J Evol Biol 25:1002–1019

Futuyma DJ (2005) Evolution, 2nd edn. Sinauer, Sunderland, Mass

Grafen A (1984) Natural selection, kin selection, and group selection. In: Krebs, J R, Davies, N B (eds.) Behavioural ecology: an evolutionary approach, 2nd edn. Sinaur, Sunderland, Mass, pp 62–84

Hanusch H, Pyka A (eds.) (2007) Elgar companion to Neo-Schumpeterian economics. Elgar, Cheltenham and Northampton, Mass

Kerr B, Godfrey-Smith P (2009) Generalization of the Price equation for evolutionary change. Evol 63:531–536

Kingsolver JG, Pfennig DW (2007) Patterns and power of phenotypic selection in nature. BioSci 57:561–572

Kingsolver JG, Hoekstra HE, Hoekstra JM, Berrigan D, Vignieri SN, Hill CE, Hoang A, Gibert P, Beerli P (2001) The strength of phenotypic selection in natural populations. Am Nat 157:245–261

Knudsen T (2004) General selection theory and economic evolution: the Price equation and the replictor/interactor distinction. J Econ Method 11(2):147–173

Lande R, Arnold SJ (1983) The measurement of selection on correlated characters. Evol 37:1212–1226

Metcalfe JS (1994) Competition, Fisher's principle and increasing returns in the selection process. J Evol Econ 4(4):327–346

Metcalfe JS (1997) Labour markets and competition as an evolutionary process. In: Arestis P, Palma G, Sawyer M (eds) Markets, employment and economic policy: essays in honour of Geoff Harcourt. Routledge, pp 328–343
Metcalfe JS (2002) Book review: Steven A. Frank. 1998. Foundations of social evolution. J Bioecon 4:89–91
Metcalfe JS, Ramlogan R (2006) Creative destruction and the measurement of productivity change. Revue de l'OFCE 97:373–397
Nelson RR, Winter SG (1982) An evolutionary theory of economic change. Harvard University Press, Cambridge, Mass and London
Okasha S (2006) Evolution and the levels of selection. Oxford University Press, Oxford
Price GR (1972) Extension of covariance selection mathematics. Annals Hum Genet 35:485–490
Price GR (1995) The nature of selection. J Theor Biol 175:389–396
Rice SH (2004) Evolutionary theory: mathematical and conceptual foundations. Sinauer, Sunderland, Mass
Schumpeter JA (2000) Briefe/Letters. Mohr, ed. U. Hedtke and R Swedberg, Tübingen
Syverson C (2011) What determines productivity? J Econ Lit 49(2):326–365
van Veelen M, García J, Sabelis MW, Egas M (2012) Group selection and inclusive fitness are not equivalent; the Price equation vs. models and statistics. J Theor Biol 299:64–80
Wright S (1932) The roles of mutation, inbreeding, crossbreeding, and selection in evolution. In: Proceedings of the 6th international congress of genetics, vol 1. Brooklyn Botanic Garden, Brooklyn, pp 356–366

The Evolution and Impact of China's Regional Policy: A Study of Regional Support Policy for Western China

Xiang Deng, Zheng Lu, and Xuezheng Chen

Abstract By examining the socioeconomic and political background, we show how China's regional policy was affected by various factors. We do this in different periods of time, accounting for the conditions in different regions to get an understanding of the policy and how it has evolved over time. From an evolutionary economics perspective, we evaluate the strengths and weaknesses of the regional support policy for China's western regions, specifically their impact on the economic and social development in these regions. We illustrate the path of change which the regional support policy for the western regions has followed. Using this perspective, we explore the links between evolutionary economics and regional policy changes in China.

1 Introduction

Regional development has always been a fascinating subject, much like the question of a nation's rise and fall. There is a growing body of literature on regional development and regional policy since 1990s. Barro and Sala-i-Martin (1991) examined the convergence across regions within the neoclassical growth model. Acemoglu and Robinson (2009) revitalized the well-known approach that seeks to better understand the historical origins of institutions and their importance for long-term economic growth. Fujita et al. (1999) explored the important role of history, increasing returns and path-dependency, in regional development, which is called the New Economic Geography. Boschma and Martin (2010) and others have made encouraging progress in this field by introducing new spatial and evolutionary elements. Gradually, the key notions from Evolutionary Economics, such as historic events, selection, path-dependency, chance, innovation and increasing returns, gradually enter the research on economic geography and regional development. Nonetheless, from the perspective of Evolutionary Economics, there are still many

X. Deng • Z. Lu (✉) • X. Chen (✉)
School of Economics, Sichuan University, Wangjiang Lu 29, 610064 Chengdu, People's Republic of China
e-mail: dengxiang@scu.edu.cn; zlu@scu.edu.cn; xzchen@scu.edu.cn

A. Pyka, J. Foster (eds.), *The Evolution of Economic and Innovation Systems*, Economic Complexity and Evolution, DOI 10.1007/978-3-319-13299-0_6

questions relating to the Regional Support Policy (RSP), both in terms of decision-making process and its impact. In this paper, we will primarily focus on the following three questions: (1) What is the connection between RSP decision-making and the economic and political institutions at the time these policies were determined? (2) How does RSP respond and adapt to the changing economic, social and political environment? (3) What is the impact of RSP on regional economic and social development?

In this paper, we present the regional development strategy and policy adopted by the Chinese government, and study the factors leading to the selection of RSP over a wide time frame. China is now the second largest economy, and her regional development strategy has experienced a rapid and dramatic evolution since 1949. Since 1949, China has gone through three stages with distinct regional development strategy. The first stage (1949–1978) is called the "Balanced Development" stage, which followed the former Soviet Union model in its institution selection and political decisions. Its objectives were to achieve a balanced development across all regions. The second stage (1979–1991), known as "Non-balanced Development", sought to promote the development of those regions with special advantages. In this stage, political elites played a decisive role and institutional reform was a major objective. The third stage (1992-present) is called the "Coordinated Development" stage. In this stage the primary objective is the acceleration of the development of underdeveloped regions in order to reduce regional disparities. These regional policy choices for the western regions are, of course, influenced by political, military and social considerations to some extent.

This paper also explores the possible links between Evolutionary Economics and regional policy change, through a study of regional policy for western China.[1] From the perspective of Evolutionary Economics, including historic events, path-dependency, innovation and institutional change, we enable a better understanding of the evolution and impact of China's regional policy on the western regions.

The rest of this paper is organized as follows. Section 2 analyzes the evolution of China's regional policy for the western regions between 1953 and 1977. Section 3 studies the evolution of regional policy since 1978 and the third "GO WEST". Section 4 reviews policy instruments of the Western Development Strategy (WDS) since 1999. Section 5 discusses the economic performance of Western China and the impact of WDS; Finally, Sect. 6 concludes.

[1]In this paper, Western China refers to 12 provincial administrative regions including Inner Mongolia, Guangxi, Chongqing, Sichuan, Guizhou, Yunnan, Tibet, Shaanxi, Gansu, Qinghai, Ningxia and Xinjiang. Moreover, mainland China is divided into four parts in terms of the official economic regionalization at present. Besides Western China, other three regions are Eastern China (includes Beijing, Tianjin, Hebei, Shanghai, Jiangsu, Zhejiang, Fujian, Guangdong and Hainan), Central China (includes Shanxi, Anhui, Jiangxi, Henan, Hubei and Hunan) and Northeastern China (includes Liaoning, Jilin and Heilongjiang).

2 The First Two Waves of "GO WEST"

2.1 The First Wave of "GO WEST": 1953–1962

When the Communist Party of China (CPC) came to power in 1949, the Soviet Union was the one of the few countries that acknowledged the new Chinese government and established diplomatic relations with China. Devastated by decades of the anti-fascist war and the civil war, China's economy and industry lagged far behind the Soviet Union and other industrial nations around the world. However, the new Chinese government led by CPC aimed to change this and set China on the path to becoming one of the world's economic and political superpowers.

Following the lead of the Soviet Union, the new government of China adopted a highly centralized economic system and introduced her own 'Five-year Plan' in 1953, mainly aiming at the nationalization of private enterprises and the development of heavy industry. Hence, it became a priority for China to increase the production of steel, iron and coal, all of which are largely concentrated in the inland regions.[2] Moreover, the start of the Korean War and the threat of continuing conflict with the Kuomintang regime in Taiwan led to the "neutralization" of the Taiwan Strait by the US Navy. This led to the further isolation of China and stimulated a military build up in eastern regions. Hence, it was not possible for coastal regions of Eastern China to capitalize on their geographic advantage to establish business relations with foreign countries.

All of these political and economic constraints led to the decision of the Chinese government's implementation of "Balanced Development Strategy (BDS)", favoring development in inland China. Under this strategy, during the "1st Five-year Plan" (1953–1957) and the "2nd Five-year Plan" (1958–1962), the Chinese government introduced regional development policy to promote economic development in Western China and Central China. Western China was undergoing the first wave of the "GO WEST" campaign.

Guided by BDS, national resources were primarily redistributed to northeastern regions and the western regions. Most of the national investment capital and projects were allocated compulsively to the northeastern, central and western regions by the central government. For instance, 68 % of key projects were allocated to the inland regions in the 1st Five-year Plan period, while only 32 % were allocated to coastal regions (Lu and Xue 1997). Furthermore, from 1953 to 1957, the share of investment in capital construction for Western China increased from 21.63 to 29.1 %, while the share for Eastern China dropped from 48.26 to 39.04 % (see Fig. 1).

[2]*Source*: Natural Resources, http://www.gov.cn/test/2005-07/27/content_17405.htm

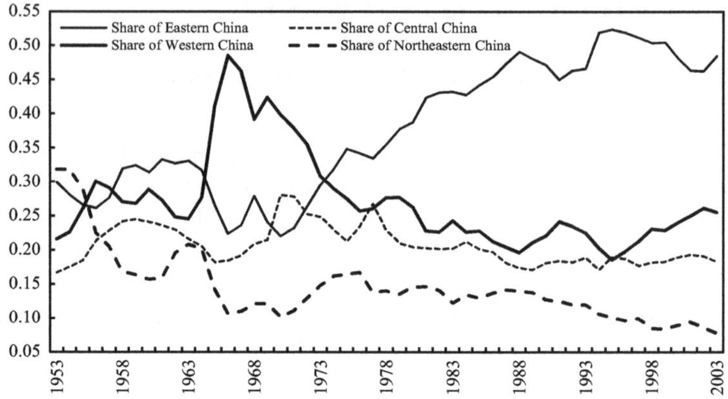

Fig. 1 Investment in capital construction in China. *Source*: Calculated based on the data from *Statistic on Investment in Fixed Assets of China (1950–2000)* and *China Statistical Yearbook* (2001–2004)

2.2 The Second Wave of "GO WEST": 1964–1975

In the late 1950s and early 1960s (the period of the 2nd Five-year Plan), both China's internal and external situations deteriorated dramatically. The implementation of the adventurous policy of "the Great Leap Forward" greatly distorted individual incentives: both agriculture and industrial production suffered dramatic contraction, resulting in a great famine between 1959 and 1962. The 1st two Five-year Plans' objectives were achieved only in part. China's foreign relations also experienced substantial deterioration, mainly due to the increasing hostility between the Soviet Union and China and the US-led military intervention in the Vietnam War.

Facing these problems, Mao Zedong's government made it an urgent task to implement a large-scale relocation of industries to western China. This dramatic shift of the regional development policy came about after the special session of the CPC in August 1964. In this session, Mao proposed that factories, especially those military industrial firms in coastal regions, should be relocated to the western regions to protect them from potential military strikes. Following Mao's proposal, the CPC decided that most of the new projects should be allocated to the western regions and most of the capital should be invested on "third front construction", which primarily contributed to the economic development in Western China.

In the early 1960s, China's national defense followed the strategy of three fronts from the coast to the interior by CPC leaders (see Fig. 2). Third front construction led to a massive investment program started in 1964 in Western China, in particular Sichuan, Guizhou, Yunnan, Gansu, Qinghai, Ningxia, and a part of Shanxi. The objective of the program was to build a range of industrial bases in the remote areas of the western regions to prepare against the potential of war and famine (Naughton 1988).

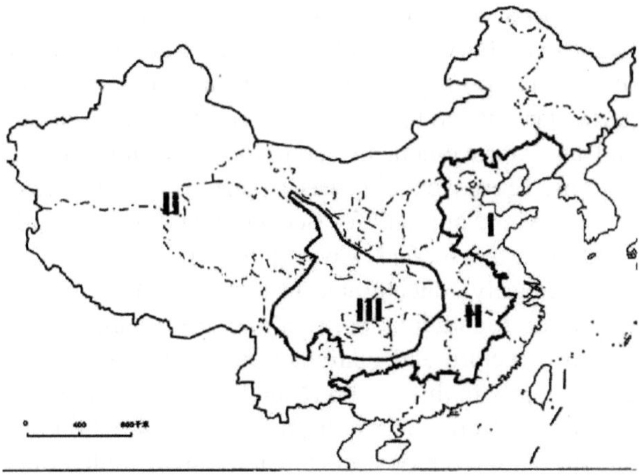

Fig. 2 Map of "Three Fronts" construction in China. *Source*: http://jianxiaochao88.blog.163.com/blog/static/31002020081022105814526

During the period of the third front construction, Mao launched the Cultural Revolution, a radical and violent political movement. In this period, production activities almost came to a halt in every part of China. Third front construction can be divided into two phases. The first phase corresponded with the 3rd Five-year Plan (1966–1970) and its strategic focus was on the southwest regions. The second phase, corresponding with the 4th Five-year Plan (1971–1975), focused primarily on Hubei and Henan, which nowadays are considered as Central China. From 1963 to 1970, Western China's Capital Construction investment share rose sharply from 24.5 to 39.84 %, while Eastern China's share decreased from 39.8 to 26.3 %. In particular 44.4 % and 32.5 % of the large and medium sized national projects were located in Western China in the 3rd and 4th Five-year Plan periods respectively. This is a considerable increase on the 20 % and 22.7 % in the 1st and 2nd Five-year Plan periods.[3]

2.3 An Evaluation of the First Two Waves of "GO WEST"

It is clear that the first wave of "GO WEST" laid a basic industrial foundation in Western China. Heavy industry, such as equipment manufacturing, aerospace and steel, grew significantly during this period. However, this campaign actually resulted in a serious loss of efficiency. Many industries were transplanted into the western regions without the basic foundations for their development, being moved from coastal regions with much better infrastructure.

[3]Data is from National Bureau of Statistics (2002) and Statistics on Investment in Fixed Assets of China (1950–2000). Beijing: China Statistics Press.

The first wave "Go West" coincided with the costly political movement of "the Great Leap Forward" and the resulting great famine between 1959 and 1962, both of which seriously compromised many objectives of the 2nd Five-Year Plan. In particular it failed to deliver a successful industrial relocation to the western regions and an improvement in economic conditions in backward areas in the western regions. Moreover, this was a period of heavy loss in terms of both economic efficiency and human life (Becker and Ghosts 1998; Dikotter 2010).

During the second wave of the "GO WEST" period, capital investment was also primarily concentrated in the western regions. This consolidated the modern industrial foundation built in the first campaign. With the great development in infrastructure and manufacturing industries, economy of Western China grew considerably in this period (Naughton 1988). Between 1952 and 1978, there were a significant decline in the disparity in industrial output between the western regions and the coastal regions, and the hinterland's industrial output share rose from 30.6 % in 1952 to 39.1 % 1978.

However, the mandatory allocation of resources to the western regions was largely inefficient. According to Lu and Xue (1997), China accumulated approximately RMB 400 billion of capital assets between 1953 and 1980. However, only RMB 250 billion of these capital assets brought some real economic effect, some of which was merely transient. Moreover, Gao (1989) showed that the capital output ratio in the period of third front construction was only 0.217, much lower than the rate 0.338 for the period of the 1st Five-year Plan.

The first two "GO WEST" campaigns showed that the willingness of a leader, together with a high degree of arbitrary power for policy makers could dramatically change the geographical distribution of various economic resources and facilities (Boschma and Lambooy 2001). However, this change was not sustainable because it was achieved at a great cost of economic and social efficiency, similar to what happened in the former Soviet Union. More importantly, under the highly centralized economic system, economic agents, such as local officials, firm managers and households, hardly had any freedom to learn or select, nor were given any incentive to do so. The only action open to them was to engage in sabotage and passive resistance and to express discontent with central government orders.

In Mao's era of extremely centralized political power, the government forcefully broke the trajectory of path-dependent socioeconomic development, but it turned out to be devastating for the overall economy and for regional development. When excessive political and military objectives are involved in the design of regional economic development strategy, it becomes almost inevitable that the overall economy and the individual regions will suffer from tremendous efficiency losses. The inland regions, including the western regions, gained some relative economic advantages and benefits in the short run because of BDS, compared with the eastern regions. Nonetheless, they were unable to escape the problems engulfing China's wider economy, as the entire economy was distorted and devastated by the inherent weaknesses of BDS and a series of costly political movements between the late 1950s and 1970s.

3 The Evolution of RSP Since 1978 and the Third "GO WEST"

Following Mao's era, China's regional policy can be classified into two phases: the first phase was from 1978 to 1991 when China's economic development was guided by the Non-balanced Development Strategy; the second phase was from 1992 to present, the Coordinated Development Strategy, which can be further divided into two sub-periods: 1992–2000 and 2000 to the present.

3.1 Non-balanced Development Strategy: 1978–1991

After the death of Mao and the defeat of 'the Gang of Four' in 1976, Deng Xiaoping, a moderate CPC leader with rich experience in managing the state economy, gradually emerged as the de facto leader of China in 1977.[4] Deng's leadership removed the political obstacles for major economic reform and adjustment of the regional development strategy.

In the late 1970s China was in great need of foreign capital and production technologies in order to revitalize the Chinese economy and improve economic efficiency. The coastal regions, compared with the inland regions, have advantages in attracting foreign capital and technologies, due to their geographic location and large numbers of overseas Chinese from these regions.

Moreover, as a result of excessive focus on the development of heavy industry, light industry was too weak to meet the needs of Chinese people. Nonetheless, with a significant improvement in foreign relations since the middle 1960s and a relatively peaceful environment in the late 1970s (Khadiagala 1982), promoting the development of light industry became increasingly important for China's economy. Compared with the inland regions, the coastal regions have strong comparative advantages in developing light industry. This peaceful environment also created precious pre-conditions for the coastal regions to re-establish international trade relations with other countries and areas and to attract foreign capital and technologies.

In order to reconstruct the Chinese economy and restore the legitimacy of the CPC regime damaged by the poor economic performance and costly political movements, the CPC regime had no choice but to shift its focus from political ideology to economic development. This shift was endorsed by the de factor leader Deng in the late 1970s (Heberer and Schubert 2006; Holbig and Gilley 2010). The CPC leaders also realized that the excessive state control of economic activities was one of the major factors contributing to the low labor efficiency in agricultural and industrial production and looked to address this problem.

---

[4]*Source*: "1977: Deng Xiaoping back in power". BBC Online, 22 July 1977.

Under Deng's leadership, China began to reform its economic system and implement the opening-up policy (i.e. Reform and Opening-up). The core of Deng's reform was known as "decentralization and interest concessions", which meant that governments would give households, firms and local governments some degree of autonomy. Deng's reform primarily focused on institutional rearrangements and the introduction of appropriate incentive mechanisms.

With the introduction of the new incentive mechanisms, households, firm managers and local officials were motivated to innovate like institutional entrepreneurs. For example, several peasants in Anhui Province introduced the so-called "Household Contracted Responsibility System", and some managers in state-owned enterprises experimented with this "contracted system" in Chengdu. In addition, the central government took measures in order to encourage local government officials to actively participate in economic management and promote economic development. It carried out fiscal decentralization, allowing local governments to retain more of the revenue generated in the local economy (Gao et al. 2009). Finally, the evaluation of government officials began to focus more on economic performance, although the political power was still highly centralized. The new partially decentralized fiscal system is called "informal federalism of Chinese style" by some researchers (Jin et al. 2005).

This fiscal decentralization provided a rather effective incentive mechanism to encourage the government officials to shift their focus from costly political movements to economic activities. This led them to put a greater emphasis on protecting the local economy, facilitating a certain degree of privatization, and promoting economic development. Since the early 1980s, the Chinese people were gradually allowed more freedom in migrating between different areas in China. The 'voting by feet' (Tiebout 1956) mechanism increased the competition between government officials in different areas. As a result, local government officials started to play an important role in the introduction of RSP, in order to bring about desirable policy that privileged their region, and to attract more projects, fund and personnel.

In the late 1970s, facing a dire economic environment, large numbers of residents in Guangdong Province fled from their hometowns to overseas areas or countries, including Hong Kong, Macao and southeast Asian countries.[5] In order to stop the illegal emigration of local residents and revitalize the local economy, Xi Zhongxiong and other leaders of Guangdong at the time, proposed the introduction of Special Economic Zones (SEZs). SEZs would be entitled to a new economic management system with more economic freedom and more conducive to business and economic activities than that in the rest of mainland China.

The proposal to introduce SEZs was supported by the CPC leaders Zhao Ziyang and Deng Xiaoping. In 1980, the central government established special economic zones in Shenzhen, Shantou and Zhuhai in Guangdong Province, and Xiamen in Fujian Province. All these cities achieved tremendous success in establishing

[5] *Source*: 'Forgotten stories of the great escape to Hong Kong', (HE Huifeng, 13 January 2013), http://www.scmp.com/news/china/article/1126786/forgotten-stories-huge-escape-hong-kong

foreign business relations and promoting local economic development from the early 1980s onwards (Graham and Wada 2001).

In the early 1980s, after decades of isolation, the Chinese government severely lacked experience and the skills needed for the development of a new economic system and the establishment of foreign business relations. In the absence of experience and relevant regulations for the new economic activities, the introduction of SEZs provided a valuable testing ground for the Chinese people and government to acquire and absorb knowledge for participating in new economic activities, and gradually adapt to the changing economic and social environment. This was a critical step to break away from the trajectory of the old economic and political models, and set out on a path to a new economic and social model with more freedom and higher efficiency.

The introduction of SEZs signaled the central government's abandonment of the balanced development strategy, and adopting instead a non-balanced regional strategy that favored coastal regions with their relative advantages to develop faster than inland regions, so as to promote overall economic growth. For example, the eastern coastal regions enjoyed preferential policies regarding investment, taxation and land use.

From 1978 to 1991, the Chinese economy grew rapidly, while the benefits from the reform and opening-up largely flowed into the coastal regions, especially those entitled to preferential policies. For this reason, regional policy in this period was called "Non-balanced Development Strategy". However, the reform in this period encountered some problems, such as the market disorder arising from the dual-track price system, local protectionism, market segmentation and especially from the rising conservatism and recentralization that took place around 1990 (Montinola et al. 1996; Lewis and Xue 2003; Cai and Treisman 2006).

After a comprehensive assessment of the reform achievements and issues in the 1980s, Deng Xiaoping and his allies launched a campaign to transform the planned economy into a market-oriented system in 1992. At the same time, partially as a response to the inland local governments' increasing discontent at the excessive policy privileges given to the coastal regions, the central government proposed an idea of "Coordinated Development" to allow the "Opening-up Policy" to spread gradually to the lagging regions.

3.2 *The First Stage of Coordinated Development Strategy: 1992–1999*

The implementation of 'Coordinated Development Strategy' could be divided into two stages: the first stage is from 1992 to 1999 and the second one is from 2000 to the present time. For the second stage, our discussion will focus on the period from 2000 to 2010, considering the availability of data.

During the first stage, the central government presented an idea of coordinated development, but there were no specific measures implemented, due to the state's limited fiscal capacity. During the second stage, the government introduced specific measures and supporting policies such as the Western Development Strategy (2000), the Northeast Area Revitalization Plan (2003) and the Rising Strategy of Central China (2006).

An all-round opening-up not only enabled lagging regions to obtain equivalent preferential policy support, but also improve their competitiveness against the coastal regions to some extent (Gao and Tong 2008). With the deepening of reforms and the acceleration of marketization and globalization, foreign and domestic capital, human resources and industries began to cluster in coastal regions, particularly in the Yangtze River Delta, the Pearl River Delta and the Bohai Bay.

Although the disparity in policy support had been eliminated, the positive effects of opening-up policy in the central and western regions were much less significant than those in eastern regions (Guo et al. 2002). The policy privileging coastal areas in the 1980s helped the eastern regions reinforce their first-mover advantage over the other regions. As a result, regional disparities increased sharply in the early 1990s (Démurger 2001; Deng 2002; Fan and Sun 2008; Fan et al. 2010). The eastern regions not only enjoyed advantages in light industry, but also gradually caught up with and surpassed the inland regions in heavy industry in the 1990s.

3.3 *Coordinated Development Strategy: 2000–2010*

Relying on relative advantages on the level of economic development, the eastern regions were able to capitalize on economic disparities to the detriment of the western regions. Attracted by more job opportunities, higher wage levels and better living conditions, large numbers of workers left their hometowns in the western regions, and migrated into the towns and cities of the eastern regions, especially into the coastal cities in the 1990s. As a result, the development of the western regions was hindered by a severe and continuous lack of labor. Furthermore, large amounts of various raw materials, such as coal, iron ore and logs, were transferred away from the western regions into the eastern regions at rather low prices, whereas the industrial products from the eastern regions were sold into the western regions at profitable prices (Xiao et al. 2010).

Facing these economic disadvantages and the overwhelming competition from the eastern regions, the local governments in the western regions adopted many protectionist measures (Bai et al. 2004). As a result, economic conflicts between different regions rose steadily during 1990s. Moreover, there is an obvious trend of resemblance in industrial structure, disregard of great differences in economic, social and natural conditions in different regions (He et al. 2008). This led to a sharp increase in transaction costs for cross-region economic activities and a tremendous loss of overall economic efficiency.

In 1994, China government embarked on the reform of the tax sharing system between the central government and the local governments, through which the central government gradually strengthened its fiscal capacity. China's central government realized it was time to take practical measures to accelerate the development of the lagging regions, and to reduce the regional disparities and tackle the problems resulting from those disparities. In 1999, the Chinese government launched the third wave of the "Go West" campaign, known as WDS. This led to the implementation of some concrete policy measures by the Chinese State Council in October 2000, so as to promote the economic development in Western China. By 2010, WDS had been in effect for 10 years. In June 2010, the CPC Central Committee and the State Council announced a new policy guideline, which adjusted and intensified policy measures and extended the key preferential policy for 10 more years. We will explain WDS in more detail in the following two sections.

4 Policy Instruments of WDS

4.1 Fiscal Policy

Preferential taxation is one of the major policy instruments of WDS. Enterprises in the western regions, whether domestic-funded or foreign-funded, are entitled to a preferential enterprise income tax rate of 15 % (the normal tax rate is at 25 %), as well as a tax reduction or a tax exemption of value added tax and resource tax. In particular, new-founded enterprises can obtain tax exemption if they operate in western China in the following sectors: transportation, power, water conservation, postal service and electronic equipment. In addition, in order to attract more FDI, tariffs and import value added tax for imported equipment are exempted under certain conditions. Moreover, for key infrastructure projects, local or central governments may introduce a special preferential tax arrangement. For example, almost all types of taxes were exempted for the Qinghai-Tibet Railway project.

The central government also increased its transfers to local governments in Western China. Between 2000 and 2005, it gradually increased general transfer payments to the local governments in Western China, and these payments in this period amounted to RMB 404.4 billion and accounted for 52.6 % of the total transfer payments by the central government (Ye 2006). The increase in total transfers (including general transfers and special transfers) reflected that fiscal transfers by the central government tended to go to the western regions. In 1999, 29.01 % of the central government's fiscal transfers were allocated to Western China, while in 2010 the percentage reached 39.42 %.

As for state investments by the central government, the distribution of national key projects and national bonds tended to favor the western regions since 2000. In the first decade (2000–2010), the central government launched 143 key projects, either located in or relevant to the western regions. The total investment of these projects amounted to over RMB 2,874.2 billion, covering various socioeconomic sectors, including infrastructure construction, ecological environmental protection, rural development, education, medical treatment and public health. From 2001 to 2010, the average annual growth rate of the state budget for investment in fixed assets in Western China was 30.76 %, much greater than that in any other region. National bonds also played an important role in WDS: about 40 % of the revenue from long-term national bonds was invested in the western regions each year. The revenue from bonds was primarily devoted to the construction and improvement of infrastructure (SIC 2005; Ye 2006).

Moreover, the central government, local governments and the People's Bank of China (PBC) promulgated several measures to: (a) encourage financial institutions, especially national policy banks to augment loans for supporting the western regions' development, (b) attract foreign banks to establish branches in Western China, (c) facilitate the participation of private capital in the construction of financial services institutions, and (d) promote the establishment and development of village banks, finance companies and rural fund cooperatives in western rural areas.

4.2 Guiding Policy

"Guiding policy" is a supplementary policy instrument. The guiding policy provides: (1) guidance to investment of foreign and private capital; (2) incentive mechanism to encourage high-level personnel to work in the western regions; (3) guidance to financial institutions in order to augment loan support; and (4) encouragement of the eastern developed regions to provide aid to the western regions.

In 2002, the National Development and Reform Commission (NDRC) promulgated "Several Opinions on Promoting and Guiding Private Investment", which suggested that local governments should vigorously support private investment in high-tech projects. The NDRC also released the 'Catalogue of Priority Industries for Foreign Investment in the Central-Western Regions', in order to guide the investment of foreign capital. In 2002 the Central Committee of the Communist Youth League of China and the Ministry of Education jointly launched the "Go West College Graduates Volunteer Program", in which college graduates were recruited every year, to serve as volunteers to work in western backward areas for 1–2 years, primarily in the fields of education, health care and poverty reduction. Between 2003 and 2010, this program recruited more than 90,000 volunteers to work in the western regions. The program also encouraged college students to obtain employment in those regions after graduation from courses.

In 2002 the central government implemented a "Ten-Year Plan for Developing Talented People in the Western Regions". The objectives included: (1) the development of education in poor regions in Western China, (2) an increase in personnel exchange and interaction between Eastern and Western China, and (3) the assignment of outstanding civil servants from central, eastern and midland governments to work in the western areas. Official data shows that from 2000 to 2010, 3,528 civil servants from western local governments were assigned to work in central and eastern local governments temporarily as a means to improve their administrative ability.

4.3 Interregional Mutual Aid Promotion Policy

There are two types of interregional mutual aid promotion policy. The first one is called Hand-in-Hand Aid (HHA) or Counterpart Support Policy. Under HHA, in order to promote the development of a region or an industry, the relevant governments establish a mutual aid relationship or partnership between different regions or industries based on each other's advantage. The central government will consider the opinions of local governments but has the final say in "who aids who" and "how to aid". HHA policy is concerned with various aspects of economic and social development, such as infrastructure construction, education, industrial development, technical assistance and direct capital investment. China has implemented four large HHA programs to date and the beneficiary areas are the Three Gorges reservoir area, Tibet, Xinjiang and the Earthquake Hit Areas in Sichuan, all in Western China.

The second type is the "East–west Interaction" policy (EWI) issued in 2007. Economic entities from the eastern regions and the western regions jointly promote the cross-regional flow of production factors by exploiting their comparative advantages. The central government encourages enterprises in eastern regions to invest in the western regions, but this policy, unlike HHA, is voluntary.

4.4 Specific and Differentiated Support Policy for Each Region

The policy and measures discussed in the above four subsections, serve as general guidelines to support the western regions. The western regions include vast areas at different development levels, with diverse development strengths and weaknesses. To address these differences, the central government worked out a specific and differentiated support policy for different areas. To date, the central government has announced specific policy measures for each of the 12 provinces or autonomous regions, except Shanxi province. Examples include the "poverty reduction policy" for Guizhou, the "post-disaster reconstruction plan" for Sichuan, the "leapfrog development plan" for Tibet.

It is worth noting that the details of RSP are usually drafted by the local governments with support from experts in relevant fields. They are then submitted to the central government and discussed by the representatives from both the central government and local governments. More often than not, in order to achieve the desired support policy, the local governments will mobilize various resources and utilize all available channels to lobby relevant officials in the central government, and even resort to some informal measures or secret transactions with these officials. For example, local governments usually set up "Liaison Offices" in Beijing, which serves as a regular channel for them to lobby or bribe the high ranking officials in the central government.

5 The Impact and Limitations of WDS and Policy Suggestions

5.1 Performance After 1978

China began to enjoy rapid and stable growth following her transition from a highly centralized planned economy to a market-oriented economy in 1992. The average annual growth rate of China's GDP was as high as 10.12 % between 1979 and 2010, while the average rates of the Eastern, Central, Western and Northeastern areas were 10.79 %, 9.98 %, 9.57 % and 8.5 % respectively. Before the implementation of WDS, the economic growth of the western regions was slower than that of other regions. However after the implementation of WDS, the western economy entered a period of rapid growth with an average annual growth rate of 13.58 % between 2000 and 2010, growing faster than Central and Northeastern China. In 2006, Western China overtook Eastern China in term of growth rate, becoming the fastest-growing region.

Rapid economic growth following the implementation of WDS led to a steady and significant increase in the GDP share of Western China. In the 1980s, the nominal GDP share of Western China fluctuated around 20 %, and then decreased rapidly to 17.09 % in 2003 from the early 1990s. It began to rise again in 2004 and reached 18.63 % in 2010. The GDP per capita of Western China also grew much faster following the implementation of WDS. From 1991 to 2000 the average annual growth rate of real GDP per capita was only 6.6 %, compared with 13.26 % from 2001 to 2010. Western China's ratio of GDP per capita to national GDP per capita rose from 61.24 % in 2000 to 71.28 % in 2010.

As we can see from the Theil index in Fig. 4, regional disparities in China decreased sharply in the 1980s, whereas they began to rise in the early 1990s (see Fig. 3). This may be partially due to the reforms in 1980s, such as the "household contract responsibility system" in rural areas and the "contract system" in state-owned factories. The reforms had a more profound impact on economic and social development in inland regions.

Moreover, due to the "China's fiscal decentralization reform in 1990s", local protectionism and market segmentation became a dominant strategic choice for many local officials in different areas of China. As a result, it became more difficult for the labor force, capital and other resources of production to cluster in those relatively developed areas. This is one of the key factors contributing to the relocation of many

Fig. 3 Real GDP share and GDP per capita of Western China (1979–2010). *Note*: *GDP per capita* $= GDP_t/AP_t$, and $AP_t = (P_t + P_{t-1})/2$, where P_t is the population at the end of period t, and AP_t is the average population of period t

labor-intensive enterprises into the inland regions or offshore areas, such as Vietnam, Cambodia and Laos, since the early 2000s. The relocation of the labor-intensive enterprises, the increase in the living cost in the eastern regions, and the very limited capacity of the employers in eastern regions to raise wages, led to large numbers of workers from inland regions leaving the eastern regions (Golley 2007). This new spatial division of labor began to emerge since around 2005.

In 1992, the central government introduced the Coordinated Development Strategy. However, due to the limited fiscal capacity of the central government after fiscal decentralization, the western provinces could not obtain sufficient financial support. Furthermore, beginning in 1992 China embraced market integration and globalization, and the coastal regions became much more attractive than inland regions, in terms of foreign investment and labor force. The coastal regions thus benefited from a geographic advantage, a larger market scale, more skilled labor and a greater concentration of industry, all of which enlarged the economic disparities between the coastal regions and the western regions.

WDS is one particular policy response to China's increasing regional disparities in the 1990s. However, as we can see from Fig. 4, the trend of enlarging disparities continued until 2005, despite the implementation of WDS in 1999. The turning point was around 2005, after which disparities gradually decreased between 2005 and 2010. This may be due to a time lag for the impact of regional policy. The fundamental factors leading to the convergence of economic development started to really kick in around 2005. These factors included the rising cost of labor and land,

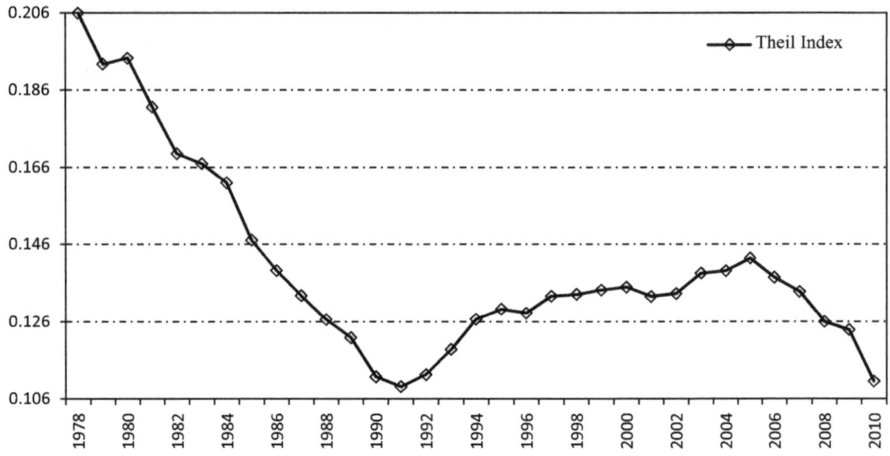

Fig. 4 Evolution of China's regional disparities (Real GDP per capita). *Source*: Data from *China Statistical Yearbook* (1985, 1990, 2000, 2012)

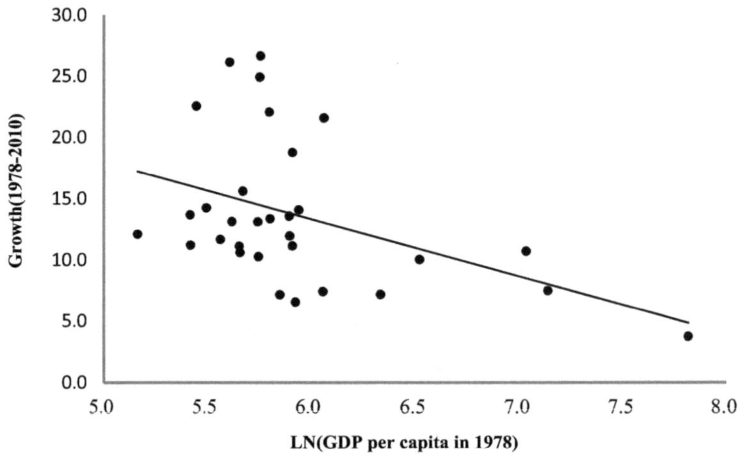

Fig. 5 Absolute convergence across 31 regions in China (1978–2010). *Source*: Data from *China Statistical Yearbook* (1985, 1990, 2000, 2012)

as well as the acceleration of industrial transfer from the coastal to the central and the western regions. Although there could be various other factors contributing to the convergence of economic development in different regions, it is safe to infer that the implementation of WDS played an important role in this process. As for absolute convergence across regions, Fig. 5 shows results for China that are similar to those seen in the US, Japan and European countries (Barro and Sala-i-Martin 1991).

5.2 *Limitations and Negative Effects*

The previous analysis shows that WDS has obtained some notable achievements and encouraging results. Nevertheless, we should not neglect the following main limitations and unsatisfactory aspects of the design and implementation of WDS.

(I) Standardized State Aid and Evaluation System The approach of WDS attempts to promote local industries with comparative advantages, through a catalogue of priority industries reflecting geographic differentiation. It is a regional development policy characterized by a generalized preferential system for Western China. Within such a state aid system, both leading regions and backward regions in Western China benefit from the same preferential policy, and so was much more effective at dealing with disparities across than within regions (Fan et al. 2010). Additionally, uniform aid policy does not address the problem of disparity between the real economic development levels of various regions in Western China.

Support policy for the western regions was supposed to be chosen with diverse natural and geographic conditions, economic foundations and comparative advantages all in mind. Instead, current support policy treats different areas in Western China in the same way. In contrast, European RSP is much better designed and implemented to reflect different socioeconomic conditions in different regions, which should be a valuable example for China to follow. Following the practices of the European RSP, Western China could be divided into several territorial units according to the level of economic development, the resources and the environmental carrying capacity. Then the central government would be able to implement different support policy for different areas.

WDS also lacks a thorough evaluation system for the policy and its projects. There are some problems with the investment process, such as misappropriation, diversion, interception, wasteful spending and corruption. For example, an audit on a highway construction project in Luojiang county of Sichuan province revealed that the local government seized most of the land compensation fund (about RMB 14.1 million) meant for the farmers, but only 4.5 % of the total amount (RMB 0.65 million) was actually paid to them. The remaining amount was turned into a local fiscal support fund managed by the local government. Another audit on the "Returning Grazing Land to Grassland" project in five provinces in Western China also found that RMB 40.68 million project fund was seized by the local government, and a RMB 64.62 million project fund was misappropriated by a local government (NAO 2006). Currently, the central government simply arranges unscheduled monitoring and auditing on some key projects, with no standardized and regular approach to monitor and evaluate the implementation of the projects under WDS.

(II) Deterioration of Environment Inefficient resource utilization, lack of appropriate planning and over-exploitation has led to a serious waste of resources and environmental damage. The ecological environment in Western China has been deteriorating rapidly since the late 1990s. The government has undertaken several

projects in an attempt to slow the rate of environmental deterioration. These projects, such as "Returning Farmland to Forests", "Returning Grazing Land to Grassland", "Natural Forest Protection", and "Soil and Water Conservation", have not achieved their objectives. Despite the improvement in the environment of a few areas in Western China, the overall situation is still deteriorating. (Sun et al. 2012), Liu (2011) stated that the soil erosion in Western China accounted for more than 80 % of the national amount, and the desertification area in Western China accounted for more than 90 %.

(III) Excessive or Inappropriate Investments in Infrastructure Improving infrastructure in the western regions is the core part of WDS. The central government budgets allocate enormous funds every year to address the lack of infrastructure in these regions. However, an analysis of the program's performances in the past 10 years revealed some seriously inappropriate and redundant infrastructure projects. For example, in some provinces, almost all second-tier cities have built or are building regional airports. In fact, demand in some of these small cities is not large enough to justify the construction of an airport. According to Chen (2010), over half of the airports in Western China are operating at a loss.

Furthermore, under the current construction pattern, most of the social and economic benefits created by infrastructure construction actually flows out of the western regions, instead of benefiting these regions. Firstly, these projects generate a high demand for engineering equipment largely produced in the eastern regions. Secondly, some key projects, such as the "West–east Electricity Transmission" and the "West–east Gas Transmission", were introduced to transfer raw materials and energy to eastern regions at a very low price. Some upstream industries located in the western regions, receive only a small part of the benefits, while most of them are seized by eastern regions. Finally, key projects for Western China are managed by those state-owned key enterprises, which means a large proportion of the income tax will be paid to the central government instead of to the local governments.

(IV) Underinvestment in the Public Service Sectors Under WDS, large amounts of capital have been invested in the western regions; however, there is still severe underinvestment in various public service sectors in these regions, especially in education and public health care. This is one of the major obstacles for the improvement in well-being of the population in Western China. In the 1990s and early 2000s, China's health financing system gradually decentralized to the lowest administrative level, the survival of the public health care system became more and more reliant on the service charges and other revenues generated by the hospitals and other health care institutions. Although since 2006, there has been a reverse on this trend, because a large proportion of the population in the western regions still could not afford the burden of health care.

In terms of education, the western regions lag far behind all the other regions. A large proportion of the population are scattered in vast mountainous areas or prairies in Western China, which dramatically increases the difficulty in enhancing the overall education level of the population in the western regions. Also, current education-enhancing schemes for the western regions are largely carried out in the style of political movements, and there is not a consistent and sustainable plan supported by continuous necessary scale of investments or financial transfer.

(V) Limited Impact on Job Creation and Attracting Labor With an increase in living costs in the relatively developed eastern regions and the weak capacity of the employers to raise wages, large numbers of workers originally from the western regions returned home from the eastern regions from the mid 2000s. Although some labor-intensive enterprises in inland regions absorbed some of the labor force driven out of the coastal regions, there is still a large proportion unemployed either voluntarily or involuntarily. The rise in the unemployment rate not only hinders the improvement in the living standards of the Chinese population, but also results in huge socioeconomic losses and poses a potential threat to social and economic stability. WDS currently primarily focuses on improving the infrastructure in the western regions, and creating more GDP in these regions. It does not attach enough importance to creating more job positions appropriate for workers with different educational backgrounds and different skill levels.

Since the 1990s, the vast majority of the health care and education resources have been concentrated in the eastern regions. This relative under-development in the western regions' health and education systems further enlarges the disparities between China's east and west. Without significant improvements in the overall public sectors, especially health care and education systems, it will be very difficult for the western regions to attract and retain the necessary labor force, especially highly educated or highly skilled workers. This is a major obstacle for increased economic development in the western regions.

5.3 Policy Suggestions

At present, President Xi Jinping and Premier Li Keqiang insist that WDS is still an important part of the national development strategy. The design and implementation of an appropriate WDS is still very important for Chinese society. Obviously, both the central government and the local governments in western regions have their own interests to consider. The central government gives more weight to the overall national development strategy, in terms of energy, ecology and social stability. The local governments in western regions want more policy support and transfers from both the central government and the eastern regions. Hence, the central government and local governments need to find the right balance through negotiation and compromise.

The WDS should be further refined and standardized with more monitoring and a better evaluation system for the specific policies. This improvement would help ensure that the policy will be well designed and properly implemented, and that any resulting problems could be quickly detected. Timely detection of problems would enable policy makers to revisit the policy and make adjustments quickly as necessary. Moreover, the policy makers should pay close attention to those regions threatened by ethnic conflict, such as Southern Xinjiang and the Kham region in Tibet. These regions require more caution in making and implementing RSP. Policymakers must consider not only the economic impact, but also the impact on the politics and religious beliefs of the native minority group.

Central-local relations is a vital issue and has been one of the core issues for the CPC regime since Mao's era. Actually, the central-local relations issue can be traced back to the time of China's first empire, the Qin Dynasty. However, governments have had very limited success with addressing it. In the absence of an institutionalized federal system and genuine local autonomy, the central government has always swung back and forth between decentralization and centralization. Without strong institutions and effective contracts between the central government and local governments, it is probably not possible to change this recurring pattern. Thus, WDS could be reduced to a tool of the central government to use to strengthen its control over the western regions, or to appease the discontent of the local government and ethnic groups.

Finally, WDS has had a relatively limited impact upon the public service sectors, like education and health care. The government officials have not focused enough on investment and financial support for the public sectors. The government officials' evaluation system may be the primary reason. The development of public service sectors is barely considered in the evaluation and promotion of government officials. As a result, they may be responding to an incentive to promote short run GDP growth at the expense of society and the environment, showing little regard for education, health care and the well-being of the population. This problem exists in every part of China, including the western regions. Therefore, in order to make WDS more responsive and adaptive to different social and economic conditions, the Chinese government needs to introduce a new evaluation system that holds government officials accountable for long-term economic and social development, particularly for improvements in the education, health and well-being of the local population.

6 Conclusions

In this paper, we discuss regional policy changes with a focus on China's Western Development Strategy (WDS), from the perspective of evolutionary economics. Some of the key concepts of evolutionary economics may help explain the factors and logic underlying the evolution of China's regional policy.

First, the institutional changes and the regional policy adjustment almost occur simultaneously in China, indicating that the Chinese political and economic system deeply affects its regional policy for Western China. It is worth noting that political events and movements play a decisive role in RSP for Western China, breaking up the path dependent trajectories of economic development in western regions. Our examples include the Great-leap-forward, the Sino-Soviet Confrontation, the Cultural Revolution and the Reform and Opening-up strategy.

Second, given the highly centralized regime in China, in which supreme power is held by the central government. The central government and CPC leaders design the blueprints for national economic development and decide which regions are entitled to RSP in different periods, based on their assessment of: (a) the political, economic and social situations, (b) the evaluation of the previous RSP, and (c) various objectives that may be achieved with the implementation of new RSP. The evolution of RSP is a process of trial-and-error, learning and adapting to changes in the political, economic and social situations.

Third, RSP can play a decisive role in the development of the regional economy and national economy. When these policy measures were based on excessive political and military objectives, instead of economic conditions and considerations, these measures would be rather inefficient in promoting regional economic development, while their negative impact could be destructive and long-lasting. On the contrary, RSP based on regional economic and geographic conditions and advantages, tend to have a stronger and longer positive impact on the development of regional economy. For example, the central government granted the Kashi area privileging RSP equivalent to policy privileges given to Shenzhen in Guangdong province, after a 2009 incident in Xinjiang Autonomous Region, known as the "the 'July-5th Incident". This policy was implemented in order to address the discontent of the native Uyghur people and to quickly stabilize the local political and social situation. Nevertheless, without the necessary economic, geographic and social conditions in this area, it is unlikely that this regional support will achieve its objectives, or successfully change the economic and social development trajectory.

Fourth, the local governments play a critical role in determining RSP. In order to obtain desirable RSP, the local governments mobilize various resources and resort to all available channels to influence the central government. Zhou (2007) discussed a model of competition between government officials in China, called the "Promotion Tournament Model", in which local government officials learn and compete with each other[6] and simulate successful development paths. For example, observing the success of the economic and social development in the special economic zones, a number of other cities asked the central government for policy support for their own "special economic zones". In Western China, immediately after the introduction of the "Liangjiang New Area" project in Chongqing in 2009, Sichuan government officials urgently requested policy support for the 'Tianfu New Area' project in Sichuan. The interaction between the central government and the local governments, and competition and cooperative learning among local governments have played an important role in the evolution of RSP since the early 1980s.

Last, the trend toward convergence is a result of the combined impact of various market factors, geographic factors, and policy factors. Therefore, we should be cautious in the selection of RSP and be aware of the importance of timing. We also need to better evaluate RSP and its impact, especially when the impact is negative.

[6]The local government officials compete with each other in various aspects, including taxation, land use and fee reduction etc.

Acknowledgements The authors would like to thank the anonymous referees for their constructive and helpful comments on an earlier draft of this paper. We are obliged to Prof. William Platz, Prof. Lei Zhang and Mr. James Massy for helping improve the language in this paper. The authors are grateful for the financial support from the National Natural Science Foundation of China, No. 70773078 and No. 71173149 for Xiang Deng, and the Scientific Research Foundation of Sichuan University, No. YJ201342 for Zheng Lu and No. YJ201353 for Xuezheng Chen.

References

Acemoglu D, Robinson JA (2009) Economic origins of dictatorship and democracy. Cambridge University Press, New York

Bai CE, Du YJ, Tao ZG, Tong SY (2004) Local protectionism and regional specialization: evidence from China's industries. J Int Econ 63(2):397–417

Barro RJ, Sala-i-Martin X (1991) Convergence across states and regions. Brook Pap Econ Act 1:107–182

Becker J, Ghosts H (1998) China's secret famine. Henry Holt, New York

Boschma RA, Lambooy JG (1999) Evolutionary economics and economic geography. J Evol Econ 9:411–429

Boschma R, Martin R (2010) Handbook of evolutionary economic geography. Edward Elgar, Cheltenham

Cai H, Treisman D (2006) Did government decentralization cause China's economic miracle? Word Politics 58(4):505–535

Chen S (2010) Regional airports construction is speeding up. China Business News, p A14. 7 July 2010

Démurger S (2001) Infrastructure development and economic growth: an explanation for regional disparities in China. J Comp Econ 29:95–117

Deng X (2002) Decomposition of China's regional disparity and its implications, J Sichuan U (Soc Sci Edi) 02: 31–36

Dikotter F (2010) Mao's great famine: the history of China's most devastating catastrophe, 1958–62. Bloomsbury Publishing Plc, London

Fan CC, Sun M (2008) Regional inequality in China, 1978–2006. Eurasian Geogr Econ 49:1–20

Fan S, Kanbur R, Zhang X (2010) China's regional disparities: experience and policy. Department of Applied Economics and Management Working Paper 2010–03, Cornell University.

Fujita M, Krugman P, Venables AJ (1999) The spatial economy: cities, regions and international trade. MIT Press, Cambridge

Gao C (1989) The theory and practice of China regional economic development. Liaoning Economic Plan Research No. 2

Gao X, Tong C (2008) Gradual evolution of China's regional policies over the past three decades. Tribune Study 24(12):41–45

Gao PY, Sun GF, Zhang DK (eds) (2009) China tax reform during the past 30 years: retrospect and prospect. China Financial and Economic Publishing House, Beijing

Golley J (2007) China's Western development strategy and nature versus nurture. J Chin Econ Bus Stud 5:115–129

Graham EM, Wada E (2001) Foreign direct investment in China: effects on growth and economic performance. In: Drysdale P (ed) Achieving high growth: experience of transition economies in east Asia. Oxford University Press, Sydney

Guo T, Lu D, Gan G (2002) China's regional development policy and its sound effects on the economic development of coastal Zones and Central & Western areas over the past two decades. Geogr Res 21(4):504–509

Hanusch H, Pyka A (2007) Manifesto for comprehensive neo-schumpeterian economics. Hist Econ Idea 15(1):23–41

He CF, Liu ZL, Wang L (2008) Economic transition and convergence of regional industrial structure in China. Acta Geogr Sin 63(8):807–819
Heberer T, Schubert G (2006) Political reform and regime legitimacy in contemporary China. ASIEN 99:9–28
Holbig H, Gilley B (2010) Reclaiming legitimacy in China. Polit Policy 38(3):395–422
Jefferson GH, Hu GZ, Su J (2006) The sources and sustainability of China's economic growth. Brookings Pap Econ Act 2006(2):1–47
Jin HH, Qian YY, Weingast B (2005) Regional decentralization and fiscal incentives: federalism, Chinese style. J Public Econ 89:1719–1742
Khadiagala GM (1982) Chinese foreign policy in the 1970s: a decade of change. Open Access Dissertations and Theses, Paper, 5187
Lewis JW, Xue L (2003) Social change and political reform in China: meeting the challenges of success. China Q 176:926–942
Liu Y (2011) Development of the western regions and the Great-leap-forward development of Xinjiang. Social Science Academic Press, Beijing
Lu D, Xue F (1997) 1997 China's regional development report. The Commerce Press, Beijing
Montinola G, Qian Y, Weingast BR (1996) Federalism, Chinese style: the political basis for economic success. World Polit 48(1):50–81
NAO (National Audit Office) (2006) Auditing report 2006 No. 3. National Audit Office of P.R. China, Beijing. 26 May 2006
Naughton B (1988) The third front: defense industrialization in the Chinese interior. China Q 115:351–386
SIC (China State Information Center) (2005) Extraordinary five years: the Five-years progress of Western Development Strategy. Special Report of Five-years Western Development. http://www.chinawest.gov.cn/
Sun D, Zhang J, Zhu C, Hu Y, Zhou L (2012) An assessment of China's ecological environment quality change and its spatial variation. Acta Geogr Sin 67(12):1599–1610
Tiebout C (1956) A pure theory of local expenditures. J Polit Econ 64(5):416–424
Whalley J, Xin X (2010) China's FDI and non-FDI economies and the sustainability of future high Chinese growth. China Econ Rev 21:123–135
Xiao CM, Sun JW, Ye ZY (2010) The evolution of China's regional economic development strategy. Study Pract 22(7):5–11
Ye X (2006) China increases western development investment. People's Daily Overseas Edition, p 4. 6 Sept 2006
Zhou LA (2007) Governing China's local officials: an analysis of promotion tournament model. Econ Res J 53(7):36–50

Part II
The Evolution of Innovation Systems

Evolution: Complexity, Uncertainty and Innovation

Peter M. Allen

Abstract Complexity science provides a general mathematical basis for evolutionary thinking. It makes us face the inherent, irreducible nature of uncertainty and the limits to knowledge and prediction. Complex, evolutionary systems work on the basis of on-going, continuous internal processes of exploration, experimentation and innovation at their underlying levels. This is acted upon by the level above, leading to a selection process on the lower levels and a probing of the stability of the level above. This could either be an organizational level above, or the potential market place. Models aimed at predicting system behaviour therefore consist of assumptions of constraints on the micro-level – and because of inertia or conformity may be approximately true for some unspecified time. However, systems without strong mechanisms of repression and conformity will evolve, innovate and change, creating new emergent structures, capabilities and characteristics. Systems with no individual freedom at their lower levels will have predictable behaviour in the short term – but will not survive in the long term. Creative, innovative, evolving systems, on the other hand, will more probably survive over longer times, but will not have predictable characteristics or behaviour. These minimal mechanisms are all that are required to explain (though not predict) the co-evolutionary processes occurring in markets, organizations, and indeed in emergent, evolutionary communities of practice. Some examples will be presented briefly.

1 Introduction

This paper will attempt to show how the ideas of complexity, evolutionary processes, uncertainty and innovations are all inextricably bound up together. If a system can be reduced to a set of fixed mechanical interactions, providing a predictable, stable and non-innovative future, then it is not complex, not evolutionary and not uncertain. It is also not interesting, and in addition not what we encounter and must deal with in real

---

P.M. Allen (✉)
Complex Systems Management Centre, School of Management, Cranfield University, Beds, MK43 0AL, England, UK
e-mail: p.m.allen@cranfield.ac.uk

A. Pyka, J. Foster (eds.), *The Evolution of Economic and Innovation Systems*,
Economic Complexity and Evolution, DOI 10.1007/978-3-319-13299-0_7
Reprinted from Journal of Evolutionary Economics, 24(2), Springer 2014.

life. Ecologies, families, groups, neighbourhoods, firms, organizations, institutions, markets and technologies are all complex in themselves and also sit within and among other complex systems. Instead of 'equilibrium' we find a multi-level, co-evolutionary mass of interconnected learning entities, within which pending and actual innovation is a permanent feature (Allen 1990).

As a physicist I was let loose believing that things could be modelled – and that the way to do this was to:

1. Establish the components of the situation under study
2. Try to take into account the interactions between these components.

The result would be a mechanical representation that would predict the behaviour of the system from any particular initial condition. Clearly, this kind of mechanical model is based on the renowned views of Newton, whose model of the planetary system revolutionised science and society. These ideas have permeated and driven science since then. The extraordinary success of technology then suggested that 'scientific ideas' could and should be used in biology, ecology and human systems, and that undoubtedly great things would be achieved. As a physicist, I also had been given a strong faith in the idea that: Components + Interactions = Predictive System.

Modelling, in my view, therefore appeared to provide the proper basis for decision making and policy support. Represent the situation as a system, calibrate it on reality, and then use it to predict the different possible impacts of particular interventions. This is probably the basic thought behind all scientific advice that is sought by decision and policy makers.

But people can think. They are *not* cogs in a machine, but people with differing roles and power, each of whom is attempting to decide what would be a good idea and how best to pursue it. And a social system is full of potential consumers and suppliers of products, services, policies and interventions. Each person is exploring and reflecting on their experiences and attempting to learn from them. This gives the system an underlying flexibility and inventiveness which means that a mechanical representation of average behaviours and types present at a given moment will inevitably fail over time. At any moment there will be average behaviours for particular sectors of activity, but over time competition and synergies within the system will lead to an evolution of the behaviours of the different players present. New technologies, new goals, new practices and new desires will grow in the system as some old ones disappear. Evolution will occur. Over time the differences between reality and any past, fixed, representation of behaviours will become large, and our actions erroneous. So, how do we construct an evolutionary model – a model capable of changing its own variables, interaction mechanisms and values of its underlying elements? In order to see this we need to study the assumptions that must be made in moving from 'evolutionary reality' to a 'mechanical model' of the behaviour of the current system.

2 Models: successive assumptions and uncertainties

What are the assumptions that we make in 'modelling' in order to 'understand' and predict the behaviour of the system under study? At a given moment we may identify the different types of element that are interacting, and make them 'the' variables of our model. The model dynamics changes the numbers of these different types as a result of their interactions between, for example, consumers, producers, products, services, prices and costs that are present initially. If the model is mechanical then the choice of variables, the interactions and parameters will remain fixed, while reality will evolve. Changing patterns of desirability, of cost and profit, and of production and sales will lead to the growth and decline of firms, changing patterns of consumption and to the failure of some firms and the growth of others. The real system will reflect the differential success or failure of innovations, firms and activities. So we need to take into account the fact that each population or economic sector is itself made up of diverse elements and that this micro-diversity changes over time as a result of the successes and failures that actually occur. This reflects both the detailed characteristics of the individuals or firms and also by the luck of events. If some characteristics make the individual or firm more vulnerable than others, for example, then these will be the first to go. Therefore, over time the numbers of vulnerable individuals decrease with respect to the fitter ones, thus changing the nature of the 'average' individual of that type. This means that within each type of variable identified in a model, the mechanisms of experimental micro-diversity within it will automatically provide exploratory, innovating capacity that will allow adaptation of existing types and also produce entirely new variables from successful, innovative types.

Clearly, in order to predict the exact behaviour of a complex system we might think we need to know; the different types of element present, the particular micro-diversity within of each of these, their precise locations and interaction characteristics and their internal moods and workings – an infinite depth of knowledge. But of course, not only is this not possible, but it would also fail to predict behaviour! This is because of 'emergence'. In reality, elements join together to form collective entities and things around us are characterized by structure and organization at various scales. Over time, the performance of the system' results not just from the elemental behaviours but also the structures of which they are part. The phenotype is not the genotype. Structures with various forms and symmetries possess emergent capabilities which accord differential successes over others. Micro-diversity includes these different collective entities and organizations and so innovations occur at different levels of structure, breaking previous symmetries with consequences that are completely unknowable! Life itself is the result of the emergent properties of folded macro-molecules such as proteins, and their emergent capacity to reproduce imperfectly.

Molecules, elements and systems can adopt new morphologies that break some previous symmetry leading to emergent features, capabilities, and functionalities at the level above. New variables (new types) can occur and occupy new dimensions of 'character space'. Any particular mathematical model or representation of a system, developed at a given moment, will be in terms of the existing current taxonomy and capabilities. But in reality, both the capabilities and the taxonomy will themselves be evolving and changing over time. This is why 'reality and the model' will diverge over time! As the wonderful example of origami demonstrates, not only can changes occur that modify the average interaction parameters between individuals, but also 'folding' – new forms, technologies, techniques and practices - can lead to entirely new emergent properties and dimensions of performance (Allen 1982). This means that the assumption of structural stability cannot be taken for granted.

And selection may depend on the emergent properties at the 'upper level' and not be able to select upon exploratory changes occurring at the lower level.

In the case of economic situations, interacting suppliers, distributors, retailers and potential consumers, will over time drive the evolution of products, their costs, qualities and capabilities. Human agents will be reflecting and experimenting with their various approaches, technologies and ideas in their different roles as producers, suppliers and consumers. Clearly, the strength and success of these innovative flows will depend on the 'regimes' operating in the organizations concerned. So, there are important local conditions that affect this. Firstly, there is the possibility of individuals being able to think new thoughts, and here the richness of the local cultural and technological environment will feed new ideas. Secondly, there has to be a freedom, and mechanisms, by which new ideas, techniques and technologies can be tried out and tested. These are underlying conditions of endogenous externalities that really will be important in allowing evolutionary change to occur. Again any model that has fixed products, costs, prices and consumer preferences will rapidly be overtaken by the changing reality created by the evolving firms. Clearly the simplistic ideas of 'homogeneous goods' and knowledge of pay-offs from different possible, as yet untried strategies, are quite ludicrous.

Schumpeter had the genius to see that markets were not mechanical systems of robotic producers and consumers giving rise to equilibrium markets of homogeneous goods with maximal profits for producers and maximum utility for consumers. He saw that what mattered was what came into the system and what went out. His phrase for this was "Creative Destruction", and this the same view as that coming out of complexity science. Both Darwin and Schumpeter saw and spoke a truth which has taken a long time for Science to come to terms with (Figs. 1, 2 and 3).

Today, we can examine carefully the successive assumptions that are made by people wishing to 'understand' and 'model' system behaviour, moving from totally undefined description through evolving structurally unstable systems, to deterministic mechanical representations to stationary states and attractors. In Fig. 4 as we move to the right from Reality (on the left) we come to successively simpler, more understandable and less detailed representations of that reality. And although Reality, on the left, may evolve qualitatively over time, adding new variables and structures, the models on the right of Fig. 4 cannot. They can only 'run' but not 'evolve'. So if we monitor 'reality' against our models, then we shall be forced to create successive modified dynamical systems – which we shall only be able to do

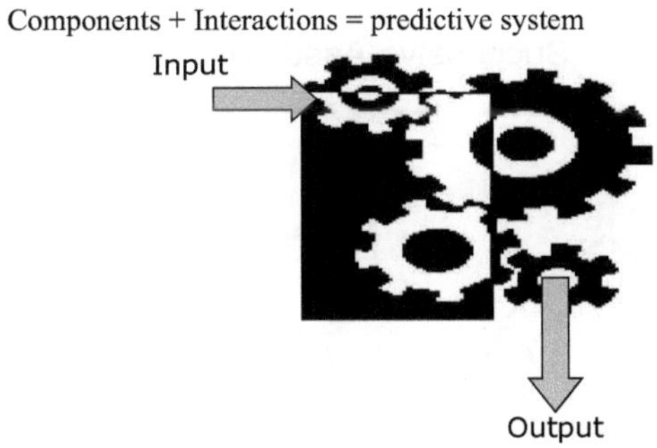

Fig. 1 A situation is represented by a series of connected components that can predict output from any input

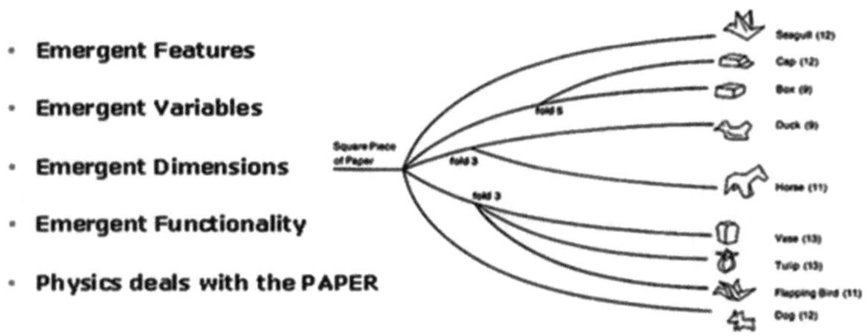

Fig. 2 Origami illustrates the reality of emergence as symmetry breaking leads to new 'dimensions' of performance, and variables and selection change qualitatively

post-hoc. In other words, in an evolving world, our representations will always be pictures of the past!

In science, understanding and prediction are achieved in practice by making successive assumptions concerning the situation under study. This means that we exchange uncertainty about the system for uncertainty about the truth of our assumptions. If no assumptions are made then we are in the realm of narrative, where we are limited in our ability to learn or generalise or predict. When we make lots of assumptions we have simple clear predictive models but are uncertain whether our assumptions are still true. Uncertainty is an irreducible fact.

2.1 Assumption 1 – the boundary

This is that the problem we are interested in has a boundary distinguishing what is inside the system and what is in the environment. In fact it may not be clear where exactly this lies and so we really proceed by choosing an 'experimental' boundary and seeing whether the model that results is useful. In fact this first assumption is

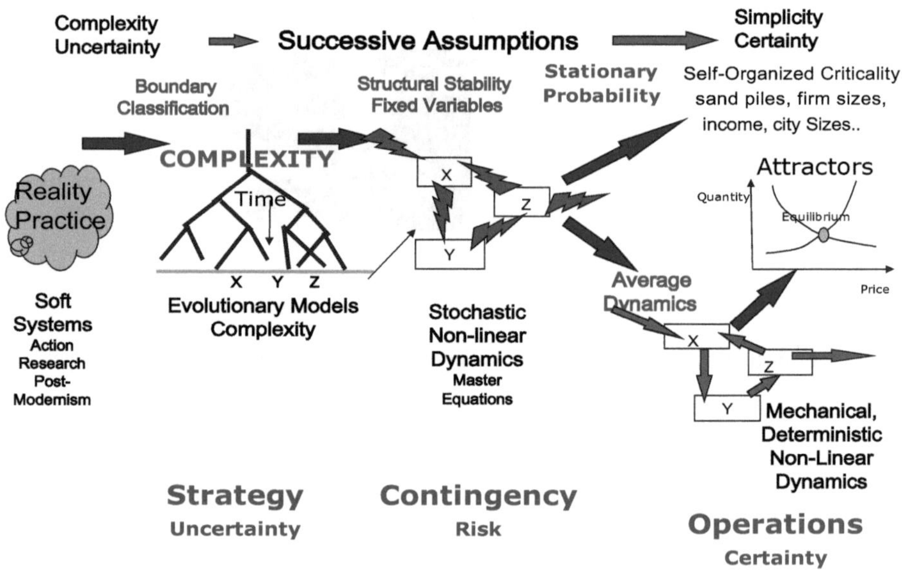

Fig. 3 This shows the successive assumptions required to arrive at different interpretive frameworks to understand and model system behaviour

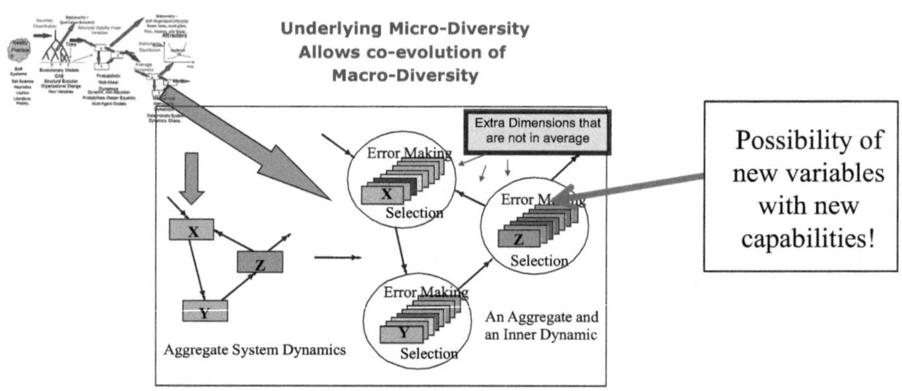

Fig. 4 Each population type can 'move' within the multi-dimensional 'character space' as a result of the differential success of its micro-variants. Each type can also discover new dimensions of emergent behaviour and hence new variables

actually tied up with the second, because the boundary can also be defined as being the decision to include or exclude a particular element or variable from the 'model' and leave it in the 'environment'. One important result that we find for complex systems is that they can possess emergent behaviours that connect them to new variables and entities that previously were not in the system. In this way, one of the important properties of a complex system is that it can itself change the boundary of the system. This means that the modeller must be sufficiently humble to admit that the initial choice of a boundary might need revision at some later time. The point is that 'modelling' is an experiment that seeks a representation that is useful.

2.2 *Assumption 2 – evolutionary complex models – qualitative change*

The second assumption concerns that of 'classification' in which we decide to label the different types of thing that populate our system. This might be firms or organizations, people classified according to their jobs, their skills or professional activities; so in this way we specify the variables of the system and we hope that the changing values of these variables will allow an answer to our questions about the system. We must face the fact that for example, market systems have changed qualitatively over time and that the taxonomy of the system will also change in the future. Different elements that were present have disappeared and new ones will appear in the future.

Social and economic systems such as markets have all evolved and changed over time as innovations, new technologies, new practices and markets have emerged. New types and activities emerge and others leave. Over time qualitative evolution occurs and the system is not structurally stable in that the variables - and therefore the equations describing the mechanisms and processes at work within it - can change. The key point here is whether or not the micro-diversity makes the system structurally unstable.

The point here is that instead of discussing 'a' mathematical model of a complex system, evolutionary change and structural instability lead us successively to a series of qualitatively different models. If a fixed set of dynamic equations might be thought to describe a particular system, then over time structural instabilities occur and a new set of equations will be required to describe the new system. So, these first two assumptions do not lead to any single mathematical model of the system, but instead to an open, diverging series of possible mathematical models that correspond to an evolving system with changing taxonomy. If we think of our assumptions as corresponding to 'constraints' on what the elements in the system can do, then we see that with only these two first assumptions the elements, and the organizations they are part of, are still free to change. Thinking again of the origami forms, the differential success of the elements may well result from their emergent 'upper level' forms and features, and 'selection' therefore can no longer act directly on the lower level details of the paper from which the different origami forms are made. But this in turn means that explorations, experiments and errors at the lower level of the paper are not directly visible to selective forces coming from outside and therefore cannot be stopped from happening. Only if a lower level change affects the emergent, upper level features will external selection operate and lead to the amplification or rejection of a particular change. The internal freedom and the endogenous externalities, lead to the emergence of new types of element, and to successive new systems. Structural stability is not guaranteed when that much freedom is present in the system.

This multi-level reality means that evolution cannot be stopped. This is because 'selection' cannot get at the internal levels directly, but only indirectly through the relative performance at the level above. So, providing there is diversity and freedom at the level of individuals, and people are not forced to keep silent or to conform to existing ideas, then new ideas will occur and some will be tried out. This may also be enhanced by the presence of rewards for successful new ideas and an ambience of encouragement for their conception. Since this will occur somewhere then any stable period of interacting forms will always eventually undergo an instability, after perhaps a long period of protected 'exploration' at the genotypic level below. We see that phenotypes carry the emergent properties of genotypes, and that selection only operates clearly on phenotypes. The phenotype 'shields' the genotype's internal details from immediate view and in this way ensures that experimentation and drift will definitely occur at the lower level. This is an absolutely vital point. Novelties, potential innovations and new ideas need to be nurtured and protected within an organization until they are ready to face the outside world.

We see that internal 'micro-diversity' will be increased constantly at the lower level by probabilistic events, the encounters between different types of individual and local freedom. But it will be decreased through the differential success of the diverse individuals. And this is the mechanism by which the overall 'average' moves in the multidimensional space of the phenotypes, responding to changing environment and also co-evolving with the other types. The 'dynamical system' is changing qualitatively as well as quantitatively, as new variables appear and others disappear. The system is structurally unstable in that its very constitution can and does change over time.

This is the reality of 'creative destruction' that Schumpeter discussed. Instead of arguing that markets are characterized by the optimized behaviour of producers and consumers, that has already led to equilibrium, what really mattered over time was the inflow of innovations (new types) and the disappearance of old ones. So Schumpeter divined correctly that classical and neo-classical market views were really pitched at the wrong time-scale, and looked at the wrong things. What he understood was that what really mattered was the evolutionary process in which innovations, new types of economic activities and technologies invaded the system usually replacing old ones.

2.3 Assumption 3 – probabilistic dynamics

But, if an economist or academic wishes to make money from his models then they must come up with a predictive model. In moving to the right of our fundamental diagram of Fig. 3 the next assumption therefore is that our system is structurally stable—the variables, taxonomy, types of individual or agent do not change.

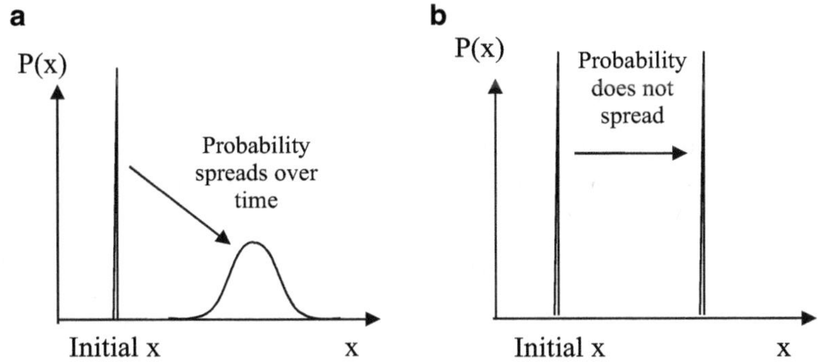

Fig. 5 (**a**) If all possible sequences of events can happen the probability spreads and uncertainty increases. (**b**) If only the most probable events can occur the 'clean' dynamic trajectory is deterministic

Our model will now describe the changes in numbers of a given set of types of individual or agent. It will be assumed that no new variables can emerge. The changing values of these variables result from the rates of production, sales, growth, declines and movements in and out of the system. But the underlying rates of the different microscopic, local events can only be represented by probabilities of such events occurring. These stochastic events lead to probabilistic equations—the Master or the Chapman-Kolmogorov equations. These govern the changing probability distribution of the different variables. They allow for the occurrence of *all possible sequences of events,* taking into account their relative probability, rather than simply assuming that only the most probable events occur (Fig. 5).

The collection of all possible dynamical paths is taken into account in a probabilistic way. But for any single system this allows into our scientific understanding the vital notion of 'freedom', 'luck' and 'uncertainty' in its behaviour. Although, a system that is initially not at the peak of probability will *more probably* move towards the peak, it can perfectly well move the other way; it just happens to be *less probable* that it will. A large burst of good or bad luck can therefore take any one system far from the most probable average, and it is precisely this constant movement that probes the stability of the most probable state. Such probabilistic systems can 'tip' spontaneously from one type of solution/attractor to another. It also points us towards the very important idea that the 'average' for a system should be calculated from the distribution of its *actual* possible behaviours—not that the distribution of its behaviour should be calculated by simply adding a Gaussian distribution around the average. The Gaussian is a distribution much loved of economists which expresses the spread of random shots around a target. In reality though, the actual distribution is given by the full probabilistic dynamics and can be calculated precisely. It will in general have a complicated mathematical form, and will be changing over time according to the probabilistic dynamics.

2.4 *Assumption 4: either a) or b)*

a) Assume the Probability is Stationary:

The assumption that the probability distribution has reached a stationary state leads to the idea of the non-linear dynamics leading to 'self-organized criticality' and to the power law structure that often characterizes them.

b) Probability remains sharply peaked: System Dynamics

Instead of a) we can look at the 'average' dynamics of the system and see where this leads. The full probabilistic dynamics is a rather daunting mathematical problem of the changing probability distributions over time. However, much of the uncertainty can be taken away as if by magic by changing slightly the question that is being asked of the model. The change is so slight that many people simple do not realize that the problem has been vastly simplified by the artifice of making this particular assumption.

Instead of asking 'what can actually happen to this system?' (requiring us to deal with all possible system trajectories according to their probability), we can ask 'what will most probably happen?' then we have a much simpler problem. We do this by assuming that only the most probable events occur; that things actually happen at their average rates. Most people do not realize the magnitude of the difference between these two questions, but it is the difference between a heavy set of probabilistic equations describing the spreading and mixing of possible system trajectories into the future, to a representation in which the system moves cleanly into the future along a single, narrow trajectory. This simple deterministic trajectory appears to provide the perfect ability to make predictions and do 'what if' experiments in support of decision or policy making. It appears to tell us exactly what will happen in the future with or without whatever action we are considering taking. These sorts of models are called 'system dynamics' and are immensely appealing to decision makers since they seem to provide predictions and certainty.

They appear to predict the future trajectory of the system and therefore seem attractive in calculating the expected outcomes of different possible actions or policies. They can show the effects of different interventions and allow 'cost/benefit' calculations. They can also show the factors to which the real situation is potentially very sensitive or insensitive, and this can provide useful information. But systems dynamics models are deterministic; they still only allow for one solution or path from a particular starting point.

Despite the limitations of such models, their 'predictions' allow comparisons with reality and can reveal when the model is failing. Without this, we might not know that the system had changed! And so this provides a basis for a learning experience where the each model is constantly monitored against reality to see when something has changed.

2.5 *Assumption 5 – solutions of the dynamical system*

The final assumption that one can make to simplify a problem even further is to consider not the System Dynamics itself as it changes over time, but the possible long term solutions of the dynamical equations—the 'attractors' of the dynamics. This means that instead of studying how the system will run, one looks simply at where it might 'run to'. Of course, non-linear interactions can lead to different possible 'attractors'—equilibrium points, permanent cycles, or chaotic attractors. This could be useful information – at least for some time.

But, of course, over longer times, the system will evolve and any set of equations will become untrue, and the possible attractors will also. In reality there is a trade-off between the utility and simplicity of predictions, and the strength of the assumptions that are required in order to make them. Of course, it is much easier to 'sell' a model that appears to make solid predictions. Because of this scientists often have had to underplay the real level of uncertainty and doubt about the possible consequences of interventions, actions, technologies and practices, allowing the seemingly solid business plans and policy consequences to be presented as persuasively as possible. In any case, usually people wish to hear clear statements that imply knowledge and certainty and find the actual uncertainty and risk much more disturbing. People will often prefer a lie that comforts to the uncomfortable truth.

In giving advice it is of critical importance to know how long the assumptions made in the calculations may hold. This is how long the actual complexity and uncertainty of 'reality' can be expected to remain hidden from view. Of course, believers in 'free markets' can get around this problem by simply stating that whatever occurs is by definition the best possible outcome. But if we wish to give advice to particular players within the system then we will need to develop models that can explore possible futures as well as possible.

This section has focused on the importance of micro-diversity in a system, which provides an automatic range of possible innovations and responses to threats. At any given time, of course, we would not be able to 'value' different types of micro-diversity, since we would not know which would in fact be important for some future problem. A theory based on the evolutionary emergence of micro-diversity, and the way that evolution itself adjusts its range (The Theory of Evolutionary Drive) was developed some time ago (Allen and McGlade 1987; Allen 1988) but has not been much commented upon, even by evolutionary economists. Instead of a complex system being successfully described by any fixed set of components and mechanisms we see that the system of components and mechanisms is not fixed, but is itself changing with the events that occur. As the system runs, so it is changed by its running.

3 Modelling human systems

Behaviours, practices, routines and technologies are invented, learned and transmitted over time between successive actors and firms, and we shall discuss how the principles of Evolutionary Drive can be used to understand them.

3.1 Emergent market structure

Since the "invisible hand" of Adam Smith, the idea of self-organization has been present in economic thought (e.g. Veblen (1898)). However, towards the end of the 19th century mainstream economics adopted ideas from equilibrium physics as the basis for understanding. This led us to neo-classical economics that was strong on very general and rigorous theorems concerning artificial systems, but rather weak on dealing with reality in practice. Today, with the arrival of computers able to "run" systems instead of us having to solve them analytically, interest is burgeoning in complex systems simulations and modelling. Complex systems thinking offers us an integrative paradigm, in which we retain the fact of multiple subjectivities, differing perceptions and views, and indeed see this as part of the complexity, as a source of creative interaction and of innovation and change. Building the model is in itself extremely informative—since it shows us mechanisms and ideas that were not apparent.

For example, in building the model we quickly find that a decision rule that expands production when there are profits and decreases it when there are losses will not allow firms to launch a new product, since every new product must start with an investment - a loss. However, in the real world, firms are created and new products and services are developed. Therefore the "equation" governing the increase or decrease of production volume cannot be based on the actual profits made instantaneously. This point is discussed in (Allen and Strathern 2004).

The next idea we could use in the model could be that an agent would use "expected" profits to adjust their production volume. So, firms moving into a new market area must be doing so because, they think that on balance their investment cost will be more than balanced by future profits. However, if we try to put this in our model we find that it is actually impossible for an agent to calculate expected profits for different pricing strategies because he does not know the strategies of other firms. Profits in each firm will depend on the products and prices of other firms and none of them know what the others will do.

Of course we could use the sort of neo-classical economics idea which would say that if firms are present then they must be operating with a strategy that maximises profits. And if no firms ever went bankrupt then we might have to accept such an idea—but in reality we know that many firms do go bankrupt and therefore cannot have been operating at an optimal strategy. An examination of the statistics concerning firm failures (Foster and Kaplan 2001; Ormerod 2005) shows us that whatever it is that entrepreneurs or firms believe, they are quite often completely wrong. The bankruptcies, failure rates and life expectancies of firms all attest to the fact that the beliefs of the founders, managers or investors are often not correct. In trying to build our model we are faced with the fact that firms cannot know what strategy will maximize profits. The market is not the theatre of perfect knowledge but instead is the theatre of possible learning.

By participating, players may find strategies, products, and mark-ups that work. Schumpeter (1962) was correct. The actual market is a temporary system of interacting firms that have entered the market and have not yet gone bankrupt. Some firms are growing and others shrinking. But with the entry into the market of new firms and products will come innovations and innovative organizations, and so over time the 'bar' will be raised by successive 'generations' of firms. Instead of supposing 'magical entrepreneurs and consumers' with perfect information and knowledge, our model shows us how real agents may behave with knowledge limited to what is realistically possible. They cannot calculate strategies and behaviours that fulfil (magically) the assumptions of (touchingly naïve) neo-classical economists. Our model shows us the many possible, market trajectories into the future. None of these correspond to a 'global' optimum (maximum profits and utility) and indeed there is no global agent to oversee the process. Each different trajectory is a possible future history of the system and will bring corresponding winners and losers, and particular patterns of strategies, imitations and routines.

The complex, evolutionary market model has been presented before (Allen et al. 2007a; Allen 2001).

Figure 6 shows us the model's structure. There can be any number of interacting firms, but in the examples we employ there will be up to 18 present at any given moment. The internal structure of each firm is represented in the illustration labelled "firm 1". Production has fixed and variable costs, that depend on the quality of the product. It also needs sales staff to sell the stock to potential customers. On the right of the figure, there are three different types of potential customer, and we have chosen here to distinguish between three groups differing in their price sensitivity. The point is that potential customers are sensitive to the price/quality of the different products on offer, and so will be attracted differentially to the different firms competing in the market place, thus creating the 'selection mechanism'. Profits from sales allow increased production and pay off any debts. In this way, our model provides an evolutionary theatre within which competing and complementary strategies are generated, tested and retained or rejected.

The firm tries to finance its growth and avoid going near its credit limit. If it exceeds its credit limit then it is declared bankrupt and closed down. The evolutionary model then replaces the failed firm with a new one, with new credit and a new strategy of price and quality. Again this firm either survives or fails. The model assumes that managers want to expand to capture their potential markets, but are forced to cut production if sales fall. So, they can make a loss for some time, providing that it is within their credit limit, but they much prefer to make a profit, and so attempt to increase sales, and match production to this.

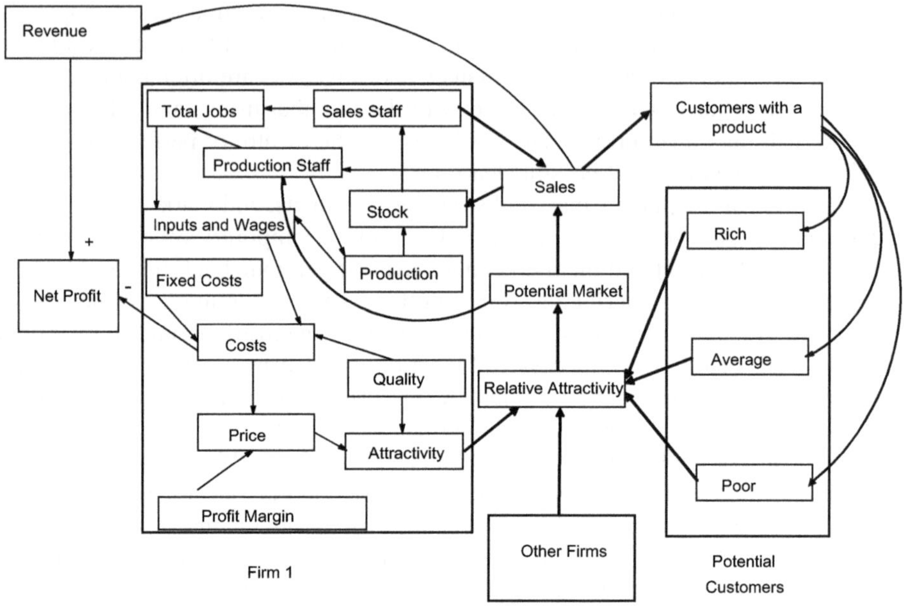

Fig. 6 An evolutionary market model

Our model is somewhat different from those of others (March 1991, 2006; Rivkin 2000; Rivkin and Siggelkow 2003, 2006, 2007; Siggelkow et al. 2005) and indeed from those inspired by Nelson and Winter (1982). In such models instead of modelling both the supply the demand sides as we have, the demand side performance of a product is inferred in an abstract way, and is generally given some randomness. Here, we model explicitly both supply and demand, though in a relatively simple manner, and the 'uncertainty' resides in the impossibility of the firm agents knowing beforehand what the real pay-off will be for a given price/quality strategy. Silverberg and Verspagen (1994), have also developed a model that is closer to ours.

3.2 Exploring the three meta-strategies

Running the model tells us that it is not the exact fixed strategy of a firm that matters. It is how successfully it can be changed if it isn't working! Learning what works for you is what matters, though the 'success' of any particular behaviour will always be temporary.

The question that we want to investigate is how firms change their strategies (quality, mark up, publicity, research etc.) over time and in the light of experience.

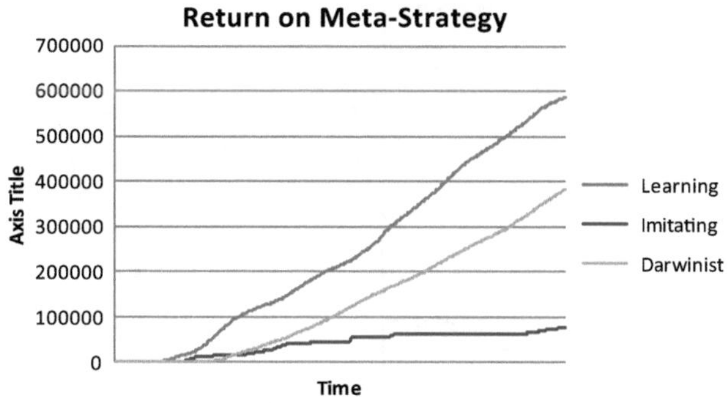

Fig. 7 For 10 different random series, the average performance of the learning, copying and intuition meta-strategies are clearly quite different

We now consider the results of running a model with 18 competing firms with three different ways (meta-strategies) to CHANGE what they are doing. They can be:

- **Learners** - test the profits that would arise from small changes in quality or price, and move their production in the direction of increasing profits.
- **Imitators** - move their product strategy towards that of whichever firm is currently making most profits.
- **Darwinists** - adopt a strategy 'intuitively' and then stick with it.

In the simulations here we study the interaction and outcomes of 6 learning firms, 6 imitating firms and 6 Darwinists. Any firm that goes bankrupt is replaced by another with the same meta-strategy but starting from a different initial position. We can then run our model repeatedly and see how well the three meta-strategies (Learning, Imitation, Darwinist) perform.

If we repeat the simulations for different random sequences (seeds 1 to 10) then we find the overall results of Fig. 7. This is the average outcome arising from ten simulations, but with different initial and re-launch choices. The message from Fig. 8 seems clear. Learning by experiment is the best meta-strategy. Using intuition and individual belief (Darwinist) is good, and imitating winners is the least successful meta-strategy. Imitators seem to arrive late to a strategy, and then suffer the competition of both the original user and that of other imitators. We can calculate the spread of results obtained by the different meta-strategies. There is some overlap of outcomes and so in a particular case we can probably never say with absolute certainty that the 'learning' strategy will 'definitely' be better than the others, only that it will 'most probably' be better than the others. If a manager owned the simulation model, then it would still not guarantee they definitely win, but only increase the probability of winning.

This result shows clearly the 'limits to knowledge' (Allen et al. 2007a), that future trajectories and strategies of other firms cannot be known, and therefore that there cannot be a corresponding 'perfect' strategy. This puts a real limit on any predictive 'horizon' which may be until the next firm changes its strategy,

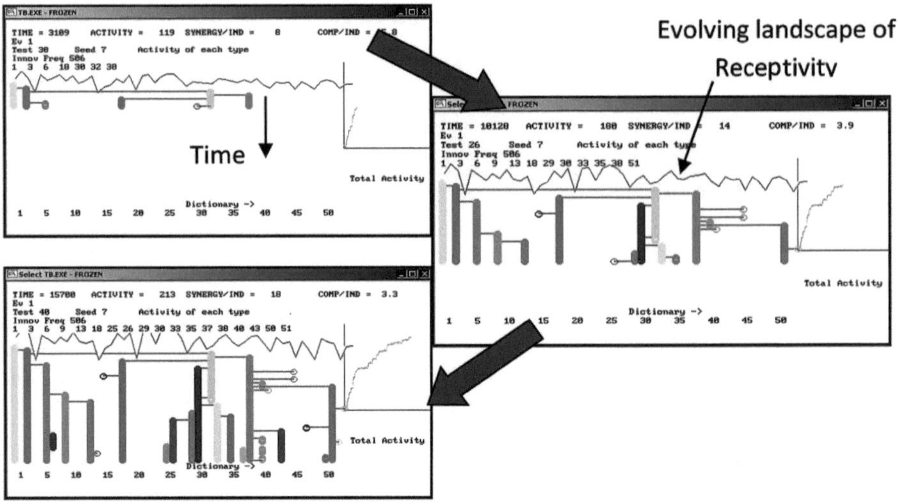

Fig. 8 Successive moments (t = 3000, 10000 and 15000) in the evolution of a particular firm. The evolutionary tree of the organisation emerges over time

or if it is pursuing a meta-strategy (of learning or imitating for example) how this will change over time. This example is limited to a discussion of innovations concerning the quality and price of a product or service, but the model can equally well look into more ambitious innovations of technology or research. Our model shows us that the basic process of "micro-variation" and differential amplification of the emergent behaviours is the most successful process in generating a successful market structure, and is good both for the individual players and for the whole market, as well as its customers (Metcalfe 1998).

3.3 Organizational evolution

In discussing how firms change their performances through product and process innovation, we can refer briefly to an example that has been published before (Allen et al. 2007a, b). Changing patterns of practices and routines are studied using the ideas of Evolutionary Drive. For a particular industrial/business sector we find a "cladistic diagram" (a diagram showing evolutionary history) showing the succession of new practices and innovative ideas within a particular economic activity. This idea looks at organizational change in terms of the emergence of particular 'bundles' of practices and techniques with performances that allow survival in the market. The ideas come from McKelvey (1982, 1994), McCarthy (1995), McCarthy et al. (1997).

For the automobile sector the observed bundle of possible 'practices', our "dictionary", allows us to identify 16 distinct organisational forms – 16 bundles of practice that actually exist:

- Ancient craft system; Standardised craft system; Modern craft system
- Neocraft system; Flexible manufacturing; Toyota production
- Lean producers; Agile producers; Just in time
- Intensive mass producers; European mass producers;
- Modern mass producers; Pseudo lean producers; Fordist mass producers
- Large scale producers; Skilled large scale producers

Cladistic theory calculates backwards the most probable evolutionary sequence of events. The key idea in the work presented here is to use a survey of manufacturers that explores their estimates of the ***pair-wise interactions*** between the practices. In this way we can 'predict' the synergetic 'bundles' of working practices and understand and make retrospective sense of the evolution of the automobile industry.

The evolutionary simulation model examines how the random introduction of new practices and innovations is affected by the changing 'receptivity' reflecting the overall effects of the positive or negative pairwise interactions. As a result of the particular sequence of attempted additions particular bundles of practices and techniques emerge that correspond to different organizational forms.

The model can generate the history of a particular 'firm' which launches new practises randomly, and grows where there is synergy between the practices. Figure 8 shows us one possible history of a firm. The particular choices of practices introduced and their timing allows us to assess how their performance evolved over time, and also assess whether they would have been eliminated by other firms.

Overall performance of each firm is a function of the synergy of the practices that are tried successfully in the context of the other evolving firms. The particular emergent attributes and capabilities of the organisation result from the particular combination of practices that constitute it. Different simulations lead to different organizational structures. The actual emergent capabilities and qualities that would be desirable for any particular firm cannot be predicted in advance, since the performance of any particular organization will depend on that of the others with which it is co-evolving. So, we cannot pre-define a desired structure through some pre-calculated rationality. Firms, markets and life are about an on-going, imperfect learning process that both creates and requires uncertainty.

3.4 Emergent supply chain performance

These ideas were applied to the study of the aerospace supply chain (Rose-Anderssen et al. 2008a, b). The aerospace supply chain actually needs a series of different capabilities if it is to succeed. They are:

1. Quality
2. Cost Efficiency

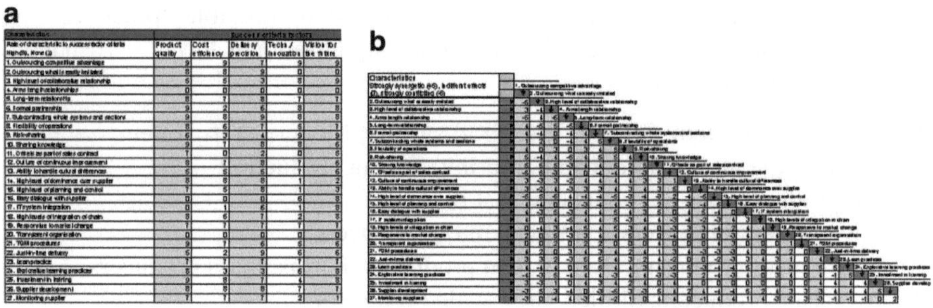

Fig. 9 (**a**) Scores for the 27 practices for 5 qualities (**b**) The pair interactions

3. Reliable Delivery
4. Innovation and Technology
5. Vision.

The stage in the life cycle of the product, or the market situation, determines what mix of these is required as the platform or product moves from design and conception, through initial prototyping and production to an eventual lean production phase. In addition 27 key characteristics or practices were identified that could characterize supply chain relationships. A questionnaire was formulated to enquire into the opinion of important individuals within these key aerospace supply chains in order to understand better the underlying beliefs that affect the decisions concerning the structure of supply chains. The questionnaire considered the intrinsic improvement of a given practice and the possible interaction between pairs of practices. The details have been given elsewhere but we can summarize in Fig. 9.

The important point about the evolution of systems is that they concern both the elements inside a system, that constitute its identity, and also the external environment in which they are attempting to perform and the requirements that are perceived for successful performance.

Our model then explores the random launching of practices under different performance selection criteria corresponding to our five basic performance qualities. The practices retained are on the whole synergetic. We can look at the patterns of synergy that have been selected, Fig. 10.

Knowledge of the effects of interaction can therefore be of considerable advantage in creating a successful supply chain. Even if the pair interaction terms are considered to be 50 times smaller than the direct effects of a practice there are still synergy effects of up to 75 %. This shows the importance of considering the systemic, collective effects of any organization or supply chain. It is another example of the 'ontology of connection' and not that of 'isolation'.

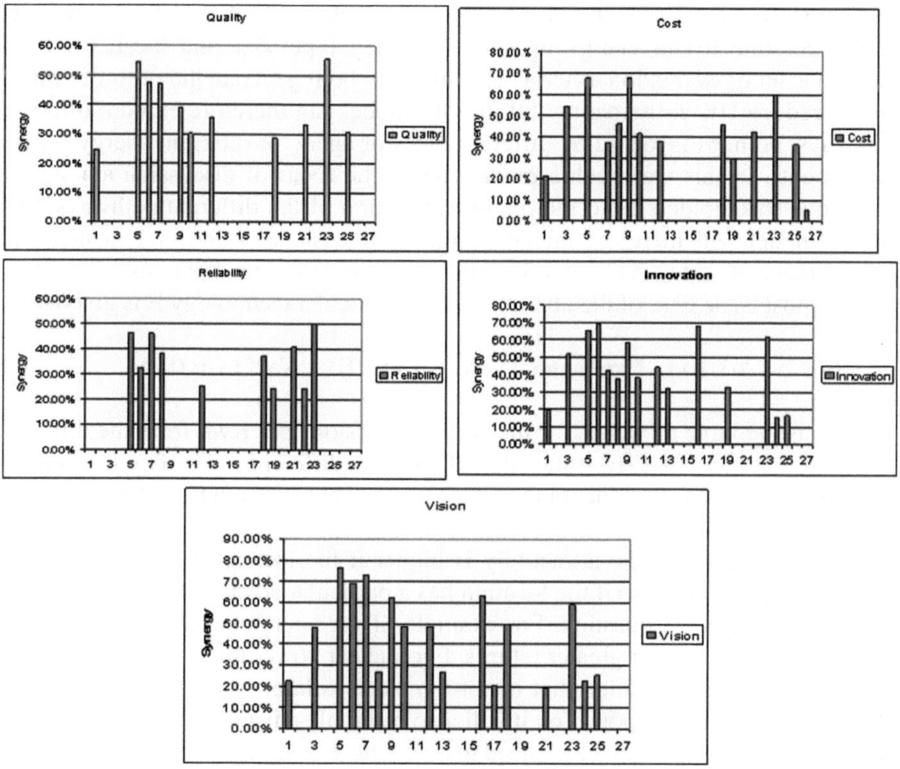

Fig. 10 The increased performance for the five dimensions showing where the strong synergies are

3.5 *Simple self-organizing model of UK electricity supply and demand*

Another important area of application concerns the future of the UK electricity supply. The model is based on an earlier 'self-organizing' logistics model (Allen and Strathern 2004) in which the structure of distribution systems emerged from a dynamic, spatial model.

We shall briefly summarize the main points. One of the main ideas adopted in order to reduce our carbon emissions is to 'electrify' transport and heating as well as all the current uses. This means that, unless we accept a radical change in lifestyle (e.g. almost no travel, or heating!), over the next 40 years electricity supply must approximately triple! And at the same time we must decrease our carbon emissions by 80 % of their 1990 value. This means that in large part we will have to add new, carbon light capacity across the country. The problem we are examining here therefore is that of 'when to put what, where' in the intervening years between now and 2050.

The model therefore first makes an annual calculation of the relative attractivity of the possible list of energy investments—their type, size and location—for a particular set of evaluation criteria. The aim is to both generate the power required and to reduce UK emissions by 80 %. Our model can therefore explore different pathways, perhaps favoured by different types of agent, of different energy supply investments. In this way such a model can be the focus of discussion among the numerous stakeholders as to the relative attraction of the different pathways. Our choice model will therefore include a multi-dimensional value system that will reflect financial costs, CO2 reduction and other possible considerations.

The most basic core of the attractivity of a particular technology E is given by:

$$A(i, E) = \text{Exponential}\{-\text{Va1}^*\text{CO2}\,(E) - \text{Va2}^*\text{LCE}\,(E)\} \quad (1)$$

CO2(E) is the table of values for the carbon emissions per Kwh from the different energy sources and LCE(E) is the table of costs for different types of generation per Kwh. Va1 and Va2 reflect the relative importance that we attach to carbon reduction and to financial cost.

In addition though, the attractivity is higher if the location i has a high stress (demand/supply) and also if the location has a particular advantage or disadvantage for the technology in question. For example, if the source is wind power, then a windy location offers far greater returns. For nuclear power there will be a need for cooling water and a location that is not too close to large populations and that as already has had nuclear power on it will also be highly advantageous. Similarly, for coastal power, (tidal or wave) we need to be on the coast but also some stakeholders may view the ecological impact of a tidal barrage (such as the Severn Barrage for example) to outweigh the value of the electricity generated. We can also allow for the 'saturation' of a zone as a function of capacity that is already installed. So, there is a limit to how many wind farms one can put in a zone, and waste and biomass incineration require populations or land to provide the raw materials. Each location also has its own 'predispositions' that affect its attractivity. The environmental impacts of the energy production can be the corresponding carbon emissions (kgs of CO2 per kWh of electricity) but could also represent radiation risks, noise, or impact on wild life.

Generally speaking however, the most common factor taken into account by actual decision makers will be financial costs. At the micro-level, however, local decisions concerning solar, wind and CHP schemes would continue reducing to some extent the supply stresses present.

In this preliminary version of the model, the geographical space for the simulations was 100 points representing the UK. The model starts from the actual situation in 2010 and then looks at the annual changes brought about by: end of service closures, closures of coal capacity, new capacity either gas, nuclear, Wind (on or Off shore), marine, biomass and solar, the continual growth of demand

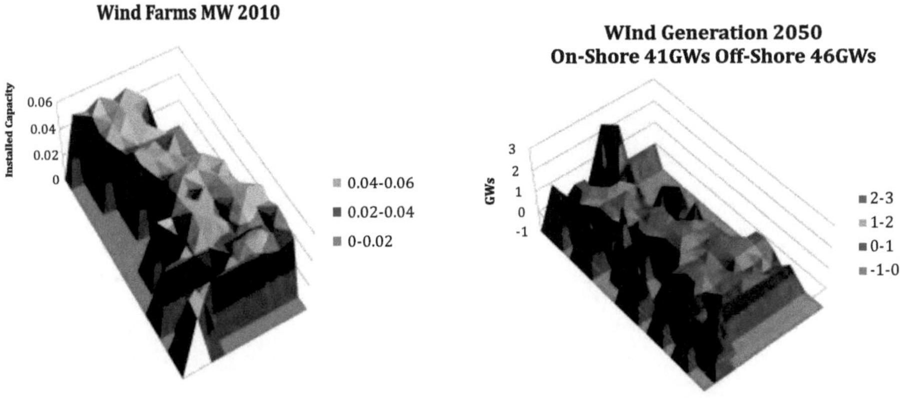

Fig. 11 Growth of wind generation from 7.5 GWs in 2010 to 87 Gws by 2050

and of local schemes for solar, wind and CHP. Each year the model makes the changes/investments suggested by the relative attractivity, in a particular type of generation technology, at a given place. It then recalculates the pattern of supply and demand. However it also calculates the CO2 emissions and if the supply is deviating too much from the trajectory towards an 80 % reduction by 2050, then the attraction of low carbon generation increases compared to higher emission technologies. In this way the system is guided towards achieving the policy aims. The costs involved take into account the transmission losses in corresponding to the spatial pattern of generation and of demand. Our model can therefore help to create how a more ‘compact’ pattern of generation.

To cut emissions by 80 % while increasing electricity production three-fold means that we must add a great deal of low carbon generation capacity (Wind, Hydro, Nuclear). Running the model generates the changing spatial distribution of generating capacity of different kinds. In Fig. 11 we show a result for wind generation under one particular scenario.

In this run the model shows us that off-shore rises steadily to 46 GWs and on-shore spreads widely across the landscape rising to 41 GWs by 2050. So much wind power raises the problem of intermittency and of the need for standby capacity or storage to ensure continuity of supply. Clearly, the larger the geographical spread of wind generation the lower the coherence of intermittency.

The model can be used to explore different possible ways of achieving the required 2050 situation Fig. 12 and can also be used to rapidly explore the effects of new technologies or changing costs of different types of generation. Simple models of complex systems can be useful for rapid, strategic explorations.

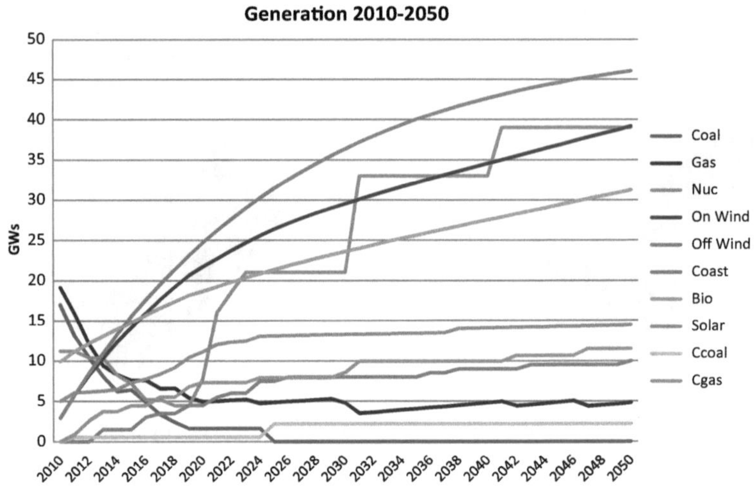

Fig. 12 One model outcome for different types of generation 2010–2050

4 Conclusions: living and learning

In trying to deal with the world we develop an 'interpretive framework' with which we attempt to navigate reality and to understand opportunities and dangers. This is really a set of beliefs about the entities that make up reality and the connections that exist between them. We see that this is really a qualitative 'model' and perhaps, sometimes, this can even be transformed into a quantitative mathematical model. But over time, our interpretive frameworks are constantly tested by our observations and experiences. Our beliefs provide us with expectations concerning the probable consequences of events or of our actions and when these are confirmed then we tend to reinforce our beliefs. When our expectations are denied however, we must face the fact that our current interpretive framework – set of beliefs – is inadequate. But there is no scientific method to tell us how to modify our views. Why is it not working? Are there new types or behaviours present? Or are their interconnections incorrect? Importantly however, there is no scientific, unique way to change our beliefs. In reality, we simply have to experiment with modified views and try to see whether the new system seems to work 'better' than the old.

In addition, when our expectations are thwarted, we can only draw on our beliefs and experiences to decide 'how to change our ideas'. This may suggest to us which of our beliefs are most likely mistaken, whose ideas or comments we should trust and listen to, and who's we should discard. Of course, some people may be happy to take on new ideas every day, while others may choose never to modify their beliefs, feeling that the increasing evidence of inadequacy is merely a test of their faith. Figure 13 was originally drawn so as to represent 'the honest scientist' seeking the truth. But it was pointed out to me that in reality people are much more complex than that. Although some people may learn, others will simply find

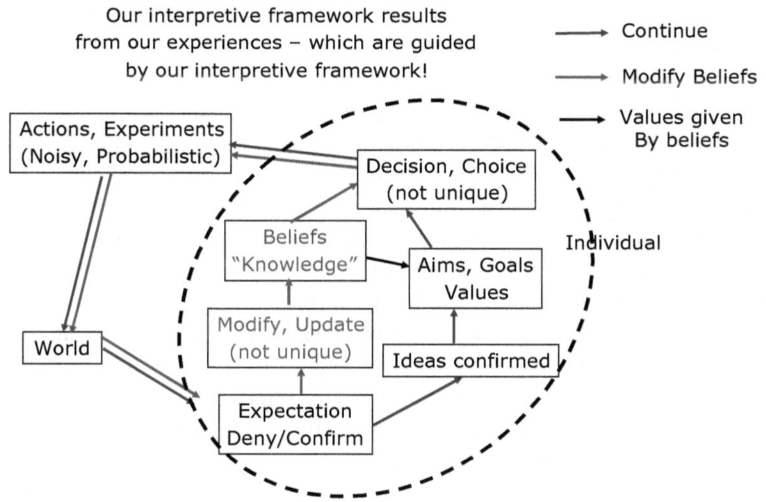

Fig. 13 Experiences confirm or deny the expectations we have that are based on our interpretive framework

reasons to ignore or reject any evidence that is contrary to their current beliefs or may detract from their own status or prestige. So micro-diversity encompasses not only the different interpretive frameworks people may have, but also how willing and equipped people are to change their beliefs and understanding and to adapt to what is happening. Complexity therefore suggests a 'messy cognitive evolution' in which some people change their beliefs and models, generating different behaviours and responses, which lead to differential success. This allows some beliefs and interpretive frameworks to evolve with the real world, as they are tested and either retained or dropped according to their apparent success. It is therefore clearly very important for an organization that wants to 'learn', to have employees that are willing to participate honestly in the learning process. This implies firstly that individuals are diverse and that the local organizational ambiance encourages open exchanges and discussions. It probably requires continual disagreement and rivalry among staff, but within a recognition of the overall good of the organization. This all points to the idea that we should really be looking at actions and events as "experiments" that test our understanding of how things work. Clearly, given the lack of any clear scientific method on how to change one's own beliefs, many may simply adopt the views of their preferred group, and simply mimic their responses without, necessarily, understanding the basis of these. This may explain the importance of 'social networks', and the 'wisdom' or 'idiocy' of crowds.

From these discussions we can derive some key points about evolution in human systems.

- Evolution is driven by the noise/local freedom and micro-diversity to which it leads—meaning that not only are current average 'types' explained and shaped by past evolution but so also are the micro-diversity and exploratory mechanisms around these.

- There is a selective advantage to the power of adaptation and hence to the retention of noise and micro-diversity generating mechanisms.
- This means that aggregate descriptions will always only be short term descriptions of reality, though useful perhaps for operational improvements
- Successful management must 'mimic' evolution and make sure that mechanisms of exploration and experiment are present in the organization. These are endogenous externalities. Though they are not profitable in the short term they are the only guarantee of survival into the longer term
- History will be marked by successive models of complex, synergetic dynamical systems: for products it is bundled technologies; for markets it is certain bundles of co-evolving firms; for organizations it is bundles of co-evolving practices and techniques; for knowledge more generally it is bundles of connected words, concepts and variables that emerge for a time.
- Living systems create a world of connected, co-evolving, multi-level structures, at times temporally self-consistent and at other times inconsistent.

The world viewed through 'complexity' spectacles is unendingly creative and surprising. Some surprises are serendipitous, others are unpleasant. We need to explore possible futures permanently in order to see when problems may occur or when something unexpected is happening. And we need to do so openly, allowing our assumptions, mechanisms and models to be studied, criticized and improved, so that we can react quickly. So, we are part of the system that we study, and the world, and its complexity will continue evolving with us as part of itself. We cannot be objective and there will be multiple truths. Even the past, where we might imagine certainty might exist, can be interpreted in a multiplicity of ways.

This new understanding of the world might appear to say that the complexity of the world is such that we cannot find a firm base for any actions or policies, and so we should perhaps just pursue our own self-interest and let the world look after itself. In many ways this would resemble behaviour resulting from belief on the 'invisible hand' of neo-classical economics. But this would be a false interpretation of what we now know of complexity. We know that we must operate in a multi-level, ethically and politically heterogeneous world where both wonderful and terrible things can happen. The models discussed here provide us with a better view than before of some possible futures, and allows us to get some idea of the likely consequences and responses to our actions and choices. We could even imagine 'Machiavellian' versions of complexity models that contained several layers of expected responses and countermoves on the part of the multiple agents interacting. Complexity tells us that our understanding of the system may be good for the short term, reasonable for the medium but will inevitably be inadequate for the long. It also tells us that sometimes there can be very sudden major changes—such as the 'financial crisis' of 2007/8. This means that policies should always consider resilience as well as efficiency or cost, as the one thing we do now know is that systems that are highly optimized for a single criteria such as profits or costs will crash at some point. Creative destruction data tells us that most firms fail quickly, some enjoy a period of growth, but all eventually crash (Foster and Kaplan 2001).

The other reason to develop and use complex systems models to reflect upon and formulate possible policies and interventions is that when a plan is chosen and put into action, the model can be used to compare with reality. Then unexpected deviations and new phenomena can be spotted as soon as possible and plans and models revised to explore a new range of possible futures.

In this complex systems' view then, history is still running, and our interpretive frameworks and understanding are partial, limited and will change over time. The most that can be said of the behaviour of any particular individual, group or organization in an ecology, a socio-cultural system or a market, is that its continued existence proves *only* that it is *not dead yet*—but *not* that it is optimal. Optimality is a fantasy that supposes the simplistic idea of a single 'measure' that would characterize adequately evolved and evolving situations. In reality there would always need to be 'sub-optimal' redundancies, seemingly pointless micro-diversity and freedom if long term survival is to occur. In reality there are multiple understandings, values, goals and behaviours that co-habit a complex system at any moment, and these change with the nature of the elements in interaction as well as with their changing interpretive frameworks of what is going on. There is no end to history, no equilibrium and no simple recipes for success. But, how could there be?

Acknowledgments Some of the work described in this paper was supported by the EPSRC Research Grant EP/G059969/1(Complex Adaptive Systems, Cognitive Agents and Distributed Energy (CASCADE))

References

Allen PM (1982) Evolution, modelling and design in a complex world. Environ Plan B 9:95–111
Allen PM (1988) Dynamic models of evolving systems. Syst Dyn Rev 4(1–2):109–130
Allen PM (1990) Why the future is not what it was. Futures 22:554–570
Allen PM (1994) Evolutionary complex systems: models of technology change. In: Leydesdorff L, van den Besselaar P (eds) Chaos and economic theory. Pinter, London. ISBN 1 85567 198 0 (hb) 1 85567 202 2 (pb)
Allen PM (2001) A complex systems approach to learning, adaptive networks. Int J Innov Manag 5(2):149–180. ISSN 1363-9196
Allen PM, McGlade JM (1987) Evolutionary drive: the effect of microscopic diversity, error making & noise. Found Phys 17(7):723–728
Allen P, Strathern M (2004) Evolution, emergence and learning in complex systems. Emergence 5(4):8–33
Allen PM, Strathern M, Baldwin JS (2007a) Complexity and the limits of learning. J Evol Econ 17:401–431
Allen PM, Strathern M, Baldwin JS (2007b) Evolutionary drive: new understanding of change in socio-economic systems. Emergence, Complexity and Organization 8(2):2–19
Foster R, Kaplan S (2001) Creative destruction. Doubleday, New York
March JG (1991) Exploration and exploitation in organizational learning. Organ Sci 2(1):71–87
March JG (2006) Rationality, foolishness and adaptive intelligence. Strat Manag J 27:201–214

McCarthy I (1995) Manufacturing classifications: lessons from organisational systematics and biological taxonomy. J Manuf Technol Manag- Integr Manuf Syst 6(6):37–49. ISSN: 1741-038X
McCarthy I, Leseure M, Ridgeway K, Fieller N (1997) Building a manufacturing Cladogram. Int J Technol Manag 13(3):2269–2296. ISSN (Online): 1741-5276 - ISSN (Print): 0267-5730
McKelvey B (1982) Organizational Systematics – Taxonomy, Evolution, Classification. University of California Press, Berkeley, Los Angeles, London. ISBN 0520042255
McKelvey B (1994) Evolution and organizational science. In: Baum J, Singh J (eds) Evolutionary dynamics of organizations. Oxford University Press, pp 314–326. ISBN13: 9780195085846, ISBN10: 0195085841
Metcalfe JS (1998) Evolutionary economics and creative destruction. Routledge, London. ISBN: 0415158680
Nelson R, Winter S (1982) An evolutionary theory of economic change. Harvard University Press, Cambridge
Ormerod P (2005) Why most things fail. Faber and Faber, London
Rivkin J (2000) Imitation of complex strategies. Manag Sci 46(6):824–844
Rivkin J, Siggelkow N (2003) Balancing search and stability: interdependencies among elements of organizational design. Manag Sci 49(3):290–311
Rivkin J, Siggelkow N (2006) Organizing to strategize in the face of interactions: preventing premature lock-in. Long Range Planning 39:591–614
Rivkin J, Siggelkow N (2007) Patterned interactions in complex systems: implications for exploration. Manag Sci 53(7):1068–1085
Rose-Anderssen C, Ridgway K, Baldwin J, Allen P, Varga L, Strathern M (2008a) The evolution of commercial aerospace supply chains and the facilitation of innovation. Int J Electron Cust Relationship Manag 2(1):307–327
Rose-Anderssen C, Ridgway K, Baldwin J, Allen P, Varga L, Strathern M (2008b) Creativity and innovation management 17(4):304–318
Schumpeter J (1962) Capitalism, socialism and democracy, 3rd edn. Harper Torchbooks, New York
Siggelkow N, Rivkin JW (2005) Speed and search: designing organizations for turbulence and complexity. Organ Sci 16:101–122
Silverberg G, Verspagen B (1994) Collective learning, innovation and growth in a boundedly rational, evolutionary world. J Evol Econ 4(3):207–226
Veblen T (1898) Why is economics not an evolutionary science. Q J Econ:12

Intentionality and the Emergence of Complexity: An Analytical Approach

Félix-Fernando Muñoz and María-Isabel Encinar

Abstract Emergence is a generic property that makes economies become complex. The simultaneous carrying out of agents' intentional action plans within an economic system generates processes that are at the base of structural change and the emergence of adaptive complex systems. This paper argues that goals and intentionality are key elements of the structure of rational human action and are the origin of emergent properties such as innovation within economic complex systems. To deal with the locus and role of goals and intentionality in relation to the emergence of complexity we propose an analytical approach based on agents' action plans. Action plans are open representations of the action projected by agents (as individuals or organizations), where the means (actions) and objectives (or goals) are not necessarily given, but produced by agents themselves.

> We may therefore feel justified in treating economic systems as a relatively new class of manifestations of a general evolutionary principle of building systems by making selective connections between elements of existing systems. We may also feel justified in seeking to analyse the structure of each system without investigating its elements in detail. However, when we encounter human-based systems an important modification of the neo-Darwinian version of this principle is required: neither random genetic mutation nor selection by differential genetic inheritance is appropriate. We must introduce intentionality. (Loasby 2012: 837)

1 Introduction

Economics focuses on the parts of action that are rational (even in contexts of true uncertainty) and involves the allocation of scarce means to goals. Thus economic actions, and actions in general, are configured and deployed on the basis of reasons for acting (Searle 2001; Bratman 1987 [1999]). Rational action is first planned and

F.-F. Muñoz (✉) • M.-I. Encinar
Departamento de Análisis Económico: Teoría Económica e Historia Económica, Universidad Autónoma de Madrid, 28049 Madrid, Spain
e-mail: felix.munoz@uam.es; maribel.encinar@uam.es

A. Pyka, J. Foster (eds.), *The Evolution of Economic and Innovation Systems*, Economic Complexity and Evolution, DOI 10.1007/978-3-319-13299-0_8
Reprinted from Journal of Evolutionary Economics, 24(2), Springer 2014.

then carried out in interaction with other agents within a system and in accordance with the corresponding plans of action. Of course, not all human action is planned -feelings and emotions may play a very important real role in an individual's action- and planned actions may produce unintended consequences. However, as far as economists are concerned, the main focus is on the part of the action that is the result of deliberation and choice as Mises (1949) pointed out.

Economic agents interact in economic complex systems. In recent decades there has been an increasing amount of literature in which the economy is considered to be an evolving complex system (Anderson et al. 1988; Blume and Durlauf 2006). Amongst others, important examples include the Santa Fe Institute, a large part of evolutionary economics (Witt 2003) and literature on innovation systems (Antonelli 2011). There are many factors that lead to the emergence of complexity in human interaction systems.[1] Some of these factors depend on agents' heterogeneity -their basic characteristics differ in terms of original endowments such as learning capabilities, size, location, etc. This said, agents also differ in their goals and intentionality. In the area of social sciences, psychology and neuroscience, etc., the concept of "intentionality" (which dates back to Brentano (1874))[2] has also gained momentum: in the last ten years, the number of articles and other papers containing the term 'intentionality' in their *title*, *keywords* or *abstract* has grown immensely. For example, between 2002 and 2011, the number of papers referenced in the ISI-Thompson and Scopus databases totaled 1161 and 1704 respectively. However, it is rare to find the connection between both semantic fields, i.e. "intentionality" + "economics" and the topic seems to be marginal in economics in comparison with neuroscience, for example.

Some economists celebrate the fact that intentionality (and other "folk psychology" terms (Hands 2001)) tends to disappear in economics. However, in recent years the debate about the role of purposeful action, intentionality and the elements that encourage action and knowledge has been revived in this field, at least among evolutionary economists (see for example Hodgson and Knudsen 2007, 2011; Levit et al. 2011; Nelson 2007; Vanberg 2006; Witt 2006).[3] Some authors have used different analytical approaches to highlight the need to associate intentionality with economics and position it at the base of the explanation of economic processes as processes that generate complexity (Antonelli 2011; Muñoz et al. 2011; Rubio de Urquía 2003; Levit et al. 2011; Wagner 2012 among others).

This chapter's main concern is to understand the sources and the process of economic change. More specifically, it investigates the role of agents' intentionality in the generation of economic processes that give rise to complex adaptive systems.

---

[1]Emergence is a key generic property that makes economies become complex (Harper and Endres 2012).

[2]A good classic precedent in philosophy is Ascombe (1957). An interesting approach quite complementary to ours is Bratman's (1987 [1999], 1999). (See also Bratman et al. (1988).) An interesting review is Zimmerman (1989).

[3]In a quite related field, Arthur (2007, 2009) has stressed the purposeful character of (actions that give rise to) invention and technical development.

As will be shown, agents' goals and intentionality play an essential role in explaining the emergence of complexity in economic systems. Thus, economic dynamics may be understood as the process for the generation, selection and attempted implementation in the interaction of agents' *intentional action* -and not only choices (Lane et al. 1996)- and their consequences.

Accordingly, we use an action plan approach (Encinar and Muñoz 2006). This approach allows us to establish micro-foundations (Felin and Foss 2009) that give rise to phenomena and processes such as the intentional orientation of projective action, the continuous appearance, dissemination and retention of novelty in economics, creative responses (Antonelli and Ferraris 2011; Kelly 1963: 8) and entrepreneurship, evolutionary capabilities (Cañibano et al. 2006), etc., that otherwise have no place in an eminently static approach (*a*-temporal, in the sense of Shackle (1972, 1977)). The fact that an unseen or unheard-of event arises from the interaction of these intentional dynamics is another matter. Nevertheless, this does not discount the fact that a key source of complexity lies in the agents' intentionality: intentionality has a systemic structure capable of producing unexpected events. The generation, dissemination and use of knowledge is fundamental for explaining the complexity of economic processes (Loasby 1999), however it is not sufficient to provide a full explanation of these phenomena. We claim that the intentionality-knowledge binomial lies at the base of complexity and evolution.

The structure of the paper is as follows: in Section 2, we present the conceptual base of the action plan and the analytical approach to develop our main argument, which links intentionality to agents' action plans. Section 3 proposes an analytical representation of agents' action that allows us to identify both the locus for intentionality and the necessary connections between the formation and the carrying out of plans in interdependent contexts. Section 4 examines the role of intentionality and its dynamic consequences in terms of production of new realities (novelties) and emergent properties. It is shown that intentionality is a sufficient (but not necessary) condition for the emergence of new properties within complex systems. The chapter ends with some concluding remarks.

2 Intentionality and agents' action plans

Economic agents interact in economic systems that are of an evolving complex kind; economies are non-ergodic systems; economic processes are historical (North 2005) and agents plan and deploy their courses of action in a context of radical uncertainty (Knight 1921). In this context, the claim that an agent's action is rational means that it is configured and deployed on the basis of reasons. That is to say that an agent's action is, essentially, planned; i.e.: in accordance with action plans. Action plans consist of the projected intentional sequence of actions that lead to goals (Rubio de Urquía 2011: 414; see also Miller et al. 1960) posed in a future (imagined in the sense of Loasby (1996)) time.[4] An agent's action plan may then be interpreted as an "analytical" template or guide for action that connects different kinds of elements projectively (that is, towards an imagined future) in accordance with the agent's intentionality: something that is to be reached (objectives or goals) is connected with actions that lead to it. These plans are drawn up by individuals, and they are inherent to them. There may also be plans that outline the action and coordinate the objectives of groups of people (all kinds of organizations).[5] Action plans are *open representations* of the action projected by the agents (as individuals or organizations), where the means (actions /resources) and objectives (goals) are not given as suggested by Robbins (1932), but rather are the results of the agents' own planning activity. The plans drawn up intentionally by the agents are those which, when carried out in interdependent contexts, configure social and economic dynamics (Muñoz and Encinar 2007): their consequences transform the agents themselves as well as the physical-natural, but above all human environment in which they interact.[6] When agents evaluate the consequences of their interactions they may perceive (or not) the inconsistencies of their plans and revise (fully, partially or not at all) their configurations, and, eventually, learn. The dynamics of interaction generates complexity because of this feedback mechanism. The consequence is a restless mechanism (Metcalfe et al. 2006) of economic change, which in this context means the (economic) dynamics of endogenous structural change are capable of inducing or generating novelties.

Not all human action is planned: the actual action of an individual comprises both *planned action* and *unplanned action*. Unplanned action is not something of residual or trivial importance that is inaccessible to scientific knowledge. In fact feelings and emotions play a very important and real role in an individual's action. However, as previously stated, our main interest lies with the part of the total action resulting from deliberation. Moreover, planned action brings in a number of fundamental dynamic elements that enable us to understand, for example, the dynamic role played by the intentionality of the action, a phenomenon which we can analyze in detail, as the following section shows.

2.1 Action plans

The concept of an action plan incorporates a number of important elements for explaining rational human action. Two of those elements are the objectives and projective nature of the action. The bonds between means and goals logically depend

[4]Fuster (2003, 2008) physiologically locates action plans in the prefrontal cortex of humans.

[5]For example a family's travel plans, the business or production plans of a company, etc.

[6]The concept of action plan has been used with different formalization by economists as diverse as Lachmann (1994 [1976]), Keynes (1936), Hicks (1939), Stackelberg (1946 [1943]), Barnard (1938), Debreu (1959), Penrose (1959), Malinvaud (1999), Boulding (1991), etc.

on what the agents know or think they know, i.e. on what we refer to as their cognitive dynamics (which we will refer to as *CD*). *CD* refers to the understanding agents have of reality, where this understanding is condensed into representation systems made by agents (according to scientific-technical representations). *CD* also refers to beliefs in terms of what this reality *is* like and to the evolution of this understanding.

However, plans are established intentionally according to the objectives and targets that agents wish to achieve. These objectives and targets guide the action and give it *meaning*. Therefore, we can distinguish analytically between agents' perception of what reality is like or could be like in the future - agents' *CD*- and their conception of what reality should be: their ethical dynamics, referred to as *ED*. Together with socio-cultural dynamics (*SD*),[7] in which the agents deploy their activity, both dynamics modify the content and form of the plans and, consequently, generate new realities. These realities stand as a contrast between what has previously been conjectured (in the sense of Popper (1972)) in the agents' action plans (*ex ante*) and what they (*ex post*) understand as what has actually happened. The compared *balances* between expectations and events (may) activate review mechanisms (learning) of the agents' plans and the way in which they are formulated.

As shown below, economic dynamics can be understood as the process for the generation, selection and (attempted) interactive implementation of agents' action plans and its consequences. The alteration of intentionality implies that agents' action plans are internally modified and that the interactive implementation of the new plans generates new realities. Indeed, the introduction of new objectives alters not only the spaces of objectives but also induces new types of knowledge, capabilities and actions.

Let p^i_{th} represent the action plan h of an individual i at the time t. The plan p^i_{th} consists of executing in t actions a^i_{th1} and a^i_{th2}, to reach in $t + 1$ the goal $G^i_{(t+1)h1}$ and, also in $t + 1$, executing actions $a^i_{(t+1)h3}$, $a^i_{(t+1)h4}$ and $a^i_{(t+1)h5}$, to finally achieve the objective $G^i_{(t+2)h2}$ in $t + 2$. The hierarchy of goals is as follows: $G^{i*}_{(t+2)h3}$ is the main goal and $G^i_{(t+2)h2}$ and $G^i_{(t+1)h1}$ are both lower level goals.

From a theoretical point of view, an action plan p^i_{th} can have, in general, any projective linkage structure. These linkages are represented in Fig. 1 by arrows indicating the direction -intention- of the action to an objective. The linkages can include estimates of probability (both 'objective' and subjective probability) or conjecture, all kinds of conditionalities (also including strategic plans); feedbacks; etc. Of course, the plan p^i_{th} may be defined incompletely by the agent. In that case, the plan p^i_{th} may include connections or actions that are not fully specified, pending future specifications.

Many outstanding features and properties of personal action plans can be known in relation to internal, logical or material consistency and ex ante and ex post

[7]Culture, defined as in North (2005), plays a fundamental role in economic change.

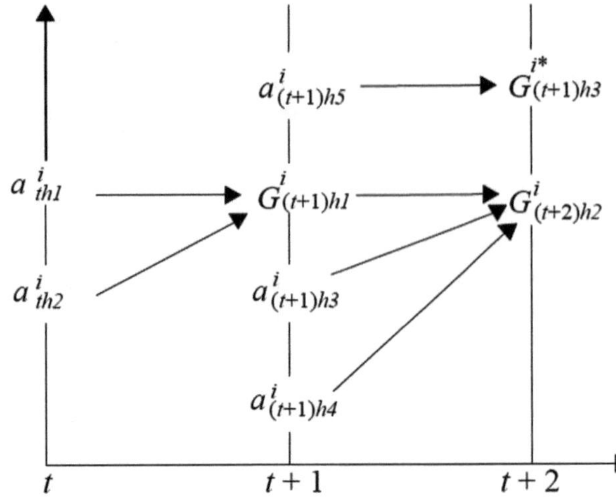

Fig. 1 Example of an action plan

feasibility (see Bhattacharyya et al. 2011; Sen 1993). Moreover, plans may involve a hierarchical structure of goals that can include a wide variety of contents: from low-level hierarchical determination (no goal is worth much more than another) to high-level hierarchical determination. Thus, the structure of a plan's goals can be inconsistent insofar as one or more of the goals contained in the plan may be incompatible with other goals within the same plan.[8]

The hierarchical structure of goals allows for a simple representation: Fig. 1 shows both a sequence and a hierarchy of goals. For example, in $t + 2$, the goal $G^{i*}_{(t+2)h3}$ occupies a higher hierarchical position than $G^i_{(t+2)h2}$, this being represented by drawing the former above the latter.

2.2 *Bundles of action plans*

In general, agents try to deploy several action plans; we will refer to this set of action plans as a bundle of action plans, B^i_t. Figure 2 illustrates a bundle of action plans B^i_t.

The bundle represented in Fig. 2 comprises three action plans and four periods of time: t to $t + 3$. At time t, the projected action relative to the individual i is based on these three plans. The chart has some intersections that are not empty between plans because they have elements (both means and goals) in common. Accordingly, for example, action a_{t13}, located in terms of time at time $t + 1$, inherent to plan 1, is also

[8]Investigation cannot pre-exclude plans that contain systems of goals that are internally inconsistent. In fact, these kinds of plans may form part of the reality under study and constitute an interesting field of study in themselves. See for example Encinar (2002).

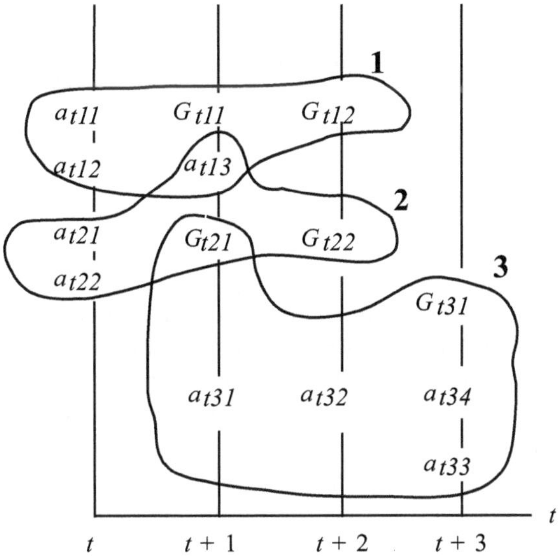

Fig. 2 Bundle of action plans B_t^i

necessary for achieving target G_{t22} inherent to plan 2. In addition, the bundle B_t^i has a projective horizon of three periods, but not all the plans have the same duration in terms of reference time and not all the plans start and end at the same times in this reference time.[9]

3 An analytic representation of agents' action

Despite the fact that goals can be treated analytically as static elements, intentionality is inherently dynamic. Intentionality is understood as the tendency towards a goal that first appears in the individual's mind as a purpose. This definition of intentionality is closely linked to the concept of plan. Intention is the determination of will in accordance with a purpose. Additionally, intention is what makes it possible to differentiate between the purposes of individuals (or groups of individuals) and their mere desires. The latter do not necessarily activate subjects' actions or, therefore, their intentions. However, the conception of purpose activates

[9]As far as plans are components of a bundle, and are intrinsically linked together forming a whole course of action, each pattern of bundling may be understood as an attempt at tentative modularization of action by the agent. The plans that form the bundle (three plans in Fig. 2) would be themselves quasi-decomposable modules of a higher level "system" of actions-goals –the bundle- that would direct the future course of action of the agent. For the meaning of quasi-decomposability and modularization see, respectively, Simon (1962) and Langlois (2002).

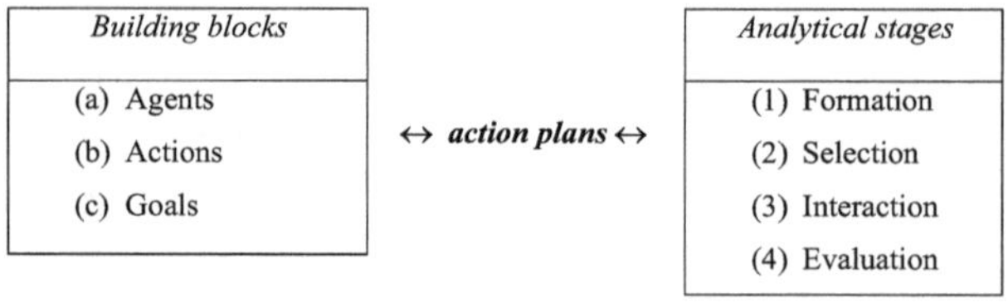

Fig. 3 Constitutive elements of the model

behavior and actions that focus on their achievement through intention and will.[10] Agents can be distinguished on the basis of their knowledge and skills, but also by the purposes they pursue. All this leads to agents being able to introduce a wide variety of changes in the environment through their actions, altering other agents' space of action.

This section proposes a model of agent action in order to identify the necessary connections between the formation (constitution) and interactive implementation of intentional plans and the production of new realities and emergent properties that change the landscape of the system. The model has the advantage of offering a summarized representation of the elements that configured the projected action by agents, its interactive implementation and its transformation into real (external/observed) action. The model has three building blocks -agents, actions/means, and goals- that are connected in action plans, and four analytical stages (see Fig. 3) –formation; selection; interactive implementation and evaluation of the consequences of action plans.

3.1 The (evolutionary) stages of agent action[11]

1. *Formation*: The first stage in the model of agent action is the process by which individuals form their *bundles* of individual action plans, in each instant of time t, B_t^i. From these bundles of plans B_t^i, agents establish a hierarchy, determine some of them as possible, $\tilde{B}_t^i$, and choose the bundle, $\hat{B}_t^i$, that best

[10]The new goal psychology represents a step forward in the integration of motives for action with psychological theories, generally cognitive, on human action. The links are the very goals or objectives of the action. See various chapters in the *Oxford Handbook of Human Action* (Morsella et al. 2009), especially those included in part 2 (dedicated to the activation, selection and expression of action) and in Moskowitz and Grant (2009). On motivation in Economics see Frey and Jegen (2001) and Gerschlager (2012).

[11]Subsections 3.1 and 3.2 are grounded and develop the approach by Rubio de Urquía (2005) introducing *intentionality* within the analytical framework.

satisfies their objectives.[12] Logically, the relation between these bundles of plans is: $\tilde{B}_t^i \subset B_t^i$, $\hat{B}_t^i = \max\{\tilde{B}_t^i\}$, where $\left\{B_t^i, \tilde{B}_t^i, \hat{B}_t^i\right\} \neq \emptyset$.

In each instant of time t, the specific content of B_t^i is shaped by means of the current agent's set of beliefs, values, attitudes, representations of reality that the individual i holds at that time t. We will refer to this set as the agents *ensemble* of beliefs, etc. -or simply the ensemble- E_t^i.[13] Both the elements and the relationships between them contained in the ensemble are the result of the previously mentioned ethical, cognitive and socio-cultural dynamics (ED_t^i, CD_t^i and SD_t respectively) of the agents. In particular, SD_t, which includes the general environment (including institutional settings, technologies, habits and rules, etc.) within which agents are inserted and deploy their actions. The ensemble E_t^i supports the subjective domain of planning, i.e., how the world is made; what is possible and what is not; what is known and what is not, in relation to the past, present and future; what the individuals acting can do; what is best and what is worst for these individuals; what they want and what they do not.[14] In short, E_t^i defines the subjective possible courses of action and provides elements of valuation for organizing them in relation to what should be, what is desired and what is preferred by the agent at each time t. This concept of ensemble is quite similar to Bratman's (see Bratman et al. 1988) conception of belief/desire/intention (BDI) architecture. For Bratman the (BDI)-architecture includes fair representations of agent's beliefs, desires, and intentions. However,

[12]This bundle in a neoclassical account would roughly correspond to the bundle that maximises some objective function (utility, profits, etc.). However, in a more general (and realistic, that is, where true uncertainty prevails) framework the agent chooses bundles that "meet targets of adequacy rather than pinnacles of attainment" (Earl 1983: 78–81). It is very interesting to compare our analytical stages with those proposed respectively by Earl and Potts. The former (Earl 1983: 149–150) presents a multistage process in which the agent proceeds sequentially as follows: (1) problem recognition (a failure to match up to aspirations), (2) search of (not given) courses of action, (3) evaluation of possible sequels of particular choices, (4) choice itself, (5) implementation (often difficult and partially accomplished), and (6) assessment (the agent examines to which extent what was decided was achieved). Potts (2000: 120–123) addresses the problem of acting in a non-integral space. Agents must form conjectures as a solution by means of searching among adjacent possibilities which relationships may solve (are more promising ways of solving) their particular problems. The 'decision cycle' that makes these operations possible consists of four separate components: {LIST, CONSTRUCT, RANK, SELECT}. The main point in Potts' proposal is that, for him, these conjectures are the agents' preferences (note the conjectural character of action plans).

[13]The ensemble refers to the "reality" such as it is conceived by the agents in order to produce their action.

[14]The term "beliefs" refers to the set of conceptions, representations and knowledge to which the individual is faithful. In general, beliefs imply evaluation criteria that organize the projective action and the action of decision among alternatives and value judgments. "Values" is understood as the set of valuation criteria effectively used by the individual to projectively organize the action and issue value judgments. The possible difference between the valuation criteria implied by the beliefs and those effectively used in practice must be acknowledged. Values include tastes and preferences. "Attitudes" refers to stable features that introduce determination in certain aspects.

the ensemble also includes the set of representations of reality that the individual i holds at a specific time t: it defines the subjective projective space of action of the individual i at each time t. Whereas in Bratman's approach agents' intentions are structured into larger plans, in our approach, intentionality is the source that *structurally* and *temporally* orders the contents of those plans; that is, intentionality generates the "library" of notional actions required to reach the goals pursued by the agents, giving sense and rationality, to their actions. Thus our approach allows us to deal with intentionality as the last source of rationality of actions.

2. *Selection*: Each ensemble E_t^i contains a structure of alternative planned action possibilities that *denotes intentionality*. After considering different planned possibilities, the individual selects one bundle $\hat{B}_t^i$ at each instant t, and begins to execute the actions (and reach the goals) corresponding to that instant t. In other words, at time t, the individual (organization) adopts one of the possible courses of action, the bundle $\hat{B}_t^i$ by means of an active decision which, among other elements, implies closing the hierarchical structure of all the alternatives of action with regard to the agent's ensemble, E_t^i. The ensemble *generates* the selected bundle:[15]

$$E_t^i \rightarrow \left\{\hat{B}_t^i\right\}$$

This process of selection is internal to the agent's subjective domain of action.

3. *Interaction*: From individual planned action to individual observable action. It is by means of the simultaneous carrying out of plans in interdependent contexts that planning connects to observable action. It is at this stage when, on one hand, *intentionality emerges* and produces external reality and, on the other, it is possible to show the analytical link between the micro- (individual) and meso-level. This is the crucial stage in which action is deployed interactively, producing instants of reality and the historical consequences of action –those that are captured in ordinary statistical measures, etc.

4. *Evaluation*: Moreover, interaction reveals which parts of the plans of interacting agents within a system are or are not compatible, and it retains ex post which parts of goals and courses of action considered ex ante as possible have been successful. In other words: agents examine whether or not their conjecture (the bundle of plans) was correct and thereby whether their goals have been attained. If evidence is in some sense unsatisfactory agents would revise how they form

[15]In our approach, the symbol → neither represents a logical relationship (for example a material conditional if-then relationship) nor a mathematical function that relates two (or more) variables (as is the case of a production function, for instance). It designates a *mode* -that is, a conventional sign- of representing a necessary causal relationship among theoretical structures. Quite a different issue is that in some very specific circumstances it is possible to characterize parts of a theory of human action by means of proper (not imposed) mathematical structures as is the case of neoclassical economics under highly restrictive theoretical assumptions.

their plans in order to try and do so otherwise.[16] Thus, as long as plans are being developed they are evaluated and processes of learning are triggered. Interaction generates a process of selection external to the agent.

In order to develop these ideas, we need to open up the internal production of action "the black box" via a sequence of two intermediate steps:

Step 1: Let s_t^i be the state of the individual i at instant t, which comprises the state of the individual in biological and mental terms; his/her individual dynamics ED_t^i and CD_t^i, as well as everything that is external to the individual and may play a role in his/her actions.[17] Let be δ^i a kind of *operator* that binds together ED_t^i, CD_t^i and SD_t; with both the agent's state s_t^i and the state of the non-human environment at t, u_t; that is, with (s_t^i, u_t). Thus, the formation of δ^i includes the dynamics ED_t^i, CD_t^i and SD_t, the sequence of personal ensembles of i before the time t and "what it is", including "what it has been". By means of δ^i the ensembles E_t^i and the bundles of plans $\hat{B}_t^i$ are continuously being formed by the individual i at time t. Thus:

$$\delta^i \left(s_t^i, u_t\right) \rightarrow \left\{E_t^i\right\} \rightarrow \left\{\hat{B}_t^i\right\}$$

Step 2: Let A_t^i denote the action really deployed by the individual i at instant t and α^i denote the system of relations that binds together the final action exercised A_t^i and the action planned in bundle $\hat{B}_t^i$ for the individual i at time t; in other words:

$$\alpha^i \left(\hat{B}_t^i\right) \rightarrow A_t^i$$

The dynamic α^i is based on the personal principles related to the relationship between planned action and unplanned action. Thus, the unplanned action forms part of what is indicated in α^i.[18] It is when the agent deploys A_t^i that *intentionality emerges*, when we shift from the individual planned action to the individual observed action.

The process of interactive implementation of plans partly configures the economic dynamics –transforming the external (objective) reality as well as the internal (subjective) realities of agents. This process depends not only on how plans are internally formed, and on their structure and content, but also on the results of interaction. Figures 4 and 5 summarize these ideas.

---

[16] This stage is rather similar to the one that Earl (1983: 150) has called "assessment" in his multistage process model of choice.

[17] The agent's state may include explicitly the agent's "biography"; the set of all the states of all the individuals other than i prior to time t that may influence the agent.

[18] They could be unplanned actions due to, for example, the use of routines, rules, procedures and behavioural habits, which also generate consequences, expected or otherwise, in action.

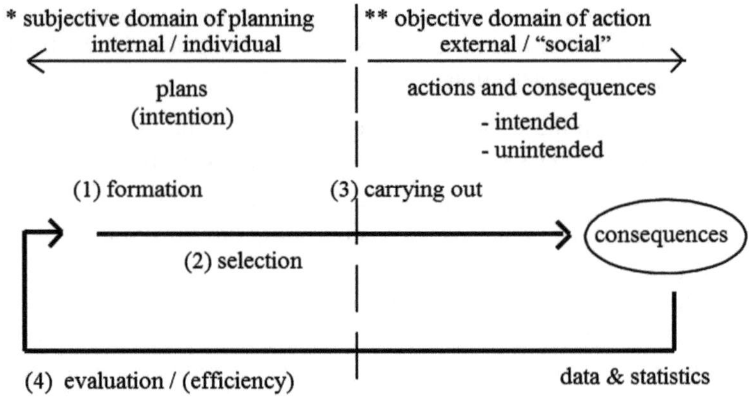

Fig. 4 The subjective and objective domains of action

$$s_t^i \rightarrow \boxed{\delta 1^i(s_t^i,u_t) \rightarrow (E_t^i,\hat{B}_t^i) \rightarrow \delta 2^i(\hat{B}_t^i)} \rightarrow A_t^i \quad = \quad \boxed{< s_t^i, A_t^i >}$$

Fig. 5 Extended and resumed representations of agent action "*black box*"

3.2 Interaction with n-agents

At each instant of time t, there are n_t agents in the economy.[19] According to their previous states and what they understood as their own current state, economic agents generate their own instantaneous personal ensemble, E_t^i. Therefore, at each instant t there is a set of personal ensembles $E_t^i : \{E_t^1, E_t^2 \ldots E_t^{n_t}\}$. Depending on their own E_t^i, and by means of δ^i, each agent produces a set of bundles of potential courses of action $E_i^t \rightarrow B_i^t$, and selects a bundle of action plans -which corresponds to the planned courses of action that each individual tries to deploy, $\hat{B}_t^i : \left\{\hat{B}_t^1, \hat{B}_t^2 \ldots \hat{B}_t^{n_t}\right\}$. Both the set of all projected bundles of action plans (imagined and deemed as possible by agents) B_t^i and its subset of selected bundles of action plans $\hat{B}_t^i$ imply intentionality.

However, for the selected action plans that give rise to action, the operator α^i, mediates, producing the actual action of each agent i at each instant of time t : $\{A_t^1, A_t^2 \ldots A_t^{n_t}\}$. Finally, the action deployed by each agent in the economy together with each agent's own state at $t, s_t^i : \{s_t^1, s_t^2 \ldots s_t^{n_t}\}$, interact. As a consequence of that interaction, the dynamics of generation of new individual states (including new knowledge, beliefs, attitudes, etc.) is produced, transforming both human and non-human environments, (new artefacts, institutions, u_t, etc.). In turn, the dynamic for

[19] At t it may be that $n_t \geq n_{t-1}$ or that $n_t < n_{t-1}$.

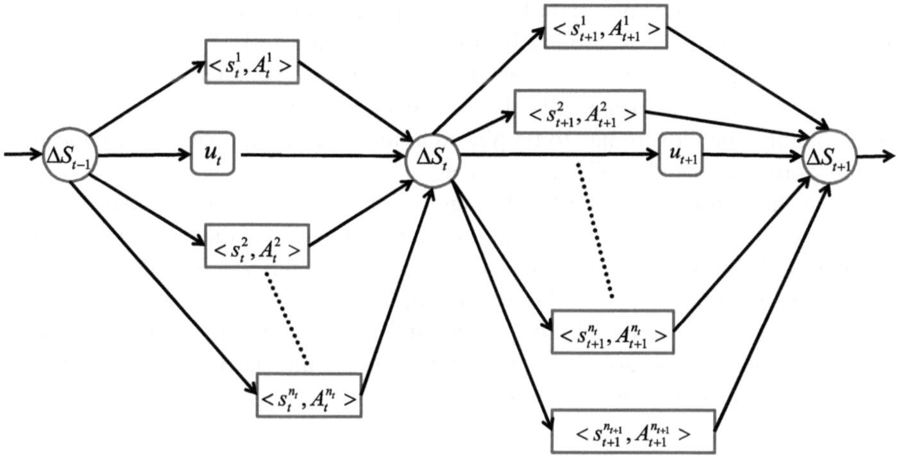

Fig. 6 A representation of the structure of agent interaction

the generation of agents' states 'returns' new states for the individuals and non-human environments that re-nourish the formation and interactive implementation of the action in the next instant $t+1$.

Figure 6 shows the interactive implementation of action, represented by ΔS_t. It is at this stage when agents interact and produce new instants of reality.

Finally, the form adopted by ΔS_t depends on the decision of the modeller. Thus, ΔS_t may include networks of agents, functional relationships without structural change, etc.

3.3 *Action and economic theory*

Obviously, planning is not economic action -as shown by the difference between $\hat{B}_t^i$ and A_t^i. Planning is a part of action (an activity itself), but not the kind of action that is truly relevant for economics.[20] Economic theory has usually focused on the analysis and development of models based on a special version of the dynamic δ understood as an optimization principle. This version of δ operates over a hierarchized set B_t^i and a subsequent subset (hierarchized and deemed possible) $\tilde{B}_t^i$ of the latter, and selects $\hat{B}_t^i$.

As all bundles of action plans depend –in our approach- on the pre-existence of E_t^i, -because E_t^i projects the space of action of agents- it may be concluded that usual economic theorizing takes (at least implicitly) the agents' ensembles as

[20]How individuals set goals, etc., is very important for other disciplines such as psychology. (See for instance, Ajzen 1991; Miller et al. 1960; Moskowitz and Grant 2009).

given or for granted. (For example, in the case of usual consumption theory, the preferences over the consumption bundles are fixed a priori). The 'closure' of the economic models is indeed necessary for the analysis of open systems, as Loasby (2003) has shown so masterfully. If we are interested in assigning any role for intentionality, the closure has to be placed at the level of E_t^i, where the *choosable* (in the words of Shackle 1977) is produced.

When the action projected by the agent is being deployed, planned action is "transformed" into actual action. As we have pointed out, this transformation is the base of the production of 'actual' human action; in other words, the production of instants of reality. This transformation requires the analytical concurrence of the dynamic α. The production of the specific (and complete) reality of the agent is not completed until the operation of α, which triggers the interactive implementation of the action that is at the base of complex phenomena.

4 Intentionality and the emergence of complexity

Emergence is a generic property that makes economies become complex. The emergence of complexity within an economic system is not (necessarily) intentional; but depends on the agents' intentions, even though what happens is not necessarily what is being sought by agents. Observed actions can differ from what was intentionally sought -when they were projected actions- although this is compatible with the fact that intentionality is present in the analytical structure of action. The question about where and when new properties emerge may be addressed as follows. New properties emerge because agents: (a) discover or invent *new* actions; and/or (b) discover or "invent" *new* objectives; and/or (c) rearrange previously existing actions and goals in a *new* way. Agents implement all these new or revised actions and/or goals into *new* plans[21] and try to deploy such action plans in interaction with other agents and the external environment. Thus, revised actions consist of introducing entirely new actions linked to existing objectives (a radical understanding of novelty (Witt 1996)) or changing (or cancelling) the links between actions and objectives; revised objectives consist of introducing entirely new ones or of changing the hierarchy of already existing objectives. However, it is as a consequence of the simultaneous carrying out of actions in interdependent contexts (ΔS) that novelties emerge.

Thus, the emergence of novelties can be both (1) the result of an agent's internal dynamics $\left(\text{that reproduce new } E_t^i, \hat{B}_t^i \text{ and } A_t^i\right)$, and/or (2) the result of interaction processes between agents. The former refers to conscious and *intentional* acts

[21]New in the sense of "unheard-of".

undertaken by agents; the latter refers mainly to unexpected products of interactions among action plans.[22]

Once new properties emerge, they fuel the processes of structural change as a necessary consequence as agents incorporate them into their space of action – $\{E_t^i\}$ and $\left\{\hat{B}_t^i\right\}$. Regardless of where novelties emerge, if they have any effect it is because, by necessity, novelties are incorporated into agents' action plans, producing specific actions, A_t^i, and novelties are disseminated through the interaction of agents' action plans.[23] When agents evaluate the results of interactions and learn, they perceive (or perhaps not) the inconsistencies of their plans and revise (fully, partially or not at all) their configurations, as feedback for their ensembles $\delta^i(\cdots) \rightarrow \{E_t^i\} \rightarrow \left\{\hat{B}_t^i\right\}$. The consequence of this interaction is a restless mechanism that generates continuous structural change.

Once the structural components of the model have been specified and extended to *nt*-agents -$\left(E_t^1 \cdots E_t^{nt}, \delta^1 \cdots \delta^{nt}, \alpha^1 \cdots \alpha^{nt}\right)$-, the process of economic change acquires full meaning, generating the states $\left(s_t^i, u_t\right), \forall i$: when any structural element changes, novelties emerge and then at least a new bundle of action plans (B_t^i) is configured. In the model, intentionality is located in the ensemble (E_t^i) and deploys its logic through the interaction of the revised agents' plans. Revised action plans, in which novelty has already emerged, induce economic change giving rise to processes of novelty-dissemination. Revised action plans are a source of complexity as far as they feed the generation of the renewed variety characteristic of evolutionary processes. Intentionality is a sufficient –but not necessary- condition for the emergence of new properties within complex systems.

Finally, interaction leads to the general dynamic of production of social and economic reality and (due to the appearance of all kinds of novelties -creative responses, unexpected consequences of actions, rationed action, positive or negative externalities, path-dependency, etc.) breaks down the sequences of the effective implementation of action plans, and triggers a dynamic of constant disequilibrium. These disequilibria do not lead to chaos, but rather generate complexity in the system of agents in interaction and in the non-social medium. According to the responses (positive or negative feedback (Miller and Page 2007)), systems stabilize or increase/decrease their degree of complexity. The logic of this entire mesh of

[22]Owing to this, novelties cannot be uncaused causes as Hodgson (2004, chap. 3) suggests: the ultimate cause is the intentionality of agents. In an example provided by Schumpeter's (2005 [1932]) Mantegna's innovations could be interpreted as a conscious and individual act undertaken by the painter; the 'Renaissance style' produced unexpected innovations in painting as a result of painters interactions.

[23]As has been said above, in economics the simplest example of ΔS is a perfect-competition market; in this structure of interaction –in which agents, agents' goals, and structure of interaction do not change- the consequences ΔS are expressed in terms of the complex of produced and consumed quantities and the equilibrium price. Of course ΔS may be more complex: we may think that there is rationing equilibria (Benassy 1986; Malinvaud 1977); non-market interactions (Schelling 1978); network effects (Katz and Shapiro 1994); etc.

interaction is more evident in specific case studies. Moreover, this logic appears more clearly when the level of analysis chosen by the theory is between the micro-meso and meso-macro levels (Dopfer 2011; Dopfer et al. 2004).[24]

5 Concluding remarks

This paper argues that intentionality is a key element of the structure of rational action and that it is at the origin of emergent properties within economic complex systems. The argument is consistent with the role that the categories of intentionality -such as belief, goal, intention, collective intentionality, etc.- have in cognitive sciences, artificial intelligence and social philosophy, as well as in the explanation of individual and collective behavior and the emergence of institutions (Baldwin and Baird 2001; Grosz and Hunsberger 2006; Malle et al. 2001; Metzinger and Gallese 2003).[25] Intentionality -an agents' feature of representations by which they are about something or directed at something (Searle 1995)- is linked to goals and in order to deal with the locus and role of goals and intentionality in relation to the emergence of complexity we have developed a model based on agents' action plans.[26]

There are many factors that lead to the emergence of complex properties in human interaction systems. Some of these factors depend on the fact that agents are intrinsically heterogeneous -their basic characteristics differ in terms of original endowments such as learning capabilities, size, location, etc. Even so, intentionality is a key factor for understanding the dynamics of human complex adaptive systems; although this factor tends to blur or even disappear in Economics. In many models, agents are portrayed as automata that are unable to implement the intentional pursuit of their interests (Rosser 2004). As a result, the main source of novelties usually remains obscured and, as Antonelli (2011) claims, the theory of complexity does not yet provide an analysis of the endogenous determining factors of the system's features.

The action plan framework presented in the foregoing sections allows for alternative uses. Our purpose in this chapter has been to shed light on the endogenous link between intentionality and the emergence of complexity in Economics. Thus, the

---

[24]Examples include the analysis of the origin and evolution of techno-economic innovation systems, the emergence of technological clusters, the evolution of institutions, etc.

[25]The role of beliefs, etc. has been recognised in economic theory. Recently, Acemoglu has pointed out that the fundamental causes of economic growth are luck, geographical differences, institutional differences and "cultural differences that determine individuals' values, preferences and beliefs" (Acemoglu 2009: 20).

[26]It must be stressed that the aim of this chapter is not to offer a technical solution to a particular problem. It is an analytical proposal intended to make tractable North's (2005) and Loasby's (2012) challenges, i.e.: to erect scaffoldings (analytical frameworks) that allow us to deal with human interaction and the sources of complexity (and structural change) -scaffoldings being able to accommodate, at the same time intentionality and different "ecologies of plans" (Wagner 2012).

main use of this approach here is to locate and understand the role of intentionality in explaining dynamic processes such as the emergence of novelty and structural change that are typical of complex systems. This approach also provides another important analytical use: it constitutes a natural place for intrinsically dynamic topics, such as Schumpeter's (2005 [1932]) "creator personality" (entrepreneur) and his role for explaining economic development. The Schumpeterian entrepreneur is the analytical subject who is *especially* capable of introducing new objectives, new actions or new relationships between actions and objectives, into his action plans; in other words, he offers creative responses to new situations (Schumpeter 1947a, b). The creator personality is especially capable of generating novelty and, therefore, of stimulating development. In all, novelty depends on the intentionality of agents. The fact that an unexpected event arises from the interaction of intentional dynamics is another matter. However, this does not eliminate the fact that its origin is intentional. Of course the creative reaction of each agent is not actually a one-off event that takes place in isolation in time and space, but rather a historic process in which the sequence of feedback plays a key role (Arthur 1990, 2007).

Acknowledgments The authors would like to thank two anonymous referees for their very useful comments and suggestions as well as to Professor Rafael Rubio de Urquía, Carolina Cañibano and David Harper, for their valuable advises.
The authors acknowledge the scientific support from the 'Instituto de Investigaciones Económicas y Sociales Francisco de Vitoria' and Universidad Autónoma de Madrid. The usual disclaimers apply.

References

Acemoglu D (2009) Introduction to modern economic growth. Princeton University Press, Princeton

Ajzen I (1991) The theory of planned behavior. Organ Behav Hum Decis Process 50:179–211

Anderson PW, Arrow KJ, Pines D (1988) The economy as an evolving complex system. Addison-Wesley, Reading

Antonelli C (2011) The economic complexity of technological change: knowledge interaction and path dependence. In: Antonelli C (ed) Handbook on the economic complexity of technological change. Edward Elgar, Cheltenham, pp 3–59

Antonelli C, Ferraris G (2011) Innovation as an emerging system property: an agent based simulation model. J Artif Soc Soc Simul 14(2):47

Arthur WB (1990) Positive feedbacks in the economy. Sci Am 262:92–99

Arthur WB (2007) The structure of invention. Res Policy 36:274–287

Arthur WB (2009) The nature of technology. What it is and how it evolves. Free Press, New York

Ascombe GEM (1957) Intention. Basil Blackwell, Oxford

Baldwin DA, Baird JA (2001) Discerning intentions in dynamic human action. Trends Cogn Sci 5(4):171–178

Barnard C (1938) The functions of the executive. Harvard UP, Cambridge

Benassy JP (1986) Macroeconomics: an introduction to the non-walrasian approach. Academic, London

Bhattacharyya A, Pattanaik PK, Xu Y (2011) Choice, internal consistency and rationality. Econ Philos 27(2):123–149

Blume LE, Durlauf SN (eds) (2006) The economy as an evolving complex system, III: current perspectives and future directions. Oxford University Press, Oxford
Boulding K (1991) What is evolutionary economics? J Evol Econ 1(1):9–17
Bratman ME (1987 [1999]) Intention, plans, and practical reason. CSLI Publications, Standford
Bratman ME (1999) Faces of intention. Cambridge University Press, Cambridge
Bratman ME, Israel DJ, Pollack ME (1988) Plans and resource-bounded practical reasoning. Comput Intell 4(3):349–355
Brentano F (1874) Psychologie vom empirischen Standpunkt. Duncker & Humblot, Leipzig
Cañibano C, Encinar MI, Muñoz FF (2006) Evolving capabilities and innovative intentionality: some reflections on the role of intention within innovation processe. Innov Manag Policy Pract 8(4–5):310–321
Debreu G (1959) Theory of value. An axiomatic analysis of economic equilibrium. Cowles foundation monograph, p 17
Dopfer K (2011) Evolution and complexity in economics revisited. Papers on Economics & Evolution Max Planck Institute of Economics, Evolutionary Economics Group, Jena
Dopfer K, Foster J, Potts J (2004) Micro–meso–macro. J Evol Econ 14(3):263–279
Earl PE (1983) The economic imagination. Towards a behavioural analysis of choice. Wheatsheaf Books, Brighton
Encinar MI, Muñoz FF (2006) On novelty and economics: Schumpeter's paradox. J Evol Econ 16(3):255–277
Encinar MI (2002) Análisis de las propiedades de "consistencia" y "realizabilidad" en los planes de acción Una perspectiva desde la teoría Económica. Universidad Autónoma de Madrid, Madrid
Felin T, Foss NJ (2009) Organizational routines and capabilities: historical drift and a course-correction toward microfoundations. Scand J Manag 25:157–167
Frey BS, Jegen R (2001) Motivation crowding theory. J Econ Surv 15(5):589–611
Fuster JM (2003) Cortex and mind Unifying cognition. Oxford University Press, New York
Fuster JM (2008) The prefrontal cortex, 4th edn. Academic, Amsterdam
Gerschlager C (2012) Agents of change. J Evol Econ 22:413–441
Grosz BJ, Hunsberger L (2006) The dynamics of intention in collaborative activity. Cogn Syst Res 7:259–272
Hands DW (2001) Reflection without rules. Economic methodology and contemporary science theory. Cambridge University Press, Cambridge
Harper DA, Endres AM (2012) The anatomy of emergence, with a focus upon capital formation. J Econ Behav Organ 82(2–3):352–367
Hicks JR (1939) Value and capital: an inquiry into some fundamental principles of economic theory. Clarendon Paperbacks, Oxford
Hodgson GM (2004) The evolution of institutional economics. Routledge, London
Hodgson GM, Knudsen T (2007) Evolutionary theorizing beyond lamarckism: a reply to Richard Nelson. J Evol Econ 17(3):353–359
Hodgson GM, Knudsen T (2011) Agreeing on generalised Darwinism: a response to Pavel Pelikan. J Evol Econ 1–10
Katz ML, Shapiro C (1994) Systems competition and network effects. J Econ Perspect 8(2):93–115
Kelly GA (1963) A theory of personality. W.W. Norton, New York
Keynes JM (1936) The general theory of employment, interest and money. MacMillan, London
Lachmann L (1994 [1976]) From Mises to Shackle. An essay on Austrian economics and the kaleidic society. In: Lavoie D (ed) Expectations and the meaning of institutions. Essays in economics by Ludwig Lachmann. Routledge, London, pp 218–228
Lane D, Malerba F, Maxfield R, Orsenigo L (1996) Choice and action. J Evol Econ 6(1):43–76
Langlois RN (2002) Modularity in technology and organization. J Econ Behav Organ 49:19–37
Levit G, Hossfeld U, Witt U (2011) Can Darwinism be "Generalized" and of what use would this be? J Evol Econ 21(4):545–562. doi:10.1007/s00191-011-0235-3
Loasby BJ (1996) The imagined, deemed possibe. In: Helmstädter E, Perlman M (eds) Behavioral norms, technological progress, and economic dynamics. Michigan University Press, Michigan, pp 17–31

Loasby BJ (1999) Knowledge, institutions and evolution in economics. Routledge, London
Loasby BJ (2003) Closed models and open systems. J Econ Methodol 10(3):285–306
Loasby BJ (2012) Building systems. J Evol Econ 22(4):833–846
Malinvaud E (1977) The theory of unemployment reconsidered. Blackwell, Oxford
Malinvaud E (1999) Leçons de théorie microéconomique (4e édition). Dunod, Paris
Malle BF, Moses LJ, Baldwin DA (eds) (2001) Intentions and intentionality: foundations of social cognition. The MIT Press, Cambridge
Metcalfe JS, Foster J, Ramlogan R (2006) Adaptive economic growth. Cambridge J Econ 30(1):7–32
Metzinger T, Gallese V (2003) The emergence of a shared action ontology: building blocks for a theory. Conscious Cogn 12:549–571
Miller GA, Galanter E, Pribram KH (1960) Plans and the structure of behavior. Holt, Rinehart and Winston, New York
Miller JH, Page SE (2007) Complex adaptive systems. Princeton University Press, Princeton
Mises L (1949) Human action: a teatrise on economics. Yale University Press, New Haven
Morsella E, Bargh JA, Gollwitzer PM (eds) (2009) Oxford handbook of human action. Oxford University Press, New York
Moskowitz GB, Grant H (eds) (2009) The psychology of goals. The Guilford Press, New York
Muñoz FF, Encinar MI (2007) Action plans and socio-economic evolutionary change. RePec: Working Papers in Economic Theory, Universidad Autónoma de Madrid (Spain), Department of Economic Analysis, Madrid
Muñoz FF, Encinar MI, Cañibano C (2011) On the role of intentionality in evolutionary economic change. Struct Chang Econ Dyn 22:193–203. Reprinted in Dopfer K & Potts J (eds.) The New Evolutionary Economics (Vol. I, pp. 57–67. Cheltenham, UK: Edward Elgar, 2014)
Nelson RR (2007) Comment on: dismantling Lamarckism: why descriptions of socio-economic evolution as Lamarckian are misleading, by Hodgson and Knudsen. J Evol Econ 17(3):349–352
North DC (2005) Understanding the process of economic change. Princeton University Press, Princeton
Penrose ET (1959) The theory of the growth of the firm. Blackwell, Oxford
Popper K (1972) Conjectures and refutations. The growth of scientific knowledge, 4th edn. Routledge & Kegan Paul, London
Potts J (2000) The new evolutionary microeconomics. Complexity, competence and adaptive behaviour. Edward Elgar, Cheltenham
Robbins L (1932) An essay on the nature and significance of economic science, 2nd edn (1969). Macmillan, London
Rosser JB (ed) (2004) Complexity in economics. Methodology, interacting agents and microeconomic models. Edward Elgar, Cheltenham
Rubio de Urquía R (2003) Estructura fundamental de la explicación de procesos de 'autoorganización' mediante modelos teórico-económicos. In: Rubio de Urquía R, Vázquez FJ, Muñoz FF (eds) Procesos de autoorganización. IIES Francisco de Vitoria-Unión Editorial, Madrid, pp 13–96
Rubio de Urquía R (2005) La naturaleza y estructura fundamental de la teoría económica y las relaciones entre enunciados teórico-económicos y enunciados antropológicos. In: Rubio de Urquía R, Ureña EM, Muñoz FF (eds) Estudios de Teoría Económica y Antropología. IIES Francisco de Vitoria-AEDOS-Unión Editorial, Madrid, pp 23–198
Rubio de Urquía R (2011) La economía española y lo urgente: operar en los fundamentos. In: Velarde J (ed) Lo que hay que hacer con urgencia. Actas, Madrid, pp 411–438
Schelling T (1978) Micromotives and macrobehaviors. Norton, New York
Schumpeter JA (2005 [1932]) Development. (Translated and with an introduction by Becker MC, EBlinger HU, Hedtka U and Knudsen T). J Econ Lit 43(1):112–120
Schumpeter JA (1947a) The creative response in economic history. J Econ Hist 7(2):149–159
Schumpeter JA (1947b) Theoretical problems: theoretical problems of economic growth. J Econ Hist 7:1–9

Searle JR (1995) The construction of social reality. Free Press, New York
Searle JR (2001) Rationality in action. MIT Press, Cambridge
Sen AK (1993) Internal consistency of choice. Econometrica 61(3):495–521
Shackle GLS (1972) Epistemics and economics. Cambridge University Press, Cambridge
Shackle GLS (1977) Time and choice. In: Proceedings of the British Academy, pp 309–329
Simon HA (1962) The architecture of complexity: hierarchic systems. In: Proceedings of the American philosophical society, pp 467–482
Stackelberg H (1946 [1943]) Principios de Teoría Económica [Grundzüge der theoretischen Volkwirschaftslehre] Spanish edition augmented, and revised by the author. Instituto de Estudios Políticos, Madrid
Vanberg VJ (2006) Human intentionality and design in cultural evolution. In: Schubert C, Wangenheim Gv (eds) Evolution and design of institutions. Routledge, Oxford, pp 197–212
Wagner RE (2012) A macro economy as an ecology of plans. J Econ Behav Organ 82(2–3):433–444
Witt U (1996) Innovations, externalities, and the problem of economic progress. Public Choice 89:113–130
Witt U (2003) The evolving economy. Edward Elgar, Cheltenham
Witt U (2006) Evolutionary concepts in economics and biology. J Evol Econ 16(5):473–476
Zimmerman M (1989) Intention, plans, and practical reason. Philos Phenomenol Res 50(1):189–197

Isolation and Technological Innovation

Peter Hall and Robert Wylie

Abstract Despite its importance as a formative influence in evolutionary biology, the notion of isolation has received relatively little attention in evolutionary economics and its application to technological innovation. This paper makes the case that isolation, in many guises, is a pervasive and permanent feature of the economic landscape and that its implications for technological innovation deserve further analysis. Isolation and potential implications for innovation are discussed in the early part of the paper and case studies of two military innovations are then used to illustrate the value of explicitly recognising various forms of isolation in explaining observed aspects of innovation process and outcomes.

1 Introduction

The role of isolation in technological innovation is yet to be fully researched and understood. Yet isolation has been a formative element in evolutionary biology and some innovation scholars have suggested that it might play a key role in launching new technological trajectories (Schot and Geels 2007). Compared with other fundamental assumptions of the modern synthesis in biology, the disruptive potential of isolation has received relatively little attention in the innovation literature. And for those wary of the value of analogies with biological evolution, it would seem to require no more than an acknowledgement of the systemic nature of innovation to warrant research into isolation, particularly in the neo-Schumpeterian framework of evolving complex systems with multiple contributions and connections.

This paper takes the position that incorporating the element of isolation more explicitly in the analysis of technological innovation offers the prospect of insights into the process that might otherwise have been overlooked. To show that this is a

P. Hall (✉) • R. Wylie
School of Business, University of New South Wales, Canberra, Australia
e-mail: p.hall@adfa.edu.au

A. Pyka, J. Foster (eds.), *The Evolution of Economic and Innovation Systems*, Economic Complexity and Evolution, DOI 10.1007/978-3-319-13299-0_9
Reprinted from Journal of Evolutionary Economics, 24(2), Springer 2014.

live issue, we note first that different strands of the innovation literature have taken quite different positions on the implications of isolation, though other terms may often be used to talk about the concept. This leads naturally to a discussion of the meanings of the concept and an analysis of what we see as its potential usefulness in understanding innovation processes. Acknowledging an injunction of Levit et al. (2011), we do not seek to advance a "top-down" general theory of isolation but seek rather to work "bottom-up" and seek to illuminate how isolation of different kinds and degrees has had demonstrable consequences through the use of a comparative case study of direct technology selection.

2 Existing perspectives

Isolation only rarely appears in the literatures of economics and innovation as a formative, analytic concept but is more often used descriptively without specific definition. Schot and Geels (2007: 13) are unusual in adopting the term explicitly as an analytic structuring device and use it to indicate one dimension of a relationship between a "niche" and an existing socio-technical regime. For them, isolation denotes the existence of spatial, social or cognitive separation. If spatial, the isolation indicates geographic separation or distance; if social, a disjunction between the characteristics of existing products and the preferences of specific social groups; if cognitive, a failure by existing suppliers to supply a potential market on the correct or erroneous grounds of insufficient promise. It is more common, however, to find the term applied more informally, as in Levinthal (1998), who talks (p. 222) about "a relatively *isolated* niche" (italics ours) without defining what, exactly, isolation might mean. The qualifier "relatively" also suggests that, like, Schot and Geels (ibid), Levinthal believes isolation is a matter of *degree*, implying that viewed as a variable, the concept is not seen as binary but continuous.

In many contexts, isolation is viewed as a less-than-desirable state. In economic analysis, a state of isolation - as an attribute of a country or economic units within it - is regarded as undesirable for the sacrifice of gains from trade that such a state implies. In connection with potential gains specifically from innovation, evidence suggests that R&D stocks in distant economies have a much weaker effect on a nation's total factor productivity than R&D stocks in countries closer to home (Redding and Venables 2002). In relation to innovation systems, connectedness is seen as both necessary and desirable for bringing together the many and varied contributions of diverse agents required to facilitate successful outcomes. From this perspective, isolation of agents from each other is viewed as an impediment to innovation, as are barriers to knowledge transfers from one sub-system to another. Reflecting this viewpoint, the open innovation approach to innovation thinking (Chesbrough 2006) has gained favour at the expense of the traditional "closed" approach. From another - and evolutionary - perspective, isolation allows the survival of relatively inefficient or lower-quality processes and products after superior versions have emerged elsewhere (Mokyr 1990: 278).

But there are more nuanced perspectives. If isolation permits inferior products and processes to exist temporarily, what is important is not so much a snapshot of the distribution at any moment as the dynamics determining whether isolation is likely to preserve inferiority for a long period or not. In some eyes, isolation from existing socio-technical systems can be viewed as a necessary, if not sufficient, condition for establishing new technological trajectories in the first place, in all probability, however, implying initial developments will yield relatively inferior products and processes (Levinthal 1998; Schot and Geels 2007; Lopolito et al. 2013). In this view, creating isolation in the form of "protected spaces" is a more pressing issue to facilitate the early stages of development than acting on concerns about insulation from competition.

Another view suggests that the degree of isolation may be at least as important as the fact. In this case, it is the cognitive form of isolation that is invoked, where cognition "denotes a broad range of mental activity, including proprioception, perception, sense making, categorization, inference, value judgments, emotions, and feelings" (Nooteboom et al. 2007: 1017). Actors in the innovation sphere are recognised as having heterogeneous life experiences and to understand and evaluate the world differently - with the consequence that "cognitive distance" exists between them. Applied to innovating firms and their performance in technology-based alliances, there is argued to be an inverted U-shaped relationship between cognitive distance and innovation performance. This perspective implies optimal cognitive distance: a high degree of cognitive isolation would be associated with low levels of innovation performance but eradicating cognitive isolation among a community of alliance members would be counterproductive.

Enough has been said here to demonstrate that the existing literature has recognised the relevance of isolation to innovation but that different perspectives on it are fragmented and attribute to it varying implications for innovation performance. We now turn to a treatment of our own, drawing on existing work but seeking to introduce a degree of systematization.

3 Isolation: conceptual and definitional issues

In this section, we address questions of meaning and definition, examining the objects or items identified as isolated, the degree and means of their isolation, and the proximate causes of isolation.

At the core of the idea of isolation is *separation* or lack of connection, a notion that has been applied to physical objects (as with islands in geography) or substances (chemistry); or systems generally, when logically possible connections are absent. Almost always left implicit is that isolation is, by construction, a *relationship*. It makes only incomplete sense to say that "Item A is isolated". Logically, Item A is isolated *from*, so to understand the meaning of the statement fully, we need a reference point for comparison. We need to know that Item A is separated from or lacks connection with another item or group of items, and that it or they are similar enough to it in kind for a comparison to make sense. While the idea of isolation must logically involve a lack of connection between or among objects or items, that does not explain why we do not view as equivalent statements, "Item A is isolated from B", and "B is isolated from Item A". We believe this puzzle deserves further attention, but we do not think that anything significant rests on its resolution for the analysis of innovation and isolation. We believe it more important to consider the *entities, separating factors and types, degree and durability of isolation, its causes,* and *its implications for innovation.*

Entities of many kinds can be in a state of separation from each other: pieces of land, populations of animals, groups of human beings, electrical and electronic components, decision-making agents in economic and social systems (e.g., individuals, and individual households and firms), groups of firms, markets, domains of application of a given technology, etc. When we talk about isolation, we need to be clear what entity is being referred to and note that isolation can occur at many levels.

Given the entity in question, the factor or feature that separates it or is the reason for its lack of connection to other similar entities can also vary widely. It is the generic description of the *separating factor* that determines the nature or *type* of the isolation in any particular case. Channels and other bodies of water separating an island and mountain ranges separating human social groups are geographical (strictly, physical geographical), so the isolation in these cases is geographical. A wall is a physical barrier to communication among prisoners, so the isolation is physical. In economic and innovation systems, separating factors may be geographical or physical, and, as noted in our earlier review, social or cognitive. In some cases, one form of isolation may coincide with another, as with geographical and linguistic separation in human populations; in others, a specific form of isolation may be observed in the absence of any other form of isolation, as with social separation rooted in religious belief within a given geographical and otherwise undifferentiated social environment.

It is not difficult to think of specific examples of separating or isolating factors in economic and innovation systems: e.g., agents lacking information about potential trading partners and opportunities, government policy on or regulation of trade (e.g., import controls), and the costs of interacting and transferring knowledge (i.e., transaction costs). What quickly emerges, however, is that the isolation of economic and innovation entities may take many and varied forms. Our examples might be called informational isolation, policy or political isolation, and transaction-cost isolation. They could also be subsumed or aggregated within the more general terms "social" or "cognitive" - but there can be a risk of burying insight in the process.

Isolation is not necessarily a binary variable - though in the case of a broken electronic circuit, for example: "broke is broke". In many cases, however, the *degree* of isolation varies: greater distance of an island from land may lead us, for example, to talk of a "more isolated" island. In non-geographic or non-physical cases, degree or extent is more difficult to define and measure. The "social" isolation of Schot and Geels may be amenable to precise calibration if: (1) the product involved can be defined exclusively in terms of measurable constituents such as those seen on the packaging of foodstuffs; (2) the preferences of actual and potential consumers can be expressed exactly and exclusively in relation to those constituents. But consumer preferences have as much to do with perceptions, image and taste as with the physical content of foodstuffs. And many products possess or lack appeal for reasons (like status) that are only indirectly or partially related to physical or performance characteristics.

Of particular interest to scholars who believe history counts, isolation may be more *durable* in some cases than others. When we turn to cause (see below), duration of isolation may be a key criterion for determining whether significant effects appear or not, depending on how quickly change processes occur under isolated conditions.

On the question of *cause*, the separating factors noted above may be viewed as the *proximate* causes of the instances of isolation we observe, but a full causal explanation requires more. If agents lack information on the potential benefits of interaction, why is that so? If governments regulate trade, what is their purpose? It is important to note that some of these causes are the result of conditions *exogenous* or *external* to the individual actors and groups involved but some of them are *self-imposed*. Isolation arising from information poverty based in wilful ignorance is isolation as much as that arising from externally determined information deprivation. But knowing the difference makes a big difference to how one understands particular cases and what to do about them.

More generally, the current state of isolation of an entity may reflect: (i) a past external shock or force on a larger whole that separated the entity from it; (ii) an internal process within a larger pre-existing system that caused it to fragment; (iii) in a social system, a choice by the entity to separate itself (secede) from the larger entity; (iv) a deliberate act by "authorities" in a pre-existing social system to expel or excommunicate the entity. Some of these states have been precipitated by events exogenous to the now-isolated entity and others have resulted from choices by decision-makers within the isolated entity and isolation can, thus, be considered self-imposed and endogenous.

4 Implications for economics and innovation

We take innovation to mean the process by which new products and production processes are developed and introduced to market or use. The process may involve much or little development of new technological knowledge but will always call for using knowledge in ways not seen before - at the level of world, nation or firm. Innovation calls for many and diverse contributions of which invention, adding to the existing stock of technological knowledge in the form of new ideas, perhaps developed through research, is only one. Invention may, but often does not, lead to innovation. Once introduced, innovations themselves may prove successful or otherwise. If successful, innovations diffuse over time, usually undergoing modification, refinement and segmentation along the way.

In the previous section, we noted that isolation takes many forms and applies at various levels of aggregation. But innovations also take many forms and, at any moment, may be farther from or closer to reaching the point of first use or market entry, and may have been more or less developed and refined since initial introduction. Various classifications of innovation exist. An approach that we find useful distinguishes both between the maturity of *technological solutions* already operating within a given lineage and the maturity of the *domains* in which technological solutions might be *applied* (Gregor and Hevner 2013). Immaturity in both dimensions defines "inventions", a high level of maturity in both dimensions points to innovation incremental or routine in nature, characterised as "adoption". The case of "exaptation" involves co-opting technology already mature in (i.e., adapted to) one domain of application and putting features of it to work in a different domain where such technology has not as yet been used, as when compact disks developed to record and replay sound was put to use in storing data for computers (Dew et al. 2004: 73). The remaining case is "improvement" - working on a relatively immature technological solution in a mature application domain to find better ways of doing things, i.e., a process of adaptation.

Thinking in terms of cost, risk and uncertainty, we would argue that invention in these terms is, in general, the most uncertain and potentially costly form of innovation. Though exaptation is also uncertain, the cost of *reusing* existing technologies, albeit in a different or new domain of application, should - usually - be relatively low compared with creating them de novo (Dew et al. 2004: 81). Straightforward adoption should, at most, carry a little risk and imply least cost of the four. Improvement will be riskier than adoption but may or may not in specific cases be more costly than exaptation, depending on the obstacles encountered along the road which, ex ante, will be partly unknown to the agents involved.

Turning to cause and effect, no *general* case exists to say that isolation is a necessary condition for innovation: there are too many forms of isolation and too many types of innovation for that to be uniformly true and examples abound of co-operation, team work and collaboration in all of the variants of innovation noted in the previous paragraph. It is more common, in fact, for scholars to argue that innovation *requires* interaction and for us the interesting question whether, in fact, that must always be true - and if not, why not. In other words, when, if ever, is isolation an important factor or even the most important - for the whole innovation process or a part of it, and for some parts rather than others? We divide answering that question into two parts, the first relating to isolation exogenous to innovating agents and the second to agents' self-imposed isolation.

(a) Exogenous isolation

In this case, the isolation of an economic environment, or population, or decision-making unit occurs for reasons over which those in the isolated entity had no choice. Thus, they may be isolated for geographical, political or social reasons by the choices and actions of others, or isolated "at birth", as it were, and as yet unconnected.

To consider whether exogenous isolation *prompts* innovation that would not otherwise have occurred, we note that stimuli to innovate may arise either from an isolating *event* or in the context of a *state* of isolation. If an exogenous event suddenly causes isolation, the separation may: (i) in and of itself *require* innovation within the newly isolated context (e.g., to produce essential goods that were previously available from external sources, but no longer are); (ii) set in motion processes of gradual change, initially almost imperceptibly, as techniques inherited from earlier, non-isolated times are *adapted* to the conditions specifically associated with the newly formed domain of application (Levinthal 1998). If an environment is "born isolated" - as often occurs when new domains of application arise (Levinthal 1998), that may set in motion adaptive processes, as noted above, or possibly innovative efforts to forge and extend connections that do not initially exist.

The first key point here is that the isolated entity or population lacks or is denied access to the stock of and developments in technology (knowledge, artefacts, institutional support) available elsewhere. In extreme cases (e.g., through political sanctions backed by military action), an isolated population may be denied all such access; in other cases, access may be denied selectively (for example, a superpower may discriminate between close and favoured allies and other states when determining the extent of access it gives to its home-grown military technology) or made available, but only at higher cost. Equally important in determining the implications and consequences of isolation, however, is that the isolated entity retains access to the stock of technological knowledge, capabilities and artefacts which lie within its own control. How it proceeds by way of innovation depends on the applications it sees as being most important for its needs and how well fitted is the technology it already possesses for meeting those needs. We now consider the particular *types of innovation* we think likely to arise.

In the case of what they perceive as essential requirements, populations or nations will put a high priority on technological applications that permit those requirements to be met. The same will be true of producer organisations in relation to performance characteristics they consider essential. When a sudden isolation of population (or organisation) leaves it dependent on the technology that remains under its control and at its disposal, its innovation response will depend on the applicability of that technology to the essential requirement. If its applicable technological solutions are lacking or very immature, decision-makers may conclude there is no option but invention: isolation prompts attempts to develop entirely new solutions if technology that addressed essential requirements in the past is now no longer available. On the other hand, if features of the existing available technology lend themselves to new uses for which they were not originally designed, exaptation would be another alternative. Improving the existing available technology would be a possibility only if it had been designed to address the essential requirement in the first place and offered the prospect of rapid development rather than gradual adaptation.

Only a minority of technological solutions, however, are developed to meet essential requirements: many meet preferences expressed with varying degrees of intensity by larger or smaller sub-groups in a population. If a community becomes isolated, its preferences may take a path of evolution divergent from that that would have occurred in the absence of isolation. If, as is common, preferences change slowly, the resulting shift in market environment will be gradual and the forms of innovation induced by isolation are likely to be incremental improvements - building on existing knowledge to find better ways of meeting preferences as preferences change. Even gradual change in preferences may, on occasions, find value in exaptation, however, since even modest changes in preferences over the *characteristics* of goods, a la Lancaster, might best be met with substantial qualitative changes in the goods themselves. In either case, the path of change will track the way preferences evolve in ways distinctive of the isolated environment, reflecting the specific resources available in that environment.

In the case of isolated organisations, the issue is choice of production technique able to support survival. If isolation implies absent or weak competition, decision-makers will face little threat or incentive to do more than undertake incremental or routine innovation consistent with learning-by-doing - and they may not even do that. The technique(s) that happen to be initially available and applied in a newly isolated environment will tend to determine the subsequent path of technological evolution for that unit. When we observe states of longstanding isolation, technological innovation in each isolated production unit will thus have followed a cumulative path determined by the conditions and resources peculiar to the isolated environment in which they operate rather than those elsewhere. Some units may be more efficient than others but the isolation of each of them permits the relatively inefficient and their relatively inefficient techniques to survive for longer than if they had not been isolated.

(b) Self-imposed isolation

Isolation is self-imposed when decision-making agents choose to isolate themselves, their organisation or their economic domain from their broader environment. Here the key isolating event is a conscious decision by an individual, management or government to operate separately: as an individual relative to the rest of a group of community; as a firm relative to other suppliers in its industry; as a nation relative to other countries or the rest of the world. As in the case of exogenous separation, the event may, of itself, prompt innovation, or change the direction of innovation. Much depends on the technology base remaining under the control of the entity when it separates and the pressures of essential requirements and preference structures.

At the level of individuals, isolation may be self-imposed more readily in the case of invention than in forms of innovation requiring more resources and more diverse inputs. "The inventor is ultimately alone in his or her attempt to make something work", says Mokyr (1990: 11). Further, start-up innovators will often choose isolation, in this case from capital markets, rather than surrender control. On the other hand, later-stage development work on applications and commercialisation, by contrast, calls for a more diverse range of inputs (some of which individual enterprises may need to source externally) and much larger investment (which may require joint ventures and links to capital markets).

A different argument relating immature technology to isolation appears in the literature of technological transitions and innovation niches (Schot and Geels 2007; Genus and Coles 2008; Lopolito et al. 2013). Here self-imposed isolation appears in the guise of socioeconomic spaces that institutions or organisations choose to protect to permit inventions (in the hope of radical innovations) to be developed and tested when normal market mechanisms would lead a novel approach to be rejected. Business incubators and government -funded defence technology facilities offer examples.

While this discussion tends to suggest that isolation is a characteristic of - and may facilitate - innovation with relatively immature technology, it is neither necessary nor sufficient for innovation of that kind. In the case of invention, research and design teams as much as individuals are commonplace working on new technology in large corporations. Lockheed Martin's Skunk Works producing revolutionary aerospace designs since World War 2 is a good example. When technological solutions mature, there are, equally, prolific examples of firms that make a strategic choice for isolation from potential collaborators or suppliers when they monopolise the use and development of a dominant design through IP protection or abandon R&D joint ventures to run their competitive race alone. Such examples suggest that it is not so much the range and cost of resources that yield isolation but, importantly, that firms *choose to isolate themselves* because of the perceived prospects of *appropriating returns* on innovation investments greater than they believe would accrue if they shared more or were more connected. The same may apply to governments.

5 Potential net benefits

What influence does exogenous isolation have over the *value or net benefit* of innovation? We have hypothesised that, in general, invention is potentially the most costly and also most uncertain of the innovation types. But there seems no way of knowing in advance whether, *in particular cases* aimed at generating an innovative technological solution (in isolated conditions or not), exaptation or improvement might not turn out less successfully and more expensively than invention. On the other hand, will isolation make every form of innovation more uncertain and/or costly than it would have been in the absence of isolation? Will it make each and every instance of innovation less certain and more costly? Will it make the totality of innovation in the isolated environment less certain and more costly than in the absence of isolation? Clearly, the answers to these questions will depend heavily on the particulars of the technologies and resources in the isolated environment; and in cases where isolation is longstanding, what adaptation has occurred since the initial isolating event. These particulars need to be compared with those that decision-makers would have confronted in the absence of the isolating event or in a putative alternative world where isolation was removed. We suggest that the answers to the questions cannot, logically, resolve into a bland certainty that isolation will always produce inferior outcomes. We also suggest that perfectly general conditions supporting the value of connectedness cannot be derived. We need, instead, to look at particular cases and to pursue these matters further we seek empirical evidence in the case studies that follow.

6 From general argument to evidence

Our starting point is that isolation, as a positive matter, remains a widely observed feature of economic life - in some cases arising from circumstances beyond the control of decision-makers but, in many, actually adopted as a strategic choice. What we have argued to this point is that such isolation often has consequences for innovation, both in terms of prompting innovation that would not otherwise have occurred and in terms of shaping the path of innovation to take forms and directions it would not otherwise have taken. This seems to us too important to be lost in the tide of argument supposing and supporting connectedness. We have said much less about whether we think innovation under isolated conditions is more beneficial than in a more connection-rich environment though if isolation prompts or shapes innovation to more closely meet the preferences of sub-populations who would otherwise have been ignored, there does seem to us to be the starting point for an argument, in some cases, in its favour.

While we do not claim to be able to formulate a *general* principle of the impact and effects of isolation, we think there is value in following the advice of Levit et al. (2011) to mimic the approach of evolutionary scholars in biology and work from the ground up by exploring specific cases. We have chosen to examine two military innovation cases since they seem to offer a natural basis for a research question. The two innovations relate to a similar body of technological solutions, radar, and were developed in two countries, Australia and Sweden, of roughly equivalent levels of economic development, in each case with aspirations to be "middle-level" military powers. The two innovations turned out very differently in terms of cost, time to delivery and exportability (a proxy for quality) and it is interesting to ask why. The differences could be explained in a variety of ways but in this paper we argue that isolation in each case played a role - in quite different ways - in prompting and shaping the innovation experiences of the two countries. It is this role we seek to focus on.

This study of defence innovation should be of interest to scholars of innovation more generally for other reasons. At the macroeconomic level, understanding of economic growth in the USA and beyond has benefited from analysing the contributions of military innovation (Ruttan 2006); in relation to economy-wide spillovers and externalities, Eliasson (2010) discusses aerospace innovation in Sweden; in relation to the process of economic evolution, government defence procurement offers insight into selection directly over technologies rather than indirectly, through market mechanisms, over the goods technology produces (Dosi and Nelson 1994); and the role of the military in constructing "protected spaces" for the development of strategically important innovations has been recognised in relation to research on technological transitioning (Schot and Geels 2007).

7 Case study

7.1 Australia

1. The innovation: JORN over-the-horizon radar

The Australian case relates to the desire of Australian governments to exploit the ionospheric refraction of certain radar frequencies to meet a requirement for surveillance of the continent's vast northern maritime approaches. In Fig. 1 (adapted from Sinnott (1988), p. 210) we show how a high-frequency (HF) signal, broadcast from a radar transmitter, can be refracted by the ionosphere sufficiently to illuminate a target area of the earth's surface. Objects in the target area will scatter the incident radar illumination in all directions. A small amount of that incident radiation is refracted back via the ionosphere where it can be detected by an appropriately configured radar receiver.

Ionospheric refraction of HF radar can, in principle, be used to detect both aircraft and surface ships at ranges typically of 1,000–3,000 kms. But because the ionosphere is not entirely predictable, effective OTHR operation requires real time monitoring of the ionosphere in order to determine which frequencies and radar parameters should be used to illuminate a given area of the earth's surface to best effect. Radar signal strength falls off with increasing distance between radar and target and targets like aircraft are very small compared to the area illuminated. The faint return from the target must be extracted from a mass of radio noise and 'clutter'.

We now turn to the Australian OTHR innovation process. In the 1960s, as a serendipitous by-product of efforts to track the re-entry of ICBMs into the earth's atmosphere, US, UK and Australian scientists had begun investigating

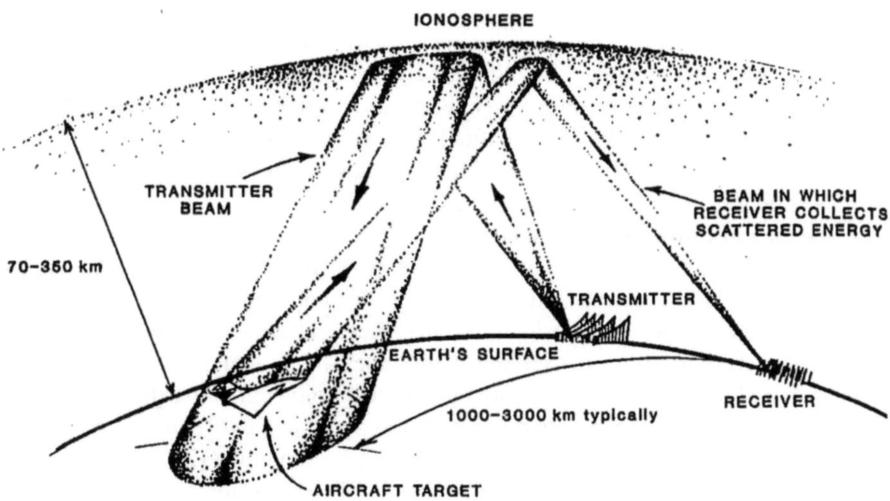

Fig. 1 Detection of over-the-horizon target by ionospheric refraction of HF radar signals

the use of ionospheric refraction of HF radar signals to detect potentially hostile aircraft well beyond the horizon. An Australian scientist, John Strath, convinced the Australian government to investige the refractive behaviour of the ionosphere over Australia. The resulting project (Geebung) established that in contrast to ionospheric conditions elsewhere, the ionosphere over Australia was sufficiently stable to permit the consistent refraction of high frequency (HF) radar signals required to detect targets at least 1,000 kms away.

Subsequent research established the feasibility of detecting aircraft at ranges of 1,000–3,000 kms and of detecting and tracking them by steering the radar beam. However, this was not sufficient to establish general perceptions of OTHR as superior to all other broad-area surveillance technology solutions such as airborne early-warning and control (AEWC) aircraft. The two factors leading to selection of the OTHR solution over the alternatives were, firstly, the enthusiastic political sponsorship of OTHR by the then-minister for Defence, Kim Beazley, a champion of the technology for its potential to underpin defence "self-reliance", the central element of Australian strategic thinking at the time and, secondly, an anticipated cost advantage of OTHR compared to AEWC aircraft. A formal decision to acquire the network of radars required - to be known as the Jindalee Operational Radar Network (JORN) - was made in 1986.

In the ensuing procurement process, the search for suppliers was, as a matter of policy, confined to Australian businesses, albeit with the requirement that they would team with suitable overseas companies. The motivating idea here was to foster the development of a cadre of "national champions" able to provide the domestic industrial component of defence self-reliance. The government-owned telecommunications provider, Telecom (later Telstra) was awarded the contract (with GEC Marconi as its principal sub-contractor) in 1991 but was replaced in 1997 by a joint venture between the Australian company Tenix and the US company Lockheed Martin.

The innovation itself, the functioning system, entered service in 2003 at an estimated total cost of AUD 1.24 billion, 17 years after the decision to proceed and 12 years after the initial contract was awarded. It has since operated successfully (McNally and Cronin 2006) and benefited from upgrades built on learning-by-doing and learning-by-using. The specific technology has not, however, been taken up by defence and security organisations outside Australia.

2. Aspects and dimensions of isolation

Physical isolation is a well-recognised feature of Australia's geography, surrounded as it is on all sides by sea, and distant from the imperial nation, Britain, that - in its formative years -established colonies there, offered the principal markets for its primary exports, and supplied it for much of its history with technology, capital and skilled labour. The economic and technological consequences of such geographical isolation have been described, among others, by Blainey (1966), Todd (1995), Barlow (2006), Battersby and Ewing (2005), Battersby (2006) and McLean (2013). But, an aspect of the country's physical isolation not, to our knowledge, invoked in earlier work relates to the ionospheric conditions over Australia.

The ionosphere over the earth's equator is relatively stable compared to the ionosphere over the planet's magnetic poles. In using ionospherically refracted radar signals to monitor the Australian continent's northern maritime approaches, Australian scientists took advantage of, firstly, the nation's location south of the equator and of, secondly, the equatorial ionosphere's stability over the region of primary Australian strategic interest to the nation's north. Australia's geo-strategic circumstances encouraged it to make greater use of OTHR compared to many other countries of the world, particularly in the northern hemisphere. These circumstances exogenously define a dimension of the physical environment that sets Australia apart, and positions it differently, from other nations where essential strategic requirements include over-the-horizon visibility of potentially hostile movements.

Australia is no stranger to self-imposed isolation and for much of the 20th century, Australian manufacturing operated behind protective tariffs only since the 1980s largely (though not completely) dismantled. In the sphere of defence, however, self-imposed isolation took a more specific form in the period of formative thinking about JORN, a political commitment to "self-reliance", which meant establishing and maintaining armed forces able to defend Australia without relying on combat forces of other countries. Self -reliance also had an industrial dimension which privileged Australian manufacturers over overseas suppliers in the interests of defence. Self-reliance was enthusiastically espoused by the Labor government elected in 1983 and remained current in defence white papers throughout the period of JORN's development. In JORN's case, moreover, Australian defence planners considered the innovation to be too strategically important to be shared with any but the closest of allies. Australian defence planners placed even the limited market for JORN off limits and declined to permit Australian companies to promote the system to potential overseas buyers.

3. Implications of isolation for innovation

Australia's ionospheric isolation - in the form of ionospheric conditions separate from those over nations facing similar strategic challenges - was a key exogenous characteristic of the environment in which this defence innovation was conducted. Australian scientists considered the OTHR technology developed by the US (which had to contend with much more demanding ionospheric conditions) less than ideal for Australia's more benign conditions. Hence, if Australia envisaged adopting an OTHR-based solution to its broad area surveillance requirement, it needed to either undertake or commission R&D and system development tailored to its specific circumstances something close to invention in terms of the schema suggested earlier. However, the exogenous isolation we have identified here was a necessary rather than sufficient condition for the innovation process to go ahead - given that AEWC aircraft able to undertake broad-area surveillance were available in international defence markets. For JORN to proceed, it had to be specifically chosen as a way ahead and supported with sufficient and durable funding.

The JORN project offered the prospect of achieving the strategically vital objective of broad-area surveillance over Australia's northern maritime approaches, though it was known to be potentially high-risk and high-cost (Gilligan 1984) consistent with our argument earlier that 'invention' in the usage adopted here is likely to give rise to such implications. The Australian government decided to proceed nonetheless with JORN under conditions of self-imposed isolation, i.e., to do it indigenously, partly because, simply, it was believed that the nation had the capability to do so provided it could leverage overseas expertise. It was also believed that implementing JORN would give Australia technological independence from overseas suppliers of essential defence systems (at a time when denial of access to key elements of military technology was a high-level concern to Australian governments) and that it would contribute to building the sophisticated indigenous defence industry base seen as a necessary element of self-reliance. These factors prompted the then-Minister of Defence to promote and fund the project, despite its budgetary cost and the availability of alternatives.

The commitment to indigenous implementation (i.e., self-imposed isolation) also shaped the innovation process that followed the decision to proceed. The Australian Government insisted on giving the lead in the contract to local industry, with visibly detrimental consequences. Work undertaken in Geebung and Jindalee A and B showed that Australian government scientists and engineers were equipped to take a sophisticated idea to the point of establishing technical feasibility. However, initial efforts by Australian companies to implement JORN as a full-scale functioning system were hampered by their lack of prior experience, resulting in technical difficulties, cost escalation and sluggish progress. By 1996, 80 % of the JORN prime contract target price had been spent, 80 % of the schedule had elapsed, but only 20 % of the system's configuration items had passed the critical design review stage. (McNally 1996). It was only when self-imposed isolation was relaxed and Lockheed Martin expertise brought to bear that progress on the project gathered speed and was completed.

Exogenous and self-imposed isolation thus provided the impetus that moved the JORN innovation beyond the stage of a potentially "good idea' that would never have been exploited. Self-imposed isolation also fostered the indigenous capacity to support and upgrade the system, but at the price of a 6 year schedule overrun and a cost blowout of over 50 % when compared to the estimates at the time of the original contract.

7.2 Sweden

1. The innovation: ERIEYE airborne over-the-horizon radar

ERIEYE is an airborne early warning system, i.e., a radar mounted on an aircraft to collect information about potential threats and provide early warning of attack. By elevating the transmitter on an aircraft, the radar can cover a much larger area than is possible from a ground-based system like JORN - which, instead, uses the ionosphere as a mirror. As an innovation, ERIEYE grew out of a Swedish Materiel Administration (FMV) commission in 1978–80, inviting the Swedish communications equipment manufacturer L.M. Ericsson to investigate the feasibility of adapting an existing radar (the PS-46/A radar developed for the JA-

37 Viggen aircraft) to meet changing Air Force surveillance radar requirements. Ericsson's investigations analysed the feasibility and utility of combining the existing radar with an electronically scannable antenna, enabling the rapid shifting and reconfiguration of the radar beam required for airborne early warning but without mechanical movement of the antenna itself.

The 1978–80 Ericsson studies suggested that combining radar and active phased array antenna technologies in a "pod" mounted outside an aircraft offered a potential solution to Air Force requirements. In 1985, FMV engaged Ericsson to develop a technology demonstrator based on their "pod" concept to confirm the studies' conclusions and refine assessment of the risk involved. This involved: (i) an example of exaptation, combining an established technology (the PS-46/A surveillance radar) with a new technology (active scanned array antennas) to create a new application (in this case an airborne early warning system); (ii) an example of technology improvement, the maturing of an immature technology (gallium arsenide integrated circuitry) to the point at which it could be applied to solve a problem (the rapid tuning and manipulation of radar beams to enable the detection and tracking of small, fleeting targets in a cluttered environment).

Flight testing of the Ericsson demonstrator began in 1990, 5 years after the initial design work for the demonstrator. The demonstrator performed so well that FMV authorised procurement of long lead items in 1989, before concluding a contract with Ericsson for full scale production of ERIEYE in 1993 (Lonroth 2010) The Swedish Air Force accepted ERIEYE into service in 1997, a little over a decade after FMV and Ericsson decided to invest in the demonstrator. The ERIEYE innovation constituted a major enhancement of Sweden's air defence capability, until then primarily ground-based. Typically, ERIEYE can detect fighter-sized targets at about 350 kms range, nearly twice that of ground-based systems already described.

In terms of resources invested, this advance was achieved at an overall cost of perhaps AUD180 million. In 1992, FMV awarded Ericsson a AUD171.5 million contract (SEK 1,200 million at 2012 exchange rate) to supply six ERIEYE radars for the Swedish Airforce (Jane's 2012), i.e., the number required to provide the coverage of Sweden's Baltic approaches considered necessary in the Cold War. To this amount should be added the AUD6.1 million (SEK43 million) FMV paid to Ericsson for the ERIEYE prototype.

The collapse of the Soviet Union removed the pressing strategic incentive for the Swedish Air Force to procure additional ERIEYE systems. But ERIEYE attracted overseas buyers and Ericsson and, later, SAAB continued to develop and adapt the ERIEYE technology along a trajectory shaped by the requirements of particular export customers as diverse as Brazil, Mexico, Greece, Thailand and Pakistan.

2. Aspects and dimensions of isolation

Sweden's isolation was substantially self-imposed and reflected past decisions that had been taken with political intent. Sweden had adopted apolicy of armed neutrality dates as early as 1838, after which Sweden sought to convince its neighbours, notably Russia and the USSR, that it would remain neutral in any war. To this end Sweden ostentatiously avoided entering into military alliances in peace. But Swedish governments recognised that the viability of Sweden's armed neutrality policy depended on Sweden convincing other countries that it had both the will and the ability to defend its sovereignty. In establishing a credible defence capability Sweden's choices were shaped initially by its World War Two experience, when its initial inability to obtain overseas technology was followed by Germany withholding technology until Sweden complied with its demands. After World War Two, Sweden sought to develop, as far as practicable, indigenous solutions to its military capability requirements so as to avoid compromising its policy of non-alignment in peace and neutrality in war by having to negotiate the release of advanced (especially US) technology.

Sweden's armed neutrality led it to make air defence choices which not only reduced the utility of non-Swedish airborne surveillance systems but also implied a degree of technological isolation. For example, runways at military bases were designed to be too short for use by either Warsaw Pact or NATO aircraft. Similarly, the US-sourced Grumman E2-C Hawkeye AWEC aircraft would have needed expensive modification to link into Swedish command and control arrangements and a major adjustment of Sweden's concept of air defence operations.

3. Implications of isolation for innovation

For a country separated from a potentially hostile Soviet Union only by the Baltic and Finland, armed neutrality in a Cold War context required from Sweden a rapid-response capability against the threat of missile or military aircraft attack from the east. This, in turn, was the prompt for a superior surveillance system and, if required, the technological innovation to achieve it.

As noted earlier, airborne systems offered a detection range much superior to ground-based coverage (in the absence of OTHR which offered no solution in the turbulent ionospheric conditions relevant to Swedish defence). Sweden did not possess such a system in the late 1970s though, in principle, it could have entered the international defence market and sought to have one developed. But self-imposed isolation in the form of armed neutrality created a strong preference to resource the development of such systems locally while, as noted above, existing airbase arrangements heavily constrained the usefulness of the overseas-sourced airborne surveillance solutions that were available. Such conditions naturally tended to shape a preference for indigenous innovation.

The specifics of the direction innovation then took reflected the technological capabilities that Sweden had available to it at the time of the decision to develop an airborne surveillance radar - crucially a legacy of Sweden's longstanding commitment to neutrality (a form of self-imposed isolation). Because of Sweden's strategic policy stance, its government had historically given priority to its national industry as the source of its military supplies and the Swedish defence industry base was, as a consequence, well attuned to the strategic requirements of the government and had developed production and innovation capabilities fitted to them. Development and production specifically of radar in Sweden was concentrated at Ericsson which, as Sweden's predominant manufacturer of communications equipment, had produced radio and telephone communication systems for the Swedish Armed Forces during the 1940s. Ericsson's radar division then became Sweden's prime repository of radar expertise (both military and civilian) through the Cold War period and

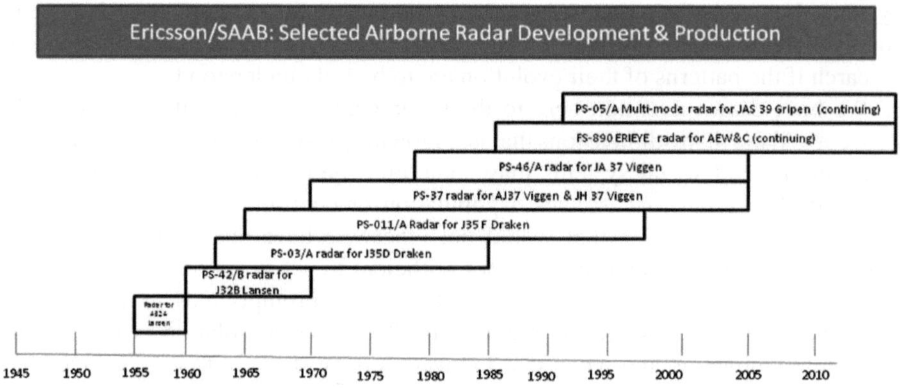

Fig. 2 Ericsson/SAAB: selected airborne radar development and production

successive programs of specifically airborne radar developments at Ericsson/SAAB are illustrated in Fig. 2 (adapted from SAAB 2005).

As Fig. 2 suggests, Swedish airborne radar development constitutes a clear technological trajectory, initiated by Ericsson's production under license of French CSF radars in the late 1950s and sustained by its ability to overlap successive programs of radar development and production to meet the progressively more demanding requirements of successive generations of Swedish fighter aircraft. When the Swedish Government addressed the Air Force's need for earlier warning of Soviet airborne assault, it could turn to a component of its indigenous industry and technology base that possessed a stock of accumulated knowledge and manufacturing experience relevant to the purpose. The specifics of the ERIEYE system reflect a government decision to resource Ericsson to be the innovator. And in that context, Ericsson's particular stocks of accumulated knowledge and experience inevitably shaped the technological details of the final outcome. ERIEYE was not so specifically moulded to Swedish conditions that it could not be used elsewhere. Isolation during development did not impede subsequent diffusion since the technology proved adaptable in other environments and the producer was keen to sell and reap profit on sales - and was not inhibited by government from doing so.

8 Conclusion

In this paper we have argued that isolation has been a relatively neglected dimension of analysis in the study of the economics of innovation, evolutionary and otherwise. Isolation, however, appears in its many forms to be a pervasive element of systems of all kinds, and to have real and important consequences. We are sympathetic to arguments promoting the potential benefits of connectivity in economic and social systems, but we believe that isolation will continue to be a feature of such systems for the foreseeable future and that its causes and consequences deserve ongoing research if the patterns of their evolution are to be fully understood.

We have drawn attention here to the separatedness that lies at the core of the concept and the many dimensions that isolation may take. And we note that isolation in economic and social systems may sometimes be exogenous but is often self-imposed. The event that isolates a population or decision-making unit may, we argue, prompt innovation that would not otherwise have occurred. However, an isolating event is neither necessary nor sufficient to set in motion a new bout of innovation, and innovation processes that isolation prompts may or may not be beneficial. Ongoing research is required to clarify when isolation is most likely to prompt innovation and when that innovation is most likely to be beneficial. As Mokyr (1990) has said, there may be "no one-line explanations here, no simple theorems' (p. 299) - because a range of exogenous social, economic and political factors in the environment may be needed for inventions to be developed into successful innovations, and even when such conditions exist, the technological ideas they would nurture might not arise. We would add that innovation also takes many forms and that isolating events may prompt some forms of innovation more readily than others.

Whether isolation prompts beneficial innovation depends importantly on the direction innovation takes once initiated. That direction will be determined, in part, by the specific nature of the isolation that characterises the environment in which the innovation evolves - and, ultimately, how innovation reshapes that environment. In the case of technological innovation, a key point is that the isolating event becomes relevant when it denies a population or decision-making entity access to technological knowledge and artefacts which would be available to it if it had maintained or were able to achieve ongoing connection with the system of which it was, or might form, a part. When such access is denied, or is unavailable, the isolated entity must build on what it had at the point of separation and the direction innovation takes will reflect uniquely what it does with what it had to start with.

We accept that top-down, general theorising about evolutionary issues raises serious methodological questions. Thus, in this paper, we have turned to specific cases to take a bottom-up approach to seeking insight into the influence of isolation on innovation processes and outcomes. The cases are drawn from the sphere of defence, an area that has proved fertile for the study of innovation in the recent past but is particularly well suited for a discussion of the implications of isolation.

In brief, we have shown that in two comparable cases - military exploitation of radar for broad area surveillance in Australia and Sweden - isolation made a difference. Exogenous (ionospheric) isolation in Australia played an influential role in prompting government commitment to an initially science-driven innovation, JORN over-the-horizon radar. In the absence of such isolation, it is hard to believe that preferences for the already-available AEWC system would not have held sway. In Sweden, self-imposed isolation in the form of a choice for armed neutrality led the government to focus on indigenously available technology when it came to consider its choice of surveillance systems. This, in turn, led to a solution suggested by an existing technological trajectory built on longstanding cumulative innovation at Ericsson. In the absence of a history of self-imposed isolation, Sweden may not in the past have made the infrastructural investments that prevented it from considering other airborne radar technologies that could have been adopted instead of ERIEYE.

Once the initial decisions were made, politically self-imposed isolation in accordance with defence "self-reliance" took JORN along a path of implementation that proved more costly and less productive than had been anticipated. As subsequent arrangements involving Lockheed Martin demonstrated, the process would likely have been less expensive and delivery less tardy had there been greater readiness to recognise the potential inadequacy of indigenous managerial capability in relation to advanced technology implementation in the first place. By way of contrast, Sweden's choice of indigenous development and implementation led it to a supplier already highly experienced in undertaking such projects.

Acknowledgments The authors gratefully acknowledge Stan Metcalfe for his stimulating insights and support over many years; comments on earlier versions of the paper from seminar participants at INGENIO, Polytechnic University of Valencia, especially Jordi Molas Gallart, and at the 14th International Schumpeter Society Conference, Brisbane, especially Ulrich Witt; and the most helpful critiques of two anonymous referees. The authors take full responsibility for all views expressed and analysis undertaken in the paper.

References

Barlow T (2006) The Australian miracle: an innovative nation revisited. Picador, Sydney

Battersby B (2006) Does distance matter? The effect of geographic isolation on productivity levels. Treasury working paper 2006-3 (April). Australian Treasury, Canberra

Battersby B, Ewing R (2005) International trade performance: the gravity of Australia's remoteness. Treasury working paper 2005-3 (June). Australian Treasury, Canberra

Blainey G (1966) The Tyranny of distance: how distance shaped Australia's history. Sun Books, Melbourne

Chesbrough H (2006) Open business models. Harvard Business School Press, Cambridge, MA

Dew N, Sarasvathy SD, Venkataraman S (2004) The economic implications of exaptation. J Evol Econ 14:69–84

Dosi G, Nelson RR (1994) An introduction to evolutionary theories in economics. J Evol Econ 4:153– 172

Eliasson G (2010) Advanced procurement as industrial policy: the aircraft industry as a Technical University. Springer, New York, London

Feist GJ (1998) A meta-analysis of personality in scientific and artistic creativity. Pers Soc Psychol Rev 2(4):290–309

Gilligan M (1984) A report to the secretary and CDF on over-the-horizon radar, executive summary. (Unpublished.)

Genus A, Coles A-M (2008) Rethinking the multi-level perspective of technological transitions. Res Policy 39(9):1436–1445

Gregor S, Hevner A (2013) Positioning and presenting design science research for maximum impact. MIS Quarterly

Jane's radar and electron warfare systems (2012) Jane's Information Group, Alexandria, VA

Levinthal D (1998) The slow pace of technological change: gradualism and punctuation in technological change. Ind Corp Change 7(2):217–247

Levit GS, Hossfeld U, Witt U (2011) Can Darwinism be generalized? and of what use would this be?J Evol Econ 21:545–562
Lonroth C-G (2010) Interview with R. Wylie, Stockholm
Lopolito A, Morone P, Taylor R (2013) Emerging innovation niches: an agent based model. Res Policy 42:1225–1238
McLean IW (2013) Why Australia prospered: the shifting sources of economic growth. Princeton University Press, Princeton
McNally R (1996) Jindalee operational radar network (Performance Audit No 28, 1995–96). Australian National Audit Office, Canberra, p 21
McNally R, Cronin C (2006) Acceptance, maintenance and support management of the JORN System (Audit Report No 24, 2005–06), Australian National Audit Office, January 2006. Available at http://www.anao.gov.au Accessed 18 April 2006
Mokyr J (1990) The lever of riches: technological creativity and economic progress. Oxford University Press, New York
Nooteboom B, Haverbeke WV, Duysters G, Gilsin V, van den Oord A (2007) Optimal cognitive distance and absorptive capacity. Res Policy 36:1016–1034
Redding S, Venables A (2002) The economics of isolation and distance. Nord J Polit Econ 28:93–108
Ruttan V (2006) Is war necessary for economic growth? Military procurement and technological development. Oxford University Press, Oxford
SAAB (2005) PS-05/A advanced aviation multi-mode radar. Available at http://www.saabgroup.com/Global/Documents%20and%20Images/Air/Sensor%20Systems/PS%2005_A/PS05_100422.pdf. Accessed 28 August 2011
Schot J, Geels F (2007) Niches in evolutionary theories of technical change: a critical survey of the literature. J Evol Econ 17:605–622
Sinnott D (1988) The Jindalee over the horizon radar system. In: Ball D (ed) Air power: global developments and Australian perspectives. Pergamon Press, Rushcutters Bay
Todd J (1995) Colonial technology: science and the transfer of innovation to Australia. Cambridge University Press, Cambridge

The Emergence of Technological Paradigms: The Evolutionary Process of Science and Technology in Economic Development

Keiichiro Suenaga

Abstract While the prospects for the world economy, especially advanced economies, are uncertain, and the fundamental solutions to important problems such as environmental problems have not yet been found, the emergence or development of new technological paradigms is expected. The emergence of technological paradigms is a most important phenomenon in economic development. In this paper, the relationship between science and technology will be classified using four diagrammatic models, and the hierarchy of technological paradigms and the characteristics of each hierarchy will be clarified in order to consider the emergence of these technological paradigms. In addition, this paper mentions the implications for the corporate strategy of R&D, science and technology policy, and economic theory.

1 Introduction

While the prospects for the world economy, especially advanced economies, are uncertain, and the fundamental solutions to important problems such as environmental problems have not yet been found, the emergence or development of new 'technological paradigms' is expected. The concept of 'technological paradigms' was introduced by Dosi (1982), and has been a great influence on the development of evolutionary economics, etc. (e.g. see the special section of *Industrial and Corporate Change*, 2008, vol. 17 (3), "Technological Paradigms: Past, Present and Future"). Thirty years have passed since Dosi's paper was published, but the potential of this concept is not exhausted. In the meantime, while science has been playing an increasingly important role in the emergence of technological paradigms, the so-called 'new economics of science' has accomplished surprising advances during the last several decades. However, the emergence of technological paradigms has not yet been clarified. Although Dosi (1982) discusses the economic, institutional, and social factors through which technological paradigms are selected

K. Suenaga (✉)
Faculty of Economics, Josai University, 1-1 Keyakidai, Sakado, Saitama, Japan
e-mail: od03008@yahoo.co.jp

A. Pyka, J. Foster (eds.), *The Evolution of Economic and Innovation Systems*,
Economic Complexity and Evolution, DOI 10.1007/978-3-319-13299-0_10

from existing scientific knowledge, he does not fully consider the factor of the emergence of technological paradigms. It is necessary for economists, particularly neo-Schumpeterian and evolutionary economists, to pay attention to the factors and processes of the emergence of technological paradigms, which are very important in economic development. In this paper, the relationship between science and technology will be classified via some diagrammatic models, and will be further discussed. In particular, the paper focuses on the emergence of technological paradigms, and explores the factors and processes involved in this emergence. Moreover, it pays particular attention to the hierarchy of technological paradigms, clarifying the characteristics of each hierarchy, and considers the ways in which the paradigms have emerged, based on a diagrammatic model.

1.1 Differences Between Science and Technology

Science aims to provide an elucidation of natural phenomena, while the purpose of technology is to create artifacts. Moreover, scientific knowledge is much more codified than technological knowledge, and much technological knowledge is implicit in experience and skill (e.g. Dosi 1982). However, not all scientific knowledge is necessarily codified, and tacit knowledge, which cannot be codified, also plays an important role in many cases. Nevertheless, generally speaking, scientific knowledge is easier to spread compared to technological knowledge.

Advances in science build mainly on already existing scientific knowledge (scientific papers cite other scientific papers much more frequently than patents), while advances in technology build mainly on technological knowledge (e.g. patents cite other patents much more frequently than scientific papers) (Price 1965; Stokes 1997; Pavitt 1998).[1] Furthermore, academic institutions dominate advances in science, while business firms do so for advances in technology (e.g. Pavitt 1998).

> One of the main purposes of academic research is to produce codified theories and models that explain and predict natural reality. To achieve analytical tractability, this requires simplification and reduction of the number of variables.... On the other hand, the main purpose of business research and development is to design and develop produceable and useful artefacts. These are often complex, involving numerous components, materials, performance constraints and interactions, and are therefore analytically intractable.... Knowledge is therefore accumulated through trial and error. As a consequence, the methodologies of 'experiments' in the two types of laboratories are often very different (Pavitt 1998, p. 795).

[1] When discussing advances in science and technology, it is necessary to divide each stock and flow clearly. That is, existing scientific or technological knowledge is a 'stock', and advances in scientific or technological knowledge are a 'flow'. Although the knowledge of science or technology is a state function and it can accumulate, the progress of science or technology is a process and is transitional. [With regard to this paragraph, see also Kline (1990) and Stokes (1997)].

Scientists are concerned with the discovery and publication of new knowledge, but they are not concerned with its application. On the other hand, the concern of technologists or engineers is the practical application of knowledge and professional recognition, and not the publication of knowledge (Price 1965; Freeman and Soete 1997). Relatively speaking, scientists (or academic institutions) act with the aim of achieving social rewards, such as a reputation, rather than economic rewards, such as profit.[2] On the other hand, engineers (or businesses) act with the purpose of earning economic rewards rather than social rewards (Merton 1973; Dasgupta and David 1994; Pavitt 1998; Bach and Matt 2005; Yamaguchi 2006; Aghion et al. 2009).[3]

1.2 Relationship Between Science and Technology

Price (1965) argues that science and technology are two subsystems which develop autonomously, and he uses the metaphor of two dancing partners that have their own steps although dancing to the same music.[4] Freeman and Soete (1997, p. 15) point out that this relationship between science and technology has changed since the nineteenth century, and sometimes they are 'cheek to cheek'. That is, the relationship between science and technology has become much more intimate, and the professional industrial R&D department is the cause and consequence of this new intimacy. With respect to the relationship between science and technology, Brooks (1994) uses the metaphor of two strands of DNA which can exist independently, but cannot be truly functional until they are paired.

According to Rosenberg (1990), one of the reasons why some firms do basic research is to resolve practical problems and/or to exploit the first-mover advantage. Moreover, it is extremely difficult to distinguish between basic research and applied research, and the relationship between them is highly complex. As contributions which science gives to technology Brooks (1994) mentions: it provides a direct source of ideas, it is a source of tools and techniques, it aids development of new human skills, etc., and as contributions which technology gives to science: it is a fertile source of novel scientific questions, and a source of otherwise unavailable instrumentation and techniques.

Kuznets (1966) indicates the importance of applying science to economic production as the main characteristic of modern economic growth, but does not suggest that modern technological innovation is triggered by scientific discovery. Rosenberg (1982) also insists that technological knowledge has preceded scientific knowledge, and that, even in industries founded on scientific research, practical experience with the new technology often precedes scientific knowledge.

---

[2]Needless to say, scientists may obtain economic rewards through IPR or academic spin-offs.

[3]Although there are many engineers who do not personally operate for economic reward, they aim for the economic reward of their company.

[4]It goes without saying that Price did not deny that science and technology have interacted.

However, it is particularly important to mention that the relationship varies, subject to the stage of industrial development: the role of science is more important in the initial stage of industrial development. Dosi (1988) points out that scientific knowledge plays a crucial role in opening up new possibilities for major technological advances, and that in the twentieth century the emergence of major new technological paradigms has frequently been directly dependent on and directly linked with major scientific breakthroughs. However, although at least the first ten years of the history of the semiconductor industry were characterized by a crucial inter-relationship between science and technology, the distance between the two has increased since the 1960s. Basic semiconductor technology has become established and its development path no longer needs a direct 'coupling' with 'Big Science' (Dosi 1984, p. 28).

1.3 Diagrammatic Illustrations of the Relationship Between Science and Technology

Some studies have tried to express this relationship between science and technology in a diagram.[5] Kline (1990) argues about the relationship between science and technology by using the 'revised chain-linked model'. Kline points out that science contributes to innovation only in the KITS (Knowledge Interface of Technology and Science) of the revised chain-linked model; the research which is born from KITS is not as difficult as the research which is produced from scientific knowledge; the problems extracted from KITS are connected with advances in science and mathematics. Kline's model demonstrates that scientific and technological knowledge are intertwined in the production process from the point of market discovery up to the point of sales.

Stokes (1997) also discusses the relationship between science and technology, based on 'a revised dynamic model'. Existing understanding can bring about improved understanding through pure basic research, and existing technology can produce improved technology through purely applied research and development. Furthermore, science and technology are semiautonomous, and are only loosely coupled. However, they are at times strongly influenced by each other, with 'use-inspired' basic research often cast in the linking role. The use-inspired basic research is also known as 'Pasteur's quadrant'. Through use-inspired basic research, existing understanding can bring about improved understanding and/or technology, and existing technology can produce improved understanding and/or technology.[6]

[5]Although Chesbrough (2003) illustrates the relationship between science and technology (research and development) in order to compare 'closed innovation' with 'open innovation', the relationship takes a linear form in his model.

[6]Stokes's model does not illustrate the technological paradigms.

Yamaguchi (2006, 2008) illustrates innovation processes in a two-dimensional diagram, an 'innovation diagram', plotting the concepts of 'knowledge creation' on a horizontal axis and the concepts of 'knowledge realization' on a vertical axis. According to him, 'knowledge creation' means to discover things which nobody knows, and the intellectual workings for the discovery are termed as 'science'. On the contrary, 'knowledge realization' refers to intellectual workings to realize feasible things by collecting and integrating scientific and technological knowledge, and the intellectual workings are limited to workings of 'technology'. In this diagram, science and technology are not a unified evolutionary system, but a chain of their actions forms an evolutionary system. In addition, in his diagram, science is located in 'soil', because it is not economically valued.

By using the concepts of technological paradigms and technological trajectories, Dosi (1982) argues about the processes by which technology is chosen from existing scientific knowledge.[7] Cimoli and Dosi (1995) attempt to illustrate technological paradigms and technological trajectories by plotting two factors of production on vertical and horizontal axes. However, the relationship between science and technology is not illustrated in a model.

In Sect. 2, based on Yamaguchi's innovation diagram which is partly amended, the relationship between science and technology is classified into four models. Suenaga (2011) clarified the hierarchy of technological paradigms and the characteristics of each soil layer, based on the analysis of Yamaguchi (2006) with regard to the transistor and MOSFET. However, the discussion is refined and the relationship between the four models and the emergences of technological paradigms are considered in Sects. 3 and 4 respectively to clarify. Finally, Sect. 5 concludes the article and points out some theoretical and political implications.

2 Diagrammatic Models of Science and Technology

This section discusses the relationship between science and technology based on a revised model of Yamaguchi's innovation diagram. Yamaguchi's model has not been developed in the neo-Schumpeterian tradition, and thus it could be further developed by utilizing neo-Schumpeterian research results.

Although he uses the concepts of 'knowledge creation' and 'knowledge realization', the intellectual workings for 'knowledge creation' are called 'science' and the intellectual workings for 'knowledge realization' are called 'technology', so that we

[7] A technological paradigm is a '"model" and a "pattern" of solution of *selected* technological problems, based on *selected* principles derived from natural sciences and on *selected* material technologies'; a technological trajectory is 'the pattern of "normal" problem solving activity (i.e. of "progress") on the ground of a technological paradigm' (Dosi 1982, p. 152).

use the terms, 'science' instead of 'knowledge creation', and 'technology' instead of 'knowledge realization'.[8]

In this section, based on Yamaguchi's innovation diagram, the relationship between science and technology is classified into four models. These are the Price model, which analyses the autonomy of science and technology, the Bush model, which focuses on science-driven technological progress, the Rosenberg model, which is based on technology-driven scientific progress, and the Dosi model, which considers the relationship between science and technology from the viewpoint of technological paradigms and trajectories.

2.1 Autonomy of Science and Technology

Figure 1 represents the case where science and technology autonomously develop. Existing scientific knowledge (S) advances through scientific research etc. ($S \rightarrow S'$). Advances in scientific knowledge are indicated by a rightward arrow in soil because they are not valued economically. Existing technological knowledge (T) advances through technological development etc. ($T \rightarrow T'$). This is illustrated as the upward arrow above the soil. Here, the case in which science and technology autonomously develop, as shown in Fig. 1, is referred to as the 'Price model', after Price (1965).

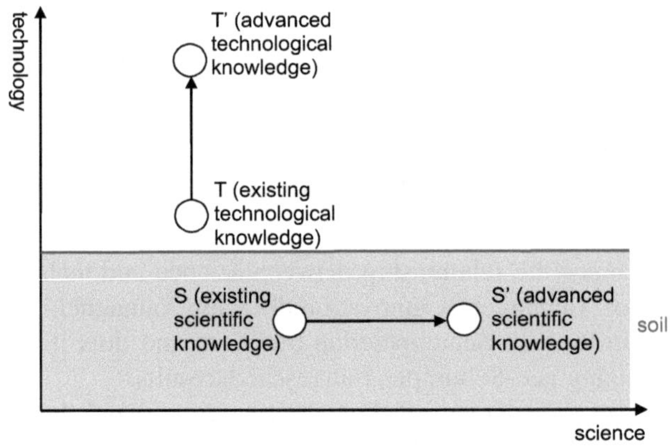

Fig. 1 Price model: a case in which science and technology autonomously develop. *Note*: Although this figure is described, based on the innovation diagram of Yamaguchi (2006), I distinguish between existing scientific knowledge and technological knowledge

[8]Although, in Yamaguchi's diagram, technology, such as the refinement method of a hermetic art, and knowledge of a chemical reaction are contained in 'knowledge creation', they are not contained in 'science' in this paper.

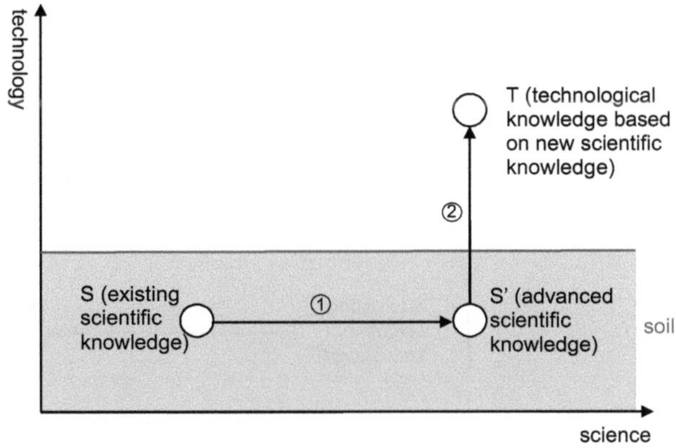

Fig. 2 Bush model (linear model): science → technology. *Note*: This figure expresses the characteristics of a linear model, based on Yamaguchi's innovation diagram

2.2 Science-Driven Technological Progress

Although science and technology develop autonomously, they are not completely independent. Regarding the relationship between science and technology, although Freeman and Soete (1997) describe it as 'cheek to cheek', and Brooks (1994) uses the metaphor of 'two strands of DNA', what is the actual relationship like in detail? Figure 2 illustrates the case in which advances in scientific knowledge ($S \rightarrow S'$) bring about advances in technological knowledge (T). The circled numbers indicate the order of the relationship between science and technology. This relationship is generally called a linear model. In this paper, this model is called the 'Bush model', after Bush (1945), who is regarded as a representative advocate of the linear model.[9]

2.3 Technology-Driven Scientific Progress

Figure 3 shows a case where existing technological knowledge triggers advances in scientific knowledge, and then scientific understanding encourages further advances in technology. As Rosenberg (1982) points out, technological knowledge without scientific understanding exists in many cases, and the existence of technological knowledge (T) promotes scientific understanding ($S \rightarrow S'$). Furthermore, advanced scientific knowledge (S′) enforces advances in technological knowledge ($T \rightarrow T'$). For example, although Duralumin was brought into existence by an engineer's trial and error, the associated scientific understanding only came about much later. In addition, scientific understanding drives the advances in Duralumin technology (Rosenberg 1982). In this paper, this model is called the 'Rosenberg model'.

[9]The problems of the Bush model (linear model) are pointed out in Sect. 4.

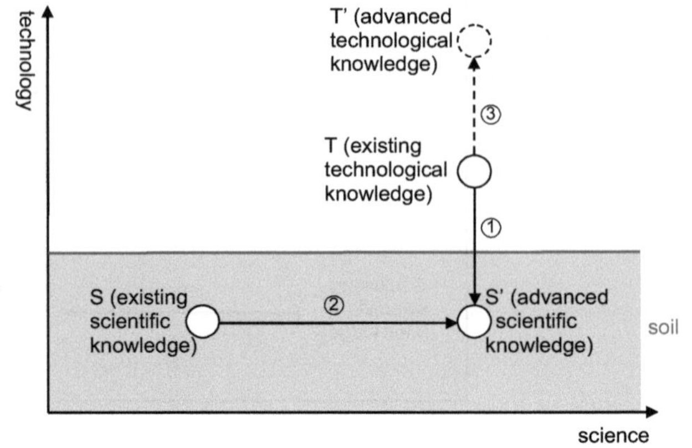

Fig. 3 Rosenberg model: technology → science (→ technology). *Note*: This figure illustrates the view of Rosenberg (1982), based on Yamaguchi's innovation diagram (2006)

2.4 Technological Paradigms and Trajectories

Dosi (1982) tries to capture the relationship between science and technology from the viewpoint of technological paradigms and trajectories. Figure 4 illustrates Dosi's 'technological paradigms' and 'technological trajectories' (1982). With regard to Dosi's (1982) definitions, this paper defines 'technological paradigms' as 'a "model" and a "pattern" of a solution to *selected* technological problems, based on *selected* scientific knowledge', and defines' technological trajectories' as' the progressing process of technological knowledge, based on a technological paradigm'.[10] Although Dosi, given the stock of scientific knowledge, discusses the process whereby technology is selected from existing scientific knowledge, scientific progress such as progress from S_1 to S_2 is illustrated in this figure. Advanced scientific knowledge, S_2, may induce new technological knowledge, T_2, such as the Bush model, or may be triggered by existing technological knowledge, T_2, according to the Rosenberg model. Therefore, Fig. 4 includes both the Bush model and the Rosenberg model. In Fig. 4, technological paradigms are expressed as a dotted line, and technological trajectories are illustrated as upward arrows within technological paradigms. The model which shows the relationship between science and technology, as shown in Fig. 4, is called the 'Dosi model' here.

[10]Whether these advances are improvements along a technological trajectory or a shift in paradigm, with new technological trajectories emerging, depends on whether the 'selected scientific knowledge' as the basis of the technological trajectory is new or not (even if scientific knowledge precedes technological knowledge as in the Bush model, or technological knowledge precedes scientific knowledge as in the Rosenberg model).

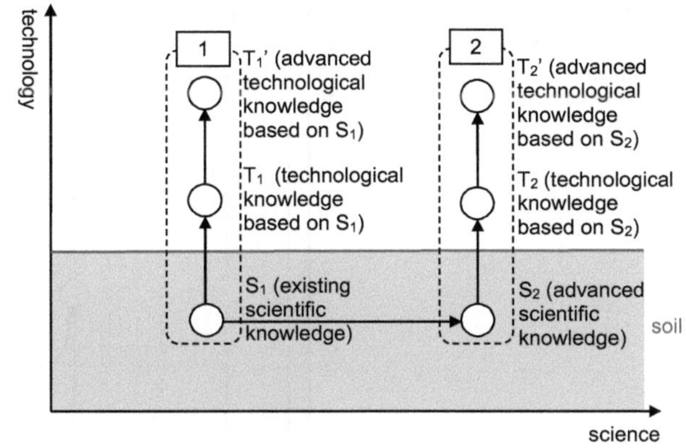

Fig. 4 Dosi model: Technological paradigms and technological trajectories. *Note*: This figure illustrates the view of Dosi (1982), based on Yamaguchi's innovation diagram (2006)

3 The Hierarchy of Technological Paradigms

The discussion in this section is based on the Dosi model, and considers the hierarchy of technological paradigms (Fig. 5). Although advances in scientific knowledge have been located in soil up to this point, there are various layers of soil. For example, in the process by which the semiconductor industry came into being and developed, while the academic framework itself changed from classical electromagnetics (3-a), the basis of tube technology, to quantum mechanics (3-b), the basis of semiconductor technology, there were also advances in science within the academic framework of quantum mechanics. For example, although the transformation of operating principles from current injection (2-a), the basis of bipolar transistor technology, to field effect (2-b), the basis of FET technology is based on the specific academic framework of quantum mechanics, it is less significant than the transformation of the academic framework. Moreover, the transformation of connection methods from point type (1-a) to junction type (1-b) is less significant than the transformation of the operating principles, because point and junction type are based on a specific operating principle, current injection. With regard to the diagram above, the transformation of the academic framework is described as being located in the deeper layer of soil (referred to here as the third layer), while the transformation of the operating principles is located in a middle layer of soil (referred to here as the second layer), and the transformation of the connection methods is located in a shallower layer of soil (referred to here as the first layer).[11]

As already mentioned, the 'technological paradigms' in this paper are 'a "model" and a "pattern" of a solution to *selected* technological problems, based on *selected* scientific knowledge'. This '*selected* scientific knowledge' sometimes refers to the *selected* academic framework, such as quantum mechanics. However, it sometimes

[11]See also Suenaga (2011) for the discussion in detail.

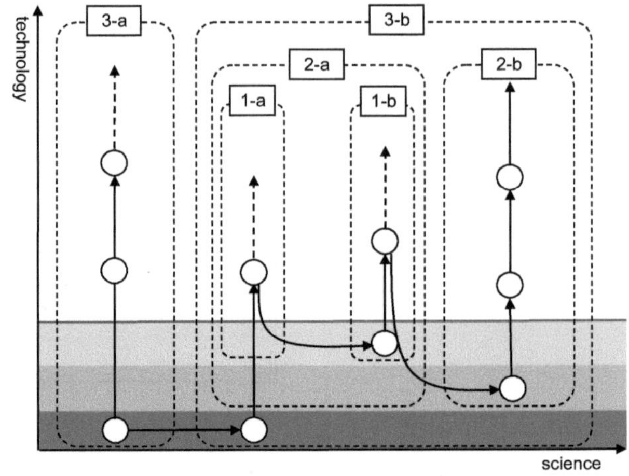

Fig. 5 Soil layers and hierarchy of technological paradigms

refers to the *selected* operating principles, such as current injection within the academic framework, and it sometimes refers to the *selected* connection methods, such as point type and junction type, within the operating principles such as current injection.

Advances in scientific knowledge in the third layer form more extensive technological paradigms (e.g. '3-b'), advances in scientific knowledge in the second layer form middle-sized technological paradigms (e.g. '2-a', which is included in '3-b'), and advances in scientific knowledge in the first layer form smaller technological paradigms (e.g. '1-b', which is included in '2-a'). As a result, layers are also formed in technological paradigms when a difference in the dimension (the depth of soil) of scientific knowledge exists.[12]

[12]Therefore, it can also be interpreted as follows: If seen from the 3rd layer, the change from '1-a' to '1-b' and the change from '2-a' to '2-b' will be the technological trajectory in the technological paradigm '3-b'. If seen from the 2nd layer, the change from '1-a' to '1-b' will be the technological trajectory in the technological paradigm '2-a'. If seen from the 1st layer, the change from the grown junction method to the alloy junction method will be the technological trajectory in the technological paradigm '1-b'. According to this interpretation, whether a specific change is an improvement along a technological trajectory or a shift in paradigm, with new technological trajectories emerging, depends on the layer from which it is seen. Moreover, although the scientific knowledge can also still be classified in detail, it will be enough just to clarify the existence of the hierarchy of scientific knowledge, or a technological paradigm, since the purpose here is to discuss essentials.

Of course, an old technological paradigm and a new technological paradigm may coexist. The vacuum tube and the semiconductor coexist, and the same may be said about the bipolar transistor and MOSFET. Moreover, science and technology affect each other mutually, and the chain (co-evolution) of science and technology forms an evolutionary system. For example, the invention of the point contact type transistor, based on the discovery of Walter H. Brattain and John Bardeen, led to William B. Shockley's scientific knowledge about the junction type transistor, and the grown junction technology was based on Shockley's scientific knowledge. Furthermore, the invention of MOSFET also led to advances in scientific knowledge about the quantum Hall effect by Klaus von

Table 1 Soil layers and technological paradigms/scientific knowledge

1st layer: Connections		1-a Ge point/ Point	1-b Ge junction/ Junction	
2nd layer: Operating principles		2-a Bipolar/ Current injection		2-b FET/ Field effect
3rd layer: Academic frameworks	3-a Tube/ Electromagnetics	3-b Semiconductor/ Quantum mechanics		

Source: This table is the revised version of Suenaga (2011)

Table 1 sums up the characteristics of technological paradigms and scientific knowledge regarding the basis of each technological paradigm. Although Table 1 is drawn from the example of the transistor and MOSFET, the same argument can also be developed in other examples. That is, layers are formed in the soil, and the hierarchy of technological paradigms based on these layers is built, although the characteristics of each layer may differ.[13] In this way, by clarifying the characteristics of the hierarchy of technological paradigms or soil layers, part of the method of producing new technological paradigms may become clear.

4 The Emergence of Technological Paradigms

How do new technological paradigms emerge? According to the Bush model (linear model), there are advances in scientific knowledge which have the possibility of producing a new technological paradigm. However, there are many cases where an advance in scientific knowledge does not produce a new technological paradigm. Moreover, there is a time-lag until advances in scientific knowledge produce new technological paradigms; sometimes this happens quickly (or almost immediately), and in other cases it takes a long time (tens of years or more than that). However, as there is much criticism about this, it is insufficient to just understand advances in scientific knowledge and new technological paradigms in terms of linear relationships (for example, Dosi 1982; Kline 1990; Stokes 1997; Nightingale 1998). Many economic factors affect advances in scientific knowledge, and the

Klitzing. That is, science provides the technological sources of a scientific question, technology also does so, and various feedback mechanisms exist between science and technology (also refer to Sect. 1.2).

[13]Although we need to analyze the various examples, Yamaguchi's analyses (2006, 2008, 2009) about the Industrial Revolution and other cases are extremely interesting.

complexity and the uncertainty of the relationship between science and technology may be overlooked in the Bush model. In the Rosenberg model, the emergence of technological paradigms happens without scientific knowledge (understanding), and the solidity of technological paradigms increases with advances in scientific knowledge (understanding). Thus, the relationship between science and technology is not a one-way thing, and a chain of science and technology forms an evolutionary system, with science and technology having a mutual influence. Nevertheless, as time goes by, the importance not only of existing scientific knowledge but advances in scientific knowledge increases. In order to produce new technological paradigms which have great potential, advances in scientific knowledge are needed at deeper layers.

Dosi (1982) discusses the economic, institutional, and social factors through which technological paradigms are selected from existing scientific knowledge. For example, the marketability, potential profitability, and labor-saving capability of technological paradigms, and industrial and social conflict, have an influence on the process by which technological paradigms are selected.[14] In this process, although the market plays a certain role, it is almost impossible to predict the long-term performance of technological paradigms. Therefore, it is not an approach like neoclassical economics (including endogenous economic growth theory) that is needed, but one like evolutionary economics (including Dosi et al.).[15] Although it is necessary to generalize as regards the factors and process of the emergence of technological paradigms through various case studies, one might not be able to find anything like a general theory of the emergence of technological paradigms, as Cimoli and Dosi (1995, p. 254) point out.

Basically, if the possibility is high that technological trajectories will develop under a specific technological paradigm, the incentive to look for other technological paradigms decreases. On the other hand, if there is a low possibility that the technological trajectories will develop, the motivation to seek other technological paradigms increases.[16] Moreover, if there is a high possibility that scientific knowledge will progress, the possibility that other technological paradigms can be selected increases. On the other hand, if the possibility is low that scientific knowledge will progress, the possibility that other technological paradigms can be selected decreases. The frequency of the emergence of technological paradigms

[14]For example, the Middle Eastern conflict affects the direction for seeking alternative energy sources. Although Dosi (1982, p. 156) mentions that 'scope for substitution ... is limited by the technology which itself defines the range of possible technological advances', Yamaguchi's model suggests that advances in scientific knowledge which generate new technological paradigms have an important role.

[15]In this process, lock-in effects or path-dependency have an important influence.

[16]About this phrase; see also Freeman and Perez (1988). 'It is only when productivity along the old trajectories shows persistent limits to growth and future profits are seriously threatened that the high risks and costs of trying the new technologies appear as clearly justified' (p. 49).

increases as the layer becomes shallower, and the potential for new paradigms increases as the layer becomes deeper.[17]

What kind of corporate strategy or policy is needed in order to generate new technological paradigms? One important point in this regard is how to combine science and technology, since this combination plays an important role in creating new technological paradigms. Although science and technology have mutually independent characteristics, they are strongly influenced by each other. In a situation where new technological paradigms are needed, how both are combined becomes important. In particular, in order to create technological paradigms based on deeper layers, 'a field' which straddles between academics or between organizations may be needed.

Regarding this field, Yamaguchi (2009) suggests the concept of 'a field of resonance'.[18] According to him, the key to what new technological paradigm emerge depends on whether those who find the existential desire for 'advances in scientific knowledge' and 'advances in technological knowledge' can succeed in resonating this desire in a realistic place which can transmit tacit knowledge... Such a place is called the 'field of resonance'.

Of course, there will be cases where those who have the existential desire for 'advances in scientific knowledge', and those who have the existential desire for 'advances in technological knowledge' are the same people,[19] and cases where both are alive at completely different times and places. Nevertheless, as already mentioned, the importance of not only existing scientific knowledge but advances in scientific knowledge increases as time goes by, and the importance of sharing a 'field' where both can transmit tacit knowledge is increasing.[20]

Table 2 generalizes the state of 'a field of resonance' to each soil layer of Table 1. According to the level (soil layer) at which the actor tries to create the technological paradigms, the person, organization, and scientific knowledge required for the field of resonance are different, although the state of optimal field of resonance changes with the characteristics of industry and the times. When considering the methods of research and development, or the policy of science and technology, it is important to recognize the hierarchy and characteristics in each such level.[21]

---

[17]This is an important factor for long business fluctuations.

[18]Refer also to Nonaka and Takeuchi (1995) in regard to the role of the 'field' in knowledge creation. They analyze the 'field' for changing tacit knowledge into explicit knowledge in the SECI model of knowledge creation.

[19]See also Rosenberg (1990) in regard to this example. Rosenberg also discusses the relationship between scientific knowledge and technological knowledge in detail.

[20]The reason the transistor was created in the Bell laboratory was that many specialists in various academic realms worked in the same field, transmitted tacit knowledge, and drew inspiration from each other. 'All in all, the people playing a major role at one time or another in the work which led to the transistor discovery may have numbered about thirteen' (Nelson 1962, p. 560).

[21]For example, this argument is also related to arguments such as 'More Moore', 'More than Moore', and 'Beyond CMOS'. Let me define 'More Moore' as 'to pursue micro-fabrication on silicon CMOS', 'More than Moore' as 'to create new value through combinations of technology',

Table 2 Soil layers and field of resonance

1st layer: Connections	Various connections based on selected principles
2nd layer: Operating principles	Various theories based on selected academy
3rd layer: Academic frameworks	Various academies, various frameworks

5 Conclusions: Some Theoretical and Policy Implications

In Sect. 2, the relationship between science and technology is discussed in a number of models, based on Yamaguchi's innovation diagram. The models are the Price model, which pays attention to the autonomy of science and technology, the Bush model, which focuses on science-driven technological progress, the Rosenberg model, which is based on technology-driven scientific progress, and the Dosi model, which considers the relationship between science and technology from the viewpoint of technological paradigms and trajectories. There are various ways of viewing this relationship, and we should discuss it from various points of view, taking into account economic development, corporate strategy, and S&T policy.

Section 3 focuses on the hierarchy of technological paradigms in order to describe the emergence of technological paradigms. Additionally, by clarifying the characteristics of each layer of technological paradigms and scientific knowledge, it proposes a conceptual framework to create technological paradigms. The scientific knowledge which is the foundation of technological paradigms consists of deeper layers forming the academic framework, and shallower layers forming the operating principles and connection methods. Furthermore, technological paradigms, which are based on the layer of scientific knowledge, exist hierarchically, and constitute a complex system. In order to come up with strategies and policies to create technological paradigms, we should make a structure of human and material resources and organizations considering the hierarchy of technological paradigms.

Although the integrated model of this paper is, in some respects, "impressionistic", it is an interesting model which illustrates the evolutionary process of economic development. Although many economists, such as Kuznets (1966), have emphasized the role of science on economic development, we can explicitly consider the relationship between science and technology, and the one between technological paradigms and economic development, based on the integrated model. Though the relationship between science and technology is not uniform, a chain of science

and 'Beyond CMOS' as 'to bring forth new devices based on new connections or principles'. Although they do not necessarily correspond completely, it follows that 'More Moore' and 'More than Moore' represent paradigm-sustaining innovation. New devices based on new connections are paradigm-disruptive innovation in the first layer, and new devices based on new principles are paradigm-disruptive innovation in the second layer. Finally, paradigm disruptive innovation in the third layer is a device based on an academic framework, which is different to quantum mechanics (referred to here as 'Beyond Quantum').

and technology forms technological paradigms, and the hierarchical development of technological paradigms results in industrial and economic development.

While traditional economic growth theory demonstrates the process of economic growth by plotting the capital stock per capita on a horizontal axis and the output per capita on a vertical axis, Cimoli and Dosi (1995) illustrates technological paradigms and technological trajectories by plotting two factors of production on vertical and horizontal axes. Although this paper considers the process of economic development by plotting science and technology on both axes, disregarding factors such as capital and labor, on which orthodox economics places significance, this is not wrong when discussing the long-term process of economic development. The essential factors in economic development are science and technology, rather than capital and labor which neoclassical economic growth theory focuses on. Moreover, the process of economic development is an evolutional process rather than an equilibrium process, and its process cannot be described using numerical formulae.

Nevertheless, this paper has a problem of theoretical imperfection. Simply speaking, scientists (or academic institutions) act with the aim of social rewards, and advances in science are a function of the input to scientific research. On the other hand, engineers (or business firms) act with a view to earning economic rewards, and advances in technology are a function of the input to technological development. Although science and technology develop autonomously, both are complexly intertwined, as already mentioned above. As a result, although it is difficult to be theoretically explicit about the totality of the relationship between the two, it is possible to theorize about the relationship, to some degree, by classifying some models, as in this paper.

The process by which science and technology form a chain in various ways, and the process through which technological paradigms are selected and developed, are just evolutionary processes. Technological paradigms which are not suited to the economic environment in the short term might be disregarded, even if they have long-term potential.

Moreover, although this research has elucidated the hierarchy of technological paradigms by clarifying the hierarchy of scientific knowledge, the existence of the hierarchy is a factor that brings short-, middle-, and long-term economic fluctuations.[22] In addition, by clarifying the hierarchy of technological paradigms, the continuity and discontinuity of an industrial development can be discussed.

Schumpeter (1934, p. 66), in the explanation of new combinations, refers to the 'introduction of a new method of production, that is one not yet tested by experience in the branch of manufacture concerned', and states that it need by no means be founded upon a discovery that is scientifically new. Although he refers to a new method of production based on a discovery that is scientifically new as a new combination, the discovery in itself is not endogenous in his model. However, we have to endogenise 'advances in science' to theorize the essence of economic

[22] See also the discussions about techno-economic paradigms and long waves, such as Freeman and Perez (1988).

development, even if scientific knowledge precedes technological knowledge as in the Bush model, or technological knowledge precedes scientific knowledge as in the Rosenberg model.

Large central laboratories such as the Bell laboratory of AT&T used to play a significant role in the emergence of technological paradigms (in particular, based on deeper layers). However, because of the greater mobility of skilled researchers, the increased knowledge in society as a whole, and the development of venture capital, it is difficult for a central laboratory in a large company to create new technological paradigms (based on the third layer).[23] How companies efficiently produce new technological paradigms in an era of open innovation is an important topic for the collaboration of industry-academia management. Moreover, how science and technology are bound together is also a crucial problem from the viewpoint of the policy of science and technology.

According to the soil layer of technological paradigms which the organization aims to create, the proportion and level of human and material resources, the organization, and the scientific knowledge required for the field of resonance differ.[24] In particular, it is necessary to develop a management framework and policies for producing new technological paradigms based on the third layer. Many organizations all over the world are challenged with this difficulty, and then such case studies are a subject that should be studied further in the future.[25]

Acknowledgements The author is grateful for the valuable comments and suggestions of Eiichi Yamaguchi, Kazuo Sakai, Tim Minshall, Hans-Jürgen Engelbrecht, Thanh Le, Dengjian Jin, and all participants at the 2nd International Symposium on Innovation Strategy at the University of Cambridge, at a session of the 14th International Schumpeter Society at the University of Queensland, and at the Meeting on Higher Education for the Next Generation. The comments of anonymous referees are also gratefully acknowledged. I am especially indebted to Fumitaka Nakamura for his profound advice. All remaining errors are my own.

References

Aghion P, David PA, Foray D (2009) Science, technology and innovation for economic growth: linking policy research and practice in 'STIG Systems'. Res Policy 38:681–693

Bach L, Matt M (2005) From economic foundations to S&T policy tools: a comparative analysis of the dominant paradigms. In: Llerena P, Matt M (eds) Innovation policy in a knowledge-based economy, ch. 1. Springer, Berlin, pp 17–45

Brooks H (1994) The relationship between science and technology. Res Policy 23:477–486

[23]See Chesbrough (2003) about open innovation.

[24]This is related to the discussion about the relationship between diversity and innovation.

[25]Suenaga (2012) examines the role of local government, focusing on IMEC in Belgium. In Japan, central government plays a significant role in implementation of science and technology policy and declines the degree of globalization about research and development in Japan. The example of IMEC has significant implications for Japan.

Bush V (1945) Science the endless frontier. United States Government Printing Office, Washington, DC
Chesbrough H (2003) Open innovation: a new imperative for creating and profiting from technology. Harvard Business School Corporation, Boston, MA
Cimoli M, Dosi G (1995) Technological paradigms, patterns of learning and development: an introductory roadmap. J Evol Econ 5:243–268
Dasgupta P, David PA (1994) Toward a new economics of science. Res Policy 23:487–521
Dosi G (1982) Technological paradigms and technological trajectories. Res Policy 11:147–162
Dosi G (1984) Technical change and industrial transformation: the theory and an application to the semiconductor industry. Macmillan Press, London
Dosi G (1988) Sources, procedures, and microeconomic effects of innovation. J Econ Lit 26:1120–1171
Freeman C, Perez C (1988) Structural crises of adjustment, business cycles and investment behaviour. In: Dosi G et al (eds) Technical change and economic theory. Pinter Publishers, London, pp 38–66
Freeman C, Soete L (1997) The economics of industrial innovation, 3rd edn. Routledge, London
Kline SJ (1990) Innovation style in Japan and the United States: cultural bases; implications for competitiveness. Stanford University Press, Stanford
Kuznets SS (1966) Modern economic growth: rate, structure and spread. Yale University Press, New Haven
Merton RK (1973) The sociology of science: theoretical and empirical investigations. The University of Chicago Press, Chicago
Nelson RR (1962) The link between science and invention: the case of the transistor. In: Nelson RR (ed) The rate and direction of inventive activity: economic and social factors. Princeton University Press, Princeton
Nightingale P (1998) A cognitive model of innovation. Res Policy 27:689–709
Nonaka I, Takeuchi H (1995) The knowledge-creating company: how Japanese companies create the dynamics of innovation. Oxford University Press, New York
Pavitt K (1998) The social shaping of the national science base. Res Policy 27:793–805
de Solla Price DJ (1965) Is technology historically independent of science? A study in statistical historiography. Technol Cult 6:553–568
Rosenberg N (1982) Inside the black box: technology and economics. Cambridge University Press, Cambridge
Rosenberg N (1990) Why do firms do basic research (with their own money)? Res Policy 19:165–174
Schumpeter JA (1934) The theory of economic development. Oxford University Press, Oxford
Stokes DE (1997) Pasteur's quadrant: basic science and technological innovation. Brookings Institution Press, Washington, DC
Suenaga K (2011) The soil layers of innovation diagram. Paper presented at the Doshisha University Graduate School (in Japanese)
Suenaga K (2012) The role of local government in an era of open innovation: an analysis based on the example of a Flemish government-funded NPO. J Urban Manag Local Gov Res 27(2):1–10
Yamaguchi E (2006) Innovation: paradigm disruptions and fields of resonance. NTT Publishing (in Japanese)
Yamaguchi E (2008) Industrial revolution as paradigm disruptive innovations. Organ Sci 42(1):37–47 (in Japanese)
Yamaguchi E (2009) What is 'Mekiki-ryoku' of technology. Nikkei Tech-On, Feb–Mar (in Japanese)

Policy Exploration with Agent-Based, Economic Geography Methods of Regional Economic Integration in South Asia

Hans-Peter Brunner and Kislaya Prasad

Abstract Parts of Asia continue to enjoy high economic growth—this rapid growth however does not extend to all regions of Asia, and within geographic regions growth disparities remain high. This paper features applied and complex models for regional economic development. In a pioneering approach that makes explicit the complex connections needed to spur growth in trade, this South Asia-focused study details a unique method to assess how Aid for Trade (AfT) investments interact with agents of economic change, such as consumers and producers and traders of intermediate and final goods and to evaluate their potential to reduce the cost of bringing more products to more markets. Furthermore, it presents a new tool for policy makers to foster regional economic integration and pursue the overarching development objective of more inclusive growth across a region. The paper shows how modeling restructuring across geographies can visualize policy choice hitherto unseen and unrecognized.

The models exhibit structural changes in the regional South Asia economy through the decreases in intra-regional trade transaction costs which are influenced by a set of investment based policy choices. The cost reduction pattern and the nature of non-linear and distributed interactions between the geographic elements of the agent-based system allow it to functionally restructure itself over time. When low growth sections of the regional economy are integrated into evolving regional and global trade networks and agent-based relationships, the benefits of high economic growth are extended to low growth sections of a regional economy, as is made visually apparent in Geographic Information System (GIS) map-based simulations. The paper will review representations of regional development models

---

The authors are solely responsible for the content, and do not speak for the respective institutional affiliate(s).

H.-P. Brunner (✉)
Asian Development Bank, 6 ADB Avenue, Mandaluyong 1550, Metro Manila, Philippines
e-mail: hbrunner@adb.org

K. Prasad
Robert H. Smith School of Business, University of Maryland, College Park, MD 20742, USA
e-mail: kprasad@umd.edu

A. Pyka, J. Foster (eds.), *The Evolution of Economic and Innovation Systems*,
Economic Complexity and Evolution, DOI 10.1007/978-3-319-13299-0_11

in terms of their assumptions (peeled away like an onion) and in terms of their level of complexity, very much in the tradition of Peter Allen's classification system. Traditional mechanical models of regional economic development assume away structural change with the assumption of completeness of network connections among agents in the system, thereby imposing a simplifying homogeneity on economic agents that significantly reduces explanatory power.

1 From Simple to Complex Economic Growth and Development Models: Allen's Peeling of the Onion

The non-equilibrium modelling approach to spatial economic and demographic change has been developed as the result of advances originating in the natural sciences of open, complex systems (Nicolis and Prigogine 1977; Haken 1977; Prigogine and Stengers 1987). These ideas led to a series of developments and applications in the fields of urban and regional modelling (Allen and Sanglier 1978, 1979a, b, 1981a, b, c; Allen 1981, 1982, 1984; Allen et al. 1983, 1985, 1986, 2007; Sanglier and Allen 1989). These developments have been described in Allen (1997). Allen's (1997) publication represents a major milestone as it leads the way towards models of geographic economic systems evolution. The elements of complexity thinking in social and economic systems, so introduced, are well characterized in *The Handbook of Evolutionary Economic Geography* (Martin and Sunley 2010). More recently, models are significantly advanced with diverse economic agents on the map, within and across economic geographies which are linked in networks of interaction (Brunner and Allen 2005). *The Handbook of Evolutionary Economic Geography* (Boschma and Martin 2010) further outlines the distinguishing features of an evolutionary approach to economic geography. Such approach combines population dynamics where heterogeneous agents compete for economic resources, with a networked interaction among them in an economic landscape, to the effect of restructuring the complex economic system. The evolution of a population of agents is conveniently modelled within an economic geography, then in the application of the evolutionary theory of international trade (Brunner and Allen 2005), economic geographies are linked via exchange mediated by transaction and transport costs to see how that affects the dynamics within economic geographies. Such network approach with the emergence of new transaction connections reflecting the essence of complex systems in geography, follows also from Foster (1993, 1994, 1997), Metcalfe (1997, 1998), Potts (2001), Metcalfe and Foster (2004), Metcalfe et al. (2006).

The behaviour of complex systems offers a rich set of concepts with which to begin a new reflection on human systems. In this new view, non-equilibrium phenomena are much more important, and offer a new understanding of the natural emergence of structure and organization in systems with many interacting individual elements. These ideas are relevant to any system that is the result of evolutionary processes where innovation and selection have been played out over time. This leads

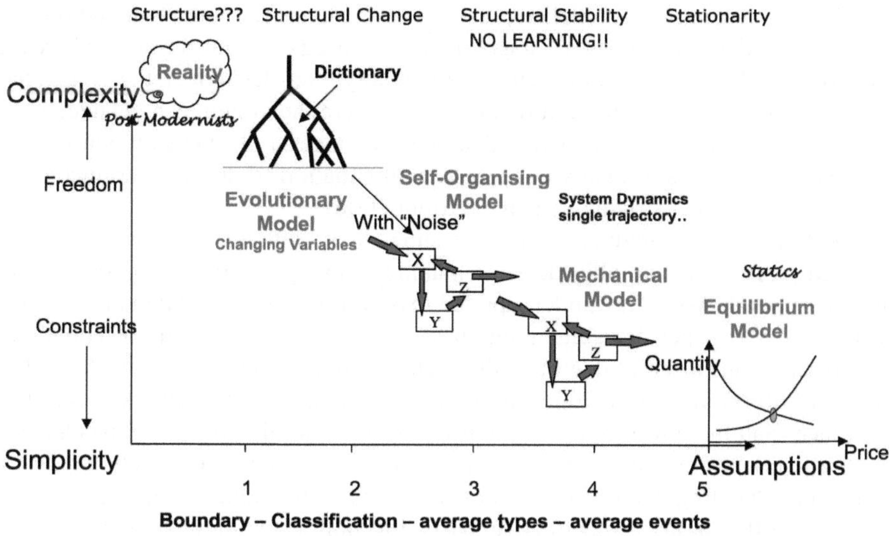

Number – stage of model	Assumption made	Resulting model
1	Boundary assumed	Some local sense-making possible; no structure, descriptive;
2	Classification assumed	Open-ended evolutionary models; math algorithms and multi-agent;
3	Average types	Non-linear equations, structure and networks;
4a	Stationarity	Self-organized criticality; equilibrium;
4b	Average events	Mechanical equations
5	Stationarity	Catastrophe theory, attractors, equilibrium;

Fig. 1 The different kinds of model that arise from successive assumptions [*Source*: Allen et al. (2007)]

to new models of regional economic systems that show how the dialogue between the two levels—individual and aggregate—generate successive spatial structures with characteristic patterns and flows.

One defining contribution of Allen has been the diagrammatic representation of model types on the complex and restrictive assumptions plane. "Models" are our simplified representations of reality. Bar-Yam (1997) defines complexity at a chosen scale of reality in terms of how much information is necessary to describe the observation of reality at that scale. It is the reduction of reality via restrictive model assumptions that allows the observer to introduce sufficient order to help describe and understand reality (Fig. 1).

Complex systems and models represent a co-evolutionary behaviour and organization, beyond the "mechanical" stages 4 and 5 focused on "equilibrium", where the locations and behaviours of the actors are mutually inter-dependent, the system has many possible responses to perturbations, and where the system can change, adapt and maintain rich, diverse and varied strategies (stages 1–3). General equilibrium models in contrast, are mainly concerned with situations that create no incentives for agents for further structure change (Arthur 2006).

The key objective here is however to show, how complex systems of the kind outlined, can be used in policy decision making in a very specific set of geographies in eastern South Asia. The models applied to South Asia and exhibited in following sections of the paper are simulations based on non-linear systems of equations, incorporating in different degree multi-agent behaviour and math algorithms. The view of sub-optimal behaviours, imperfect information and networks, mistaken inferences and the power of creativity is contrasted with the traditional mechanical representations of human systems. Section 2 of the paper details this methodological contrast by "peeling Allen's onion of assumptions." The higher complexity models discussed offer a new, quantitative basis for policy exploration and analysis, allowing us to take into account the longer-term implications for the system as a whole. For instance, the choice of analytical framework and of concepts not only helps in selecting the best use of funds by international agencies, but facilitates international economic development intervention more likely to lead to desirable outcomes. Section 3 presents the two higher complexity analytic and computational frameworks of model simulations for the conduit of policy experiments. Section 4 concludes.

2 Peeling the "Onion of Assumptions" for International Economic Trade Theory

Brunner and Allen (2005) in their book present development policy experiments with the help of complex system, evolutionary trade models. Such models combine the mathematic, numeric approach where differential equations determine macroeconomic outcomes, with a logic (time-indexed) sequence model which defines the trade network interaction of heterogeneous economic agents at the micro level. Development intervention is enacted at the meso-(institutional) level of a hierarchically structured economic system. In those experiments trade is foremost influenced by the policy induced change in *capability* of economic agents to engage in trade. Economic agents use their trading power to buy further technological capability. A technological progress function is used. Trade is productivity driven and the evolutionary trade models in this book link productivity change to structural differences occurring in terms of export product variety and quality. Structural changes in trade are linked to increases in employment, incomes, and in growth rates. In the models, export success feeds back into a positive loop, or (non-linear)

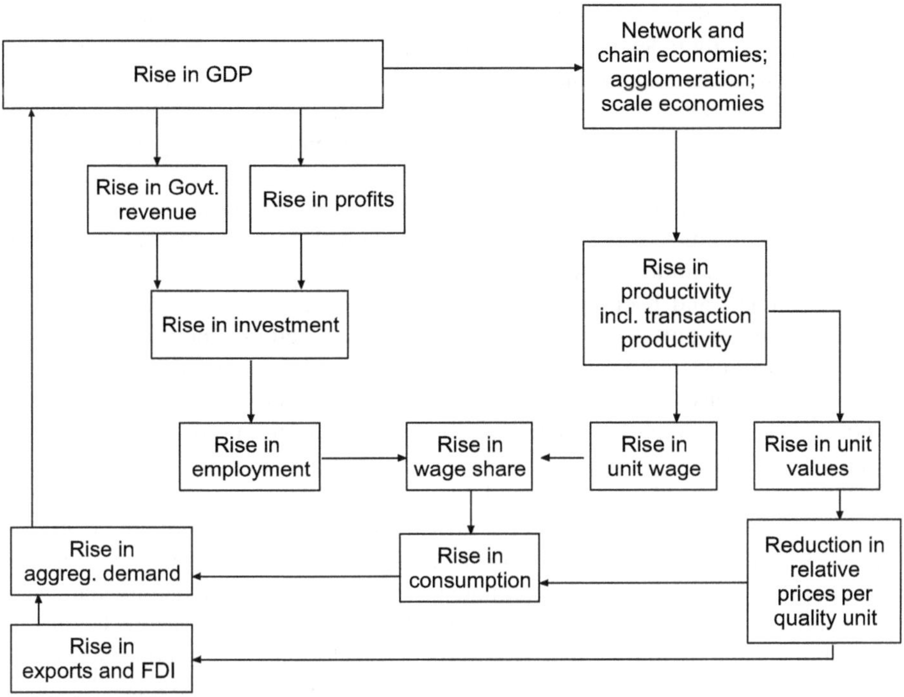

Fig. 2 A stylized feedback model of economic growth and international trade

autocatalytic process of increased productivity leading to increasing economies of scale and agglomeration effects, and as stylized in Fig. 2 [adapted from Saccone and Valli (2009) and Brunner and Allen (2005)]. This figure is a representation of positive and negative feedback components of the well-known Verdoorn law, where increasing (cost and quality) competitiveness depends on the relationship between wage growth and productivity growth, and fast productivity growth depends on fast output growth in an open trade environment, and fast output growth leads to more exports with increased competitiveness.

'Autocatalysis' refers to "any cyclical concatenation of processes wherein each member has the propensity to accelerate the activity of the succeeding link" (Ulanowicz 1999: 41–55). Autocatalysis in an economic system presumes a variety of economic actors (= vertices or nodes of a network) interacting in a network of economic links. The network structure of interaction will be detailed in a following section. For some time now, economists have used positive and negative feedback loops to model the autocatalytic nature of economic change (Arthur 1990). Brunner (1994) has formalized mechanisms underlying the creation of populations of economic actors such as firms leading to macroeconomic change. Productivity change is driven by fluctuating population size in an institutional setting for economic rules.

Another part of this feedback cycle of structural change needs detailed scrutiny. A rise of productivity leads to a rise in unit values. Unit values provide a reasonable measurement of vertical product differentiation due to additional features or quality that high-wage producers are able to add to their products (Helble and Okubo 2008; Greenaway et al. 1995). Vertical product differentiation is very pronounced in sectors which allow producers (firms as agents) to produce goods of very different quality. As it is, quality is produced by high wage producers in high income developed economies, which are able to produce with high capital and technology intensity by combining those factors with highly productive labor (Cadot et al. 2008; Hummels and Klenow 2005). Higher (unit) prices indicate per quality unit and increases in unit values are the result of productivity increases, including increases in transaction productivity. Structural change is about the establishment of economic measures and conditions that allow movement closer to those areas of product space in which firms can exploit markets through product differentiation at the high quality and price spectrum. For structural change, countries' firms and economic agents need to add capabilities. This is reliant on productivity growth. Such move in product space can occur in developing economies through integration into production chains which are anchored to a lead firm that finally assembles a vertically integrated and differentiated product at the high quality and price spectrum in a high income consumer market. We call this strategy leading to structural change in product space the vertical transformation of product space.

High quality products are also highly networked Kali and Reyes 2007) as they come with many additional features—that is these are complex goods that require equally complex production chains. With the lowering of transport and transaction costs due to technology change in the transport and communications sectors, and due to infrastructure investment, production chains have increasingly evolved in geography, which is in real space. Conversely studies have shown that inadequate infrastructure impedes horizontal diversification as market access remains difficult and costs of exploring new markets stay high (Cadot et al. 2008). For regions and countries, which produce at the lower quality and lower cost, structural change means to move into product components (and services) which are incorporated into high quality products in sectors with high vertical product differentiation. However, such move is only possible if entry into production chains is easy and can occur at low transport and transaction costs. Structural change thus also means the integration of production chains in the region and the linkage of the regional part of the production chain to the global portion(s) of the production chains.

Another facet of a structure change is for economies to diversify horizontally within the product space—an increase in the variety of trade. Greater variety can go hand in hand with vertical integration, as a greater variety also allows for increasing the focus on products that are highly vertically integrated. Diversification in product space leads to increased opportunities for growth, less vulnerability to economic disruptions (Bacccetta et al. 2009) and is shown to increase average unit values in exports and hence induces positive feedback in the growth model (Feenstra and Kee 2004). However such diversification is difficult when country exports are very concentrated, and hence when firms possess a limited range of capabilities.

The benefits from diversification, and from acquisition of capabilities increase substantially the more capabilities are already present, and the more diversified country exports are (Hausmann and Hidalgo 2010).

Transaction productivity is low in poor and small economies remote from key markets. A high cost of market access makes integration into production chains difficult, it lowers incomes and growth. Regional integration through logistics, information network and connectivity improvement can increase the 'virtual' size of an economy as trade with neighboring countries increases. This leads to substantial benefits from scale, network and agglomeration economies (Winters 2009). Again this leads to a rise of unit values in exports, and thus to income and GDP growth. Once unit values are high, the cost of transportation per weight unit decreases relative to its value.

3 Complexity in Regional Economic Development: Computing It on the Asia Map

In the previous sections, we have portrayed Allen's onion-layered assumptions leading to new approaches to policy analysis. The distinctive features of this paper's approach include the following: (1) policy experiments are conducted within a computational framework; (2) economic outcomes for a region of interest are assessed in the context of a simulation of the economy where, in particular, the actual geography is explicitly represented; (3) heterogeneous interacting agents are situated in this geography and their interactions with other agents are constrained by the characteristics of transportation and communication networks that are used to represent the connectivity and cohesiveness of the economy; (4) the evolution of this system is governed by rules of behavior of the agents which can be used to incorporate, in addition to networks, nonlinearities, feedback systems, technology change, and other features that give rise to complex dynamics.

A properly implemented version of such a model gives us a very powerful tool for policy analysis. Once calibrated with the economic data for a region, such a simulation model becomes a tool for the assessment of the *ex-ante* impact of policies (for instance, investments in the transportation infrastructure of a region). Policy alternatives can then be compared using a variety of metrics, leading to more rational choices. A beneficial consequence of the fact that the model is explicit about geography means that the output of the simulation gives us a detailed picture of the regionally disparate impact of infrastructure investments.

We illustrate the richness of our approach, which has moreover been tested "in the field," by discussing two large-scale applications. The general approach outlined here also undergone refinement in light of the experience gained from the applications. The first application is in northeastern India, and the second is for a broader swathe of South Asia, including Bangladesh, Bhutan, Nepal, and parts of eastern India (combined this is named the South Asia Sub-regional Economic Cooperation region, or SASEC). In preparation of ADB operations, the northeastern part of South Asia's economy (comprising Bangladesh, Bhutan, Nepal and the eastern part of India, an area with a population of more than 300 million people) has been modeled on a map (Global Development Solutions 2006, with New England Complex Systems Institute, and Applied Agents under ADB technical assistance, 2011). All major economic activities expected to be affected by trade related transport/logistics and trade supply chain capacity building to firms in the region have been quantified and located on a scaled geographic grid of cells or tiles of this map [see Brunner and Allen (2005) and Bosker et al. (2010)]. This map provides the crucial input for the simulation models described below. Both applications involve infrastructure investments whose effects stem from their impact on the connectivity networks. This choice of investment was driven by the interests of ADB, but the methodology is applicable to a wide variety of alternative policy experiments.

3.1 Northeast India

Economic agents are approximated as actors in networked geographic space. Each geographic cell in a cellular automaton (CA) establishes trade with the neighboring cells (or 'tiles'—cells and tiles are used here in the same way and are interchangeable), mainly based on the productive capability of an export-oriented firm within the cell. Put into an agent space of the CA, the economic model combines a numerical mathematical model with a logic time-indexed sequence of agent states. Each geographic space thus produces output and consumes at the same time. Producers earn rent for their efforts. Consumers earn wages. Movement of goods between cells is costly, and depends on distance and on the condition of institutional and physical infrastructures. Within cells, movement cost is assumed negligible. Production and consumption can temporarily diverge in a particular location, thus leading to diverging prices and to trade with neighbors. Firms compete with other firms in the same sector, and get selected for their success. Firms cooperate across cells in networks of suppliers of inputs, knowledge providers, consultants, marketing, industry and service cooperatives and associations. Trade networks emerge. The whole combination of factors in a variety of trade services is characterized by a combined "transaction technology", which is incorporated in export unit values of South Asian exports to OECD countries (import data of the OECD countries). Transaction technology or productivity measures the overall cost of trade, from cell to cell over distance. Emerging trade networks encapsulate knowledge leading to high productivity measured in high export unit values. In evolutionary trade theory (Brunner and Allen 2005) variation and selection among agents re-coordinates knowledge. Development intervention is directed at structure change.

Brunner and Allen (2005) demonstrate technically the interconnection of numeric model portions with logic model portions under an algorithm. Geographic interventions can be abstracted and represented as a network of vertices with logistic links. Vertices can be positioned on a digital map via a matrix of x and y coordinates (location matrix).

Going back to the northeastern part of India, economic interaction of actors (firms by size, formal labor, sectors and output, income and distribution, all by location and districts) has been mapped across space, along transport and trade corridors and networks (also linked to the rest of the world). Similarly, in an extended model, financial and information interactions among economic players can be mapped via adjacency matrices. This is a matrix that represents economic interaction among agents as 'ones' or 'zeroes', 1 stands for an interaction (which can also be weighted in terms of strength), and 0 for no interaction, hence the vertices are not adjacent. 'Hubbing' or 'clustering' can also be expressed in matrices, specifically coefficient matrices, where cells are filled with positive or negative numbers, representing locations where economic actors attract activity (positive cells), or repel activity (negative cells).

In our initial application, two economic interventions are timed and coordinated, one in logistics/transport infrastructure and the other one in reducing the transactions cost of trade between economic nodes and along transport corridors (value chain development, or competitiveness increase of small and medium enterprises), and when only logistics/transport infrastructure investment is undertaken in isolation (Fig. 3). For each of the simulations, the maps in the top panels represent the spatial distribution of labor and employment. Purple represents available agricultural jobs, blue available high quality jobs. Dark green represents labor in agricultural jobs and light green labor in high quality jobs. Red represents unemployed labor. Time progresses from the left to the right and the panels below the maps are taken from immediately before the intervention, and then at intervals after the intervention to show the effect of the intervention.

The differences in terms of impact between the two projected approaches and scenarios are stark. A combined logistics/infrastructure and value chain improvement intervention for small and medium enterprises can double export and production, double qualified labor wage levels, and significantly reduce unemployment in the remote region. On the map, over time the employment benefits become more dispersed geographically (the sea of light green dots expands). In the second scenario, there are hardly any export production gains (there is actually a visible "emigration of resources" effect from intervention), less income and employment gains, and those employment gains remain concentrated on the map. This is a powerful demonstration of the effect of higher complexity policy making which is only made possible when a model provides higher dimensional design space to the policy maker in an easily accessible and understandable, interactive and visual way.

3.2 SASEC Study

Expanding the area of policy interest to the economic integration of Bangladesh, Bhutan and Nepal with eastern parts of India, another agent-based model is undertaken (ADB 2011). Policy experiments here take the shape of soft and

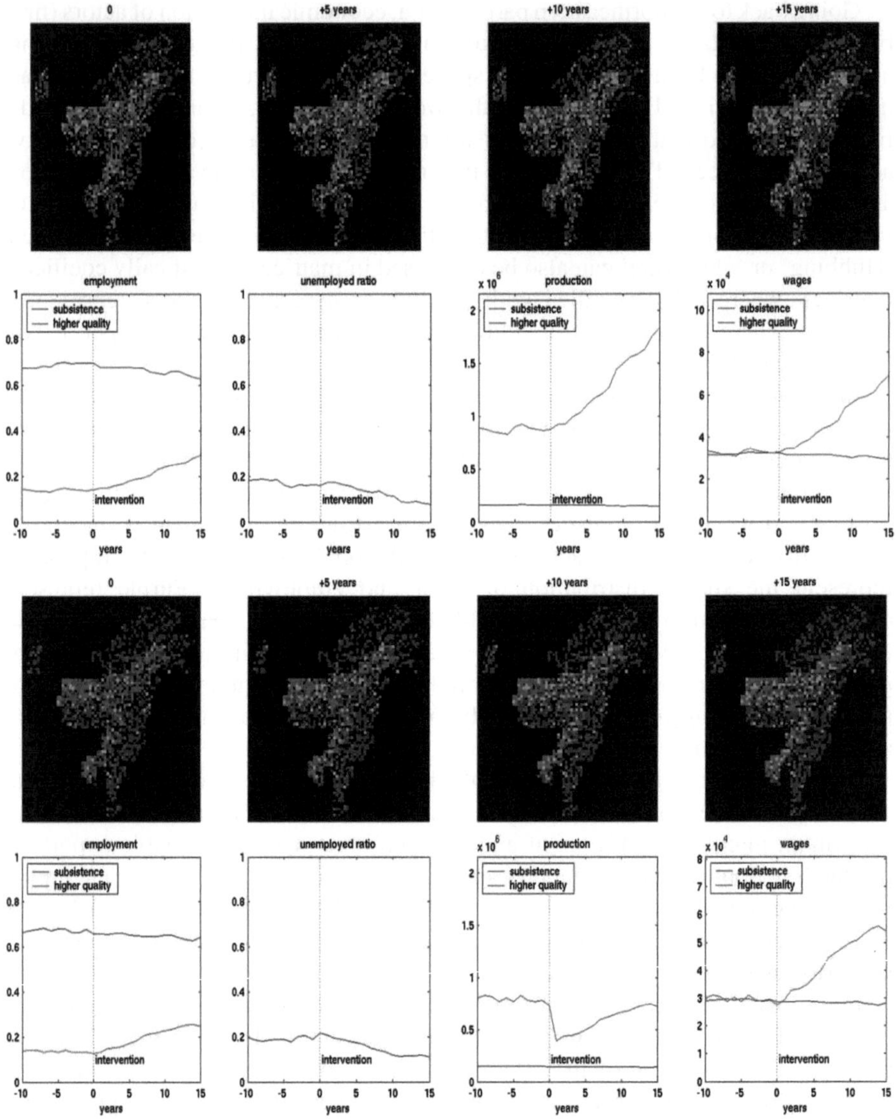

Fig. 3 Scenario 1—Trade cost reduction with competitiveness and supply capacity increase. Scenario 2: Trade cost reduction without competitiveness increase. [*Source*: GDS-NECSI (2006)]

hard infrastructure investments that facilitate trade across regions. Our model as situated in Allen's layered assumptions framework—detailed in the Appendix—is further characterized and detailed in Rossi-Hansberg (2005). A difference is that we consider out of equilibrium dynamics where the evolution of the system is guided by the choices of optimizing agents and leads to a reorganization of the spatial pattern of production. As discussed above with the CA approach, an application platform simulates the effects of investment scenarios, one scenario with infrastructure/logistics investment only, the other one adding value chain building investment, on an economic map. Impact is measured in terms of per capita income, and we are able to index this by location on the map. Full dynamic simulation movies, showing the changes of income on the map over time, are available.

In this case just like in the previously mentioned CA approach, the study region is divided into economic cells or 'tiles'. These tiles then are populated with economic agents. The model is calibrated using essential demographic data (population). Agents produce (with land and labor), 'consume' leisure and final goods, work within their economic 'tiles', and trade across tile borders at a cost. The model includes intermediate goods, whose production can be geographically separated from that of final goods (allowing for the representation within the model of non-trivial value chains). The underlying mathematical model is detailed in the Appendix (ADB 2011). A land-use parameter plays an important role, as it constrains production expansion beyond a certain available land in an economic tile (and is also an input into the determination of land rents). The non-linearity of the model can be increased by changing a production (learning) spillover parameter, or a productivity parameter γ, from 1, to a number different from 1, thus inducing agglomeration and dis-agglomeration or accelerated growth patterns across geography (refer to Eqs. (3)–(6) in Appendix). In the particular simulations undertaken for policy advisory purposes, this further increase in model complexities was not deemed to be the focus of advice, hence these model parameters were set to 1 for time being. This is one way in which improvements in technological capabilities—a crucial ingredient in development—can be incorporated into the model. While improvements in human capital through training programs, and direct technology transfer programs, are not part of the current model the model, could be adapted to include these.

Trading occurs because of price differences across economic tiles, as agents shift their demand to tiles which produce at lower prices, and which have to be lower inclusive of trade transaction costs when traded across economic tiles. When goods are traded across tiles a fraction of the goods value is lost as trade transaction cost, and this fraction increases with distance and transportation time, and with the type of good, be the good perishable (time-sensitive) or non-perishable. The cost data that underlies this study for calibration was gathered from primary sources: ground experts provided information on travel times and freight costs, which are reflective of the current condition of the transportation and trade infrastructures. Trade continues to the point when prices are driven by demand to a level such that it is no longer profitable to trade across tiles. The lowering of trade transaction costs due to geographic investments, leads to a restructuring of the regional economy as the degree of completeness of the trade networks changes. A spatial reorganization of production occurs, and this is associated with changes in wages for labor, rents for land and profits from business ventures (and consequently, incomes). An important lesson from this model was that the greatest gains of investments need not be geographically proximate to the location of the investments.

The model can be used for comparison in two ways. First, policy makers can examine the incremental effects of infrastructure investments in terms of gains in per capita income. Policy makers, who will be aware of the costs of the investments, can then determine if benefits justify costs. Second, in case there is a choice between two alternative investment projects, policy makers can compare the gains in income and costs under the alternatives. Third, policy makers which come from different political constituencies can see the (geographic) distribution of gains and losses from structural change, and thus they can be enabled to strike better compensation bargains among themselves to ensure that their constituents share more evenly in the cost and benefit distribution across the geographic region. The simulation methods require that we calibrate against a benchmark—how the economy would perform without additional infrastructure and trade investments.

Three specific scenarios are simulated:

(S1) A benchmark scenario in which economic activity with existing (present day) network of roads and trains is simulated
(S2) Economic activity after enhancement of the transport network in (S1) with a set of non-perishable [NP], trade supporting infrastructure investments
(S3) Economic activity after a full set of investments including both the non-perishable infrastructure of (S2), and additional investments in perishable [P] trade supporting infrastructure improvements (e.g. refrigerated or automated warehouses or distribution centers).

Comparisons between the three scenarios S1–S3 can be made both in final outcomes (incomes, etc.) and in dynamics leading up to steady state. The results are described at the level of administrative districts, at the level of individual tiles, and at the aggregate level for the entire population affected. We are interested primarily in how much per capita income increases. Policy makers may also be interested in the interregional distribution of income and in mitigating disparities, as well as in trade flows and volumes. The model could also potentially be adapted to examine environmental impact of transport corridors and industrial activity reorganization. In the study and this paper the focus is on incomes, and their geographic distribution. For clarity of display in a static, non-digital medium such as this paper, it is best to show the differences between the S1, S2, S3 simulations. The difference in income is observed at the ending time step in each scenario to measure growth achieved through investment. Scenario S1 (benchmark) is compared to Scenario S2 (non-perishable investments only) (GIS Map 1), S2 is compared to S3 (perishable and non-perishable investments) (GIS Map 2), and the overall growth from S1 to S3 is calculated (GIS Map 3). Each map displays actual district boundaries, regional color-coding, and geographic centroid dots. The size and color of the dots in the figures below now represent the magnitude of observed *change* in ending income (computed as average ending income from scenario $N + 1$ *minus* average ending income from scenario N) for each district. Note that dots that change from red to pink are still improving, but at a lower rate.

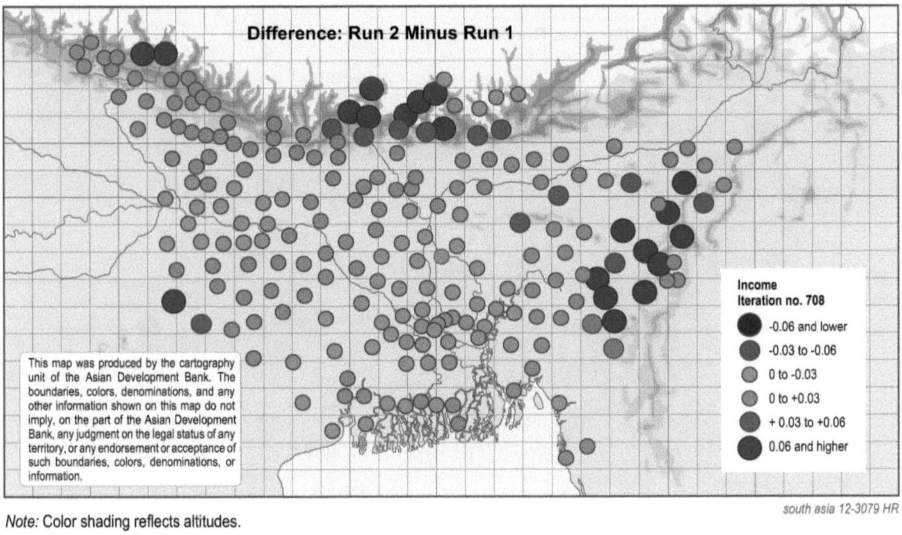

GIS Map 1 District-income income growth above baseline S1, due to S2 investments

The level of infrastructure investment in S2, in comparison to S1, leads to higher incomes in some districts (especially peripheral districts), and incomes continue to increase between the mid-point and end of the run. The full investment package (S3) shows further income increase beyond those observed in S2, with all districts experiencing income increases by the end of the run.

GIS Map 3 shows the *change in* Income from baseline (S1) generated by the full implementation of the Pand NP sets of investments (S3).

Three central conclusions are: *no district is significantly worse off after full investment, most districts show measurable improvement in income, and many districts in the economic periphery enjoy dramatic improvement.*

Figure 4 shows increases in income obtained in scenario S3 (P and NP investments) over the levels measured in baseline scenario S1—e.g. the growth in income attributable to the complete investments considered here. The results are disaggregated by tile, and shown over time from model initialization until steady state. Overall income growth is positive for most tiles, despite initial turbulence due to simultaneous implementation of all investments. Substantial variation *between* tiles in income gains can also be observed.

Last, the table shows in an exemplary manner per country per capita (Purchasing Power Parity, or PPP) income increase due to S2 and S3 sets of investments. The numbers show very significant increases income, and overall aggregate outcome,

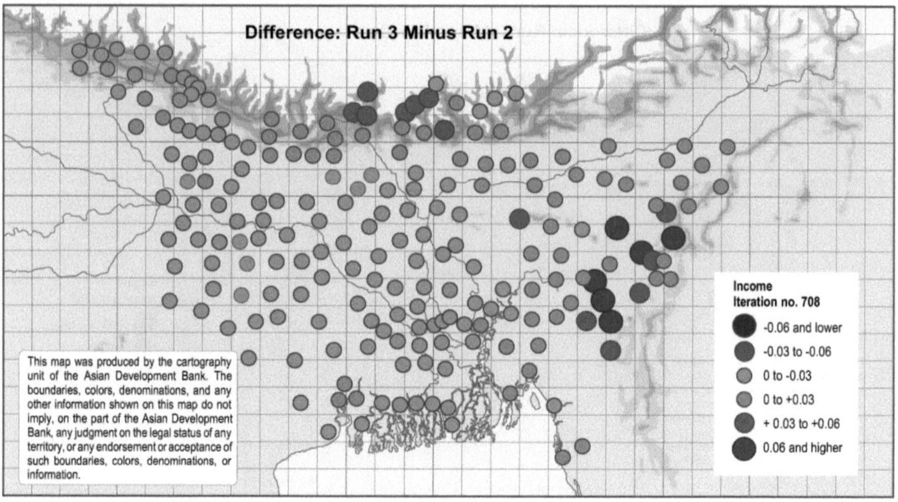

Note: Color shading reflects altitudes.

GIS Map 2 District-income income growth above S2 due to S3 investments

on the high population level in region of over 300 million people, is high at annual $6–7 billion (PPP). The outcome is particularly pronounced in the northeastern part of India, confirming the results visualized in the previous northeastern India focused model simulation. Output tables have also been produced for trade flow increases (Table 1).

This type of simulation as in the northeastern parts of South Asia can be moved further in terms of complexity and explanatory power for the practitioner. Economic development interventions can then be evaluated one by one for their economic and geographic impact. This can be done visually in a software application and interface, where development practitioners insert their development intervention, and give details about the dimension of the intervention. For instance a road and logistics connection will establish an extra link between network nodes, and thus lower transaction costs because the distance from one agent to another is shortened. This can be programmed in an adjacency matrix form where the cells represent not 'ones' or 'zeroes', but actual distances between nodes or the length of the link. 'Distance' can also reflect real distance and its quality and capacity (Allen 1997: 163). Once the intervention is made the computer software could recalculate the network connection between agents, and use this to develop forecasts of economic outcomes.

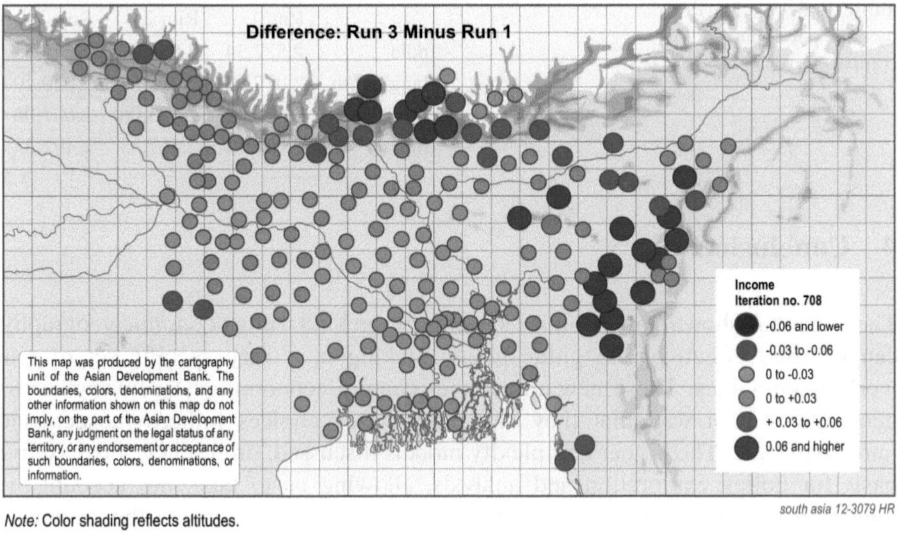

GIS Map 3 District-income income growth above baseline from full AfT investment package [*Source*: ADB (2011)]

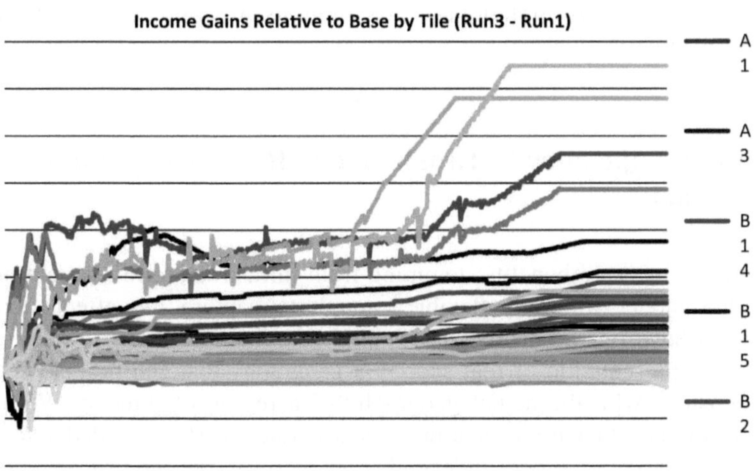

Fig. 4 Income gains relative to base tile [*Source*: ADB (2011)]

Table 1 Per capita (PPP) income, per country, comparing runs

	Run 1	Run 2	Run 3
India	2,522.34	2,554.26	2,574.03
Bangladesh	2,027.54	2,028.80	2,030.49
Nepal	2,575.61	2,603.06	2,607.06
Bhutan	2,431.13	2,467.33	2,492.33

4 Conclusion

The paper has shown how complex systems of the kind using economic geography, can be used effectively to guide policy making in a very specific set of real world geographies. These new approaches capture economic restructuring across geographies in a way that they can offer policy choices hitherto unseen and unrecognizable. The higher complexity models discussed, offer a new, quantitative basis for policy exploration and analysis, allowing us to take into account the longer-term implications for the system as a whole. For instance, the choice of analytical framework and of concepts not only helps in selecting the best use of funds by international agencies, but facilitates international economic development intervention more likely to lead to desirable outcomes. The movement in the social sciences towards application of complexity and evolutionary models and approaches, and away from stationarity assumptions, was well anticipated in Allen's seminal 1997 publication.

Appendix: Adjacency Network of Tile-Based Economies in the Model

To accurately measure benefits stemming from infrastructure investment projects, we need a model which is flexible enough to capture the effects that such investments have on the spatial distribution of economic activity. This requires an explicit representation of real space—a geography that can be matched along key dimensions with the actual geography of a region of interest. We model a number of markets that are located in this space. Each market is called a *tile* (which may be thought of as a local independent economy). The area of a tile is small enough for transportation costs within the tile to be assumed negligible. Production, consumption and trade can take place within tiles. Trade can also occur *between* tiles. However, costs of transportation must be taken into account for inter-tile trade. Infrastructure investments will then affect the spatial distribution of economic activity (i.e. the production and consumption of each good at the different locations) by changing the cost of transportation between tiles.

Our approach, which draws among others upon the model of Rossi-Hansberg (2005), will be first to specify the economy of a tile and identify relative prices in the absence of trade. For the tile economy, we assume Walrasian market-clearing. We then allow individuals in different tiles to trade taking into account price differences. In the context of trading behavior, we assume that heterogeneous, autonomous, and boundedly rational agents interact in explicit space and time, following rules that are sensible though not fully rational (as is characteristic of agent-based models). Each tile is populated with individuals who consume goods, and are also the owners of the firms that produce these goods. Although we can, in principle, allow for heterogeneity in incomes and preferences, due to data availability issues we assume identical Cobb-Douglas utilities, and take incomes within tiles to be equal (but allow for differences in incomes across tiles). Our model has an intermediate good (X_I), and two goods that enter the utility function—the "final" good (X_F) and leisure (L). There is a fixed total labor endowment for each person (A_L) and Labor supplied can be computed from leisure choice as $N \equiv A_L - L$.

The demand function for final good in a given tile can be computed from the utility function. Once we aggregate across individuals we get the demand curve in Eq. (1).

$$X_F = \alpha_s A_X \frac{M}{P_F} \tag{1}$$

The parameter α_s is a population scale factor; M is the total income of households in the tile; A_X captures relative preference for the final good (X_F); and relative preference for leisure is captured by $(1 - A_X)$. Income (M) is the sum of wages and rents:

$$M \equiv wA_L + \Pi\omega_i$$

(Π is the combined profits of all firms, and ω_i is the individual's share—this will be taken to equal $\omega_i \equiv 1/\alpha_s$, but different ownership patterns are also feasible). Individual utility maximization also allows us to compute the total labor supply in the tile:

$$N = \alpha_s \left(A_X A_L - (1 - A_X) \, {}^{\Pi}\!/_{w} \right) \tag{2}$$

Labor is assumed to be immobile across tiles but mobile across sectors.

There are two produced goods—the final good and the intermediate good. Both require land and labor for production. Additionally, the final good also requires the intermediate good. Since the intermediate good is tradable, the production of the final good can be spatially dispersed. The intermediate good could be produced in one tile, and then transported to another tile where it is used to produce the final good. We let θ_I denote the fraction of land in tile s used for the production of the intermediate good and θ_F the fraction used for the final good. Let S be the total area of the tile. We assume CES Production functions. Where values of key parameters (such as the elasticity of substitution) are unavailable, we make plausible assumptions. The final good output per unit of land is:

$$X_F = \gamma^F \left(N^a + C^a\right), \quad \text{where } a \in (0, 1)\,.$$

We compute the derived demand for labor and intermediate good (wage is w, the price of the final good is P_F, and the price of the intermediate good is P_I). Standard calculations then yield, for the demand for labor and the intermediate good:

$$N_F = \theta_F S\left(aP_F\gamma^F\right)^{\frac{1}{1-a}} w^{\frac{-1}{1-a}} \tag{3}$$

$$C = \theta_F S\left(aP_F\gamma^F\right)^{\frac{1}{1-a}} P_I{}^{\frac{-1}{1-a}} \tag{4}$$

The output of intermediate good output per unit of land is given by the production function:

$$C = \gamma^I \left(N^d\right), \quad \text{where } d \in (0, 1)$$

Derived demand for labor is:

$$N_I = \theta_I S\left(dP_I\gamma^I\right)^{\frac{1}{1-d}} w^{\frac{-1}{1-d}}$$

And total demand for labor is $D_L = N_F + N_I$. Given the technology above we can determine the supply functions of intermediate and final goods:

$$C = \theta_I S\left(\frac{w}{d}\right)^{\frac{-d}{1-d}} \left(\gamma^I\right)^{\frac{1}{1-d}} \left(P_I\right)^{\frac{d}{1-d}} \tag{5}$$

$$X_F = \theta_F S\left(\frac{1}{a}\right)^{\frac{-a}{1-a}} \left(\gamma^F\right)^{\frac{1}{1-a}} \left(P_I{}^{\frac{a}{1-a}} + w^{\frac{a}{1-a}}\right) P_F{}^{\frac{a}{1-a}} \tag{6}$$

Rental income for each unit of land is calculated as the profit per unit of land for the type of firm that occupies the land. Profits for final and intermediate good firms (at equilibrium values of prices and quantities) $\pi_F = \theta_F S\left(P_F\gamma^F\left(N_F{}^a + C^a\right) - wN_F - P_I C\right)$ and $\pi_I = \theta_I S\left(P_I\gamma^I\left(N_I{}^d\right) - wN_I\right)$.

Since that demand and supply for each good has been characterized, we can compute market clearing prices within a tile (P_F, P_I, and w). We use a zero finding algorithm, which searches for prices that make all excess demands zero, to compute equilibrium (relative) prices.

Inter-tile differences in prices induce trade. This will definitely be the case if transportation costs are zero—but trade will also occur if the advantages of a lower price outweigh the costs of transportation. We illustrate our methodology using a two tile model. Our key assumption is that costs follow the iceberg model (i.e.

some fraction of goods are lost in transportation, and this fraction increases with distance and transportation time). The costs can depend upon the nature of the good as well. As we may imagine, perishable goods are more likely to be sensitive to transportation time. As goods proceed through the value chain they are transported, and processing can change the costs (by changing the characteristics of the good—e.g. by making a good non-perishable). New infrastructure has the effect of changing costs. Clearly, a bridge across a river will reduce transportation costs by changing distance as well as time spent in moving goods between points on two sides of the river. Similarly, refrigeration facilities will change the rate at which perishables depreciate. Such investments have an effect on the geographical distribution of production and consumption through their effects on transportation costs.

Suppose P_F is higher in Tile 1. Then some people in Tile 1 will buy from Tile 2, where prices are lower. Our assumption is that these people shift their market participation to another market. Costs act like a tax—some units of the good are taken away (but unlike a genuine tax, are destroyed). We will move the entire demand curve of an individual in Tile 1, and shift the total demand curves in Tile 1 and Tile 2 by appropriate amounts. This individual's purchases in Tile 2 are subject to a tax, whereas there is no tax in Tile 1. Any market price in Tile 2 buys the agent a fraction r less. This fact needs to factor into the decision regarding which market to participate in. An individual can buy at price P_F^1 in Tile 1, or P_F^2 in Tile 2. At the lower price, the agent could buy more, pay the tax, and still come out ahead. The effects can be computed using the following logic. View the inverse demand function $-P_F = A_X \frac{M}{X_F}$—as the maximum willingness to pay for the last unit (X_F) purchased. Then for any unit, the agent would be willing to pay only a little less. If he is willing to pay \$100 for the last unit in Tile 1, he is willing to pay only \$100(1$-r$) in Tile 2, because he is only getting (1$-r$) units to consume. $X_F = (1-r)\,A_X \frac{M}{P_F}$ is the individual's demand when buying from Tile 2, and this needs to be added to the total demand in Tile 2. $X_F = A_X \frac{M}{P_F}$ is the individual's demand in Tile 1, which needs to be subtracted from the total demand there. We continue to shift individuals until the price differential is such that, accounting for the tax, it is no longer worthwhile to buy in the cheaper market. The easiest approach would be to compare buying one unit at price P_F^1 versus (1$-r$) units at price P_F^2. The effective price per unit in Tile 2 is $P_F^2/\,(1-r)$. We also allow for inter-tile trade in the intermediate good. In both cases, trade will erase price differentials, although prices will differ in equilibrium because of transportation costs.

The graphs in Fig. 5 depict the results of a simulation with two tiles that differ only in the population scale parameter. Note the convergence in prices at equilibrium. The remaining differences are a result of the cost (5 % of goods are lost in transit). The two-tile model generates a number of useful qualitative results, such as (1) the pattern of trade (exports and imports) between the two tiles, (2) the pattern of production and consumption in each tile, (3) comparisons between inter-tile trade and autarky (especially, effect on income and consumption), (4) shifts in patterns due to production externality, and (5) the impact of infrastructure changes that shift transportation costs. Generalization to multiple tiles and calibration with

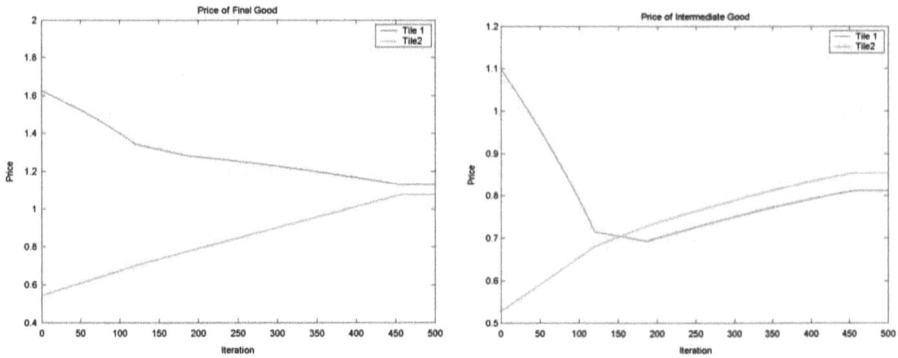

Fig. 5 Convergence of prices in the two tile model

real data is both important and complicated. However, the two tile model illustrates all the key conceptual principles involved.

References

Allen P (1981) The evolutionary paradigm of dissipative structures. In: Jantsch E (ed) The evolutionary vision: toward a unifying paradigm of physics and the social sciences, AAAS Chosen Symposia. Westview Press, Boulder

Allen P (1982) Evolution, modelling and design in a complex world. Environ Plann B 9:95–111

Allen PM (1984) Self-organisation in human systems. In: Jurkovich R, Paelinck JHP (eds) Problems in interdisciplinary studies. Gower, Aldershot, pp 105–132

Allen P (1997) Cities and regions as self-organising systems: models of complexity. Gordon and Breach, Amsterdam

Allen P, Sanglier M (1978) Dynamic models of urban growth. J Soc Biol Struct 1:265–280

Allen P, Sanglier M (1979a) A dynamic model of urban growth. J Soc Biol Struct 2:269–278

Allen P, Sanglier M (1979b) A dynamic model of growth in a central place system I. Geogr Anal 11(2):256–272

Allen P, Sanglier M (1981a) Urban evolution, self-organization and decision making. Environ Plann A 13:167–183

Allen P, Sanglier M (1981b) A dynamic model of a central place system II. Geogr Anal 13(2):149–164

Allen P, Sanglier M (1981c) A dynamic model of a central place system III—the effects of frontiers. J Soc Biol Struct 4:263–275

Allen P, Engelen G, Sanglier M (1983) Self-organising dynamic models of human systems. In: Frehland E (ed) Synergetics—from microscopic to macroscopic order, Synergetics Series. Springer, Berlin

Allen P, Sanglier M, Engelen G, Boon F (1985) Towards a new synthesis in the modelling of evolving complex systems. Environ Plann B Plann Des 12:65–84, Special Issue

Allen P, Engelen G, Sanglier M (1986) Towards a general dynamic model of the spatial evolution of urban and regional systems. In: Hutchinson D (ed) Advances in urban systems modelling. Plenum, New York

Allen PM, Strathern M, Varga L (2007) Complexity: the evolution of identity and diversity. Working Paper

Arthur B (1990) Positive feedbacks in the economy. Sci Am 262:92–99
Arthur B (2006) Out-of-equilibrium economics and agent-based modeling. In: Judd K, Tesfatsion L (eds) Handbook of computational Economics, vol. 2: Agent-based computational economics. Elsevier, North-Holland
Bacccetta M et al (2009) Exposure to external shocks and the geographical diversification of exports. In: Newfarmer R, Shaw W, Walkenhorst P (eds) Breaking into new markets—emerging lessons for export diversification. World Bank, Washington, DC
Asian Development Bank (2011) South Asia strategic framework for aid for trade roadmap. Technical Assistance Report, Manila
Bar-Yam Y (1997) Dynamics of complex systems. ISBN 0-201-55748-7
Boschma R, Martin R (eds) (2010) The handbook of evolutionary economic geography. Edward Elgar, Cheltenham
Bosker M et al (2010) Adding geography to the new economic geography: bridging the gap between theory and empirics. J Econ Geogr 10(6):793–823
Brunner HP (1994) Technological diversity, random selection in a population of firms, and technological institutions of government. In: Leydesdorff L et al. (eds.), Evolutionary economics and chaos theory. ISBN 1-85567-198-2
Brunner HP, Allen PM (2005) Productivity, competitiveness and incomes in Asia—an evolutionary theory of international trade. ISBN 1-84376-585-3
Cadot O, Carrere C, Strauss-Kahn V (2008) Export diversification: what's behind the hump?' CEPR discussion paper DP6590. Centre for Economic Policy Research, London
Feenstra R, Kee HL (2004) Export variety and country productivity. NBER WP no. 10830, Cambridge, MA
Foster J (1993) Economics and the self-organization approach: Alfred Marshall revisited. Econ J 103:975–991
Foster J (1994) The self organization approach in economics. In: Burley S, Foster J (eds) Economics and thermodynamics: new perspectives on economic analysis. Kluwer, Boston, pp 183–202
Foster J (1997) The analytical foundations of evolutionary economics: from biological analogy to economic self organization. Struct Change Econ Dyn 8:427–451
Global Development Solutions with New England Complex Systems Institute [GDS-NECSI] (2006) Northeastern states trade and investment creation initiative. Final Report for Asian Development Bank. Manila
Greenaway D, Hine R, Milner C (1995) Vertical and horizontal intra-industry trade: a cross industry analysis for the United Kingdom. Econ J 105(433):1505–1518
Haken H (1977) Synergetics, First of the synergetics book series. Springer, Berlin
Hausmann R, Hidalgo CA (2010) Country diversification, product ubiquity, and economic divergence. Harvard Kennedy School Faculty Research Working Paper 10-045
Helble M, Okubo T (2008) Heterogeneous quality firms and trade costs. Policy Research WP no. 4550, World Bank
Hummels D, Klenow PJ (2005) The variety and quality of a nation's exports. Am Econ Rev 95(3):704–723
Kali R, Reyes J (2007) The architecture of globalization: a network approach to international economic integration. J Int Bus Stud 38(4):595–620
Martin R, Sunley P (2010) Complexity thinking and evolutionary economic geography. In: Boschma R, Martin R (eds) The handbook of evolutionary economic geography. Edward Elgar, Cheltenham
Metcalfe S (1997) Evolutionary concepts in relation to evolutionary economics. Queensland University. Discussion Paper 226
Metcalfe S (1998) Evolutionary economics and creative destruction. Routledge, London
Metcalfe S, Foster J (eds) (2004) Evolution and economic complexity. Edward Elgar, Cheltenham
Metcalfe S, Foster J, Ramlogan R (2006) Adaptive economic growth. Cambridge J Econ 30(1): 7–32
Nicolis G, Prigogine I (1977) Self-organization in non-equilibrium systems. Wiley, New York

Potts J (2001) The new microeconomics. Edward Elgar, Cheltenham
Prigogine I, Stengers I (1987) Order out of Chaos. Bantam Books, New York
Rossi-Hansberg E (2005) A spatial theory of trade. Am Econ Rev 95(5):1464–1491
Saccone D, Valli V (2009) Structural change and economic development in China and India. Dept. of Economics WP 7/09, Univ. of Turin
Sanglier M, Allen P (1989) Evolutionary models of urban systems: an application to the Belgian Provinces. Environ Plann A 21:477–498
Ulanowicz R (1999) Life after Newton: an ecological metaphysic. BioSystems 50:127–142
Winters A (2009) Regional integration and small countries in South Asia. In: Ghani E, Ahmed S (eds) Accelerating growth and job creation in South Asia. World Bank, Washington, DC

Coping with System Failure: Why Connectivity Matters to Innovation Policy

Lykke Margot Ricard

Abstract This chapter is concerned with policy and the role of the European Technology Platforms as new experimental policy tools for structuring change. The problem discussed here concerns a change in the current European energy system towards a better integration of low-carbon technologies enabling it to reach its climate goals for 2020. The chapter's research strategy stresses the importance of relations rather than the determinism of technology or ideas. As a result, the chapter's structural analysis shows how firms in the modern European economy work, on a collective level, from within the political system to create new institutional structures in the economy. A major social network analysis examines how connectivity in two specific European 'technology' platforms' networks has changed and evolved in relation to researching the solutions to solving major societal problems, and therefore has also driven innovation towards new business opportunities. The analysis shows how connectivity and network relations play an important role in innovation, as opposed to arm-length anonymous interactions as presumed in mainstream economic thinking.

1 Introduction

This chapter is concerned with policy and the role of the European Technology Platforms (ETPs) as new experimental policy tools for enhancing European innovation performance and competiveness. It presents an evolutionary economic perspective on the industry-led ETPs, which are becoming widely adopted by the European Commission. The chapter is positioned within the discussion about innovation systems and system thinking. The discussion's contribution to system thinking works as a contraposition to the idea of market failure, which has been the dominating rationale for policy intervention, and hence the basis for science and technology policy. Since the ETPs formal recognition by the European Commission in 2004, the ETPs have rapidly emerged in Europe; from one in aeronautics in

L.M. Ricard (✉)
Department of Society and Globalization, Roskilde University, Roskilde, Denmark
e-mail: Lykker@ruc.dk

A. Pyka, J. Foster (eds.), *The Evolution of Economic and Innovation Systems*,
Economic Complexity and Evolution, DOI 10.1007/978-3-319-13299-0_12

2001 to 33 platforms in 2013.[1] The ETPs are designed to be industrially driven by members on a voluntary basis. However, the ETPs are not a technology platform in the physical sense, but more a knowledge sharing 'strategic platform' and a focal point for EU policy makers, industry, and academia. They have become a meeting place for industrial companies getting-together with R&D communities in order to identify the most important technological research and development necessary for enabling key technologies to solve societal challenges.

In 2008, there were nine platforms dealing with energy technologies, and seven of these were officially appointed key technologies for achieving certain policy goals or increase competitiveness in a certain sector, and they became a part of the European Strategic Energy Technology Plan (the SET-Plan). This was a turning point in that ETPs in key energy technologies came to play a key role in this information system. The rational was clear as it was important to get the main stakeholders onboard, namely the firms capable of commercializing new technologies as they were seen as a missing actor group among the applicants in the EU framework programs (Tostmann, European Commission, personal communication, 2010).

The nine ETPs dealing with energy technologies were to deliver a 2020 roadmap clarifying the long-term development in the trajectory of low carbon technologies. This was to contribute to the coordination of available funding schemes, and create certainty for investors (Gagliardi, TPWind project manager, personal communication, 2010). Furthermore, they were to form a joint technology initiative or a flagship program, today called European Industrial Initiatives. The information coming from the roadmaps would then feed into the SET-Plan as market information as shown in Fig. 1.

This chapter frames the emergence of the ETPs and sees institutions as purposeful designs. Unfolding these platforms in time and place provides us with important knowledge for policy learning. The chapter is positioned within the discussion of innovation system as flows of knowledge and interactive learning between technology users, producers, and policy makers. The analysis is framed by the idea of system thinking. It therefore takes up the discussion of the innovation system as a dynamic open system, and not limited by national, regional or technological boundaries, and furthermore positions its system thinking as a contraposition to the market-failure rationality of science and technology policy. Both ideas are considered to be rationales behind policy interventions with the implication that each paradigm is open to different policy instruments (Metcalfe 1994). The system perspective opens up to a rationality that sees problems of innovation as problems of missing actors or missing problems, rather than as markets that seem to fail. One of the propositions in innovation (systems) is that the connectivity between key-actors evolves in relation to a certain problem Loasby (2001) and Metcalfe et al. (2005), and as time goes by, interaction is established or even dissolved (Lundvall 2007).

On the basis that ETPs serve as sources of information for EU policy makers, and the theoretical underpinnings presented in Sect. 2; this chapter argues that the

[1] http://cordis.europa.eu/technology-platforms/individual_en.html

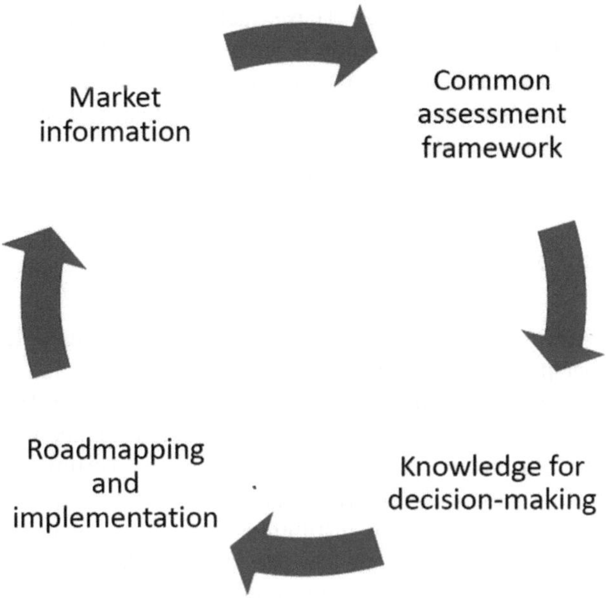

Fig. 1 The SET-plan's information system. *Source*: www.setplan.be

main objective of the ETPs is to involve industry in the EU framework programs as they are seen as missing actors, and in this way the ETPs are tools to cope with a system of innovation failure. Given these facts, changes (in connectivity) in the ETPs network are likely to be determined by the search for a solution to a problem which has emerged.

The study is limited to two specific ETPs, both in topical energy technologies namely wind energy (TPWind) and carbon capturing and storage technology enabling zero emissions at fossil fuel power plants (ZEP). Wind energy is projected to play a huge role in contributing to reaching the EU targets for renewable energy of 20 % of total energy production by 2020, while the carbon capture and storage technology is part of the transition solution towards a sustainable energy system, as projections by the Intergovernmental Panel of Climate Change (IPCC) and the International Energy Agency (IEA) forecast that renewables alone will not ensure a 80–90 % emission reduction (from the 1991 level) by the year 2050. The following cases of the TPWind and the ZEP are not representative for all ETPs, but they are representative of the policy rationality behind the ETP design (being industry-led).

The examination is driven by the main research question: Are the networks of the two specific ETPs (connectivity) changing in ways that make sense when solving the presumed problems. In this context the problems are of commercialization and technical character in why the wind and carbon capture and storage technologies (CCS) are not reaching the market in time to contribute to reaching the EU's 2020 climate targets. The choice of social network analysis as a research method is justified and developed in the theoretical discussion, followed by a brief presentation of the ETPs, the data gathering, the method and the structure of the analysis (i.e. the data matrix). These sections are then followed by the social network analysis, where the study of connectivity is based on an event network using the software tool Ucinet 6 (Borgatti et al. 2002). The analysis is followed by the chapter's findings, discussion, and conclusion. The chapter furthermore highlights the policy implications.

2 Theory and Conceptualization

Within the last decade, EU policy has changed its political instruments and perspective from science to technology policy and, most recently, from science to innovation policy as highlighted in Lundvall (2007) and Lundvall and Borras (2006). The difference between traditional science policy and technology policy is that the latter is characterized by a more instrumental focus on national prestige and economic objectives. Nevertheless, it includes the same institutions such as universities, research institutions, technological institutes and R&D laboratories. Technology policy has a wider focus on the advancement and commercialization of sectorial technical knowledge, e.g. the linking of universities with industry. Thus, the commercialization of technologies is a step towards an innovation policy perspective. A great difference is that the innovation policy perspective has a broader focus which comprises not just the university and technology sectors but also overall innovative performance, which includes the business communities.

Innovation policy and innovation systems seem to have a mutual historical development with an explicit shift in perspective from systems of production towards systems of innovation.

2.1 Innovation Systems and Evolutionary Properties

The idea of innovation systems, especially national systems of innovation (NIS), goes back 20 years, and within the last decade the terminology of system thinking has been widely adopted by the European Commission, OECD and national governments (Metcalfe and Georghiou 1998). The criticism has been raised that the concept of the national innovations systems in a globalized economy is too narrow, and scholars have added more types of innovation systems including sectorial, technological and regional innovation systems to set the boundary (Edquist 2005). The various concepts all address important issues related to systems thinking, and it is obvious that a theory needs to combine work at different levels of aggregation Dofper et al. (2004) when it comes to the supra-national level. However, most recently the system of innovation concept has received strong criticism from the transitional research community. A criticism of its theoretical status as much research has focused on benchmarking or comparative analysis with the dynamic aspects being reduced to focusing on the emergence of new systems or industries and less on the changes from one system to another (Geels 2004). The innovation system research community itself (Lundvall 2007; Edquist and Hommen 2008; Doggson et al. 2011) has argued that too much of the policy focus has been on optimal performance, where there is in fact great variety in both system characteristics, and in the 'wider setting' in which the system is operating.

This chapter claims that to fully understand the innovations system approach, it is important to understand evolutionary economics on which it is based; it stands in opposition to mainstream economic theories (i.e. neoclassic). According to Nelson (1995), neoclassical growth theory has been constrained by the fact that it is based on mechanical concepts of equilibrium (Nelson 1995), whereas an evolutionary economic theory builds on uncertainties, expectations and a 'systematic selection mechanism', which together lead to a broader understanding of what is actually happening at the micro level to understand the various levels of aggregation a the macro level; it allows us to see the variations among firms and technologies (Nelson 1994, 1995: 71; Nelson and Winter 1982). The essence of the innovation system concept is the co-evolution of organizations, knowledge and institutions (Freeman 1995; Lundvall et al. 2002; Lundvall 2007; Freeman and Soete 2009). The important works of Carlsson and Stankiewicz (1991) and later (Malerba et al. 1997; Malerba 2002) which introduced the concept of sectorial innovation systems addressing the varieties in institutional frameworks according to the technology involved and stage of maturity. As Malerba (2002: 259) states more in-depth research is needed on the dynamics and change of innovation systems, for example to explore how sectorial innovations system emerge and what the link or links with previous systems are. A research gap recently supported by Doggson et al. (2011).

Metcalfe (1994) presents Freeman and Lundvall's concept of the (N)IS as an antidote to the concept of market failure that has been the dominate rationality for science and technology policy. As a policy concept, it suggests innovation problems are system failure problems (Doggson et al. 2011). The strength of the innovation system idea is that it focuses on connections within boundaries and includes the role of universities. When Lundvall (2007: 95) reflects upon the (N)IS being around for more than 20 years, he points to the need of giving more emphasis to the distribution of power, to intuition building and to the openness of innovation systems.

The theoretical point of departure of innovation systems, and also an important assumption deduced from this theoretical discussion, is that an innovation system needs to be seen as an open system (Lundvall 2007). The specificity may be technological, but the innovation system approach also implies some sort of systemic innovation, meaning that changes in one part of the system also necessarily lead to changes? In other parts of the system (Langlois and Robertson 1995). This is the thought behind seeing the economy as a system (Metcalfe 2011). These examples of attributes are some of its evolutionary properties where the concept of market failure falls short, and one of the theoretical points that this research is investigating namely that it seems relevant to include both systemic and evolutionary properties in innovation policy.

In 1988 Metcalfe said "*Technologies do not compare in the literal sense. Only firms compete, and they do so as decision-making organizations articulating a technology to achieve specific objectives within a specific environment*" (Metcalfe 1988: 568). His point being that it is the difference in creativity and the development in creativity that generates the variety in technologies, without which, competition cannot operate. Technological development is largely embedded in social relations that exist in technology users, producers, and institutions that shape the development of collective frames around the meaning of new technologies (Kaplan and Tripsas 2008). Basically, we do need to gain better understandings of technological development, innovation, and the embedded resources of key players or the degree to which firms are enmeshed in social networks, in other words embedded, as Granovetter (1985) claims.

2.2 Social Networks

The idea of embeddedness was first articulated by Karl Polanyi in his book *The Great Transformation* from 1944. The idea is that economic relations among individuals and organizations are embedded in actual social networks and do not exist in abstract idealized markets (Granovetter 1985). This is also related to the moral economy and to Marxist thought. "The problem of embeddedness" was written by Granovetter in (1985); his theory stresses the importance of relations, and is in contrast to reductionist theory that focuses on individuals alone. It also contrasts with explanations using variables, where structure seems to be the connecting variables rather than actual social entities (Granovetter 1994). One method that stresses the importance of relations is social network analysis (SNA). It is a structural analysis that is widely used in the social and behavioral sciences, as well as in economics, market and industrial engineering. SNA presents approaches explaining social behaviour and institutions by referring to relations among actual social entities; examples being communication among members of a group, between organizations or transactions between corporations (Wasserman and Faust 1994).

The SNA method is chosen in this study as it provides both a visual and mathematical analysis of mapping relationships between the platforms' represented organizations that form a network of ties. With a network consisting of the ties between actors, it is possible to analyze it, thus finding the 'most important organizations' based on different types of centrality; in this case 'degree' and 'betweenness'. The following brief definitions of centrality measures are modified from Wasserman and Faust (1994) and orgnet.com/sna (accessed, March 2012):

Degree Actor centrality is defined as the most active actor, the one with the most ties to other actors in the network. This is the 'busy bee', one of the most active nodes in the network, a 'connector' or a 'hub' and perhaps also one of the most visible nodes in the network.

Betweenness These are the 'brokers' in the network or possibly the entrepreneurs as they are located in between important actors and play a powerful role in the network; they are the ones controlling the outcomes in the network. They are 'decision makers' and are seen as the 'high influencers', as they have the best location in the network.

Without the 'connectors', the 'brokers' or 'the high influencers', there would be no network; if these important nodes were removed, the connectivity would be dissolved, resulting in a collapse of the network. The theoretical discussion suggests one more aspect that needs keeping in mind when focusing on innovation networks is the idea of novelty, of open systems, or being open to new entrants.

Network, Trust and Innovation Network theory provides further theoretical underpinning to innovation (systems). Homogeneous individuals tend to cluster (Granovetter 1973); and after a period, they tend to think much alike, making innovation slower (Burt 1992). In contrast, Powell (1990) points to the positive advantage of homogeneous groups as the higher level of trust makes it easier to sustain the network-like relations. Though there might be clusters in a network, Burt (1992) maintains that between the clusters, the individuals are heterogeneous, and when somebody mediates between the clusters, innovation seems to increase. Large networks entail clusters and may even feature a core and periphery structure, meaning that these networks possibly "*entail a dense, cohesive core and a sparse, unconnected periphery*" (Borgatti and Everett 1999: 375). The core in the network is seen as a dominate cluster, and compared to its core, the periphery has fewer connections. The core is then defined by those organizations that have a high frequency of interaction and often participate in the same events. Therefore, if this structure exists, organizations can then be placed into two groups: either the tightly interconnected group at core, or the relatively disconnected group on the periphery. The analysis using the Ucinet 6 software (Borgatti et al. 2002) is based on a genetic algorithm using equations 2 and 4 from Borgatti and Everett (1999); it simultaneously fits a core/periphery model to the data network, and identifies which organizations belong in the core and which belong in the periphery. The fit is a correlation based on the density measurement, which in a valued network is the total of all values divided by the number possible ties. In the core and periphery structure, the "*fit function is the density of the core block interactions*" (Borgatti and Everett 1999). Consequently, the number of newcomers, and their distribution—whether in the core or in the periphery—provides us with proxy questions for measuring the dynamics in the network.

3 Data and Methods for Case Analysis

3.1 Data

Following the conceptual framework of dynamics, innovations systems and social network theory that economic interest are embedded in social relations, I apply SNA to study how connectivity changes in two technology platforms over a 4–5 year period (given time for evolutionary properties to emerge).

Data is based on historic membership of two specific platforms, the ZEP and the TPWind. Two points in time are chosen: before and after the members had identified barriers to fulfilling the common vision and the sector research agenda. The data is gathered as to create a valued network as to identify which organizations that meet on a more frequently basis. This is done by applying the formal organizational structure for each point in time with the membership list, i.e. which organization is represented in which working group, steering committee etc.

The data on how the platforms were organized were gathered from different sources, and pieced together:

- The platforms' secretariats provided recent membership lists.
- Data on Steering Committees of TPWind, Advisory Council of ZEP, and organizational structures of ZEP and TPWind were gathered from key documents of the two platforms: The common vision, the strategic research agenda, and the market deployment document.
- Data on working groups in TPWind were collected through the TPWind secretariat, EWEA.
- Data on membership of working groups and a taskforce group appointed later in ZEP were gathered through access to minutes taken of these meeting during 2005–2012. The data I needed on membership before the appointment of the ZEP secretariat was handled by Triarii BV. However, minutes, attendance lists and other documents, after the transformation to taskforces, were available at the member section of ZEP's website: www.zeroemissionsplatform.eu, to which I was granted access.
- All data were cross-checked in order to validate my data, using these different sources, and complementary interviews were conducted with Head of DG Energy, European Commission, chairmen, and project managers.

Going through all these sources, I ran into missing data on who were the members of ZEP's Working Group 3, "Infrastructure and Environment", in November 2006. By investigating key documents, I was able to gather some data on the chairman from the Bellona organization and some members of this working group. The working group data were then gathered through personal correspondence with the chairman, and via email in order to fill in the missing information on additional members. The preliminary list of members was made on the basis of existing minutes and thereafter cross-checked in order to validate my data. The membership data structured by name of organization was then entered on Excel data sheets, which revealed missing names of firms or non-exiting organizational names. This was then investigated through Google searches and Wikipedia to capture the history of mergers. All these data were double checked with minutes taken from steering committee and group meetings accessed through ZEP's and TPWind's websites before I achieved a complete data set for the two platforms at two points in time.

3.2 *Method: Using Social Network Analysis*

The research question is not whether there was a change or not, but how the ETP's network were changing. In the two policy platforms selected for investigation, the numbers of individual members have stayed the same over a 4–5 year span; being close to a limit of a 100 individual members in TPWind and to a limitation of 200 members in ZEP. Change in networks is therefore based on data concerning which organizations the individual members were representing at the given time, and to which event(s) the members were assigned, i.e. steering committee, working groups etc. Such information provides the data for an event network (two mode network), making it possibly to investigate the relations between organizations-and-organizations (and not the individual members), based on co-occurrence, a valued network (converting it to a one mode network). This provided data for a social network analysis of TPWind and ZEP, over a 4–5 year period.

Having two complete sets of data for two periods in time, before and after research of the solution to the problem emerge, makes it possible to investigate changes in connectivity among the organizations. Two elements of social network analyses, using a valued network, are supportive in this investigation; the changes in centrality and a cluster analysis testing for a core/periphery split. The following analyses are:

I. **Changes in influence (informal leadership and power)**, performing a centrality analysis calculating multiple centrality measures such as degree and betweenness.
II. **A core/periphery split**, referring to the theoretical discussion of clusters/cliques in the social network analysis and the relation to innovation as an open system. Firstly, one checks for a clear core/periphery split (goodness of the fit = a correlation with magnitude of .70 and greater, but below 1). Secondly, performing a simple core/periphery partition to compare the two networks over time: how ties were organized and to detect newcomers in total as a measurement of dynamics.

Affiliation Network Creating a network based on co-membership is accomplished through creating an affiliation network, which is a two-mode network (two sets of 'actors': actors and events). In this case, which organization that sits in which working group, steering committee in the platform. Let me first define what I mean by nodes. First, I have a set of actors that consist of a number of organizations (names of organizations $N = \{n_1, n_2, \ldots..n_g\}$), as the first of the two nodes. The second node is the events; in this case, the Steering Committee (SC) in TPWind and the working groups (WGs). In ZEP, it is the Advisory Council (AC) and the working groups, which I denote as $WGs = \{wg_1, wg_2, \ldots wg_h\}$. In general, this means that an actor is affiliated with an event: if the actor belongs to the event—in this case, if an organization is a member of working groups, the following rule applies:

$$\text{Oij} = \begin{cases} \text{1 if the organization i is affiliated with the WGj;} \\ \text{0 if otherwise} \end{cases}$$

Table 1 The data matrix for the two mode network

Name on organization	SC	WG1	WG2	WG3	WG4	WG5
E.ON	0	0	1	1	0	0
Statoil	0	1	1	0	0	1
Bellona	1	0	0	0	1	1
Vattenfall	1	1	1	1	1	0

Table 2 Sociomatrix—rows treated as a one-mode network

Rows/rows organization	E.ON	Statoil	Bellona	Vattenfall
E.ON	_[a]	1	0	2
Statoil	1	_[a]	1	2
Bellona	0	0	_[a]	2
Vattenfall	2	2	2	_[a]

[a]The self-ties are regarded as meaningless in this context. The diagonal entries are treated as undefined and are ignored in computations (Borgatti et al. 2002: 360)

It can then be said that an affiliation network is "... *information about subsets of actors who participate in the same social activities*" (Wasserman and Faust 1994: 294). Thus, we create a simple matrix, with a row for each of the organizations and a column for each of the working groups, WGs, following dichotomous coding to create the affiliated networks. The design of the matrix using the organizational categories forming the membership of the platforms could then be developed using Ucinet for analysis (Borgatti et al. 2002) (Table 1).

Analytically, the duality means that we can study the ties between organizations or between events (Steering Committee's and Working group). As we are interested in the relation between organizations, we choose to create a one-mode network based on the names of the organizations, the rows (an affiliation matrix).

In a one-mode network, two organizations are linked as pairs, if they are both affiliated with the same sub-group. We can then refer to the relationship between the organizations as co-attendance, co-membership, and co-occurrence.

For example (Table 2);

I. Leadership and power: With the matrix now consisting of the ties between organizations, we can analyze it as if it were a one-mode network (one type of 'actors': organizations-organizations), thus finding the 'most important organizations' based on the different types of centrality, degree and betweenness. When the data is based on co-membership, and there are organizations that meet on a more frequently basis, it is reflected in the network now being a valued network. Patterns from the first analysis of the two platforms showed changes in networks towards distributed power; moving from 'a few' to 'more than a few' leaders with equal centrality measures. It therefore seemed reasonable to check the networks for a clear core/periphery split.

II. Core/periphery: The size of population in the four network analyses was set accordingly to the number of organizations in the network—between 88 and 124 organizations. To test the robustness of a clear split of the data into a core/periphery structure, the algorithm was run a number of times; the number of iterations was set to 50 and checked for finding a goodness of the fit to have a correlation factor with a magnitude of .70 or greater, and below 1. A density matrix is calculated for the two group positions in the network. When the network is partitioned, the routine finds the values within and between the blocks, also called cohesion density. For a valued network it is the total of all values divided by the numbers of possible ties. "*The density of the network is simply the average value of the binary entries and so density and average value are the same*" (Borgatti et al. 2002). This is the same as finding the average tie strengths in the blocks.

Hereafter, the networks could be investigated in relation to the theories of network and innovation (system); Granovetter (1973), Powell (1990), Burt (1992), Lundvall (2007) and Metcalfe (1994). This part of the analysis is strongly related to the idea of innovation systems as open systems. The degree of openness of the system is then measured by newcomers: are there any newcomers? If yes, how many are there in total and how are these newcomers distributed? Newcomers in (1) core, (2) periphery, (3) organizations moving from periphery to core, and (4) from core to periphery? These measurements together with the centrality measurements will tell us about the dynamics in the platforms. An in-depth analysis is presented in the following section.

4 Analysing the Two European Technology Platforms

4.1 TPWind Over a 4-Year Period

TPWind was launched in 2006 with broad policy backing; however, it was the project UpWind funded by the 6th EU Framework program that brought the network together to establish the platform (Hjuler, DTU Wind, Coordinator of UpWind, personal communication, 2009). This project was the preliminary step for developing the network that should lead TPWind. The project included 43 partners from industry and research communities within Europe. Behind the UpWind application were European Wind Associations (EWEA) and the European Academy of Wind Energy (EAWE), and these organizations still play a strong supporting role today.

The main industrial actors in the TPWind project include large wind turbine manufacturers, and also small firms i.e. with expertise in aerodynamics. The vision that wind energy will cover 12–14 % of EU's electricity consumption by 2020, with a total installed capacity of 180 GW, which is seen as the main driver. By 2030, the vision is to increase the installed capacity to 300 GW. TPWind has declared that it will also assess the overall funding available to carry out this work, from public and private sources.

In November 2007, TPWind decided to focus much more on the barriers to including more wind power in the grid and expanding towards offshore wind power plants. This was a result of a common visioning and road mapping solution, which recognized the high potential of utilizing the wind power resource at sea. As size of the turbines matters at sea, the solution was also the answer to an innovation trend to make wind turbines, rotors and blades larger and thus more effective, which would be an outcome of the UpWind project. Bigger turbines would of course demand greater geographical safety distances to their neighbors' backyards. Thus, moving offshore would avoid one of the strongest public challenges, the Not-In-My-Backyard challenge (The NIMBY challenge).

At that time, TPWind's organizational body consisted of an executive committee, steering committee and seven working groups (WGs)–WG1: Wind Conditions; WG2: Wind Power Systems; WG3: Wind Energy Integration; WG4: Offshore Development and Operation; WG5: Wind Markets and Economics; WG6: Wind Policy and Environment; and a WG7: Finance. This was the original organizational structure as it had evolved since October 2006.

Then, after the first publication of the strategic research agenda and common vision, the organizational structure changed, starting in November 2007, into the organizational structure that forms it today, in November 2011. It now comprises the steering committee and the WGs–WG1: Wind Conditions; WG2: Wind Power Systems; WG3: Grid Integration: WG4: Offshore; WG5: Environment and Deployment. The main changes are in the working groups. A complete dataset was gathered on the membership of each of the working groups and the steering committee. Now, the executive committee consists only of three individuals who are also members of the steering committee, which consists of 24 individuals. The steering committee is the official management body; the executive committee could be excluded, since it is captured in the steering committee.

TPWind's Changes in Leadership and Power

The network based on the data from 2007 and the data from 2011 can then be visualized using Netdraw (Borgatti et al. 2002). In Fig. 2, the two networks are visualized. Even though the total population of organizations has diminished slightly from 91 in 2007 to 88 in 2011, the networks have not only grown in size, but in density and in changed in structure making the organizations more connected and collaboration high.

The betweenness measurement is then added to the analysis. In Fig. 2 the measurement indicating who are the 'the high influencers' is then added to the visualization, thus adding more information as the networks have grown not only more organizations, but also with more organizations being better positioned in the networks. More high influencers as these are being positioned between important organizations. These are the brokers, the high influencers, the informal decision makers or possibly the entrepreneurs as their new position are filling-in what Burt (1992) framed as a structural hole. This tells us that the power has become more evenly distributed since 2007, as the power is shared between more organizations.

TPWind November 2007

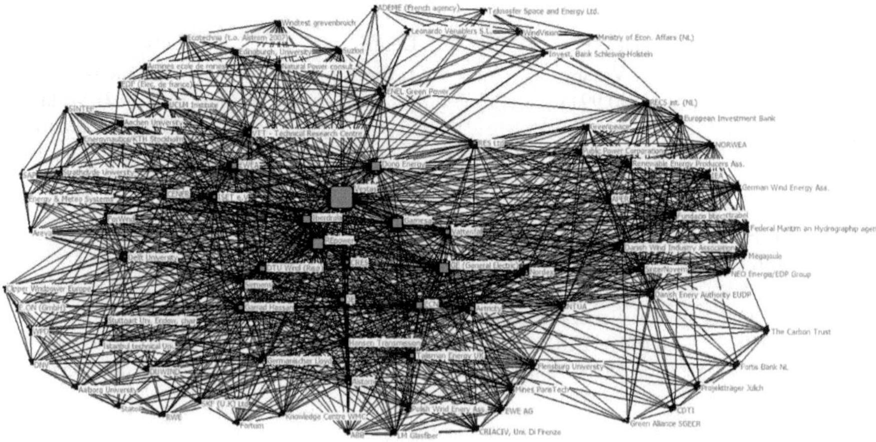

TPWind November 2011

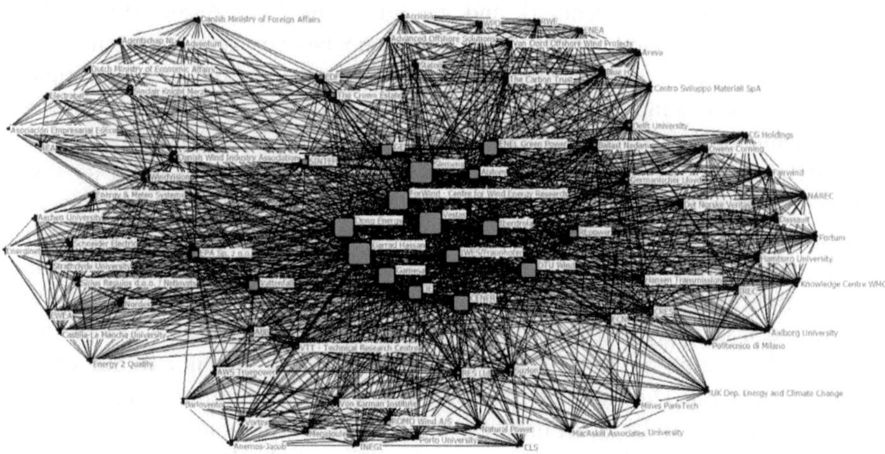

Fig. 2 Visualization of TPWind network—2007 (*top*) and 2011 (*bottom*). * Nodes are organizations. The sizes of nodes are set proportional with betweenness measures: also known as the high influencers

Table 3 presents a top-five in calculations of both betweenness (high influencers) and degree (connectors) so as to compare the changes in power. It tells us that Vestas, a Danish wind turbine manufacturer, had the leadership in the beginning of its establishment up to 2007, closely followed by Gamesa, a Spanish wind turbine manufacturer.

Hereafter, in 2011 a much stronger focus on offshore wind power plants made Siemens Wind Power an important and powerful player in the network. The power was now evenly distributed between Vestas, Siemens and Garrad Hassan, the last

Table 3 Changes in TPWind's 'leadership' (top 5, centrality)

2007		2011	
Degree	Between	Degree	Between
1. Vestas (86,000)	1. Vestas (530,991)	1. Siemens (88,000) Vestas Garrad Hassan	1. Siemens (171,807) Vestas (Garrad Hassan)
2. Gamesa (72,000)	2. Repower (226,779)	2. DONG Energy ForWind (84,000)	2. DONG Energy ForWind (147,588)
3. General Electric (GE) (69,000)	3. Gamesa (211,168)	3. DTU Wind (80,000) CENER Iberdola	3. DTU Wind (113,781) CENER Iberdola
4. Repower DONG Energy (64,000)	4. General Electric (GE) (220,160)	4. 3E (76,000)	4. ENEL Green Power (99,934)
5. Iberdola (54,000)	5. DONG Energy (173,682)	5. ENEL Green Power (72,000)	5. 3E (94,895)

also being part of the secretariat, which is evenly divided between DTU Wind at Technical University of Denmark and the European Wind Association (EWEA) that is the European wind industry's interest group. Not surprisingly, Siemens Wind Power is particularly strong in manufacturing offshore wind turbines, and Siemens industries in producing electrical control systems, which are needed for the wind power plants. Both Vestas and Gamesa seem to have been falling behind the aggressive offshore strategy focusing on their expertise in manufacturing onshore wind turbines. In May 2012, Gamesa announced that the Spanish manufacturer's first offshore prototype was ready to be launched, and Vestas had indeed played catch-up with its competitors since the early annunciation of the 7 MW offshore wind turbine, which output was later increased to the 8 MW offshore prototype (biggest wind turbine ever), securing its position. In second place, Dong Energy, a Danish utility company that within the last 3 years has focus on specializing in building offshore wind power plants. During the period of study, the Danish utility company moved from its fifth place to be a fast mover in building offshore wind farms, and closing in on the leadership of the manufactures. The change in leadership therefore seems to change, when problems change, following skills and experience in new strategic directions.

TPWind's Core/Periphery Over a 4-Year Period

The analyses run for the 91 organizations in 2007 and for the 88 organizations in the sample for 2011 were iterated 50 times. In both networks, there was a partition of a core and periphery, placing organizations in the two groups. Results are shown in Table 4.

Results show that there are relations between core and periphery; these are of average tie strengths 0.163 in 2007 and 0.949 in 2011. And there are relations among those in the periphery, however, these are few and weak relations—their relations

Table 4 Core/periphery split of TPWind—group densities

TPWind 2007–2011	Nov. 2007	Nov. 2011
Size of population[a]	91	88
Size of core/periphery[a]	23/68	17/71
Frequency[b]	8	6
Average tie strengths[c] in core	1.617	3.551
Average tie strengths[c] in periphery	0.456	0.238
Average tie strengths[c] from core to periphery (symmetric)	0.163	0.949

[a]Number of organizations
[b]Total number of events; SC, WG1, WG2...
[c]Group densities or the same as average tie strengths in the blocks

Table 5 TPWind transition matrix

	Nov. 2011, P = 88				
Nov. 2007 P = 91	(Number), %	Core (18)	Periphery (70)	Out	Out in total (48) 52.7
	Core (23)	(14) 60.8	(5) 21.7	(4) 17.4	
	Periphery (68)	(2) 11.1	(22) 31.4	(44) 64.7	
	New	(2) 11.1	(43) 61.4	New in total (45) 51	

are on average 0.456 in 2007 and 0.238 in 2011. Notably, there are relations among those in the core, many and strong—their relations are in average 1.617 in 2007 and 3.551 in 2011.

Comparison of the two results of the partition showed that the core has become denser. It gives an indication of how the network is structured around 23 organizations in 2007 and 17 hardworking organizations in 2001 with the strengths of many weak ties. This indicates that there are members that meet more frequently over time, but it also indicates that the density from core to periphery is higher—making mobility easier in moving from core to periphery and from periphery to core.

How many members are the same? How many members are new? How many have moved to the periphery, and who is out? The transition matrix in Table 5 is based on the results from the core/periphery split. By performing a structured account, it was possible to track changes. The count included the newcomers and therefore provides a dynamic picture of changes in TPWind over a 4-year time span.

Of the 23 organizations in the core in 2007, only 14 remain the same, accounting for 60.8 %. Five of those in the core in 2007 moved in 2011 to the periphery, while four organizations are out of the network. In total, there are 45 new organizations in the network, accounting for more than a 50 % change in the network, which means that 48 organizations had left the network.

An example of a newcomer is Norwegian Veritas (DNV): The company had moved into the wind industry using its existing knowledge of offshore energy and its maritime history to specialize in standards of offshore wind turbines. Another example is IWES, the Fraunhofer Institute for Wind Energy and Energy System Technology, which is especially strong in offshore wind and a newcomer entering the core in 2011. This research institute was founded in 2009 as a merger of smaller research institutes in Germany. Others are Risoe, the wind research flagship of Denmark that merged with Technical University of Denmark in 2007; and Ecotechnia', which was a Spanish wind turbine manufacturer in the periphery in 2007 but sold the same year to Alstrom for 350 million euros. This made it possible for Alstom to enter the wind industry with the model 'Alstrom Echotecnia' as their most powerful offshore wind turbine. The examples are innumerable. Some of the changes are due to natural life cycles, where individuals representing an organization are retired or simply change jobs. This a natural selection process, where skills and experience are transferred via job markets.

4.2 ZEP Over a 4-Year Period

The Zero Emission Fossil Fuel Power Plant Platform, also known as ZEP, deals with the Carbon Capture and Storage (CCS) Technology. The focus of ZEP is on deployment of CCS; therefore, the vision is also commercial. CCS should be commercially available before 2020, enabling fossil fuel power plants to be part of the low carbon economy (Christensen, Chief Geologist of Vattenfall, personal communication, 2009). ZEP is mainly driven by industry and includes large utility companies, suppliers, oil and gas companies and specialized smaller engineering companies involved in chemical processes. The platform was formed in October 2005 with an Advisory Council consisting of 25 individuals, which composes the management body. The five working groups (WGs) are WG1: Plants and CO_2 Capture; WG2: CO_2 Use and Storage; WG3: Infrastructure and Environment; WG4: Market, Regulation and Policy; WG5: Communication and Public Acceptance.

At the end of 2006, the finalizing of the strategic research agenda and strategic deployment documents was an eye-opener that required restructuring the working groups (Christensen, Chief Geologist of Vattenfall, personal communication, 2009, 2010; Sweeney, ZEP chairman, VP of Shell, personal communication, 2011). The main challenges were that of commercial viability, public acceptance and storage liability. A shift in focus from development to implementation was required, and approximately from March 2007, the working groups were divided into four taskforces—TF1: Technology; TF2: Demonstration and Implementation; TF3: Policy and Regulation; TF4: Public Communication. Call for qualified applicants for each taskforce was made in 2007 via the ZEP platform and network.

ZEP's Changes in Leadership and Power

The networks of 2006 and 2011 can be visualized, again using Netdraw. In Fig. 3, the networks are visualized, and the visual comparison shows a network that has grown extensively, not only in size with more organizations and ties, making the organizations more connected, but it has also become a much denser network,

ZEP November 2006

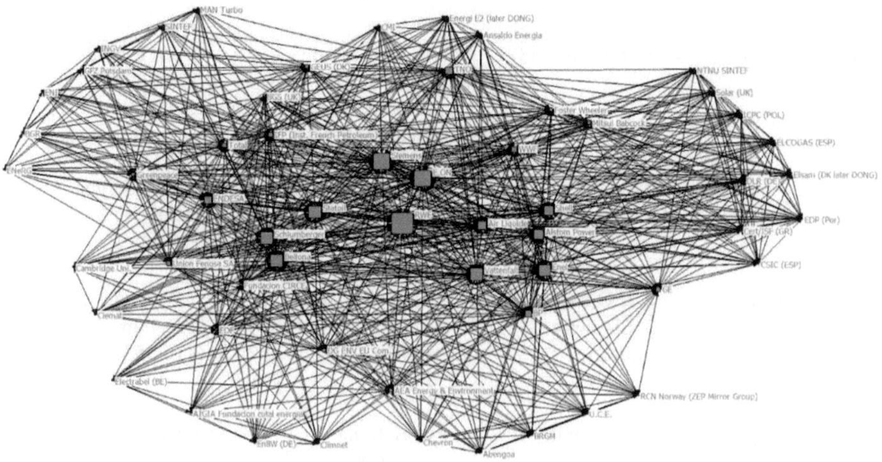

ZEP November 2011

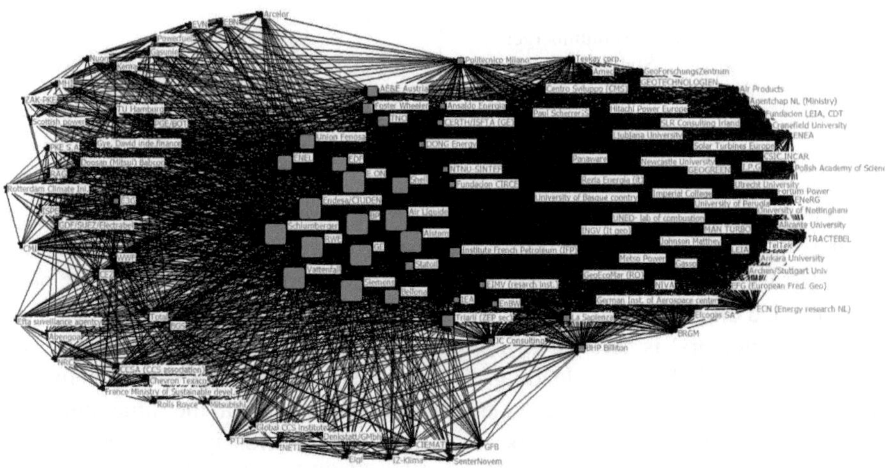

Fig. 3 Visualization of ZEP Network—Nov. 2006 (*top*) and Nov. 2011 (*bottom*). * Nodes are organizations. The sizes of nodes are set proportional with betweenness measures: also known as the high influencers

indicating high collaboration. The betweenness centrality measure is then added to the visualization in order to find the brokers.

In Fig. 3 the nodes are set to be proportional with the analysis of 'betweenness' measures. This measurement is also known as pointing out the 'brokers' in the network, the high influencers or even the entrepreneurs as they are connecting important organizations or filling out a structural whole (Burt 1992).

Table 6 Changes in ZEP's 'leadership' (top 5, centrality)

November 2006		November 2011	
Degree	Between	Degree	Between
1. RWE (1.018)	1. RWE (0.058)	1. Air Liquide Alstrom BP E.ON Endesa General Electric RWE Schlumberger Siemens Vattenfall (124,000)	1. Air Liquide Alstrom BP E.ON Endesa General Electric RWE, Schlumberger Siemens Vattenfall (165,17)
2. E.ON (0.947)	2. E.ON (0.045)	2. Shell (116,000)	2. Shell (125,081)
3. Vattenfall (0.895)	3. Siemens (0.042)	3. EDF (115,000) ENEL Union Fenosa	3. Bellona (110,853)
4. Schlumberger Statoil Bellona (0.860)	4. Vattenfall (0.033)	4. Bellona (114,000)	4. EDF (107,080) ENEL Union Fenosa
5. Enel (0.842)	5. Schlumberger Statoil Bellona (0.031)	5. AE&E Austria Foster Wheeler (107,000)	5. AE&E Austria Foster Wheeler (72,744)

To learn how the network has grown, the changes are detected through investigating the changes in 'leadership' through centrality measures. From the visualization of the betweenness, set as proportional with size of nodes, it is clear that the power is distributed differently. In Table 6, a top five in betweenness (high influencers) and degree (connectors) is calculated in order to compare the changes in power. This tells us that RWE Power, a leading UK integrated Energy Company owning and building power utilities, had the leadership in 2006, and was at the same time a very active organization in the network. This position was closely followed by E.ON and Vattenfall. The network in 2006 was strongly driven by utility companies. In 2011, the network was driven by more companies sharing the 'leadership' and thus functioning as connectors, brokers and high influencers.

Results presented in Table 6 show the changes in leadership; that new fast movers are Air Liquide, a world leader in gas processes for industry; Alstom, a global power supplier generating a quarter of the world's power; British Petroleum, a global oil and gas company that is also an innovator in biofuels and renewables but basically explores oil and gas, refines them and turns them into products; E.ON, a large utility company; Endesa, a large Spanish utility company; General Electric, also a large power supplier; Schumberger, a leading supplier of technology and management to customers working in oil and gas; Siemens, a large company supplier of products along the process chain from power generation to fuel-gas cleaning and CO_2 capture; Vattenfall, a large Swedish utility company; and Shell, a

Table 7 Core/periphery

ZEP 2006–2011	Nov. 2006	Nov. 2011
Size of population[a]	58	124
Size of core/periphery[a]	17/41	21/103
Frequency[b]	6	5
Average tie strengths[c] in core	3.029	3.557
Average tie strengths[c] in periphery	0.277	0.436
Average tie strengths[c], core to periphery (Symmetric)	0.867	1.080

[a]Number of organizations
[b]Total number of events; AC and WG1, WG2... in 2006 and AC and TF1, TF2... in 2011
[c]Group densities or the same as average tie strengths in the blocks

large oil company. Also Bellona, a Norwegian NGO, which does have sponsors from the industry but is quite open about it. Moreover, Norway has a strong oil and gas industry and is one of the few European countries that actually earn a large income from exporting oil and gas. These changes in connectivity are not surprising as they fit with the greater focus on climate change and reduction in CO_2 emissions. They also show a very collaborative network with strong players capable of investing in demonstration plants, which was one of the key problems in focus, since this change.

ZEP's Core/Periphery Over a 5 Year-Period

The analyses run for the 58 organizations in 2006 and for the 124 organizations in the sample for 2011 were iterated 50 times. In both networks, there was a partition of a core and a periphery, placing the organizations in the two groups.

Results in Table 7, show that there are relation between core and periphery. These are on average tie strengths 0.867 in 2006 and 1.080 in 2011. Furthermore there are relations among those in the periphery, however, these are few and weak and or on average 0.277 in 2006 and 0.436 in 2011. Notably, there are many and strong relations among those in the core and are on average 3.029 in 2006 and 3.557 in 2011.

A comparison, surprisingly, shows that core density is almost status quo—the network has from the beginning been based on key organizations (or key players) with a high frequency of interaction. The analysis of core/periphery presents a structured account of which organizations are in the core, how many are the same, how many are new, how many have moved to the periphery, and who is out. The figures also include the newcomers and therefore provide a picture of changes in ZEP over a 5-year time span. The calculations of the transition matrix, shown in Table 8, are based on the total population of 58 organizations in November 2006 and 124 in November 2011.

Results in Table 8, shows that in total, ZEP has a steady core of *88 %, while there is expansion of new members in the network (58/124) close to 46 %. Accounting for the expansion of the members in the core gives a core solidness of **66 % and therefore a dynamics of 34 %, while periphery has a dynamics of 58 %. The number of newcomers, including the organizations that move from core

Table 8 Transition matrix of ZEP, Nov. 2006–Nov. 2011

	Nov. 2011, P = 124				
Nov. 2006 P = 58	(Number), %	Core (21)	Periphery (103)	Out	Total
	Core (17)	(14) *88, **66	(2) 2	(1) 2	Out in total (16) 26
	Periphery (41)	(5) 24	(21) 51	(15) 15	
	New	(2) 10	(80) 64.5	New in total (82) 66	

*Indicates number divided by number of organizations in core 2006, while **indicates the number divided by number of organizations in core 2011

to periphery and from periphery to core (82 organizations), is close to a dynamics of 66 %. One example of an organization that has left the ZEP are Greenpeace, which changed its strategy to support only renewables. Even though, on the one hand, ZEP mainly consists of large firms—which seem natural since the main focus is on large-scale demonstration plants to prove viability. On the other hand, it does include many engineering companies specializing in chemical processes related to gasses like hydrogen and solar power. Techniques of CO_2 removal: post-combustion, pre-combustion, and oxy-fuel techniques are ironically related to the techniques of solar power and oxygen processes in hydrogen and fuel cells. These techniques may be a solution to make CCS cost competitive, or perhaps it is the other way around? Because that is the thing about innovation—we never really know.

5 Findings

I investigated the organizational structure of the ETPs between two given periods, before 2007 and 2011, to test if there were any dynamics in the innovation systems. To systemize the analysis, I recording all the changes in the member structure, and to analyze the results, I created a 'transition matrix' to count the changes in the core and periphery of the networks during the period. This also helped me visualize the results and show the changes and number of newcomers in the transition process.

Mapping all the members over this period of time showed that small firms also participated, but when they later left in 2011, the newcomer was a large incumbent firm. Following the lead, it turned out that one example taken from TPWind was Ecotechnia, a Spanish wind turbine manufacturer that was in the core/periphery in 2007 but was sold the same year to Alstrom for 350 million euros, making it now possible for Alstom to enter the wind industry with the 'Alstrom echotecnia' model as their most powerful turbine. Alstrom then entered the core of TPWind in 2011 as one of the high influencers. Another example shows that it is not only firms that change, but also institutions. Riseo, the Danish national laboratory for renewable energy, was part of the core in 2007; it later merged with Technical University of Denmark and thus the university entered the core in 2011 as a connector and a broker.

Our learning from the case study of the ZEP platform, with its focus on the issue of zero emission from fossil fuel power plants, tells a story of a network evolving around a certain problem. In this context, the companies and institutions are highly linked to other organizations, not only within the technological domain, but also to NGOs, banks, and policy experts. Collaboration and knowledge sharing is high, despite superior technology and competitive advantage. The stakes are higher for driving the CCS-technologies forward with the narrow window of being commercially viable in 2020 than they are for holding on to knowledge—knowledge sharing and learning is therefore pushed to a much more effective level by aligning forces and sharing vision. Elegant as the flocking instinct itself in a flock of birds, the incumbent firms in both wind and CCS are to be considered as key-players in driving the technology further. The evolutionary perspective tells the story over time of how the network has core-players, who are the connectors (degree), the influencers (betweenness), and thereby the informal decision makers, how it changes, and how the management body changes over time. Some firms and research institutions are taken over by a larger organization and the structure change. And some firms, or even NGOs, leave the ETPs, because cohesion is not achieved. As mentioned, an example of this is Greenpeace, which was a co-member of ZEP from 2005 to 2007. Its move being a member of the periphery to being outside makes sense since their current strategy is no carbon at all. In line with the industry's member of ZEP, this eye-opener of public and political acceptance of CCS also changed the organizational structure (Sweeney, ZEP chairman, Shell, personal communication, 2010). Another example mentioned was the strong and dominating network location in TPWind 2007 of Vestas, the large Danish wind manufacturer, followed by Gamesa, the Spanish manufacturer. In 2011, the network position came to be shared with Siemens Wind Power, another large wind turbine manufacturer, as the direction of the innovation moved towards offshore wind power plants. The manufacturers' positions are closely followed by utility companies, showing a stronger demand pull effect.

This is an historical perspective on how the positions in the two networks change and seemingly take advantage of the evolutionary benefits that the network provides. Combining knowledge and skills, which is necessary in a knowledge-specialized society, where organizations and individuals tend to be very specialized. Collective action in technological development, which allows spillovers to small and larger companies/research institutions, and increases the effectiveness of the industrial innovational efforts. When taking the technologies to the commercial stage, the small companies are usually not equipped to deliver. This problem brings up the relevant topic of the role of the large firms in driving innovation, and very much relates policy to the Schumpeter Mark II type of innovation (Schumpeter 1942). It is however, a step towards entrepreneurship at the collective level, where key players work collectively on researching the solution to a societal problem and driving it towards innovation.

6 Discussion

The methodology demonstrates a social network analysis situated within the idea of evolutionary economic analytical framework and the idea of dynamic systems of innovation providing theoretical underpinnings to the rationales in innovation policy.

The value of this study, which provides results of a structural change analysis, provides a detailed organizational network analysis undertaken to map and compare the organizational networks in two Technology Platforms at two time points, to understand how they have changed and evolved.

This analysis was undertaken as a core/periphery analysis over time—examining changes between two important periods of time—just before a period of organizational change due to changes in problems and in the core/periphery of the network. Obviously, one cannot simply measure the functionality of a network at one given time and draw policy conclusions based on one measurement at a given time, because the network's connectivity seems to be constantly changing along with the identification of the emerged problem. Furthermore, the analysis showed changes in influence, in the informal leadership of the platform at the collective level. Certainly, there is a chairman, but the 'actual' leadership of the platform is in network theory the high influencers (those high on betweenness measurement). The author therefore chose to investigate the whole structure, including working groups and task forces. The 'real' decision makers, those with a network location between important actors, and therefore those who play a powerful role in the network, are still in the core, but the organizations change positions in being leaders (of innovation), following skills and vision according to strategic direction. In both platforms, there are changes in the core and the periphery and many newcomers. The analysis therefore supports the Metcalfe et al. (2005) assumption that the connectivity in innovation systems evolve around certain problems. When there is a change in the problem, connectivity changes accordingly to this strategic direction for solving the problem. The analysis also seems to support the open system theory, thus emphasizing the importance of newcomers, which also includes the mobility of organizations that move between core and periphery.

However, the limitations are clear that this does not say anything about future transformation, since knowledge discovery and innovation are not a linear process. What it does tell us, in this case, is that the technological trajectories are shaped by the organizations by their path dependency, innovation capacity, discovery of new rules, interests and power to mobilize the resources needed. If the promising technology fails to deliver, thus from a system perspective it could therefore be concluded that a problem is perhaps missing, or a stakeholder group is missing (i.e. universities, industry, citizens); or maybe the technology is simply not that promising. Networks are constantly changing. The measurements only reflect the activities at the given time, and the analysis is too sparse to generate the measurements on the basis of technology policy. But, it shows that longitudinal studies are much more interesting from an evolutionary perspective, as they tell the story of how a specific innovation revolves around certain problems and how connectivity change according to interest and organizational capability—a so-called learn-and-adapt knowledge process.

System thinking and market failure perspectives on technology policy are inherently distinct. Encouraging and supporting the establishment of networks around central technologies that can change current systems involves a 180° turn from the idea of market failure. A policy perspective based on this idea would see opportunities as simply being out there for firms to discover, whereas system-thinking policy would see connectivity between organizations and institutions as the important infrastructure for shaping and creating opportunities.

These new innovation policy instruments are also an introduction to new mechanisms in the European economy, since their presence and recognition, and the strong voice of the industry, change the rules of the game. This investigation shows how firms work from within the political system to create new business opportunities *and* institutional structure in the European economy.

Based on the findings of the analysis, this chapter argues that connectivity in systems of innovation revolves around certain problems. In the case of the CCS technology, connectivity in the early phase of the study evolved around technological problems. However, after the formation of the ZEP platform, which brought key stakeholders together, it was clear that the main obstacles were and still are political and public acceptance of CO_2 storage, proof of its viability, and advising about and advocating for regulatory frameworks (Sweeney, Executive Vice-president, Shell, ZEP's chairman, personal communication, 2011).

The TPWind platform's vision of 2020 involves the expansion of the wind industry to move off shore, which will solve the public acceptance problem of the NIMBY challenge. At the same time, it will make the wind resource more efficient. Connectivity will change as knowhow and knowledge regarding reducing costs comes from competing industries. Since the oil and gas industry has a huge amount of experience with off-shore power platforms, there is good reason for collaboration at the collective level (Kruse, TPWind chairman, Siemens, personal communication, 2010). The findings of the case studies of TPWind and ZEP revealed a paradox of collective innovation and vision sharing versus firms seeking asymmetric information. This paradox also shows that pragmatic action at the collective level and firms seeking to maintain their competitive advantage relate very closely to the system thinking in the innovation system and evolutionary thinking. A basic assumption within evolutionary economics and the innovation system perspective is that firms do not innovate in isolation, which is strongly related to reducing risks. The way the systems evolve relates to connectivity and the agents working around certain problems. Sometimes the problems change, or the agents find that the problem they are working with is not really the problem; rather there is another problem and, systemically, the connectivity changes.

Transferring the theoretical concept of system thinking to the ETPs is much related to the notion of fitness. The ETPs are examples of the restless search to solve problems of scarcity, but this is also what constitutes innovation, and within an embedded refinement of the understanding of differential growth. The study initiates a quest for more research in this direction, moving from entrepreneurship at the individual level to also include studies at the collective level so as to reveal how connectivity evolves and change over time.

7 Conclusion

The ETPs are new instruments of innovation policy, and using the concept of systemic innovation, these new institutions change the rules of the game. The social network analysis of the formal structure of new policy tools like the ETPs tells us something about key institutional characteristics, but also how innovation systems are constantly changing. In other words, how firms and institutions work from within the political system to create new business opportunities and institutional structures in the economy, while shaping and unfolding technological trajectories around specific major societal problems.

The findings therefore support the theoretical assumptions that the research aimed to investigate, namely that it is relevant to include both systemic properties and evolutionary properties in technology and innovation policy, that if you change the rules of the game that define the order, you naturally also change that order on which the rules are based, thus creating a new instituted frame within which systems can evolve, this is co-development. Hence, the system perspective does provide an alternative to the idea of market failure that has been the dominating rationale for policy intervention in science and technology policy. It also tells us that the innovation policy perspective based on system thinking has implications in terms of new instruments. The implications of these are yet to be discovered, but so far this study points to the following: firms and institutions work *from within* the political systems to create their own futures by constantly challenging the path being followed (analogous to Schumpeter (1942) creative destruction), and systems of innovation have key players or core innovators. These players have strong power and act according to their interests but are socially accepted as key players, connectors, brokers and decision makers, based on their capabilities (interest, knowledge, and skills). From the study of the two ETPs, it also seems relevant to conclude that the common vision serves as an interest device, a selection mechanism of who is inside and outside of the platforms.

In conclusion, the system failure perspective works as a set of lenses, where the term 'system' is not referred to as a something mechanic, neither in public policy as something that can be created or managed, but more in term of what theory is supposed to do, to organize and focus the analysis, providing a set of lenses, and seeing the research object that could not be understood without these ideas. This is the contribution that this author wishes to make.

8 Implication for Innovation Policy

Instead of seeing opportunities as something which are simply out there for the firms to explore, this framework sees the importance of connectivity in a highly specialized knowledge economy. Innovation policy instruments may be seen as supportive in establishing infrastructures and mobility for organizations, institutions and firms in their exploration of innovation opportunities. Interest, knowledge and skills are key drivers of key stakeholders, and must be dealt with in a transparent manner. For reaching the EU policy goals of 2020 it seems highly effective to team up with such powerful players, but one may question the ETPs' life span as they fulfill their purpose (enhancing competition) as wells as their political status as the platforms are not democratic.

Firms differ in creativity, but over time, especially incumbent firms develop strong path dependencies, if these experimental platforms can enhance the technology transfer between organizations, they are important. However, identifying the high risk areas in R&D; that later serves as information in the SET-Plan and implemented in the Framework Programs must always be an open process. Open to changes in the proclaimed problem as well as to the research to the solutions, and therefore also open to interaction being established or even dissolved. Seeing systems of innovation as open system is a key issue in innovation policy, as it is the diversity in creativity that creates the variety in which competition operates—not the selection.

Acknowledgement The author is indebted to helpful comments from discussant and participants at the 14th International Schumpeter Society Conference, 2–5 July, 2012, Brisbane, hosted by the University of Queensland, and for the valuable reports given by two anonymous referees, as well as to the editors of this special book. Remaining errors and omissions in this chapter are with the author only.

References

Borgatti S, Everett M (1999) Models of core/periphery structures. Soc Networks 21:375–395
Borgatti SP, Everett MG, Freeman LC (2002) Ucinet for windows: software for social network analysis. Analytic Technologies, Harvard, MA
Burt RS (1992) Structural holes: The social structure of competition. Harvard University Press, Cambridge, MA
Carlsson B, Stankiewicz R (1991) On the nature, function and composition of technological systems. J Evol Econ 1:93–118
Doggson M, Hughes A, Foster J, Metcalfe S (2011) Systems thinking, market failure, and the development of innovation policy: the case of Australia. Res Policy 40(9):1145–1156
Dofper K, Foster J, Potts' J (2004) Micro-meso-macro. J Evol Econ 14:263–279
Edquist C (2005) Systems of innovation: perspective and challenges. In: Fagerberg J, Mowery D, Nelson R (eds) Oxford handbook of innovation. Oxford University Press, Oxford
Edquist C, Hommen L (2008) Small country innovation systems: globalization, in change and policy in Asia and Europe. Edward Elgar, Cheltenham

Freeman C (1995) The national system of innovation in historical-perspective. Cambridge J Econ 19:5–24
Freeman C, Soete L (2009) Developing science, technology and innovation indicators: what we can learn from the past. Res Policy 38:583–589
Geels FW (2004) From sectoral systems of innovation to socio-technical systems: insights about dynamics and change from sociology and institutional theory. Res Policy 33(2004):897–920
Granovetter MS (1994) Structural analysis in the social science (Series ed.). In: Wasserman S, Faust K (eds) Social network analysis. Cambridge University Press, Cambridge
Granovetter MS (1985) Economic action and social structure: the problem of embeddedness. Am J Sociol 91(3):481–510
Granovetter MS (1973) The strength of weak ties. Am J Sociol 78(6):1360–1380
Kaplan S, Tripsas M (2008) Thinking about technology: applying a cognitive lens to technical change. Res Policy 37:790–805
Langlois N, Robertson PL (1995) Firms, markets and economic change. Routledge, London
Loasby BJ (2001) Time, knowledge and evolutionary dynamics: why connections matter. J Evol Econ 11:392–412
Lundvall B-A (2007) National innovation systems—analytical concept and development tool. Ind Innov 14:95–119
Lundvall B-A, Borras S (2006) Science, technology, and innovation policy. In: Fagerberg J, Mowery DC, Nelson RR (eds) The oxford handbook of innovation. Oxford University Press, Oxford, p 656, Business and Economics
Lundvall B-Å, Johnson B, Andersen ES, Dalum B (2002) National systems of production, innovation and competence building. Res Policy 31:213–231
Malerba F, Orsenigo L, Peretto P (1997) Persistence of innovative activities, sectoral patterns of innovation and international technological specialization. Int J Ind Organ 15:801–826
Malerba F (2002) Sectoral systems of innovation and production. Res Policy 31:247–264
Metcalfe JS (1988) The diffusion of innovation: an interpretative survey. In: Dosi G, Freeman C, Nelson R, Silverberg G, Soete L (eds) Technical change and economic theory. Printer Pubishers, London, New York, p 560–591
Metcalfe JS (2011) Capitalism and evolution. Paper presentation at the GROE workshop: evolutionary thinking and its policy implications for modern capitalism, Hertfordsire University, 22–23 Sep 2011
Metcalfe JS (1994) Evolutionary economics and technology policy. Econ J 104:931–944
Metcalfe JS, Georghiou L (1998) Equilibrium and evolutionary foundations of technology policy. In: OECD. 1998 New rationale and approaches in technology and innovation policy. STI Rev Spl Iss 22:75–100
Metcalfe J, James A, Mina A (2005) Emergent innovation systems and the delivery of clinical services: the case of intra-ocular lenses. Res Policy 34:1283–1304
Nelson R (1995) Recent evolutionary theorizing about economic change. J Econ Lit 33(1):48–90
Nelson R, Winter S (1982) An evolutionary theory of economic change. Harvard University Press, Cambridge, MA
Nelson R (1994) The co-evolution of technology, industrial structure and supporting institutions. Ind Corp Chang 3(1):47–63
Powell W (1990) Neither market nor hierarchy—network forms of organization. Res Organ Behav 12:295–336
Schumpeter JA (1942) Socialism, capitalism and democracy. Harper and Bros, New York
Wasserman S, Faust K (1994) Social network analysis. Cambridge University Press, Cambridge

Part III
Entrepreneurship and Innovation Competition

A Generic Innovation Network Formation Strategy

Harold Paredes-Frigolett and Andreas Pyka

Abstract Based on a survey of *ad hoc* cases of distal embedding in the ICT sector, some of which have contributed to reshaping entire industries, we distill a model of a generic innovation network formation strategy that we have termed "distal embedding." We find that distal embedding is an innovation network formation strategy that can be used to foster economic development and growth in knowledge-intensive industry sectors embedded in emerging regions of innovation and entrepreneurship. We also present a first "guided" implementation of distal embedding and analyze it using our model.

1 Introduction

Although there is today wide agreement on the importance of innovation networks for the success of innovation processes and entrepreneurship in knowledge-intensive industries, as recently documented by two of the most comprehensive studies of the networks of Silicon Valley (Castilla et al. 2000; Ferrary and Granovetter 2009), considerably less attention has been devoted to the problem of innovation network formation (Casper 2007; Kogut 2000; Powell and Packalen 2012) and its role in the success or failure of both technology start-ups and small technology firms that operate in emerging regions of innovation and entrepreneurship. In this article, we make a contribution precisely in this area by presenting "distal embedding" as a generic innovation network formation strategy especially designed to accelerate the process of growth and expansion of technology start-ups arising out of emerging

H. Paredes-Frigolett (✉)
Faculty of Economics and Business, Diego Portales University, Av. Santa Clara 797, Huechuraba, Santiago, Chile
e-mail: harold.paredes@udp.cl

A. Pyka
Economics Institute (520I), University of Hohenheim, 70593 Stuttgart, Germany
e-mail: a.pyka@uni-hohenheim.de

A. Pyka, J. Foster (eds.), *The Evolution of Economic and Innovation Systems*, Economic Complexity and Evolution, DOI 10.1007/978-3-319-13299-0_13

regions of innovation and entrepreneurship. As a theoretical foundation of the model, we use the Comprehensive Neo-Schumpeterian Economics model put forth by Hanusch and Pyka (2007).

Comprehensive Neo-Schumpeterian Economics (CNSE) highlights the importance of the innovation and future orientation not only for the industrial sector in an economy but also for the financial and the public sector. The long-term nature of the innovation processes requires for innovative firms to be embedded in stable network relationships with a heterogeneous set of partners comprising actors at the public, private, and finance pillars of the CNSE model (Hanusch and Pyka 2007). Obviously, in the creation of these innovation networks the public sector can play an active role as network trigger and network enhancer (Schön and Pyka 2012). In many instances, however, such an environment cannot be created, at least not in the short term, because of missing institutions, scarcity of resources, and a missing critical mass. As a result, a vicious circle emerges because the low performance of entrepreneurial activities does not spur economic growth, which leads to a shortage in resources to create the required institutions to support entrepreneurial activities (Saviotti and Pyka 2011). In order to get out of this unholy alliance of missing future-oriented institutions and the shortage of resources leading to the inability to set up innovative new sectors by entrepreneurial activities, we put forward a Keokuk strategy that we have termed "distal embedding." Distal embedding is an innovation network formation strategy that can be executed by actors at the three pillars of the CNSE model to drastically enhance the future orientation of a region of innovation and entrepreneurship and the actors located there.

In Sect. 2, we survey *ad hoc* cases of distal embedding as an innovation network formation strategy. In Sect. 3, we present a model of distal embedding that has been distilled from these and other *ad hoc* cases of distal embedding. In Sect. 4, we describe the implementation of a program aimed at distally embedding technology projects arising out of the emerging regions of technology innovation and entrepreneurship in Chile in complex innovation networks. In Sect. 5, we present our discussion of the present results. In Sect. 6, we present our conclusions and ideas for future work.

2 Ad Hoc Cases of Distal Embedding

In this section, we present the results of two cases of distal embedding in the ICT industry. These cases have not been based on a comprehensive set of public policies driven by governments (public pillar), or on strategic plans driven at the corporate level (industry pillar), or on the coordinated efforts of those actors providing financial backing (the finance pillar).

2.1 Case 1: Israel and Its Quest for Distal Embedding

Perhaps the most salient case of distal embedding has been implemented by Israel for very singular reasons. Israel holds one of the world's highest per-capita VC funding rates and one of the world's highest rates of investment in R&D as a percentage of GDP, has a number of world-class R&D centers producing cutting-edge IPs, and has invested in a local environment where technology entrepreneurship thrives. From this perspective, Israel is quite a departure from the situation of most countries of emerging economies. Israel's need for a distal embedding strategy stems from its geopolitical location, the lack of a large domestic technology absorption market, and the lack of access to requirements from world-class customers in key vertical markets.

The implementation of distal embedding executed by Israel is rather singular in that the distal embedding process did not take place initially by identifying an embedding node in a complex innovation network such as Silicon Valley in order to use this node as a source of embedding for start-ups arising out of Israel. In the absence of such a node, many Israeli start-ups attempted a process of "self-embedding." Since most Israeli start-ups realized the need to access the largest technology absorption markets very early on in their innovation life cycles, they "disembarked" in complex innovation networks, such as the "128 corridor" around Boston or Silicon Valley in California, in an attempt to get themselves "self-embedded" in those innovation networks. In so doing, they have been financially backed by VCs based in Israel. Not being themselves embedded in those complex networks, Israeli VCs did not meet the necessary conditions to embed the technology start-ups they funded in complex innovation networks such as Silicon Valley or the 128 corridor. As a result, the distal embedding process could not take place.

Most successful technology start-ups in Israel were initially funded by local VCs in the emerging innovation networks of Israel. Israeli VCs are insofar very unique as they have specialized themselves in funding early-stage deals, a practice that in complex innovation networks such as Silicon Valley has long become a relic of the past. Given the need for distal embedding, local VCs in the emerging innovation networks of Israel typically incorporated subsidiaries in complex innovation networks such as Silicon Valley, keeping R&D, engineering and back-office operations locally in Israel. Unfortunately, this indirect process did not distally embed the U.S. subsidiaries of Israeli start-ups in those complex innovation networks. As a result, Israeli start-ups—and the VCs that backed them—engaged in a long and tedious process of establishing and nurturing ties with other actors in complex innovation networks such as Silicon Valley on their own. Unfortunately, this process did not yield the desired results for the companies seeking the embedding because of the lack of a node actively engaged in the distal embedding process in the complex innovation network. The process of distal embedding could not unfold even in cases where these companies had advanced to the phase of exploitation in the innovation life cycle.

Despite the lack of a successful distal embedding strategy, the large number of Israeli start-ups financially backed by local (Israeli) VCs with the potential to become world-class companies has reached such a critical mass that Israel, in particular its local VC investor community, has been able to produce some compelling cases of technology companies that not only went public in the U.S. but also became leading technology vendors in the global markets. These highly visible cases have contributed to a process of establishing ties between the VC community in Israel and its counterpart in complex innovation networks such as Silicon Valley.

The events taking place in the emerging region of innovation and entrepreneurship in Israel, namely, the compelling amount and quality of technology start-ups arising out of this region in conjunction with some highly successful technology companies that went on to IPO in NASDAQ and became leading technology vendors, particularly in the ICT industry, have attracted the attention of tier-1 VCs in Silicon Valley in such a way that stronger ties between the VCs in Israel and their counterparts in Silicon Valley have now started to emerge. This reinforcing effect is contributing to the creation of "strong" ties between the local VC community in Israel and tier-1 VCs in complex innovation networks such as Silicon Valley. As a result—and after a long process that unfolded over the last two decades—the conditions for distally embedding start-ups founded in Israel and financially backed by Israeli VCs are only now beginning to emerge, thus allowing Israeli VCs to distally embed their portfolio companies in complex innovation networks such as Silicon Valley in a more formal and systematic way.

The rise of highly visible and successful technology companies out of Israel and the compelling flow of "fundable deals" arising out of that region constitute the enabling assets that Israel has been able to develop over a long period of time. This, in turn, has contributed to the VC community in Israel nurturing strong ties with tier-1 VCs in places such as Silicon Valley. As a result, Israel and its emerging technology innovation networks are now in a much better position to articulate compelling value propositions in order for processes of distal embedding to unfold in a much more straightforward manner. Ultimately, the emergence of strong ties between Israeli VCs and tier-1 VCs in places such as Silicon Valley and the 128 corridor are rendering distal embedding a viable innovation network formation strategy for Israel today.

2.2 *Case 2: Distal Embedding and the Enterprise Software Industry*

2.2.1 The Enterprise Software Industry

Another case of distal embedding emerged spontaneously in the ICT industry in connection with the millennium bug. In this second case, the Big 5 consulting companies[1] played a key role in embedding enterprise software vendors in global innovation networks. In order to understand the process of distal embedding that took place in this industry, we need to explain their business and revenue models in the early 1990s. Prior to this successful case of distal embedding, the revenue model of the enterprise software vendors consisted in selling software licenses and professional services. This second component of the revenue model required that enterprise software vendors built and grew a large professional services organization especially dedicated to deploying large integration projects based on their flagship product.

2.2.2 The Y2K Mitigation Strategies

The millennium bug gave rise to a singular event in the enterprise software industry that dominated the agenda of the information services and technology divisions of the largest corporations of the world throughout the 1990s and resulted in a process of creative destruction in the Schumpeterian sense. There were basically three strategies for large and medium-sized corporations to cope with the threat associated with the millennium bug:

1. supercharging (also referred to as turbination);
2. replacement through an in-house custom solution; and
3. replacement through a best-of-breed productized solution.

Supercharging consisted in testing existing information systems for Y2K compliance, identifying those systems compromised, and then mitigating the compromised systems through rewriting the compromised code. This strategy involved a lesser investment and consisted in engaging the services of boutique IT consultancies that specialized in solving the Y2K problem. This mitigation strategy was adopted primarily by small and medium-sized firms willing and able to assume the latent risk of failure, as in most cases there were no contractual assurances that the supercharged systems would not fail at the turn of the millennium.

Replacement through the development of a new in-house solution, although feasible in some cases for small and medium-sized companies, was not an option for large corporations that had invested massively in IT infrastructure, software, and services throughout the 1960s, 1970s, and 1980s. The Y2K agenda, which had been driven by the Big 5 consulting companies at the largest corporations of the world since the early 1990s, left little room for this strategy. Indeed, not only the costs but also the times needed to execute this second strategy at the largest corporations in tier-1 markets rendered it impractical.

[1]This is a term used to refer to the largest professional services firms that provided consulting services in strategy and management throughout the 1990s, including ICT strategy and execution, to the largest corporations of the world.

The third strategy, namely, replacement through a best-of-breed productized solution, seemed to fit well with the strategy of both the Big 5 consulting companies and the largest corporations of the world. This strategy required the Big 5 consulting companies to position themselves as independent advisors at the world's largest corporations. The Big 5 consulting companies would then advise their clients and provide them with a comprehensive solution following a three-stage process. The first stage consisted in conducting Y2K compliance studies to ascertain to what extent IT infrastructure and systems were compromised by the Y2K problem and to assess the potential business impact of not being Y2K-compliant. The second stage consisted in preparing a strategy to mitigate the problem that met the client's constraints in terms of times and costs. The third stage consisted in executing and implementing the chosen strategy. In looking at the tier-1 ICT absorption markets in the main industry verticals, it became apparent to the Big 5 consulting companies that the third strategy outlined above, namely, replacement through a best-of-breed productized solution, would not only fit well with the challenge posed by the Y2K bug but would also represent a tremendous market opportunity for them. To replace existing enterprise software systems through a best-of-breed productized solution had several advantages for large corporations, including warranties of the chosen independent software vendor as to the Y2K compliance of their product.[2] This would come along with the best business and technical advise money can buy—namely, the advise of the world's leading consulting firms. This strategy also meant that the world's leading corporations would benefit from a world-class enterprise software product, that is, a product that addressed the requirements of the largest corporations of the world in several vertical markets and was continuously updated to meet the new business and technical requirements of such a world-class client base.

2.2.3 Changing the Revenue Model of the Enterprise Software Industry

In order for the Big 5 consulting companies to participate and capitalize upon the third stage of the process outlined above, namely, the execution of the replacement strategy through a world-class productized solution, a change in the revenue model of leading enterprise software vendors was needed. The change consisted in separating the licensing from the professional services component of the revenue model. This was seen as a radical business change by many of the largest enterprise software vendors. Indeed, by the mid-1990s the entire enterprise software industry saw their business primarily as the provision of professional services. According to this model, the professional services division of any major enterprise software

[2]Though these warranties were often limited contractually to the amount of licenses under the contract and did not cover the integration of their product with existing infrastructure, the vendor's "client referenceability" provided in most cases enough assurances to prospective clients in lieu of actual legal warranties.

vendor would utilize the product developed by the engineering and marketing divisions as a way to differentiate their services and drive not only licensing but also professional services revenues at the customer. Although margins from the licensing business were higher, professional services driven out of several industry verticals in tier-1 technology absorption markets took the lion's share of revenues in the entire enterprise software industry.

Many of these vendors, especially those with global reach that had a strong track record of growing a global professional services division, were unwilling to undertake such a radical change in their revenue models due to the dilemma of creative destruction. Smaller enterprise software vendors that operated at a more regional level, though, saw the opportunity to attain global presence through access to world-class clients in tier-1 technology absorption markets that had been so far out of their reach. Unaware of the profound implications that such a radical change did entail, these smaller vendors were more willing to change their revenue models, accommodating in the process the requirements of the Big 5 consulting companies and establishing and managing strategic alliances with them.

With operations in all major technology absorptions markets in most industries throughout the world, the Big 5 consulting companies offered a selected group of enterprise software vendors two fundamental "enabling assets," namely:

1. access to world-class customers in the world's largest ICT absorption markets and
2. execution power to deploy large integration projects leveraging the professional services organization of the world's largest consulting firms.

2.2.4 Changing the Business Model of the Enterprise Software Industry

With this new revenue model and strategic alliances with a selected group of enterprise software vendors in place, the Big 5 consulting companies set out to execute the third stage of the strategy outlined above, igniting a process of hyper growth not only in terms of the professional services revenues for their IT consulting divisions but also in terms of the revenues driven from licenses for their strategic allies, the enterprise software vendors. The hyper growth in license revenues more than compensated for the reduction in professional services that the enterprise software vendors had anticipated.

Interestingly, this much-feared reduction in professional services revenues ended up not occurring. By strategically repositioning their professional services divisions as strategic allies of the Big 5 consulting firms, the enterprise software vendors could avoid this reduction in professional services revenues. The undeclared "new mission" of the professional services divisions of leading enterprise software vendors was to complement the teams of their strategic allies with subject matter experts in order to make sure that a process of knowledge transfer and diffusion could take place from their own professional services divisions to those of the Big 5 consulting firms. Unaware at the outset of the consequences this change in their business and revenue models would have not only for them but also for the entire enterprise software industry, the enterprise software vendors that adopted this new revenue model and successfully managed their strategic alliances with the Big 5 consulting firms saw their licensing revenues grow dramatically.

A first result of this process caused the global sale forces of the Big 5 consulting companies to develop the consultative selling skills required not only to better advise their customers on the best enterprise software solutions but also to assist their strategic allies, the enterprise software vendors, in the presales and sales efforts at the largest corporations of the world. A second—and more important—result was that the global professional services organizations of the Big 5 consulting firms did also develop the professional services competences required to deploy the product of their allies at the largest corporations of the world, releasing the enterprise software vendors from the problem of having to cope with building a global professional services organization and positioning the Big 5 consulting firms as prime contractors whenever possible. Without these strategic alliances with the Big 5 consulting companies in place this monumental task would have been necessary to deploy large-scale customization and integration projects at the world's largest corporations, especially in those industry verticals that provided the largest absorptive capacities.

In dealing with a rapidly growing customer base for the licensing business, these enterprise software vendors also saw the need to support the professional services divisions of the Big 5 consulting companies and help them in the process of deploying large IT projects based on their product in order to ensure project success and, above all, client referenceability. This "new mission" of the vendors' professional services business units contributed to repositioning them as units whose "new strategic objective" was to support their strategic allies in large-scale deployments and make sure that they (the Big 5 consulting companies) rapidly build the resources, capabilities, and competences required to successfully deploy their (the enterprise vendors') products at the largest corporations of the world. As far as the enterprise software vendors were concerned, the ideal scenario was to have a highly competent team of strategic allies able to deploy their products independently of them.

This change in revenue model resulted in the rapid growth of regional enterprise software vendors such as SAP into large and globally operating companies in a relatively short period of time, prompted a major change in the business model of these vendors, and restructured their internal organizations. The core business shifted from selling software licenses and mostly consulting services to selling primarily software licenses. A new division, the alliances division, was also created and positioned as one of the cornerstones of their new business model in order to make sure that the relationships with the Big 5 consulting companies, and other technology vendors and channel partners, were managed successfully.

2.2.5 The Dilemma of Creative Destruction

It is important to note that not all the enterprise software vendors did pass a qualification process by the Big 5 consulting companies in order for them to be eligible candidates for this process of embedding in the tier-1 technology absorption markets. Eligible candidates needed to be perceived as enterprise software vendors with a highly competitive product and a sizeable customer base in at least one tier-1 market. Executing this process of distal embedding, the Big 5 consulting companies were able to select a group of enterprise software vendors in enterprise software markets such as enterprise resource planning (ERP) and customer relationship management (CRM), to name but a few, offering them not only access to the leading companies of the world but also execution power to deploy their enterprise software solutions at these large corporations. By helping the leading corporations of the world standardize on the products of these enterprise software vendors, the Big 5 consulting companies did contribute to making these vendors world leaders as well.

In this second case of distal embedding, the Big 5 consulting companies were the "nodes" that did exert strong influence on the purchasing decisions of the largest corporations in tier-1 markets in the Americas, EMEA (Europe Middle East and Africa) and APAC (Asia Pacific). The Big 5 consulting companies exerted their influence and deployed their execution power at the largest corporations of the world in order to distally embed the enterprise software vendors in the world's complex innovation networks of the enterprise software industry. They did so because they had a vested interest in such a process of distal embedding. In this connection, it is important to note that it was only by changing their revenue model that "eligible" enterprise software vendors were able to characterize a compelling value proposition in order for the Big 5 consulting companies to have such a vested interest in executing the process of distal embedding.

Large enterprise software vendors that had invested in growing large consulting organizations were, in principle, eligible for this process of distal embedding. Indeed, many of them were seen by large corporations as markets leaders already. But they had the dilemma of creative destruction. In fact, they were unwilling to relinquish the consulting business as their core business, or at least as one of their core businesses. Such vendors did not benefit from a process of distal embedding and were not able to get distally embedded in the emerging and rapidly growing innovation networks of the enterprise software industry throughout the mid and late 1990s.

The smaller but still eligible vendors that did adopt the new revenue model were able to create a compelling value proposition for the Big 5 consulting companies. With such a value proposition in place, the Big 5 consulting companies did actively engage in the process of distal embedding, which in turn did increase the chances of such smaller vendors to drive an aggressive agenda of expansion and hyper growth across regions in the world's largest technology absorption markets. Smaller enterprise software vendors did have a crucial advantage over larger vendors due to the dilemma of creative destruction. With a large consulting organization in place that was actively engaged in deployments in tier-1 vertical markets, large enterprise software vendors that had so far dominated the enterprise software market did face the dilemma of destroying a successful revenue model and changing their organizational structure in order to accommodate the requirements of the Big 5 consulting firms. Smaller vendors were more amenable to this idea and ended up accepting such a radical change in their revenue models. They were therefore able to characterize a compelling value proposition for the Big 5 consulting firms, which in the end led to a process of creative destruction in the entire enterprise software industry.

By getting distally embedded, smaller enterprise software vendors were able to have access for the first time to requirements of large corporations in tier-1 markets in several industries and regions across the world. This not only provided access to client financing but also to requirements from world-class clients in regions of innovation that were not easily accessible to them prior to this process of distal embedding. The Big 5 consulting firms did deploy vast resources through their subsidiaries in these tier-1 technology absorption markets, providing *de facto* not only a global consultative sales force to qualify and close very large license deals for the enterprise software vendors but also the execution power required in order to successfully deploy large enterprise software integration projects at the world's largest corporations, rendering them key reference accounts in the process. As a result, enterprise software vendors that operated regionally at the beginning of the 1990s became global leaders in a relatively short period of time. This case shows the high impact the successful execution of a distal embedding strategy can entail. This new business model, and its associated revenue model, proved to be the right business model for any enterprise software vendor with the potential to become a leading vendor and dominate a segment of the growing enterprise software market.

This successful case of distal embedding, triggered by such a singular event as the millennium bug, unfolded throughout the 1990s and captured the attention of other emerging enterprise software vendors. With the turn of the millennium, this new business model began to be adopted by those emerging enterprise software vendors that qualified as good candidates for distal embedding by the Big 5 consulting firms. This case also provides evidence that distal embedding, as a generic innovation network formation strategy, can not only drive processes of high-value creation for the companies being embedded but also ignite a process of dramatic structural change in an industry. The enterprise software industry underwent such a radical change during the 1990s.

We have surveyed other cases of *ad hoc* distal embedding by analyzing the evolution of small and medium-sized technology vendors in the ICT and other knowledge-intensive industries. Our findings so far suggest that there are very similar patterns behind the process that we have termed distal embedding. This has led us to the distillation of a model of distal embedding that captures the method behind "the magic" of distal embedding. We present this model in the next section.

3 A Model of Distal Embedding

The issue of embeddedness in social structures and its impact on economic outcomes, originally raised by Milgram and Granovetter in their study of labor markets (Milgram 1967; Granovetter 1973) and later expanded to other areas of the economy (Granovetter 1985; Granovetter 2005), pervades today a number of other areas in the social sciences. Innovation and entrepreneurship are two areas that are poised to benefit from a better understanding of the importance of complex innovation networks and the role they play in the outcomes of innovation and entrepreneurial processes (Ahrweiler 2010; Ahuja 2000; Bathelt et al. 2004; Bresnahan and Gambardella 2004; Podolny 2001; Powell et al. 2005; Powell et al. 2012; Singh 2005; Sorenson and Stuart 2001, 2008; Uzzi, 1996).

If we take the position that successful processes of entrepreneurship and innovation in knowledge-intensive industries are not only determined by the entrepreneur (Schumpeter 1911) and that the success or failure of innovation and entrepreneurship in these industries is primarily the result of multiplex interactions among diverse nodes in a complex innovation network, then the problem of network formation and the embedding of economic actors in those networks should become a top priority for actors at the public, finance, and industry pillars of the CNSE model introduced in Sect. 2. In fact, the importance of developing a strategy for innovation network formation aimed at the embedding of actors in complex innovation networks should be a top priority for emerging regions of innovation and entrepreneurship.

3.1 *Distal Embedding*

We put forward the term "distal embedding" to denote the embedding of nodes of emerging regions of innovation and entrepreneurship, that is, those regions that do not present the complexity required for innovation processes in knowledge-intensive industries to succeed, in innovation networks of "distant" regions of innovation and entrepreneurship that do present the complexity required. It should be noted that distance in this context has a connotation that goes beyond geographic location and even propinquity, as this term is defined in social and organizational psychology (Festinger et al. 1950). For the purposes of our definition, the term "distal" shall entail a fundamental lack of "access to absorptive capacities." Hence, also actors geographically located in complex innovation networks could benefit from a process of distal embedding, as the case of Israel discussed in Sect. 2 shows.[3]

[3]Though U.S. subsidiaries of the Israeli start-ups were located geographically in the complex networks of Silicon Valley or Silicon Valley of the East, they were unable to get distally embedded there for the reasons explained in Sect. 2.

3.2 Embedded Nodes

In this section, we present a set of characteristics shown by emerging regions of innovation and entrepreneurship, classifying them according to the three pillars of the CNSE model. Nodes embedded in such emerging regions may qualify as potential candidates for distal embedding.

3.2.1 Public Pillar

In this section, we present some of the characteristics of emerging regions of innovation and entrepreneurship at the public pillar of the CNSE model.

Low R&D Investments as a Percentage of GDP

Most emerging regions of innovation and entrepreneurship have low R&D investments as a percentage of GDP, often below 1 %.

Lack of Future Orientation of the Educational System

This is expressed in terms of a system where actors at the public pillar either play a marginal role that has left the orientation of the educational system in the hand of actors at the private pillar of the CNSE model or lack an strategic plan aimed at promoting the creation of infrastructure and human capital and their embedding in value chains representing future growth opportunities in global markets.

Lack of Involvement of Actors at the Public pillar in Funding and/or Attracting World-Class Basic and Applied R&D Centers to Disembark in Their Region

Emerging regions generally lack the critical mass of publicly funded R&D output, comprised of generated patents and IP, required to establish linkages with industry partners and engage in successful processes of technology transfer and intrapreneurship. The lack of incentives provided by actors at the public pillar to attract the investment of world-class R&D divisions of large diversified companies and R&D centers located in complex regions of innovation does exacerbate this problem.

R&D Policies that Encourage Traditional Push Technology Transfer Models

This is often the direct result of lack of university-industry relationships in the emerging regions of innovation and entrepreneurship. In fact, pull models of technology transfer that initiate entire research agendas starting from important customer and market needs are very rare in emerging regions of innovation and entrepreneurship.

Lack of Technology Innovation Strategies at Regional or National Level

The lack of technology innovation strategies at regional and national level is often the result of following a more neoclassically inspired tactical approach that leaves the question of how to embed emerging regions of innovation and entrepreneurship in knowledge-intensive industries unaddressed. Due to the localized nature of knowledge diffusion, these development approaches often apply a "salami tactic" aimed at incrementally increasing the product space in areas that already provide a comparative advantage (Hausmann and Klinger 2006).

Innovation Policies that do not Allow Public Investing in Foreign Technology Companies Disembarking Locally

Public policies that prevent actors at the public pillar from investing public funds in foreign technology companies disembarking or wanting to disembark in emerging regions of technology innovation and entrepreneurship eliminate not only a potentially important source of knowledge diffusion and transfer but also a potential source of embedding that might otherwise contribute to the creation of more robust technology innovation networks in those regions.

3.2.2 Industry Pillar

In this section, we present some of the characteristics of emerging regions of innovation and entrepreneurship at the industry pillar of the CNSE model.

Low Private Investment in R&D

This is often due to the fact that actors at the private pillar have not yet adopted a successful outbound innovation strategy as part of their business and corporate strategy, that is, they tend to rely more on the global competitiveness of foreign technology vendors by positioning themselves as their channel partners in their local innovation networks. This inbound innovation orientation of actors at the private pillar reduces dramatically the absorptive capacities of the emerging region.

No Local Talent in Strategic Technology Management and Marketing

Technology companies located in emerging regions of innovation and entrepreneurship have often difficulties in attracting and retaining talent with the necessary management skills due to the lack of labor mobility of their local innovation networks (Ferrary and Granovetter 2009).

Lack of Competitive Strategies Based on Differentiation Through Innovation

The lack of importance that companies in emerging regions of innovation and entrepreneurship assign to innovation as a source of differentiation exacerbates the lack of absorptive capacities available to innovative technology companies arising out of these emerging regions. This is highly detrimental to local innovative companies in need of lead customers and early adopters to drive their innovations forward throughout the initial phases of the innovation life cycle.

Inbound Innovation Approaches

As opposed to outbound innovation, inbound innovation is a tactical approach based on local technology companies positioning themselves as channel partners and value-added resellers of successful foreign technology vendors.

Lack of IP Management Competences

The lack of IP management skills is often the result of a lack of a comprehensive body of IP laws combined with the inbound innovation strategies typically adopted by emerging regions of innovation and entrepreneurship, which prevents the creation of an ecosystem of actors in the local networks with an specialization in all the technical, commercial, and legal aspects of IP management.

Lack of Managerial Talent that Can Bridge the Gap Between University Base and Applied R&D and Early-Stage Technology Marketing and Commercialization

In emerging regions of innovation and entrepreneurship we do not typically find R&D divisions and marketing departments of large diversified companies and small and medium-sized enterprises working closely with research staff from research centers and universities on the development of new products, services, and market solutions. In these regions, there will be a tendency to rely on R&D, product marketing, and product development being conducted by foreign companies. This leads to a situation where the competences needed to successfully drive new product development activities cannot be developed by actors at the private pillar in these emerging regions.

Lack of Access to World-Class Clients

The lack of access to world-class clients is often, though not always, the result of a relatively small domestic market lacking the necessary absorptive capacities. The lack of absorptive capacities typically encountered in emerging regions of innovation and entrepreneurship translates into an endemic lack of access to requirements of world-class customers, which is arguably the most important asset to drive processes of high-value creation through technology innovation for companies located in those regions.

3.2.3 Financial Pillar

In this section, we present some of the characteristics of emerging regions of innovation and entrepreneurship at the financial pillar of the CNSE model.

Lack of a Local Venture Capital Industry

This is one of the most fundamental gaps in emerging regions of innovation and entrepreneurship. In fact, venture capital firms are the nodes that show the highest complexity in terms of CNT[4] metrics such as "heterogeneity," "betweenness centrality" and "multiplexity" in innovation networks (Ferrary an Granovetter 2009) and they play a key role in helping technology companies execute outbound innovation strategies and position themselves as world-class technology vendors catering to the global tier-1 technology absorption markets.

No "Enabling Assets" that May Attract Investment of Foreign Venture Capitalists (VCs) or Large Diversified Companies (LDCs) to the Emerging Region of Innovation and Entrepreneurship

Some emerging regions of innovation and entrepreneurship may have "local enabling assets" that compel actors located in complex technology innovation networks to disembark in those emerging regions. We have termed this strategy "local embedding." Contingent upon a proper characterization of such enabling assets, actors located in such emerging regions might be able to execute the local embedding strategy. Local embedding will result in knowledge being diffused

[4]CNT is an acronym that states for Complex Network Theory (Watts 2004).

and transferred to actors located in those emerging regions. Unfortunately, most emerging regions will not have such enabling assets and will not be able to attract actors located in complex technology innovation networks to disembark locally. Such regions are good candidates for distal embedding as an innovation network formation strategy. We shall point out that local embedding, though the exact opposite of distal embedding, can in some cases be executed in concert with a distal embedding strategy.

Investors Used to High Returns from Investments in Traditional Industries

This is another characteristic of many emerging regions of innovation and entrepreneurship. Many industry sectors in these regions have not yet evolved into hypercompetitive industries. Investors in these industries are often able to exert a considerable amount of control not only over the markets their companies serve but also over external stakeholders from the public sector such as governing bodies and regulatory agencies. As a result, it is not uncommon for investors in these emerging regions to invest in local entrepreneurship projects subject to low strategic uncertainties in industries that are not very knowledge-intensive and obtain much better returns than those a tier-1 venture capital firm located in a complex innovation network would consider outperforming.[5] This is highly detrimental to the local innovation systems in emerging regions of innovation and entrepreneurship for two main reasons:

1. the availability of funding for high-technology ventures is scarce and more difficult to obtain given the lack of incentives for the local investor community to invest in technology ventures and
2. the resources, capabilities, and competences usually associated with venture capital investing are simply not available to the investor community.

If investors do decide to invest in high-technology ventures, they do so lacking the knowledge about how to manage the agency and monitoring costs associated with high-risk technology ventures and are therefore unable to provide "smart money" to their portfolio companies, thus reducing the probability of success of their portfolios.

Investor Focus on Efficiency and Short-Term Financial Success Instead of Value Creation and Market Dominance

This is a corollary of the generalized orientation towards investing in low technology ventures often shown by investors in emerging regions of innovation and

[5]Over an average period of 15 years, an annualized return on investment of over 35 % is considered to be an outperforming return in the VC industry in Silicon Valley.

entrepreneurship. The resulting focus on efficiency and short-term financial success is often maintained even when investing in technology ventures. For technology ventures, the focus of investors should be shifted towards effectiveness and long-term market success. This shift proves highly problematic for traditional investors because effectiveness and long-term market success are often measured not based on short-term financial metrics but on more strategic grounds such as creating connectivity and rapid expansion in a complex innovation network, for which a set of metrics unknown to most of these traditional investors is required.[6]

Lack of Local Technology Investment Funds and Lack of Ties to Foreign Technology Investment Funds in Complex Regions of Innovation

This is in part due to the lack of incentives to form such funds often due to the high returns that investors can obtain from ventures in traditional, commodity-driven industry sectors, on the one hand, and to the lack of competences to manage technology investment funds successfully, on the other. In regions where such technology investments funds are emerging, there is typically a lack of ties with foreign technology investments funds. Knowledge gaps regarding how to manage the agency and monitoring costs associated with high-risk technology ventures are also plentiful in these emerging regions. To the extent that ties with technology investment funds located in complex innovation networks were already established, as in the case of Israel surveyed in Sect. 2, knowledge diffusion processes could unfold from complex innovation regions into these emerging regions of innovation and entrepreneurship. These processes of knowledge diffusion could contribute to closing such knowledge gaps.

3.3 Analysis of Emerging Regions of Innovation and Entrepreneurship from a CNSE Perspective

In regions embedded in national innovation systems sharing some of the characteristics discussed above, the success of outbound innovation, defined as a tactical approach aimed at the creation of world-class technology companies exporting to the global technology absorption markets, will be compromised. In these regions, there is a natural bias towards implementing inbound innovation, defined as a tactical approach aimed at importing products and services developed in more developed countries. Using these inbound innovation approaches, the most innovative companies in emerging regions of innovation and entrepreneurship tend to position themselves as value-added resellers and channel partners of the world's leading

[6] A real-options approach to evaluating technology investment portfolios seems more appropriate to measure effectiveness than traditional financial metrics.

technology companies, thus helping these foreign vendors introduce their offerings in emerging markets. Although in many of these emerging regions some of these companies can grow into large corporations using this inbound innovation approach, it will be difficult for them to adopt a peacefully co-existing outbound innovation approach via the creation of business lines with offerings that can be exported to the global markets. Most of the companies that attempt to follow an outbound innovation approach will typically fail due to lack of access to key enabling assets that are only available in complex technology innovation networks. Distal embedding is an innovation network formation strategy that can help entrepreneurs from emerging regions of innovation and entrepreneurship circumvent this problem.

3.4 The Distal Embedding Process

The distal embedding strategy consists in "embedding" a node of an emerging innovation network (EIN) in a complex innovation network (CIN). A so-called "embedding node" needs to exist in the CIN and the proper incentives need to be articulated by the EIN in order for a distal embedding process to take place. This strategy overcomes the problems that pervade EINs by way of allowing nodes embedded in EINs to access key enabling assets that are only available in CINs. In our model, we introduce a special node, the so-called "embedding node," to perform the so-called "embedding function," the key function underlying this strategy.

3.5 Embedding Nodes and Their Properties

The distal embedding strategy is based on finding and engaging a suitable "embedding node" in the CIN and characterizing a so-called "embedding function." Embedding nodes are a very special kind of node in a complex innovation network. To qualify as such, a potential embedding node needs to satisfy very peculiar conditions:

1. Unlike VCs, embedding nodes do not necessarily need to have strong ties to a wide variety of nodes in the CIN, though weak ties to a wide variety of nodes in the CIN will typically exist;
2. Embedding nodes must have strong ties to nodes that do possess these strong ties to other strongly connected nodes in the CIN, though, most notably to VCs or to nodes in the CIN with high degree of betweenness centrality;
3. Embedding nodes do not necessarily provide financing, although they can connect nodes in the EIN with nodes in the CIN that can provide such financing.

VCs are by definition potential embedding nodes in our model. In fact, a company located in an emerging region of innovation and entrepreneurship that succeeds in securing funding from a tier-1 VC in a complex innovation network would get distally embedded in such network in a straightforward way by its funding VC. Unfortunately, most technology firms located in emerging regions of innovation and entrepreneurship will not be able to receive funding from a tier-1 VC in a complex innovation network. More realistically for such technology firms, nodes embedded in the CIN and strongly connected to other nodes exerting power over investment and technology-purchasing decisions in the CIN could play the role of embedding nodes. These embedding nodes could include key reference accounts and channel partners.

3.6 Analyzing the Role of Embedding Nodes

Ferrary and Granovetter (2009) argue that due to the systemic nature of complex innovation networks, the presence or absence of a few types of nodes in an innovation network, especially those highly connected in the network, can seriously compromise the functioning of the network. Even though complex networks show resilience to changing conditions, the removal of nodes with high betweenness centrality in the network can lead to systemic failure (Callaway et al. 2000; Newman et al. 2006). The role of embedding nodes in our model is of such an importance that the absence or removal of an embedding node can lead to a systemic failure and compromise the process of distal embedding. In this section, we analyze the special role of embedding nodes. Using the five functions put forth by Ferrary and Granovetter (2009) to analyze the role of VC firms in innovation networks, we investigate the multiplex roles of embedding nodes for a successful execution of a distal embedding strategy.

3.6.1 Financing

Embedding nodes do not need to fund nodes in the EIN but should give access to nodes in the CIN that provide funding.

3.6.2 Selection

Embedding nodes select start-ups in the EIN long before distally embedding them in the CIN. They contribute to saving resources in the EIN by identifying nodes in the EIN with high potential for either regional or global competitiveness and by diffusing this information in the EIN. Distally embedded nodes that are located in the EIN undergo a selection process that saves resources in the CIN as well, particularly for VCs potentially interested in funding start-ups originating outside the CIN.

3.6.3 Signaling

Distal embedding sends a signal to nodes located in the EIN and the CIN to work with and fund distally embedded nodes both in the EIN and the CIN. Once distally embedded in the CIN, the "embedded nodes" become more likely to receive VC funding in the CIN.

3.6.4 Learning

Embedding nodes are industry veterans that accumulate and diffuse the knowledge required to create successful start-ups and provide the role of a non-funding super angel investor to nodes in the EIN. Embedding nodes also serve the process of accumulating knowledge about investing opportunities and technologies arising out of the EIN, diffusing this knowledge through the CIN.

3.6.5 Embedding

A node from an EIN that gets distally embedded in the CIN by an embedding node will get embedded in the CIN without being geographically located there. If distally embedded, nodes from the EIN are more likely to receive VC funding in the CIN and, if successful in receiving such funding, the embedding will get reinforced in the CIN. Eventually, the embedded node will have subsidiaries in the EIN or will move its headquarters there. Though the process of distal embedding can have as a result the relocation of the entire firm to the CIN, such relocation might not always be intended as end result. In some cases, the embedded node will become a globally operating company with subsidiaries in the CIN but will keep its headquarters in the EIN.

3.7 Embedding Functions

The cornerstone of the distal embedding model is the so-called embedding function. An embedding function for a node in the EIN is defined as a function performed by the embedding node in the CIN with the aim of embedding a node located in the EIN (the embedded node) in the CIN. The availability of such an embedding function depends on whether or not a "compelling value proposition" can be articulated between the embedding node in the CIN and the embedded node in the EIN that is seeking to be embedded in the CIN. In some cases, not the actors seeking such embedding provide the "enabling assets" for the embedding function to be characterized. Indeed, actors from the public or finance pillars such as government agencies or venture capital firms, respectively, can act on behalf of the embedded nodes located in the EIN and provide the "enabling assets" for this value proposition to be generated.

It should be noted that the embedding function creates a strong tie between the embedding node in the CIN and the embedded node in the EIN. Such a strong tie can be established only if a "vested interest" is created for the embedding node to engage on a long-term basis in the embedding process such that a value creation process ensues in the CIN for both the embedded and the embedding node. Both the embedded node and the embedding node need to capitalize upon this process of value creation. Invariably, the embedding node will need to embrace the risks associated with the *ex ante* possibility of failure and losses. This will make it necessary for the value proposition underlying the embedding function to provide the necessary incentives for the embedding node to assume this risk. If this is not the case, a suitable embedding function will in all likelihood not be characterized and the embedding process will not unfold in the CIN.

4 Implementing Distal Embedding

In this section, we report on the implementation of a recent program aimed at embedding high-technology projects arising out of the emerging regions of innovation and entrepreneurship in Chile in complex innovation networks. The agenda for the implementation of this program was proposed at the first international seminar on technology innovation strategies. This international seminar was the first of its kind in Chile and was organized by the Faculty of Economics and Business at Diego Portales University in Santiago de Chile with the sponsorship of the Chilean Economic Development Agency (CORFO).[7]

4.1 The Agenda

A first international seminar entitled "Towards a technology innovation strategy for Chile" took place in Santiago, Chile, in March 2011. Although general technology innovation strategies were discussed by some of the international speakers, the main focus of this international seminar was to discuss technology innovation strategies that could be applied in order to increase the regional and global competitiveness of the innovation networks emerging in some of the knowledge-intensive industry sectors in Chile. The agenda for an implementation of the distal embedding strategy presented by the first author at this seminar aimed at overcoming some of the structural gaps of the emerging technology innovation networks in Chile and identified the elements involved in the model of distal embedding discussed in Sect. 3. This seminar also contributed to initiating a series of negotiations between the Chilean

[7]CORFO is an acronym that stands for "Corporaci6n de Fomento de la Producci6n", the Chilean Economic Development Agency.

Agency of Economic Development and the embedding node proposed by the first author at this seminar (see Sect. 4.5 below). These negotiations ended up in a series of agreements between these two parties that were instrumental in creating the "Go To Market" program by the Chilean Agency of Economic Development. Although the actual implementation of this program deviates in some respects from the original implementation of distal embedding proposed at the seminar, we will analyze this implementation using the formal model of distal embedding presented in Sect. 3.

4.2 The Emerging Innovation Network

The emerging regions of innovation and entrepreneurship proposed for the implementation of the Go To Market program were entrepreneurial projects arising out the emerging innovation networks in knowledge-intensive industries in Chile. The program implemented by the Chilean Economic Development Agency deviated from the original agenda proposed at the seminar in that there was no technology or industry focus specified *a priori* for this program.

4.3 The Complex Innovation Network

The complex innovation network originally proposed at the seminar corresponded to the complex innovation networks of Silicon Valley. Such a proposal had been put forth based on the observation that many of the emerging innovation networks in Chile are arising in knowledge-intensive industries that have been pioneered by actors located in the complex innovation networks of Silicon Valley. Although rather agnostic in this regard, the program implemented by the Chilean Economic Development Agency did require that the entities acting as "facilitating entities" (corresponding to the embedding nodes in our distal embedding model) had a series of characteristics that made them "eligible entities for the program" only if embedded in complex technology innovation networks.

4.4 The Embedded Nodes

The embedded nodes corresponded to innovation projects arising out of universities, R&D centers, and small enterprises with a clear outbound innovation orientation. Eligible beneficiaries of the program, acting as "embedded nodes" according to our model, needed to comply with a series of requirements, including having a set of core IPs based on competitive technology, a clear outbound innovation orientation, a compelling value proposition, the potential to export products and services to regional and global markets, and a competent skeleton management team.

4.5 *The Embedding Node*

The implementation proposed at the seminar called for a node strongly connected in the innovation networks of Silicon Valley to play the role of embedding node. The embedding node proposed corresponded to SRI International (SRI), a contract R&D center with global headquarters in Menlo Park, California. Founded in the 1940s, SRI was an applied R&D center linked to Stanford University up until the 1960s, at which point it became an independent R&D center with no ties to Stanford University other than the fact that many of its research staff studied there. Since the emergence of the networks in Silicon Valley, SRI has been playing a major role in generating cutting-edge IPs and spinning out technology firms in Silicon Valley, some of which have gone on to IPO in NASDAQ or have been acquired by other Silicon Valley firms. SRI maintains strong ties to most tier-1 VCs in Silicon Valley. All these characteristics made SRI meet most, if not all, the criteria for an embedding node in our model. Its "strong embedding" in the complex innovation networks of Silicon Valley made SRI an ideal candidate for the role of embedding node in our model.

The Chilean Economic Development Agency ended up implementing a program that did not specify a unique or preferred facilitating entity (the embedding node in our model). Eligible candidates for the program could either select one of the facilitating entities from a list of preapproved entities or propose another entity meeting the stringent criteria stipulated by the program to qualify as facilitating entity. SRI International, the embedding node originally introduced at the seminar, was part of the list of preapproved facilitating entities and played a key role in the creation of this program, as originally envisioned at the seminar. Initial qualification meetings between the first author and management of SRI took place in California in 2010. A preliminary agenda was agreed upon to organize the first seminar on technology innovation strategies in Santiago de Chile. Upon receiving a grant from the Chilean Agency of Economic Development, the first author prepared, jointly with management and staff of SRI International, the agenda for this seminar during 2010 and 2011. The seminar took place in Santiago in March 2011 and had an attendance of over 400 small and medium-sized technology companies and entrepreneurs. Policymakers and high-ranking government officials were also in attendance. A workshop on innovation management methodologies was also organized as part of this event for a group of government officials from the Chilean Agency of Economic Development (CORFO) and a group of emerging technology companies in Chile.

4.6 *The Embedding Function*

For this particular implementation of the program, the active involvement of an actor at the public pillar in the Chilean innovation system was required. The Ministry of

Economy, and more specifically the Chilean Economic Development Agency, did play this role in the implementation of the program. Initially, the engagement model was construed as a consulting agreement whose objective was to identify and qualify prospective Chilean technology companies with the potential to export products and services to regional and global markets. In doing so, the embedding node should deploy subject matter experts to perform technical and market due diligence and select a number of qualified embedded nodes arising out of the emerging technology innovation networks in Chile. In order to fill an initial funnel with a large number of prospective companies as potential embedded nodes, this process was to be executed in two stages.

In an initial qualification process, the Chilean Agency of Economic Development conducted an initial qualification of eligible candidates. To this end, members of management and staff of this agency underwent training on innovation management methodologies. Initial training had taken place as part of the workshop organized by the Faculty of Economics and Business at Diego Portales University and SRI International in March 2011. Subsequent training was provided by SRI International throughout 2011 and 2012. After this initial prequalification of eligible candidates, subject matter experts of the embedding node jointly with staff of the Chilean Agency of Economic Development conducted further qualification in Santiago and eventually identified those qualified candidates that could act as beneficiaries of this program (the "embedded nodes" in our model). The final step consisted in selecting and bringing a group of qualified technology companies to the premises of the facilitating entity (the embedding node located in the CIN in our model) for further training and induction to processes of fund raising and early-stage commercialization.

The implementation of this program did not officially foresee any direct involvement of the facilitating entity in the full process of distal embedding, as described in our model. Although the "embedding node" did not provide any funding to this selected group of companies and did not play an active role in finding such funding either, it did play a role in providing further training on its premises and in identifying both client and investing opportunities in the complex innovation network. Contingent upon beneficiaries of the program meeting all the requirements to qualify as an "embedded node" in our model, the embedding node would be in a position to make the necessary introductions to tier-1 VC firms and help with the preparations of road shows with investors in the complex innovation network. In this particular implementation, meeting such requirements meant that the selected group of beneficiaries that underwent further training in the complex innovation network needed to be qualified by the embedding node as potential "fundable deals" for venture capitalists in the complex innovation network. Contingent upon raising a series A round with a tier-1 VC in the complex innovation network, the process of distal embedding, as defined in our model, would be performed by the VC firm without any further involvement of the embedding node.

5 Discussion

In this section, we discuss the *ad hoc* cases of distal embedding shown in Sect. 2 and also analyze the first guided distal embedding implementation introduced in Sect. 4.

5.1 Analysis of ad hoc Cases of Distal Embedding

Table 1 characterizes the distal embedding case of Israel according our model. Table 2 characterizes the distal embedding case of the enterprise software industry according to our model (in Tables 1 and 2, EIN and CIN stand for emerging innovation network and complex innovation network, respectively). As opposed to the first case of distal embedding shown in Table 1, the second case of distal embedding shown in Table 2 followed closely the model of distal embedding we introduced in Sect. 3. As a result, once all the components of the proposed model of distal embedding put forth in this article were in place, including a highly compelling embedding function for the embedding nodes, the distal embedding process unfolded rapidly and produced high-impact results in a relatively short

Table 1 Distal embedding in the case of Israel

Element	Description
EIN	Emerging regions of innovation and entrepreneurship in Israel
CIN	Silicon valley and silicon valley of the East
Embedded nodes	Start-ups financially backed by Israeli VCs in the EIN
Embedding nodes	Israeli-based VCs (in stand-alone mode through a process of self-embedding)
Embedding function	Large flow of high-quality deals with a high potential to be syndicated with tier-1 VCs in silicon valley

Table 2 Distal embedding in the case of the enterprise software industry

Element	Description
EIN	Innovation networks of enterprise software vendors in emerging regions of innovation and entrepreneurship
CIN	Complex innovation networks of the enterprise software industry, especially those located in the tier-1 ICT absorption markets in the Americas, EMEA, and APAC
Embedded nodes	Regional enterprise software vendors
Embedding nodes	Big 5 consulting companies
Embedding function	Positioning the Big 5 consulting companies as the prime contractors in charge of deployments of enterprise software solutions

period of time. In the case of software vendors such as SAP, the results were of such magnitude that the company became a world-class company and eventually the world's largest enterprise software vendor in less than a decade.

Albeit in an *ad hoc* way, this second case of distal embedding took place in one of the most industrialized regions of Europe, a region that is notorious for having formed highly complex innovation networks in several knowledge-intensive industries. This reveals an important finding, namely, that distal embedding can also be successfully executed as an innovation network formation strategy in highly developed regions of innovation and entrepreneurship. In this second case, the embedding nodes comprised of the global consulting organizations of the so-called Big 5 consulting firms caused the process of distal embedding to occur in a relatively short period of time, mobilized vast resources located outside the network in which the organization being embedded was located, and effected a transition of embedded companies such as SAP from being a regional player in a tier-1 technology absorption market in the DACH region[8] to becoming the world's largest enterprise software vendor in about a decade. This process of value creation, ignited by three highly compelling value propositions addressing important needs of the clients, the vendors, and the Big 5 consulting firms, respectively, produced also a radical change in terms of a completely new business model, and its associated revenue model, within the entire enterprise software industry. By the late 1990s, this new business model had become the *de facto* standard for any enterprise software vendor with the ambition and the potential to achieve a position of global market leadership.

Conversely, the distal embedding process executed by Israel did not follow the model proposed in this article. In the absence of a proper embedding node and an associated embedding function, distal embedding could not take place initially. The case of Israel followed a brute-force approach to self-embedding that has proven to be successful in the end due to the continuous investment and future orientation of the finance pillar in the Israeli innovation system over a long period of more than two decades, on the one hand, and some very singular events and conditions of the national innovation system of Israel, on the other. It was the rather unusual combination of these two factors that led to the creation and consolidation of a number of Israeli technology firms as global leading vendors in their respective markets in a relatively short period of time.

[8]DACH is an acronym used in German-speaking countries that stands for Germany, Austria and Switzerland.

5.2 Implementing Distal Embedding

To our knowledge, the case described in Sect. 4 corresponds to what we could construe as the first guided implementation of distal embedding. Though still too early to ascertain the final results of this process, we can drive some initial conclusions from this implementation.

As far as a successful implementation of distal embedding is concerned, the case of Chile is particularly challenging for a number of reasons. Firstly, the number of qualified deals arising out of the emerging technology innovation networks in Chile is still too small. A more active role on the part of actors at the public and private pillars of the national innovation system in Chile is required to increase the number of qualified deals. The goal of public policies at the interface of the public and private pillars should be to increase the flow of qualified deals, that is, of technology companies with the potential to get distally embedded in complex innovation networks. Secondly, incentives need to be created for the finance pillar to engage actively in the process of distal embedding. Solving the deal flow problem is one first step towards creating these incentives for the finance pillar. In fact, to the extent that the number of qualified deals increases and the successful cases of distal embedding commence to unfold, actors at the financial pillar will regard them not as isolated cases of serendipitous technology innovation and entrepreneurship with an interesting upside financial potential but rather as an emerging industry in which they need to participate.

Actors at the public pillar in Chile have already taken initial steps in this direction by setting up matching funds that provide interested actors at the finance pillar with financial incentives to create technology investment funds. Actors at the public pillar will need to redouble their efforts to create a technology investment industry and an emerging venture capital industry in Chile. We expect that the need for distal embedding in the case of Chile will arise much earlier in the innovation life cycle than in the case of Israeli technology start-ups due to the current lack of competences on the part of the Chilean investor community and their local networks to manage the agency and monitoring costs associated with high-technology ventures. This adds complexity to the implementation of distal embedding in Chile.

Finally, the embedding function in this first guided case of distal embedding is still too weak. We do not yet see the incentives for the embedding node to engage more actively in the distal embedding process. We believe that the provision of consulting fees, even on a long-term, ongoing basis, will not be sufficient incentives to characterize a strong embedding function, at least not at the present stage. If the number of qualified deals increases and actors at the finance pillar engage more actively in the process of funding a larger number of qualified deals at the early stages of their financial life cycle, then the required enabling assets might start to get generated in the emerging regions of technology innovation and entrepreneurship in Chile in order for the "robustness" of this embedding function to increase, as required by our model.

6 Conclusions

As argued by other researchers (Castilla et al. 2000; Ferrary and Granovetter 2009), the complexity of an innovation network is a key factor that determines the chances of success of processes of innovation and entrepreneurship taking place in that network. Unlike other research in this area, we focus in this article not on the study of such complex networks but on the rather elusive problem of how the process of innovation network formation takes place. Our work focuses on generic innovation network formation strategies that can be implemented to increase the chances of success of processes of technology innovation and entrepreneurship taking place in innovation networks lacking the necessary complexity. The concept of embedding plays a central role in this connection. In our model, the success of processes of outbound technology innovation driven by actors located in emerging regions of innovation and entrepreneurship will strongly depend on the possibility of these actors getting distally embedded in complex innovation networks. The economic outcomes such an actor can achieve will strongly depend on the "robustness" of the distal embedding function.

While the cases described in Sect. 2 did not follow a systematic approach to distal embedding driven by the embedded nodes, as defined in our model, they demonstrate the feasibility of distal embedding as a process of innovation network formation. The second case, in particular, is the quintessential manifestation of an *ad hoc* distal embedding process. This second case exemplifies the impact that a process of distal embedding can have on the economic outcomes of an innovation process. The magnitude of the success of this second case was predicated on the magnitude of the singular event that gave rise to the process of distal embedding, namely, the millennium bug. This singular event gave rise to a highly compelling value proposition for the embedding function to be characterized. Such a strong embedding function provided the necessary incentives for the embedding node to deploy a vast amount of resources in the execution of the distal embedding process.

We put the case that the process of distal embedding is not only relevant to companies in emerging regions of innovation and entrepreneurship, especially those that are not endowed with the local "enabling assets" required to successfully execute a local embedding strategy. Indeed, distal embedding can also be used in more complex innovation networks located in regions of technology innovation and entrepreneurship of developed countries, as exemplified by the second case of distal embedding discussed in Sect. 2.

Although we might argue that the embedded nodes involved in the cases of distal embedding analyzed in Sect. 2 were initially unaware of what mechanism was at work and how it operated, they were very much aware of the results this mechanism was producing. Albeit implemented and executed in an *ad hoc* way, these cases show that there is a mechanism at work behind the process of distal embedding. We claim that there is method behind the magic of distal embedding and that technology companies from both complex and emerging regions of innovation and entrepreneurship can benefit from understanding how the process of distal embedding works and how a distal embedding strategy can be implemented.

Our work has important implications for theories of economic development and the approaches to implementing them. Empirical evidence shows that mainstream approaches aimed at incrementally increasing the product space in areas where emerging regions of innovation and entrepreneurship do already possess comparative advantages may face a higher probability of augmenting the productivity and the knowledge pool of these regions (Hausmann and Klinger 2006; Bahar et al. 2014). Unfortunately, these approaches fail to address the problem of how to embed these regions in industry sectors in which they do not yet present such comparative advantages. For emerging regions of innovation and entrepreneurship, these are often the most attractive sectors as far as future growth and diversification opportunities are concerned. We find these "salami tactics" somewhat shortsighted and, more importantly, more prone to leading to potential dead ends due to its fundamental lack of future orientation. Although the mainstream approach in most emerging regions of innovation and entrepreneurship, we find that these neoclassically inspired tactical approaches to economic development might peacefully co-exist with a more comprehensive neo-Schumpeterian strategy of innovation network formation such as the one advocated in this article.

Our future work will focus on expanding our model of innovation network formation by postulating three generic innovation network formation strategies called "replication," "local embedding" and "distal embedding" and integrating them in a comprehensive model of innovation network formation.

Acknowledgements The first international seminar on technology innovation strategies planted a seed for the creation of the Go To Market program of the Chilean Economic Development Agency in 2011. This seminar was funded through a grant from the Chilean Agency of Economic Development and by the Faculty of Economics and Business at Diego Portales University. The first author would like to thank the Chilean Agency of Economic Development as well as management and staff of the Faculty of Economics and Business at Diego Portales University and SRI International for their support in organizing this seminar and the German Academic Exchange Service (DAAD) for a grant that supported part of the work reported in this article.

References

Ahrweiler P (2010) Innovation in complex social systems. Routledge, New York

Ahuja G (2000) Collaboration networks, structural holes, and innovation: a longitudinal study. Adm Sci Q 45:425–455

Bahar D, Hausmann R, Hidalgo C (2014) Neighbors and the evolution of the comparative advantage of nations: evidence of international knowledge diffusion? J Int Econ 92(1): 111–123

Bathelt H, Malmberg A, Maskell P (2004) Clusters and knowledge: local buzz, global pipelines and the process of knowledge creation. Prog Hum Geogr 28:54–79

Bresnahan T, Gambardella A (2004) Building high-tech clusters: silicon Valley and beyond. Cambridge University Press, Cambridge

Callaway D, Newman M, Strogatz S, Watts D (2000) Network robustness and fragility: percolation on random graphs. Phys Rev Lett 85:5468–5471

Casper S (2007) How do technology clusters emerge and become sustainable? Social network formation and inter-firm mobility within the San Diego biotechnology cluster. Res Policy 36:438–455

Castilla E, Hwang H, Granovetter E, Granovetter M (2000) Social networks in silicon valley. In: Lee C-M, Miller WF, Hancock MG, Rowen HS (eds) The silicon valley edge. Stanford University Press, Stanford, pp 218–247

Ferrary M, Granovetter M (2009) The role of venture capital firms in Silicon Valley's complex innovation network. Econ Soc 38:326–359

Festinger L, Schachter S, Back K (1950) The spatial ecology of group formation. In: Festinger L, Schachter S, Back K (eds) Social pressure in informal groups. Harper, New York

Granovetter M (1973) The strength of weak ties. Am J Soc 78:1360–1380

Granovetter M (1985) Economic action and social structure: the problem of embeddedness. Am J Soc 19:481–510

Granovetter M (2005) The impact of social structures on economic outcomes. J Econ Perspect 19:33–50

Hanusch H, Pyka A (2007) The principles of Neo-Schumpeterian economics. Camb J Econ 31:275–289

Hausmann R, Klinger B (2006) The structure of the product space and the evolution of comparative advantage. CID working paper series 128. Center for International Development, Harvard University

Kogut B (2000) The network as knowledge: generative rules and the emergence of structure. Strateg Manag J 21:405–425

Milgram S (1967) The small-world problem. Psychol Today 1:62–67

Newman M, Barabasi A, Watts D (2006) The structure and dynamics of networks. Princeton University Press, Princeton

Podolny J (2001) Networks as the pipes and prisms of the market. Am J Soc 107:33–60

Powell W, Koput K, Owen-Smith J (2005) Network dynamics and field evolution: the growth of inter-organizational collaboration in the life sciences. Am J Soc 110:1132–1205

Powell, W.W., Packalen, K., Whittington, K.B. (2012). Organizational and institutional genesis: The emergence of high-tech clusters in the life sciences, in Padgett, J.F. and Powell, W. W. (editors): The Emergence of Organizations and Markets, chapter 14, Princeton University Press.

Saviotti PP, Pyka A (2011) Generalized barriers to entry and economic development. J Evol Econ 21(1):29–52

Schön B, Pyka A (2012) A taxonomy of innovation networks. FZID Discussion Paper #42-2012. Research Centre for Innovation and Services (FZID), University of Hohenheim, Stuttgart

Schumpeter JA (1911) The theory of economic development. Harvard University Press, Cambridge

Singh J (2005) Collaborative networks as determinants of knowledge diffusion patterns. Manag Sci 49:351–365

Sorenson O, Stuart T (2001) Syndication networks and the spatial distribution of venture capital investments. Am J Soc 106:1546–1588

Sorenson O, Stuart T (2008) Bridging the context back in: settings and the search for syndicate partners in venture capital investments networks. Adm Sci Q 53:266–294

Uzzi B (1996) The sources and consequences of embeddedness for the economic performance of organizations: the network effect. Am Soc Rev 61:674–698

Watts D (2004) The new science of networks. Ann Rev Soc 30:243–270

Intellectual Property as a Complex Adaptive System

David A. Harper

Abstract This article aims to provide some elements of an evolutionary theory of property rights. It applies a systems-based capital-theoretic perspective to explain the formation and transformation of property rights structures. The approach emphasizes how entrepreneurs create capital combinations by connecting capital goods—defined widely to include property rights, such as patents—in their production plans. Their actions change complementarity relations between property rights as used in production. We treat the property rights structure as a complex adaptive system that exhibits increasing structural complexity as it evolves. Entrepreneurs discover gaps in the property rights system. As they organize production to exploit profit opportunities, entrepreneurs regroup existing intellectual property rights (IPR) into new modules, such as patent pools, that encapsulate more complex combinations of basic building blocks of intellectual property. A patent pool constitutes an interpolation of a new meso level within the macro IPR structure. We apply our framework to the first of the patent pools for digital video compression technology used in digital television and DVDs.

D.A. Harper (✉)
Department of Economics, New York University, 19 West 4th Street, New York, NY 10012, USA
e-mail: david.harper@nyu.edu

A. Pyka, J. Foster (eds.), *The Evolution of Economic and Innovation Systems*,
Economic Complexity and Evolution, DOI 10.1007/978-3-319-13299-0_14
Modified and extended version from Journal of Evolutionary Economics 24(2), Springer 2014

> There is a legal system, and it is complex and adaptive. We can leave it at that and intuit propositions that seem likely to follow, or we can dive headfirst into law's complexity to swim amidst its chaos, its feedback networks, its self-organization, its scales, its emergence, and its sheer dynamism.
>
> (Ruhl 2008: 888)

1 Introduction: The Legal Order as a Capital Structure

This paper supplies some key components of an evolutionary approach to property rights and entrepreneurship.[1] It applies a capital-theoretic perspective in order to address fundamental questions about the nature of the property rights system, its structure and operation. By portraying property as a multi-level complex structure of capital, the paper seeks to explain crucial aspects of the flux and transformation of the property rights system over time. In particular, it explores the dynamics of change in intellectual property rights at micro-, meso- and macro-levels, and it investigates the emergence of novel property rights structures, such as patent pools, that constitute a new level of economic organization within the economy-wide network of rules. It explains how changes in property rights are causally related to entrepreneurship and production. The focus is upon how entrepreneurs seek to identify gaps within the complex network of property rights and then form new connections between existing property rights to create new combinations of rules. It thereby studies important endogenous economic forces that propel the evolution of property rights and the ongoing generation of novelty.

What does it mean to say that the law in general and the system of property in particular constitute a complex capital structure? Following Fisher (1906), we define capital broadly to include any resource—whether natural, artifactual or human—that produces a flow of services that people value (see too Tobin 2005). "The importance of capital goods lies not in their physical qualities but in the service streams to which they give rise" (Lachmann 1956: 86). The upshot is that any resource qualifies as capital if it is used in a production plan. Consequently, law qualifies as capital provided that people apply it in production and view it as capable of rendering services over time that they desire. Legal rules such as property rights are, directly or indirectly, instruments of production. They function as higher-order capital goods that help produce lower-order goods (e.g. consumer goods). They derive their economic significance and their property of being capital from their use within the production plans of entrepreneurs, firms and households. Property rules are an integral part of the knowledge structure that mobilizes and guides the transformation (manufacture, transportation and storage) of materials, energy and information in the economic system.

[1] This chapter is a longer, unabridged version of Harper (2014) and contains more extensive details and citations on the connections between evolutionary economics and the law and economics approach to property.

The system of property is a structure in the sense that its heterogeneous elements are connected and interact. It is not a mere aggregate or stock. There is some patterning in the diverse array of property rights. These rules cannot be combined arbitrarily; they have to fit together and mesh with other types of inputs. They are like blocks of Lego that can be mixed and matched in particular ways to yield endless combinations. In addition, the property rights system exhibits a great deal of structural patterning at more than one level. It emerges as a nested multi-layered structure—a system of systems in which interrelated subsystems in turn consist of lower-level subsystems and connections between them.

According to this capital-theoretic conception, the property rights system has a prominent place in the realm of production, not just exchange. Property rules participate in the production process. Property law is not a stand-alone governance structure that hovers over people and transactions; it is a structure of rules and connections "installed" in a social network of economic actors and is embedded in the DNA of doing business and carrying out productive tasks. The law of property and contract are part of the core connective structure of rules that supports production and exchange in the economic system, and these two rule systems provide significant connections between entrepreneurs, consumers and resource owners. "Law exists in order to be applied; and it must be applied through some human agency" (Allen 1927: 72). Its only existence is in its applications.

Recognizing that the legal order of property is a capital structure serves to sharpen our understanding that property is also a complex adaptive system. The property rights system is:

1. Complex: it contains many heterogeneous elements that "interact in a nonsimple way" (Simon 1962: 468). The law possesses a higher order of complexity than systems involving mere application of given or acquired knowledge in that it involves interactive knowledge structures and mental models (in Foster's (2005) typology, the legal order is "fourth-order complex").
2. Adaptive: There can be change in the structure of property rights in the sense that there is some plasticity in the connections among its elements.
3. Modular: it comprises functionally differentiated subsystems (relatively stable subassemblies) that are connected to one another (Holland 2006).
4. Stratified: each module of property rights is both a system and an element of a higher-level system—that is, the structure of property rights contains multiple levels of order and interaction (Dopfer et al. 2004).
5. Knowledge-generating: the knowledge generated by the property system includes classifications meaningful to the participants in the context of the legal order (McQuade and Butos 2009; Hadfield and Weingast 2012). These classifications exist at multiple levels and adjust continuously to changing circumstances. As a kind of capital formation process, the ongoing creation of the property rights structure is a social learning process that is self-organizing and selective.

The law of property exhibits the agent-based and systemic features identified by Ruhl (2008) that qualify it as a complex adaptive system. For instance, agents in the property system are heterogeneous, consisting of several different classes (e.g. courts, legislatures, lawyers, clients); they follow local rules of interaction; and their interactions can give rise to sharp discontinuities, such as when courts overrule established precedent unexpectedly or old statutes (e.g. the Patent Act 1952) are amended significantly. The property system generates emergent features, such as the capacity to coordinate people's expectations, that cannot be reduced to the behavior of individual agents or individual property rules taken in isolation; the system exhibits path-dependence, such as when judicial interpretations build on prior cases; and the law of property organizes itself around a set of core doctrinal rules, such as the rule of first possession, that lend stability to the system over time.

Treating a system of property rules as a kind of capital is not without precedent in the law and economics literature. For instance, Coase (1960: 43–44) suggests that the right to carry out certain physical actions with a particular resource, rather than the physical resource itself, is a factor of production. To exercise a property right is to use a factor of production. Similarly, Hayek depicts abstract rules of legal order as a "kind of instrument of production" that assist people in making their individual plans so that they are better coordinated with the actions of others (Hayek [1944] 2007: 113–114).[2] Such legal rules are instrumental in the sense that they are useful for as yet unknown ends of as yet unknown people, rather than useful for particular ends of particular people. In a seminal article, Landes and Posner (1976) view the body of legal precedents as constituting a "stock of legal capital subject to depreciation" (p. 262) that generates a flow of information services that can be quantified in monetary terms. Their conception of capital is cast in a neoclassical production function and is consequently very "jelly-like": legal capital is an aggregate, measured by a scalar magnitude, that is smoothly synchronized to equilibrium requirements. More recently, Hadfield's (2012) concept of "legal infrastructure" comports well with the notion that property law is a capital structure. Legal infrastructure is a form of "socially available capital that produces a stream of services". Legal infrastructure is the "accumulated stock" of legal resources, comprising legal rules and other materials, that is produced by "legal actors"—broadly defined to include judges, legislators, regulators, arbitrators, lawyers, and other legal practitioners. Legal rules are intermediate goods produced as output by the legal sector that are available for use as inputs in other sectors (p. 25). They are "essentially economic inputs" (p. 9) to "an economic output" (p. 24).[3]

By developing the perspective that property systems are capital structures, this paper addresses two related lacunae in the economic analysis of organization and the economic theory of capital. First, it addresses the lack of emphasis in

[2] Demsetz (1967: 347) also describes property rights as an "instrument" that helps people form expectations in their interactions with others. His approach focuses upon how changes in property rights can internalize potentially relevant externalities (e.g. spillover effects). Although they differ in emphasis and the problems they address, both the capital-theoretic perspective developed in this paper and Demsetz's approach examine how property rights can coalesce into new bundles as economic circumstances change and new opportunities emerge.

[3] Other recent literature includes Barnett (2011), Foss and Garzarelli (2007), Kieff (2006) and Merges (2001).

the economics of organization on entrepreneurship as a capital-creating force in the economic system and the inattention to how entrepreneurs use legal rules as inputs in production. Transaction cost economics (e.g. Williamson 1985, 1988) tends to emphasize the exchange aspects of the firm (i.e. buying and selling of inputs and outputs) and the design of governance structures to mitigate socially unproductive rent-seeking; the role of legal inputs in production is treated in a very stylized fashion (Coase 1988; Langlois and Foss 1999). In addition, the formal property rights approach to the nature of the firm developed by Oliver Hart and his associates (e.g. Grossman and Hart 1986; Hart 1989) downplays entrepreneurship—economic agents in these models are limited to allocating given ownership rights to achieve given ends; they are not able to create new rights structures, novel contractual solutions or ingenious enforcement technologies hitherto unforeseen by the economic theorist (Foss and Foss 2000: 319, 322). To rectify this gap, this paper grounds analysis of the evolution of property rights in a systems-based theory of capital that squarely locates the function of entrepreneurs in making and revising capital combinations in a world of unexpected change (Lachmann 1956). Entrepreneurship is brought center stage; it is the driving force behind how property rights are combined and used in production. Second, the paper addresses the lack of attention given to property rights in the theory of capital (Hennings 1990). The theory of capital tends to treat the basic structure of property rights as a datum, as exogenously determined. It does not focus upon how property rules can affect the structure of production plans in the economic system as a whole. The theory of capital does not examine how the structure of legal entitlements affects who (i.e. which entrepreneur) gets to select the uses of capital goods and what decisions they make to transform, combine, regroup or scrap capital goods. It does not investigate the question of what effects changes in legal claims to productive resources have on different levels of the capital structure and the economic system.

1.1 *Objectives and Organization of the Paper*

The objective of this paper is to explain the formation, integration and transformation of property rights systems at multiple levels of complexity. We are interested in questions relating to the emergence, boundaries and internal structure of systems of property rights. We study the overall topology of the property rights system—the general connecting principles underlying the structure of the system—rather than the efficiency properties of individual property rules. The property rights system is a web-like network of rules that exhibits increasing structural complexity as it evolves. This network consists of nodes and channels through which information, materials and energy flow.

This scope of this article is limited to a positive analysis of property rights and how entrepreneurs create new structures of property rights in their capital formation activities. It is not concerned with normative questions, such as those concerned with the desirability of instituting or abolishing a patent system or questions about the legitimacy of patents. Nor is it concerned with competition policy issues, such as the appropriate antitrust treatment of patent licensing arrangements (see Carlson 1999; Lerner and Tirole 2008). Accordingly, the paper treats the patent system and other statutory regimes of intellectual property protection as antecedently existing structures that are nonetheless amenable to change. Entrepreneurs adapt to the world as they find it; they fashion new capital combinations out of the property rule systems and resources available to them. They do not start from a blank slate devoid of rules. Entrepreneurs orient their actions to existing structures of intellectual property rights in order to make their production plans, and as they form new combinations of complementary capital, they may then transform these very rights structures. Hence, the approach is in line with institutional economic approaches that proceed by successive stages to endogenize the structure of property rights (Barzel 1997; Eggertsson 1990). It is also consistent with evolutionary economic perspectives that explain the adaptive capacities of increasingly complex systems (Potts 2000).

The organization of the paper is as follows. In Sect. 2, we outline the systems-based theory of capital and its implications for entrepreneurship and economic organization (Endres and Harper 2012; Harper and Endres 2010, 2012). We focus upon those aspects most relevant for explaining the evolution of intellectual property rights. Entrepreneurs discover gaps in the property rights system—discrepancies between how rights are currently structured and how they could be profitably restructured to facilitate production of different kinds and qualities of goods and services. As they organize production and orchestrate assets to exploit profit opportunities, market-based entrepreneurs repartition and reshuffle existing property rights into novel modules. Section 3 applies this theory to investigate the emergence and structure of patent pools. We examine how entrepreneurs use private-ordering rules to form patent pools that encapsulate basic building blocks of intellectual property. Patent pools are explained as emergent capital combinations that interpolate a new meso level of order into the property rights system. We apply our framework to the first of the patent pools for digital video compression technology used in digital television and DVDs.

2 Entrepreneurship as the Causal Agent in the Transformation of Intellectual Property Rights Structures

2.1 Gaps and Obstacles in the Structure of Property Rights

This paper takes the notion of a network as the basis for its perspective on the nature of the legal order. The network comprises legal rules and connections between them. The legal order has a spatial, temporal and social structure. The network is incomplete—it contains gaps, because elements and connections are missing. For example, legal gaps can arise from the absence of property rights so that a resource is unowned, as in the classic tragedy of the commons. The law is an imperfect network rife with holes, obstacles and ill-defined pathways and nodes. Thus, the legal property rights structure is not a fully connected system located in "integral space" in which every element (e.g. agent, rule) directly affects every other element in the system. Rather, there exist clusters of local interactions: each agent interacts with only some other agents; each legal rule interacts with only some other rules (Potts 2000: 19, 25–26). Local interactions between rules generate a modular architecture in which legal rules and other legal inputs can be categorized into discrete areas even though boundaries may not always be that sharply delineated. For example, intellectual property law consists of an array of distinct legal subsystems for patents, copyrights, trademarks, and trade secrets (see Smith 2007, 2012).

There are always gaps in the system of property rights within which economic production and market exchanges occur. The property rights framework is never perfectly delineated in advance. They are always incomplete. Full specification of the rights to an asset would require that both the existing and potential owners of an asset have complete knowledge of all its valued attributes (Barzel 1997: 4; Harper 2013: 66). The potential infinity of rights makes present knowledge, on the part of both agents and the observing economist, of all possible future rights impossible. The emergence of new property rights to newly discovered attributes of assets is unpredictable in principle. Property rights are always incompletely defined because of irremediable imperfections of our knowledge and the prohibitive costs of fully specifying legal rules and regulations. In the case of individual patents, the incompleteness of property rights means that there is a gap between the de jure scope of the patent system (i.e. legal rights) and de facto, economic rights of patent holders. The incompleteness of patents and the high monitoring and enforcement costs of the patent system have the effect of tolerating and insulating some level of infringing activity. Because of irremediable imperfections of their knowledge, judges and legislators cannot make rules that anticipate all future legal and economic developments. For example, at the time when the traditional conception of property in land (which held that ownership of the ground extended from the center of the earth to the heavens) became firmly established in English common law in the late sixteenth century, no one could have foreseen the recent emergence of new technologies for use of the deep subsurface—such as heat mining and carbon sequestration (Sprankling 2008).

One of the potential obstacles or "knots" in the legal order that can impede the diffusion of patented technology is the alleged "patent thicket". Patent thickets are dense networks of overlapping and blocking intellectual property rights owned by different firms (Shapiro 2000). For example, Heller and Eisenberg (1998: 698–699) suggested that a proliferation of patents covering individual gene fragments would result in underusage of research materials and inhibit biomedical research. In the absence of patent pools, patent thickets require firms seeking to commercialize new technologies to negotiate individual patent licenses with multiple patent holders. Patent thickets can mean that there will be many conflicting claims of intellectual property ownership among many patent owners.

A patent thicket is an instance of an "anticommons" problem where the existence of multiple rights to exclude leads to "inefficient underutilization" of resources ("inefficient" relative to a zero transaction-cost benchmark) (Heller 1998). There is an anticommons problem in which no firm has an effective right to use the intellectual property but many firms have the right to veto a proposed use, resulting in an underusage of the patented invention. The patent thicket emerges because multiple firms are assigned rights of exclusion, and the exercise of these patents creates interdependencies that are not included in agents' decision-making. Each patent holder imposes external diseconomies on others who also hold exclusion rights (Buchanan and Yoon 2000: 3–4). The overwhelming rights of exclusion held by other patent holders effectively constrain and potentially eliminate each patent holder's right of use. The patent holders are not able to coordinate their actions, so that the actions of each block the actions of others. According to the anticommons thesis, the magnitude of the opportunity loss (in terms of nonrealized profits) increases with the number of firms assigned simultaneous exclusion rights related to the patented technology.

It seems that the patent thicket arises because intellectual property rights have been partitioned into too many small fragments. The patent system has been "inefficiently modularized" from the perspective of entrepreneurs and end-users (Langlois 2002: 29). Unlike cases of unified ownership, commons and anticommons situations entail rights of use and rights of exclusion that have "non-conforming boundaries" in that these rights are not exercised over a similar domain (Parisi et al. 2005: 584). If rights are cut too thin, the presence of prohibitive and asymmetric transaction costs will make it difficult to regroup rights into larger, more appropriately sized bundles. Consequently, the market will not elicit cooperation among entrepreneurs where the transaction costs of overcoming patent thickets are prohibitive.

2.2 *Entrepreneurial Regrouping of Capital Combinations That Embody Intellectual Property*

The existence of holes and obstacles in the property rights structure provide opportunities for entrepreneurship. Entrepreneurship is the "self-organizing impetus" that fills gaps, develops connections and generates ordered complexity in the property rights structure (Foster 2000: 319). Entrepreneurs are alert to profitable opportunities for voluntary market exchanges that are implicit in the status quo pattern of property rights. Whereas political entrepreneurs ("rent seekers") use the coercive powers of the state to re-allocate property rights through uncompensated transfers, market-based entrepreneurs pursue profit by trading property rights in resources through non-coercive means (Ricketts 1987: 462).[4] Entrepreneurs who

[4]This article focuses upon market entrepreneurship rather than legal or political entrepreneurship. An example of the latter is copyright owners' lobbying Congress to implement legislation (the

establish private rights or a common property regime in newly discovered, hitherto unowned and unused (or abandoned) resources are not challenging the property rights of others and no unwilling transfers are involved, so their actions qualify as market-based.

Entrepreneurs discover gaps in the capital structure—here broadly construed to include the structure of property rights. They discover holes and obstacles that could conceivably be surmounted at a profit. For example, a new kind of entrepreneur is the so-called "patent troll". These patent dealers act as intermediaries and do not use the patents they acquire in production. They discover gaps between de jure and de facto patent rights that represent profit opportunities. Unlicensed use of patented technology is extensive in commercial production because it is very costly both for technology developers to assert patents (e.g. because of high litigation costs) and for technology users to identify the patents they might be infringing.[5] The increasing number of weakly enforced rights in the patent system lures entrepreneurs who can profit by buying up these rights and then developing creative strategies for asserting them. "Patents that are worth little to their initial owners may be worth more to entrepreneurs who enjoy a cost advantage in asserting patents against users or who own complementary assets (such as large patent portfolios) that either increase the value of the patents or lower the costs of asserting them" (Eisenberg 2011: 68). These patent entrepreneurs reduce the gap between the expansive legal rights of the patent system and the narrower economic rights experienced in practice. Their actions improve market coordination relative to the status quo benchmark of legal rights (i.e. current patent law).

However, the entrepreneurial function *vis-à-vis* capital creation is not limited to arbitrage or buying and selling property. As they perceive incoherence or holes in the capital order, entrepreneurs also reorganize production. They bring together heterogeneous capital goods (defined broadly to include patents and other intellectual property rights) into new combinations, and reshuffle and dissolve existing combinations (Lachmann 1956). Capital goods used in the same production plan stand in relations of complementarity to one another. Complementarity thus derives from the particular production plan being implemented by the entrepreneur; that plan is itself derived from the entrepreneur's expectations about the future constellation of demand and supply. Entrepreneurs experiment to find better capital combinations (including better combinations of intellectual property rights) that meet the demands of the market. As they revise their production plans, entrepreneurs substitute some capital goods for others. Substitutability is a phenomenon of unexpected change and an integral part of the process of capital regrouping. Whereas

Digital Millennium Copyright Act of 1998) that increases penalties for copyright infringement on the Internet and criminalizes the circumvention of technological protection measures to control access to copyrighted works. See Litman (2001: 122–149).

[5] Willful patent infringers who rely upon high detection and enforcement costs to shelter themselves from patent assertion are capturing value through uncompensated transfer and challenging the rights of the patent owner from the perspective of the legal status quo.

"complementarity is an aspect of any given plan, substitutability is an aspect of contemplated changes in plans" (Lewin 1994: 242). Complementarity thus relates to the coherence of the capital structure, while substitutability relates to its adaptability. These relationships are not mutually exclusive alternatives. Taken together, these relationships bring order to the capital structure and help maintain order in the face of unexpected change. The construction of new capital combinations gives rise to more complex layers of capital complementarities. As the range and variety of capital goods (especially of an indivisible character) increase, the capital structure exhibits a higher degree of complexity.

2.3 Specifying Capital Combinations That Embody Intellectual Property

As they create capital combinations, entrepreneurs make decisions on the particular form of rule complexes for their enterprises. We refer to this process as *specification*. Entrepreneurs specify the architecture, interfaces and standards that pertain to these rule complexes. As they knit capital goods together into new combinations, entrepreneurs select, order and configure legal rules in particular ways to generate a specific rule structure. For example, the entrepreneur specifies the form of legal entity for organizing the venture, which explicitly codifies legal rights. At the most general level, entrepreneurs make use of abstract legal rules of property and contract and apply them to specific settings in light of their own particular knowledge and purposes. These rules exist in order to be applied and have a very wide range of potential applications. In the process of specifying rule complexes, entrepreneurs turn abstract formal rules into productive rules-in-use in actual economic contexts. They thereby plug abstract rules into operational routines and processes of production and exchange. Because abstract rules of property and contract by themselves are not sufficient to manage and coordinate the productive activities of the firm, entrepreneurs combine these rule sets with more concrete rules of organization and specific directives that fill in the gaps. Entrepreneurs' specifying activities are forward-looking and "forward-matching" in that entrepreneurs combine rules today in the expectation that the output generated by those rule combinations will be demanded by end-users in the future and sold at a profit (Endres and Harper 2012).

In the context of intellectual property, entrepreneurs make decisions about the specific legal and non-legal rules they will use in order to control their knowledge assets and capture the profits generated by their innovations. Table 1 presents a simple classification of different types of rules that provide the "atomic" building blocks from which "molecular" rule complexes can be formed. For short, we denote the vector of legal rule types as [PCSMA] and the non-legal rule vector as [NFTB]. We examine these rule structures in turn. As a first approximation, we can assume that they select legal rules of property from a fixed menu of legally sanctioned intellectual property forms: patents (P), copyrights (C), trade secrets (S) and trademarks (M) (Merrill and Smith 2000: 19–20). These property forms

Table 1 Simple taxonomy of rules for controlling knowledge assets

Legal rules	Other (i.e. non-legal) rules
Menu of legal forms of intellectual property:	[N] Social norms
[P] Patents	
[C] Copyrights	[F] Physical and location decision heuristics
[S] Trade secrets	
[M] Trademarks	[T] Technological protection measures
[A] Contractual agreements	[B] Business rules and marketing strategies

grant exclusive rights on new creations of intellectual capital, such as specific inventions, particularized expressions and source-identifying marks. The menu of property forms is a stable and distinct structural pattern.[6] From the perspective of individual entrepreneurs, the menu of legal property forms is a "relatively absolute absolute" that imposes constraints on their decision-making and capital-creating activities (Knight 1944); the menu itself is not a choice variable. However, the menu of intellectual property forms is not just a constraint on entrepreneurial action. By making available basic building blocks akin to standardized Lego pieces, it also defines useful pathways for doing things—it provides routines for "propertizing" knowledge assets (for a generalized statement of this theme, which builds on North (1990), see Nelson and Sampat (2001)). In short, the law of intellectual property comprises rules-as-routines as well as rules-as-constraints. "Structures both enable and constrain; indeed, they enable because they constrain" (Loasby 1999: 124).

Entrepreneurs can also use contract law to secure their control (exclusivity) over knowledge assets. Contractual agreements [A] can effectively extend intellectual property protection and "propertize" knowledge assets. Such contractual arrangements include inventorship assignment provisions in employment contracts (that ensure that intellectual property developed by an employee on company time are assigned to and owned by the employer), covenants not to compete in labor contracts, confidentiality agreements (with employees, customers and suppliers), technology licensing agreements and joint venture agreements. As we shall see in Sect. 3, entrepreneurs use private-ordering rules to construct higher-level structures of property rights, such as standard-setting organizations, R&D consortia, patent pools and collective copyright licensing organizations (e.g. ASCAP), which encapsulate more complex combinations of the basic building blocks of intellectual property. Unlike property law, the regime of contract in modern market economies

[6]The relative stability of the menu of property forms is a result of the *numerus clausus* principle, which limits intellectual and other property rights to a small closed class of well-defined types. (*Numerus clausus* means "the number is closed".) This legal principle discourages judges from recognizing new or customized forms of legal property rights. The principle is explicit in civil law systems and implicit in Anglo-American common-law systems (Merrill and Smith 2000: 9–11). For a critique of Merrill and Smith's assertion of the existence of a numerus clausus principle in the context of intellectual property law, see Mulligan (2013).

offers entrepreneurs a high degree of latitude in customizing the rights of parties to a contractual agreement. "Contract may be said ... to be the laboratory for what ultimately may be codified as fully fledged property rights" (Mackaay 1990: 901). It is the chief source of spontaneous rule systems. Contract law provides rules of interaction that engender functional differentiation in the capital structure—they facilitate heterogeneity in the uses of intellectual property across dispersed agents.

In order to protect intellectual property, entrepreneurs also combine the above legal rules with non-legal rules, including social norms [N], physical measures [F], and technological [T] and business [B] rules. Indeed, the law presupposes an existing structure of social relations that embodies social norms; these norms are the default backdrop that shape the negotiation of business transactions and entrepreneurial processes of adaptation (Ellickson 1991). Accordingly, entrepreneurs can make use of norm-based systems of intellectual property. These systems rely upon implicit social norms that community members hold in common, such as the non-disclosure norm among accomplished French chefs that prohibits them from passing on a new recipe to third parties without permission if the originator of that recipe reveals it to them (Fauchart and von Hippel 2008: 187). In addition, in Japan, entrepreneurs used norms of trust combined with long-term employment to substitute for formal confidentiality agreements and trade secret law (Nakoshi 1993). Apple's iPhone development project, codenamed Project Purple in its infancy, used social rules to reinforce a culture of secrecy. "The first rule of Fight Club is you don't talk about Fight Club. The first rule of Project Purple is you don't talk about the Project Purple" (Scott Forestall, a senior VP for Apple's iOS software; quoted in Guglielmo 2012).

The vector of non-legal rules also includes physical and location decision heuristics [F] to protect confidential information, such as geographical isolation of a firm or venture. For example, Apple located its iPhone development project in a locked down building in Cupertino, California, thereby insulating its members from Apple's normal R&D operations. Entrepreneurs can also secure some measure of exclusive control of knowledge assets by means of technological protection mechanisms [T] of some sort, such as encryption, copy protection and digital watermarking of software and media content, and "potting" in the microprocessing industry (i.e. physically packing or obscuring a product innovation in such a way that it makes it very difficult to remove the packaging without destroying the product). Business strategies [B] that emphasize lead-time and learning-curve advantages are of particular importance, including business techniques to slowdown competitors' use of new technology. Another business strategy is to make prior investments in certain complementary or cospecialized assets (e.g. requisite marketing services, manufacturing capacity) that must be used in conjunction with the new technology during production and commercialization of the innovation (Teece 1986: 285, 289). Marketing techniques and tying arrangements can also be used, such as restricting regular software updates and online assistance to registered users.

In their efforts to protect their knowledge assets, entrepreneurs experiment with making connections among rules. They engage in a process of discovery through a "combinatorial design space" (Beinhocker 2011). They adopt tokens of one type of rule and combine them with rules of the same or different kinds to make a more complex rule system that in turn becomes an element in a higher-level network of rules. An example will help. Thomas Edison, the great American inventor and innovator obtained patents ($p_1 \ldots p_j$) relating to motion picture cameras and other equipment, and combined them with creative contractual rules ($a_1 \ldots a_k$) to form a new organization, the Motion Picture Patents Company. This business enterprise was a rule system at a higher level that Edison and other patent holders put together to control the manufacture, distribution and exhibition of movies. When legal measures fell short, Edison also made use of social rules and connections ($n_1 \ldots n_m$) to enforce his patent claims—in particular, he used his mob connections to hire armed thugs who sabotaged film productions and destroyed motion picture equipment not licensed by MPPC (Slide 1994: 63–64) (independent filmmakers migrated west to Hollywood in part to escape such interference).

The process of assembling rule systems for protecting knowledge will depend, among other things, on the nature of the module that encapsulates the new knowledge—whether the knowledge is embodied in machines and products (physical capital), in individuals (human capital) or in the firm's organizational structure (organizational capital) or some mix of these (Gorga and Halberstam 2007). It also depends on the characteristics of the new knowledge, that is, whether it is a product or process innovation, the degree to which new knowledge is codified or tacit, teachable or non-teachable, observable in use or non-observable, and simple or complex (Winter 1987: 170). Patents, for instance, afford considerable protection on new chemical products, but are generally ineffective at protecting process innovations in most manufacturing industries (Teece 1986; Grindley and Teece 1997). Trade secrets are particularly important for some process innovations, such as industrial-commercial processes for cosmetics (Levin et al. 1987).

Complex innovations require the complex integration of different types of knowledge and rules. For instance, Google's chief legal officer, David Drummond, estimates that the smartphone might be open to a quarter of a million patent claims (Lohr 2011). Entrepreneurs mix and match different intellectual property rules to protect different aspects of a complex innovation that comprises multiple components. The entrepreneur makes a choice to patent some parts, while deciding to keep other parts as a trade secret (Menell and Scotchmer 2007: 1498, 1507; Ottoz and Cugno 2011). For example, Apple employs utility patents ($p_1 \ldots p_j$) to protect the multi-touch user interface technology of the iPhone, copyright ($c_1 \ldots c_k$) to guard against unauthorized reproduction or distribution of the phone's operating system software, trade secrecy ($s_1 \ldots s_n$) to protect source code, a raft of trademarks ($m_1 \ldots m_p$) to protect the iPhone product name and Apple's brand name and logo. It also uses license agreements to govern the purchaser's use of the software included with the iPhone as well as technological protection measures ($t_1 \ldots t_q$) such as encryption and signing devices that function as access and copy controls to the iPhone's computer software. Hence, different types of intellectual property rules can stand in a relation of complementarity in the context of the same production plan. The emergent effect of the network of both legal and non-legal rules assembled by the entrepreneur determines the entrepreneur's actual power to control the use of intellectual property and to appropriate the returns. In other words, it is the structure of the emergent heterogeneous rule network that determines the entrepreneur's *economic* property right to his knowledge assets (in Barzel's (1997) sense of the term).

Matching the configuration of property rights to the nature of the technology, and ultimately, the constellation of end-user demand involves a process of trial and error-elimination over time. Entrepreneurs will only ever try out a very small subset of possible rule combinations and their decision process relies upon sufficiency criteria rather than optimality. The learning process is very definitely not one of instantaneous discovery of a fully formed idea about how to configure property rights to protect a clearly defined technology, all of whose attributes are well known to the entrepreneur. Rather, entrepreneurial discovery is a dynamic problem-solving process that takes place in real time and under conditions of structural uncertainty (Harper 1996). Over time, entrepreneurs must try to adapt the combination of IP rules that will add value to their productive ventures as technology and market conditions change. In order to hone appropriability mechanisms, entrepreneurs actively experiment in a piecemeal fashion with the elements of the property rights mix. They also improvise in response to the actions of competitors and adapt to changes in technology that result in existing "fences" becoming more permeable (e.g. "fence-cutting" inventions such as encryption circumvention measures).

2.4 *Appraising Capital Combinations Embodying Intellectual Property*

As they create and adjust IP rule complexes, entrepreneurs engage in forward-looking evaluations of the net benefits of alternative capital combinations. This process is referred to as *appraisal*. These appraisals are acts of the mind. The appraisal constitutes a relationship between the evaluating mind and the capital combination evaluated; it does not inhere in the combination or its measurable attributes (Lachmann 1977: 92, 156). Appraisals require an entrepreneurial mind-set oriented toward profit-and-loss accounting and the comparison of monetary costs and benefits. Capital combinations involving intellectual property are thus appraised according to the profit flows that they are expected to make. They are appraised according to the value of what they are anticipated to produce. Hence, the actual direction of value imputation excludes cost-based methods, which claim to value intellectual property on the basis of development expenses already incurred to produce it. In practice, real-world entrepreneurs employ a range of approaches for valuing patents and patent-protected projects, such as discounted cash flow (DCF) analysis, binomial decision tree analysis, real option-pricing models and hybrid methods (see Martin and Partnoy (2012) for a critical review of current approaches used by market participants to value patents). No matter which valuation technique is used, entrepreneurial expectations are a crucial part of any appraisal because the appraisal is undertaken at a point in time when the corresponding final goods (e.g. final output embodying the patented technology) and associated sales revenues are still yet to emerge in the future. Given the heterogeneity of their expectations and circumstances, different entrepreneurs will have different valuations of the same capital good or capital combination. Any given entrepreneur's appraisal depends on "who s/he is, what s/he knows and whom s/he knows" (Sarasvathy and Dew 2013: 290). With intellectual property, it is most unlikely that the same patent or patent portfolio would receive the same appraisal by different entrepreneurs because a patent's value is highly dependent upon local context of use: "The worth of a patent ... depends upon who wants to use it, for what commercial or other purpose, in what market (or litigation setting), and under what set of economic and legal constraints" (Phelps and Kline 2009: 168). As van Triest and Vis's (2007) case study of patent valuation shows, appraisal requires local knowledge of market conditions, competitors and relevant technological developments. The particular purposes to which entrepreneurs put patents depend not only upon their expectations about the future but also on their judgments of the relevance of past experience to this future. In their appraisal of IP combinations, entrepreneurs also try to take account of the plans of other entrepreneurs whose future actions complement or compete with their own because they will influence the value of the final goods to be generated (Lewin and Baetjer 2011: 341). Thus, appraisals involve forming guesses about others' perceptions of patent value and hence the interaction of entrepreneurial minds (heterogeneous mental models):

> Owners and users [of patented technology] may ... draw inferences about each other's perceptions of value from observing willingness or reluctance to incur costs in asserting or clearing rights. Patent owners decide how much to spend monitoring infringements and asserting their rights, thereby signaling how valuable they consider their patents to be. Users give signals about the value that they place on technology through their responses to assertions of rights [i.e. assertions of patents against users by patent owners] and through their own investments in patent searching and clearing rights. These signals may help owners and users to decide when bargaining over licenses is worthwhile.
> (Eisenberg 2011: 66)

Furthermore, in the portfolio-driven era of patenting, entrepreneurs base their patenting decisions upon appraisals, not of individual patents in isolation, but of portfolios of complementary patents and the synergistic benefits they generate. Other things being equal, patents that are linked together by genealogical relationships over time (i.e. because they build on the firm's same underlying technology) are valued more highly than a set of stand-alone patents (Liu et al. 2008). Interrelatedness among the firm's patents confers broader protection of its underlying intellectual property and strengthens its ability to appropriate the returns from its innovation. It is to the theme of the emergent properties of patent pools that we turn in the next section.

3 Patent Pools as Emergent Combinations of Property Rights at the Meso Level

A patent pool is an organization set up to combine multiple patents owned by multiple entities into a single portfolio.[7] The patents are bundled into a single licensing package that is offered to pool members and third parties. The relevant patent holders are usually for-profit firms, but not exclusively (e.g. Columbia University is a member of the MPEG-2 patent pool). In effect, patent pools enable a collection of firms "to combine their patents *as if* they were a single firm" (Lampe and Moser 2011: 1; emphasis added). Though differentiated, the patents are related by significant technological properties, whether product- or process-based. For instance, the MPEG-2 patent pool encapsulates a large share of the essential patents required to implement core MPEG-2 technology for compressing and transmitting audio-visual information for over-the-air digital television, digital cable TV and DVD products. ("MPEG" stands for the Moving Picture Expert Group, a standard-setting working group of the International Organization for Standardization.) The boundary of the pool is not fixed once and for all, but provisional, mutable, incomplete and semi-permeable and continually subject to adjustment and revision. For instance, what began as an agreement among nine patent holders to combine 27 patents required to meet the MPEG-2 technical standard has evolved over time into a capital structure containing more than 900 patents worldwide from 27 different companies (MPEG LA 2011).

In terms of the taxonomy in Table 2, a patent pool is a planned organization. It is a deliberate creation of relatively few individuals and relies upon formal organized enforcement. It is a purposeful combination of individual patents that is the product of entrepreneurial agency. For instance, the entrepreneurial driving force behind the formation of the MPEG-2 patent pool was provided by sophisticated lead users of the patented technology rather than existing owners of MPEG-2 patents. In particular, the idea for a patent pool originated within Cable Television Laboratories (hereafter "CableLabs"), a non-profit R&D consortium of cable television system operators. Its chief operating officer, Baryn Futa, was an intermarket operator who bridged structural holes in the social structure of the market by forging important connections between users (cable operators) and MPEG-2 patent holders (mainly hardware manufacturers) through his role as chair of the MPEG Intellectual Property Rights Working Group (Voorhees 1995b; Yoshida 1997). CableLabs meets all of von Hippel's (1996) criteria for qualifying as a "lead user" of an innovation: as the research arm of the cable-TV industry, it was at the forefront of emergent market and technological trends for mass-scale implementation of digital compression technology, its members experienced strong needs that would later become more

[7] "Patent pool" is not actually a legal technical term, so its meaning is not defined by law (United States v. Line Materials, 333 US 287, 313, n. 24 (1948) in Klein 1997: 3). A patent pool is different from cross-licensing, in which firms agree bilaterally to license their intellectual property to each other and retain control over it.

Table 2 Dimensions of intellectual property rule systems

Mode of origin \ Nature of rule system	Orders (i.e. systems of abstract, end-independent rules)	Organizations (i.e. systems of concrete, end-dependent rules)
Spontaneous	Common law of trade secrets Copyright at common law (non-statutory law created by state courts) (Balganesh 2010) Common law of publicity rights (relating to commercial use of one's identity or persona) "Shop right" doctrine Norm-based intellectual property systems (Fauchart and von Hippel 2008)	Codification and harmonization of trade secret law of different states (Uniform Trade Secrets Act) Statutory patent and copyright regimes over time (e.g. Patent Act 1952, America Invents Act 2011, Copyright Act 1976, Copyright Term Extension Act 1998 ("Mickey Mouse Protection Act"))[a]
Planned	Open source software development projects (e.g. Linux operating system) Standard-setting organizations Secondary markets in patents (including online auctions) Clause in US Constitution on patents	Patent pools Bilateral cross-licensing agreements Patent portfolio under a single firm's control Development contracts, patent licenses Confidentiality agreements Industry associations for protecting intellectual property (Hermitte 1988) Economic Espionage Act 1996

Source: The dimensions of classification of the table, but not its content, are derived from Vanberg (1989) and Langlois (1992)

[a]Statutory intellectual property regimes are classified here as spontaneous organizations (upper right-hand cell) rather than planned organizations because they have changed so frequently in ways that could not have been anticipated by their founders, giving their evolution an organic character over long time periods

general in the future, and they expected major benefits from using the new technology in terms of increased services (quality, security and interactivity) and lower video distribution costs.

Although it is embedded within an abstract system of general legal rules of property, a patent pool is constituted and maintained by rules of organization that are relatively concrete and oriented toward specific common goals. In the case of the MPEG-2 pool, the common goal was to establish a licensing entity whose mission was to foster reasonable and nondiscriminatory access to intellectual property rights necessary for global implementation of digital television (CableLabs 1995). To develop the licensing entity's organizational structure, Baryn Futa managed to build a consensus for a voluntary patent pool that employed a traditional royalty model for licensing MPEG-2 patents. The MPEG-2 pool was originally created through a network of four formal agreements that established boundary rules (e.g. rules specifying how patent holders enter and leave the pool, and procedures for adding and removing patents from the portfolio), position rules (e.g. rules specifying the different roles of the independent licensing administrator, licensors and licensees), authority or choice rules assigning action possibilities to each position and determining the level of decision-making control, scope rules (e.g. rules delimiting the portfolio license's authorized fields of use), information rules governing who communicates what with whom, and payoff rules (e.g. rules specifying the amount and allocation of royalties).[8] In specifying these organizational rules for the pool, entrepreneurs repartitioned and rebundled existing patent rights and formed new connections among them; they repackaged rights into new parcels and reallocated them among the relevant parties. In our capital-theoretic framework, such a reshuffling of entitlements to knowledge-based resources constitutes a form of capital regrouping. It results from an adaptive entrepreneurial process of "remodularization" that specifies a new architecture of intellectual property rights and a new set of interfaces between owners and potential users of knowledge resources. In the MPEG-2 pool, the patent holders in the pool retain their high-level residual rights of control over their intellectual property (including the right to offer independent bilateral licenses outside the pool), but they grant the licensing administrator the necessary legal rights to be able to license their patents to third parties over the useful life of the patents (Horn 2003: 121). The patent pool thereby coalesces day-to-day decision rights into the hands of the licensing administrator (known as MPEG LA) that has a comparative advantage in managing the licensing of intellectual property. It effectively moves decision rights to those with the superior knowledge and expertise in making decisions over access to the package of knowledge assets. Although the licensing administrator is not a patent owner, it has de facto control over the diffusion of the patented technology and can capture economies of specialization and of scope in administering this and other portfolio licenses for other patent pools.

Although a patent pool results from a well-articulated plan and purpose, there is a sense in which the patent pool, as a meso-level technological platform for multiple industries, becomes a system of rules characterized by an *intermediate* degree of abstraction (as defined by Whitman 2009). The patent pool fills the gap between end-independent abstract rules of property (that are highly general, pertaining to all persons in all circumstances) and specific concrete purposes. It abstracts from the details of many small-scale bilateral licensing contracts (that are highly specific to the details of idiosyncratic deals) in order to provide a portfolio license that serves as a common point of orientation for numerous users of that

[8]The classification of rules in this paragraph draws upon Ostrom et al.'s (1994) study of rules and common-pool resources. For a discussion of how Ostrom's proposed set of institutional design principles for managing common-pool resources derives from foundational evolutionary principles, see Wilson et al. (2013).

patented technology. The portfolio license becomes a meso-level focal point for certain types of transactions around which potential users can orient their production plans (Lachmann 1971). The MPEG-2 patent pool, for instance, provides a stable orientation scheme for over 1,400 licensees. It thereby facilitates the coordination of diverse concrete purposes of these licensees, ranging from television broadcasting based on MPEG-2 to consumer-electronics manufacturing for DVDs and digital TV. We do not know beforehand by whom and in what way the licenses will be used. Third parties can use the rules to help them predict the behavior of those with whom they interact and reduce the likelihood of infringing others' patents and subsequent litigation. As a modular interface and meso-level structure, the patent portfolio license encapsulates a common solution to a recurring problem and repackages it for reuse with multiple licensees (Langlois 1999).[9] The license agreement is a form of "congealed knowledge" about effective business practices ("ways and means") for carrying out productive tasks (Veblen 1908). It is a replicable template that embodies knowledge of standardized legal solutions for guaranteeing the implementation of complex licensing agreements and for resolving disputes.

The creation of a patent pool meets all the preconditions that Menger (1950) identified for capital formation. The patents are available in the present for combination in future time periods; they possess real properties that bestow causal powers and they are capable of being organized in a production process; individuals have command over potentially complementary patents for an extended time period; and individuals have knowledge of causal connections between patents and the satisfaction of human needs (Harper and Endres 2010: 33). A patent pool also exemplifies Menger's idea (1950: 55, 159) that forbearance may actually be an economic good that can be turned into capital when it is combined with other goods. It will be recalled that like other entitlements backed by property rules, patents provide a set of high-powered enforcement options, including shutdown injunctions and enhanced (i.e. supracompensatory) damages, to deter transfers of entitlements without the owner's consent. By refraining from rushing to enforce its own patent, each pool member acts in a manner that increases the totality of means at the disposal of other pool members. Forbearance from patent enforcement by a patent holder functions as a kind of capital good for each other member in the pool and the mutual coordination of decisions of forbearance creates a complex capital combination that promotes production.

Patent pools are an excellent example of how the capital structure interpolates new levels of organization within itself as it differentiates and evolves. The patent

[9]Widespread use of the portfolio license agreement across firms at the meso level increases its value because reusable contract terms are an important source of economies of scope and network effects. "Legal advice, opinion letters and related documentation will be more readily available, more timely, less costly, and more certain" (Klausner 2010: 761). This is especially so in the case of the MPEG-2 licensing administrator, which manages several other patent pools, including three separate pools for high-definition digital video coding standards (i.e. MPEG-4 AVC, VC-1 and MVC) used by Blu-ray Disc products and other formats. Legal knowledge developed and embodied in the MPEG-2 license has been carried over to these other portfolio licenses.

Table 3 Intellectual property rights as a multi-level pattern of capital

Level of economic order	Type of capital pattern embodying intellectual property	Examples	Potential for entrepreneurial connections
Mega (L^5)	Arrangement of all patents in the global economy	Worldwide patent network	↑
Macro (L^4)	Arrangement of all patents in the economy as a whole	Overall patent network in the United States	
Meso (L^3)	Patent pools among firms	MPEG-2 patent pool, patent pools for MPEG-4 (Part 10) and other high-definition video compression standards, two DVD pools, two pools for Blu-ray Disc products	
Enterprise (L^2)	Patent portfolio at the firm-level (actually used in production)	Sony's patent portfolio (more than 33,000 US patents)	
Micro (L^1)	Individual patents (potentially available for use in production)	Sony's patent for a "Moving image compressing and recording medium and moving image data encoder and decoder" (US 5,343,248) which includes 11 claims	
Nano (L^0)	Individual claims within a patent	The 11 claims in Sony's US patent no. 5,343,248: e.g. claim 1 is a "moving image data decoder for receiving and decoding a data stream including frames of compressed image video data . . . "; claim 2 is "an apparatus for encoding an interlace-scanned moving image video signal to form a video data stream"	

pool is an interpolation of a new meso level of economic organization within the macro IPR structure. The macro IPR structure comprises a network of property rules that establish boundaries on the intellectual resources that can be secured for private use (Calabresi and Melamed 1972). Table 3 reveals that systems of intellectual property comprise multiple levels, and in the case of patents, the system ranges from the nano level of individual patent claims to the mega level of the global patent network. The table shows that the formation of a patent pool is partly determined by processes at lower levels of individual patents and firms' portfolios and at the higher macro level of the economy-wide patent network. That is, patent-pool formation emerges from the interaction between processes occurring at adjacent levels of

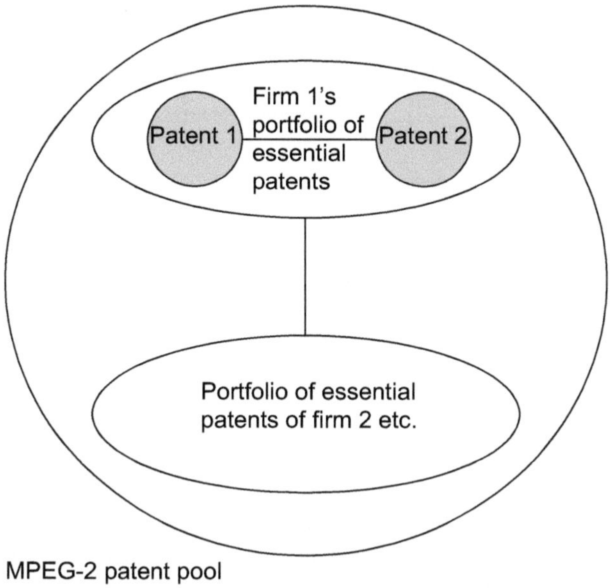

Fig. 1 Multi-level structure of capital embodying intellectual property

economic order. Both lower and higher levels enable and constrain processes of entrepreneurial combination and adjustment at the meso level; they have an effect on the dynamics of how entrepreneurs put the pool together and modify its boundaries and internal structure over time. Entrepreneurs construct a patent pool from the "bottom" up by connecting standard building blocks of intellectual property—namely patents. They form firm-level portfolios of essential patents in a particular technological field, which they may then connect to similar portfolios of other firms to create a patent pool, which may in turn be connected to other pools to create ever more complex structures. They thereby create and configure capital out of what intellectual property already exists. See Figs. 1 and 2. Individual patents at the micro level offer many possible permutations or initiating conditions for the emergence of new patent portfolios and patent pools and other capital structures embodying intellectual property. In order to form the patent pool, entrepreneurs combine the rights to exclude of many individual, closely related patents (e.g. essential patents required to practice the MPEG-2 standard) and thereby provide the pool with broader exclusionary power in its particular technological domain. Each patent gives its owner the legal right to exclude others from making, using, selling or importing a product or service embodying the claimed invention in the absence of a license. [10] The patent holder has the right to exclude others from the scope of the

[10]Individual patents only give patent owners rights of exclusion, not affirmative rights to use their intellectual property. "Ownership of a patent does not entitle one to do anything, including making

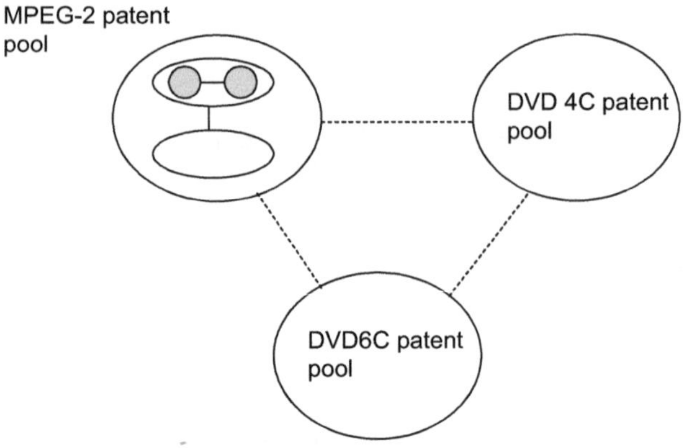

Fig. 2 Complementarity relationships between patent pools for digital video optical media

claims of the patent. "The claims of a patent are its boundaries, defining the scope of exclusion" (Chiang 2010: 523).[11] The patent pool combines the exclusionary power of its constituent elements.

The entrepreneurial participants who put the MPEG-2 pool together perceived a major gap between what was available (the current structure of property rights) and what could be achieved (the potential restructuring of essential patents into a patent pool). They saw that a gap in the existing capital structure stood in the way of improving digital media services for end-users and lowering costs. Overlapping patents, potential legal disputes over MPEG-2 intellectual property rights and royalties, and the credible threat of production-stifling injunctions for patent infringement were jeopardizing widespread adoption of MPEG-2 technology and the development of digital television (Krause 1994; Voorhees 1995a). Cable-TV operators also saw that the formation of a patent pool would enable them to exploit the untapped capacity of their existing capital structure at enterprise and meso levels—namely, the higher bandwidths (data rates) available to deliver higher image resolution and picture quality to their customers (CableLabs 1995). They could see that a reorganization of property rights into a pool would enable them to

---

the invention. Patent ownership only allows the owner to stop others from doing certain acts without the owner's permission" (Hays 2008: 502). The uses to which patent holders can put their intellectual property are determined by other areas of law, such as criminal laws and public safety laws (Kieff and Paredes 2004: 188).

[11]The claiming system of patent law requires patent holders to articulate the boundaries of their invention by the time of patent issuance, usually by listing the necessary and sufficient characteristics of the invention (Fromer 2009). The claims comprise technical descriptions of the process, machine, method, or matter contained in the original patent application. The scope of the exclusion right of an individual patent depends upon legal rules of "patent claim construction" (i.e. the methodology for interpreting the patent's meaning).

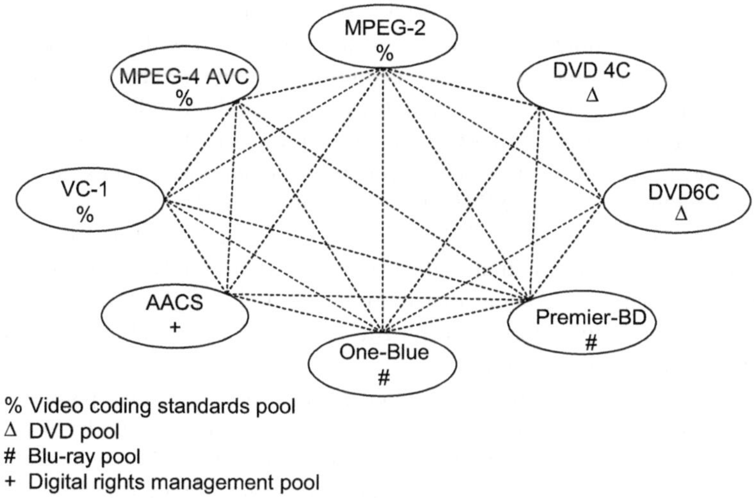

Fig. 3 Evolving complexity in the network of patent pools for digital video optical media

use MPEG-2 technology to capture profit opportunities from supplying video-on-demand and digital TV services on a wide scale.

The MPEG-2 pool did not mesh instantaneously and smoothly into the overall capital structure—it had to compete with and displace existing meso-level capital combinations that embodied older modes of production and distribution based on analog video and analog television. The formation of the MPEG-2 pool also facilitated the formation of other patent pools at the meso level that are related to the DVD standard. MPEG-2 compression technology made it possible to store an entire movie on one 12 cm optical disc and spurred the adoption of DVD-Video. In practice, the implementation of the DVD standard involves two mutually exclusive patent pools—the 4C pool overseen by Philips and the DVD6C Licensing Group administered by Toshiba. In order to manufacture products compliant with the DVD standard, entrepreneurs need to obtain licenses from both pools so that the two pools are complementary to each other in production (Layne-Farrar and Lerner 2011: 295). Furthermore, these two pools are also complementary to the MPEG-2 pool because DVD videodiscs and recorders use MPEG-2 compression. See Fig. 2. Hence the complementarity relation is not limited to the capital combination of a single firm but extends outwards and upwards through the level-structure of capital.

With the evolution from DVD to Blu-ray technology, the network of patent pools has become increasingly complex, as the number and variety of elements and connections have grown. Figure 3 shows how, through an entrepreneurial connection-making process, more and more patent pools can become linked through relationships of complementarity in production (indicated by the dotted lines). There are currently two patent pools for Blu-ray Disc products: One-Blue and Premier BD, formerly known as BD4C Licensing Group. Here again, as with DVD, making products compliant with the Blu-ray standard requires licenses from both pools. Moreover, given that Blu-ray Disc devices are backward-compatible with the various DVD standards in order to ensure integration with DVD-Video, these devices must include patented DVD technology (Peters 2011: 38). Furthermore, because the Blu-ray specification mandates support for three video coding standards (MPEG-2, MPEG-4 AVC, and VC-1), manufacturers of Blu-ray players, recorders and drives need licenses from the corresponding patent pools for these standards, all of which are administered by MPEG LA. (3D Blu-ray products require an additional license from MPEG LA for the MVC video coding standard.) Finally, because the Blu-ray specification also mandates the use of the Advanced Access Content System (AACS), a standard for content distribution and digital rights management, both device-makers and replicators pressing Blu-Ray discs will need a license from the AACS Licensing Administrator.

As we have seen, patent pools are emergent networks of related patents within a technological field. A patent pool is not a mere aggregate (i.e. stock) of patents. It consists of patents in relations to each other. The properties of a patent pool depend critically upon how it is organized and how its elements interact. Patent pools have internal structure. Patents stand in relations to one another, and these relations have a direction. If *a* and *b* are two non-identical patents, the state of affairs *a* blocks *b* is quite different from the state of affairs *b* blocks *a*. In the case of the aircraft manufacturers' pool established in 1917, for instance, the Wright brothers' patent (issued in 1906) for their wing-warping mechanism could block the production of planes using Glen Curtiss's patented improvements (issued in 1916), but the Curtiss patent did not block the production of planes using the Wright patent, provided production did not include Curtiss's patented wing flaps (Bittlingmayer 1988).

Patent pools possess emergent properties and produce significant synergistic effects. For example, they improve qualitative coordination of complementary activities by helping parties to link and mesh their expectations and production plans. More specifically, they can potentially generate knowledge-related benefits by speeding up the development and diffusion of new technology. "For patents, the whole is greater than the sum of its parts. The true value of patents inheres not in their individual worth, but in their aggregation into a collection of related patents—a patent portfolio" (Parchomovsky and Wagner 2005: 5–6). The strategic advantages of patent portfolios and patent pools are more than just additive. The broader scope of exclusivity from pooling related patents yields benefits to patent holders that differs in kind from those conferred by a mere stock of unrelated patents. Parchomovsky and Wagner (2005) identify several emergent effects from purposeful combinations of distinct but related individual patents, including facilitating subsequent in-house innovation, coordinating related technological developments, avoiding costly litigation, improving bargaining and defensive positions with respect to competitors, enhancing ability to attract capital investment, reducing uncertainty related to technological, competitive, market and legal developments, and increasing voice in the politics of patent reform.[12]

Indeed, patent pools fulfill all the formal conditions for emergence that economic patterns must satisfy to qualify as emergent phenomena (Harper and Endres 2012): (1) *material realization* (patent pools are realized in physical structures and processes)[13]; (2) *coherence* (patent pools are not a mere aggregate but a systemic whole); (3) *non-distributivity* (a patent pool possesses global qualitative coordination properties absent from its parts); (4) *structure dependence* (their systemic properties depend upon the connective structure and organization of patents and other rules). In addition, patent pools exhibit extra-strength versions of diachronic and synchronic emergence, which require that patterns possess one or more additional features: (5) *genuine novelty* (a patent pool is a genuinely novel structure that is qualitatively different from the individual patents from which it emerges); (6) *unpredictability in principle* (as the first patent pool in US history, the Sewing Machine Combination (1856–1877), could not be predicted or logically deduced through a rational procedure); and (7) *irreducibility* (the systemic properties of a patent pool, such as its economic value, do not follow from the properties of individual patents in isolation or in smaller, simpler patent portfolios). The economic value of a coherent patent pool or portfolio is greater than the sum of the values of the individual patents if each were separated from the others.

4 Conclusion

Even if some property rights are created and granted by the state, entrepreneurs in the market are the ultimate arbiters of how property rights are applied and used in production. Entrepreneurs are the major causal agents in the transformation of legal rules-in-use and their actions form and change production complementarities between legal rules. Legal rules do more than just structure exchange relationships among economic agents. They are an integral part of the productive capabilities of the economic system and participate in productive processes. They are part of

[12]The "economics jury" is still out when it comes to determining the empirical effects of patent pools on innovation (Lampe and Moser 2010; Joshi and Nerkar 2011; Flamm 2013). But it seems clear that a simple analysis of patent statistics is not sufficient. Rather, it is important to examine the specific content and structure of the rules of organization that form patent pools, to trace changes over time in how pools are organized, and to employ direct measures of innovation in product markets rather than indirect correlates of innovation, such as patenting metrics. As Flamm (2013: 45) concludes: "The clear implication is that organizational details matter: no single conclusion is likely to fit all cases. As theory seems to predict, the empirical effects of patent pools on innovation are likely to be ambiguous, dependent on the historical and institutional particulars of the pool and the industry it affects".

[13]According to Cheung (1982: 49), a key element of the patent system is an "observability conversion". In order to protect an idea with a patent, it is necessary to convert the idea into an observable product or process and to draft a patent claim that sets boundaries for the idea.

the knowledge structure that captures energy to select, transport and transform materials into new forms. Like all capital goods, property rights are combinatorial, relational, structural and heterogeneous. Entrepreneurs mix and match legal rules and property forms and combine them with other types of rules (including social norms and technological rules) in order to protect knowledge assets and organize production. Entrepreneurs identify gaps in the meshing of the capital structure. Because they face structural uncertainty, new combinations of rights are seldom if ever perfect; they are all based on fallible entrepreneurial conjectures about the future. The making of new combinations precedes their selection by the market and their matching with the wishes and needs of consumers. Entrepreneurs continually reshuffle property rights in response to changes in technology and market conditions. Rebundling property rights is not a one-off event but an ongoing process that takes time. Entrepreneurs create more complex structures of property rights by means of sequential adjustments in capital combinations and rule complexes. Like other capital patterns, the property rights structure undergoes continual transformation as a result of these piecemeal entrepreneurial experiments. In addition, as entrepreneurs fill gaps in the capital structure, they at once open up other gaps elsewhere in the network. Each new clustering of property rights not only produces synergistic effects but also generates new, unforeseeable opportunities for other entrepreneurs to rebundle rights and regroup capital. The endogenous process of capital formation is ceaseless and open-ended, and does not converge to a predetermined end state. Thus, in the capital-theoretic approach, the network of entrepreneurs' production plans exerts an ongoing causal influence on the overall structure of property rights. Production plans and property rights structures are reciprocally related in that entrepreneurs' production plans are constrained by pre-existing legal structures and then capable of transforming those rights structures.

Theories of property rights that ignore multilevel patterning and the interactions of phenomena at different temporal and spatial scales are going to be deficient. We have shown that the idea of a capital combination is useful for reexamining the nature of property rights in general and the structure of intellectual property rights in particular. A production module (the capital combination) rather than an exchange relation (the transaction) forms the basic unit of the analysis. Unexpected changes in productive processes always imply remodularization and regrouping of property rights. They entail changes in encapsulation boundaries, revisions in the modular decomposition of entitlements, and changes in connections and levels of property rights.

The interpolation of new levels of property rights (such as patent pools) arises from specific combinatorial acts that create capital. It occurs as a result of capital formation. The combinatorial creation of patent pools conforms to what Abler (1989) calls the "particulate principle" of self-diversifying systems. This principle maintains that generative recombination of system elements must be based on regrouping particles rather than on blending constituents. Adaptive processes of self-organization and selection in the patent system are based upon dynamically stable discrete units (forms of intellectual property). Even after they are combined into higher-level structures, such as patent pools, the original patents (i.e. the "particles") continue to be identifiable perceptually rather than blend with each other.

Future research should apply the capital-theoretic perspective to study the coordination of rules (and associated coordination processes) in the legal system, and particularly the intellectual property regime. It is necessary to examine the impediments to the adaptation of rules at different levels of the legal order of property, and to identify where and how coordination processes can break down. We are particularly interested in the sources of what Dopfer and Potts (2008) call "deep coordination failure". This kind of failure results from poor fit between rules—not only dysfunctional but also missing connections between legal rules.

Another item on the agenda of future research is to draw out the implications of the approach for the co-evolution of law and economic systems. This requires examining the nature of the coupling relationships between the law and the market economy—the peculiarities of the interactions and feedbacks between these two multi-layered systems. We are particularly interested in how a discontinuous change in one system, especially at a lower level (such as a structural break in the norms of legal practitioners), can percolate upwards to generate a new level of structure that is interpolated into the existing legal order and how this can impact the economic system. It would be interesting to investigate how entrepreneurial dynamics in the legal system (e.g. norm innovation, novel litigation strategies) can reverberate on market dynamics, and vice versa.

Acknowledgments The author is indebted to two anonymous referees for constructive suggestions for improvement. I would also like to thank participants at the following seminars and conferences where the paper was presented: the Colloquium on Market Institutions and Economic Processes, Department of Economics, New York University, April 2012; the Annual General Meeting and study day of the Law and Economics Association of New Zealand (LEANZ), Wellington, June 2012; session 5A on Complex Systems of the 14th International Schumpeter Society Conference, Brisbane, Australia, July 2012; and the annual conference of the Society for the Development of Austrian Economics, New Orleans, November 2012. I would particularly like to thank Karen Bradshaw Schulz, Tony Endres, Lew Evans, Roel Kramer, William Lenihan, Stuart McDonald and Thomas Pontani for informative discussions and comments. Any remaining errors are the author's.

References

Abler WL (1989) On the particulate principle of self-diversifying systems. J Soc Biol Struct 12(1):1–13

Allen CK (1927) Law in the making. Oxford University Press, Oxford

Balganesh S (2010) The pragmatic incrementalism of common law intellectual property. Vanderbilt Law Rev 63(6):1543–1616

Barnett JM (2011) Intellectual property as a law of organization. South Calif Law Rev 84(4):785–857

Barzel Y (1997) Economic analysis of property rights, 2nd edn. Cambridge University Press, Cambridge

Beinhocker ED (2011) Evolution as computation: integrating self-organization with generalized Darwinism. J Inst Econ 7(3):393–423
Bittlingmayer G (1988) Property rights, progress, and the aircraft patent agreement. J Law Econ 31(1):227–248
Buchanan JM, Yoon YJ (2000) Symmetric tragedies: commons and anticommons. J Law Econ 43(1):1–13
CableLabs (1995) MPEG IPR Backgrounder. Available at: http://www.cablelabs.com/news/pr/ipr_backgrounder.html. Accessed 30 Aug 2013
Calabresi G, Melamed AD (1972) Property rules, liability rules, and inalienability: one view of the cathedral. Harvard Law Rev 85(6):1089–1182
Carlson SC (1999) Patent pools and the antitrust dilemma. Yale J Regul 16(2):359–399
Cheung SNS (1982) Property rights in trade secrets. Econ Inq 20(1):40–53
Chiang TJ (2010) Fixing patent boundaries. Mich Law Rev 108(4):523–575
Coase RE (1960) The problem of social cost. J Law Econ 3(October):1–44
Coase RE (1988) The nature of the firm: influence. J Law Econ Org 4:33–48
Demsetz H (1967) Toward a theory of property rights. Am Econ Rev 57(2):347–359
Dopfer K, Potts J (2008) The general theory of economic evolution. Routledge, London
Dopfer K, Foster J, Potts J (2004) Micro-meso-macro. J Evol Econ 14:263–79
Eggertsson T (1990) Economic behavior and institutions. Cambridge University Press, Cambridge
Eisenberg RS (2011) Patent costs and unlicensed use of patented inventions. Univ Chicago Law Rev 78(1):53–69
Ellickson RC (1991) Order without law: how neighbors settle disputes. Harvard University Press, Cambridge
Endres AM, Harper DA (2012) The kinetics of capital formation and economic organization. Camb J Econ 36(4):963–980
Fauchart E, von Hippel E (2008) Norms-based intellectual property systems: the case of French chefs. Organ Sci 19(2):187–201
Fisher I (1906) The nature of capital and income. Macmillan, New York
Flamm K (2013) A tale of two standards: patent pools and innovation in the optical disk drive industry. NBER Working Paper No. 18931
Foss K, Foss NJ (2000) Theoretical isolation in contract theory: suppressing margins and entrepreneurship. J Econ Methodol 7(3):313–339
Foss NJ, Garzarelli G (2007) Institutions as knowledge capital: Ludwig M. Lachmann's interpretative institutionalism. Camb J Econ 31(5):789–804
Foster J (2000) Competitive selection, self-organisation and Joseph A. Schumpeter. J Evol Econ 10:311–328
Foster J (2005) From simplistic to complex systems in economics. Camb J Econ 29(6):873–892
Fromer JC (2009) Claiming intellectual property. Univ Chicago Law Rev 76(2):719–796
Gorga E, Halberstam M (2007) Knowledge inputs, legal institutions and firm structure: towards a knowledge-based theory of the firm. Northwest Univ Law Rev 101(3):1123–1206
Grindley PC, Teece DJ (1997) Managing intellectual capital: licensing and cross-licensing in semiconductors and electronics. Calif Manag Rev 39(2):1–34
Grossman SJ, Hart OD (1986) The costs and benefits of ownership: a theory of vertical and lateral integration. J Polit Econ 94(4):691–719
Guglielmo C (2012) The Apple vs. Samsung patent dispute: 20 talking points. Available at: http://www.forbes.com/sites/connieguglielmo/2012/08/21/the-apple-vs-samsung-patent-dispute-20-talking-points/3/. Accessed 30 Aug 2013
Hadfield GK (2012) Legal infrastructure and the new economy. I/S J Law Policy Inform Soc 8(1):1–59
Hadfield GK, Weingast BR (2012) What is law? A coordination account of the characteristics of legal order. J Legal Anal 4(2):471–514
Harper DA (1996) Entrepreneurship and the market process: an inquiry into the growth of knowledge. Routledge, New York

Harper DA (2013) Property rights, entrepreneurship and coordination. J Econ Behav Organ 88:62–77
Harper DA (2014) Property rights as a complex adaptive system: how entrepreneurship transforms intellectual property structures. J Evol Econ 24(2):335–355
Harper DA, Endres AM (2010) Capital as a layer cake: a systems approach to capital and its multi-level structure. J Econ Behav Organ 74(1–2):30–41
Harper DA, Endres AM (2012) The anatomy of emergence, with a focus upon capital formation. J Econ Behav Organ 82(2–3):352–367
Hart O (1989) An economist's perspective on the theory of the firm. Columbia Law Rev 89(7):1757–1774
Hayek FA [1944] (2007) The road to serfdom: text and documents. University of Chicago Press, Chicago
Hays T (2008) The exhaustion of patent owners' rights in the European Community. In: Takenaka T (ed) Patent law and theory: a handbook of contemporary research. Edward Elgar, Cheltenham, pp 501–518
Heller MA (1998) The tragedy of the anticommons: property in the transition from Marx to markets. Harvard Law Rev 111(3):621–688
Heller MA, Eisenberg RS (1998) Can patents deter innovation? The anticommons in biomedical research. Science 280(5364):698–701
Hennings KH (1990) Capital as a factor of production. In: Eatwell J, Milgate M, Newman P (eds) Capital theory. W.W. Norton & Company, New York, pp 108–122
Hermitte MA (1988) Histoires juridiques extravagante: la reproduction végétale. In: L'homme, la nature et le droit. Christian Bourgois, Paris, pp 40–85
Holland JH (2006) Studying complex adaptive systems. J Syst Sci Complex 19(1):1–8
Horn L (2003) Alternative approaches to IP management: one-stop technology platform licensing. J Commer Biotechnol 9(2):119–127
Joshi AM, Nerkar A (2011) When do strategic alliances inhibit innovation by firms? Evidence from patent pools in the global optical disc industry. Strateg Manag J 32:1139–1160
Kieff FS (2006) Coordination, property, and intellectual property: an unconventional approach to anticompetitive effects and downstream access. Emory Law J 56:327–438
Kieff FS, Paredes TA (2004) The basics matter: at the periphery of intellectual property. George Washington Law Rev 73(1):174–204
Klausner M (2010) Corporations, corporate law, and networks of contracts. Virginia Law Rev 81(3):757–852
Klein JI (1997) Cross-licensing and antitrust law. Address before the American Intellectual Property Law Association, May 2, San Antonio, Texas
Knight FH (1944) The rights of man and natural law. Ethics 54(2):124–145
Krause R (1994) Cable Labs explores licensing to stem MPEG patent imbroglio. Electron News, 2 May
Lachmann LM (1956) Capital and its structure. G. Bell, London
Lachmann LM (1971) The legacy of Max Weber. The Glendessary Press, Berkeley
Lachmann LM (1977) Capital, expectations, and the market process. Sheed Andrews and McMeel, Kansas City, KS
Lampe R, Moser P (2010) Do patent pools encourage innovation? Evidence from the nineteenth-century sewing machine industry. J Econ Hist 70(4):898–920
Lampe R, Moser P (2011) Patent pools and the direction of innovation: evidence from the 19th-century sewing machine industry. NBER working paper no. 17573
Landes WM, Posner RA (1976) Legal precedent: a theoretical and empirical analysis. J Law Econ 19(2):249–307
Langlois RN (1992) Orders and organizations: toward an Austrian theory of social institutions. In: Caldwell BJ, Boehm S (eds) Austrian economics: tensions and new directions. Kluwer, Dordrecht, pp 165–192

Langlois RN (1999) Scale, scope and the reuse of knowledge. In: Dow SC, Earl PE (eds) Economic organization and economic knowledge: essays in honour of Brian J. Loasby, vol 1. Edward Elgar, Cheltenham, pp 239–254
Langlois RN (2002) Modularity in technology and organization. J Econ Behav Organ 49:19–37
Langlois RN, Foss NJ (1999) Capabilities and governance: the rebirth of production in the theory of economic organization. Kyklos 52(2):201–18
Layne-Farrar A, Lerner J (2011) To join or not to join: Examining patent pool participation and rent sharing rules. Int J Ind Organ 29(2):294–303
Lerner J, Tirole J (2008) Public policy toward patent pools. In: Jaffe AB, Lerner J, Stern S (eds) Innovation policy and the economy, vol 8. University of Chicago Press, Chicago, pp 157–186
Levin R, Klevorik A, Nelson R, Winter S, Gilbert R, Griliches Z (1987) Appropriating the returns from industrial research and development. Brook Pap Econ Act 3:783–831
Lewin P (1994) Knowledge, expectations, and capital. The economics of Ludwig M. Lachmann: attempting a new perspective. Adv Aust Econ 1:233–256
Lewin P, Baetjer H (2011) The capital-based view of the firm. Rev Aust Econ 24:335–354
Litman J (2001) Digital copyright. Prometheus, New York
Liu K, Arthurs J, Cullen J, Alexander R (2008) Internal sequential innovations: how does interrelatedness affect patent renewal? Res Policy 37(5):946–953
Loasby BJ (1999) Knowledge, institutions and evolution in economics. Routledge, New York
Lohr S (2011) A bull market in tech patents. New York Times, 16 August
Mackaay E (1990) Economic incentives in markets for information and innovation. Harv J Law Public Policy 13(3):867–909
Martin S, Partnoy F (2012) Patents as options. In: Kieff FS, Paredes TA (eds) Perspectives on commercializing innovation. Cambridge University Press, Cambridge, pp 303–326
McQuade TJ, Butos WN (2009) The adaptive systems theory of social orders. Stud Emerg Order 2:76–108
Menell PS, Scotchmer S (2007) Intellectual property law. In: Polinsky AM, Shavell SM (eds) Handbook of law and economics, vol 2. Elsevier, Amsterdam, pp 1473–1570
Menger C (1950) Principles of economics (trans: J. Dingwall and B. F. Hoselitz). Free Press, Glencoe, IL. Original German edition published in 1871
Merges RP (2001) Institutions for intellectual property transactions: the case of patent pools. In: Dreyfuss R, Zimmerman DL, First H (eds) Expanding the boundaries of intellectual property: innovation policy for the knowledge society. Oxford University Press, Oxford, pp 123–166
Merrill TW, Smith HE (2000) Optimal standardization in the law of property: the numerus clausus principle. Yale Law J 110(1):1–70
MPEG LA (2011) MPEG-2 patent portfolio license briefing (12/3/11 version). Available at: http://www.mpegla.com/main/programs/M2S/Documents/m2sweb.pdf. Accessed 4 Jun 2012
Mulligan C (2013) A numerus clausus principle for intellectual property. Tennessee Law Rev 80, pp. 235–290
Nakoshi H (1993) New Japanese trade secret act. J Pat Trademark Off Soc 75(August):631–644
Nelson RR, Sampat BN (2001) Making sense of institutions as a factor shaping economic performance. J Econ Behav Organ 44(1):31–54
North D (1990) Institutions, institutional change, and economic performance. Cambridge University Press, Cambridge
Ostrom E, Gardner R, Walker JM (1994) Rules, games, and common-pool resources. University of Michigan Press, Ann Arbor
Ottoz E, Cugno F (2011) Choosing the scope of trade secret law when secrets complement patents. Int Rev Law Econ 31(4):219–227
Parchomovsky G, Wagner RP (2005) Patent portfolios. Univ Pennsylvannia Law Rev 154(1):1–77
Parisi F, Schulz N, Depoorter B (2005) Duality in property: commons and anticommons. Int Rev Law Econ 25(4):578–591
Peters R (2011) One-Blue: a blueprint for patent pools in high-tech. Intell Asset Manag (September/October): 38–41

Phelps M, Kline D (2009) Burning the ships: intellectual property and the transformation of Microsoft. Wiley, Hoboken
Potts J (2000) The new evolutionary microeconomics: complexity, competence and adaptive behaviour. Edward Elgar, Cheltenham
Ricketts M (1987) Rent-seeking, entrepreneurship, subjectivism, and property rights. J Inst Theor Econ 143:457–466
Ruhl JB (2008) Law's complexity: a primer. Georgia State Univ Law Rev 24:885–911
Sarasvathy SD, Dew N (2013) Without judgment: an empirically-based entrepreneurial theory of the firm. Rev Aust Econ 26(3):277–296
Shapiro C (2000) Navigating the patent thicket: cross licenses, patent pools, and standard-setting. Innovat Pol Econ 1:119–150
Simon H (1962) The architecture of complexity. Proc Am Philos Soc 106(6):467–82
Slide A (1994) Early American cinema. Scarecrow, Metuchen
Smith HE (2007) Intellectual property as property: delineating entitlements in information. Yale Law J 116(8):1742–1822
Smith HE (2012) The modularity of patent law. In: Kieff FS, Paredes TA (eds) Perspectives on commercializing innovation. Cambridge University Press, Cambridge, pp 83–116
Sprankling JG (2008) Owning the center of the earth. Univ Chicago Law Rev 55(4):979–1040
Teece DJ (1986) Profiting from technological innovation: implications for integration, collaboration, licensing and public policy. Res Policy 15(6):285–305
Tobin J (2005) Fisher's "The nature of capital and income". Am J Econ Soc 64(1):207–14
van Triest S, Vis W (2007) Valuing patents on cost-reducing technology: a case study. Int J Prod Econ 105(1):282–292
Vanberg V (1989) Carl Menger's evolutionary and John R. Commons' collective action approach to institutions: a comparison. Rev Polit Econ 1(3):334–360
Veblen T (1908) On the nature of capital. Q J Econ 22(4):517–542
von Hippel E (1996) Lead users: a source of novel product concepts. Manag Sci 32(7):791–805
Voorhees M (1995a) New video technology faces mega-licensing woes. MPEG II may be open, but it's also highly proprietary; CableLabs tries to create voluntary patent pool. Information Law Alert 3(3), 14 February
Voorhees M (1995b) Use-based MPEG royalty may have merit depending on how it's done, says Futa. Information Law Alert 3(8), 28 April
Whitman DG (2009) Rules of abstraction. Rev Aust Econ 22:21–41
Williamson O (1985) The economic institutions of capitalism. Free Press, New York
Williamson O (1988) The logic of economic organization. J Law Econ Organ 4(1):65–93
Wilson DS, Ostrom E, Cox ME (2013) Generalizing the core design principles for the efficacy of groups. J Econ Behav Organ 90S:S21–S32
Winter SG (1987) Knowledge and competence as strategic assets. In: Teece DJ (ed) The competitive challenge: strategies for industrial innovation and renewal. Ballinger, Cambridge, pp 159–184
Yoshida J (1997) MPEG LA serves as model for pooling patents. Electr Eng Times, 18 August

Entrepreneurial Catch Up and New Industrial Competence Bloc Formation in the Baltic Sea Region

Gunnar Eliasson and Pontus Braunerhjelm

Abstract 1990 saw the break up of the Soviet political system. The liberated, but poor formerly planned economies were left on their own to restore their institutions to that of an open market organization. Even though roughly on par with the Nordic countries before being annexed, 50 years of Soviet isolation had left the formerly planned Baltic Sea Region (BSR) economies in an industrially backward state. Critical market institutions did not exist, and corruption made normal business life impossible. *Catch up with Western industrial economies therefore became a policy priority*.

During the 1970s also the industrialized BSR economies had introduced elements of centralized planning that restricted free entrepreneurial activities. By the Soviet

Revised version of paper presented at the 2012 International Schumpeter Conference, Brisbane, July 2nd-5th, 2012, based on a report of us for the Baltic Development Forum (Braunerhjelm and Eliasson 2011). We see no reason to change our empirical conclusions on what has occurred since then, and the reader is referred to that report for more empirical detail, or an updating of the report in progress. This paper, which is methodological, has benefitted greatly from comments at the SNEE Conference in Mölle, Sweden, May 22–24, 2012. We are particularly grateful for the needs for clarification pointed out by Bo Carlsson and Frederic Lehmann. Thanks go to Anjit Singh's very appropriate comments to our paper at the Swedish Entrepreneurship Forum conference in Vaxholm, Sweden, August 2013. We have added a discussion in the final policy Sect. 6 on "government entrepreneurship" in the form of centralized economic coordination of the early South Korean or Japanese METI kind, and on why this alternative would not have been the right policy approach for the liberated, formerly planned BSR economies. Thanks also go to researchers at the Baltic desk at IMF, who pointed out several misinterpretations of data. We have also done our best to explain the dynamic Micro to Macro method used in the catch-up analysis better, which an anonymous referee asked for. We are grateful to Finnish ETLA, and Pekka Ylä-Anttila in particular, for providing us with a rich documentation from ETLA's research program on the BSR. Finally, interviews with economists at the Estonian, Latvian and Lithuanian branch offices of the Finnish Evli Bank, and long discussions with Henrik Westling, partner in the Bank, and earlier responsible for its corporate finance activities across the BSR, activities that have now more or less been closed down, have given us important insights in what has been going on in the BSR financial markets.

G. Eliasson (✉) • P. Braunerhjelm
Royal Institute of Technology (KTH), Stockholm, Sweden
e-mail: gunnar.elias@telia.com; pontus.braunerhjelm@entrepreneurshipforum.se

A. Pyka, J. Foster (eds.), *The Evolution of Economic and Innovation Systems*,
Economic Complexity and Evolution, DOI 10.1007/978-3-319-13299-0_15

collapse stagnation had therefore also brought the need for entrepreneurship onto the policy agenda of Western BSR nations. Institutional obstacles to economic progress were gradually being dismantled. Historic developments in the BSR have therefore accidentally staged a unique *economic policy experiment. Using a competence bloc based method of identifying the role of the entrepreneur in observed macroeconomic catch-up, we can distinguish between the relative roles in economic progress among the BSR economies of improvements in local entrepreneurial environments, and of individual entrepreneurial action.* We found that successful catch-up among the formerly planned BSR economies still has a long way to go, and that *policy focus should be set on improving the local entrepreneurial environments* to support both new firm formation for long run development, and to encourage immediate FDI for short term effects. Significant obstacles to trade and ownership transactions, however, remain across the BSR. Hence, *success in catch-up should be expected to differ significantly among the BSR countries.*

We propose a *policy competition* among the transition countries *in improving their entrepreneurial environments* to beat each other in long run catch-up performance, that will benefit both catch-up of individual economies, and growth of the entire BSR economy.

1 Catch-up With Wealthy Neighbors Through Entrepreneurship

We study the macro economic development of individual national economies in the Baltic Sea Region (BSR) from a micro economic perspective, taking advantage of their different developments from a base in very contrasting entrepreneurial environments in the post Soviet liberalization 1990s. We are talking about a total economy with some 90 million inhabitants, covering an area roughly the size of one third of the US, and including eleven economies, or parts of economies, bordering on the Baltic.

Historically, the BSR has, however, been an institutionally fairly homogeneous economy, integrated economically and culturally through the sea lanes of the Baltic. The Baltic trading routes of the Hanseatic League of the fifteenth century in fact define the integration pattern quite well. After WWII the BSR was broken up into a dual economy, consisting of a poor Soviet block of centrally planned economies, on the one hand, and the industrially advanced economies Finland, Denmark, Germany and Sweden, on the other.

1990 saw the break-up of the Soviet political system. The liberated, but poor formerly planned economies were left on their own to restore their institutions to that of a market organization. *50 years of Soviet isolation had prevented producers there from learning about rapidly expanding new industrial practices in the west*, and left the formerly planned BSR economies in an industrially backward state. Critical market functions did not exist, and corrupt institutions made normal business life impossible (Eliasson 1998). C*atch up with Western industrial economies therefore became a policy priority.*

Coping With Unequal Progress: A Policy Problem and a Research Opportunity During the 1970s also the industrialized BSR economies had introduced elements of a centralized agenda in their industrial policy repertoires in the belief that it would improve economic performance. "Planning" focus was on supporting big firm growth, coupled with a lack of attention to the role of a viable commercial climate. Policies to support "plans" by definition meant institutional encouragement of big firms, through for instance tax favors, restrictions on free entrepreneurial activity, and disincentives for new business formation and SME growth. By the time of the Soviet break-up, stagnation had however brought an awareness of the role of entrepreneurship in growth onto the policy agenda of Western nations. Obstacles to economic progress were gradually being dismantled. But some ambitious welfare economies had suffered from reduced opportunities to learn and to innovate. The destructive "delearning" influence of centralized policy ambitions had affected the actors in the financial commercialization markets in particular (Eliasson and Petersen 2013). So the problems of catch-up that we address are also relevant for at least some of the advanced economies of the BSR. Could some "mixed" Western economies with large and rigid public production of welfare services even have got stuck with problems similar to those of the formerly planned economies?

Before the Soviet occupation the formerly planned Baltic economies, excepting Russia and Poland, were institutionally and industrially roughly on par with Denmark, Finland and Sweden. The industrial backwardness of the formerly planned economies at the time they were liberated was therefore due to constraints on entrepreneurial initiatives, broadly defined, that limited the competitive market dynamics that we associate with macro economic growth, limitations imposed by the Soviet Union.[1] So by definition there was a policy task of some magnitude to undo that heritage, and we should still be able to take advantage of the fact that historic developments in the BSR have accidentally staged an *economic policy experiment that allows us to distinguish between the relative roles in economic progress of improvements in local entrepreneurial environments and of individual entrepreneurial action.* The key question therefore is how the agents of markets have been mobilized to overcome the obstacles to catch-up left behind by centrally directed policy.

To answer that question a method to link the entrepreneurs to their observable outputs has been derived. The role of entrepreneurial entry in macro economic growth through competitive selection of innovation supplies, is explicitly linked to various features of a competence bloc that determines the dynamic efficiency of such selections. In this sense this is therefore a methodological paper. For the empirical analysis we draw on the detailed statistical documentation in Braunerhjelm and

[1]We are grateful to Anjit Singh for very appropriately pointing out that we had failed to mention the successful record of "Government dictatorial entrepreneurship" that took, for instance, South Korea onto a fast long term growth path, an observation that is also relevant for the current policies of making the Chinese economy catch-up with Western industrial performance. Since our policy proposal in the final Sect. 6 comes out very differently from that, we address that policy alternative in that later context.

Eliasson (2011) and updates. Empirical research, and simulations on the Swedish evolutionary Micro firm to Macro model furthermore suggest that growth through new firm formation initially is a very slow process that may however suddenly, and seemingly unexpectedly, gain momentum. Such a sudden wave of expansion, furthermore, is typically uneven and moved by a few entrepreneurial winners. The import of new technology through FDI is the fast way to achieve that stimulus in catch-up, but the indigenous emergence of a few entrepreneurial winners is the only sustainable catch-up formula for the very long run. Both forms of entrepreneurship, however, benefit from the same positive entrepreneurial climate. *Policy focus should therefore be set on the local entrepreneurial environments, but success in catch-up should still be expected to differ significantly among the formerly planned BSR economies.*

The Role of Entrepreneurs in Catch Up: The Research Problem

The role of entrepreneurs in closing the still significant gaps in per capita incomes between the rich industrialized, and the poor and formerly planned Soviet economies in the BSR is the main theme of this empirical analysis. To catch up on what was lost in economic performance and economic wellbeing during 50 years of Soviet isolation and central planning, some form of entrepreneurship is needed by definition. Catch up, however, is not a matter of more investment and more labor input of the same as before. *Catch up by definition has to take place through entrepreneurial entry of new and superior actors and/or through innovative entrepreneurial action that takes existing business firms up their value chains* ("intrapreneurship"). Both are very long term evolutionary processes that in the advanced industrial economies of the post WWII period have occurred predominantly through innovative product development, rather than through rationalization and cost competition (Eliasson 1987).[2] Catch-up to Western industrial performance of the formerly planned economies is one thing, but it will be a tougher race for those economies if their industrially wealthy neighbors have also been moving ahead on an entrepreneurial wave of their own. And how can innovative entrepreneurship occur in economic environments that lack both the requisite technical, management, marketing and other commercial competences, and the critical supporting institutions (Eliasson 1993, 1998; Eliasson et al. 1994). To understand that we distinguish between change in the environment in which the entrepreneurs operate, on the one hand, and the entrepreneurial capabilities of individual actors, on the other. Do the various economies of the BSR possess different endowments of innate entrepreneurs that need to be awaken, and will generate unequal national economic growth outcomes, or are the innate entrepreneurial endowments more or less equally distributed, so that the national growth outcomes will depend on how vigorously

[2]This in turn relates to the current discussion about globally increasing inequality. Are the economies of the world economy converging long term onto the same national standards of living, as was believed not long ago (Dollar and Wolff 1988), or diverging (Pritchnett 1997; Eliasson 2007; Braunerhjelm 2008; Ballot and Taymaz 2012; Piketty 2014). The industrial dynamics of the BSR pits those two hypotheses against each other.

policies to improve local entrepreneurial environments are carried out? The working hypothesis is that distributions of individual and latent entrepreneurial capacities are the same, and that environmental differences are what matter, not least when it comes to attract "imports" of entrepreneurial knowhow through FDI.

Economic growth has to be based on particular kinds of industrial knowhow, and takes place in entrepreneurial environments rich in supporting infrastructure, both in scarce supply, or not existing, in the formerly planned economies. *Lack of statistically significant catch-up, notably in recent years, might therefore be interpreted as failure on the entrepreneurial policy agenda, i.e. institutional set up.*

The formerly planned BSR states have tried different approaches, and experienced different difficulties of unloading their Soviet heritage. Some, for instance Estonia, have reduced corruption from the extreme state prevailing in the Soviet Union at the time of break up, to the extent that they now rank almost on par with modern Western economies. Russia, on the other hand, remains were it was in the beginning of the 1990s according to the Transparency International Corruption Perception Index. Similarly, during the same period, the advanced BSR economies have more or less unloaded the socialistic elements of their welfare experiments. The opportunity costs of industrial subsidy programs to temporarily shelter employment at doomed firms, notably shipyards, were simulated[3] and found to be extremely large (Carlsson 1983a, b; Carlsson et al. 1981; Bo et al. 2014). Credit market regulation that reduced access to finance for new firms and SMEs have been politically abandoned, in reality, however, we should add, largely as a result of the globalization of financial markets. High and distortive taxes that favored growth through self financing in big firms in traditional markets, and discouraged SME growth into new markets have been reduced. A generally anti-entrepreneurial political climate had been largely dismantled by the beginning of the new millennium, and been replaced by political concerns about the distributive impact of globalization (Braunerhjelm et al. 2009). Since the BSR setting thus offers *a unique opportunity to study the macroeconomic outcomes of several comparable national economic policy experiments*, we identify and distinguish between four forms of entrepreneurship: (i) Imports of new technology through FDI, (ii) New business establishment, (iii) Innovative recombinations of incumbent actors over private equity markets, and (iv) Improved entrepreneurial environments through policy.

FDI contributions and massive lay offs to restore entrepreneurial life in the "business" colossuses so typical of former Soviet economies were often suggested, but rarely found workable (Eliasson et al. 1994). On FDI based catch-up we distinguish between: (a) Local companies that buy into western firms to complement or upgrade their technology portfolios on the one hand, and (b) Western firms that invest in catch up countries, either through greenfield investments, or through the acquisition of incumbent firms.

[3]On the Swedish Micro to Macro model. See further below.

We expect (b) to be typical of FDI directed to the formerly planned economies, notably to exploit their low wages, while (a) is typical of the exchange of FDI between the industrialized Western economies.

Large Income Gaps Define Both Opportunities and Social Problems
Defining the BSR area

The BSR economies, as we define them, have about 90 million inhabitants and cover an area roughly the size of 3.5 million square kilometers, or somewhat more than one third of the area of the US. If the Baltic Sea could be regarded as an inland sea that ties the Baltic states together culturally, politically and commercially, which has some economic and historic merits to it, the geographical area becomes enormous. The BSR, as we define it, includes, on the one hand, the formerly planned economies of Estonia, Lithuania, Latvia and Poland, the coastal region of St. Petersburg and Kaliningrad (formerly Königsberg) and Belarus, with together some 60 million inhabitants, with very low per capita incomes. On the other side we find the wealthy industrial economies of Finland, Northern Germany, Denmark, Norway and Sweden, together with a population of some 30 million, and significantly higher per capita incomes. *Such differences should define a great industrial potential should the economies be opened up for spontaneous market directed specialization,* provided the associated reallocation of resources can be institutionally and politically accommodated.

The statistical definition of the BSR that we use is perhaps not the best one.[4] Germany, for instance, includes the Baltic rim of both the former West Germany and the former East Germany, which despite enormously costly attempts at integration, still exhibit significant characteristics of their different pasts. With the Baltic as the historic, cultural and economic "integration theme", Norway may look as an outsider. Historically, however, Norway was part of the Hanseatic trading area that was integrated through trade across the Baltic, as was England. Some studies (e.g. Eliasson 2000a; Partanen 1998) even see a trade potential in the wider "Northern Dimension" that includes also North West Russia, a political concept introduced in the late 1990s by the Finnish Government.

We will argue that access to a common and growing BSR market for specialized subcontractor services is especially important for long run growth in the entire BSR, and for the catch-up of the formerly planned economies in particular, since developed such markets constitute critical breeding grounds for the evolution of new large companies. This resource reallocation potential will however not be fully

[4]We have been very careful not to draw conclusions where the details of the national economic classifications matter. From the point of view of our Baltic theme, the interesting region to study would also includes a significant part of the upstream river economies of Russia and (above all) Germany, which could today, as in the past, be integrated through trade across the Baltic, i.e. if the needed physical infrastructure (for instance harbor facilities) could be mobilized through governmental initiatives and entrepreneurship. For practical, and also to some extent for analytical reasons we have decided to stay as much as possible with the definitions used by the Baltic Development Forum in their State of the Region Report (2011), in which we participated.

realized until the still remaining significant obstacles to across border trade in the formerly planned Baltic economies have been removed.

We compare policies in the different countries of the BSR in terms of the categories of what we call the theory of an Experimentally Organized Economy (EOE) and of competence blocs (see next section), and relate them to levels of catch-up. The EOE features a Schumpeterian Creative Destruction process of growth through competitive selection, while the competence bloc defines the dynamic efficiency of that same selection. Special attention is paid to the role of environmental improvement in attracting FDI.

2 Theory and Hypothesis Formulation[5]

Entrepreneurship in some form is key to successful catch-up, and therefore also to our analysis, but an elusive phenomenon that has been difficult both to define and to integrate in economic theory and econometric analysis. Standard neo-classical theorists have simply assumed the phenomenon away, and been happy to treat the entrepreneur as a stochastic phenomenon and/or as the output of R&D based innovation production functions. By our definition, on the other hand, entrepreneurial inputs cannot be determined *ex ante*, but the entrepreneurial output can be observed and *measured ex post* (see further supplement). We therefore have to expect systematic differences between ex ante plans and ex post realizations, differences that should be expected to systematically influence growth (Eliasson 2014). Similarly, business firms are *experimental entities* that pursue individual and often unique strategies, that in many ways exhibit entrepreneurial qualities (Eliasson 1992, 1996: Chap. 3). So entrepreneurial catch-up will have to be experimental in nature, both as such, and as a consequence of policy. Thus mistakes will occur both at the micro business and the macro policy levels. To understand the reasons for observed different rates of catch-up among the formerly planned BSR economies, therefore, *the analysis has to be taken down to the micro market level.* This will take us out of the neoclassical model into an Austrian or Schumpeterian economic world, or as we prefer to call it, into an *experimentally organized economy (EOE),* the dynamics of which is moved by the ex ante unpredictable plans of the elusive *entrepreneurs* (see supplement).

We make a special point of departing from the mainstream linear Schumpeterian, or national innovation systems model, and, as well from the related neoclassical macro model, in favor of a non linear Schumpeterian growth theory embodied in a micro based EOE in which *commercialization agents intermediate the transformation of innovative technology supplies into growth. This resource*

[5]This is a methodologically oriented paper. Most of the empirical material supporting our conclusions is found in Braunerhjelm and Eliasson (2011), and in a current updating of that report under way.

demanding commercialization phase plays a critical role in the growth outcome of new technology introductions, that normally fail to materialize altogether without commercialization support (Eliasson 2003a).

The Neglected Entrepreneur of Economic Theory

We propose the theory of the EOE to be a realistic and useful alternative to explain what is going on in the BSR to both the neoclassical macro model, and the related innovations systems model. Both the latter make technology inputs the direct mover of growth. The theory of the EOE, on the other hand, places focus on *entrepreneurship and the commercialization of innovations*, and features endogenous growth through two dynamic modules defined at the micro market level; (1) Schumpeter (1942) *creative destruction* through the four stylized investment mechanisms of Table 1, that move the economy through endogenous entry (entrepreneurship), competition and selection, and (2) the *competence bloc* of Fig. 2, which defines the technical, commercial and institutional environment that comes in between innovation supplies and the commercialization of innovations. The competence bloc therefore governs both the dynamic efficiency of innovation selection and, consequently, also macroeconomic growth.

Three analytical categories are needed to determine the explicit role of entrepreneurs in the theory of an Experimentally Organized Economy (Eliasson 2005a: 37): The entrepreneurial *behavior* of individuals and businesses, the *environment* in which these entrepreneurs operate, and its supporting institutions, and finally, the growth or welfare outcomes (the *result*).

The entrepreneurship needed for our catch-up analysis appears in this model, either in the form of new actors, incumbent actors that reorganize for new tasks, or through entrepreneurial competence imports (FDI). Literature mostly refers to FDI as a channel of technology and spillover contributions (See e.g. Branstetter 2000). In effect, however, such technology contributions affect the receiving economy (or the Micro to Macro model) as indigenous entrepreneurial inputs.[6] Entrepreneurship per se, however, carries little interest if not related to some "welfare" outcomes. So we make catch-up the politically desired policy objective.

Table 1 The four mechanisms of Schumpeterian creative destruction and economic growth—going from micro to macro in an experimentally organized economy

1	Innovative entry enforces (through competition)
2	Reorganization
3	Rationalization
	or
4	Exit (shut down and business death)

Source: Eliasson (1996: 45)

[6]Branstetter (2000) makes the additional point that spillovers go both ways, both from investing firms to indigenous firms, and from indigenous firms to investing firms. The latter, however, is most common when FDI occurs between advanced economies, where investing international firms often function as global intelligence organizations that tap into foreign technology networks (Eliasson 1991c).

Growth Through Schumpeterian Creative Destruction: Going from Cases to Macro Across Markets

The model of Schumpeterian Creative Destruction stylized in Table 1 endogenizes growth through endogenous entrepreneurial entry induced by profit expectations. Entry puts competitive pressure on incumbent actors and forces them to reorganize, rationalize or exit. Experimental selection of actors occurs. This is the principal endogenous evolutionary mechanism of the empirically implemented evolutionary Micro to Macro growth model that may lead to growth, stagnation or decline depending on environmental circumstances. Competitive destruction, for instance, may be faster and more forceful than new business creation, because of, for instance, weak commercializing conditions, leading to economic decline (Eliasson 2009a).

The Micro to Macro model endogenizes non-linear aggregation from cases to macro over dynamic markets, that gives it particular, and empirically relevant systems properties that are lacking in standard neoclassical models. Endogenous entrepreneurial entry, business reorganization and rationalization of incumbent production organizations, and exit (death) of failing businesses are the four necessary and sufficient micro categories of endogenous industrial evolution in the EOE.[7]

Actors in the Micro to Macro model react to expected price change by adjusting their supplies ("quantities"), and market prices respond to those quantity changes in an iterative fashion. The Micro to Macro model is therefore self-regulating through endogenous market supplies and demands of, and on individual firms. It cannot be solved for an external equilibrium steady state, *which should not be possible in an evolutionary model*. The ongoing dynamics hence never ceases.[8] This model has been implemented on a Swedish firm based national accounts database and calibrated on Swedish data, and is therefore empirical (Albrecht et al. 1992; Taymaz 1991b). Simulation experiments on this model will be referred to in support of the analysis to follow.

---

[7]Each category is represented by at least one module that interacts through markets with all other modules in the Swedish Micro (firm) to Macro model. This makes it possible for us to discuss growth, or the absence of growth in BSR economies directly in terms of the dynamics of that model.

[8]Selection through endogenous price and quantity determination in markets is the main non-linear feature which generates non-reversible trajectories that depend in the long term on seemingly insignificant circumstances. Complexity makes the long run virtually unpredictable as to composition, even if something might be said on macro categories such as GNP growth. Table 1 presents the taxonomy of endogenous growth. Endogenous entry sets the model economy in growth motion through competition, by forcing less productive incumbent firms to raise performance through reorganization or rationalization, or, if unsuccessful, to die (exit). Since entrepreneurial entry is endogenous (Eliasson 1991b; Eliasson et al. 2004, 2005: 333ff; Taymaz 1991a, b; Braunerhjelm et al. 2010a, b), this means that loading the model with the case data that we discuss, the macro economic growth consequences for the model economy can be calculated, conditional on the initial empirical micro macro structure of Swedish industry, and calibrated coefficients governing the market dynamics of endogenous growth processes. Non linear, initial state dependent models normally exhibit what is nowadays often called *chaotic* behavior (Eliasson 1977, 1978, 1991a; Eliasson and Taymaz 2000).

The Micro to Macro model still features all the characteristics of static computable general equilibrium (CGE) models, or so called new growth models of for instance Aghion and Howitt (1992) and Pakes and Ericson (1998), that can be made to appear as special cases of the Micro to Macro model if its dynamic, notably its highly non-linear specifications that determine selections processes and structural change are removed (Eliasson 1991a).

Entrepreneurial selection drives the transformation processes in the EOE through *new firm formation* that enforces *innovative reorganization* of incumbent firms to cope with the new competition, or *rationalization* or *exit*.[9] Each form requires different entrepreneurial capabilities and supporting environments, most of them not available in the formerly planned economies.

Entry is the creative function of Schumpeterian creative destruction in Table 1. Exit is the destructive part that releases resources for superior and growing actors. Business death is therefore as important a part of the growth process as the other three items in the table. Holding back exit for social reasons, or preventing overstaffed firms from shedding labor are safe ways to reduce growth.

Competence Bloc Analysis and the Entrepreneurial Environment

Competence bloc theory defines the dynamic efficiency of selection in the EOE. A competence bloc lists the minimum of different actors functionally defined[10] with complementary competencies (Fig. 2) needed to create, identify, support, finance and take winning projects on to industrial scale production and distribution, either by way of new firm entry, or through firm reorganization, both being acts of innovation and entrepreneurship.

The customer plays a prominent role in competence bloc analysis. *In the long run no better products will be developed and put on the market than there are customers sufficiently competent to appreciate their qualities and willing to pay for them.* The customer is often directly involved in product innovation, and notably so in advanced military procurement. Then *customer competence enters as a characteristic of technology supply* (Eliasson 2011). In Burenstam-Linder (1961) the advanced customers appear as a comparative advantage of rich industrial economies.

A competence bloc has to be *vertically complete* to be capable of creating, identifying and supporting winners all the way to industrial scale production and distribution. In economies with incomplete commercialization competence (see Fig. 2), but with proficient technical innovators, foreign investors often pick up the value potential of winning technologies cheaply and move them up to more profitable

[9] Also see Andersson et al. (2012) who show that entry still affects productivity among incumbents after several years, the delayed productivity effect, a dynamical systems effect that was "theoretically" demonstrated to exist, and be significant, in early simulation experiments on the Swedish Micro to Macro model (Eliasson 1978: 52ff).

[10] The reader should observe that the actors are *functionally defined*. In reality actors may integrate two or more functions. Innovation and entrepreneurship, for instance, may be integrated within one actor.

levels on their value chains (Eliasson 2000b, 2011). A particularly serious deficiency is the absence of industrially competent venture capitalists (Eliasson 2003b, 2005b), and that deficiency for obvious reasons was, and still is, a major problem in the formerly planned economies. Complete downstream commercialization support is needed for the technology potential to be indigenously exploited. Being vertically complete, however, is not sufficient. Diversity of competence inputs are required. The competence bloc has to be *horizontally sufficiently varied to make the right matching of technology and commercialization competencies possible*. Then *critical mass* has been reached, and the competence bloc has become an *attractor* of new business entrants. New entrants then face a highly competitive market environment and soon exit, if not up to the competition. This defines a *spillover generator*, and endogenous growth has been achieved (Eliasson 2003a, b; Acs et al. 2009). *Actors are then subjected to a maximum of competent and varied evaluation that minimizes the risk of losing winners,* and losers are more effectively competed out of business. A conceivable winner can therefore confidently continue its search for resources. Ex ante all entrepreneurs of course will have to consider themselves winners. Why should they otherwise try? If an ex post winner, resources will be provided and the loss of winners (business failure) will be minimized. A competence bloc that has reached critical mass so defined will function as an endogenously developing *regional attractor* (Eliasson 2003a).

The Role of Institutions

Institutions regulate incentives and competition in markets (North 1990). For each individual actor these institutions, and all other actors together define its business or commercial environment. Allocations occur within hierarchies, or over markets (Coase 1937; Williamson 1975). The latter requires the existence of efficient property rights protection to make trade in *intangible technology assets* possible, or the allocation process will come to a halt (Eliasson and Wihlborg 2003). In the competence bloc of Fig. 2 these transactions take place in the venture capital and private equity markets. Hence, competence bloc theory can also be used to determine the outer limits of the firm where market allocation becomes *dynamically* more efficient than internal hierarchical allocation by management (Eliasson and Eliasson 2005, 2009). Functioning markets for trade in intangible assets are not well developed in most of the industrial economies, and have a very long way to go to be established in the formerly planned economies of the BSR.

Institutions may facilitate, ease or block market processes. Institutions regulate both the creative destruction process of Table 1, and the allocation dynamics of the competence bloc in Fig. 2. Incentives to enter the market, rules for leaving the market, and for laying off people during a business reorganization are all part of the legal, cultural and contractual framework of an economy.

Inconsistent laws, corrupt business practices and red tape make business life unpredictable and risky and hinder entrepreneurship, as do labor market laws that slow the reorganization of failing businesses. Institutions define, limit and influence the freedom to act in markets (Nyström 2008, 2010; Braunerhjelm and Eklund 2014). *Government is responsible for the functioning of many of these institutions, and therefore plays an important role in determining the entrepreneurial environment of a national economy.* The potential for influencing that environment is also the main policy focus of our analysis.

Particularly *important for comparing the formerly planned economies with the regulated welfare economies of the BSR is the degree of centralism imposed on the economy through policies.* The market functions, linking actors vertically and horizontally in competence blocs, can be more or less regulated. *The degree of internalization of functions of competence blocs within one national hierarchy therefore also determines the degree of central regulation of the entrepreneurial environment of an economy.* There is the possibility that central planning may be superior to disorderly market coordination of a macro economy, as was generally believed in the early post WWII period. We recognize that possibility under conditions of very good predictability, as may be the case in a less developed economy, the policy makers of which are vigorously aiming to catch-up with superior economies ("South Korea" in the mid sixties), but not in an advanced industrial economy where complexity rules and growth primarily occurs through unpredictable innovation and entrepreneurship. Then the conditions of good predictability are no longer there. If policy makers still pursue central coordination into a development phase where individual innovative entrepreneurs should have been allowed a free play, the economy may get stuck for decades in an inferior stagnation phase ("Japan" during the last 20 years. See further policy Sect. 6 and Ballot and Taymaz 1998).

In simulation experiments on the Swedish Micro to Macro model Antonov and Trofinov (1993) imposed two forms of centralism on the actors of the model economy (Keynesian demand and neoclassical central planning directives).[11] They compared the long run outcomes with the free decisions processes of the original Micro to Macro model specification, where firms could concoct any perception of its future based on their past experiences. In the medium term some improvement in macro economic performance of central coordination could be registered. In the very 30 year *long run the free market scenario came out on top in terms of macroeconomic growth, because unhindered exploration of perceived opportunities meant that some firms came upon opportunities that had gone undiscovered in the policy constrained scenarios.*

Improved macro performance, however, always came at the cost of a higher rate of business failure. This is also the theoretical bottom-line of the Experimentally Organized Economy that the Swedish Micro to Macro model approximates. Entry and exit go hand in hand in a dynamically efficient firm turnover process, and in the dynamic setting of the Micro to Macro model an "optimal" very long term turnover rate can be estimated (Eliasson et al. 2005). Faster growth and/or recovery of growth, therefore, comes with a social cost associated with the needed faster labor turnover. That cost can however be mitigated by the right institutions and/or policies (Eliasson 2009a, b). Institutions, therefore, impact on the categories of both creative destruction, and the resource allocations across the competence bloc *by*

[11]Based on forecasts of such models that were reestimated every quarter on the quarterly data generated in the Micro to Macro model simulations.

orienting incentives, directing competition and reducing (or raising) uncertainty, and allowing an explicit role for the policy maker to influence the economy without direct interference with the micro decision processes (See further Eliasson 2005a: 38, 44ff, 74ff). In our empirical analysis we therefore explicitly link institutional characteristics of each BSR economy to the various categories of Schumpeterian creative destruction in Table 1, to determine the components of output change, and then to the various categories of the competence bloc in Fig. 2, that make up the entrepreneurial environment of the local economy, to be able to say something on the consequences for macro economic growth and catch-up. The question is; Can the balance between positive creation and necessary, but politically and socially unpopular destruction be softened by policy?

The Balance Between Creation and Destruction Cannot Be Fine Tuned by Policy

Exits are needed to release resources, notably human capital, for expanding businesses. This is a critical element of Schumpeterian creative destruction and Micro to Macro growth dynamics. Creation and entry and destruction and exit go hand in hand, and simulation experiments on the Micro to Macro model that features growth through selection, as in Table 1, suggest that there is a maximum parallel rate of entry and exit, or turnover of firms that maximizes long term sustainable growth (Eliasson et al. 2005).

Achieving the right balance between creation and destruction therefore also defines the optimal reallocation of resources. Such reallocations require trade over markets in intangible assets that depends on well designed property rights protection and developed financial markets. But resource reallocations, notably of human capital, also depend on functioning markets for labor (competence) that efficiently reallocates people on new jobs. The cultural mentality of a country, an "institutional characteristic" that makes individuals accept being forced to move on to new and better jobs, and/or to take initiatives to move ahead of time, influences the speed of such processes in important ways. Attempting to fine tune that balancing act through central policy is a complex task that as far as we can see takes decision makers far beyond existing policy practice and empirical knowledge, that will certainly fail, and be turned into something worse, if attempted with ambition.

Theoretically we therefore conclude that a dynamically efficient and socially responsible catch-up policy among the formerly planned economies should be based on the understanding that policies organized through central directives and direct meddling with micro decisions, rather than improved market conditions, and pursued vigorously carries a high risk of failure. That risk is easily overlooked if "viewed through" oversimplified policy models, and can only be realistically appreciated on the basis of a systemic understanding of complex dynamic Micro to Macro processes. Policies that support market based reallocation of resources mean facing the "social transactions costs" directly in the form of an increase in the rate of labor turnover. Flexible labor markets are thus needed to make businesses absorb released labor. The complexity of the total restructuring of entire economies will, therefore, make it impossible to fine tune that machinery on a balanced growth path through policy. *Only national economies socially capable of taking the immediate crunch in the labor market will come close to anything that can be called optimal catch-up performance.*[12]

The Elusive Entrepreneur Only Becomes Visible Ex-Post, and After a Long Time
The entrepreneurial action needed to move catch-up is an elusive phenomenon. It occurs at all levels, within firms and in markets. Entrepreneurship is by definition unpredictable ex-ante and therefore not plannable, and in principle therefore also beyond analytical understanding. It is mostly treated as an exogenous phenomenon. Joseph Schumpeter (1911), for instance, used to talk about a "Deux ex machina", or the "God in the machine" that unexpectedly emerged on the stage of the Greek dramas and disturbed the action there.

If this unexpected disturber is a winner (Steve Jobs and his Iphone, which disturbed the until then dominant player in the market, Finnish Nokia), his/her success can be explained ex-post. In principle the entrepreneur could have been modeled ex-ante, if you had known all the relevant and complex circumstances involved in the entrepreneurial decision. But you don't. So, even if in principle predictable, there was only one player, the successful entrepreneur, who got it right, and dared to act. To spot this entrepreneur ex ante is therefore impossible by definition. And the right entrepreneurial action will be one out of many experiments (Eliasson 2009a). Outsiders and disturbed players will have to wait until they have learned what the entrepreneur has done. Innovation races to find the optimal innovation are therefore a misconceived idea of entrepreneurship, since the optimal innovation is indeterminate in an Experimentally Organized Economy. Then they will all be scrambling to their feet to imitate the success, dramatically reorganizing their businesses. The winners of the past may not be among the survivors. We will therefore not attempt to identify the entrepreneurs in BSR catch-up by way of ex-ante indicators, but rather look for the visible economic consequences of entrepreneurial action that cannot be related to any measured factor input. We will also have something to say on the environment where such entrepreneurs thrive and operate.

This is, however, not without its problems. The production process is replete with intangible inputs that are not easily observed, but that may be, if sufficient effort is expended. Knowledge can be systematically accumulated through R&D, and R&D investment can be measured. Measured R&D in firms, however, is largely devoted to access (globally) available technology and integrate it with their own portfolios of technology assets (Eliasson 1991c). The R&D based innovation functions that are currently the basis for a whole branch of new growth theory models are therefore misspecified, since they imply the causality that new innovative technology is created by firm R&D (Braunerhjelm et al. 2010a, b; Eliasson 2000b, 2003a, 2009a).

[12]This also means that we disassociate ourselves from the innovation systems propositions to stimulate growth through R&D subsidies (Freeman 1987; Nelson 1993 and Lundvall 1992) that replaced Keynesian demand policies when they became discredited in the 1980s as a means to restore growth and employment.

Even so, the fact that econometric analyses demonstrate very large "effects" from R&D based spillovers does not diminish the significance of such analysis. To draw conclusions on policy, however, it is necessary to know which way the causality runs. And the magnitudes involved seem to be large. This is made overwhelmingly clear in the more sophisticated versions of new growth theory, as distinct from the results of the previous empirical productivity literature (Jones and Williams 1998, 1999; Braunerhjelm 2008, 2012).

Our empirical method will now be implemented in four stages. *First*, what has occurred in the form of catch-up over the 20 years through 2009 is documented (Next Sect. 3). *Second*, the extent to which entrepreneurship has been involved is determined in terms of the theoretical categories of the EOE (Schumpeterian Creative Destruction in Table 1). This is done in Sect. 4. *Third*, an explanation of the extent of entrepreneurial inputs in each BSR economy follows in terms of the environmental and commercializing categories of the competence bloc in Fig. 2. Observed differences in the entrepreneurial environments of the different BSR economies can now be related to the ex-post determined entrepreneurial outputs. Finally, the quantitative relationships of the Swedish Micro to Macro model can be referred to to say something on the magnitudes involved, to say something on what to expect, and to derive (in Sect. 6) a policy agenda.[13] So let us therefore first take a look at the records.

3 Entrepreneurial Catch-up Takes Time: The Records

Available evidence suggests that new firm formation takes a very long time to show statistically at the macro level, a conclusion that is supported by simulation experiments on the Micro to Macro model referred to above. After some time, however, new entry may have developed critically needed diversity and mass, and the growth process may gain cumulative momentum (Eliasson et al. 2004). In the long run aggregate growth becomes dominated by a small number of successful and fast growing firms. Jagren (1988) calculated that it took on average 25 years for those very few Swedish firms that succeeded in growing big ("the winners") to reach the size of one thousand employees, and most firms in the original sample had been closed down, acquired by other firms or had simply remained small. Simulation experiments on the Micro to Macro model repeat that pattern (Eliasson 1991b)

Contraction, and falling further behind occurred in the BSR transition economies during the immediate post liberalization years after 1990, and the following recovery was slow. When manufacturing productivity levels are compared not much in the form of catch-up had been achieved by 2004 (Nevalainen 2008). Even later, through

[13]For reasons of space the following empirical analysis will have to be brief and incomplete. For full detail we refer to Braunerhjelm and Eliasson (2011), and an updated version in progress. The main point here is to explain the logic of our method in linking the empirical results to the theoretical categories of Sect. 2 above (Tables 1 and 2). For more detail on the method see the Supplement.

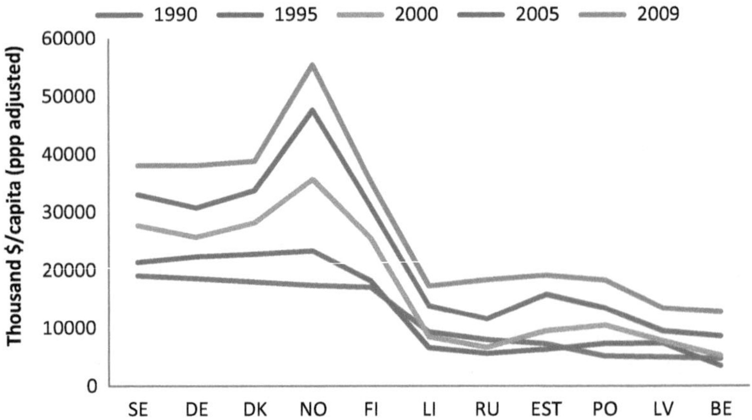

Fig. 1 Per capita income levels of the Baltic economies (PPP adjusted) 1990, 2000, 2005 and 2009. Note: The economies are ordered by decreasing per capita income in 1990 from *left to right*. The countries are in that order: *SE* Sweden, *DE* Germany, *DK* Denmark, *NO* Norway, *FI* Finland, *LI* Lithuania. *RU* Russia, *EST* Estonia, *PO* Poland, *LV* Latvia and *BE* Belarus. *Source*: The World Bank

2008, a rapid catch-up in per capita (PPP corrected) income levels, notably by Estonia, Latvia and Lithuania (See Fig. 1), was followed by a particularly deep recession in the Baltic transition economies 2008/09, which ended in a further falling behind for most formerly planned economies for the whole period through 2009. This, by definition, suggests that there has been something missing on the entrepreneurial side. In fact, the relative difference in average per capita income (adjusted for purchasing power) between the formerly planned economies and the rest of the Baltic economy did not diminish appreciably during the first decade of the new millennium. Part of the reason for that negative experience was that the wealthy industrial BSR economies had experienced a growth surge of their own, after having changed their policies in a more entrepreneurial friendly direction.

The wealthy Baltic neighboring economies have in fact outgrown both the EU and the OECD economies as a whole, and significantly caught up with North America. This makes the catch-up comparison of the formerly planned economies a bit unfair. On the other hand, the fast growing neighbors should have exercised an extra export demand pull on the formerly planned Baltic economies.

We conclude that not much of macro economic catch-up occurred during the first 10 years of freedom of the formerly planned economies in the BSR. But neither did a significant closing of the per capita income gaps between the formerly planned economies and the other Baltic economies occur during the following 10 years,[14] and preliminary updates of statistical data indicate that the same is

[14]This is a brief statement of results from the more comprehensive empirical analysis in Braunerhjelm and Eliasson (2011).

true for the following 3 years through 2012. However, and drawing on available evidence and simulation analogies, we have to recognize the possibility that *twenty years may still be too short a period to allow for the cumulative build up in some transition economies to become statistically visible.* Our theoretical considerations furthermore suggest that catch-up, when it occurs will be very unevenly distributed over the BSR transition economies. Graphically this would show in Fig. 1 as some individual country peaks for later years. Preliminary calculations on World Bank national accounts data do not indicate much of that through 2012, possibly excluding Estonia, which would also be in line with our theoretical discussion. We would also expect the oil price dependent Russian economy to have experienced significant "negative" catch up" in 2013 and 2014 in particular, even though data to confirm that proposition have not yet become available. On the whole, catch up among the industrially less developed economies appears to have met with "strong headwinds" to quote *The Economist* (Sept. 13th. 2014:24f), in the last few years

4 What Kind of Entrepreneurship Has Moved the Catch up Dynamics of the Formerly Planned BSR Economies?

The four different kinds of entrepreneurship identified in Sect. 1 can now be related to the categories of Schumpeterian Creative Destruction in Table 1. We begin (in this section) with "imports of entrepreneurial knowhow" through FDI, and the entry of new firms. Also the innovative recombination of existing firms in "private equity markets", instigated through FDI from the wealthy BSR economies is mentioned even though there is little evidence of successful such activities. The lack of local financial markets capable of intermediating such activities in the formerly planned BSR economies, means that this case of entrepreneurship also belongs to the next section on Government entrepreneurship.

FDIs Have Supported Growth in Some BSR Economies

Reorganization and upgrading of incumbent firms in transition economies to Western *standards* of competition are instances of entrepreneurship that have so far not been possible without technical and management support from industrially more competent BSR neighbors. The upgrading of incumbent firms, through the massive shedding of redundant labor, and dramatic exits of now inferior producers, furthermore, have not been a politically favored solution in the formerly planned economies. Without outside FDI support, destruction rather than industrial creation would have followed from a sudden exposure to global competition. Significant net FDI has also arrived in some formerly planned BSR economies, even though the typical pattern seems to have been a mutual exchange of FDI among the industrially advanced BSR economies. Among the formerly planned economies, however, Estonia seems to have been favored by its closeness to Finland, and Poland to Germany

Entrepreneurial New Entry and Self-Employment

Growth through new firm establishment (Item 1 in Table 1) is the conventional manifestation of entrepreneurship. It is however a growth process of much longer duration than is the case when large firms are reorganized (Item 2) to compete in new environments on the basis of new technology and competence brought in, for instance through FDI. While the same entrepreneurial environments are conducive to both, the two require very different entrepreneurial and management competencies, that were all lacking in the formerly planned economies to begin with, and still more or less is.

Statistics do not indicate significant differences in new firm entry among the formerly planned BSR countries. Subcontracting arrangements, on the other hand, seem to have mattered more for SME growth in the old than in the new EU member economies.

Germany, however, sticks out by having considerably more self-employed, and with the highest educational level for both men and women. This tallies with Blanchflower's (2004) observation that the more educated one is, the more likely one also is to benefit from self-employment, and the more satisfied with one's professional role one is. For Germany and Sweden, Blanchflower notes, this satisfaction is, however, maximized with self-employment without employees. For Sweden this observation has earlier been related to the presence of growth inhibiting institutions (Andersson et al. 1993). The same observation also suggests that self-employment in the two countries is largely the business organisational form preferred by (highly educated) professionals in the most advanced industrial economies.

The advanced industrial economies of the BSR have their own problems. In the New Emerging Economy of the increasingly globalized world great new opportunities for entrepreneurship combine with competitive challenges and a limited capacity to accommodate structural change over labor markets. New industrial technology is however increasingly demanding of salaried employees to take entrepreneurial initiatives on the job. This is in contrast with the past when employees worked for a wage with job specifications laid down by the organisation they were working in, and the equipment they were operating (Eliasson 2006a). Today's software expert, on the other hand, working in a small consulting firm, and the R&D engineer on the staff of a large manufacturing firm, have to largely define their own jobs, and are expected to take innovative initiatives. This was not a normal demand of a worker some 20 years ago. With a growing share of labor working in small companies, and/or in sophisticated service production or on their own, education and an entrepreneurially friendly work environment will matter increasingly for economic growth.

Entrepreneurial Reorganization Through Mergers & Acquisitions Across the BSR

Strategy literature has long emphasized the role of mergers and acquisitions in business learning and performance upgrading. Even though empirical literature is inconclusive on the pros and cons of such activities, the merging or taking over of Baltic firms in transition economies with, or by firms in the non-transition BSR

Fig. 2 Decision makers and markets of the competence bloc. *Source*: Eliasson and Eliasson (1996) and Eliasson (2005a: 255)

economies has very much figured in the catch—up policy discussion. Corporate finance was also a lively area some 10 years or more ago, that has significantly slowed down in recent years parallel with the recessionary cyclical development.

Statistical evidence on the role of corporate financial intermediation and sophisticated financial markets in the restructuring and reorganizing of incumbent firms in transition economies (Item 2 in Table 1 and Item 5 in Fig. 2) through takeovers by western firms is almost non existing beyond some cases, and the private equity markets needed for such intermediation are not yet to be found in the transition economies. The 1990s however opened up with an inflow of subsidiary activities of western banks into the BSR transition economies. Several specialized in intermediating an expected flow of FDI and mergers & acquisitions to take advantage of the low wages. Many of these financial ventures failed, and towards the end of the first decade of the new millennium many foreign financial activities in the BSR transition economies were being closed down, for instance by the large Swedish banks, to the tune of losses of billion of Swedish SEK. The small BSR transition economies were now argued to be too small, and hedged in by formal restrictions to serve as a platform for operations across the entire BSR. Russia was then seen as a large enough economy to be interesting, with very low taxes, but international investors have become increasingly sceptical of the high levels of corruption there and its unpredictable legal system. And current (2014) Russian power politics will not encourage western business ventures there. Favourite among investors was Estonia, even though considered too small. It had privatized early and in an open non corrupt way compared to the other transition economies. It is a member of the EMU, and is considered to offer a very friendly and favourable entrepreneurial climate.[15]

[15]As one interviewed banker responded to the question; What more could Estonia do? "Not much except patiently wait for the results".

We have also observed that inward FDI and subcontracting arrangements between western firms and firms in transition economies are correlated with closeness (Estonia to Finland and Poland to Germany). Altogether the general development in the corporate finance markets of the transition economies of the BSR touches on a pessimistic note. We make these observations because of the potential importance of across border mergers & acquisitions for the long term catch-up performance of these economies, and for further attention.

5 Environmental Differences among the BSR Economies: On Government Entrepreneurship

Government can engage in "entrepreneurship" in two ways; Through central coordinating directives and through improving the economic environment in which spontaneous entrepreneurship occurs. In the formerly planned economies individual innovation and entrepreneurship were effectively suppressed in the interest of a politically orderly Soviet State. Revival of spontaneous entrepreneurial activity therefore not only required that lacking commercialization competence be supplied. Growth through recombination and reorganization of firms through acquisitions, divestments and close downs for fast upgrading also required a legal environment that supported property rights and trade in intangible technology assets, a legal environment directly that did not exist in the formerly planned Baltic economies. These deficiencies are still largely there.

The prime motives for entering the Baltic economy (through new firm establishment, FDI or by acquisitions) from other countries have been the capturing of a local market, and/or the exploitation of low wages,[16] when the preferred action should have been an entrepreneurial build up of foreign and locally owned and operated businesses capable of catching up in technology and management prowess with Western competitors. The reasons for the absence of such entrepreneurial momentum have to be looked for in the entrepreneurial environments of the formerly planned economies, deficiencies that keep planning horizons short and promote exploitation of low wages rather than long term entrepreneurial activities. Here we can identify differences that relate to differences in catch-up.

[16]Of course, trade in technology assets and FDI cannot be clearly distinguished from one another, since FDI always involves exchange of assets over markets. FDI, however, often takes the form of direct investments of one firm in another country within its own organization, often to exploit some comparative advantage in that country, such as low wages. Trade in technology assets in specialized markets, for instance strategic acquisitions, on the other hand, is a phenomenon that is primarily, and increasingly found in the wealthy industrial economies to complement an existing technology portfolio of the firm (Eliasson and Eliasson 2005).

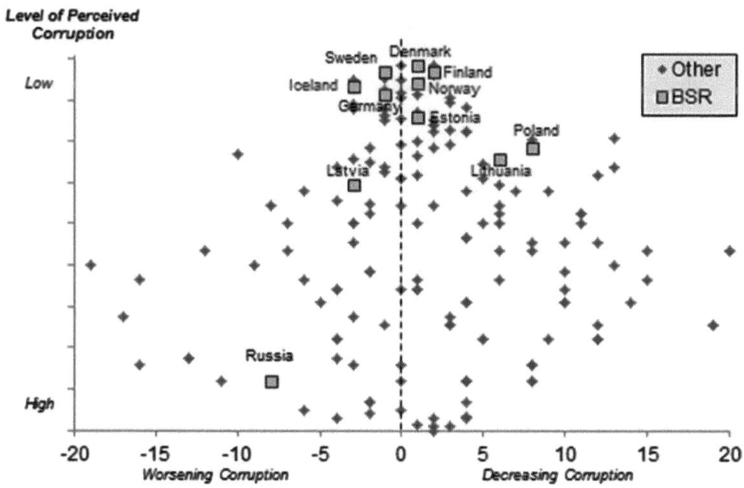

Fig. 3 Corruption perception index 2010. *Source*: Transparency international corruption perception index (2010)

Corruption and Property Rights

Even though reliable privatization measures to safeguard investors' property were missing during the first decade of liberalization, the formerly planned economies have now been significantly upgraded in that respect. Corruption has been very much reduced in all formerly planned economies, except Russia. Estonia in particular, but also Latvia and Lithuania, now rank far ahead of EU members such as Greece and Italy (See Fig. 3). However, when it comes to ease of doing business, red tape and similar negative commercial circumstances, the formerly planned economies still rank low compared to their wealthy neighbors in the BSR[17] (Table 2). We identify this as important negative circumstances in the entrepreneurial environments of these countries, and reasons both for the slow catch-up, and for the myopic compositions of investments. The elimination of such obstacles should therefore be a prime focus of political attention.

Policy and institutions in the formerly planned economies have not been entirely welcoming neither to foreign, nor to local entrepreneurship and investment, and especially so in Russia. Russia, however, has been able to thrive on its own, at least up to 2013, because of large capital gains from oil and gas that have helped its economy from slipping further behind. But raw material capital gains are not entrepreneurial inputs, and no sustainable solution to long term growth and catch-up, and may also explain why Russia has done so little to clean up its institutions. If the Russian people is interested in economic progress, and wants to see something

[17]Except that Germany comes in somewhat behind Estonia in the aggregate ranking of Ease of Doing Business 2011, because of difficulties of starting a business, and relatively less protection of investors (Table 2).

Table 2 Ease of (EO) doing business. Ranking 2011

	EO doing business (aggregate)	Starting a business	Getting a credit	Protecting in-vestors	Trading across borders	Enforcing a contract	Closing a business
Singapore	1	?	?	?	1	?	?
Denmark	6	27	15	27	5	30	5
Norway	8	33	46	20	9	4	4
Finland	13	32	32	59	6	11	6
Sweden	14	39	72	28	7	52	18
Estonia	17	37	32	59	4	50	70
Germany	22	88	15	93	14	6	35
Lithuania	23	53	46	93	31	17	39
Latvia	24	87	6	59	16	14	80
Poland	70	113	15	44	49	77	81
Russia	123	108	89	93	162	18	103

Source: The World Bank

done about it, it should be very concerned about the entrepreneurial environment of their country, characterized by arbitrary legislation, bureaucratic red tape, corrupt practices and suspect political leadership.

Political Inabilities to Weather Exits and Creative Destruction
Another related factor is the political reluctance in the formerly planned economies to manage the immediate negative social consequences of a massive shedding of redundant labor and business exits, all being needed for fast catch-up. The legal system of all of the formerly planned economies makes it difficult to close down businesses, and to lay off people. This is a social residue from the Soviet regime, where inferior economic performance and bankruptcy were unrecognized phenomena. Political impatience for immediate positive results, in addition, has disposed policy makers towards ineffective short-term measures. Here, however, important differences can be observed between the different Baltic economies. Rapid and radical measures enacted in Estonia to improve its entrepreneurial environment seem to have helped the country to receive an unproportionally large inflow of FDI.

Environmental Improvement Appears to Define a Winning Political Agenda
Having gone over the evidence we are not surprised, neither to find little evidence of significant catch-up, nor reasons that there should be. Rather, it is good enough that several formerly planned economies have kept pace with their wealthy neighbors.

The high performers in catch up have been Estonia and Poland. Despite its protectionist institutions, compared to Estonia, Latvia and Lithuania, Poland has done well. We believe Poland's proximity to Germany, large inflows of German FDIs and a large home market, help explain that.

Catch-up through entrepreneurship means that the entrepreneurial output is becoming statistically visible at the macro level. It is observed that catch up through new business formation therefore is a long winding process, taking decades to materialize, rather than years, and following a very differentiated pattern, some economies exhibiting much more success than others because of a few winning entrepreneurial businesses. The modest catch -up that we have observed in the macro statistics across the BSR, therefore, has occurred primarily in the form of entrepreneurship through FDI, and through oil rents. Catch- up varies across the economies according to the attractiveness of the local (national) entrepreneurial environment, which indicates an opportunity for policy based entrepreneurial environment improvement. In that perspective Estonia comes out favorably. The closer to a large and prospering economy with large contractor firms the better for catch-up. The Poland/Germany constellation illustrates.

In the longer (than up to now) run indigenous entrepreneurship through spontaneous new firm formation and market directed resource allocation will have to take over for significant catch-up to become statistically visible. And if our theoretical case for a slow, but eventually rapid entrepreneurially based cumulative growth process is a credible working hypothesis, Estonia would be a long term winner under our prior hypothesis. The general case, based on theoretical reasoning and the scant empirical evidence there is, is that long term success will be unevenly distributed, and based in each economy on the evolution of a small number of winners that have been successfully sorted out of a large number of business ventures. This observation also points forward to a constructive future policy focus.

6 Policy Propositions

Modern neoclassical macroeconomics emphasizes R&D based innovation supply as the engine of growth. The linear Schumpeter hypothesis, or the innovation systems proposition are similar stories in that they both feature growth driven directly by R&D generated innovations. We consider both stories falsely conceived and would not recommend R&D support to raise the rate of catch-up in the Baltic transition economies. The eastern European economies are still burdened by their communist non-market past of more than half a century. Their economic problem therefore is not to create new technology, but to commercialize whatever technologies their businesses can access. Therefore we instead emphasize the *critical support of commercializing actors* as necessary intermediaries to activate technology supply economically through entrepreneurship, new firm formation and SME growth. This non- linear early Schumpeter (1911) proposition, that we prefer, requires a Micro based Macro understanding to make sense, and *a strong policy focus on the local commercializing environments to be effective*.

Some of the BSR transition economies have adopted radically new and market friendly institutions, while others still suffer from inept institutions, unreliable property rights and unpredictable applications of the law, Russia and Belarus being the outstanding examples. There are, thus, huge differences as regards institutions, norms and traditions that govern market dynamics among the economies in the BSR, that define their entrepreneurial environments and affect their growth. As a consequence catch-up rates also differ among the Baltic transition economies, and should be expected to differ as well in the foreseeable future.

The non-transition Baltic economies, on their side, belong to the mixed economy welfare states with open markets, but also with large public sectors financed through heavy taxes, and being reined in through sometimes far reaching central direction and regulation. The latter is particularly the case with the labor markets. The public sectors of the welfare economies have long been operated as centrally planned economies with all the accompanying problems, notably when it comes to discouraging innovation and entrepreneurship, and preventing economic incentives from fostering competition and driving productivity performance. And the public sectors have grown so large relative to the total economy in most European countries as to make it a misnomer to characterize them as market economies. While the public sectors in these countries need to be opened up for free entrepreneurial experimentation and competition, the BSR transition economies are in great need of knowledge inputs in management, marketing, manufacturing production technology, and experience from working in global markets for specialist subcontractors. Hence, obstructions to entrepreneurship still remain across the entire BSR, albeit more or less depending on country. If one excludes Russia and Belarus there is however also significant historic, cultural and institutional affinity across the BSR. As a consequence we point to three critical areas for policy action of the *facilitating kind*:

1. *Industrial knowledge transfer* within the region on a much larger scale than has occurred so far is needed both to speed up growth of the entire BSR-economy, and for faster catch-up. Particularly important is that potential business winners obtain the commercializing competence support needed to grow big. Since this knowledge primarily resides outside the transition economies, the creation of attractive environments for local investment by external investors comes before other policy action. This will however require significantly increased *trade in intangible assets,* preferably over local equity markets. Since those local markets do not yet exist in the formerly planned economies, and only in the wider context of the entire BSR economy the necessary knowledge transfer will not easily be accomplished. *Facilitating the local development of more advanced markets for venture capital and private equity services in the formerly planned BSR economies should therefore be a prime policy ambition.*
2. The development of broad based markets for *specialist subcontractors is* particularly important as a platform for the evolution of large manufacturing firms from a base in SMEs (Braunerhjelm 1991). When new and small firms develop in symbiosis with large firms, the large firms will also contribute user knowledge as competent customers (Eliasson 2010). So *eliminating the many remaining national barriers to the establishment of a cross national integrated market for specialized subcontractor services* available to the entire region, should be the second policy priority.
3. Finally, since the *quality of the general entrepreneurial environment*, and its institutions, is what determines the long-run, eliminating red tape and corruption

in the formerly planned economies to facilitate entrepreneurially driven learning and resource allocations through market competition must be the overriding long-run policy focus (Andersson et al. 2012). Here each country will find itself on its own, and there is no need to wait for policy cooperation to be agreed on. Rather the opposite. The more radically, and the faster, a formerly planned economy improves its market institutions, the more FDI and talent it will attract, the more of local firm formation it will create compared to its neighbors, and the more experience from dynamically competitive global markets its firms will acquire. We therefore propose that a *policy competition* be encouraged among those countries *in opening up and improving their entrepreneurial environments* to beat each other in catch-up. This policy competition is best enacted individually, without any delaying attempts at cooperation among the competing economies and, if individually enacted in a competitive spirit, will benefit both the winners and the entire BSR economy. The outcomes of this *policy competition through institutional improvement* between the BSR economies in the form of national catch-up rates compared can be monitored. And no cumbersome political negotiations have to precede and delay policy based environmental improvement. Each country will gain from acting on its own and in its own best interests, as will the entire BSR.

If such a competition could be incited also in, and forced on the wealthy Baltic welfare economies that have long suffered from stagnating entrepreneurship and ailing big firms, a *positive sum growth game in the BSR of extraordinary dimensions might have been politically established.*

A.1 Supplement on Methodology

Baumol (1968) observed that it would probably be impossible to integrate the entrepreneur in the received static neoclassical or General Equilibrium (GE) model. And he was right. In a footnote in the same article Baumol referred to the recently published Jorgenson and Griliches (1967) as not contradicting his statement on this probable impossibility. We have used those two references to show that ex ante the entrepreneur by definition should be analytically elusive. On the other hand, what the entrepreneur has achieved ex post can be observed and measured. Neoclassical equilibrium theory is ex post based on the assumption that ex ante plans equal ex post outcomes in expectation (Eliasson 1992). Jorgenson and Griliches (1967) use the duality property of the GE model in equilibrium where factor incomes exhaust total production value. This requires a model (representation of reality) in which an external market clearing equilibrium can be demonstrated to exist. We observe that such a model will be a false representation of the dynamics of reality, and that the desired evolutionary model capable of explanation should not be structured a priorly such that all ex ante plans are optimally sorted out and all markets cleared (Eliasson 2014). As a consequence the ex post outcomes are never equal to the original plans and the optimum computed never an optimum, something Demsetz

(1969) observed and called the "Nirvana Fallacy" of neoclassical economics. *Only in such an evolutionary model, with no market clearing can a meaningfully defined entrepreneur exist* (Eliasson 1992, 2009a). Still, the Jorgenson and Griliches (1967) method allows us to obtain *biased ex post measures of entrepreneurial outcomes.*

Measuring Entrepreneurial Output

Jorgenson and Griliches (1967) method is to decompose Total Factor Productivity (TFP) growth by imputation back to the originating factor inputs, under the assumption that markets are in static full information market clearing equilibrium. Under that assumption Jorgenson and Griliches (1967) managed to more or less eliminate TFP growth, or the technical residual, which would otherwise have captured entrepreneurial output.

In static general equilibrium total costs exhaust total output value. The fact that this is not the case "in reality" has puzzled many economists. Knight (1944) meant that increasing returns, which are incompatible with the Walrasian model, were the reason. For the same reason Marshall (1919) introduced the concept of an externality, and ruled out the Walrasian model as a tool of practical analysis, but nevertheless tried to endogenize the increasing returns through his concept of an industrial district, that in modern terminology created "networking externalities." Thus Marshall removed the inconsistency of the Walrasian model very much as Romer (1986) did the same thing. McKenzie (1959) added *unmeasured capital inputs* to the discussion. Both increasing returns and unmeasured capital inputs show up as total factor productivity (TFP) change, or the mysterious time dependent technical residual in traditional production function econometrics, and therefore create unexplained value, or positive externalities. The output of entrepreneurial inputs should therefore be looked for in that residual (Eliasson 1992). Jorgenson and Griliches (1967) managed to eliminate almost all of TFP change ("the exogenous technical residual") by correcting factor inputs for quality change, for instance human capital embodied in labor, or technology embodied in hardware capital, using the duality property of the neoclassical model in static equilibrium, which was assumed to prevail. That elimination then also included entrepreneurial inputs as unmeasured (intangible) capital inputs. So in the *assumed* equilibrium entrepreneurial value creation was assumed to have been fully understood in the capital market, and the entrepreneurial value created captured by the owners. Externalities had been endogenized, and correctly priced by (the assumed) fully informed agents in the stock market.[18]

In the pure, before Jorgenson and Griliches (1967) and new growth theory, neoclassical production model quality inputs were not recorded, while their ex post

[18]This assumption is of course as far distant from reality that one can imagine. As long as you understand that this is the crucial assumption you will, however, be able to say something meaningful about ex post productivity measurements. Above all, however, the conclusions should be, that to proceed further in entrepreneurship and industrial dynamics research you have to explicitly model the ex ante ex post realization process at the micro market level (Eliasson 1992, 2009a, 2014).

consequences on value added more or less were. Hence value added was created seemingly for free, and the mysterious TFP technical residual was recorded as an externality in standard production function econometrics. The extra value added creation (an externality) benefitted some in the form of higher profits, capital gains and higher wages. It can therefore be demonstrated that *TFP change in the early production function analysis under the duality premises of neoclassical production theory is directly related to relative price change and realized capital gains* (See Eliasson 1976: 296ff, 1992 and 1996: 84ff, 114 for a mathematical derivation). Such capital gains originate partly in invisible (not recorded) entrepreneurial inputs, but also in, for instance, raw material rents. If these different sources of capital gains can be sorted out ex post the value added contribution of the ex ante invisible entrepreneur can also be observed ex post.

Our method has therefore been to link measured macro TFP growth to originating circumstances by way of the categories of the competence bloc (Fig. 2) and the micro investment categories of Schumpeterian creative destruction in macro economic growth (Table 1). Since these categories define modules in the Swedish Micro to Macro model we can also feel confident to interpret our empirical ex post macro observations in terms of the dynamics of that model, even though we have not carried out empirical Micro to Macro simulation experiments on the BSR economies. In addition Micro to Macro simulations carried out in other contexts allow us to say something on the magnitudes involved.

(So called "new growth theory" (Romer 1986, etc) endogenized the technical residual by defining the aggregate of all capital inputs as a measure of generally available knowledge that improved the productivity of other factors. General knowledge, however, could only be increased at decreasing returns. Romer's model could therefore be solved for an external equilibrium. Jones (1999), Jones and Williams (1998) found these macro models disturbingly counterfactual, and when carefully examined not really endogenizing growth. So they suggested a theoretical modification that made new ideas, or new knowledge creation, increasing in the level of knowledge already attained. If this was the case was an empirical hypothesis, that they however found consistent with empirical evidence. One way of interpreting such increasing returns in ideas production is that the more knowledge that already resides in an economy the more effectively the cloud of technology spillovers surrounding new technology development is captured and commercialized (Eliasson 2010). This, for one thing, puts the industrially developed world at an advantage over the underdeveloped or developing economies because of the large amount of general economic infrastructure knowledge already accumulated there. Second, if Keller (2001) is right, and most technology put to use in the production of industrial economies is really accessed from a global pool of technology, then this infrastructure capital is commercialization knowledge residing in business firms (Eliasson 1991c, 2010: 41f, 276ff). But all these econometric models which we tap for empirical evidence are still static, with assumed external equilibria that the models, with a now slightly larger mathematical effort than before, can be solved for. These models *represent estimated or calibrated relationships between ex post outcomes of both factor inputs and outputs* and are therefore subjected to Baumol's (1968) scepticism, and Demsetz (1969) Nirvana Fallacy.

Marshall's (1919) industrial district, on the other hand, is micro based and recognizes innovative organization of production, and therefore based on an idea very agreeable to our Micro to Macro model. In the dynamic setting of the empirical Swedish Micro to Macro model both "networking externalities", "organization" (in the form of innovative structural change) and simultaneous price and quantity determination are allowed to enter the growth analysis. Above all, the ex ante plan, ex post realization process is explicitly modeled, and allowed to influence the evolution of industrial structures and therefore giving a meaningfully defined entrepreneur a role (Eliasson 1989, 2009a, 2014).)

The Economics of a National Competition Game of Environmental Improvement

The creation of growth as reflected in entrepreneurial rents in macro production function econometrics is a true outcome of a dynamic micro based experimental selection process moved by entrepreneurial entry, enforced business reorganization to cope with the entry competition, rationalization and exit, as in the Schumpeterian creative destruction of Table 1. The dynamic efficiency of that selection in terms of maximizing long term growth is determined by the organization of commercializing actors in the competence bloc of Fig. 2.

Getting all that Micro to Macro dynamics into a national long term macro growth perspective is of course an impossible analytical, or planning task. It requires that the distributed intangible competence capital of the entire economy be put to maximum possible efficient use in the economy, a selection and allocation process of formidable proportions that is not only beyond central overview, but can only be intermediated through markets. The functions of such markets are governed by the institutions of the economy, defining property rights, the entering and enforcement of contracted obligations, the consistency and efficiency of law, and the freedom of all actors to destroy any monopoly formations of their competitors through entrepreneurial initiatives. *Government therefore has an important role in influencing the evolution of these institutions of the legal, cultural and economic environment, that define, through the competence bloc of Fig. 2, the efficiency of entrepreneurial creation and selection of winners.* Since an agreement on how that is best done through analytical persuation is a practical impossibility, *the best long term outcome is best achieved through experimentation. Since the rate of economic experimentation and competition in markets can be pushed by policy competition it also sets the Schumpeterian creative destruction process of Table* 1 *in motion.* This is also the rational foundation of the economic policy competition proposition that concluded our analysis.

Since policy experimentation, like business market experimentation, is also prone to mistakes, an improved entrepreneurial environment will raise both entry and the rate of failure. It therefore becomes more important to clear the economy of failed experiments.

Exit is the destructive part of creative destruction and releases resources for superior and growing actors. Business death is therefore as important a part of the growth process as the other three items in Table 1. So by proposing the policy competition that concluded this essay, we are also proposing to raise the destructive part of creative destruction to clear the formerly planned economies of remaining bad structures from the Soviet period. Holding back exit for social reasons, or preventing overstaffed firms from shedding labor are safe ways to reduce growth.

References

Acs Z, Braunerhjelm P, Carlsson B (2009) The knowledge spill-over theory of entrepreneurship. Small Bus Econ 32:15–30

Aghion P, Howitt P (1992) A model of growth through schumpeterian creative destruction. Econometrica 60(2):323–351

Albrecht JW, Braunerhjelm P, Eliasson G, Nilsson J, Nordström T, Taymaz E (1992) MOSES database. Research report No. 40. IUI, Stockholm

Andersson T, Braunerhjelm P, Carlsson B, Eliasson G, Fölster S, Jagren L, Kazamaki-Ottersten E, Sjöholm K-R (1993) Den långa vägen- Den ekonomiska politikens begränsningar och möjligheter att föra Sveriger ur 1990- talets kris (The long road—The limits of policy in taking the Swedish economy out of the crisis of the 1990s). IUI, Stockholm

Andersson M, Braunerhjelm P, Thulin P (2012) Entrepreneurs, creative destruction and production. entry by type, sector and sequence. Journal of Entrepreneurship and Public Policy 1:125–146

Antonov M, Georgi T (1993) Learning through short-run macroeconomic forecasts in a micro-to-macro model. J Econ Behav Organ 21(2)

Ballot G, Erol T (2012) Love thy neighbor- a simulation study on international technology spillovers and growth regimes, revised version of paper presented to the DIME Workshop, Universite Antilles Guyanes, 2–4 December 2009

Ballot G, Taymaz E (1998) Human capital, technological lock-in and evolutionary dynamics. In: Eliasson LG, Green C (eds) The micro foundation of economic growth. University of Michigan Press, Ann Arbor, MI, pp 301–330

Baumol WJ (1968) Entrepreneurship in economic theory. Am Econ Rev Pap Proc LVIII(2):64–71

Blanchflower DG (2004) Self-employment: more may not be better. Swedish Econ Policy Rev 11(2):15–94

Bo C, Eliasson G, Sjöö K (2014) The Swedish industrial support program of the 1970s revisited—A study in Micro to Macro analytical method. Paper presented to the 15th International Joseph A. Schumpeter conference, Jena Germany, July 2014.

Branstetter L (2000) Is foreign direct investment a channel of knowledge spillovers? Evidence from Japan's FDI in the United States. NBER Working Paper No. 8015 (November), NBER, Cambridge, MA

Braunerhjelm P (1991) Svenska underleverantörer och småföretag i det nya Europa (Swedish Subcontractors and SMEs Facing EC), Research report No. 38, IUI, Stockholm

Braunerhjelm P (2008) Entrepreneurship, knowledge and growth. Foundations and Trends in Entrepreneurship 4:451–533

Braunerhjelm P (2012) Innovation and growth. In: Andersson M, Johansson B, Lööf H (eds) Innovation and growth: from R&D strategies of innovating firms to economy-wide technological change, Forthcoming from Oxford University Press

Braunerhjelm P, Eliasson G (2011) Entrepreneurship and new industrial competence bloc formation in the Baltic Sea Region, in the 2011 State of the region report, Baltic Development Forum, Copenhagen

Braunerhjelm P, Johan Eklund J (2014) Taxes, tax administrative burdens and new firm formation. Kyklos 67:1–11

Braunerhjelm P, von Greiff C, Svaleryd H (2009) Utvecklingskraft och omställningsförmåga (Development strength and adjustment capacities), Final report from the Secretariat to the Swedish Government's Globalisation Council, Ministry of Education, http://www.regeringen.se/globaliseringsradet

Braunerhjelm P, Acs Z, Audretsch D, Carlsson B (2010a) The missing link. Knowledge diffusion and entrepreneurship in endogenous growth. Small Bus Econ 34:105–125

Braunerhjelm P, Halldin T, Heum P, Kalvet T, Pajarinen M, Pedersen T, Ylä-Anttila P (2010b) Large firm dynamics on the Nordic-Baltic scene. SNF, Bergen

Burenstam-Linder S (1961) An essay on trade and transformation. Almqvist & Wiksell, Uppsala

Carlsson B (1983a) Industrial subsidies in Sweden: macro-economic effects and an international comparison. J Ind Econ XXXII(1):9–14

Carlsson B (1983b) Industrial subsidies in Sweden: simulations on a micro-to-macro model. In: Microeconometrics, IUI yearbook 1982-1983. IUI, Stockholm

Carlsson B, Bergholm F, Lindberg T (1981) Industristödspolitiken och dess inverkan på samhällsekonomin (Industry Subsidy Policy and Its Macroeconomic Impact). IUI, Stockholm

Coase RH (1937) The nature of the firm. Economica, New Series IV(13–16):386–405

Demsetz H (1969) Information and efficiency: another viewpoint. J Law Econ 12(April):1–22

Dollar R, Wolff EJ (1988) Convergence of industry labor productivity. Rev Econ Stat LXX(4): 549–558

Eliasson G (1976) Business economic planning—theory, practice and comparison. Wiley, London

Eliasson G (1977) Competition and market processes in a simulation model of the Swedish economy. Am Econ Rev 67(1):277–281

Eliasson G (ed) (1978) A micro-to-macro model of the Swedish economy, Conference Reports, 1978: 1. IUI, Stockholm

Eliasson G (1987) Technological competition and trade in the experimentally organized economy. Research report No. 32. IUI, Stockholm

Eliasson G (1989) The dynamics of supply and economic growth—how industrial knowledge accumulation drives a path-dependent economic process. In: Carlsson B (ed) Industrial dynamics, technological, organizational and structural changes in industries and firms. Kluwer, Boston

Eliasson G (1991a) Modeling the experimentally organized economy—complex dynamics in an empirical micro-macro model of endogenous economic growth. J Econ Behav Organ 16(1–2): 153–182

Eliasson G (1991b) Deregulation, innovative entry and structural diversity as a source of stable and rapid economic growth. J Evol Econ 1(1):49–63

Eliasson G (1991c) The international firm: a vehicle for overcoming barriers to trade and a global intelligence organization diffusing the notion of a nation. In: Mattson LG, Stymne B (eds) Corporate and industry strategies for Europe. North-Holland, Amsterdam

Eliasson G (1992) Business competence, organizational learning and economic growth—establishing the Smith-Schumpeter-Wicksell connection. In: Scherer FM, Perlman M (eds) Entrepreneurship, technological innovation, and economic growth: studies in the Schumpeterian tradition. University of Michigan Press, Ann Arbor, MI

Eliasson G (1993) The micro frustrations of privatization in economies in transition. In: Genberg H (ed) Privatization in economies in transition. ICMB, Geneva

Eliasson G (1996) Firm objectives, controls and organization—the use of information and the transfer of knowledge within the firm. Kluwer, Boston, MA

Eliasson G (1998) From plan to market. J Evol Econ 34:49–68

Eliasson G (2000a) The Baltic economic potential—competence blocs, firm strategies and industrial policy. In: Alho K (ed) Economics of the Northern dimension. ETLA-Taloustieto oy, Helsinki

Eliasson G (2000b) Making intangibles visible- the value, the efficiency and the economic consequences of knowledge. In: Buigues P, Jacquemin A, Marchipont JF (eds) Competitiveness and the value of intangible assets. Edward Elgar, Cheltenham, pp 42–71

Eliasson G (2003a) Global economic integration and regional attractors of competence. Industry and Innovation 10(1):75–102

Eliasson G (2003b) The Venture Capitalist as a Competent Outsider in Kari Alho-, Jukka Lassila- and Pekka Ylä-Anttila, 2003, Economic Research and Decision Making, ETLA-Taloustieto oy, Helsinki.; An earlier version was published under the same title by Stockholm: KTH, TRITA-IEO R 1997: 06

Eliasson G (ed) (2005a) The birth, the life and the death of firms-the role of entrepreneurship, creative destruction and conservative institutions in a growing and experimentally organized economy. The Ratio Institute, Stockholm

Eliasson G (2005b) The venture capitalist as a competent outsider, Chap. IV. In: Eliasson G (ed) The birth, the life and the death of firms-the role of entrepreneurship, creative destruction and conservative institutions in a growing and experimentally organized economy. The Ratio Institute, Stockholm

Eliasson G (2006) From employment to entrepreneurship. J Ind Relat 48(5):633–656

Eliasson G (2007) Divergence among mature and rich industrial economies—the case of Sweden entering a new and immediate economy, Chap. 8. In: Hämäläinen T, Heiskala R (eds) Social innovations, institutional change and economic performance. Cheletenham, Northampton, MA/Helsinki, Edward Elgar/Sitra

Eliasson G (2009a) Knowledge directed economic selection and growth. Prometheus 7(4)

Eliasson G (2009b) Policies for a new entrepreneurial economy. In: Cantner U, Gaffard JL, Nesta L (eds) Schumpeterian perspectives on innovation, competition and growth. Springer, Berlin

Eliasson G (2010) Advanced public procurement as industrial policy—aircraft industry as a technical university. Springer, New York, NY

Eliasson G (2011) Advanced purchasing, spillovers and innovative discovery. J Evol Econ 21(1–4):121–139

Eliasson G (2014) The failed Austrian Swedish school connection. Paper presented at the International Joseph A. Schumpeter Conference in Jena, Germany, 27–30 July 2014

Eliasson G, Eliasson Å (1996) The biotechnological competence bloc. Revue d'Economie Industrielle 78(4 Trimestre):7–26

Eliasson G, Eliasson Å (2005) The theory of the firm and the markets for strategic acquisitions. In: Cantner U, Dinopoulos E, Lanzilotti RF (eds) Entrepreneurship. The new economy and public policy. Springer, Berlin

Eliasson G, Eliasson Å (2009) Competence and learning in the experimentally organized economy. In: Bjuggren PO, Mueller DC (eds) The modern firm, corporate governance, and investment. Edward Elgar, Cheltenham

Eliasson G, Peterson C (2013) On the experimental restructuring of a regional economy—a post deregulation experience in Northern Sweden. Paper presented to the entrepreneurship forum August 22–23 conference on regulation, entrepreneurship and firm dynamics, Vaxholm, Sweden

Eliasson G, Taymaz E (2000) Institutions, entrepreneurship, economic flexibility and growth—experiments on an evolutionary model, in Cantner – Hanush – Klepper, 1999, Economic evolution, learning and complexity—econometric, experimental and simulation approaches. Physica, Heidelberg

Eliasson G, Wihlborg C (2003) On the macroeconomic effects of establishing tradability in weak property rights. J Evol Econ 13:607–632

Eliasson G, Rybczynski T, Wihlborg C (1994) The necessary institutional framework to transform formerly planned economies—with special emphasis on the institutions needed to stimulate foreign investment in the formerly planned economies. IUI, Stockholm

Eliasson G, Johansson D, Taymaz E (2004) Simulating the new economy. Struct Chang Econ Dyn 15:289–314

Eliasson G, Johansson D, Taymaz E (2005) Firm turnover and the rate of macroeconomic growth, Chap. VI. In: Eliasson G (ed) The birth, the life and the death of firms-the role of entrepreneurship, creative destruction and conservative institutions in a growing and experimentally organized economy. The Ratio Institute, Stockholm, pp 305–356
Freeman C (1987) Technology policy and economic performance. Pinter, London
Jagrén L (1988) Företagens tillväxt i ett historiskt perspektiv. In: Örtengren J, Lindberg T, Jagren L, Eliasson G, Bjuggren PF, Björklund L (eds) Expansion, avveckling och företagsvärdering i svensk industri—en studie av ägarformens och finansmarknadernas betydelse för strukturomvandlingen. IUI, Stockholm
Jones CI (1999) Growth: with or without scale effects. Am Econ Rev Pap Proc 89(May):139–144
Jones CI, Williams JC (1998) Measuring the social returns to R&D. Q J Econ 113(4):1119–1135
Jones C, Williams JC (1999) Too much of a good thing? The economics of investment in R&D. NBER Working Paper Nr 7283 (August), NBER, Cambridge, MA
Jorgenson DW, Griliches Z (1967) The explanation of productivity change. Rev Econ Stud XXXIV(3):249–282
Keller W (2001) International technology diffusion. NBER Working Paper No 8573 (October), NBER, Cambridge, MA. Published 2004 in J Econ Lit 42:752–782
Knight FH (1944) Diminishing returns from investment. J Polit Econ LII(1):26–47
Lundvall B-Å (1992) National systems of innovation. Pinter, London
Marshall A (1919) Industry and trade. Macmillan, London
McKenzie LW (1959) On the existence of general equilibrium for a competitive market. Econometrica 27(1):30–53
Nelson R (ed) (1993) National systems of innovation: a comparative study. Oxford University Press, Oxford
Nevalainen A (2008) Development of labor productivity in Estonia 1995–2004—an international comparison. In: Industry engines 2018 (2008)
North D (1990) Institutions, institutional change, and economic performance. Cambridge University Press, Cambridge
Nyström K (2008) The institutions of economic freedom and entrepreneurship: evidence from panel data. Public Choice 136:269–282
Nyström K (2010) Business regulation and red tape in the entrepreneurial economy. CESIS, KTH Stockholm
Pakes A, Ericson R (1998) Empirical implications of alternative models firm dynamics. J Econ Theory 79(1):1–45
Partanen A (1998) Trade potential around the Baltic rim: a two-model experiment. ETLA Discussion Paper No 645. ETLA, Helsinki
Piketty T (2014) Capital in the twenty-first century. Belknap, Cambridge, MA
Pritchnett L (1997) Divergence big time. J Econ Perspect 11(Summer):3–17
Romer PM (1986) Increasing returns and long-run growth. J Polit Econ 94(5):1002–1037
Schumpeter JA (1911) Theorie der Wirtschaftlichen Entwicklung, Dunker und Humblot, Jena. English edn, 1934, The theory of economic development: an inquiry into profits, capital, credit, interest and the business cycle, Vol. XLVI, Harvard University Press, Cambridge, MA
Schumpeter JA (1942) Capitalism, socialism and democracy. Harper & Row, New York, NY
State of the Region Report 2011 of the Baltic Development Forum
Taymaz E (1991a) MOSES on PC: manual, initialization, and calibration. IUI Research Report Nr 39. IUI, Stockholm
Taymaz E (1991b) Calibration, Chap. III. In: MOSES on PC: manual, initialization, and calibration. IUI Research report nr. 39. IUI, Stockholm
Williamson OE (1975) Markets and hierarchies: analysis and antitrust implications: a study in the economics of internal organization. Free Press, New York, NY

Absorptive Capacity and Innovation: When Is It Better to Cooperate?

Abiodun Egbetokun and Ivan Savin

Abstract Cooperation can benefit and hurt firms at the same time. An important question then is: when is it better to cooperate? And, once the decision to cooperate is made, how can an appropriate partner be selected? In this paper we present a model of inter-firm cooperation driven by cognitive distance, appropriability conditions and external knowledge. Absorptive capacity of firms develops as an outcome of the interaction between absorptive R&D and cognitive distance from voluntary and involuntary knowledge spillovers. Thus, we offer a revision of the original model by Cohen and Levinthal (Econ J 99(397):569–596, 1989), accounting for recent empirical findings and explicitly modeling absorptive capacity within the framework of interactive learning. We apply that to the analysis of firms' cooperation and R&D investment preferences. The results show that cognitive distance and appropriability conditions between a firm and its cooperation partner have an ambiguous effect on the profit generated by the firm. Thus, a firm chooses to cooperate and selects a partner conditional on the investments in absorptive capacity it is willing to make to solve the understandability/novelty trade-off.

1 Introduction

This paper presents a new theoretical model of absorptive capacity and cooperation between firms. The aim is not to completely capture the motivations for cooperation; rather, we focus on a very specific effect, that is, knowledge sharing or what

A. Egbetokun
Graduate College 'Economics of Innovative Change', Friedrich Schiller University and Max Planck Institute of Economics, Jena, Germany

I. Savin (✉)
Graduate School of Economics and Management, Ural Federal University, Mira 19, 620002 Yekaterinburg, Russian Federation
Bachstrasse 18k Room 216, 07743 Jena, Germany
e-mail: ivan.savin@uni-jena.de

A. Pyka, J. Foster (eds.), *The Evolution of Economic and Innovation Systems*, Economic Complexity and Evolution, DOI 10.1007/978-3-319-13299-0_16
Modified and extended version from Journal of Evolutionary Economics 24(2), Springer 2014.

De Bondt (1996) termed the "voluntary exchange of useful technological information". In this sense our model shares the features of Cowan et al. (2007) model of bilateral collaboration where firms form alliances purely based on the production of shared knowledge.

Inter-firm cooperation for learning and innovation has become more common in recent years, mainly due to rapid technological progress and changes in the business environment. Quickly advancing technological knowledge and rising costs of R&D make it virtually impossible for any firm to maintain in-house all the capabilities and knowledge required for production. Moreover, increasing specialisation creates a situation where firms occupy relatively narrow positions in the knowledge space. Consequently, firms often need knowledge [1] that lies outside their core competence. The formation of alliances with other organisations has proven to be an effective way to access external knowledge to complement endogenous capabilities (Powell and Grodal 2005; de Man and Duysters 2005; Brusoni et al. 2001; Bamford and Ernst 2002; Powell 1998).

For such alliances to have the desired effects, firms require absorptive capacity to understand and apply knowledge generated elsewhere. This capacity is developed by investing in R&D (Cohen and Levinthal 1989, henceforth CL).[2] Moreover, the effectiveness of alliances is known to have an inverted 'U'-shaped relation with cognitive distance. In alliance formation, therefore, firms need to balance between their technological heterogeneity and overlap with potential partners (Nooteboom 1999). This creates a proximity trade-off and has been a major focus in the recent literature.[3]

However, other issues are also important. Reciprocal terms of cooperation require a firm to share some of its knowledge with the partner in order to gain access to the latter's knowledge base (Fehr and Gächter 2000). This is like a 'two-edged sword': if the partner can learn faster and is more capable to innovate, a firm then runs the risk of making its partner better at its own expense. For this reason, voluntary spillovers or appropriability conditions between cooperation partners become a very critical factor to consider in cooperation. For the same reason, a firm will take the R&D efforts of its potential partner seriously since that is the main source of absorptive

[1]Henceforth, knowledge in this sense includes technologies that firms use in innovation. Innovation refers to a technically new product which develops as an outcome of R&D (see the Oslo Manual, OECD 2005). Consequently, by R&D profit we imply profit due to innovation.

[2]Although recent studies have argued that absorptive capacity, being a multidimensional concept, is not fully proxied by R&D or staff quality alone (Flatten et al. 2011; Zahra and George 2002), we assume that a significant portion of it is embodied in R&D performance. Therefore, our conceptualisation of absorptive capacity in this paper derives mainly from a firm's R&D investments.

[3]Some studies (e.g., Cantner and Meder 2007; Mowery et al. 1996) have also shown that cognitive proximity reduces over time. This affects the learning and innovation potential of an alliance and reduces the likelihood that the same partners will cooperate in the next period. This dynamic is important and we address it in a subsequent paper.

capacity. When these are combined with the challenge of cognitive distance, an important practical question arises: when is it better for a firm to cooperate?

In this paper, we approach the question from a theoretical perspective by looking at the contribution of absorptive capacity (driven by cognitive distance, appropriability conditions and external knowledge) to firms' R&D profit. To do this, we develop a model of inter-firm cooperation in which partners increase their knowledge stock by sharing complementary knowledge. The amount of external knowledge absorbed depends on absorptive capacity, and the new knowledge affects firm performance through innovation-driven profit. For a representative agent, we examine the conditions under which a cooperative strategy is superior to non-cooperation in terms of profit generated.

Two things set our model apart. First, a firm develops absorptive capacity not as a side-effect of total R&D but by devoting a share of its total R&D budget explicitly to it. This creates an investment trade-off. Second, accounting for cognitive distance allows us to distinguish voluntary spillovers within an alliance from other forms of external knowledge. With these elements, we are able to modify the original absorptive capacity model of CL for the context of inter-firm alliances. We use that to study how cooperation affects firm performance in terms of profit. The analyses in the present paper treat cognitive distance as exogenous. This simplification allows us to focus on the specific effect in which we are interested, that is, how the profits of a representative firm evolve with regard to its cooperation strategy. In a follow-up paper (Savin and Egbetokun 2013), we extend our model to analyse the dynamic scenario in which firms' absorptive capacity and their cognitive distance are affected by past decisions.

This study contributes to understanding cooperation and R&D investment preferences of companies and, therefore, has important theoretical and practical applications. The theoretical predictions of our model are more relevant in the context of interactive learning, and our comparative results offer some practical insight on alliance formation decision-making.

2 Literature Overview

Technological progress develops along certain trajectories within a given technological paradigm. Each of these trajectories contains some technological opportunities which are either intensive or extensive. In the former case, companies explore opportunities on a particular trajectory by investing in own R&D. In the latter case, firms make use of external knowledge generated by other firms and public research. For this, however, at least a share of the external knowledge must not be a private good (i.e., not appropriated by the owner). The magnitude of this share depends on the effectiveness of the mechanisms by which knowledge is protected—the appropriability conditions (Dosi 1982). In the literature, there is a long discussion on the trade-off between knowledge spillovers and appropriability conditions starting from Arrow (1962). It is argued that spillovers create a negative appropriability incentive. Reducing the innovation rent, large spillover possibilities result in lower (than optimal from a social point of view) level of R&D investments. However, due to the heterogeneity of companies, knowledge transfer via these spillovers contributes to technological progress and can be beneficial for recipient firms (de Fraja 1993). Those spillovers are nevertheless only effective if the recipient of knowledge has a sufficient capacity to absorb it.

Absorptive capacity, that is the ability to value, assimilate and apply new knowledge, was originally conceptualised by CL as a byproduct of a firm's R&D efforts. By allowing the firm to complement its own knowledge with incoming spillovers, this capacity enhances a firm's problem-solving ability (Kim 1998). Zahra and George (2002) extended the concept of absorptive capacity by differentiating between potential and realised absorptive capacity. Potential absorptive capacity involves the acquisition and assimilation of knowledge spillovers, while realised absorptive capacity guarantees the application of this knowledge through the development and refinement of routines that facilitate its transformation and exploitation.

As already hinted, spillovers generally arise from two sources: public and private R&D. Compared to public R&D, spillovers from private R&D are often not easily accessible. Moreover, in the context of today's rapidly changing and highly competitive business environment, spillovers from other firms' R&D sometimes provide more relevant complementary resources. Thus, firms often feel the need to engage in cooperation with other firms to gain access to such knowledge spillovers. In this context, both dimensions of absorptive capacity are at work. Potential absorptive capacity helps the firm to identify an appropriate partner and learn from it, while realised absorptive capacity enables the firm to deploy the knowledge acquired in innovation which enhances profit. Indeed, recent empirical work on inter-firm learning and alliances has shown that firms with higher absorptive capacity tend to benefit more from external knowledge (e.g., de Jong and Freel 2010; Lin et al. 2012).

When a firm engages in cooperation, in addition to involuntary spillovers from other sources it can also appropriate voluntary spillovers from its partners (Gulati 1998). But securing access to voluntary spillovers through partnerships has a potentially negative side effect because of the reciprocity that characterises cooperative arrangements. In exchange for accessing a (potential) partner's knowledge stock, a firm also needs to open up its own knowledge base (Fehr and Gächter 2000). Consequently, spillovers from the firm's R&D efforts do not only reduce its own appropriation, they potentially improve its competitor's R&D performance.[4] This is a 'cost of partnership' which constitutes another form of the negative appropriability incentive. This negative incentive is lowered because the partner firm does not possess perfect absorptive capacity to appropriate all the spillovers (CL, pp. 575–576; Hammerschmidt 2009, p. 426). Thus, what a firm worries about is not necessarily the total spillovers it generates, but how much its partner can absorb,

[4]This argument is important for our model and will be applied later in modeling the firm's profit.

that is, the effective spillovers which increase as the absorptive capacity of this (competing) partner increases.[5] Moreover, the firm also benefits from cooperation because it has access to a pool of knowledge larger than just its own, particularly when the partner holds complementary technological knowledge thereby creating a higher potential to innovate.

The relative value of knowledge spillovers can be represented by the distance between partners.[6] If the distance is small, companies well understand each other and there is much less uncertainty (Lane and Lubatkin 1998), but there might be no new knowledge to learn and, hence, there is the risk of lock-in. In contrast, if the distance is large, the knowledge has higher novelty but is too difficult to absorb and coordination problems may arise (Boschma 2005). This leads to the optimal cognitive distance hypothesis which has been the subject of many studies. The consensus in the empirical literature is that technological or cognitive proximity between cooperation partners has an inverted 'U'-shaped relation with the value of learning the partners obtain (or, alternatively, the innovative potential of the alliance) (Lin et al. 2012; Gilsing et al. 2008; Nooteboom et al. 2007; Wuyts et al. 2005). An understandability–novelty trade-off exists such that effective learning by interaction is better accomplished by limiting cognitive overlap while securing cognitive proximity.[7]

The discussion so far is based on a perception of absorptive capacity as a passive by-product of R&D investments made to generate inventions. However, it can be argued that the allocation of R&D resources is not a simple and unidirectional decision. A distinction can be made between absorptive R&D and inventive R&D. Absorptive R&D refers to the investments made to benefit from knowledge spillovers while inventive R&D is the effort made by a firm to generate original knowledge (Hammerschmidt 2009; Cantner and Pyka 1998). This distinction reflects the difference between "the exploration of new possibilities and

[5]In our model we are concerned with firms competing on the same technological trajectory. In the extreme case that the cooperating partners operate in different industries, competition between them is mostly negligible. In this case, spillovers do not constitute a disincentive to cooperation and R&D investments (Cantner and Pyka 1998, p. 374).

[6]Distance, in this sense, includes not only cognitive distance but also organisational, social, institutional and geographical ones (Boschma 2005). For instance, Dettmann and von Proff (2010) demonstrated that organisational and institutional proximity facilitate patenting collaboration over large geographical distances. Wuyts et al. (2005) demonstrated that, depending on the industry, organisational and strategic proximity are sometimes more important in the formation of alliances. And the literature on economic geography is coherent on the relevance of geographic distance in knowledge transfer; the greater the distance, the more knowledge decays (Boschma 2005). Nevertheless, since our study is concerned with knowledge sharing, it is more appropriate to concentrate on cognitive distance.

[7]In a dynamic sense, cognitive overlap tends to increase with cooperation intensity (Mowery et al. 1998). Thus, it is expected that a firm will reconsider its cooperation decisions depending on cognitive distance. Alliances may be discontinued when partners become too close and previously discontinued alliances may be re-formed if the partners have become sufficiently distant in terms of their knowledge endowment.

the exploitation of old certainties" (March 1991, p. 71)[8] as well as the common classification of R&D into basic and applied research. As Cassiman et al. (2002) showed, by doing basic R&D a firm can effectively access incoming knowledge spillovers which then help to increase the efficiency of own applied R&D.

In this sense, absorptive capacity is no longer a passive by-product of R&D, but an explicit part of the firm's strategy. This strategic necessity is even more important when the external knowledge source (from which a firm desires to learn) is not close to its prior knowledge. This is also true when the knowledge, such as that which comes from universities and research institutes, is not directly applicable to the needs of the firm. In this case, CL (p. 572) argue that a firm's capacity to appropriate the knowledge increases as the firm invests more in R&D. This argument is extended with the distinction between inventive and absorptive R&D; it can now be noted that it is not routine R&D but explicit investments in the form of absorptive R&D that facilitates the build-up of absorptive capacity. At the same time, firms need to build up a certain level of capacity to generate own knowledge through inventive R&D.[9] Consequently, firms are faced with the strategic decision of how to optimally allocate resources between inventive and absorptive R&D, which, though complementary, are mutually exclusive. This constitutes an investment trade-off that holds important implications for a firm's learning abilities and cooperation preferences.

Historically, modeling studies have treated the R&D investment and cooperation decisions of firms only with respect to exogenous spillovers (see De Bondt 1996, for an overview). Typically, such spillovers, especially when they are symmetric, have a negative effect on strategic R&D investments. At the same time, they incentivise firms to engage in cooperation and to make bilateral investment commitments. Later models account for absorptive capacity and show that technological heterogeneity, as reflected in relatively high (exogenous) spillover rates, incentivises the build-up of absorptive capacity (Hammerschmidt 2009). Even when spillovers are endogenous, as is the case in the model of Cantner and Pyka (1998), allocating more resources to absorptive R&D as spillovers increase tends to be a more profitable strategy when compared with other strategies such as the one in which the firm concentrates purely on invention. A limitation of these studies is their

[8]Even in this framework the understandability–novelty trade-off exists. In the context of exploitation, wherein firms are concerned with improving their performance along the same technological trajectory, a high level of mutual understanding is required to reduce transaction costs (Drejer and Vindig 2007; Cantner and Meder 2007). Notwithstanding, since technological opportunities within a certain trajectory tend to decrease continuously according to Wolff's law (Cantner and Pyka 1998), firms seek for more explorative or extensive opportunities, the aim of which is to generate novelty. Consequently, increasing cognitive distance positively influences the value of interactive learning because it raises the novelty value of technological opportunities as well as the possibility of novel combinations of complementary resources. This is, however, only possible as long as the partners are close enough to understand each other.

[9]This is a mechanism that assures the presence of reciprocal incentives for cooperation (Kamien and Zang 2000; Wiethaus 2005).

failure to account for strategic alliance formation as a way for firms to access complementarities, pool knowledge resources or innovate jointly.

In more recent models (Cowan et al. 2007; Baum et al. 2010), alliance formation is driven by its probability to succeed in terms of knowledge generation and innovation, as well as the proximity of the potential partner. Among other things, the models present knowledge sharing as a major motivation for alliance formation. In particular, even in the absence of any social capital considerations,[10] empirically founded network characteristics such as repeated alliances, transitivity and clustering can be observed. However, these models treat absorptive capacity as an exogenous parameter which is similar for all firms in the network. Although our model shares some of their features, an important contribution we make is that absorptive capacity is not modeled exogenously. In contrast, it is endogenous and is influenced by the two trade-offs described earlier. Ultimately, cooperation decision is driven by proximity considerations, endogenous absorptive capacity and the cost of partnership in terms of the knowledge spillovers that a potential partner can absorb.

3 The Model

In the model, a total of N firms compete within a defined knowledge space. A firm seeks to maximize its profit from generating innovations. It does this by developing absorptive capacity to gain from knowledge spillovers while also maintaining own inventive R&D. Consequently, the firm needs to decide how to allocate its R&D investments between own invention and the development of absorptive capacity. Knowledge spillovers arise voluntarily through inter-firm cooperation and involuntarily from non-cooperative sources. The decision on investment allocation is affected by cognitive distance (from both types of spillovers); larger distances correspond to higher resource heterogeneity or novelty potential but also to larger investments required to absorb them. For the analyses in this paper, these distances are given exogenously.[11] Each firm resolves the investment trade-off and makes a cooperation decision. This decision is influenced by cognitive distance, R&D investments and appropriability conditions. We are particularly interested in the conditions under which cooperation is superior to non-cooperation. To study this, we compare the R&D investments and profits for a representative firm when it engages in R&D cooperation and when it does not.

[10]This means that technological fit, rather than social capital factors like trustworthiness and embeddedness, is a major causal force behind alliance formation (Baum et al. 2010). Firms will select partners from whom they can learn significantly and for specific (short-term) purposes. In this sense, multiple partnerships may not be necessary and firms stop their partnership search once they find a technologically fit partner.

[11]In the dynamic setting that we analyse in Savin and Egbetokun (2013), cognitive distance changes according to the innovation success and learning of the firms.

Some important assumptions are to be noted. Firstly, in making their cooperation decisions, firms consider only their short term potential profits. This assumption reflects firms' behaviour when the frontier of knowledge is rapidly extending, in which case the pressure to innovate quickly is high, or when productive activities require a rapidly expanding knowledge base, in which case firms need to cooperate so as to gain access to complementary knowledge (Cowan et al. 2007).

Secondly, firms only select one partner and conduct one R&D project at a given period. This is a simplifying assumption that improves the tractability of the model, allowing us to focus exclusively on knowledge sharing between unique pairs of firms, and is computationally more feasible. The cost of scanning the environment is incurred by all firms and is therefore not considered in the analyses.

Thirdly, the reliability and trustworthiness of potential partners is not taken into account in the selection of cooperation partners. This follows partly from the short-termism with which firms approach partner selection. In addition, since the potential partners both have reciprocal incentives for cooperation, their likelihood to misbehave is significantly lower. Otherwise, firms can simply discontinue the partnership in the next period preventing an access to their voluntary spillovers.

Finally, firms are assumed to have perfect information about the knowledge base of other firms.[12] This assumption appears to be rather strong and is in contrast with the common perception that firms have imperfect information about partners' knowledge and motivations (Oxley 1997). However, it finds justification in the fact that the capabilities and strategic focus of potential partners can be easily assessed through massive information that is freely available. For example, a firm's patent portfolio (which can be freely accessed online) contains significant information on its knowledge stock and market value (Hall et al. 2005). Thus, patents constitute a comprehensive representation of the knowledge space in an industry. Note also that investments in screening and understanding this knowledge (e.g., by hiring patent lawyers) can be considered as a separate share of a firm's R&D budget, further justifying the distinction in R&D investments applied in the model. In addition, there are several other channels through which reliable information can be obtained, for example, scientific and technical articles, hiring, and informal networks (see footnote 3 in Baum et al. 2010, for more details on this).

3.1 R&D Investments

In accordance with CL, we consider R&D investments as an instrument to stimulate absorptive capacity. However, we consider this capacity to be not a by-product of the

[12]This does not necessarily eliminate the risks associated with innovation. First, firms need to be able to understand the information available, an endeavour which is by itself costly and risky. Then, innovation still runs the risk of failing, irrespective of how well-informed firm's cooperation decisions are.

total R&D investments but of a separate share of it. Thus, we distinguish between investments directly in R&D that exploit identified technological opportunities (rdi_i) and investments for exploring the environment for technological development (aci_i), together forming total R&D spending (RD_i)[13]:

$$RD_i = rdi_i^t + aci_i^t = \rho_i^t RD_i + (1 - \rho_i^t) RD_i . \tag{1}$$

This investment trade-off is shaped by learning incentives including the potential quantity and complexity of external knowledge.

3.2 Knowledge Generation

In line with CL, firm i's stock of knowledge in period t (k_i^t) is increased by a quantity comprising the firm's own direct investment in R&D and externally generated knowledge which, in turn, consists of other firms' R&D (rdi_h^t) and knowledge generated by public institutions (ek):

$$k_i^t = \left(rdi_i^t\right)^{\xi} + ac_i^t \left(\delta_n \sum_{h \neq i} rdi_h^t + ek^t \right), \tag{2}$$

where $\xi \in (0, 1)$ is a parameter which defines the rate of return to inventive R&D, $\delta_n \in (0, 1)$ reflects the fraction of knowledge not appropriated by firms and $ac_i^t \in (0, 1)$ is the degree to which firm i can absorb external knowledge, i.e. absorptive capacity. The summation term in (2) assumes no cooperation between firms, hence no voluntary knowledge spillovers. All firms want to ensure that the value of δ_n is as low as possible.

However, within a cooperative context the situation is different. Besides involuntary spillovers (δ_n), firm i can also appropriate voluntary spillovers (δ_c) from its strategic partner. Thus,

$$k_i^t = \left(rdi_i^t\right)^{\xi} + ac_i^t \left((\delta_c + \delta_n) \sum_{j \neq i} rdi_j^t + \delta_n \sum_{j \neq h \neq i} rdi_h^t + ek^t \right), 1 > \delta_c > \delta_n > 0$$

The term $\delta_c + \delta_n$ reflects total spillovers available to a cooperating firm and is always below 1. In a dyadic relationship, only one partner j is present, and it can be assumed that all involuntary spillovers available are included in the total external

[13] We abstract from production and the market by treating the R&D budgets as exogenous. In this way, the focus of the model is narrowed to the firm's investment and cooperation decisions, and innovation.

knowledge ek.[14] Therefore,

$$k_i^t = \left(rdi_i^t\right)^{\xi} + ac_i^t \left(\delta_c rdi_j^t + ek\right). \tag{3}$$

As stated earlier, we assume that firms have a perfect knowledge about the distances to their potential partners and about their R&D budgets. Now, since any particular firm takes a decision on the investments in R&D based on the investment decision of its potential partner, we assume that in any given period each firm forms an expectation, considering the investment decision of the partner to be equal to, e.g., the average from the last few (σ) investment allocations made by the partner[15]:

$$E^i(\rho_j^t) = \frac{\sum_{\iota=1}^{\sigma} \rho_j^{t-\iota}}{\sigma}. \tag{4}$$

With the analysis of a representative agent and exogenous cognitive distance, no interaction of firms is considered and the equality in (4) simply translates into an assumption of perfect knowledge about the partner's investment allocation (i.e., $E^i(\rho_j) = \rho_j$).[16]

External knowledge, ek, is set as the total inventive R&D investment of companies (N firms in total) in the knowledge space which the firm i can potentially understand, rescaled by the parameter of involuntary spillovers,[17] $\delta_n \in (0, 1)$:

$$ek^t = \delta_n \sum_{i \neq h=2}^{N} rdi_h^t. \tag{5}$$

In the meantime we drop the time argument t to remove the notion of dynamics.

[14]This follows partly from our focus on dyadic partnerships. In this sense, knowledge spillovers from other firms not in the dyad and from public organisations together constitute technological opportunities for the dyad.

[15]The exact number of periods constituting a reasonable expectation is best validated in a simulation model (Savin and Egbetokun 2013).

[16]However, in the dynamic setting that we simulate subsequently, (4) necessarily introduces some uncertainty as the expectation of firm i will not necessarily coincide with the actual investment decision of firm j, which, in turn, is based on its own expectation about firm's i decision: $E^i(\rho_{j,t}) \neq \rho_j = f(E^j(\rho_{i,t}))$.

[17]This fraction is determined by the appropriability conditions which include the patent system in a particular industry and the efficacy of secrecy or other forms of protection of firm j's internal knowledge.

3.3 Absorptive Capacity

Absorptive capacity (ac_i) is dependent on two variables: (i) the distance ($d_{i\cdot}$) between firm i's knowledge base and external knowledge available and (ii) the investments in absorptive capacity (aci_i) made by the firm. Cognitive distance d_{ij} is modeled as the Euclidian distance between the stock of knowledge of the two partners i and j ($\nu_{i.}$ and $\nu_{j.}$), which are independently and randomly attributed to the firms from the interval [0, 1]:

$$d_{ij} = \sqrt{(\nu_{i1} - \nu_{j1})^2 + (\nu_{i2} - \nu_{j2})^2}. \tag{6}$$

We choose a two-dimensional space for a better visualization of results. As earlier mentioned, for the present analyses cognitive distance is given exogenously. In a separate dynamic analysis we allow the distance to vary depending on cooperation intensity.

As explained earlier, shared knowledge is the main motivation for alliance formation between any two firms i and j. Following Wuyts et al. (2005), this knowledge can be represented as the mathematical product of its novelty value (which increases in cognitive distance) and understandability (that respectively decreases in cognitive distance):

$$an_{i,j} = (\alpha d_{ij})(\beta_1 - \beta_2 d_{ij}) = \alpha\beta_1 d_{ij} - \alpha\beta_2 d_{ij}^2, \tag{7}$$

And accounting for the stimulating role of investments in absorptive capacity (aci_i):

$$an_{i,j} = \alpha\beta_1 d_{ij}(1 + aci_i^{\psi}) - \alpha\beta_2 d_{ij}^2 = \alpha\beta_1 d_{ij} + \alpha\beta_1 d_{ij} aci_i^{\psi} - \alpha\beta_2 d_{ij}^2, \tag{8}$$

where $\psi \in (0, 1)$ reflects the efficiency of absorptive R&D. This investment essentially causes an upward shift in understandability for any given d_{ij} and has decreasing marginal returns. Since the aim of the firm is to maximise the knowledge it absorbs given its current level of absorptive capacity, we proceed by considering absorptive capacity as a function of the knowledge absorbed by i from cooperation with j. Specifically, it is presented as $an_{i,j}$ normalized by its maximum value:

$$ac_{i,j} = \frac{\alpha\beta_1 d_{ij} + \alpha\beta_1 d_{ij} aci_i^{\psi} - \alpha\beta_2 d_{ij}^2}{\frac{1}{4\alpha\beta_2}\left[\alpha\beta_1(1 + aci_i^{\psi})\right]^2} \in [0, 1] \tag{9}$$

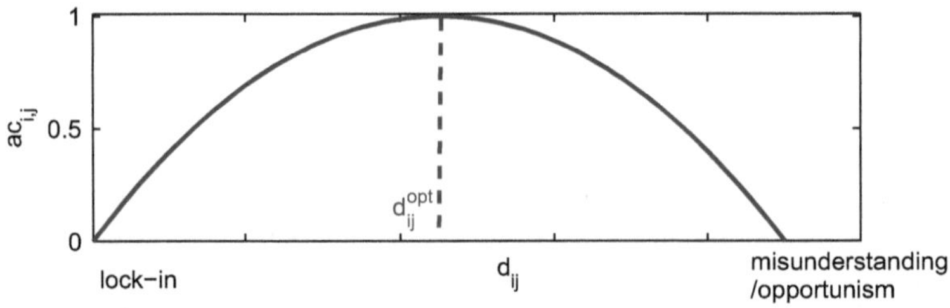

Fig. 1 Absorptive capacity function

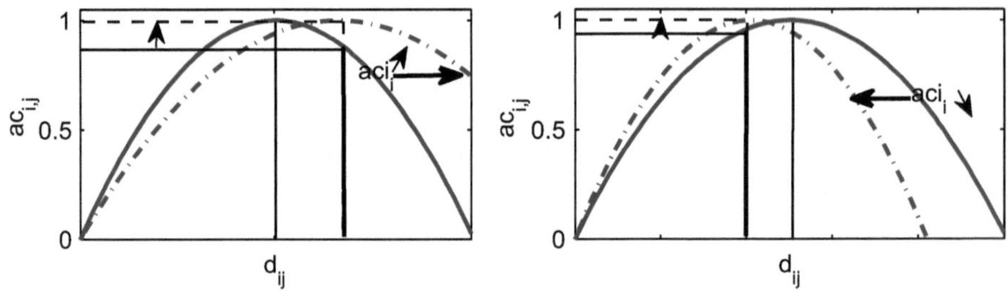

Fig. 2 Dynamics in absorptive capacity function. As company i increases its investments in absorptive capacity (aci_i), the optimal distance to its cooperating partner increases. Thus, for the larger distance, i has a higher absorptive capacity by increasing its investments (*left plot*). The opposite is true for the lower distance (*right plot*)

A larger d_{ij} increases the marginal impact of aci_i on absorptive capacity ($\frac{\partial ac_{i,j}}{\partial aci_i\,\partial d_{ij}} > 0$), which corresponds with CL (p. 572).[18] In contrast, the effect of d_{ij} on $ac_{i,j}$ is ambiguous: for a given value of aci_i, it is positive ($\frac{\partial ac_{i,j}}{\partial d_{ij}} > 0$ and $\frac{\partial^2 ac_i}{\partial d_{ij}^2} < 0$) until a certain optimal distance is reached and negative ($\frac{\partial ac_i}{\partial d_{ij}} < 0$) otherwise (Fig. 1). The maximum of the inverted 'U'-shaped function shifts right (left) with increasing (decreasing) aci_i (Fig. 2), allowing a firm to adopt its absorptive capacity to the actual distance from its cooperation partner. The latter characteristic corresponds to the empirical fact that investments in absorptive capacity raise the optimal distance between cooperation partners (de Jong and Freel 2010; Drejer and Vindig 2007).

It is clear from (9) that when $d_{i.} = 0$ absorptive capacity equals zero. This is because if there is no difference between firm i's own knowledge and the external one, the novelty value is zero even if understandability is maximal. In this way, absorptive capacity ($ac_{i,.}$) is modeled explicitly at the level of interactive learning[19];

[18]Note that while cognitive distance is symmetric (i.e. $d_{ij} = d_{ji}$), $an_{i,j}$ and $ac_{i,j}$ are asymmetric. This is because the investment trade-off is not solved by the two companies identically (i.e. absorptive R&D investments are not necessarily the same for the two companies).

[19]This is similar to the conceptutalisation by Lane and Lubatkin (1998) of absorptive capacity as 'a learning dyad-level construct'.

and it captures not only the ability to understand external knowledge, but also the ability to explore the environment and to identify novel knowledge.

It should be noted that the cognitive distance of firm i from external knowledge ek (i.e. d_{iek}) is not necessarily the same as that from firm j (i.e. d_{ij}). In this study we consider it as the average distance to all other firms in the knowledge space:

$$d_{iek,t} = \frac{\sum_{i \neq k=2}^{N} d_{ik}}{N-1}, \tag{10}$$

so that the maximum distance to the external knowledge does not exceed the maximum distance to a single potential partner in this space. Thus, for the same level of absorptive R&D, the absorptive capacity directed on each of the two sources of spillovers will be different.[20] When this is accounted for, (3) transforms into:

$$k_i = rdi_i^{\xi} + ac_{i,j}\left(\delta_c rdi_j\right) + ac_{i,ek}\left(ek\right). \tag{11}$$

Therefore, one should not misinterpret ek as any sort of knowledge which can be transferred automatically. Like voluntary spillovers, the involuntary ones—though codified—also require the effort of absorption: a firm has to have sufficient absorptive capacity to identify and assimilate this new knowledge.

Without an R&D partner, the knowledge to be generated by firm i is different (ek is the only source of external knowledge):

$$k_i^{\text{generated alone}} = rdi_i^{\xi} + ac_{i,ek}\left(ek\right) \text{ as } \delta_c = 0. \tag{12}$$

3.4 *Innovation and Profit*

Innovation is perceived as a process which involves recombination of heterogeneous resources. Thus, the size of a potential innovation is defined by the amount of knowledge (k_i) generated. When the firm does not form a partnership, its profit (Π_i) is not affected by voluntary spillovers. In a partnership, however, the profit of the firm decreases proportionally with the amount of knowledge spillovers ($ac_{j,i}\delta_c rdi_i$) that the partner can absorb (which is essentially a constituent part of k_j that reduces the appropriability of k_i). This is in contrast to CL where Π_i is reduced proportional to the knowledge generated by the partner (k_j).[21] This 'cost of partnership' or, in the words of CL, 'effect of rivalry' affects the choice of an R&D partner. To avoid the problem of increasing Π_i for $ac_{j,i}\delta_c rdi_i < 1$, we introduce a 'natural' leak-out

[20] As in (9), $ac_{i,ek} = f(d_{iek})$.

[21] Recall that in CL $\frac{\partial \Pi_i}{\partial k_i} > 0$, $\frac{\partial \Pi_i}{\partial k_j} < 0$ and $\frac{\partial \Pi_i}{\partial k_i \partial k_j} < 0$.

that is fixed and equal to 1.

$$\Pi_i = \begin{cases} k_i^{\text{generated in cooperation}} / \left(1 + ac_{j,i}\delta_c rdi_i\right) & \text{if } i \text{ has a partner } j, \\ k_i^{\text{generated alone}} & \text{if } i \text{ has no partner.} \end{cases} \tag{13}$$

One way of interpreting the profit function in case of partnership in (13) is a split of property rights over a certain invention (new technology) converted into a monetary value. Since this technology may be used in different applications, the split is not necessarily exact; however, appropriation of rights over the invention is reduced by the amount of spillovers to a competing partner. Thus, the functional form suggested can have a meaningful (although not necessarily exclusive) economic interpretation and also follow the assumptions on the functional form from CL (see above). In general, the variable Π can be interpreted as an incremental innovation based on a new recombination of knowledge resulting from a firm's continuous R&D effort and from which the firm derives profits.[22] Therefore, henceforth (13) is referred to as profit and used in our study as a main indicator of firms' performance.

4 Optimal Decision Making

In the following we discuss the optimal strategy of firm i in (i) solving the investment trade-off and (ii) forming a partnership. Our interest is in how absorptive capacity (derived from R&D resource allocation, ρ_i), cognitive distance (d_{ij}), appropriability conditions (δ_c) and technological opportunities (ek) affect the benefits from cooperation. To study this, we resolve the investment trade-off for a representative firm in two scenarios (cooperative and non-cooperative) and compare the results in terms of innovative profit.

4.1 Investment Trade-Off

For certain levels of the distance d_{ij} that maximises understandability and novelty, firm i is incentivised to invest in absorptive R&D to maximise the amount of external knowledge absorbed. The trade-off that the firm faces is how to optimally distribute its total R&D investment between the creation of own knowledge and the improvement of absorptive capacity. This necessitates a comparison of the marginal returns to each type of investment with respect to the profit gained. Absorptive R&D begins to pay off when it generates a marginal return that is equal to that of inventive R&D:

$$\frac{\partial \Pi_i}{\partial aci_i} = \frac{\partial \Pi_i}{\partial rdi_i} \tag{14}$$

[22] Once we address the dynamics of firms in the knowledge space, the notion of radical innovation will also be required. However, for the sake of brevity we do not include its discussion in this study.

Using (13), (12), (11), (9) and (1), we obtain (see Appendix 1 for derivation) the condition for the R&D investment that satisfies (14):

$$\begin{cases} \mathrm{F}(\rho_i) = 0 & \text{if } i \text{ has a partner } j, \\ \mathrm{F^a}(\rho_i) = 0 & \text{if } i \text{ has no partner.} \end{cases} \tag{15}$$

As (15) is a highly complex non-linear function with multiple local minima depending on the particular set of parameter values applied, it is a non-trivial problem to find the value of ρ_i satisfying the condition.[23] For this reason we apply a heuristic optimisation technique, in particular, Differential Evolution that is able to identify a good approximation of the global optimum in (15) for different sets of calibrating parameters as long as they satisfy the conditions stated above (see Appendix 2 for details). It is important to note that this optimization is performed solely on current expected profits as it was done, e.g., by Klepper (1996). Such a short-term horizon consideration together with the uncertainties about partners' investment decision and the exact outcome of partnership matching does not allow pursuing any long-term equilibrium (which is also not our aim).

4.2 Partnership Formation

Since larger distances (until a certain optimum level) increase the marginal returns to new knowledge generated, it follows that each firm prefers to select a cooperation partner at the largest distance possible to maximise the novelty value of the R&D cooperation. At the same time, the partner choice is essentially constrained by understandability such that the firm i chooses a partner which it can also understand. In addition, the firm also takes into account the costs of partnership as a result of spillovers from its R&D efforts. Ultimately, the decision to cooperate (or not) is a profit-maximising one which depends on the potential profit generated when working alone in comparison with profit generated by cooperating with the most 'fitting' partner:

$$\max\left(\Pi_i^{\text{generated alone}}; \Pi_i^{\text{with any of the possible partners}}\right). \tag{16}$$

To this end, the simulation in the basic case can proceed as follows. First, all exogenous parameters (α, β_1, β_2, ψ, ξ, η, γ, ρ_j, δ_c, ek (the latter three can be simulated with different scenarios)) must be set.[24] This also includes a random

[23] A deterministic iterative solution (e.g., according to the fixed-point theorem) is also not applicable as the function does not necessarily always converge to a $\rho_i \in [0, 1]$ for all possible combinations of parameters.

[24] For illustrative reasons we take a single set of parameter values for two firms satisfying their constraints. In particular, $\alpha = \sqrt{2}/50$, $\beta_1 = \sqrt{2}$, $\beta_2 = 1$, $\psi = \xi = 0.4$, $RD_i = RD_j = 0.2$,

distribution of the initial stocks of knowledge ($\Rightarrow$ set d_{ij}) and aggregated R&D budgets (*RD*) for all firms.

Second, in each period one needs to solve the investment trade-off of each company ($\rho_{.}$) for all potential partners, considering the expectation about other firms' investments in R&D to be known. After that, the amount of knowledge $k_{.}$ to be generated by each company either alone (standalone mode) or in partnership with any of the firms in the knowledge space is estimated. Based on this information the most lucrative partner for each company can be selected by maximizing profit from R&D activity Π_i.

Third, although the most lucrative partner for each firm is identified, partnership formation is a non-trivial task in this model. The reason is that the incentives of a firm i to build a partnership with firm j are asymmetric: although distance between the partners is the same, the decision on the investment trade-off in R&D is individual for each company. Hence, there is no 'Nash stable network'.[25] Therefore, the model we build can be considered to be 'non-equilibrium' model basing on the functional dependencies described and following certain matching rules given below:

- *Unilateral matching*: in each period in a random order firms sequentially identify their most fitting partner. Once the partner is found, partnership is formed (i.e. the chosen firm simply adjusts its ρ to the given partner).
- *Reciprocal matching*: if firm i identifies firm j as the most lucrative cooperation partner and is itself among the 'top' 5 % of the companies with whom firm j would cooperate, then they build a partnership.
- *A 'popularity contest'*: one counts for how many firms each company is the most lucrative one, the second most lucrative, ... After that the firms are ranked according their popularity and choose a partner in the order of the ranking.

It remains for simulation experiments to decide which of the scenarios described fits best. The extensive simulation is described in Savin and Egbetokun (2013). In the following, only some illustrative results for one firm in two scenarios (cooperative and non-cooperative) are demonstrated.

4.3 Comparative Statics

In CL, absorbed external knowledge is endogenous and influenced by R&D investments, which is itself affected by the ease of learning, intra-industry spillovers

$\delta_c = 0.5$, $ek = 1$, $\rho_j = 0.5$, $d_{iek} = \sqrt{2}/1.001$ and $d_{ij} = \sqrt{2}/1.01$. These values were chosen to demonstrate on a single set of graphs the complex shape of the ρ and Π functions in response to changes in the variables of interest.

[25] 'a stable network is one in which for each agent (or pair of agents) there is a payoff maximizing decision about which link to form' (Cowan et al. 2007, p. 1052).

Table 1 Comparative static results

Effect	Cohen and Levinthal 1989	Our model
$\partial\Pi_i/\partial d_{ij}$	Positive	Ambiguous
$\partial\Pi_i/\partial\delta_c$	Ambiguous	Ambiguous
$\partial\Pi_i/\partial\rho_j$	–	Positive
$\partial\Pi_i/\partial ek$	Ambiguous	Positive

and technological opportunities.[26] The effects of the latter group of parameters are similar for both R&D investment and the payoff it generates for the firm. However, the extensions we make in our study lead to different results. First, the distinction between absorptive (aci_i) and inventive (rdi_i) R&D implies that the learning effects of research are driven by only the investments in the build-up of absorptive capacity. Second, explicitly accounting for voluntary spillovers introduces the effect of reciprocal incentives in resource allocation and partnership formation. In addition to its own resource allocation problem, each firm takes into account the investment decisions of the potential partners.

Moreover, in contrast to CL, we model in the context of inter-firm cooperation and, therefore, concentrate on cooperation decision and innovation-driven profit rather than just on R&D investments. As it is clear from comparing (1) and (13), the parameter effects on the firm's R&D investments ($\partial RD_i/\partial\cdot$) and its payoff in terms of profit ($\partial\Pi_i/\partial\cdot$) are not necessarily similar. In Table 1 we summarise our results in comparison to CL[27] focusing on the latter group of effects (since the R&D profit presents the main motivation for firms to engage in cooperation in our study), while Fig. 3 illustrates them in detail for the cooperating and non-cooperating scenarios. With reference to this figure, we elaborate on the effects of each parameter in the following subsections. Note at this point that the results (primarily, investment allocation) illustrate the optimization outcome (see (15))—a best option out of the set of alternatives, which by no means guarantees success in innovative performance for the reasons stated earlier in this chapter.

4.3.1 Cognitive Distance

As seen from the bottom leftmost plot in Fig. 3, the cognitive distance d_{ij} between cooperating partners has an ambiguous effect on R&D profits. A small distance (which does not require absorptive investments) positively affects R&D profit. This is because the firm can dedicate most of its R&D budget to invention and it suffers little or no negative appropriation in return (top leftmost plot). In this range, R&D

[26] For the sake of comparison, CL's ease of learning is analogous to our cognitive distance, intra-industry spillovers—to appropriability conditions and technological opportunities—to external knowledge.

[27] Note that by construction, in CL firm i's marginal returns to R&D have the same effect on marginal returns generated by the firm in terms of profit.

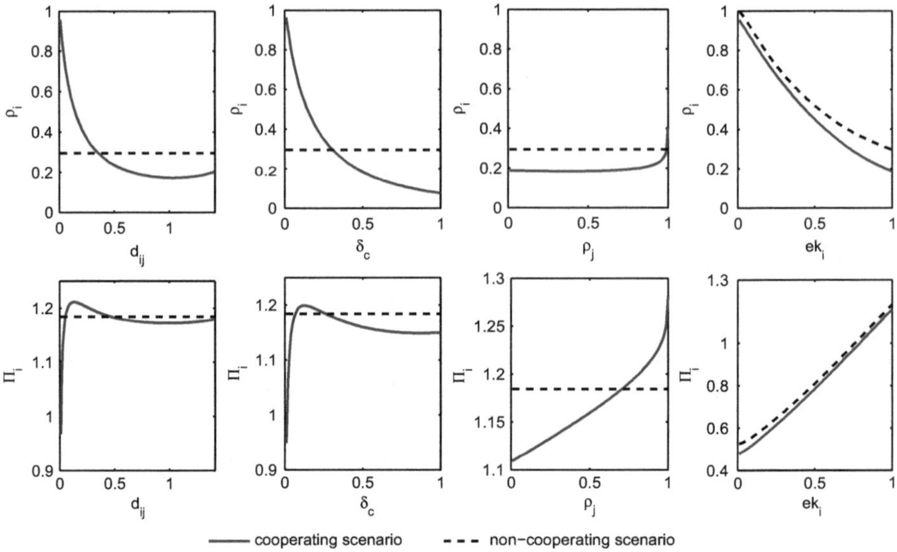

Fig. 3 Comparative statics for the investments (ρ_i) and profits (Π_i) of firms

profits in the cooperation scenario consistently increase and overtake the levels in the non-cooperation scenario because the cooperating firm can complement its own knowledge with increasingly novel knowledge from the partner. This, however, requires raising investments in absorptive capacity to maintain the gain from the partner's knowledge. Consequently, inventive R&D reduces. The R&D profits also reduce since, with increasing cognitive distance, the cost of partnership in terms of spillovers increases as well.

At a very large distance, an 'understandability problem' arises such that new knowledge cannot be absorbed as efficiently any longer. This problem cannot be overcome by simply increasing investments in absorptive capacity. In this range, increasing absorptive R&D investments becomes sub-optimal, and as a result, some resources are shifted back to inventive R&D. Clearly, the standalone strategy is more lucrative only when the distance to a potential partner is either too large (understandability problem) or too small (no novelty). For a range of cognitive distance between these two extremes, the cooperative strategy is better.

Taken together, these results imply that firms' decision to cooperate and the choice of a cooperation partner is heavily influenced by the investments they are willing to make in order to establish efficient collaboration. And in contrast to CL, where the ease of learning has a strictly positive effect on R&D investments and profit when cooperation is not accounted for, the effect of cognitive distance on profit has an inverted 'U' shape in the context of cooperation.

4.3.2 Appropriability Conditions and External Knowledge

Appropriability conditions (δ_c) and external knowledge (ek) show similar effects on the amount of knowledge generated by the firm. $\partial k_i/\partial \delta_c$ and $\partial k_i/\partial ek$ are strictly positive suggesting that the appropriability conditions in a cooperative setting as well as the amount of external knowledge raise the ability of the firm i to create new knowledge from external sources. Consequently, firm i is incentivised to reallocate its investments from inventive to absorptive R&D. More resources are devoted to absorptive capacity which generally results in a higher level of new knowledge (k_i) generated from the cooperation.

However, appropriability conditions (δ_c) and external knowledge (ek) show different effects on the R&D profits generated by the firm. In contrast to ek (which has a strictly positive effect as shown in the lower rightmost plot in Fig. 3), δ_c has an ambiguous effect on R&D profit (bottom second plot in Fig. 3). On the one hand, the firm i benefits from voluntary spillovers from its cooperation partner and experiences increasing profits. As voluntary spillovers increase, the profits rise consistently and overcome the levels in the standalone strategy. On the other hand, voluntary spillovers from i also contribute to the knowledge stock of the cooperating partner. This causes a reduction in firm i's R&D profit. The combination of these two effects leads to an inverted 'U'-shaped relationship between δ_c and Π_i. This relationship is such that the cooperation is only better for an intermediate range of voluntary spillovers. When cooperation intensity is too low, the additional knowledge gained through voluntary spillovers will be too low to justify investments made to absorb it. When cooperation intensity reaches its maximum level, the threat of large spillovers is more pronounced. In both of these latter scenarios, the non-cooperative strategy is more attractive.

The ambiguous effect of δ_c on profits is necessarily affected by the absorptive R&D budget of the partner: if it is small enough, firm i can benefit from intensive cooperation not being afraid that its partner absorbs much.[28] In contrast, if the partner has sufficiently high absorptive capacity, firm i's losses from a larger δ_c can exceed its benefits. This particular result contrasts with CL where the effect of appropriability conditions is modified by the ease of learning. In our model, the effect of cognitive distance in this respect is captured in absorptive capacity which has the inverted 'U'-shaped form representing the understandability/novelty trade-off. With a very large cognitive distance the appropriability conditions may not matter at all as the partners have difficulties understanding each other.

Since technological opportunities are equally available for both cooperating and non-cooperating firms, R&D profit in relation to ek is only dependent on the firm's absorptive capacity (see Eq. (12)). The relationship varies because of the different number of factors involved—for the cooperating and non-cooperating scenarios—

[28]For instance, setting investment decision of the partner $\rho_j = 0.75$, Π_i in the cooperating scenario shows only a small downturn and then rises consistently outperforming the non-cooperating scenario.

in the firm's optimal decision making (see Appendix 1). In particular, when the cost of cooperation is high, as in the representative case that we analyse, the non-cooperative strategy consistently yields superior performance benefits (lower rightmost plot in Fig. 3). This result is reversed at lower levels of cooperation intensity (e.g. at $\delta_c = 0.2$).

4.3.3 R&D Investments and Absorptive Capacity

The investment decision of the partner ρ_j has an ambiguous effect on firm i's investment allocation, but not on its profit (where it is strictly positive). This is because as ρ_j increases, it contributes to the pool of external knowledge i can benefit from. This creates an incentive to increase investments in absorptive capacity. However, ρ_j reaching its maximum values (close to 1) implies that the cooperating partner invests very little in the build-up of absorptive capacity. Thus, knowledge spillovers from firm i to j that can be absorbed do not present a big threat for firm i's inventive R&D any longer. This leads to a large change in i's investment allocation and, consequently, its R&D profit. In this context, the non-cooperative strategy is more lucrative only when the partner mostly invests in absorbing knowledge and not in its generation ('free rider' problem). When the partner heavily invests in invention, it is obviously better to cooperate.

5 Conclusion

In this paper we set out to model absorptive capacity within the framework of inter-firm cooperation such that the capacity of a firm to appropriate external knowledge is not only a function of its R&D efforts but also of the distance from its partner. This framework allows to account for recent empirical findings and to examine factors affecting the firm's choice on whether to engage in R&D cooperation. In comparison with the original model of Cohen and Levinthal (1989), our results show some marked differences. Besides, some insights into the cooperation and R&D investment preferences of firms are provided.

First of all, the cognitive distance between a firm and its cooperation partner has an ambiguous effect on the profit generated by the firm. Thus, a firm chooses its cooperation partner conditional on the investments in absorptive capacity it is willing to make to solve the understandability/novelty trade-off. Firms possessing a larger R&D budget have the possibility to engage in cooperation with firms located further away in terms of cognitive distance. This is in keeping with empirical studies of alliance formation (Lin et al. 2012; Nooteboom et al. 2007; Wuyts et al. 2005). If the partner is too close or too far, no efficient collaboration can be established.

Next, though appropriability conditions in the framework of cooperation also have an ambiguous effect on profits, this effect does not necessarily become greater (positive) with a larger cognitive distance as in CL. At a very large cognitive distance the appropriability conditions may not matter at all as the partners cannot understand each other. In this respect, a more important variable is the partner's absorptive capacity. In our formulation, absorptive capacity is a more complex construct presenting the interaction between a firm's absorptive R&D and cognitive distance. The larger the partner's absorptive capacity, the larger the portion of knowledge spillovers that this partner can assimilate and the more risky cooperation becomes. This complex relationship, in our view, partly explains the caution that firms have in engaging in R&D cooperation and the very detailed contracts related to the respective agreements (see, e.g., Atallah 2003). The finding that cooperation is a more profitable strategy than 'going it alone' only for an intermediate range of voluntary spillovers is consistent with an empirical finding in the literature on alliances. Intense cooperation between the same firms imply increasing cognitive overlap and reducing learning and innovation potential of the alliance (Mowery et al. 1996).

Finally, external knowledge, that is knowledge available outside the framework of cooperation, as well as the partner's inventive R&D investments have positive effects on the R&D profit. While the latter distinguishes our model from CL (where such a variable is not explicitly considered), the former demonstrates an effect that somehow contradicts CL. The reason is that according to CL where R&D investments are considered as one expense item, external knowledge reduces incentives to own R&D on the one hand, but incentivises investments for absorptive capacity on the other hand. Since we distinguish between inventive and absorptive R&D, the dynamics from CL is contained in the focal firm's reaction in investment allocation, while the total effect on the R&D profit is strictly positive. Also it is clear that the knowledge about the partner's R&D investment allocation presents an important asset for any firm in our model. Ability to foresee this split allows a company to avoid opportunistic behaviour from potential partners (i.e. 'free riders' with low inventive R&D) and better resolve the two trade-offs in their decision making (optimal cognitive distance and optimal split of investments).

The analyses in this paper have been carried out for a single representative firm. This setting has allowed us to explicitly focus on a major aim of this paper, namely, analysing the condition under which it is better to cooperate in R&D than to stand alone. Although the analyses have led to some useful results, a full-blown dynamic analysis of a population of firms is potentially more interesting. Such analysis is beyond the scope of the present paper. In a follow-up paper (Savin and Egbetokun 2013), we present a dynamic model of network formation where firms ally purely for knowledge sharing and we examine the effects of networking on firm performance.

Acknowledgements Financial support from the German Science Foundation (DFG RTG 1411) is gratefully acknowledged. Thanks are due to very helpful comments and suggestions from Uwe Cantner and Robin Cowan as well as from participants at the SPRU 18th DPhil Day in Brighton, 14th International J. A. Schumpeter Society Conference in Brisbane and 6th Summer Academy on Innovation and Uncertainty in Jena. The usual disclaimers apply.

Appendix 1: Resolving the Investment Trade-Off (Eq. 14) to Find ρ_i

The objective is to obtain values of ρ_i that satisfy:

$$\frac{\partial \Pi_i}{\partial aci_i} = \frac{\partial \Pi_i}{\partial rdi_i}.$$

Recall from (13) that in case of a partnership, where i needs to optimise its investment allocation conditional upon the partner's investments,

$$\Pi = \frac{k_i}{1 + ac_{j,i}\delta_c rdi_i}.$$

Hence,

$$\frac{\partial \Pi_i}{\partial rdi_i} = \frac{\partial(\frac{k_i}{1+ac_{j,i}\delta_c rdi_i})}{\partial rdi_i} = \frac{\xi rdi_i^{\xi-1}(1 + ac_{j,i}\delta_c rdi_i) - k_i\delta_c ac_{j,i}}{(1 + ac_{j,i}\delta_c rdi_i)^2}, \tag{17}$$

$$\frac{\partial \Pi_i}{\partial aci_i} = \frac{\partial\left(\frac{k_i}{1+ac_{j,i}\delta_c rdi_i}\right)}{\partial aci_i} = \frac{(1 + ac_{j,i}\delta_c rdi_i)\left(\frac{\partial k_i}{\partial ac_i}\right) + k_i\delta_c ac_{j,i}}{(1 + ac_{j,i}\delta_c rdi_i)^2}, \tag{18}$$

where $E^i(\rho_{j,t}) = \frac{\sum_{\iota=1}^{\sigma} \rho_j^{t-\iota}}{\sigma} \Rightarrow \frac{\partial ac_{j,i}}{\partial rdi_i} = 0$ and $rd_i = RD_i - aci_i \Rightarrow \frac{\partial rdi_i}{aci_i} = -1$. Next we set (17) equal to (18) as in Eq. (14):

$$\xi rdi_i^{\xi-1}(1 + ac_{j,i}\delta_c rdi_i) - k_i\delta_c ac_{j,i} = (1 + ac_{j,i}\delta_c rdi_i)\left(\frac{\partial k_i}{\partial ac_i}\right) + k_i\delta_c ac_{j,i}$$

and collect terms:

$$\frac{\xi rdi_i^{\xi-1}}{\left(\frac{\partial k_i}{\partial ac_i}\right)} = \frac{2k_i\delta_c ac_{j,i}}{(1 + ac_{j,i}\delta_c rdi_i)}. \tag{19}$$

Recalling the expression for k_i from (11) we obtain

$$\frac{\partial k_i}{\partial ac_i} = \delta_c rdi_j\left(\frac{\partial ac_{i,j}}{\partial aci_i}\right) + ek\left(\frac{\partial ac_{i,ek}}{\partial aci_i}\right). \tag{20}$$

Accounting for the difference in d_{ij} and d_{iek} in $ac_{i,\cdot}$ (9) we obtain the derivative of the absorptive capacity function with respect to distance as follows:

$$\frac{\partial ac_{i,\cdot}}{\partial aci_i} = \frac{4\beta_2\psi d_i.aci_i^{\psi-1}}{\beta_1(1+aci_i^{\psi})^2}\left[\frac{2\beta_2 d_{i\cdot}}{\beta_1(1+aci^{\psi})}-1\right]. \tag{21}$$

Inserting (21) into (20) accordingly:

$$\begin{aligned}\frac{\partial k_i}{\partial ac_i} &= \delta_c rdi_j\left(\frac{4\beta_2\psi d_{ij}aci_i^{\psi-1}}{\beta_1(1+aci_i^{\psi})^2}\left[\frac{2\beta_2 d_{ij}}{\beta_1(1+aci^{\psi})}-1\right]\right)\\ &+ ek\left(\frac{4\beta_2\psi d_{iek}aci_i^{\psi-1}}{\beta_1(1+aci_i^{\psi})^2}\left[\frac{2\beta_2 d_{iek}}{\beta_1(1+aci^{\psi})}-1\right]\right).\end{aligned} \tag{22}$$

Note that the absorptive capacity of firm j directed on firm i is:

$$ac_{j,i} = \frac{\alpha\beta_1 d_{ij}+\alpha\beta_1 d_{ij}aci_j^{\psi}-\alpha\beta_2 d_{ij}^2}{\frac{1}{4\alpha\beta_2}\left[\alpha\beta_1(1+aci_j^{\psi})\right]^2} \quad \text{as } d_{ij}=d_{ji}. \tag{23}$$

When (22) and (23) are inserted in (19) and the latter is rearranged, we obtain

$$\begin{aligned} rdi_i = &\frac{32\beta_2^2}{\xi\alpha\beta_1^4\left(\beta_1+\beta_1 aci_j^{\psi}-\beta_2 d_{ij}\right)\left(1+aci_i^{\psi}\right)^5}\left(\delta_c rdi_j d_{ij}\left(2\beta_2 d_{ij}-\beta_1\left(1+aci_i^{\psi}\right)\right)+\right. \\ &\left.+\ ek d_{iek}\left(2\beta_2 d_{iek}-\beta_1\left(1+aci_i^{\psi}\right)\right)\right)\frac{aci_i^{\psi-1}}{rdi_i^{\xi-1}}\left(\beta_1+\beta_1 aci_j^{\psi}-\beta_2 d_{ij}\right)\cdot \\ &\cdot\left(\frac{rdi_i^{\xi}}{4\alpha\beta_2}\left(\alpha\beta_1\left(1+aci_i^{\psi}\right)\right)^2+\alpha\delta_c rdi_j d_{ij}\left(\beta_1+\beta_1 aci_i^{\psi}-\beta_2 d_{ij}\right)+\right. \\ &\left.+\ \alpha d_{iek}ek\left(\beta_1+\beta_1 aci_i^{\psi}-\beta_2 d_{iek}\right)\right)-\frac{\beta_1\left(1+aci_j^{\psi}\right)^2}{4\beta_2\delta_c d_{ij}\left(\beta_1+\beta_1 aci_j^{\psi}-\beta_2 d_{ij}\right)}. \end{aligned} \tag{24}$$

Recall from (1) that $rdi_i = \rho_i RD_i$ and $aci_i = (1-\rho_i)RD_i$; when this is applied to Eq. (24) it takes the form:

$$
\begin{aligned}
\rho_i \;=\; & \frac{32\beta_2^2}{\xi\alpha\beta_1^4 RD_i\left(\beta_1+\beta_1\left(\left(1-\rho_j\right)RD_j\right)^{\psi}-\beta_2 d_{ij}\right)\left(1+\left(\left(1-\rho_i\right)RD_i\right)^{\psi}\right)^5} \\
& \cdot\left(\delta_c\rho_j RD_j d_{ij}\left(2\beta_2 d_{ij}-\beta_1\left(1+\left(\left(1-\rho_i\right)RD_i\right)^{\psi}\right)\right)\right. \\
& \left.+\; ekd_{iek}\left(2\beta_2 d_{iek}-\beta_1\left(1+\left(\left(1-\rho_i\right)RD_i\right)^{\psi}\right)\right)\right)\frac{\left(1-\rho_i\right)^{\psi-1}RD_i^{\psi-\xi}}{\rho_i^{\xi-1}} \\
& \cdot\left(\beta_1+\beta_1\left((1-\rho_j)RD_j\right)^{\psi}-\beta_2 d_{ij}\right)\left(\frac{(\rho_i RD_i)^{\xi}}{4\alpha\beta_2}\left(\alpha\beta_1\left(1+((1-\rho_i)RD_i)^{\psi}\right)\right)^2\right. \\
& +\; \alpha\delta_c\rho_j RD_j d_{ij}\left(\beta_1+\beta_1\left((1-\rho_i)RD_i\right)^{\psi}-\beta_2 d_{ij}\right) \\
& \left.+\; \alpha d_{iek}ek\left(\beta_1+\beta_1\left((1-\rho_j)RD_j\right)^{\psi}-\beta_2 d_{iek}\right)\right) \\
& -\; \frac{\beta_1\left(1+\left((1-\rho_j)RD_j\right)^{\psi}\right)^2}{4\beta_2\delta_c d_{ij}RD_i\left(\beta_1+\beta_1\left((1-\rho_j)RD_j\right)^{\psi}-\beta_2 d_{ij}\right)}.
\end{aligned}
\tag{25}
$$

Shifting ρ_i from the left hand side to the right one, one gets $F(\rho_i) = 0$.

Remembering that for firm i performing R&D activity without a partner $\delta_c = 0$, it is straightforward to show that for this firm (25) takes a simpler form as follows:

$$
\begin{aligned}
F^a(\rho_i) \;=\; & ek\frac{4\beta_2\psi d_{iek}((1-\rho_i)RD_i)^{\psi-1}}{\beta_1(1+((1-\rho_i)RD_i)^{\psi})^2}\left(\frac{2\beta_2 d_{iek}}{\beta_1(1+((1-\rho_i)RD_i)^{\psi})}-1\right)- \\
& -\; \xi\left(\rho_i RD_i\right)^{\xi-1}=0.
\end{aligned}
\tag{26}
$$

Appendix 2: Finding Optimal Solution for $F(\rho_i)$ and $F^a(\rho_i)$ Using Heuristics

Thanks to the recent advances in computing technology, new nature-inspired optimization methods (called heuristics) tackling complex combinatorial optimization problems and detecting global optima of various objective functions have become available (Gilli and Winker 2009). Differential Evolution (DE), proposed by Storn and Price (1997), is a population based optimization technique for continuous objective functions. In short, starting with an initial population of solutions, DE updates this population by linear combination and crossover of four different solutions into one, and selects the fittest ones among the original and the updated population. This continues until some stopping criterion is met. Algorithm 1 provides a pseudocode of the DE implementation.

Algorithm 1 Pseudocode for Differential Evolution

1: Initialize parameters p, F and Ω
2: Randomly initialize $P_i^{(1)} \in \Omega, i = 1, \cdots, p$
3: **while** the stopping criterion is not met **do**
4: $\quad P^{(0)} = P^{(1)}$
5: $\quad$ **for** $i = 1$ to p **do**
6: $\quad\quad$ Generate $r_1, r_2, r_3 \in 1, \cdots, p, r_1 \neq r_2 \neq r_3 \neq i$
7: $\quad\quad$ Compute $P_i^{(\upsilon)} = P_{r_1}^{(0)} + F \times (P_{r_2}^{(0)} - P_{r_3}^{(0)})$
8: $\quad\quad$ **if** $P_i^{(\upsilon)} \in \Omega$ **then** $P_i^{(n)} = P_i^{(\upsilon)}$ **else** *repair* $P_i^{(\upsilon)}$
9: $\quad\quad$ **if** $F(P_i^{(n)}) < F(P_i^{(0)})$ **then** $P_i^{(1)} = P_i^{(n)}$ **else** $P_i^{(1)} = P_i^{(0)}$
10: $\quad$ **end for**
11: **end while**

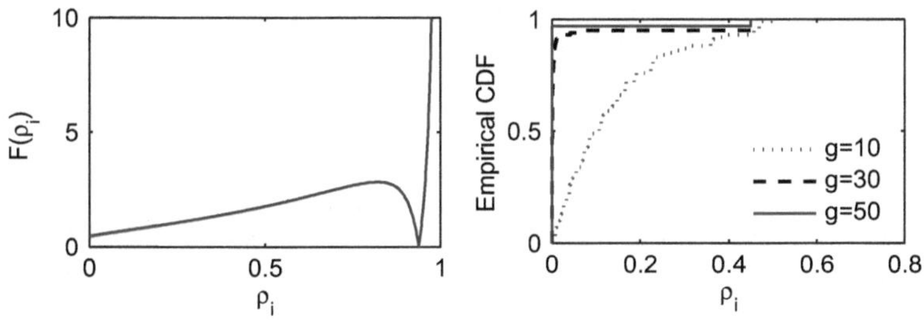

Fig. 4 $F(\rho_i)$ for different ρ_i and empirical distribution of $F(\rho_i)$ for different g

In contrast to other DE applications to optimization problems (as described in, for example, Blueschke et al. 2013), our solution is represented by a single value within $[0, 1]$ according to (1). Therefore, DE starts with a population of size p of random values drawn from $[0, 1]$ (Ω) (2:). For the same reason, current DE implementation has no need in the crossover operator (otherwise, one would have to compare $F(P_i^{(0)})$ with itself and potentially waste computational time). Tuning our DE code we set $p = 30$, $F = 0.8$ and as a stopping criterion we choose a combination of two conditions: either a maximum number of generations is reached (which is set to be equal 50[29]) or the global optimum is identified ($F(P_i^{(1)}) = 0$). To make sure that our candidate solutions constructed by linear combination (7:) satisfy our constraint on ρ_i, we explicitly check it in (8:)—and if it is not met we 'repair' it by adding/deducting one unit—before comparing its fitness with the current solutions in (9:).

As an illustration of the DE convergence for the tuning parameters stated consider Fig. 4 below. On the left plot one can see $F(\rho_i)$ simulated for different $\rho_i \in [0, 1]$, while on the right plot the cumulative density function of $F(\rho_i)$ for 100 restarts and different number of maximum generations g (10, 30 and 50) is given. Obviously, with $g = 50$ DE converges to zero (or a very close approximation of it) in almost 100 % of restarts. To ensure a good solution, therefore, we take $g = 30$ and restart

[29]At this point DE population always converges to very similar values.

DE three times. Using Matlab 7.11 on Pentium IV 3.3 GHz a single DE restart with thirty generations requires about 0.02 s.

References

Arrow K (1962) Economic welfare and the allocation of resources for invention. In: Nelson R (ed) The rate and direction of inventive activity. Princeteon University Press, Princeteon, NJ, pp 609–626

Atallah G (2003) Information sharing and the stability of cooperation in research joint ventures. Econ Innov New Technol 12(6):531–554

Bamford J, Ernst D (2002) Managing an alliance portfolio. McKinsey Q 3:29–39

Baum JAC, Cowan R, Jonard N (2010) Network-independent partner selection and the evolution of innovation networks. Manag Sci 56(11):2094–2110. doi:10.1287/mnsc.1100.1229

Blueschke D, Blueschke-Nikolaeva V, Savin I (2013) New insights into optimal control of nonlinear dynamic econometric models: application of a heuristic approach. J Econ Dyn Control 37(4):821–837

Boschma R (2005) Proximity and innovation: a critical assessment. Reg Stud 39(1):61–74

Brusoni S, Prencipe A, Pavitt K (2001) Knowledge specialization, organizational coupling, and the boundaries of the firm: why do firms know more than they make? Adm Sci Q 46(4):597–621

Cantner U, Pyka A (1998) Absorbing technological spillovers: simulations in an evolutionary framework. Ind Corp Chang 7(2):369–397

Cantner U, Meder A (2007) Technological proximity and the choice of cooperation partner. J Econ Interac Coord 2:45–65

Cassiman B, Pérez-Castrillo D, Veugelers R (2002) Endogenizing know-how flows through the nature of R&D investments. Int J Ind Organ 20(6):775–799

Cohen W, Levinthal D (1989) Innovation and learning: the two faces of R&D. Econ J 99(397): 569–596

Cowan R, Jonard N, Zimmermann J (2007) Bilateral collaboration and the emergence of innovation networks. Manag Sci 53(7):1051–1067

De Bondt R (1996) Spillovers and innovative activities. Int J Ind Organ 15(1):1–28

de Fraja G (1993) Strategic spillovers in patent-races. Int J Ind Organ 11(1):139–146

de Jong J, Freel M (2010) Absorptive capacity and the reach of collaboration in high technology small firms. Res Policy 39(1):47–54

de Man AP, Duysters G (2005) Collaboration and innovation: a review of the effects of mergers, acquisitions and alliances on innovation. Technovation 25(12):1377–1387

Dettmann A, von Proff S (2010) Inventor collaboration over distance—a comparison of academic and corporate patents. Tech. Rep. 2010–01, Working Papers on Innovation and Space

Dosi G (1982) Technological paradigms and technological trajectories: a suggested interpretation of the determinants and directions of technical change. Res Policy 11(3):147–162

Drejer I, Vindig A (2007) Searching near and far: Determinants of innovative firms' propensity to collaborate across geographical distance. Ind Innov 14(3):259–275

Fehr E, Gächter S (2000) Fairness and retaliation: the economics of reciprocity. J Econ Perspect 14:159–181

Flatten T, Engelen A, Zahra S, Brettel M (2011) A measure of absorptive capacity: scale development and validation. Eur Manag J 29(2):98–116

Gilli M, Winker P (2009) Heuristic optimization methods in econometrics. In: Belsley D, Kontoghiorghes E (eds) Handbook of computational econometrics. Wiley, Chichester, pp 81–119

Gilsing V, Nooteboom B, Vanhaverbeke W, Duysters G, van den Oord A (2008) Network embeddedness and the exploration of novel technologies: technological distance, betweenness centrality and density. Res Policy 37(10):1717–1731
Gulati R (1998) Alliances and networks. Strateg Manag J 19(4):293–317
Hall B, Jaffe A, Trajtenberg M (2005) Market value and patent citations. RAND J Econ 36(1): 16–38
Hammerschmidt A (2009) No pain, no gain: an R&D model with endogenous absorptive capacity. J Inst Theor Econ 165(3):418–437
Kamien M, Zang I (2000) Meet me halfway: research joint ventures and absorptive capacity. Int J Ind Organ 18(7):228–240
Kim L (1998) Crisis construction and organizational learning: capability building in catching-up at Hyundai motor. Organ Sci 9(4):506–521
Klepper S (1996) Entry, exit, growth, and innovation over the product life cycle. Am Econ Rev 86(3):562–583
Lane PJ, Lubatkin M (1998) Relative absorptive capacity and interorganizational learning. Strateg Manag J 19(5):461–477
Lin C, Wu YJ, Chang C, Wang W, Lee CY (2012) The alliance innovation performance of R&D alliances: the absorptive capacity perspective. Technovation 32(5):282–292
March JG (1991) Exploration and exploitation in organizational learning. Organ Sci 2(1):71–87
Mowery DC, Oxley JE, Silverman BS (1996) Strategic alliances and interfirm knowledge transfer. Strateg Manag J 17:77–91
Mowery DC, Oxley JE, Silverman BS (1998) Technological overlap and interfirm cooperation: implications for the resource-based view of the firm. Res Policy 27(5):507–523
Nooteboom B (1999) Inter-firm alliances: analysis and design. Routledge, London
Nooteboom B, Haverbeke WV, Duysters G, Gilsling V, van den Oord A (2007) Optimal cognitive distance and absorptive capacity. Res Policy 36(7):1016–1034
OECD (2005) Proposed guidelines for collecting and interpreting technological innovation data: Oslo Manual. Organisation for Economic Cooperation and Development, Paris
Oxley J (1997) Appropriability hazards and governance in strategic alliances: a transaction cost approach. J Law Econ Organ 13(2):387–409
Powell W (1998) Learning from collaboration: knowledge and networks in the biotechnology and pharmaceutical industries. Calif Manag Rev 40(3):228–240
Powell WW, Grodal S (2005) Networks of innovators. In: Fagerberg J, Mowery DC, Nelson RR (eds) Oxford handook of innovation. Oxford University Press, Oxford, chap. 3, pp 56–85
Savin I, Egbetokun A (2013) Emergence of innovation networks from R&D cooperation with endogenous absorptive capacity. Tech. Rep. 13/022, CEB Working Paper
Storn R, Price K (1997) Differential evolution: a simple and efficient adaptive scheme for global optimization over continuous spaces. J Glob Optim 11(4):341–359
Wiethaus L (2005) Absorptive capacity and connectedness: Why competing firms also adopt identical R&D approaches. Int J Ind Organ 23(5–6):467–481
Wuyts S, Colombo M, Dutta S, Noteboom B (2005) Empirical tests of optimal cognitive distance. J Econ Behav Organ 58(2):277–302
Zahra S, George G (2002) Absorptive capacity: a review, reconceptualization, and extension. Acad Manag Rev 27(2):185–203

Innovation and Finance: A Stock Flow Consistent Analysis of Great Surges of Development

Alessandro Caiani, Antoine Godin, and Stefano Lucarelli

Abstract The present work aims at contributing to the recent stream of literature which attempts to link the Neo-Schumpeterian/Evolutionary and the Post-Keynesian theory. The paper adopts the Post-Keynesian Stock Flow Consistent modeling approach to analyze the process of development triggered by the emergence of a new-innovative productive sector into the economic system. The model depicts a multi-sectorial economy composed of consumption and capital goods industries, a banking sector and two households sectors: capitalists and wage earners. Furthermore, it provides an explicit representation of the stock market. In line with the Schumpeterian tradition, our work highlights the cyclical nature of the development process and stresses the relevance of the finance-innovation nexus, analyzing the feed-back effects between the real and financial sides of the economic system. In this way we aim at setting the basis of a comprehensive and coherent framework to study the relationship between technological change, demand and finance along the structural change process triggered by technological innovation.

1 Introduction

Almost a century ago, Schumpeter (1912, 1939) argued that boom and bust cycles, inherent to the rise of innovation, are an unavoidable consequence of the way in which a capitalistic economy evolves and assimilates successive technological

We want to thank Carlota Perez, Domenico Delli Gatti, Roberto Fontana, Gennaro Zezza and an anonymous referee for their valuable comments. All remaining errors are ours.

A. Caiani (✉)
Department of Economic and Social Sciences, Marche Polytechnic University, Ancona, AN, Italy
e-mail: a.caiani@univpm.it

A. Godin
Kemmy Business School, University of Limerick, Limerick, Ireland

S. Lucarelli
Dipartimento di Scienze Aziendali, Economiche e Metodi Quantitativi, University of Bergamo, Bergamo, Italy

A. Pyka, J. Foster (eds.), *The Evolution of Economic and Innovation Systems*, Economic Complexity and Evolution, DOI 10.1007/978-3-319-13299-0_17
Reprinted from Journal of Evolutionary Economics, 24 (2), Springer 2014.

revolutions. Instead, in most orthodox macroeconomic models, technological change is treated as an exogenous stochastic shock (Castellacci 2008). Real Business Cycle Models (King and Rebelo 1999; Stadler 1994) explain the existence of persistent business fluctuations as a consequence of exogenous and unpredictable technological shocks (including negative ones), which generate fluctuating dynamics in a stochastic general-equilibrium framework grounded upon a fully-rational, forward-looking representative agent. New-Keynesian Dynamic Stochastic General Equilibrium models (Mankiw and Romer 1991; Greenwald and Stiglitz 1993), while looking instead at the role played by labor and financial market imperfections such as informational asymmetries to explain economic cycles, are nonetheless based on the same theoretical framework: when it comes to technological change, it is always treated as an exogenous shock that simply affects some coefficient of the aggregate production function. In these models, the superimposed tendency towards equilibrium (Farmer and Geanakoplos 2009) implicitly rules out any possible source of endogenous instability.

The present paper presents a Post Keynesian Stock Flow Consistent (PK-SFC afterwards) multi-sectorial model through which we aim at setting the basis of a comprehensive and coherent framework to analyze the relationship between technological change, demand and finance, along the structural change process triggered by the emergence of a new innovative sector in the economic system (i.e., similar to a Schumpeter Mark I regime). In particular, we focus on the introduction of a bundle of new, more productive investment goods, that is, of a new kind of capital good. This paper is structured as follow; this section surveys the relevant literature and highlights the aspect of novelty of our paper. Section 2 describes the model. Section 3 presents our results and we conclude in Section 4.

1.1 Innovation

Several fields of research contribute to define the background literature of the present work. A first source of inspiration is obviously represented by the literature on technological revolutions (Perez 2002), technological paradigms (Dosi 1982), and techno-economic paradigms (Freeman and Perez 1988). The common thread between these concepts is the idea that the diffusion of new technologies induces a profound change in the productive, organizational, and institutional structure of the whole economy, triggering a process of structural change. In turn, this usually exerts significant effects on investment behaviors, labor market, wealth and income distribution, thus affecting the reproduction conditions and the stability of an economic system.

In particular, the literature on Great Surges of Development (Perez 2009, 2010) has highlighted the centrality of the nexus between finance and innovation, focusing on the role played by financial capital during the successive stages of a techno-economic paradigm, and suggesting that financial instability may arise as a consequence of innovation dynamics.[1] Our paper explicitly aims at analyzing in a pervasive way the implications of technological progress by assessing the effects of innovation on different sectors and social groups during the stages of installation, deployment and exhaustion of a new techno-economic paradigm (Perez 2010). Contextually, we provide an analysis of financial markets both from the point of view of firms -looking for funding-, and from the point of view of investors -seeking remunerative opportunities-, which may help to identify the potential sources of financial instability, in particular during periods of radical technological change.

1.1.1 Innovation and demand

Our work obviously owes much to the rich evolutionary modeling literature inspired by the seminal work of Nelson and Winter (1982). For a long period, evolutionary models have mainly focused on the supply side of the economy. Since the turn of the century, these models have begun to include demand and distributive issues. In an attempt to overcome the perceived lack of *"a clear theory of other economic phenomena than technological change"* (Verspagen 2002, p.3), Neo-Schumpeterian scholars have increasingly looked at Post-Keynesian (PK) tradition.

The PK and the evolutionary approaches share similar fundamental assumptions, which facilitate their integration: fundamental uncertainty, bounded-procedural rationality, adaptive expectations, path-dependency, refusal of the reductionist approach, resulting in the famous "fallacy of composition", in favor of a holistic perspective are indeed typical elements at the base of PK models. Nevertheless, only a handful of PK authors have tried to embed innovation in their models as an endogenous factor. In particular, the impact of radical technological breakthroughs, capable of changing the entire structure of an economy as described by Schumpeter and his followers, has been almost neglected.

A first aim of the present work is to contribute to the emerging stream of literature linking Neo-Schumpeterian and PK traditions. More precisely, the paper aspires to analyze the structural change process triggered by the emergence of a cluster of innovators within a demand driven model which largely borrows from PK theory. Innovators are collected into a new sector, distinguished from old capital producers, in order to better investigate the competition process taking place between the old and new producers. The process of economic development triggered by the creation of new sectors, such as the innovative capital sector in our model, has been previously investigated by Saviotti (2004, 2008), though within a supply driven framework that left aside financial aspects.

The relationship between demand and changes in production organization structure, due to innovation dynamics, is instead at the core of the model presented in Ciarli et al. (2010). Here, changes in the organization structure affect the hierarchical

[1] This intuition has found increasing support in a number of recent empirical studies (see Mazzucato 2003; Pastor 2009, among others).

structure of wages paid to different tiers of workers, the distribution of earnings and income, and therefore aggregate demand. Yet, while their model attains stock-flow consistency on the real side, the financial side remains flawed. For example, the model does not explain how firms' temporary budget deficits are financed, nor where the money they can freely borrow on financial markets comes from. Our work attempts to overcome this drawback by providing an explicit treatment of financial markets, households portfolio choices, and firms' decisions about the funding of investments.

Within the emerging literature aiming to integrate Evolutionary and Keynesian approaches, one of the first contributions is Verspagen (2002) in which an input-output model with PK features and endogenous demand is "augmented" with evolutionary characteristics, such as the use of replicator equations to describe the evolution of some variables of interest in terms of population dynamics. Within the proposed input-output framework, technological change contributes to determine the demand from each sector for labor, capital and the intermediate goods produced by other sectors. The model thus provides an explicit and coherent representation of the real inter-sectoral relationships between the 25 sectors representing the Dutch economy, while the financial side of the economy remains unexplored.

Finally, in recent years, this mixed Evolutionary-Keynesian literature has been considerably enriched by a number of works employing Agent Based (AB, hereafter) simulation techniques (see, for example Dosi et al. 2010, 2013). At the present stage, our model adopts instead the typical aggregate perspective of PK-SFC models, subdividing the economy into macroeconomic sectors with specific functions and behaviors. The implementation of their rigorous and comprehensive accounting system is one of the most important achievements of the present work, allowing us to analyze in a pervasive and coherent way the feed-back effects between the real and financial sides the economy. Nevertheless, the adoption of a pure aggregate perspective brings about some disadvantages which will be explicitly addressed in the conclusions. We will also argue in favor of adding micro-foundations to the present SFC model along the bottom-up perspective of Agent Based Models, as a possible way to overcome these drawbacks.

1.1.2 Innovation and finance

In a capitalistic economy, the way firms finance their investment projects is crucial. Schumpeter's analysis stressed the fundamental role played by finance in fostering innovation, defining bank credit as the "monetary complement" of innovation, and entrusting banks the task of selecting "in name of the society" the people authorized to innovate (Schumpeter 1912, p.74). This explains the interest of evolutive scholars in exploring the reciprocal influence between innovation dynamics and finance. Dosi (1990) investigated how different financial set-ups may lead to different outcomes in terms of rates and modes of innovation at the industry level. A similar attention to the financial side of the economy may be found in the most recent literature on evolutionary AB models (Russo et al. 2007; Dosi et al. 2010, 2013), where this aspect is analyzed in relationship with government's fiscal policy.

Within the orthodox literature (Levine 2005) dealing with finance and growth, (King and Levine 1993a) provide cross country evidence in favor of Schumpeter's idea that the financial sector has an active role in promoting growth, opposite of what real business cycle models do. On the theoretical side, King and Levine (1993b) and Aghion and Howitt (2009) present two endogenous growth models which stress the importance of the selection function performed by financial intermediaries. However, this literature proposes to analyze the finance-innovation relationship within a framework with exogenous money and where credit is conceived as a fixed multiplier of deposits.

This approach has been criticized harshly by heterodox schools of thought, in particular by PK (see, for example, Lavoie 1992) and Circuitist scholars. Though this is not the place to deal with the critique to the deposit multiplier, it is worth noting that the formula "deposits make loans" was considered an old prejudice by Schumpeter himself (Graziani 2003, p.82). According to Schumpeter, the creation of money "ex novo" by the banking sector was the typical way in which a capitalistic society allowed entrepreneurs-innovators to enter the market. In Schumpeter's *Theory of Development* (1912) the supply of loans fundamentally depended upon entrepreneurial demand for credit, so that the stock of money was endogenously determined.

The endogeneity of money constitutes, in our opinion, a further ground of natural convergence between the Neo-Schumpeterian and the PK traditions. In the *Treatise on Money*, Keynes himself clearly described the endogenous nature of money. Prominent Post-Keynesians, such as Robinson and Kaldor, have long asserted that the money stock is endogenous. More recently, the PK-SFC approach was precisely developed around the question "where does money come from? And where does it go?" By developing a multi-sectorial model to analyze medium and long term economic cycles triggered by technological change, our paper thus aims at providing a more systematic analysis of the finance-innovation nexus.

1.2 *Of stocks and flows*

We believe that the adoption of the PK-FSC methodology can help to build a new and coherent framework to analyze the process of development described by a Schumpeter Mark I regime within a "monetary theory of production" framework as the one implicit in Schumpeter's own theory of money. This will contribute in improving our understanding of the pervasive effects generated by innovation and technological change.

The PK-SFC approach is based on the seminal works of Wynne Godley and James Tobin.[2] SFC models are consistent in that every monetary flow, in accordance with the double-entry book keeping logic, is recorded as a payment for one sector and a receipt for another sector, and every financial stock is recorded as an asset for a sector and a liability for another sector. Flows and stocks are recorded in matrices where the different sectors composing the economy are represented in their columns, while the rows show the different types of flows/stocks for each period. For consistency to hold, the sums of flows and stocks along each column and each row of the matrices must be nil.

These models thus provide an integrated picture of the real and financial sides of an economic system which allows to address fundamental questions such as: What form does personal saving take? Where does any excess of sectoral income over expenditure actually go to? Which sector provides the counterpart to every transaction in assets? Where does the finance for investment come from? How are budget deficits financed? In other words, the adoption of an SFC methodology eliminates black holes in accounting for real and nominal stocks and flows, acting as a "energy conservation principle" for economic theory. This makes PK-SFC models particularly suitable to theoretical frameworks based on endogenous money.

Nevertheless, albeit finance in its various form has been thoroughly analyzed within the PK-SFC literature,[3] the process of innovation and its relation to finance has not been investigated yet. We argue that through their rigorous and comprehensive accounting framework, PK-SFC models may significantly help to track the flows of funds resulting from the emergence of a cluster of innovations in the system, and its impact on real and financial stocks. In particular, we argue that the adoption of a multi-sectorial PK-SFC approach significantly improves our understanding of the dynamics of prices, wages, profits, income distribution, employment, and wealth across the various segments of the economy, and over time.

2 The model

The economy at hand presents two household sectors: wage earners and capitalists. Wage earners offer labor in exchange for a wage and capitalists own the firms through shares and receive dividends from firms and banks. Both sectors consume part of their income and save the rest, thus building a stock of financial wealth. While wage earners' savings are held as cash, capitalists distribute their financial wealth among four assets, money and three types of

[2]See Caverzasi and Godin (2013) for historical reviews of the emergence of SFC and Godley and Lavoie (2007) for extensive modeling examples.

[3]See, among the others, Zezza (2008), van Treeck (2009), Le Heron et al. (2012).

shares issued by each productive sector, their portfolio choice being each asset expected return rate. All productive sectors need capital to produce their own good. Consumption good firms invest either in traditional or in innovative capital goods, their choice being based on relative costs (depending on the price and productivity of each capital). Traditional capital firms produce their output using only traditional capital. Innovative capital firms produce at first with the traditional capital good,[4] while in the successive periods, they employ only innovative capital goods.

Each industry has three separate sources of finance: retained earnings, new emission of equities and bank credit. This implies that firms decide not only how much to invest but also how to finance their investment. Their financing decision is based on the pecking order theory of finance, privileging internal resources. The choice between the two kind of external finance is based on their relative costs. On the other hand, banks apply different rates of interest, on the basis of the perceived reliability of each borrower sector.

Finally, investors portfolio choices depend on expectation of dividends, capital gains and profits related to the different types of securities. In this way, the model aims at providing an explanation of technological rooted economic cycles that explicitly takes into account the interaction between real and financial sides of the economy. The adoption of an SFC framework is a key aspect in this respect since it avoids black boxes between between real and nominal variables.

2.1 Households

In each period, all households, whether they are capitalists or wage earners, decide how much to consume. Real consumption[5] level c is a function of expected real disposable income yd^e and previous period real wealth v_{-1} (2.1), with α_1 and α_2 respectively representing the propensities to consume out of income and wealth. Households form backward-looking expectations on their disposable income, by using an average over the last four periods. Expected real disposable income, defined à la Haig-Simons (Godley and Lavoie 2007), is equal to real expected income minus the inflationary impact on wealth (2.2), with p_c and π_c representing respectively consumption goods price and its rate of inflation. Nominal consumption is then

[4] Schumpeter in fact argued that *"the carrying into effect of an innovation involves, not primarily an increase in existing factors of production, but the shifting of existing factors from old to new uses"* (Schumpeter 1964/1939, p.110). Production of the innovative good takes time to come into effect. Hence the first effect of the appearance of entrepreneurial demand is an increase in the demand for traditional capital goods.

[5] We adopt the convention of using capital letters to refer to nominal variables and lowercase letters for real variables.

computed using consumption goods price. All nominal income that is not spent is saved, increasing the stock of nominal wealth ($\Delta V = YD - C$).

$$c = \alpha_1.yd^e + \alpha_2.v_{-1} \tag{2.1}$$

$$yd^e = YD^e / p_c - \pi_c V_{-1} / p_c \tag{2.2}$$

Wage earner's nominal income is composed of wages received from all industries (2.3). Wage earners save all their wealth as cash ($M_w = V_w$).

$$YD_w = W_c N_c + W_k N_k + W_i N_i \tag{2.3}$$

Capitalists' disposable income (2.4) is composed of dividends FD from all industries, as well as from banks, plus capital gains, thus accounting for their impact on capitalists' consumption behavior (Godley and Lavoie 2007, p.140). $e_{j,-1}$ and $\Delta p_{j,e}$ represent respectively the total number of shares of sector j at time $t-1$ and the variation of their price during the last period (2.5).

$$YD_c = FD_c + FD_k + FD_i + FD_b + CG \tag{2.4}$$

$$CG = \sum_{j \in c,k,i} e_{j,-1} \Delta p_{j,e} \tag{2.5}$$

Capitalists' wealth V_c is formed by the sum of cash (M_c) and equities, $V_{ec} = e_c\, p_{c,e} + e_k\, p_{k,e} + e_i\, p_{i,e}$, (2.6). Capitalists hold cash for two reasons. The first one is cash holding as a fraction β_c of consumption ($M_c^{d,c}$, 2.7). The second one is as a store of wealth ($M_c^{d,f}$) and will be described in the portfolio decision hereafter.

$$V_c = M_c^h + V_{ec} \tag{2.6}$$

$$M_c^{d,c} = \beta_c C_c \tag{2.7}$$

We assume cash to be the equalizing buffer stock.[6] Capitalists' total expected wealth V_c^e depends upon previous period total wealth, expected income and consumption (2.8). The difference between total expected wealth and money used for consumption is called expected financial wealth V_{fc}^e (2.9). Indeed, this is the amount of resources that capitalists distribute between the three equities ($V_{ec} = e_c\, p_{c,e} + e_k\, p_{k,e} + e_i\, p_{i,e}$) and money ($M_c^{d,f}$) through their portfolio choice (2.10).

[6]Following Foley (1975) and many PK-SFC authors, the level of financial assets held might not be equal to their desired level, due to discrepancies between expected income, on which consumption is based, and actual income. We thus need one asset which will absorb the difference between aggregate level and aggregate desired level. In our model, as in most PK-SFC models, cash is the buffer stock asset.

Because agents have no perfect foresight, total wealth at the end of the period (2.11) is generally not equal to expected total wealth, on which the portfolio choice was based. Being money the buffer stock, capitalists end up with an amount of cash holding (M_c^h, 2.6.A) which is not generally equal to its desired level (M_c^d, 2.12).

$$V_c^e = V_{c,-1} + YD_c^e - C_c \tag{2.8}$$

$$V_{fc}^e = V_c^e - M_c^{d,c} \tag{2.9}$$

$$V_{fc}^e = V_{ec} + M_c^{d,f} \tag{2.10}$$

$$V_c = V_{c,-1} + YD_c - C_c \tag{2.11}$$

$$M_c^d = M_c^{d,c} + M_c^{d,f} \tag{2.12}$$

$$M_c^h = V_c - V_{ec} \tag{2.6.A}$$

To define capitalists' portfolio choice, we follow a Tobinesque approach (Brainard and Tobin 1968). The system of Eqs. 2.13 to 2.16 defines how capitalists distribute their expected financial wealth between the four different assets of the economy: money and the shares issued by each productive sector. Each asset return rates will impact the distribution of expected financial wealth among the assets. The parameters of this system of equation has to respect the conditions described in Brainard and Tobin (1968) and Godley and Lavoie (2007).[7]

$$M_c^{d,f} = (\lambda_{10} + \lambda_{11} RR_m + \lambda_{12} RR_c + \lambda_{13} RR_k + \lambda_{14} RR_i)\, V_{fc}^e \tag{2.13}$$

$$e_c p_{c,e} = (\lambda_{20} + \lambda_{21} RR_m + \lambda_{22} RR_c + \lambda_{23} RR_k + \lambda_{24} RR_i)\, V_{fc}^e \tag{2.14}$$

$$e_k p_{k,e} = (\lambda_{30} + \lambda_{31} RR_m + \lambda_{32} RR_c + \lambda_{33} RR_k + \lambda_{34} RR_i)\, V_{fc}^e \tag{2.15}$$

$$e_i p_{i,e} = (\lambda_{40} + \lambda_{41} RR_m + \lambda_{42} RR_c + \lambda_{43} RR_k + \lambda_{44} RR_i)\, V_{fc}^e \tag{2.16}$$

We assume that the expected real return rate on each equity is based on a weighted sum of expectations on real capital gains (cg_x^e), real dividends (r^e) and real profit rate (rg^e), all computed relative to the sector previous period market capitalization

[7] In the model, we fix only λ_{10} while λ_{20},λ_{30},λ_{40} are endogenously determined, each one being defined equal to the ratio between the potential output of the related sector and total potential output. Hence, these parameters roughly reflect the changing weight of each industry on the whole economy. Furthermore, in order to satisfy the horizontal adding-up constraints on the 4×4 matrix of coefficients λ_{11} to λ_{44}, we adopt a more stringent symmetry constraint (see Godley and Lavoie 2007, p. 145).

(2.18–2.19). Since cash does not yield any return, the expected real rate of return on money is negative when inflation is positive (2.17).

$$RR_m = \frac{-\pi_c}{1+\pi_c} \tag{2.17}$$

$$RR_x = \zeta_1\left(\frac{1+cg_x^e}{1+\pi_c}-1\right)+\zeta_2\left(\frac{1+r_x^e}{1+\pi_c}-1\right)+\zeta_3\left(\frac{1+rg_x^e}{1+\pi_c}-1\right) \tag{2.18}$$

$$cg_x^e = \frac{CG_x^e}{e_{x,-1}p_{x,e,-1}},\ r_x^e = \frac{FD_x^e}{e_{x,-1}p_{x,e,-1}},\ rg_x^e = \frac{F_x^e}{e_{x,-1}p_{x,e,-1}} \tag{2.19}$$

The supply of equities (e_c, e_k, e_k) being determined by firms (see Section 2.2.3), prices $p_{c,e}$, $p_{k,e}$, $p_{i,e}$ are such that the market clears. Expectations on nominal capital gains, dividends and the profit rate of sector $x \in \{c,k,i\}$ are defined, for simplicity reason, as the mean over the last four periods.

2.2 Productive sectors

Our model describes an economy in which, at a certain point, a new capital good is introduced in the capital good market. Once the innovative good is produced and sold, there are two different capital goods (traditional -*k*- and innovative -*i*-) and three different productive sectors (consumption -*c*-, capital -*k*- and innovative -*i*-). We can describe a technology by the couple $\{pr_{yx}, l_{yx}\}$, that is the average productivity of capital $x = k, i$, when used in sector $y = c, k, i$, and the corresponding capital labor ratio. For simplicity reasons, we assume that the productivity of each investment good and its capital-labor ratio are the same across sectors, that is the two technologies are represented by $\{pr_k, l_k\}$ and $\{pr_i, l_i\}$. The new investment good has a higher productivity of capital $pr_i > pr_k$ and we further assume that the capital-labor ratio of the two types of capital are the same: $l_k = l_i$. Notice that this implies that the productivity of labor is higher when using the innovative good.

2.2.1 Wages and unit costs

Each sector sets its nominal wage by updating wages paid in the previous period for the difference between previous period targeted (ω^T) and realized real wage (2.20), with the exogenous parameter Ω_3 determining the speed of this correction mechanism. Targeted real wage depends on that sector labor productivity $\overline{pr_x^N}$ and $\frac{N}{LF}$, the aggregate employment rate (2.21). Productivity in each sector is determined as an average of labor productivities when using the two types of capital ($pr_k l_k$, $pr_i l_i$), weighted for the shares of workers who work on them (2.22).

$$W_x = W_{x,-1} + \Omega_3 \left(\omega^T_{-1} - \frac{W_{-1}}{p_{c,-1}}\right) \tag{2.20}$$

$$\omega^T_x = \Omega_0 + \Omega_1 \log(\overline{pr^N_x}) + \Omega_2 \log\left(\frac{N}{LF}\right) \tag{2.21}$$

$$\overline{pr^N_x} = pr_k l_k \frac{N_{x,k}}{N_x} + pr_i l_i \frac{N_{x,k}}{N_x} \tag{2.22}$$

Unit labor costs are defined as the wage bill divided by real output. Given that $N = y/(pr \cdot l)$, when only one kind of capital is used unit costs reduces to $UC = WN/y = W/(pr \cdot l)$.

In the cases of the consumption good industry and the innovative firms, two kinds of capital are used: traditional and innovative.[8] Because the innovative capital is more productive, it is reasonable to assume that firms choose first to produce using innovative goods and then, using traditional goods. We thus face a non constant unit cost function depending on total output produced. If demand for sector's x goods (y_x) is lower than the maximum level of output produced by innovative goods ($y_x^{fc,i}$, 2.23), only innovative capital is used and $UC_x = W_x/pr_i l_i$. When $y_x > y_x^{fc,i}$, both capital are used and unit costs depend on wages, employment and output. Total output is produced using both capital following Eq. 2.24 where $u_{x,k}$ is the utilization rate of traditional capital in sector x (2.25). Employment is determined through the capital-labor ratio of each type of capital multiplied by their respective utilization rates (2.26). Unit labor costs, in this case take the form Eq. 2.27, using the assumption $l_k = l_i$.

$$y_x^{fc,i} = i.pr_i \tag{2.23}$$

$$y_x = i_x.pr_i + u_{x,k} k_x.pr_k \tag{2.24}$$

$$u_{x,k} = \frac{y_x - y_x^{fc,i}}{k_x.pr_k} \tag{2.25}$$

$$N_x = \frac{i_x}{l_i} + u_{x,k}\frac{k_x}{l_k} \tag{2.26}$$

$$UC_x = W_x \frac{y_x + i_x(pr_k - pr_i)}{l_i pr_k y_x} \tag{2.27}$$

[8]In fact, the overall capital stock of the innovative sector includes both kinds of capital, till the stock of traditional capital bought when entering the market depreciated.

2.2.2 Pricing decision and investment

Prices are Kaleckian mark-up on unit labor costs (2.28). Following Lavoie (1992), the mark-up (ϕ_x, 2.29) is endogenously determined through r_x^T - the desired return on capital in sector x - expected output and expected unit costs, y_x^e and $UC_x(y_x^e)$ respectively. Expected output growth is inversely proportional to their price growth rate p_x(2.30), that is firms expect their demand to decrease when the price of their output increases, and vice-versa.

$$p_x = (1 + \phi_x)UC_x(y_x^e) \tag{2.28}$$

$$\phi_x = \frac{r_x^T(p_{k,-1}k_{x,-1} + p_{i,-1}i_{x,-1})}{UC_x(y_x^e)y_x^e} \tag{2.29}$$

$$y_x^e = y_{x,-1}(1 - \pi_x) \tag{2.30}$$

Desired productive capacity rate of growth ($g_{y,x}$, 2.31) is a function of expected capacity utilization (u_x^e, 2.32), real interest rates $rr_{l,x}$,[9] leverage level (λ_x, 2.33) and Tobin's q (q_x, 2.34).

$$g_{y,x} = \eta_0 + \eta_1 u_x^e - \eta_2 rr_{l,x}\lambda_{x,-1} + \eta_3 q_{x,-1} \tag{2.31}$$

$$u_x^e = \frac{y_x^e}{k_{x,-1}.pr_k + i_{x,-1}.pr_i} \tag{2.32}$$

$$\lambda_x = \frac{L_x}{k_x.p_k + i_x.p_i} \tag{2.33}$$

$$q_x = \frac{e_x.p_{x,e}}{k_x.p_k + i_x.p_i} \tag{2.34}$$

2.2.3 Financing decision

The financial side of our model is largely inspired by the results obtained by the ever growing empirical literature analyzing the relationship between finance and investment.[10] The common thread of these works has to be found in the observation that firms' financial structure is likely to affect their investment policies.

[9]Since firms invest in both capital goods, $rr_{l,x}$ is defined as the nominal interest rate $r_{l,x}$ deflated by capital price inflation.

[10]For an extended review of the empirical literature in this field, see Lazonick et al. (2010).

Solid arguments have been provided in favor of a pecking order theory of finance (Meyers 1984). In presence of imperfections in capital markets (e.g., information asymmetries), the cost of external finance (equity and loans) is usually high. This higher costs affect in particular young and innovative firms investing in R&D, due to the lack of collateral and the unavoidable difficulties in evaluating ex-ante their future profitability potential (Hubbard 1998). So, firms rely first of all on their retained earnings to finance investments, and resort to external financing only after they have exhausted internal resources.

While the dominance of internal finance has been widely accepted, there is no similar agreement on whether firms prefer equity issues or bank credit when looking for external finance. Mayer (1990), Hakim (1989), Vos et al. (2007) and Jarvis (2000) show that external equity seem to account only for a small portion of external finance.

On the other hand, some recent studies have highlighted how the growing importance of R&D investments may have partially changed the structure of firms' corporate finance. Mina et al. (2011) argue that the need to smooth R&D investments should lead to a preference for long term capital due to the high adjustment costs of knowledge capital, so that external equity might be preferred to bank credit. Brown et al. (2009) suggest that innovative young firms, which accounted for the 90's boom in R&D investment, almost entirely relied on internal funding or external equity through public share issues. Brown and Petersen (2009) show that stock issues by young publicly traded firms are particularly volatile and prone to stock prices movements, thus suggesting that the cost of public equity finance tends to follow the run-ups and swings in stock prices.

Therefore, while in accordance with the pecking order theory of finance we assume that firms use internal fundings as preferred source of finance, we adopt a more agnostic attitude in the definition of firms' preferences over the two sources of external finance: equities emissions and bank credit. Their shares over total external finance are then endogenously determined as a function of the rate of interest applied by banks on loans -which roughly captures the cost of credit- and past capital gains -which proxies the dependence of equity finance on stock prices dynamics in line with the observations of Brown and Petersen (2009).

Formally, we assume that firms of sector $x \in \{c, k, i\}$ always use first their profits net of interests $F_x = Y_x - W_x N_x - r_{l,x,-1} L_{x,-1}$ to finance investments. If profits are larger than their need of finance, the remaining profits are distributed as dividend, $FD_x = F_x - I_x$. If the need for finance is larger than profits, firms then have to decide how to finance the remaining part $I_{f,x} = I_x - F_x$. The share Ψ_x of investments funded by equities emission is a function of targeted return on capital (r_x^T), capital gains relative to the firm's market value, (cg_x, 2.36), and $r_{l,x}$, the interest rate on loans (2.35). The quantity e^s of new equities issued depends on firm's expected price for their equities, that we assume for simplicity equal to $p_{x,e,-1}$, the price of equities in the previous period (2.37). Finally, loans are the residual between need for finance and the quantity of funds raised by equities emission (2.38).

$$\Psi_x = \frac{1}{1+\exp\left[\psi(r^T - cg_{x,-1} - r_{l,x})\right]} \tag{2.35}$$

$$cg_x = \frac{CG_x}{p_{e,x,-1}e_{x,-1}} \tag{2.36}$$

$$e^s_x = \frac{\Psi_x I_{f,x}}{p_{e,x,-1}} \tag{2.37}$$

$$\Delta L_x = I_{f,x} - e^s_x p_{e,x} \tag{2.38}$$

2.2.4 Consumption good sector

Real demand in consumption goods is given by $y_c = c_c + c_w$. Once determined $g_{y,c}$ as described in Section 2.2.2, investment is given by Eq. 2.39.

$$inv_{y,c} = g_{y,c}y_{c,-1} + d(k_c)pr_k + d(i_c)pr_i \tag{2.39}$$

where $d(k_c)$ and $d(i_c)$ are the depreciation of, respectively, traditional and innovative capital stocks.[11]

Consumption good producers use both kinds of capital. Therefore, given the desired growth in productive capacity, they have to choose in which kind of capital to invest. Their decision is based on the relative cost of the two types of capital: $cost_k = p_k/pr_k$, $cost_i = p_i/pr_i$. However, their demand in the desired type of capital might be frustrated due to an insufficient production capacity of the producers of the desired capital. In this case, the consumption sector is forced to buy also a certain amount of the undesired type of capital in order to attain its desired growth rate.

2.2.5 Traditional capital good industry

The traditional capital good industry faces a demand depending on the investment decisions by the three productive sectors $y_k = i_{c,k}+i_{k,k}+i_{i,k}$ though $i_{i,k}$ is not nil only when innovative firms appear. Remember that traditional capital good producers only use one kind of capital, therefore they face constant unit costs. Given $g_{y,k}$, investment reduces to Eq. 2.40 as traditional capital producers only invest in traditional capital.

$$inv_{k,k} = d(k_k) + k_{k,-1}\frac{g_{y,k}}{pr_k} \tag{2.40}$$

[11] We follow Bhaduri (1972) and use a non-linear depreciation function: $d(k,t) = ke^{(t-n)}$.

2.2.6 Innovative capital good industry

When creating a new firm, entrepreneurs face the choice of how to finance their initial investment. Two solutions may be envisaged: either they resort to bank credit, or they use part of the wealth previously accumulated by their own or by others (as in the cases of joint ventures, or spin-offs from existent productive units). In the former case, new means of payments are injected into the economic system trough the new loans accorded to entrepreneurs,[12] whereas in the latter a share of financial resources already in the system is diverted from their old uses to be employed in the new productive processes. Though we recognize that both possibilities are equally relevant, both from a theoretical and historical point of view, we had to make a choice due to space and tractability reasons. Schumpeter's theory have long insisted on credit and the creation of "fiat money" in triggering the development process, defining credit as "the monetary complement of innovation". Accordingly, in the present paper, we assumed that the new sector is initially financed via credit.[13] Before entering the capital good market, innovative firms must produce their first batch of capital good. To do that, they need to buy traditional capital goods. We assume that firms and banks determine together the quantity of credit L_i that allows them to buy the amount of capital goods (k_i) required to attain an initial market share ρ, as well as a target growth rate of their productive capacity for the next period t. The exogenous parameters ρ and τ might be seen as the result of a bargain between bankers and innovators, ensuring that the firm will make profits soon enough to be able to repay part of their loans. The following system of equations determines initial output (y_i), initial stock of traditional capital (k_i), initial number of workers employed (N_i), the innovative good price (p_i), the amount of initial output that will be retained to ensure a productive capacity growth equal to t ($i_{i,i}$), and the amount that will be sold (s_i) to attain ρ:[14]

$$y_i = k_i pr_k = s_i + i_{i,i} \tag{2.41}$$

[12]Indeed, contrary to most mainstream works in which money is exogenous and credit is conceived as a multiplier of deposits (i.e., of money already in the system), the theory of endogenous money argues that money is created *ex novo* by the banking sector, dependent on demand for credit coming from the economy. This new amount of monetary means must ends up in a rise of deposits so that the reversal causal link "loans make deposits" holds. See Graziani (2003)

[13]Of course, the opposite choice could affect the results of the simulations, as the emergence of entrepreneurs could exert a different initial impact on the demand of each sector, and thus on employment, wealth and stock market prices. However, notice that in order to investigate such a case, we would only have to change our assumption concerning the initial finance of the innovative sector, while the model's structure and behavioral equations would remain unaffected.

[14]Notice that in Eq. 2.44, we assumed that the innovative sector initially pays a salary equal to that of the traditional capital sector. In the following period nominal wages will be updated following the rule already explained in Section 2.2.1

$$i_{i,i} = y_i \frac{1+\tau}{pr_i} \tag{2.42}$$

$$s_i p_i = \rho(s_i p_i + Y_{k,-1}) \tag{2.43}$$

$$p_i = \frac{W_k N_i}{y_i}(1 + \phi_i) \tag{2.44}$$

$$N_i = \frac{ki}{pr_k l_k} \tag{2.45}$$

Then, the amount of credit asked by entrepreneurs will be given by:

$$L_i = k_i p_k \tag{2.46}$$

The innovative firms sector starts producing in the next period, selling its capital to consumption good producers. The real demand they face is made up of their own investment and of the consumption good industry's investment $y_i = i_{c,i}+i_{i,i}$. Employment and unit costs follow the same rule as in the consumption good sector, since the innovative firms use both kind of capital.[15] Growth of capital stock is fixed to t until the (exogenously determined) period in which they enter the financial market, then it follows the rule presented in Section 2.2.2. Given $g_{y,i}$, investment is determined in the same way as for the consumption good sector. Before entering the financial market, all investments are financed through profits and loans. Afterwards, they follows the general rules described in Section 2.2.3.

2.3 Banking sector

Banks hold deposit accounts from both household sectors and lend cash to firms. Since we are considering a relative simple economy with endogenous money, with no government and no central banks, all the money circulating in the system (M_s) is injected through loans (L_d) and comes back to banks as deposits[16] (2.48). Banks only source of revenues are the interests paid by firms (2.47). Banks do not have any operating costs and, for simplicity, do not pay any interest on households cash deposits. All profits are distributed as dividends (FD_b) to capitalists. Banks accommodate loans requests ($L_d = L_s$). However, banks discriminate among different sectors by charging different interest rates based on the perceived risk of lending to the different sectors. Risk evaluation is proxied using the difference

[15] The innovative firms use both type of capital until the traditional capital bought in the first period of their life is fully depreciated.

[16] This is a standard result of a pure credit money system like the one described in our model (Graziani 2003).

between an exogenously determined benchmark return rate r_b and the average net-of-interest return rate on capital generated during the last 4 periods (2.49), (2.50).

$$FD_b = r_{l,c}L_{c,-1} + r_{l,k}L_{k,-1} + r_{l,i}L_{i,-1} \tag{2.47}$$

$$M_s = M_w + M_c,\ L_d = L_c + L_k + L_i,\ M_s = L_d \tag{2.48}$$

$$r_{l,x} = r_l\left(1 + \frac{1}{1+\exp[\kappa(\overline{r_x}-r_b)]}\right),\ x \in \{c,k,i\} \tag{2.49}$$

$$\overline{r_x} = \frac{1}{4}\sum_{n=1}^{4} \frac{F_{x,-n} - r_{l,x,-n}L_{x,-(n+1)}}{p_{k,-(n+1)}k_{x,-(n+1)} + p_{i,-(n+1)}i_{x,-(n+1)}},\ x \in \{c,k,i\} \tag{2.50}$$

3 Results

Table 1, in Appendix, contains a summary of the calibrated values used for each scenario. We fixed exogenous parameters such as productivity of labor and capital at realistic values. Other endogenous variables, such as capital stocks or wages, have been assigned an arbitrary, but plausible, initial value. Finally, in order to determine the value of all parameters that cannot be directly observed, such as portfolio choice parameters, we calibrate the steady state of the model so that relevant stock-flow norms such as wage share, capacity utilization and unemployment rate have realistic values.

We ran robustness check on fundamental equations such as the consumption, wage-setting and desired growth equations. These checks were conducted by simulating the model when setting the parameter to 90 % or 110 % of the value used in the baseline scenario, while keeping the other parameters constant. The results of these check can be found in Table 2, in Appendix. The conclusion of these tests is that while the steady-state depends on the parameters value, the dynamics of the model are not impacted qualitatively for most of the parameters. The two delicate cases concern the propensity to consume out of wealth of capitalists and the wage setting equation. When the capitalist propensity to consume out of wealth is set too low, it does not smooth the consumption function and renders the model too sensitive to the large income shock of capitalists. The wage setting parameters play a destabilizing role in the model by rendering the targeted real wage too responsive to aggregate employment movements, particularly the negative shock occurring when the traditional sector leaves the market. This thus depresses disposable income of workers and hence consumption. For all these cases, we observe a threshold effect which destabilizes the model when the parameter is set too high or too low. However, when changing the value of the parameter away from that threshold, the model remains stable.

3.1 *The baseline*

During each simulation, the economy faces three different shocks: (i) the emergence of the innovative capital sector and the related increase of money due to the new credit accorded to entrepreneurs; (ii) the entry of the innovative sector in the stock market; (iii) the exit of the traditional capital good sector and the related drop in capitalists' wealth, due to non performing loans.

3.1.1 The rise of innovators

The first phase, starting with the appearance of entrepreneurs (period 20), is characterized by a strong increase in aggregate demand. Indeed both consumption and investment grow as a result of (i) new demand in traditional capital goods implying more employment in the traditional sector, (ii) new employment in the innovative sector and (iii) more consumption arising from (i) and (ii), implying more employment in the consumption good sector, see Fig. 1 for output dynamics.

However, the rise in traditional capital demand is only temporary. Once entrepreneurs have set up their new production process, they start to sell it on the market. Note that the transition from traditional to innovative capital is rather smooth, and does not lead to a sudden drop in traditional capital output. This is due to two processes; (i) the innovative sector has limited output capacity and cannot fulfill all the demand arising from the consumption sector. This is reinforced by the fact that (ii) the consumption sector desires to grow and thus demands more and more capital goods.

While the rise of innovators and the decline of traditional producer is a rather long and structural process, the feedbacks between the financial and real economy imply short-term fluctuations. The ex-novo created money, initially injected into the system in the form of loans to innovators, increases the wealth of wage-

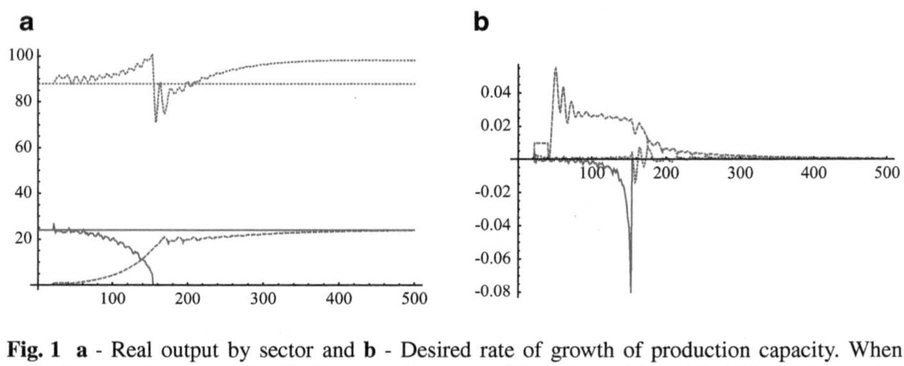

Fig. 1 **a** - Real output by sector and **b** - Desired rate of growth of production capacity. When $g_x < 0$, gross investment is nil. Consumption sector (*dotted*), traditional (*solid*) and innovative (*dashed*) capital sectors. *Straight lines* in fig.a are original levels

earners through increase of wages and employment, and the one of capitalists via increased gross and distributed profits. This leads to more liquidity entering the financial market and thus generates capital gains in both consumption and traditional capital sectors. Capital gains then feed back to the real sector, leading to increased investment (Fig. 1b) via two channels: (i) a consumption increase due to a wealth effect, triggering a new cycle of growth demand-investment-employment, and (ii) via the Tobin's q impacting investment.[17]

3.1.2 The transition between traditional and innovators

As innovative firms continue to grow in an exponential way, the situation for the traditional capital sector radically changes. The innovative sector is able to provide more and more capital goods and gains market share. This process is reinforced by the fact that the innovative sector enters the financial market in period 40, and by a decrease in investment from the traditional sector itself, due to financial aspects.

In fact, the first consequence of the innovative sector Initial Public Offering (IPO) is a boom in the investment of the innovative sector. Indeed, the innovative sector shares price rapidly rises, pulled by the increase in both gross and distributed profits, eventually rising its Tobin's q in a significant way. Furthermore, the innovative sector has used the money obtained by its IPO to partially repay its original stock of debt, thereby reducing its leverage.[18] Finally, as profits grow, the perceived reliability of innovative firms significantly improves, inducing banks to charge them a lower interest rate. All these factors add to the high rate of capacity utilization to generate sustained growth in the innovative sector. In three periods (68, 77, and 99), the level of investment is so high that retained earnings are not sufficient to fund it and firms are forced to ask for external finance.[19]

The second consequence is that the traditional capital sector market capitalization starts to fall, see Fig. 2a. The main cause for this dynamics has to be found in the process of Schumpeterian competition undergoing in the real economy. As the production capacity of the innovative sector continues to grow, the demand of traditional capital continues to fall, leading also to a fall in investment from the traditional sector. The stock of capital decreases since a constantly increasing portion of depreciated capital is no longer replaced. Furthermore, the fall in profits (gross and distributed) worsens the expected return of traditional capital sector

[17]The product of the leverage ratio for the real interest rate charged on loans is roughly constant in this phase and thus plays a minor role.

[18]This assumption is very reasonable since the innovative sector, when entering the market, used only bank credit to buy its initial stock of capital and to hire workers. Consequently, its leverage ratio was initially equal to one, by far the highest in the system (almost five times that of other sectors).

[19]It is interesting to note that in these three cases, the preferences of the innovative sectors move from external equity finance to bank loans as a consequence of the gradual reduction in the interest rate charged by banks.

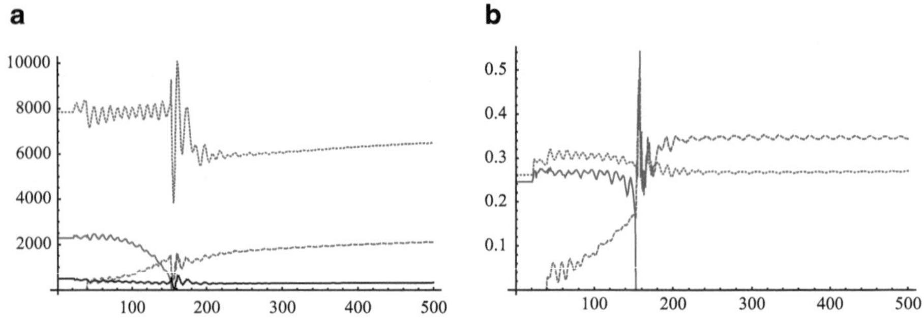

Fig. 2 **a** - Market capitalization and **b** - expected rate of return of each financial asset: money (*black*) and consumption (*gray, dotted*), traditional (*gray, solid*) and innovative (*gray, dashed*) capital sectors stocks

shares, thus generating negative expectations about capital gains which in turn further reduces expected returns, giving rise to a vicious circle (see Fig. 2b).

Beside the fall in the stock prices of the traditional capital sector, the contraction of its capital stock blows up the leverage ratio. This adds to the fact that the unrelenting reduction of profits increases the interest rate asked by banks, who are now perceiving the higher riskiness associated to the traditional capital sector, and exerts a huge negative impact on investment, notwithstanding a sharp increase in the Tobin's q and in the rate of capacity utilization due to the drop of their capital stock.[20] As its demand exponentially decreases, the traditional capital good sector goes bankrupt in period 153.

3.1.3 The fall of obsolete industries and convergence to a new Steady State

The exit of the traditional sector implies a strong shock to the economy, impacting all sectors. The default induces a non performing loan and a loss for the banking sector. This loss is transferred to banks profits that turn negative, inducing an unexpected negative income for capitalists, and a consequent drop of capitalists' wealth, see Fig. 3. The demand of consumption goods shrinks heavily (Fig. 1a) as a consequence of the contraction of capitalists' consumption,[21] and of workers' consumption, dragged down by massive unemployment increase. Wage earners' disposable income and wealth shrink (Fig. 3a and b) further reducing consumption.

[20]The interest rate increases by approximately 40 % compared to that charged at steady state, while the leverage ratio increases up to ten times between period 100 and period 153.

[21]Capitalists consumption does not fall at once since it is a function of wealth (which remains positive) and of expected disposable income (defined as the average of disposable income over the last 4 periods). Consumption remains thus roughly constant in period 153 and shrinks only in the following periods.

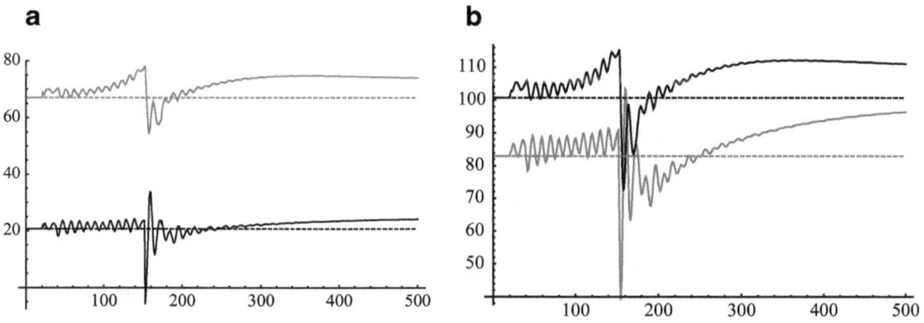

Fig. 3 **a** - Total real disposable income and **b** - real wealth of wage earners (*gray*) and capitalists (*black*). *Dashed lines* represent original levels

Furthermore, the huge loss of wealth by capitalists causes a bust of the stock market, reducing the market capitalization of the consumption sector and its Tobin's q. Consequently, $g_{y,c}$ that has been positive for many periods, now turns negative (Fig. 1b).

The shock induced by the bankruptcy of the traditional sector is only temporary. In fact, the banking sector makes negative profits only for one period and FD_b turns back positive in the next one, leading to positive income for capitalists. This tendency is only partially compensated by negative capital gains related to the contraction of capitalists financial wealth. After the initial drop, employment (and thus the disposable income of workers) starts to recover. The economy nonetheless displays a period of high volatility, mainly due to the mismatching in the timing characterizing the fall/rise of disposable income and wealth and the fall/rise of consumption. This volatility, however, tends to fade as the expectations made by capitalists and workers about their disposable income and wealth are gradually revised, thus approaching their correspondent observed values. The system then converges to the new steady state position.

The new steady state is characterized by a higher level of output. While the capital sector real output seems to converge to the previous steady state value, real output has significantly increased for the consumption sector, see Fig. 1a. In the new steady state situation, both capitalists and wage earners show a higher level of real income (Fig. 3a) and real wealth (Fig. 3b), although a slight redistribution in favor of capitalists has taken place. The employment rate is slightly below the original level. This fact is quite interesting since it means that the new technology has definitely resulted *labor-saving*, even assuming a constant capital-labor ratio for the innovative capital good, equal to that characterizing the old technology.

In the convergence towards the new steady state position, the investment function obviously plays a central role. From this point of view, it's interesting to note that while the Tobin's q of both productive sectors converge to their original levels,[22] this does not happen for the leverage ratios and the rate of capacity utilization.

3.1.4 Conclusions on the baseline scenario

The dynamics just presented show that the process of Schumpeterian competition between the two capital sectors is going hand in hand with the process of structural change of the economy. Old traditional capital has been progressively substituted by the new more innovative one, thus pushing down the unitary costs of production in both the innovative and consumption sector. At the same time, this process of "creative destruction" has pushed out of the market the traditional capital sector under the competitive pressure of entrepreneurs who finally come to dominate the market. Furthermore, our analysis highlights the complex interaction between the process of structural change taking place in the real economy and the evolution observed on financial markets.

Indeed, the dynamics of the model is definitively driven by two fundamental processes: (i) the replacement of the old capital by a new, more productive capital and (ii) financial instability arising from the emergence of a new sector. The first process is rather slow as the innovative sector is slowly building its own productive capacity, while selling the remaining part of its output to the consumption good producers.

The second process, on the other hand, is rather short. The wealth and income effects due to the introduction of new money are directly realized by both household sectors and this drives short demand cycles. Expectations are not met (at first they are too low and then they are too large), creating the first wave of financial-induced short cycles. Similarly, the second shock due to the entrance of innovative firms into the stock market increases again the volatility. Finally, the traditional sector bankruptcy, creating a massive loss to banks which is transmitted to capitalists wealth, leads to more financial instability.

Financial volatility is transmitted to the real sector via two behaviors: the consumption decision by capitalists which is based on real wealth and disposable income (which contains distributed profits and capital gains) and the investment function where Tobin's q impacts firms decision to increase or not their production capacity. In turn real economy affects financial dynamics via gross and distributed profits on one hand, and via changes in nominal wealth on the other.

3.2 More discriminative banks

This section analyzes the distributive impacts that the financial side of the economy has on real disposable income, and real output. The scenario, called *InterestRate*

[22]Or rather, the consumption sector q converges to its original value, the innovative sector Tobin's q converges to the original value of the traditional capital sector.

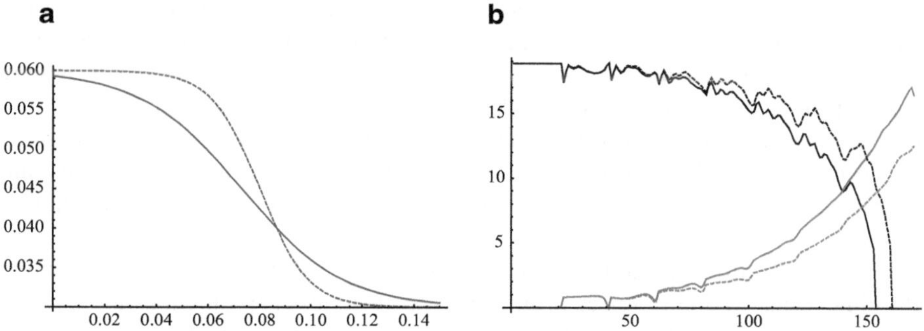

Fig. 4 **a** - Interest rate fixing curve for baseline (*solid*) and IR (*dashed*), and **b** - investment by consumption firm in traditional (*black*) and innovative (*gray*) capital for baseline (*solid*) and IR (*dashed*)

or IR, allows for banks to be more discriminative by using a steeper curve to fix the interest rate charged, see Fig. 4a. The main results of this experiment allows us to see that the traditional sector remains longer in the market (it exits at period 160 instead of 153) and that in the long run, this new curve of interest rates implies a redistribution from capitalists to wage earners and from capital good producers towards consumption good producers.

By being more discriminative, banks reduce the net profits of innovative firms who are initially perceived as riskier. This in turns reduces the growth rate of the sector in the short run and allows for traditional firms to live longer. Figure 4b shows how, in the IR scenario, the lower rate of growth of the innovative firms forces consumption good producers to invest longer in traditional capital goods.

However, the short-run impact of this different interest rate policy by banks also has an impact on the long-run. The fact that banks charge a higher interest rate for customers perceived as riskier and a lower one for the safer customer definitively implies that innovative firms obtain less funds from their IPO, due to the fact that the lower net profits realized in the the first stage of their life depress the expected return on their equities by capitalist. This implies that the debt reduction that the innovative sector can afford with the money raised through the IPO is smaller in IR than in the Baseline scenario. Furthermore, lower profits reduce the amount of internal resources to finance investment thus forcing the innovative sector to ask more external finance. Notice that, despite the higher interest rate charged by banks, the depressive effect of minor net profits and minor capital gains over the expected return rates of innovative shares, makes the share of loans over total external finance higher than in the baseline. This leads to a steady state where innovative firms have a larger level of debt than in the baseline.

Higher interest rates in the early life of the innovative sector and for the consumption sector at its steady state imply that both these sectors invest less in capital as it is perceived as less profitable. This leads to a situation where both sectors ends up with less capital stocks and a larger capacity utilization rate. This causes lower prices, since the price is computed having a fixed return rate on capital and thus if there is less idle capital, the markup on unit cost can be lower. This lower level of prices turns out to be profitable for the consumption sector as they can sell more output. Furthermore, the larger output of consumption goods more than compensates for the lower output of capital goods and total employment turns out to be larger in IR than in the Baseline scenario. Lower aggregate profits and higher wage bill imply that the wage share is slightly higher (0.67 %) in IR than in Baseline.

Finally, the market capitalization of both sectors is lower in IR than in the Baseline scenario due to lower profits. This leads to less capital gains and a lower level of financial wealth for capitalists. Since the steady state wealth level of workers is related to their income level through the consumption function, their wealth ends up higher in IR. As a result, the wealth share also turns out to be slightly favorable(0.73 %) to workers in IR. Thus, surprisingly, more discriminative interest rate settings leads to a slight redistribution from capitalists towards wage earners.

3.3 *Failure of innovators*

This section analyzes more in depth the choices made by innovative firms. We show the possibility of failure of the innovation process where innovative firms - although producing a more efficient capital - does not succeed in remaining in the market. We changed the parameters determining the entrance of innovative firms, that is the target market share when entering the market (ρ) and the fixed rate of growth pursued until entering the financial market (τ). Hence this scenario depicts a situation in which innovative firms are more aggressive when entering the market. In that scenario, called *Bigger and Faster* or BaF, $\rho = 0.05$ instead of 0.03 and t=0.013 instead of 0.01. We observe that in that case, innovative firms fail after 61 periods and leave the market.

In the BaF scenario, the innovative sector produces more output when entering the market and then grows faster for the 20 periods before its entrance on the stock market, see Fig. 5a. Obviously, this implies that the quantity of loans requested to enter the market is significantly higher in the BaF scenario than in the Baseline one and thus the innovative sector has a higher initial debt. Despite the higher debt, the leverage ratio of innovative firms tends to lower in the first periods as a consequence of the faster growth of their capital stock, financed via the higher profits allowed by the faster growth of innovators' market share. Then, as in the Baseline, the funds raised through the innovative IPO of equities in period 40 are used in the following periods to reduce the outstanding debt. However, the rise in funds collected through the innovative sector IPO is not proportional to the rise in initial debt. Indeed, while the initial credit in BaF is 172 % of the Baseline one, the BaF IPO value is only 112 % of the Baseline one, implying that a lower portion of debt will be repaid. In addition, at period 41, the final depreciation of traditional capital stock owned

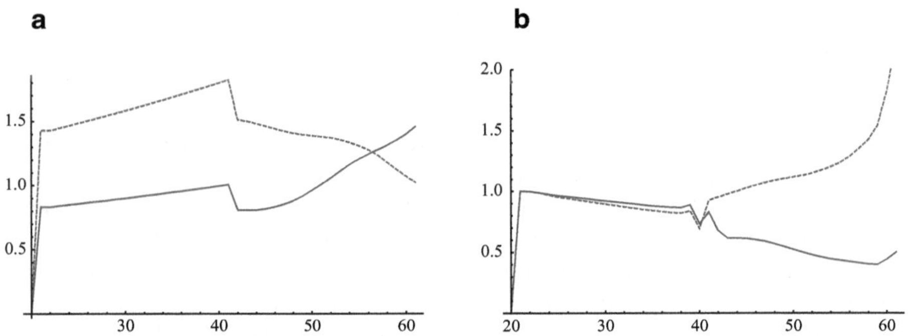

Fig. 5 **a** - Innovative sector output and **b** - leverage in the Baseline (*solid*) and BaF (*dashed*) scenarios

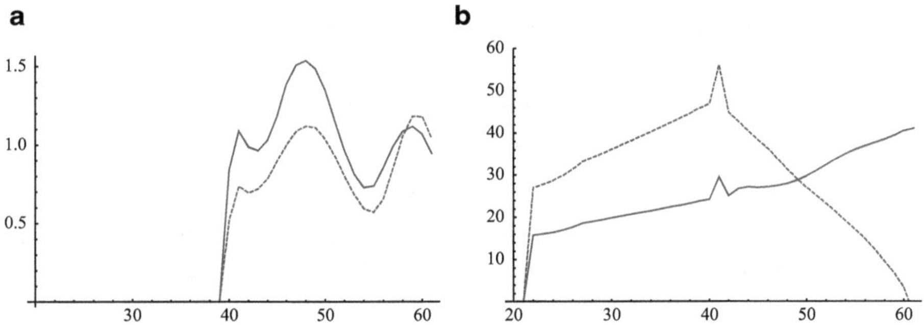

Fig. 6 **a** - Innovative sector Tobin's q and **b** - profits in the Baseline (*solid*) and BaF (*dashed*) scenarios

by the innovative sector[23] increases the leverage, just as observed in the Baseline. However, this increase is more marked in the BaF scenario due to the higher capital stock depreciating and the lower IPO value, see Fig. 5b.

Furthermore, the innovative sector Tobin's q remains significantly lower in BaF than in Baseline, because the market capitalization is lower relatively to the size of the innovative sector (i.e., the larger capital stock in BaF), see Fig. 6a. The combination of lower Tobin's q and higher leverage implies that the desired growth is dampened. While the outstanding debt is not reduced, depressed investment leads to decreasing capital, which blows the leverage ratio thus further reducing investment. As the innovative sector is not investing any more, it can sell less and less capital to the consumption sector and thus makes less and less profits. The

[23]Remember that, since we adopted an exponential depreciation function over 20 periods, rather than a less realistic linear one, the portion of capital depreciating in each period is exponentially increasing with its age.

whole dynamics starts snowballing until innovative firms stop making profits and exit the market, see Fig. 6b.

This scenario shows how a too aggressive policy by entrepreneurs, aiming to achieve rapidly a higher market share, may lead to the failure of innovators. The same innovation comes to dominate the market in the Baseline scenario while it does not in the BaF scenario. This happens due to a badly designed entrance whereas the need to grow faster induces innovators to become more indebted. This level of indebtedness should be evaluated in comparison with firms' ability to attract equity capital. Indeed, the simulations shows that even when innovative firms are making more profits, as in the BaF case, if they fail in raising enough funds to lower significantly their debt, the whole growth dynamics is then disrupted and leads to a massive failure of the innovative sector.

4 Conclusions and further developments

The experiments performed highlighted the relevance of the link between demand, finance and innovation in shaping long and short-term economic fluctuations triggered by technological change.

However, it is probably still too early to draw explicit policy implications from the model or to make a direct comparison with the results obtained by more established modeling traditions. In particular, we want to highlight some major limitations affecting the work, at the present stage. Some of them are related to the simplifying hypothesis and ad hoc assumptions that we had to make in order not to complicate further the analysis. These limits, which are in a certain measure inherent to every modeling attempt, have been already discussed throughout the paper.

On the other hand, the adoption of a pure aggregate perspective, while helping to highlight some important mechanism underlying technology rooted cycles, brings about some drawbacks. First, it contributes to make the dynamics of the model particularly crude by amplifying feedback effects and thus the impact of shocks. Entrepreneurs (i.e innovators) for example are collected in a unique innovative sector and consequently act simultaneously in a homogeneous way. Entrepreneurs thus appear *en masse* in a unique period generating a huge shock in the economic system. Similarly, the failure of an entire sector, as a consequence of the Schumpeterian process of competition among new and old producers, creates a massive and unrealistic loss for the banking sector (related to non-performing loans) and a dramatic (though transitory) peak in unemployment. This feature is also exacerbated by the fact, again related to the aggregate nature of the model that we do not account for imitative behaviors and incremental patterns of innovation.

In order to overcome these limits, we have to abandon the rigidity and the constraints imposed by the adoption of a pure macroeconomic perspective in favor of a more flexible framework, while maintaining the rigorous accountability rules implied by the PK-SFC approach. We believe that agent-based model (ABM) might prove suitable for this purpose.

Beside providing a realistic micro-foundation, another important advantage of these models is that they allow to avoid all the simplifications required in order to find a steady state. In this respect, it must also be stressed that macro-stability of a sector does not imply the micro-stability of its components. In this respect, the adoption of the bottom-up perspective of ABMs would help to highlight important features concerning the conditions determining the stability or instability of an economic system during the process of structural change triggered by innovation.

The implementation of a SFC-AB framework would also bring two further important characteristics: the possibility of different lengths of the production processes across agents, and the possibility of asynchronous decision in consumption, investment, production, and so on.

Finally, as already recognized by Schumpeter (1939, pp. 43–44) *"Aggregate conceals more than it reveals"*. The use of aggregate sectors prevents to account for intra-sectorial flows and stocks. Consequently it impedes to analyze intra-sectorial dynamics that can be of some interest, in particular when we allow for some degree of heterogeneity among agents to arise, not only across different sectors, but also within the same sector.

The possibility to explicitly account for agents' adaptive behavior during each stage of deployment of a techno-economic paradigm would thus represent a key aspect to improve our analysis of the pervasive effects of major technological shocks on both the real and financial economy. The elaboration of a SFC-AB framework along the lines just sketched above will be at the core of our future research.

A.1 Appendix: Parameters

Table A.1 Parameters

Symbol	Description	Baseline	IR	BAF
back	Number of years in the backward looking behavior	4	same	same
$\alpha_{c,1}$	Capitalists propensity to consume out of income	0.6	same	same
$\alpha_{c,2}$	Capitalists propensity to consume out of wealth	0.1	same	same
$\alpha_{w,1}$	Workers propensity to consume out of income	0.7	same	same
$\alpha_{w,2}$	Workers propensity to consume out of wealth	0.2	same	same
β_c	Capitalists share of consumption held as cash	0.3	same	same
ζ_1	Share of relative capital gain in equities return rate	0.25	same	same
ζ_2	Share of relative dividends distribution in return rate	0.375	same	same
ζ_3	Share of relative gross profit rate in return rate	0.375	same	same
λ_{10}	Portfolio choice equation (2 equities)	0.1	same	same
λ_{11}	Portfolio choice equation (2 equities)	0.208	same	same
$\lambda_{12}, \lambda_{21}, \lambda_{13}, \lambda_{31}$	Portfolio choice equation (2 equities)	−0.104	same	same
$\lambda_{22}, \lambda_{33}$	Portfolio choice equation (2 equities)	0.312	same	same
$\lambda_{23}, \lambda_{32}$	Portfolio choice equation (2 equities)	−0.208	same	same
λ_{10a}	Portfolio choice equation (3 equities)	0.1	same	same

(continued)

Table A.1 (continued)

Symbol	Description	Baseline	IR	BAF
$\lambda_{ija}, i \neq j \in \{1,4\}$	Portfolio choice equation (3 equities)	−0.104	same	same
$\lambda_{iia}, i \in \{1,4\}$	Portfolio choice equation (3 equities)	0.312	same	same
Ω_0	Real wage target, autonomous term	0.3	same	same
Ω_1	Real wage target, productivity term	0.1	same	same
Ω_3	Nominal wage adjustment rate	0.5	same	same
pr_k	Productivity of traditional capital	0.3	same	same
pr_i	Productivity of innovative capital	0.33	same	same
$l_k = l_i$	Capital-labor ratio of traditional capital	0.4	same	same
r_x^T	Return rate on capital in sector $x = c, k, i$	0.096	same	same
η_0	Growth function, autonomous term	−0.03	same	same
η_1	Growth function, capacity utilization term	0.05	same	same
η_2	Growth function, debt cost term	−1.25	same	same
η_3	Growth function, Tobin's q term	0.05	same	same
$\eta_{0,i}$	Growth function, innovative sector autonomous term	0.06	same	same
$\eta_{3,i}$	Growth function, innovative Tobin's q term	0.01	same	same
ψ_x	Equities emission parameter, $x = c, k, i$	10	same	same
n	Life length of capital	20	same	same
LF	Labour force	1000	same	same
entry	Period for entry in the financial market	40	same	same
ρ	Targeted market share for innovators	0.03	0.03	**0.05**
t	Targeted growth rate for innovators	0.01	0.01	**0.013**
r_l	Interest rate setting parameter	0.03	same	same
r_b	Interest rate setting parameter	0.073	**0.08**	0.073
κ	Interest rate setting parameter	51.28	**106.371**	51.28

IR: *InterestRate* scenario, BAF: *Bigger and Faster* scenario

Table A.2 Robustness check

Symbol	Description	90%	110%
$\alpha_{c,1}$	Capitalists propensity to consume out of income	Slower	Slower
$\alpha_{c,2}$	Capitalists propensity to consume out of wealth	KO	Slower
$\alpha_{w,1}$	Wage earners propensity to consume out of income	Slower	Faster
$\alpha_{w,2}$	Wage earners propensity to consume out of wealth	Slower	Faster
Ω_0	Real wage target, autonomous term	KO	Faster
Ω_2	Real wage target, aggregate employment term	Faster	KO
Ω_3	Nominal wage adjustment rate	Similar	Similar
η_1	Growth function, capacity utilization term	Similar	Similar
η_2	Growth function, debt cost term	Similar	Slower
η_3	Growth function, Tobin's q term	Slower	Faster

References

Aghion P, Howitt PW (2009) The economics of growth. The MIT Press, Cambridge
Bhaduri A (1972) Unwanted amortisation funds. Econ J 82(326):674–677
Brainard WC, Tobin J (1968) Am Econ Rev 58(2):99–122
Brown JR, Fazzari SM, Petersen BC (2009) Financing innovation and growth: cash flow, external Equity, and the 1990s R&D boom. J Finance 64(1):151–185
Brown JR, Petersen B (2009) Why has the investment-cash flow sensitivity declined so sharply? rising r&d and equity market developments. J Bank Finance 33-5:971–984
Castellacci F (2008) Innovation and the competitiveness of industries: comparing the mainstream and the evolutionary approaches. Technol Forecast Soc Chang 75(7):984–1006
Caverzasi E, Godin A (2013) Stock-flow consistent modeling trough the ages. Working Papers 745, Levy Economics Institute of Bard Callege
Ciarli T, Lorentz A, Savona M, Valente M (2010) The effect of consumption and production structure growth and distribution. A micro to macro model. Metroeconomica 61(1):180–218
Dosi G (1982) Technological paradigms and technological trajectories: a suggested interpretation of the determinants and directions of technical change. Res Policy 11(3):147–162
Dosi G (1990) Finance, innovation and industrial change. J Econ Behav Organ 13(3)
Dosi G, Fagiolo G, Napoletano M, Roventini A (2013) Income distribution, credit and fiscal policies in an agent-based keynesian model. J Econ Dyn Control 37-8:1598–1625
Dosi G, Fagiolo G, Roventini A (2010) Schumpeter meeting keynes: a policy-friendly model of endogenous growth and business cycles. J Econ Dyn Control 34(9):1748–1767
Farmer J, Geanakoplos J (2009) The virtues and vices of equilibrium and the future of financial economics. Complexity 14-3:11–38
Foley D (1975) On two specifications of asset equilibrium in macroeconomic models. J Polit Econ 83-2(2):303–324
Freeman C, Perez C (1988) Structural crises of adjustment, business cycles and investment behaviour. In: Dosi G, Freeman C, Nelson R, Silverberg G, Soete L (eds) Technical change and economic theory. Pinter, London and New York, pp 38–66
Godley W, Lavoie M (2007) Monetary economics an integrated approach to credit, money, income, production and wealth. Palgrave MacMillan, New York
Graziani A (2003) The monetary theory of production. Cambridge University Press, Cambridge
Greenwald BC, Stiglitz JE (1993) Financial market imperfections and business cycles. Q J Econ 108(1):77–114
Hakim C (1989) Identifying fast growth small firms. Employment Gazette 27:29–41
Hubbard R (1998) Capital-market imperfections and investment. J Econ Lit 36-1:193–225
Jarvis R (2000) Finance and the small firm. In: Carter S, Jones-Evans D (eds) Enterprise and small business: principles, practice and policy. FT Prentice Hall
King R, Levine R (1993a) Finance and growth: Schumpeter might be right. Q J Econ 108:717–738
King R, Levine R (1993b) Finance, entrepreneurship, and growth: Theory and evidence. J Monet Econ 32:513–542
King RG, Rebelo ST (1999) Resuscitating real business cycles. Handb Macroecon 1:927–1007
Lavoie M (1992) Foundations of Post-Keynesian economic analysis. Edward Elgar, Aldershot
Lazonick W, Mazzucato M, Nightingale P, Parris S (2010) Finance, innovation & growth - state of art report. Finnov Discussion Paper 1.6:44
Le Heron E, Rochon L-P, Olawoye SY (2012) Financial crisis, state of confidence and economic policies in a post-keynesian stock-flow consistent model Monetary policy and central banking - new directions in post-keynesian theory. Edward Elgar
Levine R (2005) Finance an growth: theory and evidence. In: Aghion P, Durlauf SN (eds) Handbook of economic growth. Elsevier
Mankiw NG, Romer DH (1991) New Keynesian economics, vol 2. MIT press, Cambridge
Mayer G (1990) Financial systems, corporate finance, and economic development. In: Hubbard R (ed) Asymmetric information, corporate finance, and investment. University of Chicago Press

Mazzucato M (2003) Risk, variety and volatility: growth, innovation and stock prices in early industry evolution. J Evol Econ 13:491–512
Meyers S (1984) Capital structure puzzle. J Finance 39-3:575–592
Mina A, Lahr H, Hughes A (2011) The demand and supply of external finance for innovative firms. Finnov Discussion Paper 3.5:39
Nelson R, Winter SG (1982) An evolutionary theory of economic change. Harvard University Press, Cambridge
Pastor L, Veronesi P (2009) Technological revolutions and stock prices. Am Econ Rev 99-4:1451–1483
Perez C (2002) Technological revolutions and financial capital: the dynamics of bubbles and golden Ages. Elgar, Cheltenham
Perez C (2009) The double bubble at the turn of the century: technological roots and structural implications. Camb J Econ 33-4(4):779–805
Perez C (2010) Technological revolutions and techno-economic paradigms. Camb J Econ 34-1:185–202
Russo A, Catalano M, Gaffeo E, Gallegati M, Napoletano M (2007) Industrial dynamics, fiscal policy and r&d: Evidence from a computational experiment. J Econ Behav Organ 64(3):426–447
Saviotti PP, Pyka A (2004) Economic development by the creation of new sectors. J Evol Econ 14(1):1–35
Saviotti PP, Pyka A (2008) Product variety, competition and economic growth. J Evol Econ 18(3):323–347
Schumpeter JA (1912) The theory of economic development. Harvard University Press, Cambridge, MA
Schumpeter JA (1939) Business cycle. A theoretical, historical and statistical analysis of the capitalist process. Abridged Edn., McGraw Hill, New York
Stadler GW (1994) Real business cycles. J Econ Lit 32(4):1750–1783
van Treeck T (2009) A synthetic, stock-flow consistent macroeconomic model of Financialisation. Camb J Econ 33(3):467–493
Verspagen B (2002) Evolutionary macroeconomics: a synthesis between neo-schumpeterian and post-keynesian lines of thought. The Electronic Journal of Evolutionary Modeling and Economic Dynamics, p 1007
Vos E, Yeh Y, Carter S, Tagg S (2007) The happy story of small business financing. J Bank Finance 31-9:2648–2672
Zezza G (2008) U.S. Growth, the housing market, and the distribution of income. J Post Keynesian Econ 30(3):375–401

Restless Knowledge, Capabilities and the Nature of the Mega-Firm

Harry Bloch and Stan Metcalfe

Abstract An evolutionary approach to economics recognises that the economy is an open system subject to change from within. One important evolutionary feature is the emergence of dominant firms in many important sectors of the global economy. We argue that these firms have distinguishing characteristics that contribute to their evolutionary fitness and have powerful impact on the process of innovation. We designate these firms as mega-firms.

We locate the distinctive competitive advantage of the mega-firm in its ability to cope with restless knowledge. The mega-firm imagines and then pursues its products, technology and resources. It does not take its environment as given. It develops extensive capabilities from the specialised knowledge of large numbers of individuals, thereby reaping economies through the coordination of a division of labour. Importantly, firm capabilities expand organically from the interaction of the knowledge of individuals, enhanced by introspection and creative problem solving, which provides potential protection for the firm against the ravages of creative destruction in the competitive process. Most importantly, the mega-firm organises itself to enhance innovation without destroying cohesion, which means that its structure and functions are both historically specific and changing over time. Thus, the mega-firm is a restless firm.

1 Introduction

In this essay we address a number of questions relating to the nature of the firm in modern economies. We do this using an approach that recognises the economy as an open system subject to evolutionary change from within. One important evolutionary feature is the emergence of dominant firms in many important sectors of the global economy. We argue that these firms have distinguishing characteristics that contribute to their evolutionary fitness and have powerful impact on the process

---

H. Bloch (✉) • S. Metcalfe
Curtin University, Bentley, WA, Australia
e-mail: h.bloch@curtin.edu.au

S. Metcalfe
University of Manchester, Manchester, UK

A. Pyka, J. Foster (eds.), *The Evolution of Economic and Innovation Systems*,
Economic Complexity and Evolution, DOI 10.1007/978-3-319-13299-0_18

of innovation. We designate these firms as mega-firms as they have some features earlier attributed to "megacorps" by Eichner (1976). We then pose traditional questions of "What should we expect from a theory of such firms?" and "To what extent is the form and functioning of such firms dependent on the wider set of economic contexts in which they operate?" We will show that these questions are capable of generating rather different answers to those normally associated with traditional theories of the firm.

Recognition of the development of a different species separate from the family firm of classical economics is certainly not new, with roots at least as far back as Marshall's (1920) treatment of joint-stock companies. The canal, railway and land companies of the nineteenth century certainly made their impression on the emerging industrial economy. By the second half of the twentieth century a large literature had developed that recognised the distinctive organisational and behavioural characteristics of modern large corporations, well illustrated by the Berle and Means (1932) classic, *The Modern Corporation and Private Property*. There then followed a number of theoretical contributions that built on the perceived separation of ownership and control in the large modern corporation by postulating managerial objectives as drivers of decision making. These include the aforementioned work by Eichner (1976), as well as contributions by Baumol (1958), Marris (1964) and Wood (1975).

A separate literature deals with the limits to knowledge and calculation capabilities that undermine the idea of optimisation in decision making, which applies to firms of all sizes as well as individuals. Notable early contributions are by Cyert and March (1963), Simon (1964), and Shackle (1970). A contribution with a distinctly evolutionary orientation from the same era is by Sidney Winter (2006), based on notes from a lecture in 1967 and on a RAND research paper of 1968. Here, Winter puts forth views on the requirements for a neo-Schumpeterian theory of the firm, including emphasising the importance of history, uncertainty, coordination of knowledge and the difficulties in dealing with radical change. Winter and his frequent co-author, Richard Nelson, have made important subsequent contributions to the development of the neo-Schumpeterian theory of the firm since 1967, many of which are collected in Nelson and Winter (1982). We follow in this tradition but with a particular focus on mega-firms, a sub-species of firms that we observe are particularly well suited to dealing with the evolutionary context of the modern economy. Also, our analysis focuses on the role of the internal structure and external linkages of mega-firms in the innovation process, rather than following the emphasis on the market as a selection mechanism that features in much neo-Schumpeterian literature.

Winter (2006) notes that history, dynamics and probability combine to ensure that firms differ. Firms coexist in the modern economy in a bewildering variety of sizes, scope of operations, forms of governance and strategic objectives. The vast majority of firms remain small, are privately owned and produce a limited range of products serving a narrow range of customer needs. Many of these firms have short lives, and, of those that discover longevity, a very small number grow to a size and scope of a mega-firm. In so doing, it is rarely sufficient to grow by organic means alone, rather the mega-firm achieves much of its scale and scope by transactions in the capital market, adding (and often subtracting) already existing business units in line with the development of its overarching strategies. Indeed, it is difficult to imagine the development of the mega-firm without a complementary understanding of the development of the market for corporate control. This is why, in addition to locating our subject firms in a modern economy in terms of technology and organisational innovations, we consider the instituted context of a modern economy in asking what type of firm is particularly fit in the environment there generated. Nelson and Winter (1982) provide a rich analysis of the selection mechanism that operates when firms differ and this analysis has been further developed in a substantial literature on innovation and competition as selection mechanisms.

Rather than emphasise selection, we join Richard Nelson when he famously asks "Why firms differ and why does it matter" (Nelson 1991, 2008). In general terms, the proximate differences in firm behaviour that matter are differences in the nature, design and quality of what they produce, differences in the methods they use to produce these goods, differences in the rate at which they invest to expand their capability and capacity to produce the goods, and differences in their capacity to innovate to change what they produce and the technical and business processes they use to produce and distribute it. Of course, large firms are complex organisational systems. Typically they produce more than one kind of commodity or service, often in different geographical locations, sell in different kinds of markets to customers who put their goods and services to different uses, and purchase many different kinds of input to support their production activities. Each mega-firm is typically a set of quasi-independent business units, each unit charged with a particular set of tasks, some centralised (investment planning or corporate research and development, for example), and others decentralised to the business units, such that we can conceive of the overall development of a mega-firm as a mix of developments within its constituent business units combined with the adding of new or the subtracting of existing business units under its control. These are the surface phenomena, and what we need to understand is what lies behind the content of a mega-firm's activity and why this changes as the firms develop.

The complexity of the mega-firm's organisation, the fact that it consists of multiple interdependent components connected in different ways, is the natural starting point to explain why and how these firms differ in their economic performance characteristics, the characteristics that underpin their scale, profitability, growth and innovativeness. One strand of this relates to the emergence of a sophisticated division of labour in the mega-firm and the associated capabilities, whether managerial or shop floor, to execute particular tasks and to coordinate the operation of those tasks. This is the Penrose (1959) line of capability development within an administrative framework and we shall explore it in more detail below.

But there is a perhaps more fundamental strand to contend with in explaining why task and coordination capabilities differ across mega-firms, even those working in the same trade producing broadly similar products. This is the strand that relates to the knowledge and understanding contained in the firm. The claim developed below is that activity depends on reliable belief, which is to say on knowledge that "works" in the sense that it has yet to be falsified or tested to its detriment by a rival hypothesis. If several mega-firms differ in their economic performance it is largely because they "know differently" and "conceive and solve problems differently" so we need to understand the differential processes by which firms come to know what they know and the different ways that they articulate this knowing to competitive effect. To explore this theme we must turn to the question of knowledge, information and understanding.

The firm in traditional theory operates with given technology, given products and faces given market demand and factor supply conditions that serve to constrain its behaviour. These constraints have correspondingly been the focus of analysis, particularly the comparative statics of the impact of exogenous changes in technology and factor supply conditions. What is missing is an understanding of how firms might develop from within, to use Schumpeter's phrase, how they develop endogenously and deliberatively. The modern mega-firm imagines and then pursues its products, technology and resources in an out of equilibrium fashion, it is ever transforming, never at rest because the knowledge and understanding on which it is based is never at rest. It is the archetype of Schumpeter's Mark II model of innovation by oligopolistic firms with internal research and development capability. It does not take its environment as given. It can't know the future but acts purposefully to change the constraints it faces. As Andersen (2012, pp. 646–647) notes, 'Today an important task is to operationalize the concept of macroevolution by adding microevolutionary processes that includes both innovation and selection. ... we should in this connection not ignore Schumpeter's well known Mark II model of oligopolistic competition.'

One might reasonably suggest, along with Adam Smith, that the modern economic problem is fundamentally a problem of ignorance, a problem of the limits to human understanding and its distributed nature. This is a natural consequence of intense specialisation within an ever more refined division of labour in which the fundamental scarcity relates to the limitations on human minds to conceive of and solve problems. The employees of the firm individually know a great deal but their but their knowledge is highly circumscribed and pertinent to a narrow aspect of the firm's functioning. From the wider viewpoint they are ignorant in respect to the totality of knowledge deployed by the mega-firm. How the mega-firm operates then depends on how these pools of localised knowledge are connected so that firms as complex systems may differ because of what is known within them and because the different knowings are differently connected. Connection is the province of organisation and organisation is the province of management, which is why Alfred Marshall devoted so much attention to their interdependence (Metcalfe 2007). Each firm develops its own individual way of dealing with the challenges and opportunities posed by this ignorance by pooling knowledge, pursuing new knowledge and acting on discoveries.

2 What Do Firms Know and How Do They Know It?

Like many modern evolutionary scholars, we recognise that the firm is an organisation premised upon the differentiated and distributed understandings of its present members, and that the elaborate division of labour that characterises its internal operation is reflected in the multiple kinds of internal knowing and connections with external spheres of understanding. Of course, if we were to say that a firm is knowledge based that would carry little purchase, what else could it be? All activity, all organisation, presumes some human knowing, the possession of reliable beliefs about cause and effect, and changes of activity or organisation normally follow from some change in knowing within the firm. So the issue is not the brute connection between action and reliable belief but rather the processes that generate the many different sets of reliable beliefs on which the performance of a firm is premised. Not only different kinds of knowledge are in play (chemistry versus statistical inventory control versus the characteristics of its customers, for example) but different ways of accumulating knowledge and different ways of storing and transmitting knowledge.

The chief characteristic of human knowing that we emphasise is its restless, self-transforming nature. Human beings are by nature inquisitive and although they may seek answers to the same question they will often have different answers. Indeed it is a defining aspect of success in science and enterprise precisely to formulate different answers. Humans are individuals to the extent that they think differently and are able to conjecture different answers to the same question. Different answers transform the state of knowing, such that every solution to a problem has the capacity to define further problems and the growth of human knowing becomes autocatalytic and open.

We begin to see in the light of this the fundamental reasons why firms differ. They differ because their employees conjecture differently and because the interaction and coordination between employees is organised differently. What employees conjecture differs because they are different individuals, with different capacities to understand different phenomena and different capacities to change their understandings. The firm's organisation further differentiates the learning process because of differences in the manner of learning across firms. Employees conjecture differently, they learn differently and so they imagine differently. While it might be tempting to treat the formation of conjecture as a random process, we would suggest that in fact it is a guided, path dependent process, contingent upon the particular entwining of creative ability and experience of each individual operating within the flows of information that the internal and external organisation of the firm generates.

Of course markets are organisational forms just as much as a firm is an organisational form and it was one of Marshall's great insights to see that the firm needs to match its internal organisation to generate internal economies and its external organisation to garner external economies. The two information systems have to interconnect and many of the problems that lead to the demise of firms can be traced to the imperfect interconnectedness of their internal and external organisation. In a world of distributed ignorance it is natural for things to go wrong, for a firm to find itself operating beyond the bounds of its understanding. The classic students of management such as Barnard (1938) and Drucker (1964) have always understood this point with great clarity and, as Brian Loasby (2009) has recently pointed out; this is the problem that also motivated Coase's famous analysis of the proper boundaries of a firm.

This is perhaps the most basic of the sources of business differentiation. New conjectures are constantly being added and diffused within the firm, whereas old conjectures are forgotten or even rejected. Without such a hypothesis about the dynamics of knowing it is impossible to let the firm change endogenously, impossible to conceive of innovation, and if firms conjecture differently they necessarily must come to innovate differently. Because what each firm knows is distinct and individual its knowledge is necessarily incomplete and potentially incorrect. Several consequences follow.

First, with imperfect knowledge it is impossible to avoid making mistakes in the sense of taking actions that lead to outcomes inferior to what might have been achieved on the basis of better knowledge. Thus, neoclassical equilibrium based on perfect information and Olympian rationality (possession of the same knowledge by all participants) overstates the performance to be expected from individuals, organisations or from the decentralised market. Firms can improve on the actual performance of a group of individuals by providing an environment conducive to the pooling of knowledge. All firms in a modern economy face the problem of imperfect knowledge, but it is here where the advantages of the mega-firm start to bite.

Second, much behaviour is motivated by the pursuit of knowledge through learning or discovery because, for example, new knowledge can bring greater profitability or improved working conditions. Firms contain internal and external learning networks that lead to discovery and potentially to the exploitation of these discoveries for the benefit of the group. Mega-firms are a particular feature of the modern society precisely because the exploitation of such discoveries has become critical to long-run success in a dynamic economy and the mega-firm is best able to act on discoveries in spite of uncertainty regarding the outcome.

Thirdly, differential knowledge is fundamental to understanding the distribution of individual success or failure. Hence, the control of knowledge is an important motivator of behaviour. The ability of individuals to control complex knowledge is limited. Mega-firms are better situated by size and by potential longevity to reap benefits of successfully controlling knowledge. They are also well suited to sharing the losses from failure, thereby helping to insulate individuals within the mega-firm from unfavourable consequences of uncertainty.

Let us hold to the idea that knowledge is conjecture that has been verified by experience, what does this imply about the knowledge base of any firm? The contrast is with belief, conjecture that is imagined but not verified. Knowledge and belief are states of the individual mind, but the behaviour of firms depends on joint action, on coördination within and across teams of individuals, such that it cannot be that the knowledge of the team members is randomly associated. How is it that individual knowledge and belief can be mapped over to the action of the firm? This is a matter of coordination achieved through organisation, which is particularly acute in the varied and complex activities of the mega-firm.

Coordination depends on a degree of correlation of the knowledge of the team members, that they understand their tasks in common, that when asked a question or confronted by a command they act in very similar, typically indistinguishable, ways. This is crucial, correlated behaviour is constrained behaviour, reliable behaviour that is confidently shared. The degree of sharing of course is highly uneven, depending on the context. At one level it may involve knowledge that is shared with very few others, but by degrees of generalisation we find kinds of knowing that are shared across the business department, the whole firm and indeed an entire nation. How is this necessary correlation brought about?

To understand these complex phenomena is to clarify the relation between knowledge and information. If, as we claimed above, knowledge is a property, state of, the mind, it is necessarily inseparable from the person who knows. Information, by contrast, is an expression in some form of what the individual knows, it is not knowledge per se, but rather a particular representation of that knowing. Thus, information is a public representation of private knowing that is inherently incomplete.

As is often observed, some information is expressed in codified form, in writing, in film, in sound recording and in visual demonstration (the restaurant owner better have a good sense of smell and taste too!). Codification, and the technologies on which it depends, is indeed vital for the growth of human knowing, for it creates information in durable forms, forms that can be stored and transmitted over space independently of the original act of their creation. A distinct advantage to the mega-firm is that information and communication requirements can be economised through appropriately designed organisation (Arrow 1974).

Within the firm, the requirements for effective communication of information are of two distinct kinds. On the one hand, each team requires a high level of correlated knowledge to perform specialized tasks. On the other hand, the firm as a whole requires overlapping knowledge to effect the coordination of tasks, meaning there can be gaps in correlation or at least a different degree of detail that is shared. The knowledge required for effective management of the organisation is different in detail, and perhaps in form, than that required to carry out the multitude of specialised tasks.

As we need hardly labour, information exists in many forms and is generated by widely different kinds of processes that appeal to different human senses. To interpret some new information may indeed require a considerable expenditure of time and effort in acquiring other complementary information before that new information can be read with effect. This differential capacity to transmit and receive is a fundamental aspect and consequence of the elaborate division of labour in the firm and in an economy. As pointed out above and putting it informally, individuals typically know a great deal about very little, they are trained to read some information with great facility but to be quite blind to other flows of information and the consequence is that the collective productivity of our knowledge based economy is in fact premised on large scale ignorance. We might as well speak of the ignorant society as the knowledge society for it is the feat performed in any modern economy to create wealth from knowledge by means of the widespread propagation of ignorance. There is nothing new in this claim, as Adam Smith knew very well. All of this has a considerable bearing on those approaches to the firm that treat it as an information generating and diffusing system, a system of transmitters, receptors and communication channels (Boulding 1951). The mega-firm is such a system writ large.

Moreover, as Polanyi (1958) suggests, any individual knows more than they can say and can say more than they can write. It is not necessarily the case that some forms of information are intrinsically non-codifiable, rather that, in many contexts codification would be an economic waste of resources, a process of recording very localised information soon to become obsolete. In such cases the spoken word dominates and authority, the exercise of power, is a typical correlating mechanism and it works because the messages are usually transient in their importance.

Every team-based activity will need its own language to ensure that commands are understood in the correct way, and Arrow has hinted how this system or architecture of codes is one of the major capital investments distinguishing one firm from another. Other scholars, Nonaka and Tacheuchi (1995), in particular, have stressed the importance of the tacit in internal communication processes and they are surely right to do so and thus to make clear the point that communication is more than a matter of (physical) communication channels.

Here we might add a point of some importance, given the suggestion that the boundaries of a firm are premised on a market failure in relation to the public good nature of knowledge. It is often and rightly said that information is a public good in that what is in the public domain may be accessed by many individuals other than the originator of that information and, moreover, may be used in any number of production processes. What it is not right to claim though is that the transmission of understanding can occur at zero real cost. Of course, the physical costs of transmission of information may be effectively zero but the costs of acquiring the capacity to transmit and, more fundamentally, the capacity to receive and learn from those messages is not costless. It often requires major investments in human capital. The mega-firm has this capacity writ large as well as the predilection to make this investment.

A second aspect of the interplay between information flow and the change in the distribution of human knowing is the fact that it is transformed by introspection and by reason. This is what we mean by conjecture and imagination being an independent source of further knowledge that interacts with the processes of information communication. Absent human imagination and conjecture, beliefs held within the firm would not change. No new information would be generated to challenge prevailing states of knowing, knowledge of the firm would be stationary. Innovation would not be possible without this second aspect. This is the world of the stationary state, a logical statement of what an economy could not be as long as human individuality persists.

The crucial interplay between the diversity of conjectures and the development of knowledge has a very important implication, namely that while much information flow has the effect of correlating human understanding some of it has the quite opposite effect, it de-correlates what is known. In fact our economic progress has as much depended on successive cases of decorrelation as it has on necessary correlation. Every breakthrough in science, every discovery of a lost manuscript, every invention or innovation has the effect of decorrelating the prevailing state of understanding, leading to the abandonment of prior practice and the establishment of a new consensus. That is why modern societies assign great status to the leading scientist and to the leading entrepreneur, who have much in common. They are valued because they disagreed with the prevailing state of knowing, while living in the same world as others they had the capacity to conjecture and establish that the present is not necessarily an image of the future. The successful entrepreneur is engaged in creative destruction of knowledge as well as the destruction of established market positions. As Schumpeter insisted, this is a defining feature of capitalism as it has evolved. The contrast to traditional societies, where such individuals are persecuted and their ideas suppressed, is clear, as is the difference in the rates of technical change that are achieved (Mokyr 1990, especially Chapters 7 and 8).

3 The Organisation of Knowledge and the Emergence of the Mega-Firm

For the evolutionary theory of the firm the distinction between information and knowledge presents several challenges. First, it implies that the information processes within the firm cannot be focused exclusively on correlating the understanding of its employees without risking the possibility that the firm will become ossified and overtaken by rivals who innovate. Any firm that wishes to survive must accept that, at some points in its development it has to modify or abandon in whole or in part the pattern of knowing that served it well in the past. To do this, it must establish knowledge decorrelating procedures that explicitly question its future. In any firm the pressures to adhere to what has served in the past are powerful, as it is this consistency in the application of knowledge that generates the firm's immediate performance. To challenge the status quo is to court unpopularity; to be entrepreneurial is to be subversive, to question the present understandings on which the firm operates. Schumpeter (1934) well understood in developing his Mark I model of innovation that the entrepreneurial type is rarely thanked for the fact that they have disrupted that which had worked. This is true with equal or greater force within organisations as outside, and so applies when Schumpeter (1942) recognises the shift of innovation to industrial laboratories. The mega-firm requires an effective set of processes for encouraging and protecting entrepreneurial types if they are to drive successful innovation.[1]

Secondly, the firm's present state of knowing not only enables it to read some externally generated information flows, indeed is designed specifically to do so, it also inhibits its capacity to read discordant information, precisely the information that may undermine its competitive position in its markets. As we point out above, the ability to read the external information flux requires investments in organisation and personnel, Marshall's (1920) external organisation that is needed to benefit from external economies. This external organisation has to connect with the internal organisation of the firm, not always a task that is easily accomplished. Not surprisingly, the development of effective mechanisms for handling this connection has been a key element in the emergence of the mega-firm over the past century.

What the firm can articulate on the basis of the internal distribution of knowing depends on how it is organised, on the distribution of communication channels and procedural routines that establish who can talk with whom to what effect. Important differences can be found in this regard as organisational scholars have established. Patterns of hierarchy lead to one kind of information dynamic, flatter structures, cellular forms of organisation, for example, lead to others. The point is that the evolution of the firm is deeply connected to its form of organisation. A point well recognised by Alfred Chandler (1977) in his classic discussion of the emergence of the prototypes of what we call mega-firms.

Business, like economic activity in general, is a process of problem solving but problem solving is not a finite task. Each solution typically serves to change the knowledge of those who generate it and thus to open up further problems for solution, the firm is restless because the knowings of its employees are restless. This is naturally a path dependent process and different paths lead in different directions and are traversed at different rates. Thus, mega-firms with their multi-dimensional activities and their focus on the internalisation of innovation come in many different varieties. Further, path dependency means that the fact that they differ today implies that they will continue to differ in the future—but differently.

One might be tempted to say that all of this is a matter of the growth of knowledge within and between firms but the growth metaphor is not helpful. What we have in fact is an uneven process of development of knowing qualitatively and quantitatively, some knowing is abandoned, other kinds of knowing decline in relative importance as new knowings take their place. If we see knowledge as a structure, it is a structure that changes unevenly, the idea of a balanced growth of all the elements of human knowing is indeed a strange idea.

It would be tempting to imagine that metrics can be devised to capture the different knowledge states of different firms and to a degree this is possible, patent statistics, for example, provide *prima facea* evidence that firms do indeed differ in

[1]An anonymous referee helpfully points to Drucker's (1964) example of Bell System recognising the need to shift its focus from the completion of its network to the promotion of telephone use as this new concept was deeply disturbing to many of its senior management.

what they know. But to measure more generally is to miss the point. Multiple kinds of knowledge are involved for which there is no obvious standard of reduction to a common dimension. There is no stock of knowing as if it were a homogeneous substance to match the famous "jelly or leets (steel spelt backwards)" of capital theory, rather knowledge for any firm is an organised matrix of things that are reliably known arrayed against the individuals who know them. It is naturally an uncomfortably large matrix, particularly in the case of mega-firms.

To the question "Why do firms differ?" we have answered that the differences lie in the variety of knowledge between firms. Each firm's knowledge matrix differs in the dimension of things known and the individuals who know them. Mega-firms occupy a crucial position in the distribution of matrixes across firms. Through size, scope and a focus on growth through innovation they are positioned to reap economies of specialisation that are not available to the individual entrepreneur of Schumpeter's Mark I model of development. That is fundamental, but it is a necessary and not sufficient requirement for mega-firms to be primary drivers of development in an evolutionary theory of economic change along the lines of Schumpeter's Mark II model of development.

4 Knowing and Acting in the Mega-Firm

There is a general problem in modern economies of deciding and acting in the presence of uncertainty (Levine 1997). The certainties of traditional society have been removed and replaced with an environment subject to the vagaries of restless knowledge. No matter how carefully we develop knowledge, we may be surprised by an unexpected outcome, as most action takes place in an environment of at least partial ignorance. Every action generates new information and potentially leads to a change in knowing. For understanding the nature of the mega-firm, this implies a critical distinction is between what a firm has the capability to do and what it decides to do, or in other words, between knowing and acting.

Each of the approaches mentioned in the sections above focuses on what a firm can do, but none of them mandates that a firm engage in all the activities that are within its capability (or for that matter refrains from activities outside its capabilities). When does knowledge translate into a decision to act and when does it remain an unexploited potential or, more generally, when are capabilities deployed and when not? All firms in modern societies face this question, but the larger the organisation and the more extensive its activities the more massive is the coordination problem in resolving to act.

What is known in the mega-firm extends beyond the range of things that are known by any individual within it. The mega-firm contains many individuals who know many different things and who decide and act in many different ways. The survival and performance of these firms depends greatly upon the degree of compatibility and indeed complementarity of the individual actions. Compatibility and complementarity provide coherence and coherence is essential to the effective operation of the mega-firm. Lacking coherence, the mega-firm is open to attack from both within and without. Large size and a history of successful innovation is no guarantee of a continued success or even existence, witness Lehman Brothers, General Motors and Eastman Kodak, or ICI and GEC.

Individual knowing has to be correlated to a requisite degree if a chosen task is to be implemented as desired, with the proximate expression being the emergence of routines. Routines can here be considered as templates for action. In many cases the template is rigid and doesn't permit deviation from a prescribed course of action. The division of labour can then yield gains from specialisation while minimising surprise and without the requirement of leadership. This is the task of management as opposed to leadership, providing a reliable internal environment for reaping the advantages of coordinated action. The mega-firm requires a highly developed managerial function with a substantial set of differentiated routines to deal with the range of activities with which it is engaged and the complex interrelationships that result. Chandler (1977) aptly describes this development as it applied to the development of prototype mega-firms in the US, while Williamson (1975) provides a theoretical framework for analysing the administrative structure of such firms.

Not all routines are tightly prescriptive in nature. Some guide action, but allow scope for initiative, experimentation and surprise, for example, the rules that govern the conduct of R&D in terms of the financing, choice and termination of projects. It is these routines that are particularly important for the development of the mega-firm. They are the context for learning and the generation of new knowledge. However, surprise carries danger, leading to the de-correlation of localised knowledge within the firm.

As discussed above, in the context of acting on discoveries that arise from learning and creative problem solving, firms may refrain from acting on new knowledge. When new routines displace established ones, knowledge becomes de-correlated. Action based on correlated knowledge can be widely understood and supported throughout the firm, but not so for action based on de-correlated knowledge. This is where leadership is required for action to be taken, where entrepreneurship, as in Schumpeter and Marshall, can be seen to be a special form of leadership required for implementing radical change (Witt 1998).

Care needs to be exercised in the application of leadership to overcome resistance to change when actions can lead to surprising outcomes, with some surprises having negative consequences for the firm. Where leadership is held responsible for the action, the negative outcomes may undermine confidence in the leadership and the loss of confidence is especially high among those who do not share the knowledge on which the action is based. Leadership thus requires decisions that imagine the potential gain from action against the possibility of surprises with negative consequences. Such decisions are strategic. They involve purposeful change to the scope and structure of the firm, stimulating the discovery of further knowledge and opening additional opportunities for the continuing development of the firm. It is not surprising that mega-firms with global reach and employing tens of thousands of individuals often are identified with the leadership of a single individual, such as

Bill Gates at Microsoft, Steve Jobs at Apple, Jack Welch and Jeff Immelt at General Electric or Richard Branson at Virgin.

Strategic decisions to act are taken in historical time against the background of imperfect knowledge both within the firm and of the external environment (Schumpeter 1939). Each decision has a uniqueness that defies generalisation of the type assumed in the calculus of optimisation in neoclassical economics. Two particularly extreme cases serve to illustrate the general problem.

Consider first the case where a negative surprise is a known but unlikely possibility and where the occurrence is always associated with historically specific circumstances. An example is the possibility of a catastrophic accident at a nuclear power plant, such as has occurred at Three Mile Island, Chernobyl or Fukushima. Does one refrain from building such plants because of this possibility? We can calculate an expected value of the loss associated with the accident and consider it against the expected gain from safe operation of the plant. However, the result of this calculation depends very much on the subjective probability we assign to the catastrophe. Raising the probability from 0.000001 to 0.00001 raises the expected loss tenfold, but knowledge to choose a probability in this sort of range is necessarily imprecise. Further, the occurrence of catastrophe will depend on a combination of human errors and design faults, which can't be foreseen in the specific circumstance. The usefulness of the calculation is illusory when the data on which it is based are arbitrary.

A second case is when the surprise is complete. Here, at a most basic level we have in mind the fate of firms when there are major changes in technology. For example, the shifts in motive power from human to animal to steam to fossil fuels and electricity have left many surprised firms out of business. Firms that stay with routines based on the outmoded form of motive power, agriculture with horse-drawn ploughs or steam-driven tractors, drown in the wave of creative destruction. On the other side are the firms that amass fortunes from change, who are often all too happy to claim that they correctly foresaw their success. It may be possible to undertake ex post calculations of expected value that show the decision maker has optimised, but again the calculation is illusory as it implausibly assumes knowledge is available at the time of decision when, in fact, it is only revealed as a consequence of the decision.

Leadership and entrepreneurship are responses to the absence of knowledge and, as such, are subject to dangers of ex post rationalisation. After the fact, explanations of unfavourable outcomes as the unavoidable consequences of making decisions under uncertainty may be seen as face-saving attempts to rationalise poor judgement based on inadequate knowledge. Calculating the gains and losses to firm cohesion that are associated with uncertain outcomes for a given distribution of knowledge across the firm might be possible, but the information necessary is not currently available.

The importance of leadership and entrepreneurship are well recognised in the management literature, but there is limited quantitative research into the metrics of the costs and benefits of coherence and the impact of unexpected negative consequences of decision making under uncertainty. As is generally the case with an evolutionary economy, recognition of a problem precedes its solution often by decades rather than years when the problem is complex. Learning may eventually bring the evaluation of the costs and benefits of firm coherence into the some sort of codified assessment of risk management, but that time is yet some way off.

Correlation of knowledge is but one component of forces that contribute to the cohesion in the firm. Shared knowledge may lead to shared understanding but not necessarily to shared objectives and actions. Individual interests differ across the firm, both in the narrow sense of pecuniary reward and in the broader sense of mission or purpose. Indeed, conflicting interests may actually interfere with the sharing of knowledge (Ramazzotti 2004). We have also to consider the more practical aspect of how differential knowledge connects to differential action. This is the province of the capabilities theory of the firm to which we now turn.

5 Firm's Capabilities

Utilising knowledge to undertake action requires some means of coordinating the contribution of distinctive individuals. Only individuals know, but their coordination requires them to understand some things in common. This is the problem of organisation of capabilities for effective action.

Here, we follow Penrose (1959) who is rightly recognised as providing the seminal insights into the theory of the firm in a modern economy by treating the firm as an administrative framework for developing the capabilities of a complex organisation that integrates the many levels of specialised knowledge into a functioning whole. Penrose emphasises the emergence of a sophisticated division of labour in the firm and the associated capabilities, whether managerial or shop floor, to execute particular tasks and to coordinate the operation of those tasks. The full range of firm activity is covered by Penrose, but in the modern setting it is worthwhile to emphasise areas that lie outside the production sphere, particularly the "corporate" areas of finance, information systems, human resource management, marketing and strategy. These are areas in which the explosion of the specialised knowledge of individuals, and the corresponding explosion of collective ignorance, has magnified the payoffs to complex organisations that are able to effectively coordinate individual knowledge. The Penrosian firm is the nascent mega-firm.

The Penrosian firm directs the use of bundles of resources that it either owns or rents from the market. The resources, however, are not the inputs into the productive process rather they are funds from which heterogeneous services are drawn and the services that are so drawn from any one resource depend on the other services that are available to the firm. Thus, the services derived from any given manager in a given time interval, for instance, are not simply a property of that manager but rather a potential that is to be realised, a potential that depends on the surrounding managerial team and organisational context and that, in its realisation, changes the services that are available. This is the nub of her connection between the development of the firm and the development of its managerial team, with the essential task of organisation being to act as an operator, translating the knowledge of individuals into the appropriate degree of shared understanding. As in Marshall, management is the basis of performance and management is an integrated team activity dependent on practice of working together.

The logic of firm differentiation follows immediately once we recognise the epistemic element in Penrose's theory. In order to operate effectively, the management team must develop a coherent sense of common understanding as to their respective duties and how these are coordinated in the organisation. Correlation of understanding is essential for the cohesion of the firm. But performance of any activity changes that knowing and gives rise to new understandings in the form of unexploited, latent managerial services for the firm to act upon and no two firms will develop in the same way. Thus, Penrose's firm is neither an equilibrium firm nor a uniform firm and it is this fact which makes strategy meaningful as we suggest above.

Enterprise in this scheme involves the decorrelation of understanding, the conception of alternative ways of conducting the activities of a firm and of putting the new perspectives into effect. Enterprise, like management is multi-dimensional and a given team may vary in its entrepreneurial versatility, fund raising ingenuity, ambition, and judgement in assessing and taking risks, all dimensions that impinge heavily on the development of the firm. If enterprise and innovation are at the core of what we mean by economic development, then a theory of development needs a Penrose style theory of the firm.

Penrose is quite careful to distinguish between the size of the firm and its rate of growth, or more precisely its development, when discussing the possibility of limits imposed by the difficulties of organisation. She argues there are no limits to firm size but definite limits to the rate and direction of its development. Every firm is constrained by the range of activities that can be undertaken with its existing managers and their knowledge. They will find it easier to expand in some directions than in others. Overcoming constraints to development rests on the process of integrating new managers into the firm, which requires the diversion of effort from existing managers.

In addressing the emergence of mega-firms, we view the process as more general. Penrosian firms are learning organisations. We extend this notion from the individual learning associated with the integration of new managers to collective learning associated with extending the capabilities of the organisation. Discovery through learning might send the firm off in novel directions. Of course, as suggested above, this creates tensions by challenging the correlation of knowledge on which cohesion of the firm and its effective functioning as an organisation depends. Thus, not all novel directions will be followed.

Discovery is particularly useful if the scope for expansion along the lines of existing activities is limited by the size of the market or the intensity of competition. Firms that enhance their ability to learn new things, such as through organised research and development efforts or marketing research, are that much more likely to make discoveries and alter the boundaries of their activity. Indeed, the organised pursuit of new knowledge on which to base new activities is an intuitively attractive response to the perceived limits to expansion of existing activities. The mega-firm is an organisation that largely succeeds or fails based on its ability to choose when to pursue novel directions and when to stick to its core business.

If the generation of new knowledge undermines the boundaries to the mega-firm's activities and thereby relaxes the limits on firm size, how do we place a particular mega-firm in the landscape of the economy? Government statisticians traditionally classify firms into industries based on the type of goods and services they produce, with products classified into industries generally based on related production technologies, for example, wood products, dairy products and legal services. This approach is problematic when discovery leads firms to regularly undertake new activities that don't fit within their pre-existing set of products or technologies.

An important early contribution to what we now take to be the theory of the mega-firm is by Richardson (1972), who explains the elaborate internal and external division of labour that marked the modern economy (firm). We shall say more on his contribution below, but for present purposes his key vision is to see the firm as a bundle of activities with each activity depending on the possession of specific, appropriate capabilities. He then defines capabilities in terms of "appropriate knowledge, skills and experience" that enable the firm to perform similar specialised activities, but does not allow it to engage in complementary activities that are not similar.

Penrose's view has been further developed into approaches that focus on firm competencies, dynamic capabilities and the resource-based view of the firm (Barney 1991; Dosi et al. 2002). As with the shared knowledge approach set out above, this means that the scope of the mega-firm in terms of products and technologies is fuzzy at best. Instead, the mega-firm's place in the economic landscape is defined by the competencies and resources it has for undertaking activities or, perhaps more broadly, the capabilities it can bring to bear on an activity. Even here, the boundaries to a large and complex organisation, such as the mega-firm, are subject to controversy (Ramazzotti 2004).

Of course, a firm's capabilities rest on more than just the knowledge of individuals within the firm. The practical skills of the individuals are crucial as are the firm's other tangible and intangible resources. Further, the firm's connections with other firms, individuals and organisations (governments, universities, etc.) invariably play a key role in constraining or enhancing the firm's activities. All of this immeasurably increases the complexity of the firm and makes the boundaries of a mega-firm even fuzzier (Bloch and Metcalfe 2011). Further, the changing activities of mega-firms creates difficulties for the concept of the industry and for evolutionary analysis more broadly within the economy, as the industry concept provides an ideal grouping within which to consider the working of competition as a selection mechanism (Bloch and Finch 2010).

We might add that the manner in which different mega-firms learn will be different too and this further differentiates the outcomes of their learning processes. It is not sufficient to recognise that firms are differentiated by their capabilities for capabilities are transient. Rather, what is required is to understand why the process of capability formation differs across firms. This brings us to our main concern, what is the nature of the type of organisation we refer to as a mega-firm?

6 The Nature of the Mega-Firm

In order to understand the nature of the mega-firm we need to go deeper into the process of capability formation. In particular, to ask what is it about capability formation that makes the mega-firm an effective organisation for coping with the tensions arising from the limitations of human knowing. Our discussion in prior sections suggests there are many dimensions of the influence of incomplete and constantly changing knowledge in the mega-firm.

First, the notion that mega-firms operate optimally has limited applicability. Mega-firms are inherently different in what they know, they imagine different choice sets and so they calculate different optimal outcomes even if their goals are the same. Their choices impart a strategic function in the sense that they decide on actions among alternatives for which there are no guaranteed outcomes, only imagined possibilities. Not surprisingly mistakes are made when firms follow different strategies. As Earl (1984) and Vickers (1994) argue persuasively, the treatment put forward in modern neoclassical analysis that firms only make optimising decisions about how to employ known technology to produce outputs to meet given preferences of consumers is an extremely damaging fiction.

Second, mega-firms have boundaries to their scope, which brings us to the question asked by Coase (1937) as to the boundary between firms and markets. Coase's answer is based on minimising transactions costs throughout the economy, such that internal direction is employed as long as the cost of organising the activity within the firm is less than the cost of employing a market transaction. Firms have an incentive to expand their activities under their direction when they can organise activities internally at a lower cost than buying or selling in the market. Likewise, they have an incentive to downsize when the market can provide goods or services at lower cost. Coase identifies transaction cost as the key factor affecting these incentives and suggests, in addition, that competition imposes an external discipline to ensure firms that do a better job of minimising transaction costs will displace laggards.

Incomplete knowledge plays an important role in Coase's analysis. He identifies discovering prices in the market as part of the transaction cost of using the market. With perfect knowledge, it would be possible to organise a complex division of labour through the market without incurring costs associated with collecting information and protecting against the unknown. Of course, with perfect knowledge everyone knows everything and the organisation of production and distribution can be done optimally by the self-organising market, a single firm, the state or any combination thereof. All that is required is the ability to calculate the optimal outcome. The idea of perfect knowledge is a distorting mirror in which to reflect the distinction between the firm and the market. We cannot comprehend their respective spheres of influence without recognising the limitations on and the diversity of human knowing, nor can we understand the inherent connections between economic change and the development of new and different knowing.

In reflecting on the influence of his work 50 years after the publication of the 'The Nature of the Firm', Coase (1988, p. 47) notes that his analysis was limited in its scope and that 'if one is to explain the institutional structure of production in the system as a whole it is necessary to uncover the reasons why the cost of organizing particular activities differs across firms.' Here, Coase is acknowledging that using the transaction cost approach to explaining the existence of firms has limited operational implications. We still do not know much about which activities are in the domain of the market and which are carried out through direction within the firm.

Moreover, Richardson (1972) carefully explains there are many forms of linkage between the extremes of the unitary firm and the pure market, including formal and informal contracts, supply chain alliances, joint ventures, interlocking share holdings and other forms of collaboration between buyers and sellers. Each of these forms of linkage is suitable to particular distributions of knowing and has implications for the further development of knowledge in the respective bodies. Any change in knowledge may induce a change in the pattern of linkages. Thus, innovations arise that are not even imagined at the time of the initial decision whether to use simple market transactions, full vertical integration or some hybrid arrangement that explicitly or implicitly ties the buyer and seller together for a long interval.

Richardson draws attention to the scope of activity of firms and markets. An evolutionary approach focuses the further dimension of dynamics. Neither markets nor firms are historically fixed. If boundaries depend on capabilities and capabilities are changing, as Coase comes to suggest, then we require an explanation of the process by which capabilities change. In fact, the costs of transactions through the market have in many cases fallen dramatically over time and the efficiency with which firms organise production internally has risen dramatically. Even when a competitive selection process operates to reduce aggregate transaction costs, it need not determine which of the many different configurations of the division of activities between firms and markets emerges. In fact, the outcome is historically specific, which helps to explain why different configurations are observed in different points of time and in different economies.

We argue that firms and markets play quite different roles in the modern economy, with the mega-firm playing a particular role by internalising the organisation of production and distribution in a manner well beyond the capability of the firm in traditional theory with its fixed and limited scope. The mega-firm is an administrative institution that effectively manages the pooling of knowledge wherever there are advantages from integrating specialised knowledge, thereby reaping gains from the division of labour. Markets can lead to gains from the division of labour as long as knowledge of internal processes is not required to pass between the transacting bodies. Mega-firms and markets are, to this degree, complementary and not substitutable forms of organisation. Only mega-firms have the knowledge to make the strategic decisions what to produce and how to produce it when these decisions require extensive pooling of knowledge, which is something that markets cannot do.

Here lies an essential point. Markets can transact, but only firms can innovate. The small, entrepreneurial firm may effectively innovate over the limited domain of the knowledge of a small group. In contrast, a mega-firm, in making decisions about what actions to take, conjecture the future development of current observables as they will affect its large and complex organisation and imagine, as best it can, the novelty that is inevitably generated by the developing economy and its own creative processes. In taking action to advance its own interests, the mega-firm is creative as well as reactive. In the process, it recreates itself and alters the institutional setting in which it operates. This is the essence of enterprise, namely the application of imagination beyond experience.

Schumpeter (1934) brings this insight to the fore in his analysis of economic development. Schumpeter initially identifies change as a special activity within the economy and associates it with a special agent of change, the entrepreneur, and clearly distinguishes the activity of the entrepreneur from that of management. In this Mark 1 version, the entrepreneur is typically an individual acting outside of the established industry. He is distinguished sharply from the inventor for his role is not to discover new technical opportunities but rather to introduce new business combinations into the prevailing economic structure.

As far as the economy is concerned, it is not invention but innovation that is the determining constraint on the rate of its development. Imagination is clearly central to this role, the entrepreneur conjectures, not always correctly, that the prevailing economic structure can be organised differently and has the drive and personality to implement the desired change and overcome the hostility of incumbent firms and interests in the process. In Schumpeter's account the primary role of the innovator is to successfully challenge the status quo. An economy with enterprise is an economy that is out of equilibrium, its fundamental properties relate not only to its structure but to the processes by which that structure is changing from within.

Interestingly, Schumpeter (1942) later moves the location of innovation to within the large business organisation and treats it as part of the bureaucracy of the modern economy. It is from this treatment of Schumpeter "Mark 2" that we take the key distinction between family-run firm of classical or early neoclassical economics and the mega-firm, namely the incorporation of the entrepreneurial function into the ongoing functions of management of a large and complex organisation. How does the mega-firm incorporate the entrepreneurial function? These firms need to be able to create specific capabilities by combining knowledge, skills and experience of individuals in a way that achieves specialisation and economies of scale through the division of labour. This raises the question of how mega-firms choose to organise themselves.

Change in knowledge potentially undermines the shared understanding that contributes to the cohesion, and hence, stability of the mega-firm. This is problematic because of the tension between the practices that underpin the efficiency of the firm and the quite different practices required for change. The former depends substantially upon a degree of shared understanding within the firm as to its routines, whereas the latter depends on challenging and breaking the rigidity associated with the pursuit of efficiency. The former is the domain of management in a narrow sense, while the latter is the domain of entrepreneurial imagination, of thinking through how the firm could be different with respect to activity and organisation. If the mega-firm is to be fit, it must be efficient and it must be innovative. If this tension is not resolved, the firm is unlikely to survive. This is one reason why mega-firms devote substantial effort to the integration of new knowledge within the firm.

As Penrose (1959) argues, this puts limits on the growth of the firm as the time of existing managers for integrating new managers is limited. However, there is no absolute limit on the size of the firm per se. Of course, this assumes that the routines for dealing with existing activities can be implemented with a constant level of management effort. It also assumes that the structure of the firm is sufficiently open to permit the emergence of new routines and the associated changes in management and organisation. A larger firm or more diverse firm may require a different structure to accomplish this function.

The mega-firm is also able to generate new knowledge and assimilate new knowledge generated outside the firm, bringing this knowledge to bear with existing capabilities to be able to innovate and to adapt to changing external conditions. The activities undertaken by the firm are changing over time. IBM no longer produces typewriters, but continues as an evolving organisation. There is no position of equilibrium or rest for the mega-firm. As Shackle (1970, p. 155) notes, 'The paradox of business, in its modern evolution, is the conflict between our assumption that we know enough for our logic to bite on, and our *essential*, prime dependence on achieving *novelty*, the novelty which by its nature and meaning in some degree discredits what had passed for knowledge.'[italics in the original]

There are no fixed boundaries to the mega-firm because there are no fixed boundaries to restless knowledge within the firm. The traditional analysis of firm growth through expansion of existing activities to reap static economies of scale is far too limiting for understanding the development of the mega-firm. Even diversification into related fields that utilise the firm's existing capabilities as in Penrose (1959) is too limiting. Innovation based on the connection of knowledge within a large and complex organisation can point in radically new directions, which may be supported by the firm's leadership under particular historical circumstances. This means that mega-firms often operate at the meso level creating new products, processes and, even, new markets, so they are unlikely to be fully identified with only one industry or sector of a single economy, at least not indefinitely. From our perspective, the distinguishing characteristics of mega-firms are a combination of large size, broad scope and, most especially, a history of innovation that includes development extending beyond the improvement of existing products and processes.

7 Conclusions

We consider the nature of the mega-firm, the large and complex firms that dominate modern economies. We locate their distinctive competitive advantage in the ability to cope with restless knowledge. These firms are able to develop extensive capabilities from the specialised knowledge of large numbers of individuals, thereby reaping dynamic economies through the coordination of a division of labour. Importantly, mega-firm capabilities expand organically from the interaction of the knowledge of individuals, enhanced by introspection and creative problem solving, which provides some protection for the firm against the ravages of creative destruction in the competitive process. Because the mega-firm can survive and prosper in the face of restless knowledge, it is in a position to provide security to the individuals on whose efforts the success of the firm depends.

Cohesion in the mega-firm, especially in the face of negative outcomes to decisions made under uncertainty, depends on the trust that comes from shared understanding. Yet, fully exploiting the capabilities of the firm involves action that extends beyond the domain of this shared understanding. This is especially the case with the expanded capabilities that come from learning and discovery through creative problem solving. Strategic choices must be made about how far to venture beyond the domain of shared understanding and how much effort to devote to further integration of the knowledge within the firm. This is the role of leadership and, in the case of acting on new knowledge, entrepreneurship, for which the calculus of optimisation is relevant but not sufficient. This leadership function of management incorporates the traditional role of the entrepreneur, so the mega-firm is generally an entrepreneurial firm.

The mega-firm has fuzzy boundaries in terms of activities determined by its capabilities, resources and the strategic decisions of management. Further, these boundaries are subject to change over time that is sometimes dramatic in response to developments in the rest of the economy driven by restless knowledge, as well as internally by changing personnel and other resources, by learning and by changing strategic direction. In order to survive the firm needs to maintain cohesion in the face of these forces of change. Most importantly, the mega-firm must organise itself to enhance innovation without destroying cohesion, which means that its structure and functions are both historically specific and changing over time. Thus, the mega-firm is a restless firm.

Evolutionary analysis suggests that there will be further development of the techniques of risk management, the science of leadership and other methods of dealing with the complexity facing mega-firms. However, the unlimited potential for gains from the further specialisation of labour suggests that the complexity of these organisations will increase apace. As best practice continues to develop, there will remain surprises that will undo even previously successful mega-firms. Thus, while large size and broad scope with a sharp attention to opportunities for continual innovation provide distinct evolutionary advantages for mega-firms over traditional family firms in the modern economy, they are neither infallible nor destined to live forever. Such is the power of the perennial gale of creative destruction.

Acknowledgments We thank and absolve two anonymous referees along with Jerry Courvisanos, David Levine, Peter Murmann, Richard Nelson and participants at 2012 International Schumpeter Society conference as well as seminars at University of Birmingham and the University of Manchester for productive commentary on earlier versions of this paper.

References

Andersen ES (2012) Schumpeter's core works revisited resolved problems and remaining challenges. J Evol Econ 22:627–648
Arrow K (1974) The limits of organization. Norton, New York
Barnard C (1938) The functions of the executive. Harvard University Press, Cambridge, MA
Barney J (1991) Firm resources and sustained competitive advantage. J Manage 17:99–120
Baumol WJ (1958) On the theory of oligopoly. Economica 25:187–198
Berle A, Means G (1932) The modern corporation and private property. Transaction Publishers, New Brunswick, NJ
Bloch H, Finch J (2010) Firms and industries in evolutionary economics: lessons from Marshall, Young, Steindl and Penrose. J Evol Econ 20:139–162
Bloch H, Metcalfe JS (2011) Complexity in the theory of the firm. In: Antonelli C (ed) Handbook on the economic complexity of technological change. Edward Elgar, Cheltenham, pp 81–105
Boulding K (1951) Implications for general economics of more realistic theories of the firm. Am Econ Rev 42:35–44
Chandler AD (1977) The visible hand: the managerial revolution in American business. Harvard University Press, Cambridge, MA
Coase RH (1937) The nature of the firm. Economica 4:386–405
Coase RH (1988) The nature of the firm: influence. J Law Econ Org 4:33–47
Cyert RM, March JG (1963) Behavioral theory of the firm. Prentice-Hall, Englewood Cliffs, NJ
Dosi G, Nelson RR, Winter SG (2002) The nature and dynamics of organizational capabilities. Oxford University Press, Oxford
Drucker PF (1964) Managing for success. Harper and Row, New York
Earl P (1984) The corporate imagination. Wheatsheaf, Brighton
Eichner A (1976) The megacorp and oligopoly: micro foundations of macro dynamics. Cambridge University Press, Cambridge
Levine DP (1997) Knowing and acting: on uncertainty in economics. Rev Polit Econ 9:5–17
Loasby B (2009) Knowledge, coordination and the firm: historical perspectives. Eur J Hist Econ Thought 16(4):539–588
Marris R (1964) The theory of managerial capitalism. Macmillan, London
Marshall A (1920) Principles of economics, 8th edn. Macmillan, London
Metcalfe JS (2007) Alfred Marshall and the general theory of evolutionary economics. Hist Econ Ideas 15(1):81–110
Mokyr J (1990) The lever of riches. Oxford University Press, Oxford
Nelson RR (1991) Why do firms differ; and how does it matter. Strat J Manage 12:61–74
Nelson RR (2008) 'Why do firms differ and how does it matter?' A revisitation. Seoul J Econ 21(4):607–19
Nelson RR, Winter SG (1982) An evolutionary theory of economic change. Harvard University Press, Cambridge, MA
Nonaka I, Tacheuchi H (1995) The knowledge-creating company: how Japanese companies create the dynamics of innovation. Oxford University Press, New York

Penrose ET (1959) The theory of the growth of the firm. Basil Blackwell, Oxford
Polanyi M (1958) Personal knowledge. University of Chicago Press, Chicago
Ramazzotti P (2004) What do firms learn? Capabilities, distribution and the division of labor. In: Metcalfe JS, Foster J (eds) Evolution and economic complexity. Edward Elgar, Cheltenham, pp 38–61
Richardson GB (1972) The organisation of industry. Econ J 82:883–96
Schumpeter JA (1934) The theory of economic development (trans: 2nd German ed: Opie R). Oxford University Press, London
Schumpeter JA (1939) Business cycles, vol 1, 2. McGraw-Hill, New York
Schumpeter JA (1942) Capitalism, socialism and democracy. Harper Row, New York
Shackle GLS (1970) Expectation, enterprise and profit. George Allen and Unwin, London
Simon HA (1964) On the concept of an organizational goal. Adm Sci Q 9:1–22
Vickers D (1994) Economics and the antagonism of time. University of Michigan Press, Ann Arbor, MI
Williamson OE (1975) Markets and hierarchies. Free Press, New York
Winter S (2006) Toward a neo-Schumpeterian theory of the firm. Ind Corp Chang 15:125–141
Witt U (1998) Imagination and leadership—the neglected dimension of an evolutionary theory of the firm. J Econ Behav Organ 35:161–177
Wood A (1975) A theory of profits. Cambridge University Press, Cambridge

The Role of Management Capacity in the Innovation Process for Firm Profitability

Giovanni Cerulli and Bianca Potì

Abstract This paper studies the relation between firm managerial capacity in doing innovation and firm profitability. The approach taken is at the intersection of evolutionary/neo-Schumpeterian theory and the resource-based view of the firm. Utilizing a stochastic frontier analysis, we provide a direct measure of the innovation management capacity which is then plugged into a profit margin equation, augmented by the traditional Schumpeterian drivers of profitability. We run both ordinary least squares and quantile regressions.

Results show evidence of an average positive effect of the innovation managerial capacity on firm profitability, although quantile regressions show that this mean effect is mainly driven by the stronger magnitude of the effect for lower quantiles. This means that less profitable firms (i.e. the smaller ones in our sample) could gain more from increasing managerial efficiency for innovation in comparison to more profitable (larger) businesses.

1 Introduction

The evolutionary neo-Schumpeterian theory of the firm typically assumes that the competitive performance of businesses depends on a combination of market, innovation and firm-specific factors. Early investigations of relationships in this area took a structure-conduct-performance approach, focusing on traditional Schumpeterian determinants such as market structure, firm size, company R&D and innovation effort.

However, neo-Schumpeterian scholars recognized that firms' idiosyncratic capacities to master innovation processes could have equally important weight in explaining potentials to achieve relatively better or lesser profit rates, in a given environment. This realization was in part influenced by the management field and by the resource-based theory of competitive advantage. However measuring firm capacity in managing innovation production is far harder than accounting for the

G. Cerulli (✉) • B. Potì
CNR-IRCrES, Via dei Taurini 19, 00185 Rome, Italy
e-mail: giovanni.cerulli@ircres.cnr.it; bianca.poti@ircres.cnr.it

A. Pyka, J. Foster (eds.), *The Evolution of Economic and Innovation Systems*, Economic Complexity and Evolution, DOI 10.1007/978-3-319-13299-0_19

role played by "traditional" factors, such as for example sectorial concentration, market power or scale.

The difficulties result from the immaterial and "fuzzy" nature of managerial capacities, which are approximated by variables that seem to give only a poor reckoning of the phenomenon. The problem becomes even trickier if we wish to separate the roles of "general" managerial abilities, concerning the overall management of firm divisions and activities, from the more entrepreneurial capacities specifically involved in managing innovation processes.

Papers such as those by Geroski et al. (1993) and Cefis and Ciccarelli (2005) have tried to account for the role of managerial capacity when estimating a Schumpeterian profit function, by either incorporating fixed effects (Geroski et al.), or firm-idiosyncratic elements through Bayesian random-coefficient regression (Cefis and Ceccarelli). Meanwhile, management studies have tried to capture roles in innovation by introducing proxies such as indicators of experience, education, researcher skills and firm managerial skills (Cosh et al. 2005). As one example, Bughin and Jacques (1994) explored the Schumpeterian links between size, market structure and innovation by controlling for a series of managerial factors generally thought to affect efficiency and success rates in innovation.

The problems with this literature are twofold. First, it fails to explicitly examine the company capacities in managing innovation, and instead looks more at general capabilities. Second, the studies apply only partial and contingent measures of managerial capacity. On the other hand there have been a small number of recent econometric analyses of company innovation performance (Bos et al. 2011; Gantumur and Stephan 2010) that have derived a direct measure of innovation capability by deconstructing the residual of a production function into a technological and an efficiency component. The residual term is in effect what Mairesse and Mohnen defined as "innovativeness", in their well-known paper of 2002.[1]

Continuing in this more recent line, in this work we identify a direct measure of innovation-related managerial capacities, to be plugged into a profit function along with traditional Schumpeterian determinants of profitability. The primary research goals for the study are to determine to what extent management's capacity in mastering the generation of innovations could have a driving effect on profit rates, and if complementarities with traditional factors can be detected (Percival and Cozzarin 2008). We also wish to study the role of managerial capability given situations of different levels of company profitability and/or size.

The next section of the paper presents an in-depth review of the literature. Section 3 sets out a concise explanation of the econometric model used to measure the firm's capacity in managing innovation. Section 4 presents the dataset, of over 2,000 "innovating" Italian companies, and the variables employed in the estimation

[1] "Innovativeness is to innovation what TFP (*Total Factor Productivity*) is to production. [...] Both correspond to omitted factors of performance such as technological, organizational, cultural, or environmental factors (and to other sources of misspecification errors), although TFP is commonly interpreted as being mainly an indicator of technology" (Mairesse and Mohnen 2002, p. 226).

stage. Section 5 shows the results of the analysis. First we present the results from a measure of innovation efficiency applying a stochastic frontier regression, which we call the "Innovation efficiency index" (IEI). Next we provide the results from a regression analysis of the operating profit margin (OPM) on IEI, while controlling for other variables. The intent of the analysis is to respond to the research question: "Is innovation management capacity significantly conducive to higher rates of profit, given other profit determinants?" We first use ordinary least squares (OLS) to examine to what extent the Innovation efficiency index is significantly related to the profit rate. Next we use a quantile regression (QR) to see whether the OLS results are sufficiently robust and to detect potential non-uniform patterns of the effect of IEI on OPM.

Section 6 offers a discussion of the results and of several implications for policy, management strategies and for the understanding of Schumpeterian models of competitive advantage.

2 Literature Review

The research concept stems from three strands of literature: (i) the evolutionary and resource-based approach, which offers theoretical and empirical approaches to the characterization of firms and competitive advantage (Nelson and Winter 1982; Dosi 1988); (ii) management literature, which provides empirical exploration of the role of managerial factors in firm innovation propensity and thus firm output; (iii) efficiency-frontier literature, which conceives of gauging managerial competencies in terms of the distance between the actual and the optimal innovation frontier.

2.1 Evolutionary and Resource-Based Literature

Evolutionary theory holds that the main function of the firm is the integration of resources and competencies in teams, for productive services that would not be accessible through market contracts. Following Penrose's classic (1959) argument, value creation arises from business competencies in combining and using the available resources. The differences in firm behavior create particular traits of greater or lesser competitiveness, with selection advantages reflected in profitability. At the core of this firm capabilities theory are the key concepts of synergy and efficiency. Thus the character of links between the different parts of the firm, or the internal synergy, contributes to innovative capacity. At the same time, given the possibility of increasing returns, there are grounds for searching greater efficiency in the use of the firm's assets. Nelson and Winter (1982), Winter (2003) and Teece (1984, 1986) are among the authors that explain inter-firm and intra-industry performance variability through an efficiency approach, rather than taking a market-positioning approach. Such studies stress the role and the understanding of firms' internal features as sources of competitive advantages.[2]

The relationship between market power (firm's relative size) and efficiency (making the most of available resources) as drivers of business success is a further key issue in the evolutionary perspective. Here the actual concept of innovation is introduced as a cumulative and irreversible learning process regarding the technological path (Malerba and Orsenigo 1990; Pavitt et al. 1987). This conception implies that the level of accumulated resources and capabilities plays a significant role in determining future innovation efficiency. According to Vossen (1998), large firm strengths are predominantly material, in economies of scale, scope, and financial and technological resources. It is often argued that larger firms permit greater innovation, since they enjoy greater economies of scale and scope than smaller firms (Cohen and Klepper 1996). Small firm strengths are in turn mostly behavioral, as smaller firms are generally more dynamic and flexible and can have closer proximity to the market. You (1995) suggests that efficient firm size is determined by the interaction between economies of scale, stemming from increasing returns to production technology, and diseconomies of scale, stemming from decreasing returns to organizational technology. Thus, although large firms can benefit from technological and learning economies, these may be outweighed by organizational diseconomies of scale (Zenger 1994).

Early research in this field initially focused on the role of the firm's industrial market in performance variations (Schmalensee 1985), in keeping with the assumption that industry structure drives firm conduct and in turn firm performance (Scherer 1980, p. 4; Tirole 1988). Since then, other research streams have inquired into the role of corporate ownership, or emphasized analysis at the level of business units (Bowman and Helfat 2001; Brush and Bromiley 1997; James 1998; McGahan and Porter 1997, 2002; Rumelt 1991). By far the most consistent result across these studies is that, when estimated over time, the business unit class of analysis explains the most variance in performance (Brush and Bromiley 1997; James 1998; Roquebert et al. 1996; Rumelt 1991).

A particularly interesting study in this area is by Bughin and Jacques (1994). These authors found that the positive correlation between firm market share and innovation success became significant and more robust across the various dimensions of innovation output, when controls for managerial (in)efficiency were explicitly introduced, and in this way concluded that the Schumpeterian conjecture is not rejected. However "without this normalization, the marginal effect of market share on innovation is biased downward" (Bughin and Jacques 1994, p. 658), meaning that in the specific area of managing their innovation, higher market-share firms are actually less effective, and that "systematic inefficiency is also related to

[2]An important evolution of the firm capability theory deals with dynamic capabilities. Teece (1987, p. 516) define firm dynamic capabilities as the ability to integrate and reconfigure internal and external competences/resources. These capabilities are what matters also in the case of R&D collaboration and joint ventures.

firm size" (p. 658). Thus these scholars conclude that in keeping with Schumpeterian theory, increasing firm size and market share are conducive to innovation, but on the other hand smaller firms have relative "managerial" advantages in innovation activity.

There can also be a bi-directional causality between perfect/imperfect market structures and innovation efficiency. First, because in the presence of market structures showing perfect competition, inefficient firms would be driven out of the market, and second because empirical results have shown that competition has positive effects on innovation efficiency.[3] Since competition is positively associated with higher scores in management practice, endogeneity bias will lead to underestimation of the importance of competition, as better managed firms are in any case likely to have higher profit margins. It is therefore important to explicitly use indicators of market structure in examining performance functions such as innovation, production or profit.

Based on Penrose's (1959) resource-based theory and Porter's (1980, 1985) activity-based approach, the more recent strategic view of the firm investigates the influences on firm strategy both from market structures and from internal resources and capabilities. Such studies attempt to explain the effect of strategy-structure relationships on efficiency. The literature on strategic theory is the first to incorporate a "strategic efficiency" criterion to evaluate competitive advantage. Strategic efficiency refers to the realization of sustainable competitive advantages, as strategic rents of the firm. Depending on the origin of the competitive advantages, different strategic rents can be realized. If the competitive advantage results primarily from monopolistic advantages, as argued by Porter (1980, 1985), the strategic choice depends on the generation of monopolistic rents. If the competitive advantage is primarily based on knowledge advantages due to specific resources, capabilities and competencies, Ricardian and Schumpeterian rents can be realized (Peteraf 1993; Winter 1987).

Ultimately, findings from the empirical literature on the relationship between firm size and efficiency are ambiguous, but there are indications that firm size could be one of the primary sources of heterogeneities in technical efficiency. On the one hand, large firms could be more efficient in production because they use more specialized inputs and are better at coordinating their resources. On the other hand, small firms could be more efficient because they have more flexible, non-hierarchical structures and usually do not suffer from the so-called "agency problem" (Gantumur and Stephan 2010). Size may also have an indirect effect on productivity through other variables, such as resource and capability constraints (Geroski 1998).

[3]Over time, low productivity firms are selected out and the better ones survive and prosper. But in the steady state there will always be some dispersion of productivity, as cost factors limit the number of new firms that enter the market (Bloom and van Reenen 2010).

2.2 Management Literature

The management literature includes an extensive body of studies on the impact of managerial practices on firm performance, measured in terms of productivity (Huselid 1995; Ichniowski et al. 1997; Black and Lynch 2001; for a review see Bloom and Van Reenen 2010).

Bloom and Van Reenen (2007, 2010) found that measures of monitoring, target-setting and incentivizing, as assessed via surveys, are strongly associated with productivity and other measures of firm-level performance. The question of whether there is impact from management practices precisely in the area of innovation has received less attention, although several scholars have recently explored the effects from firm organization and employment conditions on propensity to innovate and on actual success in innovation (generally represented by sales of innovative products) (Arvanitis et al. 2013).[4] Other scholars have attempted to examine managerial effects on innovation by examining mainly human resources management (HRM) practices, such as employee training, hiring criteria, teamwork, job design and employee hierarchies (Ichniowski and Shaw 2003).

There are many "partial" measures, assessing specific managerial capabilities, within the various studies of general management impact on innovation performance, although these provide very different results. Mookherjee (2006) observes that beyond such descriptive formulations, there is a general lack of theoretical models, and especially of formal models. Hempel and Zwick (2008) investigated the effects of two organizational practices, employee participation and outsourcing, on the likelihood of introduction of product and/or process innovations. They found that while employee participation is positively associated with product and process innovations, outsourcing favors innovations in the short-run, but then reduces performance in the long-run. Zoghi et al. (2010) analyzed the relationships between innovation and certain organizational practices and incentive schemes in a large sample of Canadian firms with three cross-sections. They found correlation between innovation and the factors under examination, but in many cases this was weak. Many empirical studies find different innovation results according to the type of management practice under examination: Zhou et al. (2011) for the Netherlands, Cosh et al. (2012) for UK, Chang et al. (2012) for Taiwanese firms, Jiang et al. (2012) for Chinese firms, Koski et al. (2012) for Finnish manufacturing firms, and Arvanitis et al. (2013) for Swiss and Greek firms.

Certain management studies have advanced in the direction of applying specific measures of management capability through better use of surveys (Bloom and van Reenen 2010) and the analysis of "clustered" management practices. Laursen and Foss (2003), for instance, used a synthetic index considering a combination of

[4]These scholars reported that, overall, variables representing workplace organization show highly significant positive associations with innovation propensity, and that some of them seem to be more important than other "standard" determinants of innovation, such as demand development, competition conditions or human capital assets.

human resources management practices, as revealed by principal component factor analysis, and find that this index is strongly significant in explaining innovation performance. These scholars interpreted this result as evidence of complementarities between HRM practices and innovation. Arvanitis et al. (2013) find cumulative effects from the use of HRM practices on innovation. From a certain threshold on, the effect on innovation is larger with the firm's introduction and intensive use of larger numbers of individual HRM practices. However, although both Laursen and Foss (2003) and Arvanitis et al. (2013) control simultaneously for many different aspects of innovative HRM practices,[5] several problems still remain, as follows.

(i) Other single managerial practices can impact on innovation performance, and various authors suggest additional ones as determinants of innovation performance. Indeed besides HRM practices, other traditional organizational design variables included in the theory of economics of organizations are sometimes neglected. Examples of overlooked variables include delegation, departmentalization, specialization, and others (Foss 2013). Hence a relevant problem recognized by many scholars working in this field is the possibility of "omitted variable bias", which would imply inconsistent estimates of the effects. Solutions could lie in the use of fixed-effect regression, or in the indication of a broader set of observable variables.[6]

(ii) A single management capability measure has contingent effect: it can have a positive or a negative effect, depending on the circumstances in which the firm operates. Any coherent theory of management assumes that firms will choose different practices in different environments, so that some element of contingency always arises. As an example, Van Reenen and Bloom (2007) show that firms specialize more in people management (promotion, rewards, hiring and firing) when they are in a more skills-intensive industry. The interesting question is whether practices exist that would be unambiguously better for the majority of firms. The results of the study just cited, in which certain management practices are robustly associated with better firm performance, seem to suggest that this may be the case.

(iii) There is a lack of benchmarks for understanding whether the management factors considered, and their measurement, are examples of good or bad practices. Van Reenen and Bloom (2007) developed a survey tool that in principle could be used to directly quantify management practices across firms, sectors and countries. The fundamental aim of this approach is to measure the firm's overall managerial quality by benchmarking against a series of global best practices: "These practices are a mixture of things that would always be a good idea (e.g. taking effort and ability into consideration when promoting

[5]They control the impact on: (a) the firm's innovation propensity (whether or not a firm has introduced innovations in a certain period), and (b) innovation success as measured by the firm's innovative product sales in relation to total turnover.

[6]Another problem indicated by Arvanitis et al. (2013) is reverse causality: innovative firms could in turn be more likely to adopt innovative organizational practices.

an employee) and some practices that are now efficient due to changes in the environment" (Bloom and Van Reenen 2010, p. 6). These scholars use an interview-based evaluation tool that defines and scores 18 basic management practices, from one (worst) to five (best practice). This evaluation tool was developed by an international consulting firm to target practices they believed were associated with better performance.[7] These management practice scores can then be related to firm performance (total factor productivity, profitability, growth rates, and Tobin's Q and survival rates) as well as firm size. However, as the authors themselves suggest, these correlations should by no means be understood as causal (Bloom and Van Reenen 2010).

2.3 *Efficiency-Frontier Literature*

A third body of literature, efficiency-frontier studies, states that firm innovation performance is determined not only by hard factors such as R&D employees and investment, but also by factors like management practices and governance structures (Aghion and Tirole 1994; Black and Lynch 2001; Bertrand and Schoar 2003; Cosh et al. 2005). Many management and organizational factors are found to be correlated with firm propensity to innovate. Bughin and Jacques (1994) found that in particular, synergy among firm departments, together with the effective protection of innovation, were the key factors for successful management of the innovation process. Translated into economic terms, their result means that: "innovation activity by firms may be subject to systematic inefficiencies, i.e. firms do not necessarily operate on their best practice frontier" (Bughin and Jacques 1994, p. 654).

Firm innovativeness can be defined as the ability to turn innovation inputs into innovation outputs. As such it naturally incorporates the concept of "efficiency", which in turn can be explained by technological factors on the one hand, and firm-specific managerial capabilities on the other hand (Gantumur and Stephan 2010). There are difficulties in measuring firm capabilities because of their complex, structured and multidimensional nature. In typical econometric exercises examining determinants of innovation performance (Mairesse and Mohnen 2002, 2003), the firm's innovation management efficiency is encompassed within an unobservable regression term. Mairesse and Mohnen (2002) refer to an innovation production function where, similar to the standard production function framework, differences across units (or time periods) are explained by differences (or changes) "in the inputs and in a residual that is known as total factor productivity or simply productivity" (Mairesse and Mohnen 2002, p. 226). This residual incorporates all the omitted

[7]One way to summarize firm-specific quality is to z-score each individual question and take an average across all 18 questions. Another is to take the principal factor component. This in fact provides extremely similar results to the average z-score, since they are correlated (see Van Reenen and Bloom 2007).

determinants of performance, and grasps innovativeness in a loosely-defined sense. Starting from this assumption, a recent paper (Bos et al. 2011) tested the weight of efficiency as determinant of an innovation production function, but in any case without identifying statistically significant and theoretically based components of such "efficiency".[8] The relevance of managerial (in)efficiency implies that measure of innovation inputs in an innovation production function is biased, unless there is an indicator of firm (in)efficiency. If resources are not used effectively, additional investment may be of little support in stimulating the innovation process (Gantumur and Stephan 2010).

Bos et al. (2011) studied the relationship between R&D inputs and innovative output in a sample of Dutch firms and found that over 63 % of inter-firm variation in the observed innovativeness could be attributed to inefficiency in the innovation process. "In productivity analysis it is quite common to separate (in)efficiency from technological change empirically, using stochastic frontier analysis (SFA)… In the empirical literature on the KPF (knowledge production frontier), however, researchers to date still assume, usually implicitly, that all innovation takes place at the frontier and no waste of R&D inputs occurs" (Bos et al. 2011, p. 2) These scholars use a stochastic frontier analysis, and keeping the stock of knowledge constant, draw the innovation frontier of a knowledge production function.

In another paper, Bos et al. (2007) analyzed the relation between innovation output growth and (in)efficiency by a stochastic frontier analysis (SFA) at macro level in 80 countries. The analysis relied on the usual practice adopted in cross-country growth studies, where differences in the efficient use of inputs are computed through a two-stage approach. Cross-country productivity is first retrieved as a residual from a production function estimation, and then regressed against a set of possible determinants of productivity growth. The authors comment that in the presence of inefficiency, total factor productivity indices are biased. SFA overcomes this problem, since it uses a benchmark approach for identifying the technically efficient use of inputs and production technology. Firm optimal behavior is represented by the production frontier, which is the maximum level of output the firm can achieve. The limit of this approach is the assumption of a common current technology for all firms, in all industries and countries, although the authors attempt to accommodate this assumption by accounting for cross-sectional heterogeneity.

Gantumur and Stephan (2010) also estimate an innovation frontier, but at micro level. The authors examine the innovation performance of firms as determined not only by innovation inputs, but also by productivity in innovation and factors affecting this productivity.[9] These authors noted that only a few papers in the preceding

---

[8]Other scholars have used data envelopment analysis (DEA) to estimate the innovation frontier. Zhang et al. (2003) and Coelli and Rao (2005) provide a discussion of the differences between DEA and stochastic frontier analysis (SFA). Kumbhakar and Lovell (2000) give an elaborate discussion of the development and application of SFA to efficiency measurement.

[9]The general aim of their paper is to examine at micro level the impact of external technology acquisition on the achievement of innovative efficiency and productivity, i.e. on a firm's innovation performance.

literature had studied innovative efficiency at the firm level by using quantitative approaches. Cosh et al. (2005) examined the impact of management characteristics and patterns of collaboration on firm innovation efficiency by comparing both data envelopment analysis (DEA) and stochastic frontier analysis (SFA). Zhang et al. (2003) applied the SFA approach to the R&D efforts of Chinese firms to examine the difference in efficiency among various types of ownership. Hashimoto and Haneda (2008) analyzed R&D efficiency change of Japanese pharmaceutical firms using DEA methodology. These examples are restricted to the estimation of the predicted inefficiency and use a two-stage approach when analyzing the inefficiency determinants.

3 Methodology

Proceeding from the literature review, we adopt a methodological approach based on a stochastic frontier analysis (SFA). For the SFA, the innovation output is the firm "innovative turnover" and the inputs are the innovation effort (specifically the innovation expenditures) and various control variables. Adopting such a model allows us to compute an "Innovation efficiency index" (IEI), defined as the distance between the actual realized innovative output and the potential innovative output, given the inputs of the production function considered.

The assumption behind the approach is that the complement of this difference can be suitably interpreted as the managerial capacity of firms in promoting innovation. When for the same inputs this difference is high, we can conclude that the entrepreneurial ability in combining and exploiting innovation input potential has been poor; on the contrary, when this difference is low, business ability in combining and exploiting input potential has been substantial. Thus, the Innovation efficiency index, calculated as "minus the difference between the actual and the potential innovative output", can be correctly used to approximate a direct measure of firm's innovation management capacity.

Once we have this measure in hand, we wish to respond to at least two pertinent questions. First: is innovation managerial capacity significantly conducive to higher rates of profit, given other profit determinants? And then: is this effect uniform over the distribution of the profit rate or is it unevenly spread? The aim of this paper is to shed light on these issues.

In so doing, we assume that firms are subject to the same form of innovation function (Cobb-Douglas)[10] and share the same type of knowledge inputs, but can operate at different innovation output levels. Other things being equal, firms

[10]For the sake of simplicity we do not assume other forms of the production function (e.g., the translog), or that the Cobb-Douglas regression coefficients vary across sectors.

using the same level of input(s) can produce different innovation output (i.e., innovation turnover), because of the presence of inefficiency in the innovation process. Inefficiency in turn can depend "partly on adequacy of the strategic combinations [. . .] and partly on idiosyncratic capabilities embodied in the various firms" (Dosi et al. 2006, p. 1110; see also Teece 1986).

For the dataset, we use the third edition of the Eurostat Community Innovation Survey (CIS3) for Italy, merged with firm accounting data. CIS3 provides a broad set of data on firm innovation activity, both quantitative and qualitative, including information on "organizational innovation". Furthermore both manufacturing and service companies are considered, and the survey reports on a substantial sample size of innovating firms (over 2,000). We use data on various innovative or new organizational practices from CIS3 as determinants of innovation-based managerial efficiency. When possible, inputs and outputs are taken with a delay to attenuate simultaneity.

Our experiment utilizes a two-step approach. In the first step, we estimate the direct measure of innovation-related managerial capacity (the Innovation efficiency index, IEI); in the second, a Schumpeterian profit function including IEI as predictor. To estimate IEI, we use a stochastic frontier analysis approach, starting from the equation:

$$y_i = f\left(\mathbf{x}_i; \beta\right) \cdot \eta_i \cdot \exp\left(\varepsilon_i\right) \tag{1}$$

where y_i, $\mathbf{x}_i$, η_i and ε_i represent the innovative turnover, the innovation inputs, the innovation efficiency and an error term for the *i-th* firm, given an innovation technology $f(\cdot)$. The term η_i, varying between 1 and 0, captures the efficiency of the innovation, that is, the distance from the innovation production function. If $\eta_i = 1$, the firm is achieving the optimal innovative output with the technology embodied in the production function $f(\cdot)$. Vice versa, when $\eta_i < 1$, the firm is not making the most of the inputs $\mathbf{x}_i$ employed. Because the output is assumed to be strictly positive (i.e., $y_i > 0$), the degree of technical efficiency is also assumed to be strictly positive (i.e., $\eta_i > 0$).

Taking the natural log of both sides of Eq. (1) yields:

$$\ln\left(y_i\right) = \ln\left\{f\left(\mathbf{x}_i; \beta\right)\right\} + \ln\left(\eta_i\right) + \varepsilon_i \tag{2}$$

Assuming that there are k inputs and that the production function is linear in logs, and by defining $u_i = -\ln(\eta_i)$ we have:

$$\ln\left(y_i\right) = \beta_0 + \sum_{j=1}^{k} \beta_j \cdot \ln\left(x_i\right) - u_i + \varepsilon_i \tag{3}$$

Because u_i is subtracted from $\ln(y_i)$, restricting $u_i > 0$ implies that $0 < \eta_i \leq 1$. Finally, we can assume u_i to depend on a series of covariates $\mathbf{z}_i$, so that the final form of the model is:

$$\begin{cases} \ln(y_i) = \beta_0 + \sum_{j=1}^{k} \beta_j \cdot \ln(x_i) - u_i(\mathbf{z}_i;\gamma) + \varepsilon_i \\ u_i(\mathbf{z}_i;\gamma) = \sum_{j=1}^{m} \gamma_j \cdot \ln(\mathbf{z}_i) + \omega_i \end{cases} \tag{4}$$

By estimating this equation through maximum likelihood (assuming a normal truncated distribution for u_i) we can then recover the value of η_i which represents the IEI, i.e. the firm idiosyncratic score accounting for firm capacity to suitably combine innovation inputs for achievement of innovation output, once all possible elements affecting innovation and efficiency in doing innovation are controlled for ($\mathbf{x}_i$ and $\mathbf{z}_i$). Thus, we can assume η_i as a measure of the firm innovation managerial capacity, to be used as regressor in the second step of this methodology. Here, an operating profit function of the kind:

$$OPM_i = \gamma + \gamma_0 \cdot \eta_i + \sum_{j=1}^{h} \gamma_j \cdot \mathbf{w}_i + v_i \tag{5}$$

is estimated via ordinary least squares (OLS) and quantile regression(s) (QRs), to better examine the heterogeneous response of firms to innovation efficiency gains. The set of variables contained in the vector $\mathbf{w}_i$ includes the determinants of the OPM different from η_i (i.e., industrial organization determinants, financial factors, skills and R&D competence, etc.)

4 Dataset, Variables and Descriptive Statistics

As noted, the empirical application for our study draws on the Italian Community Innovation Survey, 3rd edition (1998–2000), containing information on innovation-related variables for 15,279 Italian companies. Information from this source is merged with firm accounting data obtained from the AIDA archives on Italian companies[11] maintained by Bureau Van Dijk Electronic Publishing BV. The CIS provides information on the resources for firm innovation activity (inputs and outputs), sources of information and cooperation for innovation, and factors hampering innovation. The third edition of the survey has the advantage of providing, for the first time, a section on "organizational innovation". We make use of all this

[11] AIDA: Information Analysis of Italian Companies.

information for the reliable construction of array $\mathbf{x}_i$, $\mathbf{z}_i$ and $\mathbf{w}_i$, in order to obtain a reliable measure of η_i for estimating Eq. (5).

Table 1 presents a brief description of the three sets of variables employed in the estimation of Eqs. (4) and (5). The rationale for the choice of these variables is as follows.

1. The variables included in the array $\mathbf{x}_i$ represent typical input factors characterizing an innovation production function, i.e. expenditures devoted to fostering innovation. The in-house R&D investment (*R&D intra*) traditionally represents the major innovation input, accounting for the firm's direct effort devoted to knowledge production. Expenditures for purchasing R&D services provided by other companies (*R&D extra*) reflects in turn the amount of external knowledge sources needed for acquiring specific R&D capabilities not existing within the firm. Expenditure for machinery (*Machinery*) regards the need for fixed capital assets (tangibles), to set up, enlarge and maintain R&D productive capacity over time (i.e., labs, tools, etc.). Expenditure for acquiring technologies (*Technology*) concerns in turn investments in intangible assets, such as patents or technological licenses, and reflects the need to boost the size of the firm technological portfolio. The number of university-educated employees employed by the firm (*Skills*), represents a measure of human capital and thus of R&D skills available to the firm. Finally, some control variables are introduced to take into account the form of the company, as independent or part of a group (*Group*), its experience in doing business (*Age*), the presence of process innovation (*Process*), the sector of firm economic activity (*Sector*), its size (*Size*) and location (*Geo*). Note that the expenditures variables are expressed in logs, as a linearized Cobb-Douglas function is employed in the estimation phase.
2. The variables included in the array $\mathbf{z}_i$ represent factors explaining the company efficiency in doing innovation. The first main input is the total expenditure for innovation (*Total innovation spending*) and the second is *Skills*, since it is well recognized that efficiency is strictly linked to human capital. A series of dummies are then included, intended to account for a series of strategic behaviors adopted by companies to increase their capacity in suitably and effectively combining the heterogeneous set of innovation inputs.
3. Finally, variables in $\mathbf{z}_i$ should explain the main drivers (and controls) of company economic return (profitability). Apart from the auto-regressive components (the *Operating profit margin* at *t*-1 and *t*-2) and the *Innovation efficiency*, the other factors explaining profitability are: the size of the firm (*Turnover*), accounting for the potential existence of scale economies; *Concentration*, accounting for degree of competition and barriers to entry (Paretian rents); *R&D per capita*, surrogating the knowledge competence of the company; *Skill intensity*, representing the (relative quota) of human capital (and thus quality of the labor input); *Export intensity*, referring to the level of company external competition; *Indebtedness*, accounting for the financing structure of the company (the so-called capital structure); *Labor costs*, capturing the cost structure of the firm; a set of control dummies (*Cooperation*, *Age*, *Group*, *Sector*, *Size* and *Geo*), including also *Patent*

Table 1 Description of variables employed in the two-step procedure

Variables in **x**	
R&D intra	Log of the intra-muros R&D expenditure
R&D extra	Log of the extra-muros R&D expenditure
Machinery	Log of the expenditure for innovative machinery
Technology	Log of the expenditure for acquiring technology
Skills	Log of the number of employees with a degree
Group	Dummy: 1 = firm belonging to a group
Age	Dummy: 1 = firm set up in 1998–2000
Process	Dummy: 1 = firm doing process innovation
Sector	2-digit NACE Rev. 1 classification (both manufacturing and services)
Size	Five classes of firm size (10/49; 50/99; 100/249; 250/999; >1,000)
Geo	Three Italian macro regions (north; center; south and islands)
Variables in **z**	
Total innovation spending	Log of the total expenditure for innovation activities
Skills	Log of the number of employees with a degree
Process	Dummy: 1 = firm doing process innovation
IPRs protection	Dummy: 1 = firm improving management in protecting innovation
New strategies	Dummy: 1 = firm improving business strategies for innovation
New management	Dummy: 1 = firm improving management strategies for innovation
New organization	Dummy: 1 = firm improving internal organization for innovation
New marketing	Dummy: 1 = firm improving marketing activities for innovation
Cooperation	Dummy: 1 = firm cooperating for innovation
Variables in **w**	
Profit margin (t-1)	Operating profit margin (profit/turnover) in 1999
Profit margin (t-2)	Operating profit margin (profit/turnover) in 1998
Innovation efficiency	Firm innovation efficiency index
Turnover	Firm turnover
Concentration	2-digit sectoral concentration index
R&D per-capita	R&D per employee
Skills	Number of employees with a university degree per total employees
Export intensity	Export on turnover
Indebtedness	Stock of short and long term debt on turnover
Labor costs	Labor costs on turnover
New organization	Dummy: 1 = firm improving internal organization for innovation
New marketing	Dummy: 1 = firm improving marketing activities for innovation
Cooperation	Dummy: 1 = firm cooperating for innovation
Age	Dummy: 1 = firm set up in 1998–2000
Patent dummy	Dummy: 1 = firm applying for patents in 1998–2000
Group	Dummy: 1 = firm belonging to a group
Sector	2-digit NACE Rev. 1 classification (both manufacturing and services)
Size	Five classes of firm size (10/49; 50/99; 100/249; 250/999; >1,000)
Geo	Three Italian macro regions (north; center; south and islands)

Table 2 Descriptive statistics: continuous and binary variables

	N	Mean	Median	Std. dev.	Min	Max
Continuous						
Operating profit margin	2,094	4.73	3.31	6.60	−31.59	32.64
Innovation efficiency	2,094	0.53	0.57	0.17	0.01	0.85
Turnover	2,094	39,010	9,590	140,917	3	4,081,976
Concentration	2,094	14.92	15.17	8.98	3.24	66.41
R&D per-capita	2,094	2.35	0.49	5.09	0.00	61.75
Skills	2,094	0.11	0.05	0.16	0.00	1.00
Export intensity	2,094	24.74	10.91	28.71	0.00	100.00
Indebtedness	2,094	0.64	0.67	0.19	0.01	1.27
Labour costs	2,094	22.02	19.53	13.20	0.53	100.00
Binary						
New organization	2,094	0.65	1	0.48	0	1
New marketing	2,094	0.50	1	0.50	0	1
Cooperation	2,094	0.20	0	0.40	0	1
Age	2,094	0.01	0	0.11	0	1
Patent dummy	2,094	0.40	0	0.49	0	1
Group	2,094	0.39	0	0.49	0	1

dummy, signaling the presence of at least one patent application within the firm. This latter regressor should grasp the presence of potential Schumpeterian rents, i.e. rents due to company past innovative performance.

Tables 2 and 3 show some descriptive statistics of the variables noted above for the sample (2,094 units) used in the regression analysis (Sect. 5). Table 2 reports the continuous and binary variables and Table 3 the multi-value ones. From Table 2 it is immediately clear that some variables are very unevenly distributed: *Turnover*, for instance, has a mean of 39.01 million euros against a median of 9.59, demonstrating a very strong right-asymmetry for this variable, with few companies having a very large size. *R&D per-capita* and *Export intensity* are also asymmetrically distributed, while *Operating profit margin* and *Innovation efficiency index* are quite symmetric and bell-shaped. Looking at the binary factors (Table 2), we see that 40 % of companies have filed at least one patent, 39 % belong to a group, 20 % do innovation in cooperation, and 65 % have introduced new organizational changes for promoting innovation.

Table 3 sets out some structural characteristics of the sample. Concerning location (*Macro regions*) we see that the large majority of firms (72 %) are situated in northern Italy (the most developed region), while only around 20 % are situated in central Italy, and 8 % in the south and the islands. For *Size*, we note that the greatest share (around 45 %) are small companies (10–49 employees) with only a few very large firms (less than 3 %). Finally, the large part of the firms operate in medium-high technological sectors (28 %), and a small number in high-tech ones (13 %).

Table 3 Descriptive statistics: multi-value variables. Sample size: $N = 2094$

		Frequency	Percentage
Macro regions	North	1,519	72.54
	Center	399	19.05
	South and Islands	176	8.40
Size	10–49	933	44.56
	50–99	407	19.44
	100–249	383	18.29
	250–999	315	15.04
	>= 1,000	56	2.67
Sector	High-tech	280	13.37
	Medium-high-tech	598	28.56
	Medium-low-tech	361	17.24
	Low-tech	398	19.01
	Knowledge intensive services	234	11.17
	Low knowledge intensive services	223	10.65

5 Model Specification and Results

Not every resource (financial, labor or capital assets) spent in R&D produces the same additional innovation. Therefore the final impact on economic performance can be different, as the same R&D inputs, *ceteris paribus*, can give different innovation output due to different innovativeness.

Firm innovativeness can be defined as the ability to turn innovation inputs into innovation outputs. As such, it incorporates the concept of efficiency, which in turn can be explained by technological factors on the one hand, and managerial capabilities (which are firm specific) on the other (Gantumur and Stephan 2010). Indeed, "The meaning of the term *capabilities* is ambiguous in the literature, often seeming synonymous with competence, but sometimes also seeming to refer to higher-level routines (Teece and Pisano 1994), that is, to the organization's ability to apply its existing competences and create new ones" (Langlois 1997, p. 9). The organization's ability can also be understood as a matter of fit between the environment and the organization as cognitive apparatus (Winter 2003).

As illustrated above, the current study aims at identifying a direct measure of innovation-related managerial capabilities (efficiency), to be inserted into a profit function along with traditional Schumpeterian determinants of profitability. We apply a stochastic frontier analysis (SFA) to innovation production, which permits separation of the technological factor effect on innovativeness, from that due to managerial capability.

Consider Eq. (4): in a world without inefficiency the i-th firm will produce, on average (as the error term has a zero conditional mean), an output equal to $f(\mathbf{x}_i)$. In the study, this innovative output is explained by some of the typical innovation determinants, which are well established in the literature on economics of innovation [see among others Mairesse and Mohnen (2003)]. These are: R&D inputs, defined as intra-mural and extra-mural R&D expenditures connected to product or process innovations; acquisition of machinery and equipment; acquisition of external technology; human capital (skills); affiliation to a national or foreign group of firms; experience (age of firm); sector, size and localization dummies. We do not introduce the firm's idiosyncratic stock of knowledge because of poor information on past R&D spending (see description of variables **x** in Table 1).

The stochastic frontier analysis assumes that firms can be inefficient and produce less than $f(\mathbf{x}_i)$ for an average amount equal to $u_i(\mathbf{z}_i)$. According to Eq. (4), we estimate firm innovation inefficiency as function of: total innovation spending (including all innovation expenditures); organizational innovation, such as the introduction of new strategies, new management tools and new organization solutions; new marketing strategies; new competencies under international property rights protection (IPRs), together with employees' skills, process innovation and cooperative innovation activity (see the description of variables **z** in Table 1).

According to Table 4, the estimation of the parameters of the innovation frontier, meaning the $f(\mathbf{x}_i)$ in Eq. (2), shows that almost all variables are statistically significant and that the most relevant positive effect is given by employee skills. This means that innovation turnover is highly sensitive to human capital upgrading. Table 4 also sets out the parameters' estimate of the inefficiency function, i.e., the $u_i(\mathbf{z}_i)$ in Eq. (2). We find that the elasticity of the inefficiency function in this specification is −0.52. This means that a 10 % increase of total innovation expenditures will on average produce an increase in efficiency (or decrease in inefficiency) of about 5.2 %. It is worth noting that the other variables, although not significant, generally take the expected sign. In particular, the management innovation dummies (except "new business strategies") all take a negative sign, thus showing that they serve in the direction of reducing inefficiency. The same applies for the dummies of process innovation and IPRs protection capability, while higher labor skills and R&D cooperation present a positive (although again not significant) sign.

In short, it seems that our inefficiency function is not well explained by the organizational/managerial determinants, a finding that remains in keeping with other studies on the subject (e.g. Bos et al. 2011). However, overall the regression is highly statistically significant (see the Chi-squared at the end of Table 4), thus we can trust the model's predictions in obtaining firms' efficiency scores (i.e, the η_i).

Figure 1 plots the distribution of the efficiency scores η_i. It shows a higher frequency of firms for values higher than the sample mean (0.51), meaning a relatively larger presence of efficient firms. The distribution shows a fairly evident longer left tail with the median equal to 0.55.

Before presenting results on the operating profit margin (OPM) function, we look at its distribution and quantiles plots (see Fig. 2). These illustrate that about 90 % of firms have a positive OPM (in 2000), and that the margins are mainly concentrated between values 0 and 10; finally, 40 % of the sample is located above the OPM mean value, which is around 4.2 %.

Table 4 Stochastic frontier estimation of the innovation function (dependent variable: innovative turnover; variables are expressed in log; beta coefficients also reported; estimation method: maximum likelihood)

Equation (1)—Innovative turnover	
R&D intra	0.03***
	(0.01)
R&D extra	0.02
	(0.01)
Machinery	0.05***
	(0.01)
Technology	0.03**
	(0.01)
Skills	0.27***
	(0.03)
Group	0.33***
	(0.05)
Age	−0.06
	(0.13)
Process	−0.03
	(0.07)
Equation (2)—Innovative inefficiency	
Total innovation spending	−0.52*
	(0.27)
Skills	0.51
	(0.32)
Process	−0.89
	(0.82)
IPRs protection	−1.38
	(0.88)
New strategies	0.10
	(0.56)
New management	−0.78
	(0.68)
New organization	−0.66
	(0.66)
New marketing	−0.46
	(0.57)
Cooperation	0.79
	(0.74)
N	2,947
Chi2	2,558.25***
Log likelihood	−4,721.97

Standard errors in parentheses; $^{*}p < 0.1$, $^{**}p < 0.05$, $^{***}p < 0.01$

We now turn to examining whether the innovation efficiency, which impacts on innovation output, also has an effect on firm economic performance, by introducing the values of the efficiency scores η_i within the operating profit margin (OPM

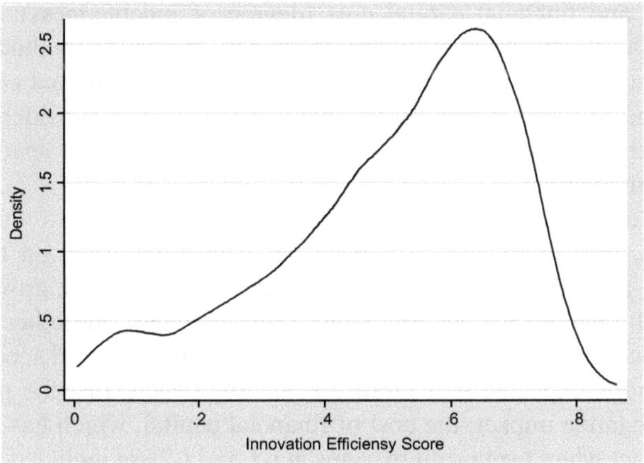

Fig. 1 Kernel estimation of the distribution of innovation efficiency scores

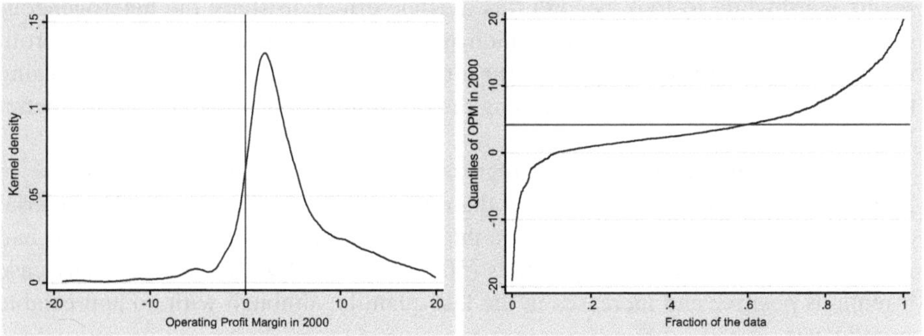

Fig. 2 Kernel estimation of the distribution and quantiles for operating profit margin (OPM) in 2000

in 2000) regression [in short we estimate Eq. (5)]. We assume that the relation between R&D activities and profit margin, *ceteris paribus*, is influenced by firms' managerial capability in innovating (as defined above), and we also introduce various explanatory/control variables for the OPM in order to get an unbiased estimate of the Innovation efficiency coefficient.

First, we estimate Eq. (5) by ordinary least squares (OLS) according to three model specifications: one not including lagged OPM realizations (i.e., the autoregressive component); one including a one-time lag (t-1); and finally, one specifying a two-time lag structure (t-1 and t-2). The other explanatory variables are: industrial structure variables, such as the level of turnover (approximating firm size and demand); industry concentration (at 2-digit sectoral level), to capture market power effects; export intensity, to grasp the type of market in which the firm operates and the level of competitive pressure; firm knowledge production capacity indicators, such as the R&D per-capita expenditures and employee skills; cost variables, such as labor cost and financial capital cost (degree of indebtedness); organizational variables, such as new forms of organization, new marketing methods, presence of cooperation in innovation; patenting activity, leading to potential commercialized innovation and property rights rent. Finally, as usual, we consider some control variables, such as firm age, affiliation to a group, sector, and spatial location in which the firm operates.

The OLS estimations are presented in Table 5. These show that in all three specifications, firm innovation efficiency has a positive effect on firm economic performance, although its marginal contribution to the OPM growth is slightly lower when the autoregressive components are included. The other factors which have a statistically significant impact on OPM in all three model specifications are, in addition to the expected past OPM levels: employee skills; the patent dummy; and, with a negative impact, the cost of financial capital, which has a less relevant marginal impact when firm profit margins at t-1 and t-2 are included.

Thus, at least at this stage, we can conclude that the managerial capacity in producing innovation has a positive effect on company profit rate. Nevertheless, it seems worthwhile to look beyond this average effect, to study the heterogeneous structure of the impact that innovation managerial efficiency has on firm profit margins. To this purpose, we perform a quantile regression (QR) analysis, using the OPM model specification including the profit margin at t-1 (that with the better F-test under OLS).

We run a number of quantile regressions at different quantiles of OPM in 2000 (see Table 6). These reveal that the marginal effect of innovation managerial efficiency is stronger and significant in the first two quantiles considered (10 % and 25 %) compared with higher quantiles (50 %, 75 % and 90 %), where in any case it remains positive and increases in the last quantile, although with no appreciable significance.

The QR analysis allows graphic inspection of the pattern of marginal effects from the Innovation efficiency index on OPM along all the OPM quantiles. Figure 3 presents the graph. Firstly, we can observe that the innovation efficiency coefficient equals the OLS coefficient[12] (represented by the horizontal dotted line) around the 20th quantile of the OPM distribution, where the effect is around 1.70. To the left of this point the effect of the innovation efficiency is stronger, even though the observation is with large confidence intervals for very low quantiles. Around the 60th quantile the effect approaches zero, and then again starts increasing for higher quantiles, although with no statistical significance.

This graph deepens our understanding regarding the impact of the innovation managerial efficiency on firm profitability. In fact while a positive effect seems to emerge on average, the QR analysis clearly shows that this finding is mainly

[12]The OLS results in Tables 5 and 6 are numerically different only because Table 3 reports standardized Beta coefficients (i.e., coefficients measured in standard deviation units), while Table 3 sets out OLS coefficients. In effect the difference is only in the unit of measurement employed.

Table 5 Operating profit margin (OPM) regression (dependent variable: OPM in 2000; estimation method: OLS; standardized beta coefficients reported)

	(1)	(2)	(3)
Profit margin (t-1)	–	0.651***	0.583***
		(0.02)	(0.02)
Profit margin (t-2)	–	–	0.114***
			(0.02)
Innovation efficiency	0.051**	0.044***	0.045***
	(0.87)	(0.66)	(0.65)
Turnover	−0.008	0.010	0.006
	(0.00)	(0.00)	(0.00)
Concentration	0.061	0.060*	0.054
	(0.03)	(0.03)	(0.02)
R&D per-capita	0.012	0.000	0.005
	(0.03)	(0.02)	(0.02)
Skill intensity	0.069***	0.042**	0.034*
	(1.01)	(0.77)	(0.76)
Export intensity	0.000	0.033*	0.024
	(0.01)	(0.00)	(0.00)
Indebtedness	−0.387***	−0.095***	−0.060***
	(0.75)	(0.64)	(0.66)
Labor costs	−0.162***	−0.005	−0.000
	(0.01)	(0.01)	(0.01)
New organization	−0.036*	−0.013	−0.021
	(0.31)	(0.24)	(0.23)
New marketing	0.000	0.010	0.014
	(0.29)	(0.22)	(0.22)
Cooperation	−0.014	−0.021	−0.024
	(0.36)	(0.28)	(0.27)
Age	−0.007	−0.009	0.005
	(1.19)	(0.90)	(0.95)
Patent dummy	0.038*	0.032*	0.040**
	(0.31)	(0.24)	(0.23)
Group	−0.038*	−0.024	−0.027
	(0.32)	(0.25)	(0.24)
N	2,113	2,094	2,071
adj. R^2	0.172	0.497	0.499
r2	0.19	0.51	0.51
F	9.80***	41.58***	40.62***

Standard errors in parentheses; $^{*}p < 0.1$, $^{**}p < 0.05$, $^{***}p < 0.01$

driven by the relatively higher effect of those firms positioned in the first quantiles (more or less from first to the 30th) of the OPM distribution. Here the effect is remarkably stronger and significant than in larger quantiles. As a consequence,

Table 6 Operating profit margin (OPM) quantile regression at different quantiles (dependent variable: OPM in 2000; coefficients reported in level)

	OLS	QR 10	QR 25	QR 50	QR 75	QR 90
Profit margin	0.62***	0.52***	0.57***	0.70***	0.72***	0.65***
(t-1)	(0.02)	(0.04)	(0.01)	(0.01)	(0.02)	(0.05)
Innovation	1.72***	2.23*	0.80**	0.52	0.61	1.22
efficiency	(0.66)	(1.26)	(0.35)	(0.36)	(0.54)	(1.51)
Turnover	0.00	0.00	−0.00	−0.00	−0.00	0.00***
	(0.00)	(0.00)	(0.00)	(0.00)	(0.00)	(0.00)
Concentration	0.04*	0.05	0.02	0.05***	0.02	0.02
	(0.03)	(0.04)	(0.01)	(0.01)	(0.02)	(0.06)
R&D per-capita	0.00	0.00	0.01	0.00	0.05***	−0.01
	(0.02)	(0.04)	(0.01)	(0.01)	(0.02)	(0.05)
Skill intensity	1.72**	0.77	0.46	1.08***	2.47***	3.84**
	(0.77)	(1.69)	(0.42)	(0.42)	(0.59)	(1.69)
Export intensity	0.01*	0.00	0.00	−0.00	0.01**	0.02*
	(0.00)	(0.01)	(0.00)	(0.00)	(0.00)	(0.01)
indebtedness	−3.30***	−0.13	−0.54	−0.85**	−4.17***	−8.10***
	(0.64)	(1.34)	(0.34)	(0.35)	(0.50)	(1.39)
Labor costs	−0.00	−0.02	0.00	0.01*	0.02***	0.02
	(0.01)	(0.02)	(0.01)	(0.01)	(0.01)	(0.02)
New	−0.19	−0.05	−0.20	−0.09	−0.17	−0.08
organization	(0.24)	(0.48)	(0.13)	(0.13)	(0.18)	(0.48)
New marketing	0.13	−0.02	0.08	0.20*	0.53***	0.73
	(0.22)	(0.47)	(0.12)	(0.12)	(0.17)	(0.46)
Cooperation	−0.35	−0.45	−0.34**	−0.01	−0.20	−0.47
	(0.28)	(0.52)	(0.15)	(0.15)	(0.21)	(0.58)
Age	−0.54	−1.00	−0.50	−0.10	−0.41	−1.05
	(0.90)	(1.65)	(0.47)	(0.49)	(0.63)	(1.70)
Patent dummy	0.43*	0.61	0.30**	0.07	0.01	0.28
	(0.24)	(0.48)	(0.13)	(0.13)	(0.18)	(0.48)
Group	−0.32	−1.56***	−0.21	0.08	0.33*	0.69
	(0.25)	(0.50)	(0.14)	(0.13)	(0.19)	(0.53)
N	2,094	2,094	2,094	2,094	2,094	2,094
adj. R^2/pseudo-R^2	0.497	0.1978	0.2370	0.3506	0.4266	0.4376
Quantile	–	−0.25	1.36	3.31	7.08	13.35
F-test	41.58***	–	–	–	–	–

Standard errors in parentheses; $*p < 0.1$, $**p < 0.05$, $***p < 0.01$

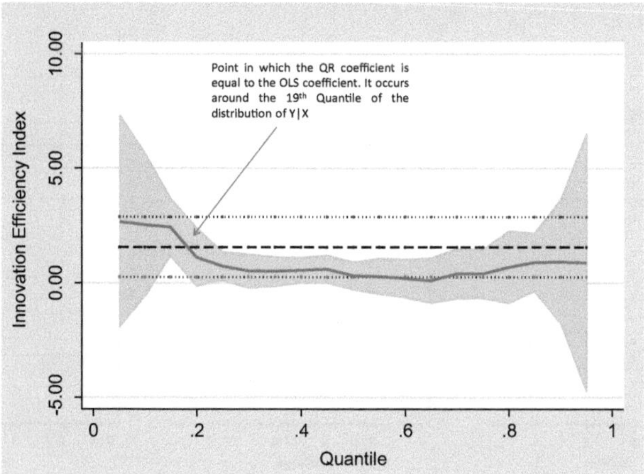

Fig. 3 Graph of the innovation efficiency index coefficient in quantile regressions: the *grey area* represents confidence intervals; the *horizontal dotted lines* refer to the OLS coefficient and its confidence interval (colour figure online)

since firms located in lower OPM quantiles are those with a negative or very small OPM, this finding states that the sensitivity of the OPM to a unit increase of innovation efficiency is stronger for firms economically more fragile (i.e., less competitive). This means that firms with relatively lower operating profit margins could experience larger benefits from implementing higher innovation efficiency than more profitable firms would.

Finally, Fig. 4 provides similar graphs for the other covariates. Three of these are interesting for brief comment. First, the profit margin at (t-1) shows an increasing pattern. This means that in the analysis, as firms become more profitable instead of less profitable, the effect of the profit margin at (t-1) increases accordingly. More profitable firms thus are more positively sensitive to past (positive) profits. Second, indebtedness shows a clear decreasing pattern, from positive to negative values. This means that the negative effect of indebtedness is basically driven by the behavior of more profitable firms, which get stronger negative values. The OPM of these firms is very sensitive to increasing debt. Third, OPM is positively sensitive to export intensity, especially for firms located in higher quantiles, meaning firms with a higher OPM. Finally, the other covariates do not seem to show any appreciably clear pattern.

Before concluding this section, it would be interesting to see whether any differences emerge at different company sizes. In this regard, Table **7** displays the effect of innovation efficiency on OPM at different quantiles, by three ranges of firm size. We immediately see that the positive effect found in the pooled regression is significantly driven by the behavior of smaller companies, and especially those characterized by low OPM quantiles. This means that firms that are smaller, and at the same time have poorer OPM performance, are those that could potentially

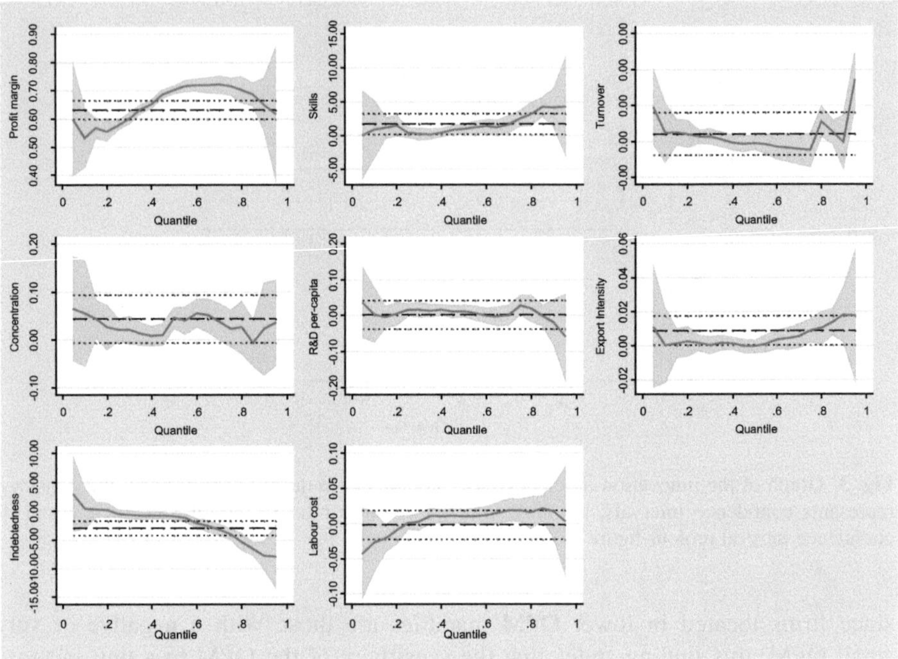

Fig. 4 Graphs of different regressors' quantile regressions coefficients: *grey area* represents the confidence interval; *horizontal dotted lines* refer to the OLS coefficient and its confidence interval (colour figure online)

Table 7 OPM quantile regressions: effect of innovation efficiency by firm size (coefficients in level)

	OLS	QR 10	QR 25	QR 50	QR 75	QR 90
Size 1 (10–49)	2.98***	4.01**	1.63***	0.39	0.62	3.09*
($N=933$)	(1.04)	(1.77)	(0.58)	(0.66)	(0.70)	(1.82)
Size 2 (50–249)	0.06	1.80	1.22*	0.30	0.87	1.09
($N=803$)	(1.71)	(3.55)	(0.67)	(0.95)	(1.20)	(6.11)
Size 3 (≥250)	−2.56	−1.03	−1.19***	−1.76***	−0.32***	−5.75***
($N=381$)	(2.06)	(0.69)	(0.00)	(0.00)	(0.00)	(1.57)

Standard errors in parentheses; $*p<0.1$, $**p<0.05$, $***p<0.01$

achieve higher benefits from an increase in innovation efficiency. This result fits with the significant negative sign of larger firms at higher quantiles. All in all it seems that as size increases, the role played by innovation efficiency in increasing profitability becomes weaker. This suggests the advisability of policies incorporating specific measures aimed at helping small companies to increase their innovative efficiency, and through this their profitability and potential growth.

6 Conclusions

The paper proves that managerial efficiency in mastering innovation is, on average, an important driver of firm innovative performance and market success, and that it complements traditional Schumpeterian determinants, such as market concentration. We have moved further along the theoretical-empirical trajectory laid out by Nelson and Winter (1982), and the resource-based view of the firm developed by strategic management literature, in proposing a direct measure of firm managerial capacity in implementing innovative products and activities.

The study has tested the significance of this direct measure of managerial capacity in a profit margin equation, augmented by the traditional competitive structural factors (demand, market concentration) and other control variables. It analyzes the role played by "innovation management efficiency" in fostering profitability, by means of an ordinary least squares and a series of quantile regressions. The model thus better clarifies the role played by companies' heterogeneous response to innovation management capacity, at different points of the distribution of the operating profit margin.

We have found evidence of an average positive effect from management efficiency, although quantiles regressions have shown that this average effect is mainly driven by a stronger magnitude of the effect for lower quantiles (i.e., for firms having negative or low-positive profitability). This means that weaker firms (in our sample those of smaller size) could profit more from an increase of managerial efficiency in doing innovation than more profitable businesses (in our sample, the larger ones).

Finally, our findings seem to suggest that the three main pillars explaining Schumpeterian comparative advantages, specifically efficiency, market concentration and skills, have different strength over the various profit margin quantiles, that is over different firm size. Higher efficiency is more relevant for small firms, market concentration is more relevant for medium firms, and human resources competencies are more relevant for larger companies.

References

Aghion P, Tirole J (1994) The management of innovation. Q J Econ 109(4):1185–1209

Arvanitis S, Seliger F, Stucki T (2013) The relative importance of human resource management practices for a firm's innovation performance, KOF Working Papers, N. 341, September

Bertrand M, Schoar A (2003) Managing with style: the effect of managers on firm policies. Q J Econ 118(4):1169–1208

Black SE, Lynch LM (2001) How to compete: the impact of workplace practices and information technology on productivity. Rev Econ Stat 83(3):434–445

Bloom N, Van Reenen J (2010) Why do management practices differ across firms and countries? J Econ Perspect 24(1):203–224

Bos J, Economidou C, Keotter M, Kolari J (2007) Do technology and efficiency differences determine productivity. Discussion paper series 07–14, Utrecht School of Economics, Utrecht University

Bos JWB, van Lamoen RCR, Sanders MWJL (2011) Producing innovations: determinants of innovativity and efficiency, preprint submitted to J Econ Growth
Bowman EH, Helfat CE (2001) Does corporate strategy matter? Strateg Manag J 22(1):1–23
Brush TH, Bromiley P (1997) What does a small corporate effect mean? A variance components simulation of corporate and business effects. Strateg Manag J 18(10):825–835
Bughin J, Jacques JM (1994) Managerial efficiency and the Schumpeterian link between size, market structure and innovation revisited. Res Policy 23(6):653–659
Cefis E, Ciccarelli M (2005) Profit differentials and innovation. Econ Innov New Technol 14(1–2):43–61
Chang YC, Chang HT, Chi HR, Chen MH, Deng LL (2012) How do established firms improve radical innovation performance? The organizational capabilities view. Technovation 32: 441–451
Coelli TJ, Rao DS (2005) Total factor productivity growth in agriculture: a Malmquist index analysis of 93 countries, 1980–2000. Agric Econ 32:115–134
Cohen W, Klepper S (1996) Firm size and the nature of innovation within industries: the case of process and product R&D. Rev Econ Stat 78:232–243
Cosh A, Fu X, Hughes A (2005) Management characteristics, collaboration and innovative efficiency: evidence from UK survey. Data Centre for Business Research, University of Cambridge Working Paper No. 311
Cosh A, Fu X, Hughes A (2012) Organization structure and innovation performance in different environments. Small Bus Econ 39:301–317
Dosi G (1988) Sources, procedures, and microeconomic effects of innovation. J Econ Lit 26(3):1120–1171
Dosi G, Marengo L, Pasquali C (2006) How much should society fuel the greed of innovators? On the relations between appropriability, opportunities and rates of innovation. Res Policy 35:1110–1121
Foss N (2013) Reflections on the explanation of heterogeneous firm capabilities. http://www.organizationsandmarkets.com/category/theory-of-the-firm/, last consulted 02/05/2014
Gantumur T, Stephan A (2010) Do external technology acquisitions matter for innovative efficiency and productivity? DIW Berlin Discussion Papers, 1035
Geroski PA (1998) An applied econometrician's view of large company performance. Rev Ind Organ 13:271–293
Geroski P, Machin S, Van Reenen J (1993) The profitability of innovating firms. RAND J Econ 24(2):198–211
Hashimoto A, Haneda S (2008) Measuring the change in R&D efficiency of the Japanese pharmaceutical industry. Res Policy 37:1829–1836
Hempel T, Zwick T (2008) New technology, work organization, and innovation. Econ Innov New Technol 17(4):331–354
Huselid MA (1995) The impact of human resource management practices on turnover, productivity, and corporate financial performance. Acad Manag J 38(3):635–872
Ichniowski C, Shaw K (2003) Beyond incentive pay: insiders' estimates of the value of complementary human resource management practices. J Econ Perspect 17(1):155–180
Ichniowski C, Shaw K, Prennushi G (1997) The effects of human resource management practices on productivity: a study of steel finishing lines. Am Econ Rev 87(3):291–313
James CR (1998) In search of firm effects: are managerial choice and organizational learning sources of competitive advantage? Paper presented at the strategic management society meetings, Fall 1997
Jiang J, Wang S, Zhao S (2012) Does HRM facilitate employee creativity and organizational innovation? A study of Chinese firms. Int J Hum Resour Manag 23(19):4025–4047
Koski H, Marengo L, Mäkinen I (2012) Firm size, managerial practices and innovativeness: some evidence from Finnish manufacturing. Int J Technol Manag 59(1/2):92–115
Kumbhakar SC, Lovell CAK (2000) Stochastic frontier analysis. Cambridge University Press, UK

Langlois R (1997) Cognition and capabilities: opportunities seized and missed in the history of the computer industry. In: Garud R, Nayyar P, Shapira Z (eds) Technological entrepreneurship: oversights and foresights. Cambridge University Press, New York, NY

Laursen K, Foss NF (2003) New human resource management practices, complementarities and the impact on innovation performance. Camb J Econ 27:243–263

Mairesse J, Mohnen P (2002) Accounting for innovation and measuring innovativeness: an illustrative framework and an application. Am Econ Rev Pap Proc 92(2):26–230

Mairesse J, Mohnen P (2003) R&D and productivity: a reexamination in light of the innovation surveys. Paper presented at the DRUID summer conference 2003 on creating, sharing and transferring knowledge, Copenhagen, 12–14 June

Malerba F, Orsenigo L (1990) Technological regimes and patterns of innovation: a theoretical and empirical investigation of the Italian case. In: Heertje A, Perlman M (eds) Evolving technology and market structure. Michigan University Press, Ann Arbor, MI, pp 283–306

McGahan AM, Porter ME (1997) How much does industry matter, really? Strateg Manag J 18(Summer Special Issue):15

McGahan AM, Porter ME (2002) What do we know about variance in accounting profitability? Manag Sci 48:834–851

Mookherjee D (2006) Decentralization, hierarchies, and incentives: a mechanism design perspective. J Econ Lit 44(2):367–390

Nelson RR, Winter S (1982) An evolutionary theory of economic change. Harvard University Press, Cambridge, MA

Pavitt K, Robson M, Townsend J (1987) The size distribution of innovating firms in the UK: 1945–1983. J Ind Econ 35(3):297–316

Penrose ET (1959) Theory of the growth of the firm. Wiley, New York, NY

Percival JC, Cozzarin BP (2008) Complementarities affecting the returns to innovation. Ind Innov 15(4):371–392

Peteraf M (1993) The cornerstones of competitive advantage: a resource-based view. Strateg Manag J 14:179–191

Porter ME (1980) Competitive strategy: techniques for analyzing industries and competitors. Free Press, New York, NY

Porter ME (1985) Competitive advantage: creating and sustaining superior performance. Free Press, New York, NY

Roquebert JA, Phillips RL, Westfall PA (1996) Markets vs. management: what 'drives' profitability? Strateg Manag J 17(8):633–664

Rumelt RP (1991) How much does industry matter? Strateg Manag J 12(3):167–185

Scherer FM (1980) Industrial market structure and economic performance. Houghton Mifflin, Boston, MA

Schmalensee R (1985) Do markets differ much? Am Econ Rev 75:341–351

Teece DJ (1984) Economic analysis and strategic management. Calif Manag Rev 26(3):87–110

Teece D (1986) Profiting from technological innovation: implications for integration, collaboration, licensing and public policy. Res Policy 15:285–305

Teece DJ (ed) (1987) The competitive challenge: strategies for industrial innovation and renewal. Harvard University Press, Cambridge, MA

Teece DJ, Pisano G (1994) The dynamic capabilities of firms: an introduction. Ind Corp Chang 3(3):537–556

Tirole J (1988) The theory of industrial organization. MIT, Cambridge, MA

Van Reenen J, Bloom N (2007) Measuring and explaining management practices across firms and countries. Q J Econ 122(4):1351–1408

Vossen RW (1998) Relative strengths and weaknesses of small firms in innovation. Int Small Bus J 16(3):88–95

Winter S (1987) Knowledge and competence as strategic assets. In: Teece DJ (ed) The competitive challenge: strategies for industrial innovation and renewal. Harvard University Press, Cambridge, MA, pp 159–184

Winter SG (2003) Understanding dynamic capabilities. Strateg Manag J 24(10):991–995

You JI (1995) Critical survey: small firms in economic theory. Camb J Econ 19:441–462

Zenger T (1994) Explaining organizational diseconomies of scale in R&D: agency problems and the allocation of engineering talent, ideas, and effort by firm size. Manag Sci 40:708–729

Zhang A, Zhang Y, Zhao R (2003) A study on the R&D efficiency and productivity of Chinese firms. J Comp Econ 31:444–464

Zhou H, Dekker R, Kleinknecht A (2011) Flexible labor and innovation performance: evidence from longitudinal firm-level data. Ind Corp Chang 20(3):941–968

Zoghi C, Mohr RD, Meyer PB (2010) Workplace organization and innovation. Can J Econ 43(2):622–639

Industrial Growth and Productivity Change in German Cities: A Multilevel Investigation

Stephan Hitzschke

Abstract The role of productivity change and city-specific characteristics on economic growth are analyzed for German cities. Productivity change is measured by the Malmquist index and its components, which are estimated by non-parametric data envelopment analysis. The nested structure as well as the interaction between industries within cities and over time is accounted for by estimating multilevel models. It is shown that there are differences for industrial growth for different cities and years. Therefore, the use of multilevel models is required. Schumpeter's creative destruction is found to hold for efficiency change on industrial growth. Efficiency change measures the catching-up to the best practice production function, reducing both value added growth and employment growth. Technological progress shifts the best practice production function and leads only to a rise in value added growth and not in employment growth. The estimations indicate a converging growth of urban industrial value added while employment growth diverges.

1 Introduction

"Why do some cities perform better than others?" remains a puzzling question in urban economics for rational actors. For example, entrepreneurs looking where to establish a new firm, consider different regional factors and might ask: Which city incorporates valuable opportunities and increases the productivity of the labor force to increase profit? Local governments are interested in how to set local variables to attract new firms within their areas and to increase the profit of the existing firms to gain more tax revenue and further increase the attractiveness of their own area. These questions are almost the same as for multicountry analyses understanding why some countries are poorer than others and do not converge as expected. Moreover, entrepreneurs have to think about settlement in different countries as well as national governments try to increase the attractiveness of their own countries for

S. Hitzschke (✉)
Department of Law and Economics, Technische Universität Darmstadt, Universitätsstraße 1, 64283 Darmstadt, Germany
e-mail: hitzschke@vwl.tu-darmstadt.de

A. Pyka, J. Foster (eds.), *The Evolution of Economic and Innovation Systems*, Economic Complexity and Evolution, DOI 10.1007/978-3-319-13299-0_20

foreign and domestic firms. This is important, especially to open economies with long-run, future-oriented governments which compete with each other.

However, these questions are in fact somewhat different in national urban decisions, in which the major economic circumstances are the same and other barriers are absent, for instance laws, political uncertainty and language difficulties. These forces are known to reduce the attitude of movements among countries and even within economic unions. Thus, altogether the decision for settlement is set by many local characteristics and is determined by various circumstances as well as being predetermined by local governmental parameter settings. By winning new companies and increasing the productivity of established industries, industries within a city grow faster. Local urban politicians try to foster industrial growth by setting the parameters of the local business environment. But what forces really affect local industrial growth? What parameter settings are optimal for local industrial growth? And is there any difference between those parameters with reference to either value added or employment growth? The goal of this work is to find answers to these questions. The analysis is rooted in the literature on urban endogenous growth that is fueled by technological improvements and their effects on the change of sectoral composition. Technological improvements are not just technical changes by the generation of new ideas, but also efficiency changes and catching-up by imitating technologies. Boschma and Lambooy (1999) present the framework of technical change in a regional context by the evolution of regional economics, called 'evolutionary economic geography' by Fratesi (2010) and Boschma and Frenken (2011).

In this analysis, value added growth and employment growth are analyzed, whether productivity change contributes to a rise or causes creative destruction. Since Schumpeter (1934, 1939) innovations as the implementation of innovative ideas are known as the major drivers of economic development. Furthermore, he emphasizes the different levels of activity, namely the micro-, meso- and macro-spheres jointly within the economic development process. In this work, the results of innovations are utilized, namely the increase in productivity and efficiency. Productivity and efficiency changes are implemented by a bias-corrected Malmquist index and its components, which are generated by the results of non-parametric data envelopment analysis, as described in Wheelock and Wilson (1999).

Additionally, the growth path estimation model is extended by local variables such as public expenditure and business taxation. These variables might have an effect on the productive performance of entrepreneurs within the city and the settlement decisions for new firms, which therefore change growth patterns. The data set contains 112 German cities with independent local political authorities over the period 1998 until 2007. Furthermore, and in tradition of urban economic analysis, the investigation contains variables for concentration, diversification and city size, and indicators related to technology and the knowledge base. The seminal paper is Glaeser et al. (1992) and the subsequent work of Henderson et al. (1995) and Henderson (1997), who estimate sector-specific regressions for different sectors, explaining employment change by local industrial and city-specific variables.

The contribution of this investigation consists of several extensions and refinements of this type of analysis. Primarily, three major extensions are incorporated. First, the role of productivity changes using bias-corrected Malmquist components estimated by data envelopment analysis is explored. Second, structural change is investigated, because aggregate economic growth is inevitably associated with structural change. Third, non-linearities are considered (i.e., interaction effects and quadratic effects) to expand the linear model to a more generalized version and to reveal the optimal conditions for future industry growth. The main refinement consists of the adoption of multilevel models to account for the nested structure of the data, the unobserved city-specific effects and to estimate unbiased estimates. Thus, these regressions are estimated by using multilevel analysis methods to account for the importance of the meso- and macro-spheres. This method allows varying coefficients on each level, which are industries as the first level, cities as the second level and time as the third level. Multilevel models include fixed as well as random effects for considering the dependency structures on each level, as explained in Raudenbush and Bryke (2002). It is possible to include exogenous variables in the estimation, which are observed at different levels, like city-specific variables as well as industry-specific variables which are nested within cities.

The purpose of this work lies in the identification of the effect of productivity and efficiency changes on value added growth and employment growth within different industries in German cities. Tests are carried out to investigate whether those effects of productivity changes vary between cities and over time. The results provide mixed evidence on the nature of the value added growth and employment growth. On average, and over all the industries included, historical changes affect value added growth and employment growth, supporting creative destruction. In addition, non-linearities seem to be characteristic features of several explanatory variables. As a consequence, some local political parameters seem to have a minimum point which leads to a decrease of value added growth and employment growth.

The work is organized as follows. The next section presents the related literature. Section 3 clarifies the data used in the estimations, and Sect. 4 gives a brief overview of the applied methods. The empirical results are presented and analyzed in Sect. 5. At the end of this work, a short conclusion is drawn in Sect. 6.

2 Literature Review

Evolutionary economic geography is classified by Fratesi (2010), who shows the connection of regional innovations and dynamics via competitiveness. He furthermore emphasizes its roots in meso-economic applications, although it is possible to extend the analyses to regional micro- as well as macro-economics. Regional innovations and their effect on competitiveness are crucial elements in evolutionary economic geography, but they also provide feedback on income growth with innovations in a dynamic process. That feedback is often used, e.g. in Gaffard (2008), who incorporates the Schumpeterian ideas of creative destruction within a Hicksian framework in which competition increases efficiency, and therefore increases the effect of innovations and growth. The creative destruction and the contributions of innovation to regional growth are theoretically implemented in dynamic analyses by Batabyal and Nijkamp (2012, 2013), in which innovations and technological progress are key divers in the regional growth path.

Frenken and Boschma (2007) build an analytical framework for the effects of innovations on firm and city growth with innovations generated exogenously. Innovations affect urban growth by increasing urban diversification. They notice that the correlation between size and innovation might be caused by the correlation between size and diversification. The positive feedback relationship is non-linear because of the routines in evolutionary economic developments. Furthermore, they incorporate negative feedback effects on urban growth, where cities and industries decline without innovations. The theoretical analysis in Martin and Sunley (2006) connects regional path dependency and lock-in effects within a region, which could be positive by stimulating innovations and increasing economic performance. It could also be negative by creating negative externalities through inflexibility and reducing economic performance, institutional hysteresis, local external economies of industrial specialization, economics of agglomeration, and region-specific institutions.

Noseleit (2013) estimates the relationship between structural change and concentration measure namely, the Gini coefficient, on employment growth for West German regions and agglomerations. He finds a negative effect of the Gini coefficient on employment growth in agglomerations and the structural change, measured by the similarity between entries and exits of firms, which has negative effect on employment growth.

Illy et al. (2011) investigate employment growth for German cities with respect to the local economic structure. They find U-shaped functional forms of specialization and size on employment growth of the free German cities for the period 2003–2007.

The necessity for different levels of activity, namely the micro-, meso-, and macro-levels, is demonstrated in Rozenblat (2012) for the agglomeration economies of firms in international cities. The importance of intercity networks is emphasized with respect to agglomeration economies, because interaction takes place between people and institutions at the micro-level. These micro-level interactions affect urban externalities by city size and growth at the meso-level. However, Rozenblat does not identify location economies emerging from cities' specialization.

One elegant way to implement different levels of activity is by using multilevel or mixed-effects models. The multilevel analysis is already a wide-spread feature, applied in different academic fields like biology, as in the various analyses assembled in Zuur et al. (2009); or sociology as variously shown in Hox (2002). So far, it is rarely implemented in economics; especially in urban economics, even the observed data are predestined for that kind of investigation. For example individuals at the same level, for instance within a city, are likely to interact and are faced with the same environmental factors, which might be observed or unobserved. Therefore, those individuals are endogenously dependent, which leads to biased estimates. This problem can be solved by mixed-effects models. Mixed-effects models are explained in Pinheiro and Bates (2000) and in Sect. 4.2 and account for each of the levels and nesting structures within the observations.

A regional multilevel model is estimated by Srholec (2010). He investigates the likelihood of innovations in the Czech Republic within a two-level Logit approach. As explanatory variables he includes a bunch of local variables, like population density, urbanization, average wage, long-term unemployment, number of murders, as well as a few other variables, and builds three factors for these. With those factors, he calculates a basic multilevel model with fixed and random effects for all factors and the intercept. Next, he extends the basic multilevel model to the so-called intercept-as-outcome model by additionally explaining the fixed effect intercept of the model. Furthermore, he generalized that model to the so-called 'slope-as-outcome' model by adding the explanatory factors for the slope estimates of each factor. In doing so, he includes all possible interaction terms to consider non-linearities. Unfortunately, he does not include any test for the model or at least any measure for the explanatory power of the model like the likelihood of the model or a resulting information criterion or likelihood ratio test. He only includes an index of dispersion that is not helpful to see whether the extensions add substantially explanatory power to the model or only increase the uncertainty of the estimates. For reasons of parsimony, likelihood ratio tests of the different models would be fruitful.

Other multilevel analyses within economics include Giovannetti et al. (2009), Goedhuys and Srholec (2010), and Srholec (2011). Giovannetti et al. (2009) analyze firm performances in Italy. They test the necessary use of the provincial level by a likelihood ratio test and conclude that the multilevel model is appropriate. They show that the effects of provincial variables like social capital have a larger effect on smaller firms than on larger firms, which still remains significant. Thus, location variables have to be considered like local governmental expenditures, as well as local circumstances like airports and other transportation facilities.

Goedhuys and Srholec (2010) perform another application of multilevel analysis within economics. They use a two-level model to analyze productivity at the firm-level within different countries. The investigation includes the stepwise approach similar to that in Srholec (2010). However, the productivity is estimated for a Cobb–Douglas production function, therefore, all the parameters of the production function have to be estimated. To derive accurate productivity measurements from the production function, all estimated parameters should be unbiased. Therefore, they apply a multilevel approach to reduce the bias resulting from the nested structure. Nevertheless, the functional form is also questionable, as indicated by analyses using translog functions as generalized versions of the Cobb–Douglas production function.

Srholec (2011) investigates the likelihood of innovations in 32 developing countries, which is similar to his analysis in 2010. He uses a two-level Logit model and finds necessary support for adoption of multilevel analysis, because country-specific variables contribute to the explanatory power for the likelihood of a successful innovation. Nonetheless, he finds no empirical evidence of an effect of population size on innovation. He records a highly significant negative estimate for the local income tax rate. Furthermore, he shows that the explanatory power soars with the random effects.

3 Data

In this analysis, a data set for 112 NUTS3-districts which are classified as free city districts (so-called 'kreisfreie Städte' or 'Stadtkreise' in Germany)[1] is used. These cities are characterized by an independent local government that determines local environmental variables within the highly restricted legislative framework, like local tax structure and expenditure on local public issues. Of course, such local governments are independent by law, but because they compete against each other their decisions depend upon the past decisions of all cities. That structure should be accounted for in the analysis. The time period for which data are available is 1998 until 2007. The data are taken from the regional database of the Statistical Offices of Germany[2] ('Statistische Ämter des Bundes und der Länder') and the INKAR database of the Federal Agency of Building and Urban Development[3] ("Bundesamt für Bauwesen und Raumordnung"). It is a balanced panel, so for all cities the number of employees and the value added is known for each sector in every year. The sectors are defined at a one-digit industry specification (WZ 2003 of the Federal Statistical Office of Germany (Statistisches Bundesamt 2003), which is a level of aggregation equivalent to the European-wide classification NACE Rev. 1.1):

CDE	wide manufacturing (including mining/quarrying, energy, and water supply)
D	core manufacturing
F	construction
GHI	private non-financial services
JK	financial and business services (finance, insurance, and real estate)
LMNOP	public and social services

Because of the minor importance of the agriculture, forestry and fishing sector in German cities, this sector (industries with code AB) has been omitted. For these economic sectors, input as output variables are required to estimate productivity measures. As Moomaw (1981) notes in criticizing how the disregard of the capital stock in Sveikauskas (1975) leads to biased estimates in productive efficiency measures, the capital stock has to be added. The capital stock for each city and the

[1] A list of the included cities is given in the Appendix.

[2] The database is available https://www.regionalstatistik.de/genesis.

[3] The database is available on CD-ROM upon request to the Federal Agency of Building and Urban Development at http://www.bbsr.bund.de.

wide manufacturing sector is computed with the perpetual inventory method (Park 1995) supposing capital stocks $cap_{j,t}$ develop as

$$cap_{j,t} = (1 - d)cap_{j,t-1} + inv_{j,t}, \tag{1}$$

with d the constant depreciation rate and $inv_{j,t}$ the city-specific investments in the wide manufacturing sector for each city j at time t. Furthermore, if investments change with constant growth rates $g_{inv,j}$, the starting capital stock at time $t = 0$, can be calculated as

$$cap_{j,0} = inv_{j,0} \cdot \frac{1 - g_{inv,j}}{d + g_{inv,j}}. \tag{2}$$

Equation (2) is the result of the capital accumulation with investments growing at a constant rate and therefore leading to an infinite geometrical series.

The data of investments in the wide manufacturing sector are also taken from the regional database of the Statistical Offices in Germany for the time period 1995–2007 in real units and are given without the energy and water supply industry. The starting capital stock is estimated for 1995. The average annual depreciation rate is set to 10 % per annum ($d = 0$), which is quite high but results in positive capital estimation caused by massive changes in investments in the first period of observation. The average growth rates of investments are calculated by the development of investment figures. Unfortunately, for some cities (Cottbus, Potsdam, and Stralsund) the growth rates of investment were shrinking by more than 10 %, caused by immense changes after German Reunification and the associated structural changes in industry. Therefore, the average growth rates for all cities in East Germany were applied, which were above minus 10 %, meaning that the denominator in Eq. (2) is positive. This results in positive starting capital stocks for all cities. Because of the higher uncertainty in the estimates of capital figures for the first years of observation, the figures should be treated with caution, especially for the first years until the starting capital stock is depreciated and the capital stock is predominately driven by last investments. However, the starting capital stock depreciated to 40 % in 2004 and thereby reduces the involved uncertainty in the input factor. The capital stock for the other industry sectors is calculated based on the capital intensity in the wide manufacturing sector for each city and the ratio of capital intensity of the wide manufacturing sector compared to the other industry sectors in whole Germany. The information is given by the OECD Database for Structural Analysis (STAN).[4] The ratio for the whole of Germany is multiplied by the calculated capital in each city.

[4]The database is available on the Internet by http://stats.oecd.org.

Population figures are taken from the regional database of the Statistical Offices in Germany. Under German registration law, a person is only added for a city if they have their principal residence within that city. So, the figure does not account for people with secondary residences in order to avoid double counting, even though many people have a secondary residence in a city and are part of its productive employees. Nonetheless, the use of the population figures for the number of inhabitants within a city is reasonable, since people who spend more than half of their time in the city are required to have their principal residence in that particular city.

Comparable studies estimate the effects of various additional variables on productivity growth by least squared methods. These analyses involve different city-specific variables, which might not have only linear effects on value added growth and employment growth. To account for the non-linear relationships proposed by Frenken and Boschma (2007), these factors are additionally included with quadratic as well as interaction terms within the linear regression, to test the significance of these terms. The factors are observed variables as, e.g., population changes (*dPop*) and the number of students within each city. For the analysis, the data has been transformed to become narrower. This is done for the number of students by taking the logarithm (ln*Stu*). However, there are several cities in the sample with no University or University of Applied Science at all, so the amount of one is added to each city, which results in positive figures for the logarithm of all students.

According to Frenken and Boschma (2007), a growing city is assumed to have negative feedback slopes on employment growth and value added growth in the industries if there is no innovative activity within the city. The number of students represents the knowledge base within the city and serves as a measure of the ability to implement and generate innovation. Therefore, a larger number of students should be correlated with larger value added and employment growth, and might interact with a technological progress measure. Additionally, I propose a variable indicating the composition of the industry within each city. Urban analyses find support for the view that homogeneous distribution for industries support the generation and flow of new ideas by the localization externalities. The Gini-coefficient (*Gini*) is calculated on the basis of employment of a more disaggregated level by ten industries, which is observed and supplied by the federal labor agency of Germany.

Furthermore, a factor for the change of the structural composition of the industries within each city is calculated by the modified Lilien-index (*SC*), which indicates to what extent the change within 1 year has taken place, and is measured by

$$SC_{jt} = \sqrt{\sum_{i=1}^{10} x_{ijt} \cdot x_{ij(t-1)} \left(\ln \frac{x_{ijt}}{x_{ij(t-1)}} \right)^2}, \tag{3}$$

with x_{ijt}, the share of industry i in city j at time t, and the sum of all industries equals one for each city and every year. This measurement is used and discussed in the literature examining structural change, e.g., Stamer (1999) and Dietrich (2009). It is a dispersion index, in which smaller sectors and sectors with lower growth are considered with a smaller weight. That structural change measure is also calculated on the basis of the employment figures of the 10 disaggregated industries.

Additionally, spatial variables implemented include the whole area as well as the share of recreational area to the total area within each city. A larger recreational area within a city enables workers to recreate faster and thereby increases labor productivity or contributes to growth.

As an additional feature, the German tax system enables every city to set its own local business tax (*BusTax*) (by setting its own so-called 'Hebesatz', a collection rate in Germany) as well as its own tax on land and buildings (*LTax*), which is by German tax law a tax on land and buildings for non-agriculture land-use (so-called 'Grundsteuer B' in Germany). On the one hand, cities with higher taxes increase the costs of living and production within that city and thereby attract firms with higher productivity. On the other hand, cities with higher income are also able to spend more on infrastructure, education, administration, and so on. Although these variables are significant in some studies, expenses on transportation facilities, tax on land and building and the recreational area share have not been proven to be significant in this investigation for German cities and have, therefore, been excluded.

All the variables are observed over the years 1997 until 2008. Descriptive statistics are given in Table 1 with the number of students measured in thousand and industrial growth rates in percentage changes.

Table 1 shows that there are many cities with a low number of students as a measure for the local knowledge base, which results in a median which is considerably lower than the mean. In addition, the standard deviation (s.d.) is very large for the number of students. Furthermore, all input variables as well as value added as output are non-negative, as required in DEA. The growth rates of gross value added have a mean and a median which are positive, meaning that on average value added is growing. Employment growth is zero on average, which indicates that there is on average no change in employment for all industries and cities. Table 1 also shows that the Gini coefficient as a concentration measure is in a narrow band. There is no extreme observation and, therefore, no absolute concentration with a city with only one industry and also no absolute equally distributed industry share. The structural change index has the value of almost zero for most cities, indicating almost no change in industry shares for subsequent years, but at least there is always some change. The descriptive statistics also show a high fluctuation among cities by massive changes in population.

Table 1 Descriptive statistics

Variable	Min.	1st Quartile	Median	Mean	3rd Quartile	Max.	s.d.
Gross value added growth	−0.829	−0.019	0.017	0.015	0.054	0.901	0.083
Employment growth	−0.330	−0.026	0	−0.004	0.018	0.571	0.047
Students	0	12.2	43.2	58.91	82.45	250.4	58.003
Population change	−20,970	−659.8	−56.5	149.7	441.2	47,880	2,939.2
Industrial Gini coefficient	0.415	0.489	0.535	0.544	0.580	0.748	0.070
Structural change	0.003	0.009	0.012	0.016	0.016	0.465	0.024

4 Theory

4.1 Productivity Change

Efficiency is measured within a non-parametric framework because the production function, which transforms inputs into outputs, is not known. Thus, a parametric setup would be questionable because of the unknown structure of the process specific for industries. Contrarily, the non-parametric data envelopment analysis solves with these problems. The non-parametric framework to measure efficiency of cities is the data envelopment analysis (DEA), which was developed by Charnes et al. (1978). Within the DEA, the observed combinations of inputs and outputs for all cities are taken into account. The aim of the DEA is to find those cities that envelop all others. These cities building the enveloping frontier represent actual best practice and thus are efficient. All other cities could improve their efficiency by either reducing inputs for the same production of outputs or by increasing the production output for their used inputs, depending on the orientation, e.g., input- or output-orientation, respectively.

A distance function for output-orientation is defined by Farrell (1957) and calculated in a linear program for each industry separately

$$\begin{aligned} \min_{\theta,\boldsymbol{\lambda}} \theta_{CRS,ij}, \\ st \qquad -\boldsymbol{y}_{ij} + \boldsymbol{Y\lambda} &\geq \mathbf{0} \\ \theta \boldsymbol{x}_{ij} - \boldsymbol{X\lambda} &\geq \mathbf{0} \\ \boldsymbol{\lambda} &\geq \mathbf{0}, \end{aligned} \tag{4}$$

where $\theta_{CRS,ij}$ is the efficiency score for industry i in city j, $\boldsymbol{Y}$ is a (1×112) vector containing all one outputs in the 112 cities, $\boldsymbol{\lambda}$ is a (112×1) vector of weights, and $\boldsymbol{X}$ is a (2×112) matrix for the two inputs in the 112 cities. The outputs are the gross value added of each of the industries investigated within the city, and the input matrix contains the two inputs capital and labor used in each industry within each city. The linear program in Eq. (4) is the most common representation. The productivity and efficiency changes are measured by an index, which is called after a similar index in Malmquist (1953). Here, the definition of Färe et al. (1992) for the index is used. The Malmquist index $MQ_{ij}(t_1, t_2)$ for two different periods in time t_1 and t_2, with $t_1 < t_2$ is defined as

$$MQ_{ij}(t_1,t_2) = \sqrt{\frac{\Delta_{ij,t_1}\left(\boldsymbol{x}_{j,t_2}, \boldsymbol{y}_{j,t_2}\right)}{\Delta_{ij,t_1}\left(\boldsymbol{x}_{j,t_1}, \boldsymbol{y}_{j,t_1}\right)} \times \frac{\Delta_{ij,t_2}\left(\boldsymbol{x}_{j,t_2}, \boldsymbol{y}_{j,t_2}\right)}{\Delta_{ij,t_2}\left(\boldsymbol{x}_{j,t_1}, \boldsymbol{y}_{j,t_1}\right)}}, \tag{5}$$

with $\Delta_{ij,t_k}\left(\boldsymbol{x}_{ij,t_l}, \boldsymbol{y}_{ij,t_l}\right)$, the distance function of industry i in city j in period t_k in comparison to the frontier in period t_l $\Delta_{ij,t_k}\left(\boldsymbol{x}_{ij,t_l}, \boldsymbol{y}_{ij,t_l}\right) = \left(\max\left\{\theta : \left(\boldsymbol{x}_{ij,t_l}, \theta \boldsymbol{y}_{ij,t_l}\right) \in T\left(t_k\right)\right\}\right)^{-1}$. The first factor in Eq. (5) measures the change of industry in city j from period t_1 to period t_2, and both relative to the frontier in period t_1. Analogously, the second factor in Eq. (5) gives the change of industry i in city j from period t_1 to period t_2, but both relative to the frontier in period t_2. Thus, the Malmquist index is the geometrical average of the productivity changes measured on the basis of the new and old frontier in period t_2 and period t_1, respectively. Values of the Malmquist index which are smaller than unity indicate decreases in productivity between period t_1 and period t_2, while values larger than unity indicate improvements in productivity between both periods. There are many different decompositions of this index. Because I am interested in the most common factors, I use the decomposition of Simar and Wilson (1999). The first decomposition of the Malmquist index is as described in Färe et al. (1992)

$$MQ_{ij}(t_1, t_2) = \frac{\Delta_{ij,t_2}\left(\boldsymbol{x}_{ij,t_2}, \boldsymbol{y}_{ij,t_2}\right)}{\Delta_{ij,t_1}\left(\boldsymbol{x}_{ij,t_1}, \boldsymbol{y}_{ij,t_1}\right)} \times \sqrt{\frac{\Delta_{ij,t_1}\left(\boldsymbol{x}_{ij,t_2}, \boldsymbol{y}_{ij,t_2}\right)}{\Delta_{ij,t_2}\left(\boldsymbol{x}_{ij,t_2}, \boldsymbol{y}_{ij,t_2}\right)} \times \frac{\Delta_{ij,t_1}\left(\boldsymbol{x}_{ij,t_1}, \boldsymbol{y}_{ij,t_1}\right)}{\Delta_{ij,t_2}\left(\boldsymbol{x}_{ij,t_1}, \boldsymbol{y}_{ij,t_1}\right)}}. \tag{6}$$

The productivity change is still the same but the effect can be observed separately. The first factor of the Malmquist index (denoted by *malm* later on) in Eq. (6) indicates changes in efficiency (denoted by *eff* later on). The second factor expresses the technological change (denoted by *tech* later on) from period t_1 and period t_2. The change in efficiency is related to the catching-up of the industry in a particular city, whereas technological change measures shifts in the technology captured by the best practice production frontier. It should be noticed, that I only use distance functions under constant returns to scale up unto this point. As used in Wheelock and Wilson (1999), the change in efficiency can be split further to

$$\begin{aligned}\Delta Eff_{ij}(t_1, t_2) = \frac{\Delta_{ij,t_2}\left(\boldsymbol{x}_{ij,t_2}, \boldsymbol{y}_{ij,t_2}\right)}{\Delta_{ij,t_1}\left(\boldsymbol{x}_{ij,t_1}, \boldsymbol{y}_{ij,t_1}\right)} &= \frac{\tilde{\Delta}_{ij,t_2}\left(\boldsymbol{x}_{ij,t_2}, \boldsymbol{y}_{ij,t_2}\right)}{\tilde{\Delta}_{ij,t_1}\left(\boldsymbol{x}_{ij,t_1}, \boldsymbol{y}_{ij,t_1}\right)} \\ &\times \frac{\Delta_{ij,t_2}\left(\boldsymbol{x}_{ij,t_2}, \boldsymbol{y}_{ij,t_2}\right) / \tilde{\Delta}_{ij,t_2}\left(\boldsymbol{x}_{ij,t_2}, \boldsymbol{y}_{ij,t_2}\right)}{\Delta_{ij,t_1}\left(\boldsymbol{x}_{ij,t_1}, \boldsymbol{y}_{ij,t_1}\right) / \tilde{\Delta}_{ij,t_1}\left(\boldsymbol{x}_{ij,t_1}, \boldsymbol{y}_{ij,t_1}\right)}\end{aligned} \tag{7}$$

with $\tilde{\Delta}_{ij,t}\left(\boldsymbol{x}_{ij,t}, \boldsymbol{y}_{ij,t}\right)$ for $t = t_1, t_2$ the distance function under variable returns to scale. The calculation of distance functions with variable returns to scale is almost the same as for constant returns to scale in Eq. (4), except for one further constraint:

$$\begin{aligned}&\min_{\theta,\boldsymbol{\lambda}} \theta_{VRS,ij}, \\ &st \quad -\boldsymbol{y}_{ij} + \boldsymbol{Y\lambda} \geq \boldsymbol{0}, \\ &\qquad \theta\boldsymbol{x}_{ij} - \boldsymbol{X\lambda} \geq \boldsymbol{0}, \\ &\qquad \boldsymbol{1}'\boldsymbol{\lambda} = 1 \\ &\qquad \boldsymbol{\lambda} \geq \boldsymbol{0}.\end{aligned} \tag{8}$$

The additional condition expressed in Eq. (8) constrains the weights to sum to unity. It is also called the convexity condition in Coelli et al. (2005). In the literature, there is a controversy about using variable returns to scale distance functions (see, e.g., Ray and Desli 1997; Färe et al. 1997). The first decomposed factor in Eq. (7) is the change of pure efficiency $\Delta PureEff_{ij}(t_1, t_2)$ and the second factor is the change of scale efficiency $\Delta ScaleEff_{ij}(t_1, t_2)$. The change of pure efficiency (denoted as *pure.eff* later on) is calculated by the ratio of the distance functions only to the variable returns to scale best practice frontier. The change of scale efficiency (denoted as *scale* later on in the estimation results) is the ratio of the scale efficiencies in period t_2 by period t_1. It is the ratio of the distance function under constant returns to scale and that under variable returns to scale at the same time as the reference observation for the frontier in that particular period. The scale efficiency change component captures the change to the most productive scale in which the variable returns to scale and the constant returns to scale frontier are equal.

In a similar way, the change in technological efficiency can be decomposed as shown in Wheelock and Wilson (1999):

$$\Delta Tech_{ij}(t_1, t_2) = \sqrt{\frac{\Delta_{ij,t_1}\left(\boldsymbol{x}_{ij,t_2}, \boldsymbol{y}_{ij,t_2}\right)}{\Delta_{ij,t_2}\left(\boldsymbol{x}_{ij,t_2}, \boldsymbol{y}_{ij,t_2}\right)} \times \frac{\Delta_{ij,t_1}\left(\boldsymbol{x}_{ij,t_1}, \boldsymbol{y}_{ij,t_1}\right)}{\Delta_{ij,t_2}\left(\boldsymbol{x}_{ij,t_1}, \boldsymbol{y}_{ij,t_1}\right)}} \tag{9}$$

$$\begin{aligned} &= \sqrt{\frac{\tilde{\Delta}_{ij,t_1}\left(\boldsymbol{x}_{ij,t_2}, \boldsymbol{y}_{ij,t_2}\right)}{\tilde{\Delta}_{ij,t_2}\left(\boldsymbol{x}_{ij,t_2}, \boldsymbol{y}_{ij,t_2}\right)} \times \frac{\tilde{\Delta}_{ij,t_1}\left(\boldsymbol{x}_{ij,t_1}, \boldsymbol{y}_{ij,t_1}\right)}{\tilde{\Delta}_{ij,t_2}\left(\boldsymbol{x}_{ij,t_1}, \boldsymbol{y}_{ij,t_1}\right)}} \\ &\times \sqrt{\frac{\Delta_{ij,t_1}\left(\boldsymbol{x}_{ij,t_2}, \boldsymbol{y}_{ij,t_2}\right) / \tilde{\Delta}_{ij,t_1}\left(\boldsymbol{x}_{ij,t_2}, \boldsymbol{y}_{ij,t_2}\right)}{\Delta_{ij,t_2}\left(\boldsymbol{x}_{ij,t_2}, \boldsymbol{y}_{ij,t_2}\right) / \tilde{\Delta}_{ij,t_2}\left(\boldsymbol{x}_{ij,t_2}, \boldsymbol{y}_{ij,t_2}\right)}} \\ &\times \sqrt{\frac{\Delta_{ij,t_1}\left(\boldsymbol{x}_{ij,t_1}, \boldsymbol{y}_{ij,t_1}\right) / \tilde{\Delta}_{ij,t_1}\left(\boldsymbol{x}_{ij,t_1}, \boldsymbol{y}_{ij,t_1}\right)}{\Delta_{ij,t_2}\left(\boldsymbol{x}_{ij,t_1}, \boldsymbol{y}_{ij,t_1}\right) / \tilde{\Delta}_{ij,t_2}\left(\boldsymbol{x}_{ij,t_1}, \boldsymbol{y}_{ij,t_1}\right)}}. \end{aligned} \tag{10}$$

The first factor in the second line measures the pure change in technology $\Delta PureTech_{ij}(t_1, t_2)$, and the second factor in the third and fourth line quantifies the change in scale of technology $\Delta ScaleTech_{ij}(t_1, t_2)$. The pure change in technology (denoted as *pure.tech* later on) is the geometric mean of the distance ratio to the variable returns to scale frontier for each time period. The change in scale of technology (denoted as *scale.tech* later on) measures the change of returns to scale for variable returns to scale technology for the two time periods. Both components include distance functions under variable returns to scale with time different observations and reference frontiers $\tilde{\Delta}_{ij,t_k}\left(\boldsymbol{x}_{ij,t_l}, \boldsymbol{y}_{ij,t_l}\right)$ with $t_k \neq t_l$. These mixed distance functions do not have to be calculable for every observation (see, e.g., Ray and Desli 1997). Computations are performed with R using the package `FEAR`, which is described in Wilson (2008).

To test whether the variable returns to scale measure is advisable, Simar and Wilson (2002) propose different non-parametric tests for returns to scale based on the bootstrap algorithms of Simar and Wilson (1998). I run two different tests, one with the mean of efficiency for all cities (used, e.g. in Cullmann and von Hirschhausen 2008), and one with efficiency for each city separately (used, e.g., in Badunenko 2010). Each test is carried out for testing first the null hypothesis of constant returns to scale against decreasing returns to scale, and second for non-increasing returns to scale against increasing returns to scale. For using the variable returns to scale measurements, both null hypotheses must be rejected. It turns out that for the means of scale efficiency over all cities, both null hypotheses can be rejected. The null hypothesis of constant returns to scale can be rejected for all industries in every year. In addition, the null hypothesis of non-increasing returns to scale is also rejected for every industry in each year. Moreover, the second test for all cities separately generally rejects both null hypotheses. Tables 2 and 3 show the results for both null hypotheses, with the percentage share of cities for which the null hypotheses cannot be rejected, depending on the sector and year.

Both Tables 2 and 3 show that the null hypotheses are not rejected in just a few cases. However, there are many cases for the second test of non-increasing returns to scale in some industries especially for financial and business services (JK) and in public and social services (LMNOP). These findings support the test, which rejects the null hypothesis of non-increasing returns to scale for all cities together.

Table 2 Results for Simar and Wilson (2002) test for constant returns to scale

Year	CDE	D	F	GHI	JK	LMNOP
1999	3	0	2	1	2	1
2000	0	0	0	0	1	1
2001	0	1	1	1	1	1
2002	2	1	1	0	1	2
2003	2	2	0	0	0	0
2004	3	0	2	0	0	1
2005	3	2	0	0	1	1
2006	1	2	3	0	1	1
2007	0	1	0	0	1	1

Table 3 Results for Simar and Wilson (2002) test for non-increasing returns to scale

Year	CDE	D	F	GHI	JK	LMNOP
1999	1	2	13	3	58	39
2000	9	9	26	4	67	33
2001	15	16	14	7	63	49
2002	23	22	34	5	59	38
2003	5	19	41	5	51	40
2004	17	21	21	7	60	45
2005	7	29	15	6	60	34
2006	4	10	20	4	57	44
2007	2	5	16	8	36	39

Therefore, the results overall indicate that the underlying production function is characterized by variable returns to scale, and that the detailed decomposition of the Malmquist index proposed by Wheelock and Wilson (1999) is possible.

Productivity change results from technological change and change in efficiency and is the observable achievement of innovative activity. In evolutionary economics, innovations are key drivers of economic growth although there is a creative destruction component of innovation, as already mentioned by Schumpeter (1934). Productivity change and its components should therefore have a positive effect on value added growth but also a negative effect on employment growth caused by of the creative destruction. Of course, the effects of innovation do not lead to a linear increasing development for the number of firms or the demand, both decline after some periods, as shown for example by Saviotti and Pyka (2004). Also concordant to Schumpeter (1939), business cycle and product life cycle developments induce a decline in economic development after an increase caused by innovations. So, the effect of productivity change on value added and employment growth depends on the considered time frame.

4.2 Multilevel Models

Economic activities take place at different levels, such as the micro-, meso-, and macro-level (Dopfer et al. 2004), and few recent econometric investigations account for this nested level structure by multilevel analysis or hierarchical model analysis. The notation of the levels in this dissertation is made according to Pinheiro and Bates (2000) and the multilevel and mixed-effects model literature, in contrast to the notation for hierarchical model analysis. The first level is the industry, as all industries are nested within the second level, which are the cities, and both levels are repeatedly measured over the third level, which is the time. This level orientation is the opposite to those sometimes found in the literature on hierarchical models (e.g., Bryk and Raudenbush 1988). It might also be possible to use the time dimension as the most nested level, as proposed, e.g., in West et al. (2007) or Tabachnick and Fidell (2007), but the data structure with the least observations within the separate industries and more observations in the city and time level reason the proposed choice of levels. Thus, the data is structured first by industries, second by cities, and third by time to calculate the multilevel models as explained in Pinheiro and Bates (2000) for the package `nlme` in R (see Pinheiro et al. 2013).

One big advantage of the analysis with multilevel models is that independence in the errors is not required. Independence is generally violated, because the objects in my case industries and cities within each level might influence each other. Furthermore, the interaction among the levels might be present, which can be taken into account within the multilevel analysis. Multilevel models enable us to include explanatory variables on each level.

Figure 1 illustrates the scheme of the multilevel model used in this dissertation.

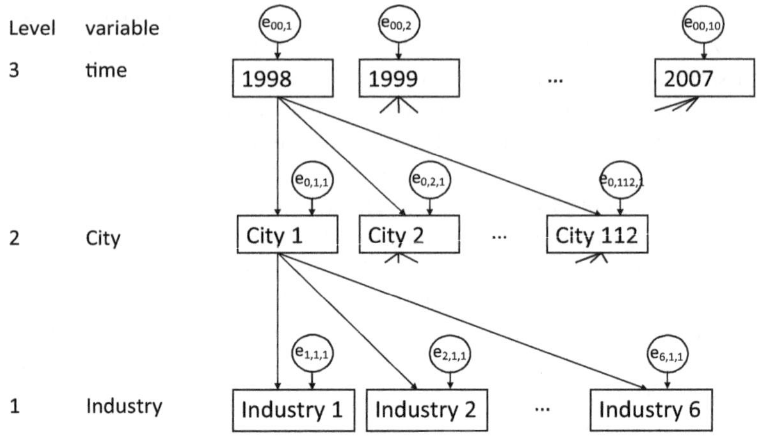

Fig. 1 Multilevel model structure

In Fig. 1, units are indicated by boxes. All units of a lower level are observed in each unit of the higher level indicated by arrows from the units to the lower level units (for convenience only to the first two and last units are shown). Several errors or unobserved factors, indicated by circles in Fig. 1 affect each of these units at every level. Within multilevel models, it is possible to account for each of the unobserved factors at each level separately by specific random effects, and thus care for the nesting structure of the units. The multilevel models are developed from the most specific model, which is the basic multilevel model with the least number of random effects and no interaction terms (see, e.g. Goedhuys and Srholec 2010 or Zuur et al. 2009). The basic multilevel model is constructed to investigate the necessity of the level structure by calculating the intraclass correlation coefficients. The basic multilevel model is then generalized by additional random effects, which allow the intercept coefficients to vary. The more generalized model is therefore called the intercept-as-outcome model. By further generalizing and allowing the slope coefficients in the model to vary by additional random effects, the most generalized model is developed, which is called the intercept-and-slope-as-outcome model. The estimations will be performed and presented in the results section in the same structure beginning with the basic multilevel model, followed by the intercept-as-outcome model and finally the most generalized intercept-and-slope-as-outcome model.

4.2.1 The Basic Multilevel Model

The basic multilevel model is the starting point for the analysis. This is comprised of the industry growth trajectories ($Y_{ijt} - Y_{ij(t-1)}$) as the level-1 model in Eq. (11). Because the endogenous variables Y_{ijt}, which are either gross value added or employment, are in logarithm, the first differences measure the growth within 1 year. Gross value added and employment are path depended and characterized as unit root processes which prevents their analysis without differentiation. To capture a growth path and measure the effect of past productivity change within an industry on value added or employment growth, the 1 year lagged growth $(Y_{ij(t-1)} - Y_{ij(t-2)})$ and the productivity change $(PC_{ij(t-2)})$ measured by the Malmquist index and its components are included as explanatory variables in the level-1 model. Because the Malmquist index and its components are correlated to each other by construction, the level-1 model includes only the Malmquist index or one component for the estimation. Therefore, a separate estimation is calculated for the Malmquist index and each component. The variation in growth parameters among industries within a city is captured in the level-2 model in Eqs. (12)–(14) by the five city-specific variables $X_{ij(t-1)}$ with $i = 1, \ldots, 5$ and their quadratic terms $X^2_{ij(t-1)}$ for every city j and time (t-1). The variation among industries and cities over time is represented in the level-3 model in Eqs. (15)–(20), as described in Raudenbush and Bryke (2002) but with the notation from Pinheiro and Bates (2000)

$$Y_{ijt} - Y_{ij(t-1)} = \pi_{0jt} + \pi_{1jt}\left(Y_{ij(t-1)} - Y_{ij(t-2)}\right) + \pi_{2jt} PC_{ij(t-2)} + e_{ijt} \tag{11}$$

with city-level equations

$$\begin{aligned}\pi_{0jt} &= \gamma_{00t} + \gamma_{01t} X_{1j(t-1)} + \gamma_{02t} X^2_{1j(t-1)} \\ &\quad + \gamma_{03t} X_{2j(t-1)} + \gamma_{04t} X^2_{2j(t-1)} + \ldots + \gamma_{010t} X^2_{5j(t-1)} + b_{0jt} \end{aligned} \tag{12}$$

$$\pi_{1jt} = \gamma_{10t} \tag{13}$$

$$\pi_{2jt} = \gamma_{20t} \tag{14}$$

and time-level equations

$$\gamma_{00t} = \beta_{000} + b_{00t} \tag{15}$$

$$\gamma_{01t} = \beta_{010} \tag{16}$$

$$\gamma_{02t} = \beta_{020} \tag{17}$$

$$\vdots$$

$$\gamma_{010t} = \beta_{0100} \tag{18}$$

$$\gamma_{10t} = \beta_{100} \tag{19}$$

$$\gamma_{20t} = \beta_{200}, \tag{20}$$

with the fixed coefficients, β, and the random coefficients, b, in the Eqs. (12) and (15)–(20), with the b_{00t} the random effect for the intercept at time-level, and b_{0jt} the random effect for the intercept at city-level. Each random coefficient, b, is assumed to be normally distributed with a mean of zero and a specific standard error σ_2 and σ_3, $b_{00t} \sim N\left(0, \sigma_3^2\right)$ and $b_{0jt} \sim N\left(0, \sigma_2^2\right)$, which has to be calculated. The remaining residual e_{ijt} is also normally distributed with a mean of zero and a constant and unique standard error σ, $e_{ijt} \sim N\left(0, \sigma^2\right)$. Altogether, this leads to the following estimation equation:

$$\begin{aligned} Y_{ijt} - Y_{ij(t-1)} = {} & \beta_{000} + b_{00t} + \beta_{010} X_{1j(t-1)} + \beta_{020} X_{1j(t-1)}^2 + \beta_{030} X_{2j(t-1)} + \ldots \\ & + \beta_{0100} X_{5j(t-1)}^2 + \beta_{200} PC_{ij(t-2)} + b_{0jt} \\ & + \beta_{100} \left(Y_{ij(t-1)} - Y_{ij(t-2)}\right) + e_{ijt} \\ = {} & \beta_{000} + \beta_{100} \left(Y_{ij(t-1)} - Y_{ij(t-2)}\right) + \beta_{200} PC_{ij(t-2)} \\ & + \beta_{010} X_{1j(t-1)} + \ldots \\ & + \beta_{0110} X_{5j(t-1)}^2 + b_{00t} + b_{0jt} + e_{ijt}. \end{aligned} \tag{21}$$

4.2.2 The Intercept-as-Outcome Model

The more generalized version is the intercept-as-outcome model. The industry-level equation for the industrial growth is the same as for the basic multilevel model in Eq. (11). The equations at the city-level are the same as the equations in the basic multilevel model, except that the coefficient of the variable of interest, which is productivity change, is randomized. Equations (12) and (13) are unchanged but Eq. (14) is modified:

$$\begin{aligned} \pi_{0jt} &= \gamma_{00t} + \gamma_{01t} X_{1j(t-1)} + \gamma_{02t} X_{1j(t-1)}^2 \\ &\quad + \gamma_{03t} X_{2j(t-1)} + \gamma_{04t} X_{2j(t-1)}^2 + \ldots + \gamma_{010t} X_{5j(t-1)}^2 + b_{0jt} \\ \pi_{1jt} &= \gamma_{10t} \\ \pi_{2jt} &= \gamma_{20t} + b_{2jt}. \end{aligned} \tag{22}$$

The time-level equations are also generalized by randomizing the coefficients in Eq. (12), which explains the intercept in the industry-level equation. Only the coefficients of the linear terms of the city-specific variables are randomized, to reduce the number of random effects; otherwise the analysis would not be computable in an adequate time. The equations for the coefficients at the time-level are:

$$\gamma_{00t} = \beta_{000} + b_{00t} \tag{23}$$

$$\gamma_{01t} = \beta_{010} + b_{01t} \tag{24}$$

$$\gamma_{02t} = \beta_{020} \tag{25}$$

$$\vdots$$

$$\gamma_{09t} = \beta_{090} + b_{09t} \tag{26}$$

$$\gamma_{010t} = \beta_{0100} \tag{27}$$

$$\gamma_{10t} = \beta_{100} \tag{28}$$

$$\gamma_{20t} = \beta_{200} + b_{20t}, \tag{29}$$

with the fixed coefficients, β, which might differ from those in the basic multilevel model because of the additional random coefficients, b, in the Eqs. (24), (26) and (29). Each random coefficient, b, is assumed to be normally distributed, with a mean of zero and a specific standard error that has to be calculated.

Altogether, this results in the simple intercept-as-outcome model

$$\begin{aligned}
Y_{ijt} - Y_{ij(t-1)} &= \beta_{000} + b_{00t} + (\beta_{010} + b_{01t})\,X_{1j(t-1)} + \beta_{020}X^2_{1j(t-1)} \\
&\quad + (\beta_{030} + b_{03t})\,X_{2j(t-1)} + \ldots + \beta_{0100}X^2_{5j(t-1)} + b_{0jt} \\
&\quad + \beta_{100}\left(Y_{ij(t-1)} - Y_{ij(t-2)}\right) + \left(\beta_{200} + b_{20t} + b_{2jt}\right) PC_{ij(t-2)} + e_{ijt} \\
&= \beta_{000} + \beta_{010}X_{1j(t-1)} + \beta_{020}X^2_{1j(t-1)} + \beta_{030}X_{2j(t-1)} + \ldots \\
&\quad + \beta_{0100}X^2_{5j(t-1)} \\
&\quad + \beta_{100}\left(Y_{ij(t-1)} - Y_{ij(t-2)}\right) + \beta_{200}PC_{ij(t-2)} \\
&\quad + b_{00t} + b_{20t}PC_{ij(t-2)} + b_{01t}X_{1j(t-1)} + b_{03t}X_{2j(t-1)} + \ldots \\
&\quad + b_{09t}X_{5j(t-1)} \\
&\quad + b_{0jt} + b_{2jt}PC_{ij(t-2)} + e_{ijt}.
\end{aligned} \tag{30}$$

4.2.3 The Intercept-and-Slope-as-Outcome Model

The intercept-and-slope-as-outcome model additionally explains the slope for the variable of interest, in my case the productivity change, which is π_{20t}. Equation (22) becomes

$$\pi_{20t} = \gamma_{20t} + \gamma_{21t}X_{1j(t-1)} + \gamma_{22t}X_{2j(t-1)} + \ldots + \gamma_{25t}X_{5j(t-1)} + b_{2jt} \tag{31}$$

with each $\gamma_{2jt}, j = 0, 1, \ldots, 5$ as a fixed coefficient $\gamma_{2jt} = \beta_{2j0}, j = 1, \ldots, 5$ except for γ_{20t} for which Eq. (29) holds. Please note, that only the linear and not the quadratic terms are added to explain variations of the effect (slope) of past productivity change on value added and employment growth, which results in the intercept-and slope-as-outcome model

$$\begin{aligned}
Y_{ijt} - Y_{ij(t-1)} &= \beta_{000} + b_{00t} + (\beta_{010} + b_{01t})\,X_{1j(t-1)} + \beta_{020}X^2_{1j(t-1)} \\
&\quad + (\beta_{030} + b_{03t})\,X_{2j(t-1)} + \ldots + \beta_{011t}X^2_{5j(t-1)} + b_{0jt}
\end{aligned}$$

$$
\begin{aligned}
&+\beta_{100}\left(Y_{ij(t-1)}-Y_{ij(t-2)}\right)+\left(\beta_{200}+\beta_{210}X_{1j(t-1)}\right.\\
&\left.+\beta_{220}X_{2j(t-1)}+\ldots+\beta_{250}X_{5j(t-1)}+b_{20t}\right)PC_{ij(t-2)}+e_{ijt}\\
=\;&\beta_{000}+\beta_{010}X_{1j(t-1)}+\beta_{020}X^2_{1j(t-1)}+\beta_{030}X_{2j(t-1)}+\ldots\\
&+\beta_{011t}X^2_{5j(t-1)}\\
&+\beta_{100}\left(Y_{ij(t-1)}-Y_{ij(t-2)}\right)+\beta_{200}PC_{ij(t-2)}+\beta_{210}X_{1j(t-1)}PC_{ij(t-2)}\\
&+\beta_{220}X_{2j(t-1)}PC_{ij(t-2)}+\ldots+\beta_{250}X_{5j(t-1)}PC_{ij(t-2)}\\
&+b_{00t}+b_{20t}PC_{ij(t-2)}+b_{01t}X_{1j(t-1)}+b_{03t}X_{2j(t-1)}+\ldots\\
&+b_{010t}X_{5j(t-1)}\\
&+b_{0jt}+b_{1jt}PC_{ij(t-2)}+e_{ijt},
\end{aligned}
\tag{32}
$$

with additional addends for the fixed effects resulting from explaining the slope. These fixed effects result from the interaction of the productivity change component and the city-specific variables. The computational details are explained in the Appendix. The intercept-and-slope-as-outcome model tests therefore whether the variation in the slope of productivity change can be explained by the other variables.

4.2.4 Model Selection

The model selection approach is similar to that in Goedhuys and Srholec (2010) and standard in multilevel analysis. First, I estimate linear models by OLS estimation and heteroscedasticity-consistent standard errors are calculated to account for heteroscedasticity in general. The heteroscedasticity-consistent standard errors are HC3 are introduced by MacKinnon and White (1985). By estimating OLS models with heteroscedasticity-consistent standard errors, it is possible to identify insignificant relationships and thus to reduce the number of coefficients which are estimated in the next steps. The OLS model is a reduced version of the intercept-and-slope-as-outcome multilevel model, which includes all city-specific explanatory variables as well as interaction terms of the city-specific variables with the Malmquist index and its components.

To compare the model fit of each model and estimation, the Pseudo R^2 of McFadden (1973) is calculated as

$$
\text{McFadden} - R^2 = 1 - \ln L / \ln L_0, \tag{33}
$$

with $\ln L$ as the log-likelihood of the actual model and $\ln L_0$ as the log-likelihood of the null model with only the intercept in the fixed effects and random effects part on each level (for multilevel models).

To verify the model and to check whether the additional variables add further explanatory power, many different measures can be used.

A general test for restrictions is the likelihood ratio test. For this, the likelihood of the more general model L_2 is divided by those of the more restricted model L_1. In general, the likelihood of the more unrestricted model is higher than the one of the restricted model. The test statistic is

$$LR = 2\ln\left(\frac{L_2}{L_1}\right) = 2\left(\ln L_2 - \ln L_1\right) \tag{34}$$

and is also always positive. Under the null hypothesis that the restricted model is sufficient, the likelihood ratio test statistic is χ^2 distributed with $k_2 - k_1$ degrees of freedom, where k_2 and k_1 are the number of parameters in the general model and the restricted model, respectively. Pinheiro and Bates (2000, Chapter 2.4) show that the test can also be performed if both models are estimated by the restricted maximum likelihood (REML). The test enables us to test random effects but also the fixed effects similar to an F-statistic in OLS estimation, depending on the reference model.

Other possible instruments for evaluating the necessity of levels and random effects include information criteria as measures of the relative goodness of fit. I use the Akaikes information criterion (AIC) as well as the Bayesian information criterion (BIC), also known as the Schwarz information criterion. The criteria are generally formulated as

$$AIC = 2k - 2\ln L$$

and

$$BIC = k\ln n - 2\ln L,$$

with the value of the log-likelihood function and k, which is the number of estimates, as well as n, the number of observations, in the BIC. The value of the log-likelihood gives the goodness-of-fit and the number of estimates to reach that goodness-of-fit is added as a positive penalty term. The penalty term is needed, because more estimates increase the goodness of fit, yet induce uncertainty and cause over-fitting. Thus, the principle of parsimony is considered by minimizing the information criteria.

The intraclass correlation coefficient is one possible instrument which is commonly used in the multilevel literature and is based on the variances of the random effects in the basic multilevel model

$$ICC_3 = \frac{\sigma_3^2}{\sigma_2^2 + \sigma_3^2 + \sigma^2}. \tag{35}$$

Equation (35) is the intraclass correlation at the third level (namely at the time-level), taken from West et al. (2007). For the second level the intraclass correlation is

$$ICC_2 = \frac{\sigma_2^2 + \sigma_3^2}{\sigma_2^2 + \sigma_3^2 + \sigma^2} \tag{36}$$

as described in Tabachnick and Fidell (2007) and discussed in Hox (2002). If the intraclass correlations are high, the correlation of the observation within that level is large. Unfortunately, there is no rule or distribution for any consideration in the test statistics.

Another way of testing the need for different levels is to look at the plots of the distribution of the observation at a specific level. The plot investigation also helps in the visualization of complicated multilevel models and is used, e.g., in Ieno et al. (2009). Generally, it is proposed for use in a protocol-based multilevel analysis as described in Zuur et al. (2009).

5 Empirical Results

The empirical investigation starts by analyzing the explanatory power and significance of the explanatory variables in a pooled setup. This pooled setup is estimated by standard OLS. Because the variables are studentized the constant term, specified as the intercept, has to be insignificant in every specification.

Table 4 shows the results of the OLS estimation for the linear models for gross value added growth on the preceding of years of value added growth, each of the components of yearly productivity change, the other explanatory variables, as well as the quadratic terms of these variables and the interaction terms of these variables, and components of productivity change. The model is similar to the intercept-and-slope-as-outcome model, but without any random effects. It helps to reduce the number of estimates, all insignificant variables are already deleted. The Gini coefficient is not significant for the gross value added and employment growth, but it is significant for gross value added and employment in absolute numbers. Therefore, the change in the Gini coefficient is tested for significance in first differences.

The results in Table 4 show many interesting features. Each column contains the estimates for one OLS estimation, with the heteroscedasticity consistent standard error below the estimates in parentheses. Each OLS estimation contains a different measurement of productivity change (*PC*). The first column A shows the results for the Malmquist index (*malm*). The intercept is not significant, with a small negative estimate of −0.0408, indicating no gross value added growth on average for an average city because the variables are standardized. The intercept is the average of the endogenous variable if every exogenous variable is zero, which stands for the average city. The next line in column A shows the results for gross value added growth lagged by one period (*dGVAL*1), which has a significant negative estimate of −0.1052. Therefore, past gross value added growth, which is also standardized,

Table 4 OLS results for gross value added growth

	A	B	C	D	E	F	G
Intercept	−0.0408 (0.029)	−0.0448 (0.0285)	−0.0416 (0.0289)	−0.0397 (0.0292)	−0.0335 (0.0284)	−0.0338 (0.0284)	−0.0448 (0.0286)
*dGVAL*1	−0.1052*** (0.031)	−0.1065*** (0.0321)	−0.1099*** (0.0314)	−0.1111*** (0.031)	−0.1063*** (0.0331)	−0.1094*** (0.0333)	−0.1062*** (0.0323)
malm	−0.0276 (0.0251)						
tech		0.0103 (0.0198)					
eff			−0.0479** (0.0239)				
pure.eff				−0.0697*** (0.0252)			
pure.tech					0.0524** (0.023)		
scale.tech						−0.0344 (0.0217)	
scale							0.0426* (0.0256)
PC.ln*Stu*	0.0193 (0.0257)	−0.0465** (0.0211)	0.0423* (0.0246)	0.0058 (0.0239)	0.0021 (0.0241)	−0.0427* (0.0251)	0.0348 (0.0333)
ln*Stu*	0.045* (0.0231)	0.0453** (0.0231)	0.0447* (0.0231)	0.0464** (0.0231)	0.0243 (0.0224)	0.025 (0.0223)	0.0465** (0.023)

(continued)

Table 4 (continued)

	A	B	C	D	E	F	G
$\ln Stu^2$	0.0352	0.0394*	0.0364	0.0369	0.0217	0.0249	0.0407*
	(0.0225)	(0.0223)	(0.0225)	(0.0225)	(0.0218)	(0.0217)	(0.0223)
PC.dPop	0.0107	−0.0166	0.0202	0.0489	−0.052**	0.0728***	−0.05**
	(0.0391)	(0.0221)	(0.0378)	(0.038)	(0.0228)	(0.0229)	(0.0241)
dPop	0.0204	0.0221	0.0185	0.0153	0.0299	0.0305	0.022
	(0.0223)	(0.0225)	(0.0224)	(0.0219)	(0.0228)	(0.0229)	(0.0221)
$dPop^2$	0.02	0.0209	0.0178	−0.0042	−0.0043	−0.0146	−0.0017
	(0.0619)	(0.0588)	(0.0652)	(0.0681)	(0.0625)	(0.059)	(0.0567)
PC.Gini	0.0591*	0.0419**	0.0323	0.039	0.0487	−0.0006	−0.0057
	(0.0302)	(0.0207)	(0.0371)	(0.0478)	(0.0298)	(0.0217)	(0.025)
Gini	0.0323**	0.0399**	0.0343**	0.0341**	0.0373**	0.0387**	0.0386**
	(0.0158)	(0.017)	(0.0165)	(0.0168)	(0.0172)	(0.0177)	(0.0176)
$Gini^2$	0.0155	0.0065	0.0104	0.0099	0.0081	0.0036	0.0042
	(0.0157)	(0.0164)	(0.0175)	(0.0183)	(0.0161)	(0.0191)	(0.0191)
PC.SC	0.028	0.0156	0.0083	0.012	0.0148	0.0014	−0.0141
	(0.0239)	(0.0223)	(0.0233)	(0.0235)	(0.0229)	(0.0276)	(0.0333)
SC	−0.1144***	−0.1177***	−0.1204***	−0.1198***	−0.1221***	−0.1208***	−0.1195***
	(0.0316)	(0.032)	(0.0314)	(0.0312)	(0.032)	(0.0318)	(0.0318)
SC^2	0.1102***	0.1075***	0.1159***	0.1153***	0.1126***	0.1146***	0.112***
	(0.0324)	(0.0331)	(0.0372)	(0.0362)	(0.0332)	(0.0357)	(0.0355)

PC.BusTax	0.02	−0.0062	0.0253	0.0027	0.0537**	−0.0272	0.013
	(0.024)	(0.0196)	(0.0212)	(0.0232)	(0.0252)	(0.0182)	(0.0208)
BusTax	−0.0299*	−0.0297*	−0.031*	−0.029*	−0.0188	−0.0234	−0.0309*
	(0.016)	(0.016)	(0.016)	(0.0159)	(0.0157)	(0.0157)	(0.0159)
$BusTax^2$	0.0337**	0.034**	0.0354**	0.0335**	0.0314*	0.0298*	0.0323*
	(0.0167)	(0.0166)	(0.0165)	(0.0166)	(0.0166)	(0.0166)	(0.0166)
ln*L*	−5518.886	−5517.6	−5517.596	−5514.262	−5364.374	−5371.791	−5520.373
R^2	0.2765	0.2766	0.2766	0.2771	0.2967	0.2958	0.2763

Significance codes: '***', '**', '*' significant up to 1, 5, and 10 %, respectively. Heteroscedasticity consistent standard errors in parentheses. R^2 is McFadden-R^2 for comparison reason leads to a catching-up of growth rates. A growth rate below the average, measured by a negative standardized growth rate, will result in a growth rate above average or a positive standardized growth rate in the next period.

The estimate for the Malmquist index is not significantly different from zero by −0.0276, indicating that the Malmquist index in total does not affect the gross value added growth. The next three rows contain the estimates for the logarithm of the number of students. Whereas the first of the three rows includes the interaction term of productivity change, which is the Malmquist index in the first column, with the logarithm of the number of students. The following row contains the linear term of the logarithm of the number of students. The last of the three rows contains the quadratic term of the logarithm of the number of students within the city. Only the linear term is significantly positive, with an estimate of 0.045, indicating that an increase in the number of students is correlated with higher gross value added growth.

The next three rows show the estimates for population change where, again, the first of these three rows gives the estimate for the interaction term of the component with population growth, the second row gives the estimate for the change in population, and the third row contains the estimate for the quadratic term of population change. All the estimates including population change are not significantly different from zero in column A.

The next three rows comprise the estimates with the change in the Gini coefficient and, as for all other variables, with the interaction term, the linear term and the quadratic term in the first, second and third row, respectively. In the case of the Malmquist index as productivity change measure in column A, the interaction term and the linear term of the change of the Gini coefficient are significantly positive, with estimates of 0.0591 and 0.0323 for the interaction term and the linear term, respectively. Thus, for an average city with all standardized variables equal to zero, gross value added growth increases by a further increase in the Gini coefficient. Therefore, gross value added growth is correlated with a stronger industrial specialization. This effect is further increased if the city has a Malmquist index which is above average.

The next three rows show the estimates for the corresponding terms of structural change variable. The interaction term of the Malmquist index and the structural change is not significantly different from zero, the linear term is significantly negative with an estimate of −0.1144, and the quadratic term is significantly positive with an estimate of 0.1102. Therefore, structural change affects gross value added growth with a U-form and a minimum point of about 0.52; for an average city the effect of the standardized structural change on gross value added growth is only positive for negative values and values above 1.04 (or values of structural change below average or with 1.04 times the standard deviation greater than the average structural change, while for structural change slightly above average the effect in gross value added growth is negative).

The last three rows in the first column contain the estimates for business tax. Similar to structural change, the linear term of business tax is significantly negative and the quadratic term is significantly positive, with values of −0.0299 and 0.0337, respectively. The U-form effect of business tax on gross value added growth is minimal at about 0.89 and is positive for standardized values of business tax below zero and above 1.78. This means that values of business tax below average and larger than 1.78 times the standard deviation above average are correlated with positive gross value added growth.

The value of the McFadden-R^2 is remarkably large for an industry pooled cross-city growth analysis, with a value of about 27 %. The next columns contain the estimates for the components of the Malmquist index, namely the technological change in column B, efficiency change in column C, pure efficiency change in column D, pure technological change in column E, scale technological change in column F, and scale efficiency change in column G. Because of the different components and the interaction terms of these with the other city-specific variables, the estimates are likely to change except for the intercept, because all variables are standardized. So, the intercept always estimates the gross value added growth of an average city with all standardized variables being zero.

Without going into too much detail, the results are explained in general without the exact estimates which can be found in Table 4. First of all, the intercept is insignificant, as expected. Secondly, past gross value added growth is negatively significant. Value added growth above average is associated with value added growth below average and vice versa, which supports the catching-up hypothesis. Thirdly, neither the Malmquist index nor the change in technology has a significant effect on value added growth, though efficiency change and its component pure change in efficiency have a negative effect on value added growth. These components measure the catching-up to production frontier by process innovations. However, the catching-up results in lower value added growth. Furthermore, pure technological change as well as change in scale efficiency have a positive effect on value added growth. Thus, a shift in the production frontier, as measured by pure technological change, results in higher value added growth. In addition, some interaction terms are significant, depending on the component. Fourthly, the structural change index and business tax have a maximum effect on value added growth because the linear term is significantly positive and the quadratic term is significantly negative. Furthermore, the number of students and the change in concentration have significant positive effects on gross value added growth.

The corresponding results of Table 4 are reported in Table 5 for employment growth.

The results for employment growth are somewhat different from those for gross value added growth, not only by higher coefficients of determination but also by different significant explanatory variables. Columns H to M in Table 5 have exactly the same structure as columns A to G in Table 4 and are, therefore, interpreted the same way simply for employment growth instead of gross value added growth. First of all, past employment growth which is above average results in positive employment growth in the next period, which indicates a divergence of employment growth for sectors in German cities. Secondly, productivity change measured by the Malmquist index is significantly negative for employment growth 1 year later. By decomposing productivity change into its components, as illustrated in Sect. 4.1, it

Table 5 OLS results for employment growth

	H	I	J	K	L	M	N
Intercept	−0.0113 (0.0251)	−0.0125 (0.0251)	−0.0102 (0.0251)	−0.0105 (0.0252)	−0.0102 (0.025)	−0.0107 (0.025)	−0.0128 (0.0251)
*dEmpL*1	0.4498*** (0.0289)	0.4463*** (0.0288)	0.447*** (0.0288)	0.4487*** (0.029)	0.46*** (0.0296)	0.4613*** (0.0298)	0.4511*** (0.0291)
malm	−0.0299* (0.0181)						
tech		0.0032 (0.0144)					
eff			−0.0391** (0.0181)				
pure.eff				−0.065*** (0.0162)			
pure.tech					0.0228 (0.0164)		
scale.tech						−0.0108 (0.0217)	
scale							0.0306 (0.0244)
PC.ln*Stu*	0 (0.0188)	0.0132 (0.0157)	−0.002 (0.0175)	−0.0247* (0.0148)	0.0302** (0.0141)	−0.0234 (0.0294)	0.0143 (0.0266)
ln*Stu*	−0.0092 (0.022)	−0.0083 (0.0219)	−0.0102 (0.0219)	−0.0093 (0.0219)	−0.0135 (0.0217)	−0.0147 (0.0218)	−0.0088 (0.022)
$\ln Stu^2$	0.0106 (0.0192)	0.0111 (0.0192)	0.0104 (0.0193)	0.0114 (0.0192)	0.0081 (0.0191)	0.0091 (0.0193)	0.0124 (0.0193)

PC.dPop	−0.0094	−0.0186	0.0044	0.0175	−0.0146	0.0093	−0.019
	(0.0241)	(0.0174)	(0.0215)	(0.0175)	(0.0169)	(0.0184)	(0.0289)
dPop	0.0483**	0.0479**	0.048**	0.0458**	0.0516***	0.0505***	0.0475**
	(0.0201)	(0.0202)	(0.0198)	(0.0204)	(0.0189)	(0.0189)	(0.0207)
$dPop^2$	0.0699**	0.0599*	0.064**	0.0606*	0.0553*	0.0584**	0.0527*
	(0.0329)	(0.0319)	(0.0321)	(0.0321)	(0.0301)	(0.0274)	(0.0294)
PC.Gini	−0.0107	0.023	−0.0234	−0.0035	0.0009	0.0192	−0.0119
	(0.0225)	(0.0154)	(0.0212)	(0.0197)	(0.0166)	(0.0192)	(0.0309)
Gini	−0.0004	0	0.0009	−0.0016	0.0025	0.0047	−0.0015
	(0.0182)	(0.0182)	(0.0182)	(0.0181)	(0.0178)	(0.0179)	(0.0181)
$Gini^2$	−0.004	−0.0013	−0.0015	−0.0045	−0.0043	−0.0043	−0.0046
	(0.0322)	(0.0326)	(0.0315)	(0.0321)	(0.0335)	(0.0335)	(0.0323)
PC.SC	0.0065	0.0028	−0.0029	−0.0019	0.0113	−0.0031	−0.0097
	(0.0094)	(0.0119)	(0.0123)	(0.0101)	(0.0123)	(0.0203)	(0.0167)
SC	−0.0937***	−0.0966***	−0.0989***	−0.0986***	−0.0913***	−0.088***	−0.0956***
	(0.0275)	(0.0276)	(0.0274)	(0.0275)	(0.0264)	(0.0268)	(0.0276)
SC^2	0.077***	0.0796***	0.0801***	0.0806***	0.073***	0.0719***	0.0771***
	(0.0263)	(0.027)	(0.026)	(0.0258)	(0.0252)	(0.026)	(0.0267)
PC.BusTax	−0.0363**	−0.0298**	−0.0016	−0.0121	0.0041	−0.0269	−0.0072
	(0.0154)	(0.0122)	(0.0138)	(0.0142)	(0.0137)	(0.0171)	(0.0146)
BusTax	−0.0301**	−0.0318**	−0.0314**	−0.0312**	−0.0275**	−0.0295**	−0.0308**
	(0.0133)	(0.0133)	(0.0133)	(0.0133)	(0.0133)	(0.0135)	(0.0133)

(continued)

Table 5 (continued)

	H	I	J	K	L	M	N
BusTax^2	0.0127	0.014	0.0127	0.0119	0.0123	0.0146	0.013
	(0.0133)	(0.0131)	(0.0132)	(0.0132)	(0.0132)	(0.0131)	(0.0132)
ln*L*	−5043.595	−5043.066	−5040.982	−5035.681	−4854.772	−4853.936	−5046.078
R^2	0.3388	0.3388	0.3391	0.3398	0.3635	0.3636	0.3385

Significance codes: '***', '**', '*' significant up to 1, 5, and 10 %, respectively. Heteroscedasticity consistent standard errors in parentheses. R^2 is McFadden-R^2 for comparison reason becomes obvious that this effect is driven only by changes in efficiency, as indicated by columns J and K. These effects are the same as for value added growth. Thus, the catching-up process seems to have a negative overall effect.

Interaction terms are only significant for business tax and the number of students. In addition, structural change has an inverted U-shaped effect on employment growth with a minimum point because the linear term is significantly positive and the quadratic term is significantly negative. The point at which structural change minimally affects employment growth is at 0.61. Therefore, standardized structural change has a positive effect on employment growth for values below zero (below average for non-standardized structural change) and for values above 1.22 standardized structural change (or 1.22 times the standard deviation of structural change above the average). Business tax is significantly negative. Thus, business tax rates below average foster employment growth, whereas business tax rates above average reduce employment growth in contrast to the effect on value added growth. Change in population has a significantly positive linear and quadratic terms, so larger growth of inhabitants within a city has even further positive effects on employment growth.

The results indicate the importance of productivity change as well as the other observed explanatory variables and the significance of some non-linear effects. Because industries are nested within cities and these are observed for many consecutive years, the results of the OLS estimation should be treated with care because the observations are correlated from the common factor within one level and some variables are only observed at lower levels. Thus, the variance was not considered correctly, which I tried to account for with the heteroscedasticity-corrected standard errors; furthermore, the estimates can be biased in the case of different slopes for each object within the levels. Therefore, multilevel analyses have to be used to gain unbiased estimates.

To test whether the levels should be considered, the residual plots of the OLS estimation can be visually analyzed at each level, as suggested by Zuur et al. (2009). The exemplary residual box plot for the city-level of the OLS estimation for gross value added growth is shown in Fig. 2 and the corresponding box plot for the time-level is shown in Fig. 3.

The equivalent residual box plots for employment growth are included in Appendix 3. As seen in the residual box plots, they change over both levels, namely the city and time. Even the variation over the years is not large but it is nonetheless present, and the variance declines over the time, indicated by narrower boxes that illustrating the interquartile range for later years. The variation should result in a relatively large intraclass correlation coefficient for the city-level and a relatively low intraclass correlation coefficient for the time-level because of smaller changes in the residual variation in the time-level.

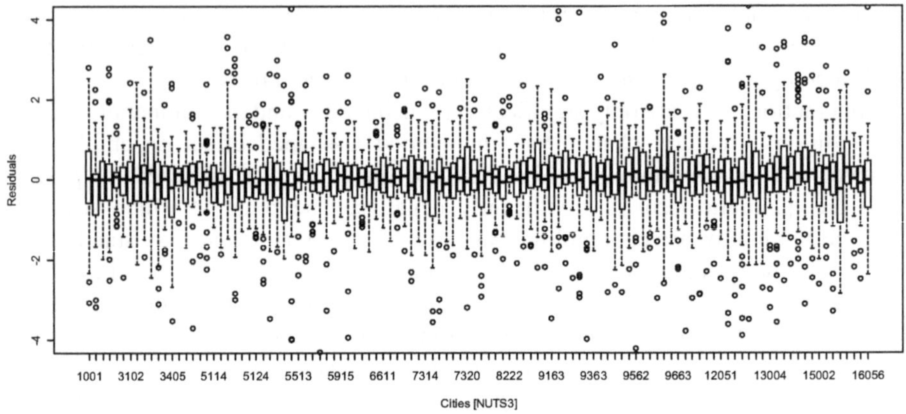

Fig. 2 Residual plot for gross value added growth at city level

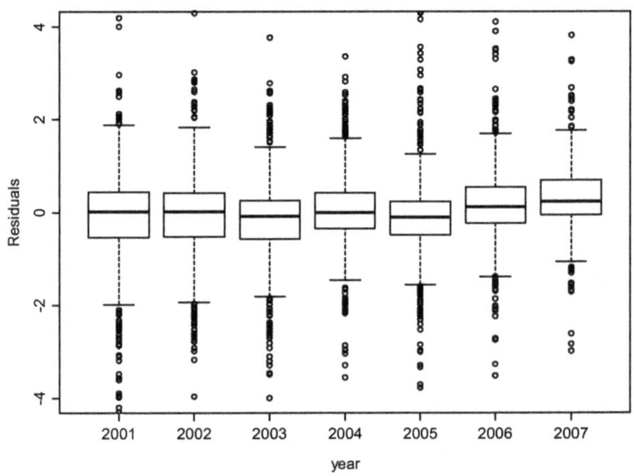

Fig. 3 Residual plot for gross value added growth at time level

5.1 Results for the Basic Multilevel Model

To detect different variations within the level and to justify the need for the incorporation of each level, the intraclass correlation coefficients have to be calculated. This is done by estimating the basic multilevel models without considering all the intercepts and slopes as being heterogeneous and all possible random effects in the different levels similar to the stepwise procedure in Goedhuys and Srholec (2010). The basic model only includes the intercepts as random. The results for the basic multilevel estimation are presented in the Tables 6 and 7.

The basic multilevel model estimations indicate different results for the necessity of the levels. On the one hand, both tables for the basic multilevel model show

Table 6 Multilevel results for gross value added growth in the basic multilevel model

	A	B	C	D	E	F	G
Fixed effects							
Intercept	−0.0359 (0.0843)	−0.0357 (0.0836)	−0.0358 (0.083)	−0.0372 (0.0828)	−0.0259 (0.0828)	−0.0265 (0.0852)	−0.0377 (0.085)
*dGVAL*1	−0.1134*** (0.0152)	−0.108*** (0.0149)	−0.1126*** (0.0151)	−0.118*** (0.0151)	−0.1086*** (0.015)	−0.1081*** (0.015)	−0.1069*** (0.0149)
malm	−0.0275* (0.0151)						
tech		0.0054 (0.0139)					
eff			−0.0262* (0.0145)				
pure.eff				−0.0587*** (0.015)			
pure.tech					0.0407*** (0.0143)		
scale.tech						−0.0462*** (0.0141)	
scale							0.0498*** (0.014)
ln*Stu*	0.0386 (0.0281)	0.0383 (0.0282)	0.0387 (0.0282)	0.039 (0.0281)	0.0154 (0.0284)	0.0152 (0.0284)	0.038 (0.0281)

(continued)

Table 6 (continued)

	A	B	C	D	E	F	G
ln*Stu*^{2}	0.0305	0.0308	0.031	0.0311	0.0148	0.0139	0.0303
	(0.0271)	(0.0272)	(0.0272)	(0.0271)	(0.0272)	(0.0272)	(0.0271)
dPop	0.0255	0.0262	0.0257	0.0253	0.038	0.0378	0.027
	(0.0231)	(0.0231)	(0.0231)	(0.0231)	(0.0235)	(0.0235)	(0.0231)
dPop^2	0.0296	0.0276	0.029	0.0337	0.0172	0.019	0.0307
	(0.0425)	(0.0426)	(0.0425)	(0.0424)	(0.0425)	(0.0425)	(0.0425)
Gini	0.0454**	0.0457**	0.0454**	0.0442**	0.0448**	0.0451**	0.045**
	(0.0185)	(0.0185)	(0.0185)	(0.0185)	(0.0185)	(0.0185)	(0.0185)
Gini^2	0.018	0.0168	0.0175	0.0186	0.0172	0.0171	0.0174
	(0.0174)	(0.0174)	(0.0174)	(0.0174)	(0.0174)	(0.0174)	(0.0174)
SC	−0.0929**	−0.0922**	−0.0926**	−0.0932**	−0.0946**	−0.0951**	−0.0917**
	(0.0427)	(0.0428)	(0.0428)	(0.0427)	(0.0426)	(0.0426)	(0.0427)
SC^2	0.0912**	0.0908**	0.091**	0.0914**	0.0925**	0.093**	0.0904**
	(0.0421)	(0.0422)	(0.0421)	(0.042)	(0.042)	(0.0419)	(0.0421)
BusTax	−0.033*	−0.0331*	−0.0332*	−0.0333*	−0.023	−0.0221	−0.0324*
	(0.0183)	(0.0184)	(0.0184)	(0.0183)	(0.0184)	(0.0184)	(0.0183)
BusTax^2	0.0301	0.0297	0.0301	0.0306	0.0247	0.0246	0.0299
	(0.019)	(0.0191)	(0.019)	(0.019)	(0.019)	(0.019)	(0.019)

Random effects						
Time-level						
Intercept	0.1898	0.1877	0.1863	0.1857	0.1856	0.1922	0.1916
City-level							
Intercept	0.2794	0.2809	0.28	0.279	0.2789	0.2786	0.2799
residuals	0.8978	0.8979	0.8977	0.8965	0.8892	0.8889	0.8966
AIC	10,992	10,995	10,992	10,980	10,698	10,696	10,983
BIC	11,093	11,096	11,093	11,081	10,799	10,796	11,083
ln*L*	−5,479.9	−5,481.5	−5,480	−5,473.9	−5,333.2	−5,331.9	−5,475.3
ICCtime	0.0392	0.0383	0.0378	0.0377	0.0382	0.0408	0.0399
ICCcity	0.124	0.124	0.1231	0.1226	0.1243	0.1266	0.1252
R^2	0.2719	0.2716	0.2719	0.2727	0.2914	0.2915	0.2725

Significance codes: '***', '**', '*' significant up to 1, 5, and 10 %, respectively. Standard errors for fixed effects are in parentheses below the estimates, for random effects standard errors are reported. R^2 is McFadden-R^2 for comparison reason

Table 7 Multilevel results for employment growth in the basic multilevel model

	H	I	J	K	L	M	N
Fixed effects							
Intercept	−0.0058 (0.1146)	−0.006 (0.1135)	−0.0057 (0.1128)	−0.0066 (0.1129)	−0.0042 (0.1105)	−0.0043 (0.1107)	−0.0068 (0.1138)
*dEmpL*1	0.4433*** (0.0141)	0.443*** (0.0142)	0.4417*** (0.0142)	0.4427*** (0.0141)	0.4555*** (0.0142)	0.4558*** (0.0142)	0.4449*** (0.0142)
malm	−0.041*** (0.0127)						
tech		0.0004 (0.0125)					
eff			−0.0422*** (0.0125)				
pure.eff				−0.0592*** (0.0128)			
pure.tech					0.0098 (0.0125)		
scale.tech						−0.0107 (0.0123)	
scale							0.0294** (0.0123)
ln*Stu*	−0.029 (0.0206)	−0.0293 (0.0206)	−0.0287 (0.0206)	−0.0284 (0.0205)	−0.0328 (0.0204)	−0.0329 (0.0204)	−0.029 (0.0205)

ln*Stu*²	−0.0012	−0.0009	−0.0006	−0.0005	−0.0038	−0.004	−0.001
	(0.0197)	(0.0197)	(0.0197)	(0.0196)	(0.0194)	(0.0194)	(0.0196)
dPop	0.0597***	0.0609***	0.06***	0.0593***	0.0639***	0.0638***	0.0608***
	(0.017)	(0.017)	(0.017)	(0.017)	(0.017)	(0.017)	(0.0169)
*dPop*²	0.0523*	0.0493	0.0514*	0.0561*	0.0464	0.0469	0.0518*
	(0.0311)	(0.031)	(0.0311)	(0.031)	(0.0305)	(0.0305)	(0.0309)
Gini	0.0527***	0.052***	0.0522***	0.0496***	0.0526***	0.0526***	0.0497***
	(0.0169)	(0.0169)	(0.0169)	(0.0169)	(0.0168)	(0.0168)	(0.0169)
*Gini*²	0.0155	0.0154	0.0153	0.014	0.0141	0.0141	0.0142
	(0.0127)	(0.0127)	(0.0127)	(0.0127)	(0.0125)	(0.0125)	(0.0126)
SC	−0.0013	−0.0006	−0.0009	−0.001	0.0036	0.0035	−0.0001
	(0.0313)	(0.0313)	(0.0313)	(0.0312)	(0.0306)	(0.0306)	(0.0312)
*SC*²	−0.0088	−0.0091	−0.009	−0.009	−0.0131	−0.0129	−0.0095
	(0.0308)	(0.0308)	(0.0308)	(0.0307)	(0.0301)	(0.0301)	(0.0307)
BusTax	−0.0352***	−0.0353***	−0.0355***	−0.0354***	−0.0313**	−0.0311**	−0.0349***
	(0.0133)	(0.0133)	(0.0133)	(0.0132)	(0.013)	(0.013)	(0.0132)
*BusTax*²	0.0065	0.0062	0.0066	0.0067	0.0054	0.0054	0.0063
	(0.0137)	(0.0137)	(0.0137)	(0.0136)	(0.0134)	(0.0134)	(0.0136)
Random effects							
Time-level							
Intercept	0.2744	0.2718	0.27	0.2702	0.2644	0.2649	0.2725
City-level							
Intercept	0.0443	0.0388	0.0444	0.0363	0.0001	0.0001	0.0227
residuals	0.811	0.8123	0.8109	0.8103	0.7954	0.7953	0.8124

(continued)

Table 7 (continued)

	H	I	J	K	L	M	N
AIC	9,890	9,900.4	9,889	9,878.9	9,525.9	9,525.8	9,894.7
BIC	9,990.7	10,001.1	9,989.7	9,979.7	9,626.4	9,626.3	9,995.5
ln$L$	−4,929	−4,934.2	−4,928.5	−4,923.5	−4,747	−4,746.9	−4,931.3
ICCtime	0.1024	0.1004	0.0995	0.0999	0.0995	0.0999	0.1011
ICCcity	0.1051	0.1025	0.1022	0.1017	0.0995	0.0999	0.1018
R^2	0.3378	0.3371	0.3378	0.3385	0.3622	0.3622	0.3374

Significance codes: '***', '**', '*' significant up to 1, 5, and 10 %, respectively. Standard errors for fixed effects are in parentheses below the estimates, for random effects standard errors are reported. R^2 is McFadden-R^2 for comparison reason

large intraclass correlation coefficients, except for the time-level for gross value added growth. Therefore, the time-level may not be kept for the estimations. The low intraclass correlation coefficient was expected to be relatively low by the residual box plots, although there is little variation and a decrease in the residual variance. However, the intraclass correlations are calculated only on the basis of the random effects of the intercepts in the basic multilevel model, even though there might be some slope variations not considered in the basic multilevel model. These results of the basic multilevel model are comparable to those results of the OLS model, except for the absence of the interaction terms with the productivity change component and the presence of random effects in the multilevel model. Therefore, these coefficients differ from those of the OLS model, not only in altitude, but also, consequently, in significance. The structure of both tables is the same as in the OLS estimation tables.

The results for value added growth in Table 6 show similar significant results to those in Table 4, with some minor differences resulting from the absence of the interaction terms in the basic multilevel model. The coefficient of the Malmquist index in column A as well as its components of efficiency change in column C fueled by change of pure efficiency change in column D and scale technological change in column F are significantly negative, with values of −0.0275, −0.0262, −0.0587 and −0.0462, respectively. The significant positive coefficient of change in pure technology (*pure.tech*) in column E is important to notice. It indicates that technological progress has a positive effect on value added growth although it is offset by the negative scale technological change.

The coefficients of the city-specific variables are the same in every estimation, because there is no changing interaction involved in any estimation. The change in the Gini coefficient is significantly positive, with an estimate of around 0.045. Structural change has a U-form effect on value added growth with a minimum of about 0.5, which indicates that a moderate change above average has the lowest effect on value added growth. The quadratic term of business tax is not as significant as in the OLS estimation. Only the linear term of business tax is significantly negative, which shows that an increase in business tax in the city has a negative effect on value added growth in that city in the next year.

A similar pattern occurs for the estimations of employment growth in Table 7. In contrast to the OLS results, in Table 5 the change in scale efficiency is significantly positive in column N. Productivity change measured by the Malmquist index affects employment growth significantly negative. That effect is caused by the negative effect of the change in efficiency which is mainly fueled by the change of pure efficiency with estimates of −0.0422 and −0.0592 in the columns J and K, respectively. The change in population has a U-form effect on employment growth with a negative minimum value at about −0.57, which indicates that a moderate change in population below the average has the smallest effect on employment growth. Additionally, the change in the Gini coefficient has a significantly positive effect on employment growth while business tax affects employment growth significantly negative, because only the linear terms are significantly different from zero for both variables. Therefore, an increase in the change of the Gini coefficient increases employment growth, whereas an increase in business tax within the city leads to a decrease in employment growth for the next year. Compared with the OLS results, structural change is not significant in the basic multilevel model.

As in the following multilevel model estimations, I am not interpreting the random effects because of sparse observations which do not affect the accuracy of fixed parameter estimates (Hox 1998, p. 150; Moerbeek et al. 2000). However, the power of the tests in multilevel models depends on the number of levels, which is only two in Hox (1998), the design of the model, number of groups within each level and the intraclass correlation as shown in Maas and Hox (2005). According to Roy et al. (2007) the sufficient sample size for longitudinal multilevel model without an attrition rate for 7 years and intraclass correlation of 10 % is 5, which is met by my data set. In the basic multilevel model the random effects are used to estimate the intraclass correlation coefficients which are about 10 % indicating correlation within each level and, therefore, the necessity of accounting for different levels.

5.2 Results for the Intercept-as-Outcome Model

The intercept-as-outcome model, additionally, has the intercepts of the basic model as random coefficients. The results for the intercept-as-outcome for gross value added and employment growth are presented in the Tables 8 and 9, respectively.

Both tables of results for the intercept-as-outcome model show similar patterns compared with those of the basic multilevel model. Table 8 presents the results for gross value added growth. Productivity change components are significant with respect to gross value added growth in Table 8, although both standard errors and estimates changed compared with the basic multilevel model. The Malmquist index and its component of efficiency change are not significant, but the more detailed components are significantly different from zero. Pure efficiency change (catching-up) and change in scale technology are significantly negative, while, again, pure technological change (technical progress) and change in scale efficiency are significantly positive on value added growth. Moreover, the significance of the change in the Gini coefficient is changed when compared with the basic multilevel model; in Table 8, only the quadratic term is significantly positive and not the linear term. Therefore, the minimum point for the effect on value added growth is zero, which is the average change in the Gini coefficient. Structural change has a U-form effect on value added growth with a minimum point at 0.5, which is the same as in the estimations of the basic multilevel model.

For employment growth, the Malmquist index, change in efficiency and change in scale efficiency are not significant. Only the change in pure efficiency remains significantly negative in Table 9 compared to Table 7. Furthermore, Table 9 shows that the business tax structure does not affect employment growth in the intercept-as-outcome model. Structural change also has a U-form effect on employment growth, with a minimum point at 0.5. Therefore, a structural change within the city below or equal to the average positively affects employment growth as well as a large

Table 8 Multilevel results for gross value added growth in the intercept-as outcome-model

	A	B	C	D	E	F	G
Fixed effects							
Intercept	−0.0285 (0.0729)	−0.0316 (0.086)	−0.0463 (0.0759)	−0.0504 (0.0738)	−0.0338 (0.0775)	−0.0309 (0.0854)	−0.0249 (0.0855)
*dGVAL*1	−0.0711*** (0.0151)	−0.0903*** (0.0148)	−0.0613*** (0.015)	−0.0718*** (0.0152)	−0.0862*** (0.0147)	−0.1103*** (0.015)	−0.1013*** (0.0148)
malm	−0.0368 (0.0314)						
tech		−0.0099 (0.0407)					
eff			−0.0261 (0.0288)				
pure.eff				−0.0766*** (0.0253)			
pure.tech					0.1025** (0.0468)		
scale.tech						−0.1121** (0.045)	
scale							0.1117** (0.0481)
ln*Stu*	0.0182 (0.0253)	0.0269 (0.0268)	0.0278 (0.0262)	0.0399 (0.0264)	0.0109 (0.0269)	0.0124 (0.0288)	0.0192 (0.0286)

(continued)

Table 8 (continued)

	A	B	C	D	E	F	G
$\ln Stu^2$	0.0166	0.0155	0.0231	0.0301	0.0059	0.0124	0.02
	(0.0235)	(0.0255)	(0.0246)	(0.0247)	(0.0249)	(0.0263)	(0.0257)
dPop	0.0163	0.0358	0.0318	0.0351	0.0532*	0.0404	0.0337
	(0.0291)	(0.0274)	(0.0289)	(0.0307)	(0.0274)	(0.0273)	(0.0278)
$dPop^2$	0.0669	−0.0029	0.0398	0.0392	−0.0047	0.0058	−0.0223
	(0.0417)	(0.0401)	(0.041)	(0.0455)	(0.0421)	(0.0436)	(0.0464)
Gini	0.0222	0.0304	0.0174	0.0229	0.0229	0.0276	0.0274
	(0.0207)	(0.029)	(0.0237)	(0.0244)	(0.031)	(0.0286)	(0.0271)
$Gini^2$	0.03*	0.0257	0.0362**	0.0234	0.0346**	0.0299*	0.0282
	(0.0157)	(0.0166)	(0.0166)	(0.0164)	(0.0169)	(0.0179)	(0.0173)
SC	−0.0925**	−0.0832**	−0.0905**	−0.0892*	−0.0966**	−0.0979**	−0.1014**
	(0.041)	(0.0412)	(0.0457)	(0.0456)	(0.0444)	(0.0444)	(0.0426)
SC^2	0.0949**	0.0836**	0.1166***	0.1253***	0.1318***	0.1104**	0.1039**
	(0.0413)	(0.0406)	(0.0451)	(0.045)	(0.0427)	(0.0439)	(0.0418)
BusTax	−0.0341*	−0.0334*	−0.0327*	−0.0391*	−0.0283	−0.0293	−0.0363**
	(0.0177)	(0.019)	(0.0185)	(0.0199)	(0.0211)	(0.0182)	(0.0178)
$BusTax^2$	0.0243	0.0197	0.0292*	0.0302*	0.0274	0.0329*	0.0278
	(0.0164)	(0.0178)	(0.0171)	(0.0173)	(0.0176)	(0.0185)	(0.018)

Random effects							
Time-level							
Intercept	0.1638	0.1961	0.1705	0.1645	0.1744	0.1936	0.1946
PC	0.0324	0.0745	0.034	0.0034	0.0876	0.0919	0.0977
ln*Stu*	0.0159	0.0115	0.015	0.0169	0.0158	0.0211	0.0256
dPop	0.051	0.041	0.0481	0.0537	0.0402	0.0362	0.0407
Gini	0.031	0.0566	0.0401	0.0427	0.0627	0.054	0.05
SC	0.0448	0.0214	0.0599	0.0592	0.0508	0.04	0.0303
BusTax	0.0194	0.02	0.02	0.0265	0.0311	0.0098	0.0095
City-level							
Intercept	0.2116	0.2674	0.2427	0.2353	0.244	0.2626	0.2497
PC	0.543	0.4158	0.4674	0.4435	0.5183	0.3163	0.3739
residuals	0.7674	0.8165	0.776	0.795	0.7967	0.8422	0.8418
AIC	10,378	10,778	10,490	10,567	10,429	10,630	10,870
BIC	10,661	11,061	10,774	10,851	10,712	10,912	11,153
ln*L*	−5,144	−5,343.9	−5,200.1	−5,238.6	−5,169.6	−5,269.9	−5,389.9
R^2	0.3165	0.2899	0.309	0.3039	0.3131	0.2998	0.2838

Significance codes: '***', '**', '*' significant up to 1, 5, and 10 %, respectively. Standard errors for fixed effects are in parentheses below the estimates, for random effects standard errors are reported. R^2 is McFadden-R^2 for comparison reason

Table 9 Multilevel results for employment growth in the intercept-as outcome-model

	H	I	J	K	L	M	N
Fixed effects							
Intercept	0.0126 (0.1112)	0.0222 (0.1267)	0.0073 (0.1148)	0.0021 (0.1115)	0.0094 (0.1112)	0.0003 (0.1109)	−0.0025 (0.1111)
*dEmpL*1	0.4347*** (0.0141)	0.4036*** (0.0143)	0.4332*** (0.0141)	0.4421*** (0.0141)	0.4503*** (0.0142)	0.4392*** (0.014)	0.4368*** (0.0139)
malm	−0.0334 (0.0218)						
tech		−0.0538 (0.1008)					
eff			−0.0278 (0.0367)				
pure.eff				−0.0515*** (0.0193)			
pure.tech					−0.0022 (0.0382)		
scale.tech						−0.0135 (0.0688)	
scale							−0.0052 (0.0597)
ln*Stu*	−0.036 (0.022)	−0.0279 (0.024)	−0.0299 (0.0229)	−0.0273 (0.023)	−0.0339 (0.0223)	−0.0283 (0.0225)	−0.0299 (0.024)

ln*Stu*^{2}	−0.0073	−0.0035	−0.0005	−0.0024	−0.0041	0.0022	0.0018
	(0.0195)	(0.0191)	(0.0193)	(0.0195)	(0.0193)	(0.0188)	(0.0189)
dPop	0.0677***	0.0626*	0.0611*	0.0586	0.0621*	0.0581*	0.0645*
	(0.017)	(0.036)	(0.0367)	(0.0377)	(0.0317)	(0.0328)	(0.0369)
dPop^2	0.0366	−0.0015	−0.0236	0.0059	0.017	−0.018	−0.0531
	(0.0315)	(0.0388)	(0.035)	(0.0396)	(0.0381)	(0.0389)	(0.0389)
Gini	0.0566***	0.0442*	0.0595***	0.0542**	0.0499**	0.0424*	0.0448**
	(0.017)	(0.0249)	(0.0201)	(0.0214)	(0.0217)	(0.023)	(0.0226)
Gini^2	0.0172	0.0295**	0.0242*	0.0245*	0.0237*	0.022	0.0223
	(0.0123)	(0.0132)	(0.0142)	(0.0146)	(0.0143)	(0.0136)	(0.0146)
SC	0.0014	−0.0053	0.0006	−0.0057	0.0006	0.0032	0.0082
	(0.0308)	(0.031)	(0.0309)	(0.0314)	(0.0309)	(0.0301)	(0.0305)
SC^2	−0.0086	0.0024	−0.01	−0.0038	0.0019	−0.0027	−0.0095
	(0.0305)	(0.0301)	(0.0302)	(0.0306)	(0.0301)	(0.0292)	(0.0297)
BusTax	−0.0369	−0.0295	−0.0333	−0.0328	−0.0306	−0.0327	−0.0284
	(0.0262)	(0.0237)	(0.0243)	(0.0231)	(0.0242)	(0.024)	(0.0251)
BusTax^2	0.0067	0.0062	0.0021	0.0041	0.0047	0.0126	0.0112
	(0.0135)	(0.0133)	(0.0134)	(0.0136)	(0.0135)	(0.0133)	(0.0132)

(continued)

Table 9 (continued)

	H	I	J	K	L	M	N
Random effects							
Time-level							
Intercept	0.2659	0.3046	0.2752	0.2667	0.2661	0.2655	0.266
PC	0.0262	0.2407	0.0797	0.0266	0.0813	0.1597	0.1351
ln*Stu*	0.0201	0.0327	0.0268	0.0264	0.0223	0.026	0.033
dPop	*NA*	0.078	0.0797	0.0821	0.0651	0.0687	0.0805
Gini	*NA*	0.0448	0.026	0.0308	0.0324	0.0384	0.0368
SC	0.0025	0.0146	0.0133	0.0134	0.0118	0.0111	0.0096
BusTax	0.0556	0.0486	0.0502	0.0464	0.0501	0.0498	0.0528
City-level							
Intercept	0.0046	0.0165	0.0223	0.0267	0.0334	0.0127	0.003
PC	0.2623	0.1192	0.214	0.1637	0.1163	0.277	0.3098
residuals	0.7765	0.7875	0.777	0.7913	0.7826	0.7515	0.7622
AIC	9,835	9,811	9,834	9,886	9,550	9,457	9,780
BIC	10,037	10,094	10,117	10,170	9,833	9,740	10,064
ln*L*	−4,885.6	−4,860.4	−4,872	−4,898.2	−4,730.1	−4,683.6	−4,845.2
R^2	0.3436	0.347	0.3454	0.3419	0.3645	0.3707	0.349

Significance codes: '***', '**', '*' significant up to 1, 5, and 10 %, respectively. Standard errors for fixed effects are in parentheses below the estimates, for random effects standard errors are reported. R^2 is McFadden-R^2 for comparison reason

structural change, which is more than 0.5 times the standard deviation above the average of all cities.

The McFadden-R^2 increases in the intercept-as-outcome models of both dependent variables. The information criteria show different results compared with the basic multilevel model. On the one hand and with respect to value added growth, both information criteria decline, except for the BIC for the estimation with change of scale technology and scale efficiency change as components (in the last two columns). On the other hand, for employment growth as an explanatory variable, the BIC always declines, compared with the basic multilevel model, but the AIC declines except for pure technological change and pure efficiency change (columns J and K in Table 9).

The intercept-as-outcome configuration clearly demonstrates that the random effect standard errors, especially for the productivity change components, are of considerable size. Thus, it would be wrong to ignore the nesting structure with both levels. Furthermore, the random effects at the time-level achieve considerably high standard errors. Unfortunately, in this estimation some random effects cannot be estimated because of the correlation at that level with the error terms and are, therefore, unavailable (NA). The likelihood ratio test statistic in Eq. (34) for the intercept-as-outcome model and the basic multilevel for value added growth reach values between 124 and 671.8, which are more than the 99 % quantile of the χ^2 distribution with eight degrees of freedom, which is about 20.1. Therefore, the null hypothesis, of no effect of the additional random effect, can be rejected on 1 % level of significance. This null hypothesis can also be rejected for the employment growth estimations, because the test statistic is still larger than the 99 % quantile with values varying between 33.8 and 172.2. The significances of the random effects indicate that the level must not be eliminated. Thus, variation in the slopes of the dependent variables is present within the levels.

5.3 *Results for the Intercept-and-Slope-as-Outcome Model*

Furthermore, I calculate the most general multilevel model, namely the intercept-and-slope-as-outcome model, which adds the higher-level variables as explanatory variables for the slope parameter of productivity change. Therefore, interaction terms of the explanatory variables with productivity change are included, as shown in Eq. (32). The results for value added growth with interaction terms are shown in Table 10 and for employment growth in Table 11.

The intercept-and-slope-as-outcome model changes the results further because of the additional fixed effects. The results in the Tables 10 and 11 are comparable with the results of the OLS estimations in the Tables 4 and 5. The interaction terms are only significant in a few cases, e.g., with business tax. Nonetheless, productivity change and the components as well as structural change, change in the Gini coefficient and business tax are significant as in the intercept-as-outcome model. Pure technological change affects significantly positive value added growth

Table 10 Multilevel results for gross value added growth in the intercept-and-slope-as-outcome model

	A	B	C	D	E	F	G
Fixed effects							
Intercept	−0.0288 (0.0727)	−0.0319 (0.0858)	−0.0462 (0.0759)	−0.049 (0.0739)	−0.031 (0.078)	−0.0298 (0.086)	−0.0241 (0.0863)
*dGVAL*1	−0.0701*** (0.0152)	−0.0902*** (0.0148)	−0.0608*** (0.015)	−0.071*** (0.0153)	−0.0873*** (0.0147)	−0.1125*** (0.015)	−0.1031*** (0.0148)
malm	−0.0437 (0.032)						
tech		−0.0142 (0.039)					
eff			−0.0281 (0.0314)				
pure.eff				−0.0776*** (0.026)			
pure.tech					0.1151** (0.0459)		
scale.tech						−0.1052** (0.0456)	
scale							0.1062** (0.0492)
PC.ln*Stu*	0.0244 (0.0288)	−0.0288 (0.0245)	0.0328 (0.0251)	−0.0039 (0.0261)	0.0016 (0.0316)	−0.0339 (0.0233)	0.0452* (0.0272)
ln*Stu*	0.0197 (0.0254)	0.0229 (0.027)	0.0263 (0.0264)	0.0397 (0.0265)	0.0098 (0.0271)	0.0113 (0.0292)	0.0192 (0.0288)

ln*Stu*²	0.0163 (0.0235)	0.0158 (0.0255)	0.0229 (0.0246)	0.0301 (0.0247)	0.0059 (0.025)	0.0132 (0.0262)	0.0213 (0.0256)
PC.dPop	−0.0004 (0.0301)	−0.0221 (0.0271)	0.0237 (0.0277)	0.0517* (0.0302)	−0.048 (0.0338)	0.058** (0.0279)	−0.0882*** (0.0289)
dPop	0.0167 (0.0287)	0.0334 (0.0286)	0.0315 (0.0291)	0.0327 (0.0314)	0.0487* (0.0288)	0.0414 (0.027)	0.0332 (0.0265)
*dPop*²	0.0707* (0.0413)	−0.0006 (0.0402)	0.0377 (0.0411)	0.0299 (0.0459)	−0.0112 (0.0425)	−0.0143 (0.0451)	−0.0535 (0.0477)
PC.Gini	0.0367 (0.0379)	0.0182 (0.0264)	0.0052 (0.0276)	−0.0014 (0.027)	0.0016 (0.0355)	−0.0133 (0.0224)	−0.0018 (0.0247)
Gini	0.0244 (0.0207)	0.0328 (0.03)	0.0176 (0.0233)	0.0231 (0.0245)	0.0215 (0.0313)	0.0266 (0.0285)	0.0283 (0.028)
*Gini*²	0.03* (0.0157)	0.0254 (0.0166)	0.0367** (0.0165)	0.0239 (0.0164)	0.0346** (0.0169)	0.0301* (0.0178)	0.0276 (0.0174)
PC.SC	0.042* (0.023)	0.0231 (0.0192)	0.0321 (0.0203)	0.0127 (0.02)	0.0173 (0.0201)	−0.0066 (0.0188)	0.0075 (0.019)
SC	−0.0901** (0.0424)	−0.0768* (0.0418)	−0.0896** (0.0444)	−0.0887** (0.0449)	−0.097** (0.0464)	−0.0978** (0.0441)	−0.103** (0.0422)
*SC*²	0.1057** (0.0427)	0.0763* (0.0412)	0.1149*** (0.0441)	0.1224*** (0.0446)	0.1391*** (0.0439)	0.1086** (0.0435)	0.105** (0.0414)
PC.BusTax	0.0254 (0.0276)	−0.0039 (0.0243)	0.033 (0.0248)	−0.0146 (0.0249)	0.1044*** (0.03)	−0.0608** (0.0239)	0.0508** (0.0257)
BusTax	−0.0326* (0.0181)	−0.034* (0.0191)	−0.0341* (0.0181)	−0.0386* (0.0201)	−0.0194 (0.0234)	−0.0322* (0.018)	−0.0381** (0.0176)
*BusTax*²	0.024 (0.0164)	0.0205 (0.0178)	0.0292* (0.0171)	0.0293* (0.0173)	0.0257 (0.0176)	0.0343* (0.0185)	0.027 (0.0179)

(continued)

Table 10 (continued)

	A	B	C	D	E	F	G
Random effects							
Time-level							
Intercept	0.1635	0.1954	0.1704	0.1649	0.1757	0.1954	0.1968
PC	0.0327	0.0682	0.0438	0.0046	0.0831	0.0927	0.1
ln*Stu*	0.0164	0.0102	0.0166	0.017	0.0154	0.0241	0.0272
dPop	0.0493	0.0438	0.0484	0.0561	0.0442	0.0349	0.0355
Gini	0.0302	0.0589	0.0386	0.0426	0.0632	0.0535	0.053
SC	0.0519	0.0248	0.0539	0.0559	0.0591	0.0376	0.0278
BusTax	0.0206	0.0187	0.0179	0.0272	0.0393	0.0067	0.0068
City-level							
Intercept	0.211	0.2675	0.2426	0.2352	0.2456	0.262	0.2487
PC	0.5437	0.4156	0.4669	0.4451	0.5108	0.3097	0.3688
residuals	0.7673	0.8165	0.7758	0.7949	0.7963	0.8425	0.8417
AIC	10,409	10,811	10,521	10,601	10,451	10,656	10,894
BIC	10,724	11,126	10,835	10,916	10,765	10,970	11,209
ln*L*	−5,154.3	−5,355.5	−5,210.3	−5,250.7	−5,175.7	−5,278.2	−5,397.1
R^2	0.3151	0.2884	0.3077	0.3023	0.3123	0.2987	0.2829

Significance codes: '***', '**', '*' significant up to 1, 5, and 10 %, respectively. Standard errors for fixed effects are in parentheses below the estimates, for random effects standard errors are reported. R^2 is McFadden-R^2 for comparison reason

Table 11 Multilevel results for employment growth in the intercept-and-slope-as-outcome model

	H	I	J	K	L	M	N
Fixed effects							
Intercept	0.0125 (0.111)	0.0219 (0.128)	0.0073 (0.1144)	0.0039 (0.1117)	0.0106 (0.1117)	−0.0002 (0.1112)	−0.0038 (0.1112)
*dEmpL*1	0.4342*** (0.0142)	0.4014*** (0.0143)	0.4331*** (0.0141)	0.4425*** (0.0141)	0.4488*** (0.0142)	0.4377*** (0.014)	0.4358*** (0.0139)
malm	−0.0374* (0.0227)						
tech		−0.0615 (0.1022)					
eff			−0.0224 (0.0374)				
pure.eff				−0.056*** (0.0207)			
pure.tech					−0.0015 (0.0415)		
scale.tech						−0.0122 (0.0699)	
scale							−0.0011 (0.0615)
PC.ln*Stu*	0.0054 (0.0193)	0.0128 (0.014)	0.0001 (0.017)	−0.0261 (0.0165)	0.0377** (0.0159)	−0.0413** (0.0207)	0.0474** (0.0237)
ln*Stu*	−0.0358 (0.0219)	−0.027 (0.0235)	−0.0297 (0.0228)	−0.0263 (0.0229)	−0.031 (0.0216)	−0.0292 (0.023)	−0.0294 (0.0243)

(continued)

Table 11 (continued)

	H	I	J	K	L	M	N
$\ln Stu^2$	−0.0078	−0.0041	−0.0005	−0.0017	−0.0036	0.0027	0.0019
	(0.0195)	(0.0192)	(0.0193)	(0.0195)	(0.0193)	(0.0188)	(0.0189)
PC.dPop	−0.0136	−0.0275*	0.0108	0.0171	−0.0196	−0.0009	−0.0005
	(0.0198)	(0.0158)	(0.0182)	(0.0183)	(0.0178)	(0.0249)	(0.0254)
dPop	0.0679***	0.0622*	0.0595	0.0568	0.0601*	0.0579*	0.0646*
	(0.017)	(0.0356)	(0.0363)	(0.0375)	(0.0321)	(0.0326)	(0.0374)
$dPop^2$	0.0418	0.0023	−0.0251	−0.0029	0.0134	−0.0157	−0.0526
	(0.032)	(0.0385)	(0.0354)	(0.0404)	(0.0388)	(0.0396)	(0.0404)
PC.Gini	0.0045	0.0168	−0.0141	0.0087	0.0042	0.0067	−0.0255
	(0.0227)	(0.0154)	(0.0198)	(0.0184)	(0.0184)	(0.0221)	(0.0276)
Gini	0.0567***	0.0445*	0.06***	0.0545**	0.0505**	0.0432*	0.045**
	(0.0171)	(0.0249)	(0.0205)	(0.0216)	(0.0214)	(0.023)	(0.0219)
$Gini^2$	0.017	0.0274**	0.0262*	0.0247*	0.0221	0.0215	0.0206
	(0.0123)	(0.0133)	(0.0145)	(0.0148)	(0.0141)	(0.0136)	(0.0143)
PC.SC	0.002	0.0258*	−0.0162	−0.0123	0.0219	0.0096	−0.006
	(0.0149)	(0.0138)	(0.0147)	(0.0135)	(0.0137)	(0.0162)	(0.0163)
SC	0.0022	−0.0038	0.0027	−0.0054	0.0055	0.0021	0.008
	(0.0309)	(0.0315)	(0.0309)	(0.0315)	(0.0309)	(0.0303)	(0.0306)
SC^2	−0.0093	0.0039	−0.0177	−0.0063	−0.0067	−0.0014	−0.009
	(0.0305)	(0.0304)	(0.0303)	(0.0307)	(0.0304)	(0.0292)	(0.0298)
PC.BusTax	−0.0368**	−0.0247*	−0.0022	−0.0131	−0.0027	−0.0183	0.0117
	(0.0185)	(0.0136)	(0.0166)	(0.0161)	(0.0161)	(0.0208)	(0.0221)

BusTax	−0.0371	−0.0312	−0.033	−0.0324	−0.0322	−0.0336	−0.0291
	(0.0255)	(0.0231)	(0.0242)	(0.023)	(0.0241)	(0.0234)	(0.0246)
$BusTax^2$	0.0065	0.0067	0.0022	0.0029	0.0039	0.013	0.0108
	(0.0135)	(0.0133)	(0.0134)	(0.0136)	(0.0135)	(0.0133)	(0.0132)
Random effects							
Time-level							
Intercept	0.2654	0.308	0.2741	0.2671	0.2672	0.2664	0.2664
PC	0.0248	0.2439	0.0797	0.0272	0.0883	0.1609	0.1378
ln*Stu*	0.0192	0.0298	0.0262	0.0255	0.0173	0.0284	0.0343
dPop	NA	0.0767	0.0786	0.0814	0.066	0.0683	0.0817
Gini	NA	0.0446	0.0279	0.0314	0.0311	0.0383	0.0345
SC	0.0028	0.0193	0.0117	0.0146	0.0106	0.0137	0.0112
BusTax	0.0535	0.0469	0.0499	0.0461	0.0497	0.0479	0.0513
City-level							
Intercept	0.0043	0.0224	0.0229	0.0288	0.031	0.0137	0.0028
PC	0.2634	0.0962	0.2169	0.1672	0.113	0.2746	0.311
residuals	0.7763	0.7892	0.7769	0.7909	0.7826	0.7516	0.7619
AIC	9,871	9,842	9,873	9,924	9,585	9,490	9,813
BIC	10,104	10,157	10,188	10,239	9,898	9,804	10,128
ln*L*	−4,898.4	−4,870.8	−4,886.7	−4,912.2	−4,742.3	−4,695.1	−4,856.7
R^2	0.3419	0.3456	0.3434	0.34	0.3628	0.3692	0.3475

Significance codes: '***', '**', '*' significant up to 1, 5, and 10 %, respectively. Standard errors for fixed effects are in parentheses below the estimates, for random effects standard errors are reported. R^2 is McFadden-R^2 for comparison reason

with an estimate of 0.1151 in column E. Therefore, technological progress has a positive effect on value added growth in German cities as expected in evolutionary economic geography. However, this effect is offset by the negative coefficient of change in scale technology in column F. Furthermore, change in pure efficiency has a negative effect on value added growth with a coefficient of −0.0776 in column D, although there are interaction terms. The effect was already observable in the basic multilevel and intercept-as-outcome model. A possible explanation is that the increase of pure efficiency and thus the catching-up to the production frontier increases the degree of competition in the market and by doing so results in a decrease of growth (Aghion and Howitt 2009, p. 92). Additional explanations are the negative feedback of firm growth in Frenken and Boschma 2007, p. 643 because the effect on gross value added is 2 years later (see Eq. (32)).

With respect to the results for employment growth presented in Table 11, the Malmquist index and the component pure efficiency change significantly affect employment growth negatively. In case of employment growth as explained variable, technological progress measured by pure technological change has no effect while change of pure efficiency in column K is significantly negative with a value of −0.056 although there are interaction terms. However, the interaction terms are even less important than in the case of value added growth. The interactions of productivity change are only significant for the number of students and business tax. Because of the insignificance of most interaction terms with productivity change, the log-likelihood does not improve and even decreases in the REML estimation, which is not best for evaluating the significance of fixed effects. This shows, that the effect of technological change and efficiency change on industrial growth does not depend on the local variables investigated.

The intercept-as-outcome model without interaction terms already generates the best results. This finding is supported by the increasing AIC and BIC, which increase for every estimation.

An evaluation of the coefficients is possible with the OLS model only because all the fixed effects are the same except that the intercept-and-slope-as-outcome model contains random effects. The likelihood-ratio test statistic in Eq. (34) with the intercept-and-slope-as-outcome model and the OLS estimates for value added growth varies between 187.2 and 729.2. Therefore, the null hypothesis of no significant level effects (no random effects) can be rejected at the 1 % level of significance and nine degrees of freedom (nine random effects are estimated). The same applies for employment growth, whose results of the test statistic vary between 225 and 378.8, which is still larger than the 99 % quantile of the χ^2 distribution of 21.7. This shows the importance of the multilevel random effects.

Furthermore, the results are proven to be robust to the elimination of insignificant variables as well as the three large cities, namely Berlin, Hamburg, and Bremen (together with Bremerhaven), which are not only free cities but also sovereign states in Germany, with further competences and a large number of inhabitants.

6 Conclusion

Because we live in an urban world with more than half of the world's population living in cities and given that most economic activity takes place in cities, it is important to know what forces foster industrial growth and to learn about the role of city-specific circumstances. In Germany, cities classified as urban municipalities have the power to influence many variables, like business tax structure and expenditure for transportation facilities. These cities compete against each other by their individual characteristics in order to attract new entrepreneurs and support established industries, increase income and tax revenue. In addition, the industrial structure is different between cities, and several analyses have observed externalities which arise by closeness and innovation in the same or a different but related industry. However, if individuals interact with each other within a city, the nesting structure should be an important feature and without its consideration econometric estimates are biased. Multilevel analyses offer the tools to solve this problem and to estimate unbiased results with corrected standard errors by accounting for the nesting structure.

It turns out that the multilevel structure is appropriate for analyzing the industrial performance of cities observed over subsequent years. The development of industries is different between different cities, offering a specific environment. Yearly productivity change as estimated with the non-parametric DEA, such as the Malmquist index and its components, affect value added growth and employment growth. In particular, efficiency change, which captures catching-up to the best practice frontier of industries, is negatively associated with both value added growth and employment growth. This can be interpreted as Schumpeter's creative destruction of innovations. Pure technological progress fosters industrial value added growth.

Furthermore, the growth path leads to an adoption of value added growth and a divergence in employment growth in German cities. Several additional forces are found to be significantly related to value added growth and employment growth. The effects are not only linear but also quadratic. For example, the structural change of the industrial composition in the cities shows a U-shaped form, indicating that both large changes in the industrial structure increase value added growth and employment growth, but also that no or lower than average structural change is fruitful. However, interactions between the exogenous variables are not found to have a significant effect on industrial growth. This implies that the effect of productivity change is independent of the other city specifics. A negative effect of industrial concentration on employment growth, as found by Noseleit (2013) for West German agglomerations over the period between 1983 and 2002, has not been found in the data set of all cities in the most recent years. Instead, only the increase of the change in industrial concentration has been found to have positive effects on value added growth and employment growth with significant quadratic terms.

A more detailed look into industry-specific results is only possible with further monitoring and information about cities over an extended period of time. Moreover, the lag structure of the variables might be refined, because decisions do not have to be based on the observations of the last year. However, to integrate more time lag structures, a larger data set is needed to be able to pass additional yearly observations. However, investigations of multilevel models remain computer- and time-intensive. Adding further random effects and levels increases the time required to calculate the models disproportionately. Future analyses of employment and value added growth model will have to close the evolutionary cycle between income growth and the generation of innovations, as shown in Fratesi (2010). Unfortunately, the Malmquist index and its components are difficult to implement as endogenous variables in such an analysis, as the result of their construction, which includes endogeneity problems analogous to those discussed in Simar and Wilson (2007) and Thanassoulis et al. (2008, p. 343).

Acknowledgements I would like to thank the participants at the 9th ACDD in Strasbourg, France, the 14th International Joseph A. Schumpeter Society Conference in Brisbane, Australia, the 9th ISNE conference in Cork, Ireland, and the 2nd ifo workshop on regional economics in Dresden, Germany, for their fruitful discussion on earlier drafts of this paper. Additionally, I would like to thank an anonymous referee and Jens J. Krüger for reading a previous version and for their helpful comments. The usual disclaimer applies.

Appendix 1: List of Cities Included (Table 12)

Table 12 Cities included with average population

City	Population	City	Population
Aachen	255,027	Kempten	61,521
Amberg	44,498	Kiel	233,806
Ansbach	40,542	Koblenz	106,998
Aschaffenburg	68,660	Krefeld	238,132
Augsburg	260,696	Landau	41,992
Baden-Baden	54,230	Landshut	60,902
Bamberg	69,776	Leipzig	499,885
Bayreuth	74,059	Leverkusen	161,072
Berlin	3,394,776	Lubeck	212,162
Bielefeld	326,375	Ludwigshafen	163,151
Bochum	386,546	Magdeburg	228,519
Bonn	311,584	Mainz	189,981
Bottrop	119,848	Mannheim	308,201
Brandenburg	74,763	Memmingen	41,157

(continued)

Table 12 (continued)

City	Population	City	Population
Bremen	545,450	Monchengladbach	261,863
Bremerhaven	117,290	Mulheim	170,506
Brunswick	245,516	Munich	1,256,420
Chemnitz	249,016	Munster	270,092
Coburg	42,109	Neubrandenburg	68,868
Cologne	976,346	Neumunster	78,651
Cottbus	105,662	Neustadt	53,815
Darmstadt	139,965	Nuremberg	495,502
Delmenhorst	75,803	Oberhausen	219,495
Dessau	80,784	Offenbach	119,003
Dortmund	588,835	Oldenburg	158,218
Dresden	490,356	Osnabruck	164,002
Duisburg	504,065	Passau	50,608
Dusseldorf	574,097	Pforzheim	118,954
Eisenach	43,931	Pirmasens	43,493
Emden	51,522	Potsdam	144,123
Erfurt	201,745	Ratisbon	129,319
Erlangen	102,921	Remscheid	116,670
Essen	586,115	Rosenheim	60,092
Flensburg	85,748	Rostock	198,844
Frankenthal	47,415	Salzgitter	108,770
Frankfurt/M	647,433	Schwabach	38,689
Frankfurt/O	65,526	Schweinfurt	54,385
Freiburg	213,741	Schwerin	97,449
Furth	112,748	Solingen	163,921
Gelsenkirchen	270,575	Spires	50,373
Gera	105,404	Stralsund	58,861
Greifswald	53045	Straubing	44,559
Hagen	198,439	Stuttgart	591,361
Halle	238,186	Suhl	43,747
Hamburg	1,741,001	Trier	100,601
Hamm	184,351	Ulm	120,140
Heidelberg	143,091	Weiden	42,744
Heilbronn	121,063	Weimar	64,299
Herne	171,745	Wiesbaden	273,603
Hof	49,198	Wilhelmshaven	83,933
Ingolstadt	120,298	Wismar	45,601
Jena	101,901	Wolfsburg	121,741
Kaiserslautern	98,896	Worms	81,425
Karlsruhe	283,809	Wuppertal	360796
Kassel	194,026	Wurzburg	132,851
Kaufbeuren	42,348	Zweibrucken	35,367

Appendix 2: Multilevel Model Estimation

In general and in the formulation of Pinheiro and Bates (2000) a three level model with two levels of random effects is written as

$$y_{ijt} = \boldsymbol{X}_{ijt}\boldsymbol{\beta}_{ijt} + \boldsymbol{Z}_{ij,t}\boldsymbol{b}_{ij} + \boldsymbol{Z}_{ijt}\boldsymbol{b}_{ijt} + e_{ijk}, \tag{37}$$

with $i = 1, \ldots, N$, $j = 1, \ldots, n$, and $t = 2, \ldots, T$, and $\boldsymbol{b}_{ij} \sim N(\boldsymbol{0}, \boldsymbol{\Sigma}_1)$, $\boldsymbol{b}_{ijt} \sim N(\boldsymbol{0}, \boldsymbol{\Sigma}_2)$, $\boldsymbol{e}_{ijk} \sim N\left(0, \sigma^2 \boldsymbol{I}\right)$. For simplification the number observations is the same for every level and group so that no observation is missing and it does not vary by lower level groups. In the mixed or random effects literature Eq. (37) is written in vector notation for all i as

$$\boldsymbol{y}_{jt} = \boldsymbol{X}_{jt}\boldsymbol{\beta}_{jt} + \boldsymbol{Z}_{j,t}\boldsymbol{b}_j + \boldsymbol{Z}_{jt}\boldsymbol{b}_{jt} + \boldsymbol{e}_{jt}. \tag{38}$$

Equation (37) and accordingly Eq. (37) incorporate $\boldsymbol{X}_{jt}$ the regressor matrix for the vector of the p fixed effects $\boldsymbol{\beta}_{jt}$, $\boldsymbol{Z}_{j,t}$ the regressor matrix for the random effects $\boldsymbol{b}_j$ of the second level, and $\boldsymbol{Z}_{jt}$ the regressor matrix for the random effect $\boldsymbol{b}_{jt}$ of the third level. The variance-covariance matrices $\boldsymbol{\Sigma}_l$ for $l = 1, 2$ and in each of the two levels of random effects have to be symmetric and positive definite and can be expressed as $\sigma^2 \boldsymbol{D}_l$ with σ^2 the variance of the error term and $\boldsymbol{D}_l$ a scaled variance-covariance matrix for the random effects of level l.

The estimation procedure is developed from the simple model with one level of random effects to two levels of random effects and can be extended by further levels of random effects.

For one level of random effects with $l = 1$ the calculation is performed as follows. The general model equation without the third level denoted with t or the second level of random effects is in vector notation

$$y_{ij} = \boldsymbol{X}_{ij}\boldsymbol{\beta}_{ij} + \boldsymbol{Z}_{ij}\boldsymbol{b}_{ij} + e_{ij}, \tag{39}$$

for $i = 1, \ldots, N$, $j = 1, \ldots, n$, and $\boldsymbol{X}_{ij}$ the $(N \cdot n \times p)$ regressor matrix for the $(p \times 1)$ vector of fixed effects $\boldsymbol{\beta}_{ij}$, $\boldsymbol{Z}_{ij}$ is the $(N \cdot n \times q)$ regressor matrix for the q random effects $\boldsymbol{b}_{ij}$. In notation for all i as vector it follows

$$\boldsymbol{y}_j = \boldsymbol{X}_j\boldsymbol{\beta}_j + \boldsymbol{Z}_j\boldsymbol{b}_j + \boldsymbol{e}_j, \tag{40}$$

for $j = 1, \ldots, n$. As Lindstrom and Bates (1988) show in general without restriction on the error term structure $\boldsymbol{e}_j \sim N\left(\boldsymbol{0}, \sigma^2 \boldsymbol{\Lambda}\right)$ where $\boldsymbol{\Lambda}$ is of size $N \times N$ and does not have to be the identity matrix $\boldsymbol{I}$

$$y_j | \boldsymbol{b}_j \sim N\left(\boldsymbol{X}_j\boldsymbol{\beta}_j + \boldsymbol{Z}_j\boldsymbol{b}_j, \sigma^2 \boldsymbol{\Lambda}_j\right), \; j = 1, \ldots, n.$$

For all j, it becomes in vector notation

$$\boldsymbol{y} | \boldsymbol{b} \sim N\left(\boldsymbol{X}\boldsymbol{\beta} + \boldsymbol{Z}\boldsymbol{b}, \sigma^2 \boldsymbol{\Lambda}\right)$$

with $\boldsymbol{Z} = \text{diag}\left(\boldsymbol{Z}_1, \boldsymbol{Z}_2, \ldots, \boldsymbol{Z}_n\right)$, $\boldsymbol{\Lambda} = \text{diag}\left(\boldsymbol{\Lambda}_1, \boldsymbol{\Lambda}_2, \ldots, \boldsymbol{\Lambda}_n\right)$ and $\boldsymbol{b} \sim N\left(0, \sigma^2\boldsymbol{\Sigma}\right)$

$$\boldsymbol{y} \sim N\left(\boldsymbol{X\beta}, \boldsymbol{D}\right), \boldsymbol{D} = \sigma^2\left(\boldsymbol{Z\Sigma Z}' + \boldsymbol{\Lambda}\right) \tag{41}$$

The likelihood function is

$$L\left(\boldsymbol{\beta}, \boldsymbol{\theta}, \sigma^2 | \boldsymbol{y}\right) = \prod_{j=1}^{n} p\left(y_j | \boldsymbol{\beta}, \boldsymbol{\theta}, \sigma^2\right). \tag{42}$$

In Eq. (42) $\boldsymbol{\theta}$ contains the unique elements of $\boldsymbol{\Sigma}$ and the parameters in $\boldsymbol{\Lambda}$ which are the variance components without exact specification (Harville 1977; Lindstrom and Bates 1990). Because $\boldsymbol{b}_j$ and $\boldsymbol{e}_j$ are independent, as Eq. (41) indicates, Eq. (42) results in

$$\begin{aligned}
L\left(\boldsymbol{\beta}, \boldsymbol{\theta}, \sigma^2 | \boldsymbol{y}\right) &= \prod_{j=1}^{n} \int p\left(y_j | \boldsymbol{b}_j, \boldsymbol{\beta}, \sigma^2\right) p\left(\boldsymbol{b}_j | \boldsymbol{\theta}, \sigma^2\right) d\boldsymbol{b}_j \\
&= \prod_{j=1}^{n} \int \frac{\exp(-\left\| \boldsymbol{y}_j - \boldsymbol{X}_j \boldsymbol{\beta}_j + \mathbf{Z}_j \boldsymbol{b}_j \right\|^2 / 2\sigma^2)}{(2\pi\sigma^2)^{N/2}} \\
&\quad \times \frac{\exp\left(-\boldsymbol{b}_j' \boldsymbol{D}^{-1} \boldsymbol{b}_j / 2\sigma^2\right)}{(2\pi\sigma^2)^{q/2} \sqrt{|\boldsymbol{D}|}} d\boldsymbol{b}_j \\
&= \prod_{j=1}^{n} \frac{1}{\sqrt{(2\pi\sigma^2)^{N/2}}} \\
&\quad \times \int \frac{\exp\left[\frac{-1}{2\sigma^2}\left(\left\| y_j - \boldsymbol{X}_j \boldsymbol{\beta} - \boldsymbol{Z}_j \boldsymbol{b}_j \right\|^2 + \boldsymbol{b}_j' \boldsymbol{D}^{-1} \boldsymbol{b}_j\right)\right]}{(2\pi\sigma^2)^{q/2} \sqrt{|\boldsymbol{D}|}} d\boldsymbol{b}_j \\
&= \prod_{j=1}^{n} \frac{1}{\sqrt{(2\pi\sigma^2)^{N/2}}} \\
&\quad \times \int \frac{\exp\left[\frac{-1}{2\sigma^2}\left(\left\| y_j - \boldsymbol{X}_j \boldsymbol{\beta} - \boldsymbol{Z}_j \boldsymbol{b}_j \right\|^2 - \left\| \Delta \boldsymbol{b}_j \right\|^2\right)\right]}{(2\pi\sigma^2)^{q/2} \,\text{abs}\, |\Delta|^{-1}} d\boldsymbol{b}_j \\
&= \prod_{j=1}^{n} \frac{\text{abs}\, |\Delta|}{\sqrt{(2\pi\sigma^2)^{N/2}}} \\
&\quad \times \int \frac{\exp\left[\frac{-1}{2\sigma^2}\left(\left\| \tilde{\boldsymbol{y}}_j - \tilde{\boldsymbol{X}}_j \boldsymbol{\beta} - \tilde{\boldsymbol{Z}}_j \boldsymbol{b}_j \right\|^2\right)\right]}{(2\pi\sigma^2)^{q/2}} d\boldsymbol{b}_j,
\end{aligned} \tag{43}$$

with $\tilde{\boldsymbol{y}}_j = \begin{bmatrix} \boldsymbol{y}_j \\ \boldsymbol{0} \end{bmatrix}, \tilde{\boldsymbol{X}}_j = \begin{bmatrix} \boldsymbol{X}_j \\ \boldsymbol{0} \end{bmatrix}, \tilde{\boldsymbol{Z}}_j = \begin{bmatrix} \boldsymbol{Z}_j \\ \boldsymbol{\Delta} \end{bmatrix}$ as pseudo data, where $\boldsymbol{\Delta}$ a relative precision factor as the Cholesky factor of $\boldsymbol{D}^{-1}$, since $\boldsymbol{b}'_j \boldsymbol{D}^{-1} \boldsymbol{b}_j = \left\| \Delta \boldsymbol{b}_j \right\|^2 = \left\| \boldsymbol{0} - \boldsymbol{0}\boldsymbol{\beta} - \Delta \boldsymbol{b}_j \right\|^2$ and therefore $\boldsymbol{D}^{-1} = \Delta' \Delta$ (Lindstrom and Bates 1990).

So the exponent is the sum of squared residuals ($\|a\| = \sqrt{a'a}$ as the norm of a matrix). Equation (43) clearly points out that the maximization of the log-likelihood requires the minimization of the quadratic norm within the exponential function within the integral. This quadratic norm includes the quadratic error terms and is therefore similar to other least squares problems except that the mean of the random effects have to be zero. To solve that least squares problem numerically the orthogonal-triangular decomposition of rectangular matrices is preferred since it provides stable and efficient results by reducing the condition, i.e. the complexity of $\boldsymbol{X}_j$ and $\boldsymbol{Z}_j$. The orthogonal-triangular decomposition uses is the QR-decomposition, with $\tilde{\boldsymbol{Z}}_j = \boldsymbol{Q}_{(j)} \begin{bmatrix} \boldsymbol{R}_{11(j)} \\ \boldsymbol{0} \end{bmatrix}$, where $\boldsymbol{Q}_{(j)}$ is a $(N+q) \times (N+q)$ orthogonal matrix $\left(Q'_{(j)} = Q^{-1}_{(j)} \right)$ and $\boldsymbol{R}_{11(j)}$ is an upper-triangular $(q \times q)$ matrix. This decomposition can be performed for every real matrix but in the case for positive elements in $\boldsymbol{R}_{11(j)}$ have to be invertible, so $\tilde{\boldsymbol{Z}}_j$ has to have full rank as for OLS regression there must not be any linear dependency structure within the random variables. Also $\tilde{\boldsymbol{X}}_j = \boldsymbol{Q}_{(j)} \begin{bmatrix} \boldsymbol{R}_{10(j)} \\ \boldsymbol{R}_{00(j)} \end{bmatrix}$ and $\tilde{\boldsymbol{y}}_j = \boldsymbol{Q}_{(j)} \begin{bmatrix} \boldsymbol{c}_{1(j)} \\ \boldsymbol{c}_{0(j)} \end{bmatrix}$. Therefore, it is also possible to orthogonal triangular decomposition (QR) of an augmented matrix

$$\begin{bmatrix} \boldsymbol{Z}_j & \boldsymbol{X}_j & \boldsymbol{y}_j \\ \boldsymbol{\Delta} & \boldsymbol{0} & \boldsymbol{0} \end{bmatrix} = \left(\tilde{\boldsymbol{Z}}_j \; \tilde{\boldsymbol{X}}_j \; \tilde{\boldsymbol{y}}_j \right) = \boldsymbol{Q}_{(j)} \begin{bmatrix} \boldsymbol{R}_{11(j)} & \boldsymbol{R}_{10(j)} & \boldsymbol{c}_{1(j)} \\ \boldsymbol{0} & \boldsymbol{R}_{00(j)} & \boldsymbol{c}_{0(j)} \end{bmatrix}$$

or

$$\boldsymbol{Q}^{-1}_{(j)} \left(\tilde{\boldsymbol{Z}}_j \; \tilde{\boldsymbol{X}}_j \; \tilde{\boldsymbol{y}}_j \right) = \begin{bmatrix} \boldsymbol{R}_{11(j)} & \boldsymbol{R}_{10(j)} & \boldsymbol{c}_{1(j)} \\ \boldsymbol{0} & \boldsymbol{R}_{00(j)} & \boldsymbol{c}_{0(j)} \end{bmatrix}.$$

The exponent in Eq. (43) becomes

$$\begin{aligned} \left\| \tilde{\boldsymbol{y}}_j - \tilde{\boldsymbol{X}}_j \boldsymbol{\beta} - \tilde{\boldsymbol{Z}}_j \boldsymbol{b}_j \right\|^2 &= \left\| \boldsymbol{Q}'_{(j)} \left(\tilde{\boldsymbol{y}}_j - \tilde{\boldsymbol{X}}_j \boldsymbol{\beta} - \tilde{\boldsymbol{Z}}_j \boldsymbol{b}_j \right) \right\|^2 \\ &= \left\| \boldsymbol{c}_{1(j)} - \boldsymbol{R}_{10(j)} \boldsymbol{\beta} - \boldsymbol{R}_{11(j)} \boldsymbol{b}_j \right\|^2 + \left\| \boldsymbol{c}_{0(j)} - \boldsymbol{R}_{00(j)} \boldsymbol{\beta} \right\|. \end{aligned}$$

Thus the integral in Eq. (43) can be expressed as

$$\exp\left[\frac{\left\|\boldsymbol{c}_{0(j)}-\boldsymbol{R}_{00(j)}\boldsymbol{\beta}\right\|^2}{-2\sigma^2}\right]\int\frac{\exp\left[\frac{-1}{2\pi\sigma^2}\left(\left\|\boldsymbol{c}_{1(j)}-\boldsymbol{R}_{10(j)}\boldsymbol{\beta}-\boldsymbol{R}_{11(j)}\boldsymbol{b}_j\right\|^2\right)\right]}{(2\pi\sigma^2)^{q/2}}d\boldsymbol{b}_j. \tag{44}$$

Note because $\boldsymbol{R}_{11(j)}$ is a non-singular, Bates and Pinheiro construct the following variable
$\boldsymbol{\phi}_j = \left(\boldsymbol{c}_{1(j)}-\boldsymbol{R}_{10(j)}\boldsymbol{\beta}-n\boldsymbol{R}_{11(j)}\boldsymbol{b}_1\right)/\sigma$ with $d\boldsymbol{\phi}_j = \sigma^{-q}\text{abs}|\boldsymbol{R}_{11(j)}|d\boldsymbol{b}_j$ to easily eliminate the integral. The integral expressed in Eq. (44) is

$$\begin{aligned}&\int\frac{\exp\left[\frac{-1}{2\pi\sigma^2}\left(\left\|\boldsymbol{c}_{1(j)}-n\boldsymbol{R}_{10(j)}\boldsymbol{\beta}-\boldsymbol{R}_{11(j)}\boldsymbol{b}_j\right\|^2\right)\right]}{(2\pi\sigma^2)^{q/2}}d\boldsymbol{b}_j\\&=\frac{1}{\text{abs}|\boldsymbol{R}_{11(j)}|}\int\frac{\exp\left(-\left\|\boldsymbol{\phi}_j\right\|^2/2\right)}{(2\pi)^{q/2}}d\boldsymbol{\phi}_j\\&=\text{abs}|\boldsymbol{R}_{11(j)}|^{-1}\end{aligned}$$

because the integral is over a standard normal distribution, which is unity over the whole range.

And because the determinant of $\boldsymbol{R}_{11(j)}$ is the sum of its diagonal elements since it is an upper-triangular matrix by construction of QR decomposition. So altogether the likelihood function becomes

$$L\left(\boldsymbol{\beta},\boldsymbol{\theta},\sigma^2|\boldsymbol{y}\right)=\prod_{j=1}^{n}\frac{\exp\left[\frac{\left\|\boldsymbol{c}_{0j}-\boldsymbol{R}_{00(j)}\boldsymbol{\beta}\right\|^2}{-2\sigma^2}\right]}{\sqrt{(2\pi\sigma^2)^N|\boldsymbol{D}|}}\text{abs}|\boldsymbol{R}_{11(j)}|^{-1}.$$

A further QR decomposition can be performed by

$$\begin{bmatrix}\boldsymbol{R}_{00(1)} & \boldsymbol{c}_{0(1)}\\ \vdots & \vdots\\ \boldsymbol{R}_{00(M)} & \boldsymbol{c}_{0(M)}\end{bmatrix}=\boldsymbol{Q}_0\begin{bmatrix}\boldsymbol{R}_{00} & \boldsymbol{c}_0\\ \boldsymbol{0} & \boldsymbol{c}_{-1}\end{bmatrix}$$

to

$$\begin{aligned}L\left(\boldsymbol{\beta},\boldsymbol{\theta},\sigma^2|\boldsymbol{y}\right)&=\left(2\pi\sigma^2\right)^{-N_M/2}\exp\left(\frac{\left\|\boldsymbol{c}_{-1}\right\|^2+\left\|\boldsymbol{c}_0-\boldsymbol{R}_{00}\boldsymbol{\beta}\right\|^2}{-n2\sigma^2}\right)\\&\quad\times\prod_{j=1}^{n}\text{abs}\left(\frac{|\boldsymbol{\Delta}|}{|\boldsymbol{R}_{11(j)}|}\right)\end{aligned}$$

with $N_n = \sum_{j=1}^{n} N = n \cdot N$ and $1/\sqrt{|\boldsymbol{D}|} = \text{abs}|\boldsymbol{\Delta}|$. The estimate of fixed effects $\boldsymbol{\beta}$ follows from $\|\boldsymbol{c}_0 - \boldsymbol{R}_{00}\boldsymbol{\beta}\|^2$ and is

$$\hat{\boldsymbol{\beta}} = \boldsymbol{R}_{00}^{-1}\boldsymbol{c}_0$$

and

$$\sigma^2 = \|\boldsymbol{c}_{-1}\|^2 / N_n.$$

Maximum likelihood estimates are then performed by setting an estimate for $\boldsymbol{\theta}$. The random effects are evaluated by

$$\hat{\boldsymbol{b}}_j(\boldsymbol{\theta}) = \boldsymbol{R}_{11(j)}^{-1}\left(\boldsymbol{c}_{1j} - \boldsymbol{R}_{10(j)}\hat{\boldsymbol{\beta}}(\boldsymbol{\theta})\right).$$

This is the best linear unbiased predictor for the random effects, where $\boldsymbol{\theta} = \hat{\boldsymbol{\theta}}$ as the maximum likelihood estimate.

Lindstrom and Bates (1988, 1990) show the computation for full maximum likelihood and restricted maximum likelihood estimation. Since the maximum likelihood estimation does not account for the loss in degrees of freedom $(N_M - p)$ the estimators are generally downward biased for example if the estimator for the variance component is $\theta_i(N_n - p)/N$ its bias is $\theta_i p/N_n$ (Harville 1977). The estimation is therefore performed with the restricted maximum likelihood estimation (REML) sometimes also called residual maximum likelihood which accounts for the degrees of freedom but results in incomparable results if the number of parameters differ. The restricted form as Laird and Ware (1982) and Ware (1985)

$$L_R\left(\boldsymbol{\theta}, \sigma^2|\boldsymbol{y}\right) = \int L\left(\boldsymbol{\beta}, \boldsymbol{\theta}, \sigma^2|\boldsymbol{y}\right) d\boldsymbol{\beta} \tag{45}$$

logarithm

$$\begin{aligned} l_R\left(\boldsymbol{\theta}, \sigma^2|\boldsymbol{y}\right) &= \log L_R\left(\boldsymbol{\theta}, \sigma^2|\boldsymbol{y}\right) \\ &= -\frac{N_n - p}{2}\log\left(2\pi\sigma^2\right) - \frac{\|\boldsymbol{c}_{-1}\|^2}{2\sigma^2} - \log\text{abs}|\boldsymbol{R}_{00}| \\ &\quad + \sum_{j=1}^{n}\log\text{abs}\left(\frac{|\boldsymbol{\Delta}|}{|\boldsymbol{R}_{11(j)}|}\right). \end{aligned}$$

As the result, the conditional estimate for $\boldsymbol{\beta}$ is

$$\hat{\boldsymbol{\beta}} = \boldsymbol{R}_{00}^{-1}\boldsymbol{c}_0$$

as the same as in the unconditional case but with $\boldsymbol{R}_{00}^{-1}$ different due to different $\boldsymbol{\Delta}$ and σ^2

$$\hat{\sigma}_R^2(\boldsymbol{\theta}) = \|c_{-1}\|^2 / (N_t - p).$$

So the restricted log-likelihood is

$$\begin{aligned} l_R(\boldsymbol{\theta}|\boldsymbol{y}) &= l_R\left(\boldsymbol{\theta}, \hat{\sigma}_{RE}^2(\boldsymbol{\theta})|\boldsymbol{y}\right) \\ &= \text{const} - (N_n - p)\log\|\boldsymbol{c}_{-1}\| - \log\text{abs}|\boldsymbol{R}_{00}| + \sum_{j=1}^{n}\log\text{abs}\left(\frac{|\boldsymbol{\Delta}|}{|\boldsymbol{R}_{11(j)}|}\right). \end{aligned}$$

In both cases the variance of the fixed effect coefficients is

$$\text{Var}\left(\hat{\boldsymbol{\beta}}\right) = \hat{\sigma}^2\boldsymbol{R}_{00}^{-1}\left(\boldsymbol{R}_{00}^{-1}\right)'.$$

The integral or respectively the sum becomes clear as soon as we rewrite the likelihood function for one level of random effects in Eq. (42) for two levels of random effects namely in my example the city level $j = 1, \ldots, n$ which is nested within the time level $t = 1, \ldots, T$, it becomes

$$\begin{aligned} L\left(\boldsymbol{\beta}, \boldsymbol{\theta}_1, \boldsymbol{\theta}_2, \sigma^2|\boldsymbol{y}\right) &= \prod_{t=1}^{T}\int\prod_{j=1}^{n}\left[\int p\left(\boldsymbol{y}_{jt}|\boldsymbol{b}_{jt}, \boldsymbol{b}_{it}, \boldsymbol{\beta}, \sigma^2\right)p\left(\boldsymbol{b}_{jt}|\boldsymbol{\theta}_2, \sigma^2\right)d\boldsymbol{b}_{jt}\right] \\ &\quad \times p\left(\boldsymbol{b}_t|\boldsymbol{\theta}_1, \sigma^2\right)d\boldsymbol{b}_t. \end{aligned} \tag{46}$$

Decomposition is constructed similar to the case with one level of random effects

$$\begin{bmatrix} \boldsymbol{Z}_{jt} & \boldsymbol{Z}_{j,t} & \boldsymbol{X}_{jt} & \boldsymbol{y}_{jt} \\ \boldsymbol{\Delta}_2 & \boldsymbol{0} & \boldsymbol{0} & \boldsymbol{0} \end{bmatrix} = \boldsymbol{Q}_{jt}\begin{bmatrix} \boldsymbol{R}_{22(jt)} & \boldsymbol{R}_{21(jt)} & \boldsymbol{R}_{20(jt)} & \boldsymbol{c}_{2(jt)} \\ \boldsymbol{0} & \boldsymbol{R}_{11(jt)} & \boldsymbol{R}_{10(jt)} & \boldsymbol{c}_{1(jt)} \end{bmatrix},$$
$$j = 1, \ldots, n,\ t = 1, \ldots, T$$

decomposition for that

$$\begin{bmatrix} \boldsymbol{R}_{11(1t)} & \boldsymbol{R}_{10(1t)} & \boldsymbol{c}_{1(1t)} \\ \vdots & \vdots & \vdots \\ \boldsymbol{R}_{11(Mt)} & \boldsymbol{R}_{1(Mt)} & \boldsymbol{c}_{1Mt)} \\ \boldsymbol{\Delta}_1 & \boldsymbol{0} & \boldsymbol{0} \end{bmatrix} = \boldsymbol{Q}_{(i)}\begin{bmatrix} \boldsymbol{R}_{11(t)} & \boldsymbol{R}_{10(t)} & \boldsymbol{c}_{1(t)} \\ 0 & \boldsymbol{R}_{00(t)} & \boldsymbol{c}_{0(t)} \end{bmatrix}$$

the profiled log-likelihood becomes

$$\begin{aligned} l_R(\boldsymbol{\theta}_1, \boldsymbol{\theta}_2 | \boldsymbol{y}) &= \log L_R\left(\hat{\boldsymbol{\beta}}_R(\boldsymbol{\theta}_1, \boldsymbol{\theta}_2), \boldsymbol{\theta}_1, \boldsymbol{\theta}_2, \hat{\sigma}_R^2(\boldsymbol{\theta}_1, \boldsymbol{\theta}_2) | \boldsymbol{y}\right) \\ &= \text{const} - (N_T - np)\log \|\boldsymbol{c}_{-1}\| - \log \text{abs}|\boldsymbol{R}_{00}| \\ &\quad + \sum_{t=1}^{T} \log \text{abs}\left(\frac{|\boldsymbol{\Delta}_1|}{|\boldsymbol{R}_{11(t)}|}\right) + \sum_{t=1}^{T}\sum_{j=1}^{n} \log \text{abs}\left(\frac{|\boldsymbol{\Delta}_2|}{|\boldsymbol{R}_{22(jt)}|}\right), \end{aligned}$$

with $N_T = N \cdot n \cdot T$ the total number of observations. Compared to the two level model, the three level model just adds the last addend for the nested higher level.

The solution is straight forward according to one level estimation.

Multilevel models are solved by EM algorithm, which is an iteration of two steps, namely the expectation and maximization (Laird et al. 1987). The data are fitted to the model within the expectation step by estimating the fixed effects, random effects, and the pseudo data ($\tilde{\boldsymbol{y}}_j$, $\tilde{\boldsymbol{X}}_j$, and $\tilde{\boldsymbol{Z}}_j$) to the current values of variance components $\hat{\boldsymbol{\theta}}$. The maximization step fits the parameter $\boldsymbol{\theta}$ of the model to the data by maximizing the likelihood to achieve new variance component parameters $\hat{\boldsymbol{\theta}}$ for the expectation step (Laird and Ware 1982; Lindstrom and Bates 1988).

As described in Laird and Ware (1982) and Lindstrom and Bates (1990) it starts by setting an initial value for $\boldsymbol{\theta}$ within the maximization-step. The error term depends on those variance components in $\hat{\boldsymbol{\theta}}$ which is straightforward $\boldsymbol{e}_j = \boldsymbol{y}_j - \boldsymbol{X}_j \boldsymbol{\beta}_j\left(\hat{\boldsymbol{\theta}}\right) - \boldsymbol{Z}_j \boldsymbol{b}_j\left(\hat{\boldsymbol{\theta}}\right)$. The expectation-step consists of estimation of the variance components namely for the error terms and the random effects, they basically are presented as in Laird and Ware (1982)

$$\mathsf{E}\left(\sum_{j=1}^{n} \boldsymbol{e}_j^T \boldsymbol{e}_j \mid \boldsymbol{y}_j, \hat{\boldsymbol{\theta}}\right) = \sum_{j=1}^{n} \boldsymbol{e}_j^T\left(\hat{\boldsymbol{\theta}}\right)\boldsymbol{e}_j\left(\hat{\boldsymbol{\theta}}\right) + \mathsf{tr\,var}\left(\boldsymbol{e}_j \mid \boldsymbol{y}_j, \hat{\boldsymbol{\theta}}\right) \tag{47}$$

and

$$\mathsf{E}\left(\sum_{j=1}^{n} \boldsymbol{b}_j \boldsymbol{b}_j^T \mid \boldsymbol{y}_j, \hat{\boldsymbol{\theta}}\right) = \sum_{j=1}^{n} \boldsymbol{b}_j\left(\hat{\boldsymbol{\theta}}\right)\boldsymbol{b}_j^T\left(\hat{\boldsymbol{\theta}}\right) + \mathsf{var}\left(\boldsymbol{b}_j \mid \boldsymbol{y}_j, \hat{\boldsymbol{\theta}}\right). \tag{48}$$

The maximization steps then use the log-nlikelihood function depending on whether estimating by maximum likelihood or restricted maximum likelihood as presented above or in Lindstrom and Bates (1990) for both estimation in general and with computational improvements in Laird et al. (1987) as implemented in current software to achieve faster convergence.

Appendix 3: Residual Plots for Employment Growth at City and Time Level (Figs. 4 and 5)

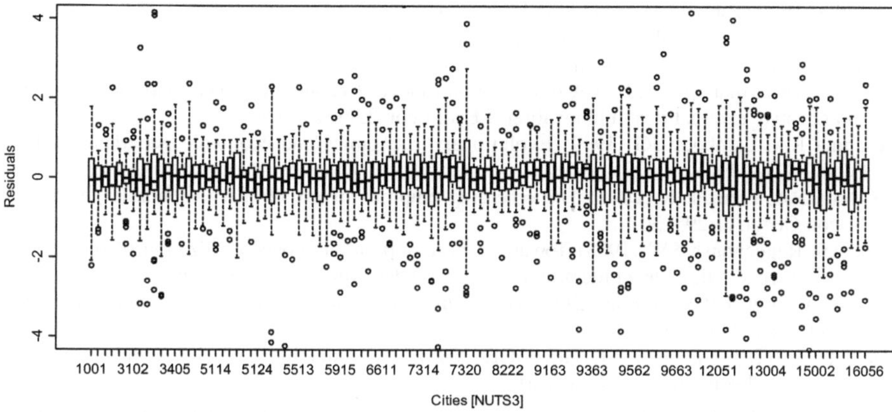

Fig. 4 Residual plot for employment growth at city level

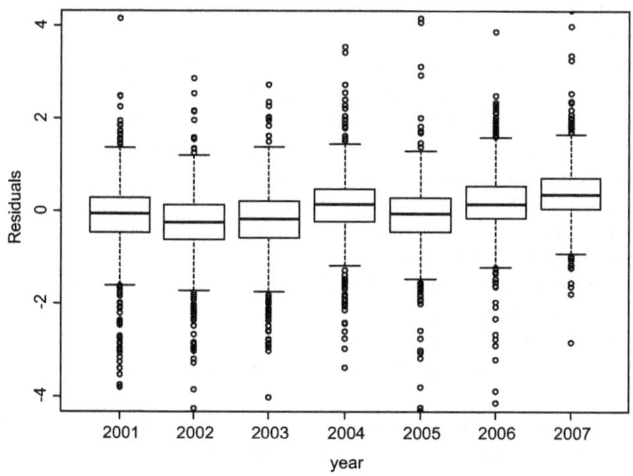

Fig. 5 Residual plot for employment growth at time level

References

Aghion P, Howitt PW (2009) The economics of growth. MIT, Cambridge

Badunenko O (2010) Downsizing in the German chemical manufacturing industry during the 1990s. Why is small beautiful? Small Bus Econ 34:413–n431

Batabyal AA, Nijkamp P (2012) Retraction of "a Schumpeterian model of entrepreneurship, innovation, and regional economic growth". Int Reg Sci Rev 35:464–n486

Batabyal AA, Nijkamp P (2013) A multi-region model of economic growth with human capital and negative externalities in innovation. J Evol Econ 23:909-n-924

Boschma RA, Lambooy JG (1999) Evolutionary economics and economic geography. J Evol Econ 9:411–429

Boschma RA, Frenken K (2011) The emerging empirics of evolutionary economic geography. J Econ Geogr 11:295–307

Bryk AS, Raudenbush SW (1988) Toward a more appropriate conceptualization of research on school effects: a three-level hierarchical linear model. Am J Edu 97:65–108

Charnes A, Cooper WW, Rhodes E (1978) Measuring the efficiency of decision making units. Eur J Oper Res 2:429–444

Coelli TJ, Rao DP, O'Donnell CJ, Battese GE (2005) An introduction to efficiency and productivity analysis, 2nd edn. Springer, New York

Cullmann A, von Hirschhausen C (2008) Efficiency analysis of east European electricity distribution in transition: legacy of the past? J Prod Anal 29:155–167

Dietrich A (2009) Does growth cause structural change, or is it the other way round? A dynamic panel data analyses for seven OECD countries. Jena Economic Research Papers 2009-034

Dopfer K, Foster J, Potts J (2004) Micro-meso-macro. J Evol Econ 14:263–279

Farrell MJ (1957) The measurement of productive efficiency. J R Stat Soc Ser A 120:253–281

Fratesi U (2010) Regional innovation and competitiveness in a dynamic representation. J Evol Econ 20:515–552

Färe R, Grosskopf S, Lindgren B, Roos P (1992) Productivity changes in Swedish pharmacies 1980–1989: a non-parametric malmquist approach. J Prod Anal 3:85–101

Färe R, Grosskopf S, Norris M (1997) Productivity growth, technical progress, and efficiency change in industrialized countries: reply. Am Econ Rev 87:1040–1043

Frenken K, Boschma RA (2007) A theoretical framework for evolutionary economic geography: industrial dynamics and Urban growth as a branching process. J Econ Geogr 7:635–649

Gaffard J-L (2008) Innovation, competition, and growth: schumpeterian ideas within a hicksian framework. J Evol Econ 18:295–311

Giovannetti G, Ricchiuti G, Velucchi M (2009) Location, internationalization and performance of firms in Italy: a multilevel approach. Universita' degli Studi di Firenze, Dipartimento di Scienze Economiche, Working Papers Series N. 09/2009

Glaeser EL, Kallal HD, Scheinkman JA, Shleifer A (1992) Growth in cities. J Polit Econ 100:1126–1152

Goedhuys M, Srholec M (2010) Understanding multilevel interactions in economic development. TIK Working Papers on Innovation Studies No. 20100208

Harville DA (1977) Maximum likelihood approaches to variance component estimation and to related problems. J Am Stat Assoc 72:320–338

Henderson JV (1997) Externalities and industrial development. J Urban Econ 42:449–470

Henderson JV, Kuncoro A, Turner M (1995) Industrial development in cities. J Polit Econ 103:1067–1090

Hox JJ (1998) Multilevel modeling: when and why. In: Balderjahn I, Mathar R, Schader M (eds) Classification, data analysis, and data highways. Springer, New York, pp 147–154

Hox JJ (2002) Multilevel analysis: techniques and applications. Erlbaum, Mahwahn, NJ

Ieno EN, Luque PL, Pierce GJ, Zuur AF, Santos MB, Walker NJ, Saveliev AA, Smith G (2009) Three-way nested data for age determination techniques applied to cetaceans. In: Zuur AF, Ieno

EN, Walker NJ, Saveliev AA, Smith GM (eds) Mixed effects models and extensions in ecology with R. New York, Springer, Chapter 20, pp 459–492

Illy A, Schwartz M, Hornych C, Rosenfeld MTW (2011) Local economic structure and sectoral employment growth in German cities. Tijdschrift voor Economische en Sociale Geografie 102:582–593

Laird N, Lange N, Stram D (1987) Maximum likelihood computations with repeated measures: application of the EM algorithm. J Am Stat Assoc 82:97–105

Laird NM, Ware JH (1982) Random-effects models for longitudinal data. Biometrics 38:963–974

Lindstrom MJ, Bates DM (1988) Newton–Raphson and EM algorithms for linear mixed-effects models for repeated-measures data. J Am Stat Assoc 83:1014–1022

Lindstrom MJ, Bates DM (1990) Nonlinear mixed effects models for repeated measures data. Biometrics 46:673–687

Maas CJM, Hox JJ (2005) Sufficient sample sizes for multilevel modeling. Methodology 1:86–92

MacKinnon JG, White H (1985) Some heteroskedasticity-consistent covariance matrix estimators with improved finite sample properties. J Econ 29:305–325

Malmquist S (1953) Index numbers and indifference surfaces. Trabajos de Estadística y de Investigación Operativa 4:209–242

Martin R, Sunley P (2006) Path dependence and regional economic evolution. J Econ Geogr 6:395–437

McFadden D (1973) Conditional logit analysis of qualitative choice behavior. In: Zaremka P (ed) Frontiers in econometrics. Academic Press, New York, pp 105–142

Moerbeek M, Breukelen GJP, Berger MPF (2000) Design issues for experiments in multilevel populations. J Educ Behav Stat 25:271–284

Moomaw RL (1981) Productivity and city size: a critique of evidence. Q J Econ 96:675–688

Noseleit F (2013) Entrepreneurship, structural change, and economic growth. J Evol Econ 23:735–766

Park WG (1995) International R&D spillovers and OECD economic growth. Econ Inq 33:571–591

Pinheiro JC, Bates D (2000) Mixed-effects models in S and S-plus. Springer, New York

Pinheiro JC, Bates D, DebRoy S, Sarkar D, R Development Core Team (2013) nlme: linear and nonlinear mixed effects models. R package version 3.1-111

Raudenbush SW, Bryke AS (2002) Hierarchical linear models, application and data analysis methods, Advanced Quantitative Techniques in the Social Science Series, 2nd edn. Sage, Thousand Oaks

Ray SC, Desli E (1997) Productivity growth, technical progress, and efficiency change in industrialized countries: comment. Am Econ Rev 87:1033–1039

Roy A, Bhaumik DK, Aryal S, Gibbons RD (2007) Sample size determination for hierarchical longitudinal designs with different attrition rates. Biometrics 63:699–707

Rozenblat C (2012) Opening the black box of agglomeration economies for measuring cities' competitiveness through international firm networks. Urban Stud 47:2841–2865

Saviotti PP, Pyka A (2004) Economic development by the creation of new sectors. J Evol Econ 14:1–35

Schumpeter JA (1934) The theory of economic development. Harvard University Press, Cambridge, MA

Schumpeter JA (1939) Business cycles. McGraw Hill, New York

Simar L, Wilson PW (1998) Sensitivity analysis of efficiency scores: how to bootstrap in nonparametric Frontier models. Manag Sci 44:49–61

Simar L, Wilson PW (1999) Estimating and bootstrapping malmquist indices. Eur J Oper Res 115:459–471

Simar L, Wilson PW (2002) Non-parametric test of returns to scale. Eur J Oper Res 139:115–132

Simar L, Wilson PW (2007) Estimations and inference in two-stage, semi-parametric models of production processes. J Econ 136:31–64

Srholec M (2010) A multilevel approach to geography of innovation. Reg Stud 44:1208–1220

Srholec M (2011) A multilevel analysis of innovation in developing countries. Ind Corp Chang 22:1539–1569

Stamer M (1999) Strukturwandel und wirtschaftliche Entwicklung in Deutschland, den USA und Japan. Shaker, Aachen
Statistisches Bundesamt (2003) German classification of economic activities, Edition 2003 (WZ 2003). Statistisches Bundesamt, Wiesbaden
Sveikauskas LA (1975) The productivity of cities. Q J Econ 89:392–413
Tabachnick BG, Fidell LS (2007) Using multivariate statistics, 5th edn. Pearson International Edition, Boston
Thanassoulis E, Portela MCS, Despic O (2008) Data envelopment analysis: the mathematical programming approach to efficiency analysis. In: Fried HO, Lovell CAK, Schmidt SS (eds) The measurement of productivity efficiency and productivity growth. Oxford, New York, Chapter 3, pp 251–420
Ware JH (1985) Linear models for the analysis of longitudinal studies. Am Stat 39:95–101
West BT, Welch KB, Galecki AT (2007) Linear mixed models: a practical guide using statistical software. Chapman & Hall/CRC Taylor & Francis Group, Boca Raton, FL
Wheelock DC, Wilson PW (1999) Technical progress, inefficiency, and productivity change in U.S. banking, 1984–1993. J Money Credit Bank 31:212–234
Wilson PW (2008) FEAR 1.0: a software package for Frontier efficiency analysis with R. Socio Econ Plan Sci 42:247–254
Zuur AF, Gende LB, Ieno EN, Fernández NJ, Eguaras MJ, Fritz R, Walker NJ, Saveliev AA, Smith GM (2009) Mixed effects modelling applied on American foulbrood affecting honey bees larvae. In: Mixed effects models and extensions in ecology with R, Chapter 19, pp 447–458
Zuur AF, Ieno EN, Walker NJ, Saveliev AA, Smith GM (2009) Mixed effects models and extensions in ecology with R. Springer, New York

A Dynamical Model of Technology Diffusion and Business Services for the Study of the European Countries Growth and Stability

Bernardo Maggi and Daniel Muro

Abstract With this study we intend to define a methodology capable to deal with the task of evaluating and planning the interdependent dynamics of growth for some European countries together with their foreign partners. To that aim we employ a nonlinear differential equations system representing a disequilibrium model based on a Schumpeterian evolutionary context with endogenous technology. We use such a model in order to disentangle the interrelationships occurring among countries for the critical variables considered. That is, we succeed in evaluating the contribution to growth of a country with respect to another one in terms of the variables involved. We address and corroborate the validity of our conjectures on the importance of the business services in the innovation and production processes by presenting also a minimal model. Further, we provide an evaluation of the convolution integral of our differential system to determine the necessary initial conditions of the critical variables for policy purposes. We then perform a sensitivity analysis to assess per each country the effectiveness of some possible efforts in order to gain stability.

1 Introduction

This paper shows how to consider in a structural, and possibly general, equilibrium context a complete dynamical analysis of an endogenous growth model with diffusion. Notably, these two issues have been dealt with in the literature under the compromise that only one of the two might be addressed satisfactorily. That is, either some aspects of the dynamics are usually missed when the structural analysis is detailed or the opposite occurs. In particular, Eaton and Kortum (1999) emphasize the difficulty to deal with both these aspects and concentrate on a

B. Maggi (✉)
Faculty of Engineering of Information, Informatics and Statistics, Department of Statistical Sciences, Sapienza University of Rome, Piazzale Aldo Moro, 5, 00185 Rome, Italy
e-mail: bernardo.maggi@uniroma1.it

D. Muro
Department of Mechanical and Industrial Engineering, University of Roma III, via della Vasca Navale 79, 00146 Rome, Italy
e-mail: dmuro@uniroma3.it

A. Pyka, J. Foster (eds.), *The Evolution of Economic and Innovation Systems*, Economic Complexity and Evolution, DOI 10.1007/978-3-319-13299-0_21

detailed description of the innovation diffusion process. Actually, they provide a complete description of such a process by making use of the patents applications data from the WIPO data base. Other literature focuses the attention on the dynamics while neglects the diffusion problems as in Jones (1995) and in the following strand of the New Economic Geography based on the seminal work of Krugman (1991a, b), Venables (1996), Englmann and Walz (1995), Walz (1996) in a two-region framework. In these works, while the transitional phases of the dynamics are fully addressed, the structure of diffusion is neglected and the relations among countries are limited to a generic analysis in which the intensity of the mutual dependence is usually represented by a defined proportion of a specific country variable on the total available for all the countries considered. Differently, in the former class of models all exchanges of inventions are fully specified. However, in order to allow for a tractable problem the analysis is confined exclusively to the steady state. This view is limiting especially from an empirical side because, though correct in principle, it drives to the possibility to estimate a dynamical problem, as it is a growth one, with only cross-sectional data as in Eaton and Kortum (1996, 1999). Neither the Dynamical Stochastic General Equilibrium approach, as in Holden (2010) or in The Anh P (2007), applied to growth and innovation succeeds in dealing with both aspects since the transition phase is discarded a priori and also the diffusion process is not implemented through appropriate functions referred to countries. Still, the estimation widely relies on the calibration of many parameters conferring a great degree of arbitrariness to the empirical analysis. Another—agnostic—approach, like that a là Keller (2002), is only grossly linked to a theory, letting the data speak on the basis of a single equation. Again—and it could not be differently—the diffusion aspect is just referred to broad definitional categories like proximity, languages etc and not to countries interaction.

We reckon that both the structure of the diffusion, consisting in the exchanges of innovations through countries interactions, and the dynamics are fundamental to assess on growth, given the intrinsically dynamical nature of the problem. We appropriately account for this aim and developed a methodology capable of answering the question of how the process of innovation of one country is affected by all other countries. But, even more, this propriety is reflected also on the other endogenous variables. This means that, in terms of growth assessment, we are capable to discern the contribution to growth for each specific variable deriving from each country. Such a result has been performed recurring to a continuous time analysis applied to several countries whose econometric counterpart is that of continuous-time panel-data. The advantage of such an approach, in solving the above described dilemma, resides in the strict connection between the theoretical and the econometric analysis in that the latter applies straightly to the theoretical—in our case—nonlinear model under consideration. This is due to the lucky circumstance that the dynamics of growth is "naturally" expressed in continuous time. Then, we first start from a set of disequilibrium equations which allows to define a nonlinear differential system. After having studied such a model we infer on the steady state which, possibly, may also not exist. The equilibrium condition therefore is an eventuality and furthermore, even if its existence may be proved, its attainability may be complex and then to be dealt with into deep. About that, following Schumpeter (1934) first and then—among others—Nelson and Winter (1982) on the evolution of the dynamic systems with endogenous technology, we are agnostic a priori on the viability of the steady state and focus on the forces that drives the economy in disequilibrium. Moreover the approximation around the steady state, and also the evolution of the system, depends on time and countries, that involves further qualifications to understand the feasibility of the equilibrium.

Another aspect which is always missed in the analysis of growth and development with diffusion is the consideration of the effect not only of the innovation activity on the production—and vice-versa—but also of its stock, which is crucial in describing the structure of the economy. In order to circumvent such an aspect, the above mentioned literature resorts to a production function based only on intermediates. Actually, the stock of technology is derived from the past and present contributions of the flow of innovations coming from all countries, which brings about a higher degree of nonlinearity in the presence of non linear behavioral functions. We correctly consider the stock of technology in the production process and account also for the connection between these two variables which is represented in our model by those business services with an intense level of knowledge (KIBS), both domestic and imported as argumented by Rubalcaba and Kox (2007). These are treated endogenously and allow us to infer on the offshoring process and its effectiveness. Moreover, the simultaneity of all the mentioned variables gains complete sense in the explanation of their interaction. In particular, knowledge intensive business services are fairly characterized by technology for the peculiarities they need in order for them to be applied and, in their turn, contribute to create new technology in the innovation sector as a consequence of their degree of specialization.

From the policy implication point of view, we are much concerned in the evaluation of how to determine in a certain future period of time a desired—and planned—outcome for a certain variable and how to control its path in order to obtain such a result. We do this by computing numerically the solution of our system and obtaining the initial conditions coherent with our targets. Further, we compute the derivative of the eigenvalues system with respect to the structural parameters of the model in order to check the changes in the stability conditions that may come from possible policy actions. Specifically, our attention is focused on the eigenvalues associated with technology, and we show a simple index capable to represent the *effort*, contributing to the dynamics, of new inventions.

Our main distinguishing features are then: (a) the definition of a methodology that accounts for the two critical aspects afore mentioned (dynamics and structure); (b) the implementation of a continuous time nonlinear estimation in an *exact* way, i.e. we estimate the solution of the differential system without approximating the continuous model to a discrete one; (c) the treatment—with a complete dynamical analysis—of the interactions among countries not only for the innovation process, but also for the other variables and, mostly, to find out the specific country contribution, in terms of each variable, to the growth path of any other country variable; (d) the sensitivity analysis of the eigenvalues (and eigenvectors) of the state-space system performed on the linearized model for all variables and for all countries; (e) the evaluation of the convolution integral of the system in order to exploit the initial conditions and to obtain a desired path for the variables of interest; (f) the capability to deal with the nonlinearity deriving from the introduction of the identity equation of technology.

Our work is organized as follows. In the second section we present the relations and the logic of the model. In the third section we comment on the econometric approach and on the estimated model. In the fourth section we present the results on the stability and sensitivity analysis. In the fifth section we perform the policy analysis. The sixth section concludes.

2 A Key Trinomial: Output, Technology and Business Services

2.1 Conceptual Framework

The logic of the model rests upon the basic concept that output grows endogenously thanks to technology but, in order to link effectively these two variables, related knowledge intensive business services (we simply refer to business services for brevity) are required. This is because technology goes hand in hand with business services for firms in order to be exploited. Still, this trinomial expresses a mutual interaction since, at the same time, services are determined by output, as usual, and technology so as to be more competitive and usable. Technology in its turn depends on output and business services for the amount requested and for its implementation. All other variables are exogenous.

We consider two models, a full and a minimal one. In the former one there are several additional exogenous variables and an endogenous one, the imported services. The comparison of these two models sheds lights to understand the importance of the offshoring activity in the convergence process. The full model was estimated first by Maggi et al. (2009)[1] but without addressing this issue and the reciprocal interactions among country variables. We start describing the full model in that it comprises the minimal one.

As usual in continuous time architecture, the variables of interest adjust themselves to their relative partial equilibrium functions which depend on the associated determinants. This means that each variable is characterized by some driving forces which may not necessarily satisfy its actual value. The driving forces of output (Y) are the basic stocks of the production function: capital (K), labor (L) and technology

[1]The model is also referred to as the SETI where the acronym stands for Sustainable Economy development based on Technology and Innovation. A first version was estimated in the recent past by Maggi B. and was the central part of a European Commission research project and later, with new advancements, the focus of the present project.

(*T*); in addition there are some peculiar variables: skilled labor (*HK*), domestic (*Sh*) and imported services (*Sm*). The driving forces of business services (both imported and exported) are: technology, output, the intensity of the use of services in the manufacturing sector deduced from I/O tables (*STR*), which represents the structure of the economy and the level of regulation (*REG*). For technology the description of the dynamics is complicated by the fact that we have combined the flow of new inventions with the deriving stock. The inventions are measured by the count of the patent citations (*Pat*) from the producer country to the receiving one. This means that new inventions of a country may be produced autonomously or acquired from abroad, determining, as a whole, the total change in technology. The innovation process is therefore a bilateral one and, by definition, accounts for the interactions among countries in such a respect, i.e. there will be an equation for any country from which inventions may be acquired. It depends on the human capital (skilled) of the receiving country (*HKR*) and of the sender country (*HKS*) that uses and produces inventions respectively, other than output and business services (*Sh* and *Sm*) as explained above. Another basic bilateral variable that defines the flow of innovation is the distance (*dist*) between two countries whose importance is expected to decrease over time (*t*). We measure it with a second order effect (*t*dist*). Actually also *HKS* is a bilateral variable because the sender country may change with respect to the receiving one. Such variables characterize the model for two reasons: first they make possible the interactions among countries, secondly, though constant over time, allow for a panel estimation. These two variables are strategic for the country characterization of the diffusion process in that, by definition, it occurs in a bilateral way. The stock of technology of one country is defined as the integral over time of the summation through countries of the innovations flows. Therefore, by construction, also for one country technology may be considered for the part imputed to another country and, as a consequence, the same applies to the other endogenous variables. In such a way we are capable to discern per each country endogenous variable the contribution to its formation and dynamics deriving from the other countries. We expect that all the explanatory variables considered exert a positive effect on the dependent variable but the regulation in the business services equations and distance in the patents equations.

An attempt to obtain this characterization is to be found in Coe and Helpmann (1995), Coe et al. (2008) and Lichtenberg et al. (1998) in which the countries interrelationships of technology are proxied by the bilateral imports drawn from the Trade-database IMF-Direction. Given the different focus, underlying the imports data, with respect to the core variable of such studies (traditionally R&D or patents) we reckon such a device a rough solution to the evaluation of technology diffusion, which might be biased by patterns reflecting different problems. Neither the agnostic approach of Keller (2002) seems to help in that the omission of any structural scheme—implied by the single equation adopted—does not allow for a satisfactory analysis in terms of hypotheses testing and policy implication.[2]

[2]Indeed, very few special cases for a single equation estimation are admissible (Hamilton 1994).

2.2 The Model

From the previous section we are left with the description of a nonlinear differential system in the mentioned variables referred to each country *j*, and accounting for the effects coming from each country *i*, of the following general form (Wymer 1997):

$$DY_{ji}(t) = f_{ji}\left[Y_{ji}(t), \Theta_{ji}\right] + D\zeta_{ji}(t), \qquad j, i = 1 \ldots n + v \tag{1}$$

where D is the first derivative operator and n and v represent the European and foreign countries respectively. Nine European countries are considered in the analysis: Austria, Germany, Denmark, Finland, France, the United Kingdom, Italy, Netherland, Sweden. Foreign countries are the United States and Japan. We consider 11 years during the pre-Union period 1988–1998 (annual data) to investigate on the solidity at the basis of the EU integration process. In fact the persistence of an uncertain European growth path might have been rooted before the joining of the Union, with particular reference to a not complete and appropriate exploitation of the new technology acquisitions of that period. We reckon that much responsibility for such a gap is due to the lack of an appropriate business services policy and, particularly, from the point of view of a greater openness towards an off-shoring process. Then, system (1) comprises 165 equations for any endogenous variable[3] and countries. As afore mentioned, the form of the differential system is that of the partial adjustment, and the nonlinearity of our model is due to the coexistence of a definitional equation of technology, expressed in original form, and the log-transformation of the variables in the other equations. The partial equilibrium functions are indicated with the exponent *pe*. They are short term behavioural equations on which the disequilibrium and then the evolution of the system depend. For simplicity of notation we omit in the following system (2) the error terms which will be commented later on:

$$\begin{cases} D\ln Y_{ji} = \alpha_j\left(\ln Y_{ji}^{pe} - \ln Y_{ji}\right) \\ \ln Y_{ji}^{pe} = \alpha_j^0 + \alpha_{ji}^1 \ln T_{ji} + \alpha_{ji}^{2sh} \ln sh_{ji} + \alpha_{ji}^{2sm} \ln sm_{ji} + \alpha_{ji}^3 \ln K_j + \alpha_{ji}^4 \ln L_j \\ D\ln Sh_{ji} = \gamma_j^{sh}\left(\ln Sh_{ji}^{pe} - \ln Sh_{ji}\right) \\ \ln Sh_{ji}^{pe} = \gamma_j^{0sh} + \gamma_j^{1sh} \ln Y_{ji} + \gamma_{ji}^{2sh} \ln T_{ji} + \gamma_{ji}^{3sh} \ln STR_j + \gamma_{ji}^{4sh} \ln ICT_j + \gamma_{ji}^{5sh} \ln REG_j \\ D\ln Sm_{ji} = \gamma_j^{sm}\left(\ln Sm_{ji}^{pe} - \ln Sm_{ji}\right) \\ \ln Sm_{ji}^{pe} = \gamma_j^{0sm} + \gamma_j^{1sm} \ln Y_{ji} + \gamma_{ji}^{2sm} \ln T_{ji} + \gamma_{ji}^{3sm} \ln STR_j + \gamma_{ji}^{4sh} \ln ICT_j + \gamma_{ji}^{5sh} \ln REG_j \\ D\ln Pat_{ji} = \beta_{ji}\left(\ln Pat_{ji}^{pe} - \ln Pat_{ji}\right) \\ \ln Pat_{ji}^{pe} = \beta_{ji}^0 + \beta_{ji}^1 (a + bt)\, dist_{ji} + \beta_{ji}^2 \ln HKS_{ji} + \beta_{ji}^{3sh} \ln sh_{ji} + \beta_{ji}^{3sm} \ln sm_{ji} \\ \qquad + \beta_{ji}^4 \ln Y_{ji} + \beta_{ji}^5 \ln HKR_j \\ DT_{ji} = Pat_{ji} \end{cases} \tag{2}$$

[3]In total we have 15 kinds of endogenous variables, comprising the definition of technology and 11 relationships for the patenting processes.

The system (2) is originally of the second order reduced to the first one by means of the identity equation, which defines—and reduces—Pat_{ij} as a first order variable. Here we represent the framework of the productive structure of the economy as one centered on innovations and related services. In fact, the leading—endogenous—elements in the production of output are services and technology which are therefore modeled accordingly. Coherently, only the bilateral exogenous variables and, consequently, all the endogenous ones are characterized by two deponents indicating the country interactions. As extensively commented in Marrewijk et al. (1997), business services may be viewed in the production process as an expression of the employment of the, say, *advanced* capital such as the ICT one. The minimal model is different from (2) for the lack of the imported business services equation and the absence of STR_j, ICT_j and REG_j as explanatory variables of services. This is crucial to test the importance of the imported business services for the convergence of the system.

3 Econometric Approach

As far as the estimation of system (2) is concerned, there are no enough data available for a characterization by the i, j deponents so that the 165 equations have to collapse to 15 during this phase. However, the implementation and the use of the model may well be extended to its full potentials thanks to the exogenous bilateral variables, researches and distances, which, therefore, revel themselves as strategic. Moreover, the dynamic properties concerning the convergence are different by countries because of the nonlinearity induced by the identity constraint of technology. In fact, the nonlinearity implies a different evaluation of the state-space matrix corresponding to system (2), according to the differences in time and space. The estimation of system (2) has been performed by means of ESCONA program by Wymer (2005), for panel data in continuous time. The estimation has been carried out having as a reference the exact solution of system (2), that is we did not use any approximation to calculate the model parameters in order to fit the model with the data and followed the *exact discrete analogue* procedure for non linear models. The procedure consists of the following steps: (I) solve system (2); (II) find the *exact* corresponding first difference system; (III) set the errors structure; (IV) implement the optimization procedure to find the parameters. (I) and (II) are solved respectively by means of the methodology based on the exponential matrices and the appropriate choices of the initial conditions.[4] As to point III) given that

[4]For these details see Gandolfo (1981).

the system comprises both stock and flow variables, our solution involves a double integration through the interval δ, from which the errors will be:

$$\xi(t) = \int_{t-\delta}^{t} \int_{0}^{\delta} e^{J[f(Y_j(\theta);\Theta_j)]} d\left(\zeta\left(t-\theta\right)\right) ds \tag{3}$$

where the exponential matrix of functions in the integral is calculated from the Jacobian of the system (1) evaluated at time t and space j, and the variance-covariance matrix is

$$\Xi_t = E\left[\xi(t)\xi'(t)\right] \quad \text{with} \quad \begin{cases} E\left[\zeta(t)\right] = \mathbf{0} \\ E\left[\zeta\left(t_1\right) - \zeta\left(t_2\right)\right]\left[\zeta\left(t_3\right) - \zeta\left(t_4\right)\right]' = \mathbf{0}, \\ \quad \forall t_1 > t_2 \geq t_3 > t_4 \\ E\left[\zeta\left(t+h\right) - \zeta(t)\right]\left[\zeta\left(t+h\right) - \zeta(t)\right]' = \Omega(h) \end{cases} \tag{4}$$

where $\Omega(h)$ is a matrix of constants.

The important property of residuals is that, because of the integrations adopted, it may also be generated by nongaussian disturbances $Dz(t)$, say Brownian motion or Poisson, even if $z(t)$ and $c\ (t)$ are of that sort. This is relevant in the studies on growth models since, as it is well known, innovations are subject to random discrete jumps.

In order to construct the likelihood function for the case of $m = 11$ countries and $p = 15$ equations, a (m^*p) matrix of m blocks, of order p is considered. Each ith block on the main diagonal represents the error covariance matrix of the p equations of country i and the off-diagonal (i, l) matrix (also of order p) is the covariance between country i and country l. The assumption made is to allow the covariances between the error terms on the equations to be non-zero and equal in each country as well as for the elements in each (i, l) of the off-diagonal matrices for pairs of countries.

The log-likelihood function of system (2), we maximize with full information, is:

$$\ln L\left(\Theta, \eta\right) = -\frac{\left(n+v\right)N}{2} \ln\left(2\pi\right) - \frac{1}{2}\sum_{t=1}^{N} \ln \det \Xi_t - \frac{1}{2}\sum_{t=1}^{N}\left(\xi_t' \Xi_t^{-1} \xi_t\right) \tag{5}$$

where h is the parameters vector of the constrained variance-covariance matrix and N is the number of observations over time.

Data on GDP, services, human capital and capital are from the OECD database.[5] Data on the bilateral exchanges of technology are from the U.S. patent office.[6] The managing of this data has involved quite some work (almost 16 millions of records!) and a special SAS code,[7] capable to retrieve and match all the correspondences one may be interested to find in the patents data, has been developed as a part of the present research. Data on regulation are from Nicoletti et al. (2000) and are referred to product market regulation.[8] Data on the structure indicator are those developed in Guerrieri and Meliciani (2005) and are based on OECD Input/Output tables.[9] Nominal data have been deflated at 1995 prices and homogenized in dollars by means of the PPP OECD index.

Table 1 reports the estimation of system (2) on the basis of the mentioned method.

As my be easily checked, all coefficients are significant and of correct sign.[10] We underline that the sum of the coefficients that accumulate in the production process is greater than 1 enabling, therefore, an endogenous growth process. Further, the business services equations are almost equal as expected but the coefficient for technology and the speed of adjustment, which are much greater in the case of imported business services. This is a clear indication that foreign business services

---

[5]More specifically, all the databases used are updated at year 2000 coherently with the estimation period, GDP is collected from the OECD Main Economic Indicators, human capital from the OECD Main Science and Technology Indicators, domestic services from the OECD STAN database and data on imported services from the OECD International Trade in Services database. Physical capital and labor are taken from the Penn World Tables. Data on ICT expenditures refer to gross fixed capital formation in Information and Communication Technologies and are taken from EUROSTAT. Distance is measured in kilometers between capitals. Given the relevance of the—knowledge intensive—business services variables we specify that they are in line with the NACE 74 classification and refer to: legal, accounting, tax consultancy, market research, auditing, opinion polling, management consultancy, architectural, engineering and technical consultancy, technical testing and analyses, advertising, other business activities [see Evangelista et al. (2013) and Muller and Doloreux (2009) for an accurate examination of problems connected to the construction of such a variable].

[6]Citations may be backward or forward if referred respectively to inventions discovered in the past or, from the point of view of the cited country, in the future. This, in case of a limited time series, may cause to neglect potential citations in the initial and final part of the period in the eventuality of discrepancy between the series and, respectively, the citing or cited patent or in case of lags in recording citations. To cope with this problem we follow the method indicated by Hall et al. (2001) where it is suggested to divide each citation by the average number of citations received by the patents of the same cohort (fixed approach).

[7]The SAS routine has been developed and implemented by Cirelli M. and Maggi B.

[8]Such an indicator is the result of a factorial analysis though several product market indicators over the years in the sample.

[9]In particular, in order to measure the intensity of the business services in the production of the manufacturing sector, we consider the use of business services on total value added for each manufacturing sector and for each country.

[10]*Beu* and *Ceu* are the constants representing the common effects in Europe for domestic and foreign business services respectively.

Table 1 Estimation results (full version)

	Explanatory variables	Parameter point estimate	Asymptotic s.e.	t
α_1	*T*	0.8020	0.0920	8.72
α_{2sh}	*Sh*	0.1056	0.0063	16.72
α_{2sm}	*Sm*	0.0790	0.0035	22.29
α_3	*K*	0.7181	0.0264	27.18
α_4	*L*	0.6871	0.0736	9.33
α	*adj. speed-Y*	0.0029	0.0011	2.57
γ_{1sh}	*Y*	0.4919	0.0138	35.59
γ_{2sh}	*T*	0.3442	0.0134	25.73
γ_{3sh}	*Beu*	5.385	0.1636	32.91
γ_{4sh}	*Regulation*	−0.3071	0.0094	32.54
γ_{5sh}	*Structure*	0.5459	0.9217	25.20
γ_{6sh}	*ICT*	0.2017	0.0126	16.01
γ_{sh}	*adj. speed-Sh*	0.0020	0.0010	2.0
γ_{1sm}	*Y*	0.4670	0.0176	26.59
γ_{2sm}	*T*	0.5517	0.0294	18.78
γ_{3sm}	*Ceu*	2.021	0.0949	21.30
γ_{4sm}	*Regulation*	−0.3153	0.0126	24.94
γ_{5sm}	*Structure*	0.4992	0.0193	25.82
γ_{6sm}	*ICT*	0.2168	0.0101	21.49
γ_{sm}	*adj. speed-Sm*	0.0031	0.0009	3.28
β_1	*(bilateral) Diffusion*	0.0136	0.0057	16.16
α	*Distance*	−0.0213	0.0181	25.52
β	*Time*	0.9570	0.0064	57.93
β_2	*HKS*	0.5351	0.0239	22.36
β_{3sh}	*Sh*	0.0921	0.0156	32.54
β_{3sm}	*Sm*	0.4612	0.0012	10.93
β_4	*Y*	0.3713	0.0016	13.56
β_5	*HKR*	0.5073	0.0268	35.73
β	*adj. speed-Pat*$_{ij}$	0.0105	0.0009	11.16

may compete with respect to domestic ones thanks to the innovation process that compensates the higher costs (not explicit in the model) associated to the import activity. In fact, due to such costs, one would have expected a smaller elasticity to technology and a slower adjustment for foreign business services in case of similar levels of performance while here this is even higher than that of domestic ones to signify that the major costs of the former are more than compensated by gains in competitiveness of the latter. An additional explanation of the growing foreign business services, with the relative offshoring process, is in the presence of the same ICT, among the explanatory variables, of the domestic business services: considering that in the estimation phase the difference between the two equations is in the dependent variable, we may reasonably asses that there is a contribution for the higher speed of adjustment of the latter due to the development of ICT of the receiving country. We interpret such a result as the confirmation of what highlighted in the study on the OECD offshoring patterns (van Welsum and Vickery 2005) where a descriptive analysis suggests and encourages to test the effect connected to ICT of the offshoring services adjustment process.[11] Moreover, given that the largest speed of adjustment is that of technology, and in such an equation the coefficient for imported business services is almost the five-hold of the domestic ones, we reckon that such facts point out a relevant contribution to the adjustment and convergence process to be attributed to an offshoring process: on the one hand foreign business services need technology to be implemented and usable abroad, on the other hand technology is much more affected by foreign business services for their—in general—higher quality. On this point two considerations have to be done. First, there is a pervasive sluggishness in the system because of the very small speeds of adjustment, in fact they represent [see for the demonstration (Gandolfo 1981)] the time required to fill the 63 % of the gap between the actual and the partial equilibrium value of the variable under consideration. Second, the speeds of adjustment, if positive, are only a necessary condition for the convergence and the stability, which are not obtained as a consequence. We will perform an eigenvalue analysis to better investigate to this purpose. However, the virtuous cycle now mentioned is certainly worthy to deserve major attention. To be confirmed of that we need more statistical analysis. In particular, if our conjecture is correct, the omission of foreign business services would probably lower the speeds of adjustment. But, to consider also the possibility that the low speeds of convergence might depend on the large number of explicative variables, as this is very often the case in continuous time (see Gandolfo 1993),[12] we eliminate some exogenous variables such as *ICT*, *REG* and *STR*. Table 2 shows that, in this second minimal case, the speeds of adjustments are much lower than before becoming practically null in some cases as for the technology equation. Here we adopted a calibration procedure for the speed of adjustment, β, which has been interrupted at the first significant result of the parameters' t-statistics, thus confirming even more our conclusion. Neither it has been helpful to drop the mentioned variables in order to increase the speed for the domestic business services which remains almost the same.

We therefore conclude, from the econometric approach, that the key trinomial is actually operating and, inside this, the offshoring activity of business services induces a peculiar virtuous process with the flow of technology.[13] We also observe that distance doesn't play a constant role with a negative decreasing effect over time.

[11]Arguably, in light of the globalization process, the natural step beyond in such a field of research is to endogenize ICT with respect business services themselves and human capital so as to control, in the adjustment process, for both the effects of feed-back and on the quality and the level of employment.

[12]The intuition is that the speeds of adjustment are on the main diagonal of the dynamic matrix, **A**, bringing about, because of that, an individual contribution to the rates of growth of the complete general solution as much small as greater is the number of the other coefficients to be estimated.

[13]In Maggi and Muro (2012) the offshoring activity is evaluated also with reference to the results obtained for the steady state.

Table 2 Estimation results (minimal version)

	Variable	Parameter point estimate	Asymptotic s.e.	t
α_1	T	0.759103	0.004811	157.78
α_2	S	0.687032	0.004155	165.35
α_3	K	0.701997	9.89E-05	7100.69
α_4	L	0.528219	0.003564	148.21
α	*(speed of adj.)*	0.000258	0.000125	2.07
γ_1	Y	0.317547	0.003625	87.6
γ_2	T	0.708908	0.005441	130.29
γ	*(speed of adj.)*	0.001889	0.000162	11.66
β_1	*diffusion*	0.015208	0.000102	149.21
β_2	S	0.100112	0.000608	164.61
β_3	Y	0.378942	0.001854	204.4
β_4	HK	0.777034	0.004769	162.95
a	*distance*	−0.02002	0.00028	71.64
b	*time*	0.994761	0.006454	154.13
β	*(speed of adj.)*	0.00005	Calibrated	

4 Stability and Sensitivity Analysis

4.1 Countries' Dynamics

We now perform a stability and sensitivity analysis, based on the full model of Table 1, to understand the relevance of the nonlinearity and the indications for economic policy purposes deriving also from the nonlinearity itself. The first thing to do is to obtain the state-space matrix, that will be, after suitable linearization, of such a form

$$D\mathbf{x} = \mathbf{A}\mathbf{x}. \tag{6}$$

We account for the nonlinearity by considering a block diagonal matrix form with one block per each country. The nonlinearity in fact implies that for any country and any time we may observe at least—as it is the case here—different blocks in which the differences are relative to the nonlinear part of the original system:

$$\begin{aligned} \mathbf{x} &= \{\mathbf{x}_j\} \\ \mathbf{A} &= \begin{bmatrix} \ddots & & \\ & \mathbf{A}_j & \\ & & \ddots \end{bmatrix} \quad j = 1, n + v. \end{aligned} \tag{7}$$

The endogenous variables and the typical block of **A** are:

$$\mathbf{x}_j = \left\{ \ln Y_j \;\; \ln Sh_j \;\; \ln Sm_j \;\; \ln Pat_j^{AU} \;\; \ln Pat_j^{GE} \;\; \ln Pat_j^{DE} \;\; \ln Pat_j^{FI} \;\; \ln Pat_j^{FR} \;\; \ln Pat_j^{UK} \;\; \ln Pat_j^{IT} \;\; \ln Pat_j^{JA} \;\; \ln Pat_j^{NE} \;\; \ln Pat_j^{SW} \;\; \ln Pat_j^{US} \;\; \ln T_j \right\}^T$$

$$\mathbf{A}_j = \begin{bmatrix}
-\alpha & \alpha\alpha_2^{sh} & \alpha\alpha_2^{sm} & 0 & 0 & 0 & 0 & 0 & 0 & 0 & 0 & 0 & 0 & 0 & \alpha\alpha_1 \\
\gamma_1^{sh}\gamma_{sh} & -\gamma_{sh} & 0 & 0 & 0 & 0 & 0 & 0 & 0 & 0 & 0 & 0 & 0 & 0 & \gamma_2^{sh}\gamma_{sh} \\
\gamma_1^{sm}\gamma_{sm} & 0 & -\gamma_{sm} & 0 & 0 & 0 & 0 & 0 & 0 & 0 & 0 & 0 & 0 & 0 & \gamma_1^{sm}\gamma_{sm} \\
\beta^{AU}\beta_4^{AU} & \beta^{AU}\beta_3^{sh} & \beta^{AU}\beta_3^{sm} & -\beta^{AU} & 0 & 0 & 0 & 0 & 0 & 0 & 0 & 0 & 0 & 0 & 0 \\
\beta^{GE}\beta_4^{GE} & \beta^{GE}\beta_3^{sh} & \beta^{GE}\beta_3^{sm} & 0 & -\beta^{GE} & 0 & 0 & 0 & 0 & 0 & 0 & 0 & 0 & 0 & 0 \\
\beta^{DE}\beta_4^{DE} & \beta^{DE}\beta_3^{sh} & \beta^{DE}\beta_3^{sm} & 0 & 0 & -\beta^{DE} & 0 & 0 & 0 & 0 & 0 & 0 & 0 & 0 & 0 \\
\beta^{FI}\beta_4^{FI} & \beta^{FI}\beta_3^{sh} & \beta^{FI}\beta_3^{sm} & 0 & 0 & 0 & -\beta^{FI} & 0 & 0 & 0 & 0 & 0 & 0 & 0 & 0 \\
\beta^{FR}\beta_4^{FR} & \beta^{FR}\beta_3^{sh} & \beta^{FR}\beta_3^{sm} & 0 & 0 & 0 & 0 & -\beta^{FR} & 0 & 0 & 0 & 0 & 0 & 0 & 0 \\
\beta^{UK}\beta_4^{UK} & \beta^{UK}\beta_3^{sh} & \beta^{UK}\beta_3^{sm} & 0 & 0 & 0 & 0 & 0 & -\beta^{UK} & 0 & 0 & 0 & 0 & 0 & 0 \\
\beta^{IT}\beta_4^{IT} & \beta^{IT}\beta_3^{sh} & \beta^{IT}\beta_3^{sm} & 0 & 0 & 0 & 0 & 0 & 0 & -\beta^{IT} & 0 & 0 & 0 & 0 & 0 \\
\beta^{JA}\beta_4^{JA} & \beta^{JA}\beta_3^{sh} & \beta^{JA}\beta_3^{sm} & 0 & 0 & 0 & 0 & 0 & 0 & 0 & -\beta^{JA} & 0 & 0 & 0 & 0 \\
\beta^{NE}\beta_4^{NE} & \beta^{NE}\beta_3^{sh} & \beta^{NE}\beta_3^{sm} & 0 & 0 & 0 & 0 & 0 & 0 & 0 & 0 & -\beta^{NE} & 0 & 0 & 0 \\
\beta^{SW}\beta_4^{SW} & \beta^{SW}\beta_3^{sh} & \beta^{SW}\beta_3^{sm} & 0 & 0 & 0 & 0 & 0 & 0 & 0 & 0 & 0 & -\beta^{SW} & 0 & 0 \\
\beta^{US}\beta_4^{US} & \beta^{US}\beta_3^{sh} & \beta^{US}\beta_3^{sm} & 0 & 0 & 0 & 0 & 0 & 0 & 0 & 0 & 0 & 0 & -\beta^{US} & 0 \\
0 & 0 & 0 & IC_j^{AU} & IC_j^{GE} & IC_j^{DE} & IC_j^{FI} & IC_j^{FR} & IC_j^{UK} & IC_j^{IT} & IC_j^{JA} & IC_j^{NE} & IC_j^{SW} & IC_j^{US} & -\sum_{i=1}^{n+v} IC_j^i
\end{bmatrix} \quad (8)$$

Where the last row, representing the identity constraint, is affected by the point of approximation, and for this reason the acronym (IC) used in that entries stands for "initial condition". All β's coefficients with an exponent indicating a country are from patents equations—even if they have been constrained to be equal.

Matrix $\mathbf{A}_j$ is quasi lower triangular so that we expect the coefficients on the main diagonal to be determinant for the dynamics of convergence and, from now, we may assess on their positive contribution given their positive value as from Table 1. As far as the values in the last row are concerned, they have been calculated by transforming the variables in the identity equation in logarithms and linearizing.

In fact,

$$dT_j = \sum_{i=1}^{n+v} Pat_{ij}$$

from which, dividing the equation for T_j and exploiting the properties of the log derivative

$$\frac{dT_j}{T_j} = \sum_{i=1}^{n+v} \frac{Pat_{ij}}{T_j}$$

or

$$\frac{d \ln T_j}{dt} = \sum_{i=1}^{n+v} e^{\ln \frac{Pat_{ij}}{T_j}},$$

which may be linearized using the Taylor series about the initial condition denoted by 0

$$\frac{d \ln T_j}{dt} = \sum_{i=1}^{n+v} \left[e^{\ln \frac{Pat_{ij}}{T_j}}\Big|_0 + e^{\ln \frac{Pat_{ij}}{T_j}}\Big|_0 \left(\ln Pat_{ij} - \ln Pat_{ij}\big|_0\right) - e^{\ln \frac{Pat_{ij}}{T_j}}\Big|_0 \left(\ln T_j - \ln T_j\big|_0\right) \right]$$

and, considering only the perturbative terms, we get

$$\frac{d \ln T_j}{dt} = \sum_{i=1}^{n+v} e^{\ln \frac{Pat_{ij}}{T_j}}\Big|_0 \left(\ln Pat_{ij} - \ln T_j\right). \tag{9}$$

Therefore the entries in the last row will be simply the ratio between the flow of inventions from the *i*th country to the *j*th one upon the stock of technology of the *j*th country, except the last entry which is referred to the total flows of inventions:

$$IC_j^i = e^{\ln \frac{Pat_{ij}}{T_j}}\Big|_0, \quad \sum_{i=1}^{n+v} IC_j^i. \tag{10}$$

4.2 *Dynamical Properties of the Model*

As regards the dynamical properties of the system (6), the second element in formula (10), being the last one on the main diagonal, will be at the same time the eigenvalue that will characterize the dynamics of the several countries considered given the innovations adopted. For this reason we name it as an indicator of the *innovative effort*, that is the more a country invest in new inventions the faster approaches the steady state, provided it exists. In this connection, there are two possibilities of evaluating the steady state for this model. A first one is to consider the estimation as referred to an average European country and, for that reason, all exogenous bilateral variables have to collapse to an averaged unilateral one; which means that the concept of distance is simply referred to "abroad" in general sense and the same for the researchers. This is equivalent to say that, from a technological point of view, foreign countries are in a unique pool to which we tap irrespectively of their reciprocal interactions. Such an approach, from one side, simplifies much the analysis for the reduction of the number of the variables considered, whilst from the treatment of the nonlinearity the difficulty increases.[14] We adopted a second approach where the countries specificities are accounted for in the model, and in particular consider as many stocks of technology as the associated patents flows are, over time and from

[14]In fact, in this case the identity constraint would impose that technology depends on the summation—through all countries—of the patents in natural numbers which on its turn—from the patents behavioral equations—depends on the log of technology. Such a difficulty has been overcome in Maggi et al. (2009) where a closed form solution has been found.

any country. In such a case the difficulty of finding a closed form solution for the steady state is referred to the much larger number of variables involved and to the fact that their convergence does not imply necessarily a country convergence, being this one the result of the summation of the country variables contributions.[15]

Maggi and Muro (2012) addresses such an issue and, after having found a closed form solution also for this second case, elaborated a MATLAB program to study the proprieties of the steady state. The results say that the dominant rates of growth are—being dominant—pretty large coherently with the double convergence process under which the variables have to go: one ordinary and a second one due to aggregations.

This said, we can assert that the steady state does exist and the study of the convergence depends on the eigenvalues of the linearized state-space matrix and on their sensitivity to the structural model parameters. We preformed such an analysis using CONTINES program by Wymer (2005). Here below in Table 3 we report the eigenvalues for all countries. From the 1st to 14th they are almost equal through countries, admitting some small roundings, while the 15th is country specific.[16] It easy to check that it identifies with the last element in the main diagonal and therefore with the initial condition of the rate of change for technology. Moreover, from the eigenvectors analysis the relevant element, in the general complete solution of the technology dynamics, is the one referred to this eigenvalue. Unfortunately there is not the same clear cut for the first three eigenvalues being equally relevant, in the general complete dynamic solution, for output and services both imported and exported. It is also observable the correspondence between the speeds of adjustments of the patents equations and the eigenvalues even if only for 10 of them, whilst the 11th couples with the one of the stock of technology. Several observations are to be drawn. First, we obtain all stable eigenvalues even if the first one is very close to zero.[17] Therefore the model is stable and the initial conditions we used for the approximation (steady state) may be considered also as equilibrium conditions. Second, we are not assessing on the significance of the eigenvalues because of the nonlinearity of the model. In fact, given the relationship between the state-space matrix and the eigenvalues it is always possible [see Wymer (2005) manuals and Gandolfo (1981)] to construct a t-test for the eigenvalues but in our case a new

[15]This means that if we consider a variable Z for an hypothetical country composed of K parts ($k = 1, \ldots, K$) with the following dynamics per each: $Z_{k,t} = Z_1 e^{z_1 t} \ldots Z_K e^{z_K t}$, the Z rate of growth (r.o.g.) will be $\frac{\dot{Z}}{Z} = \frac{\sum_{k=1}^{K} z_k Z_k e^{z_k t}}{\sum_{k=1}^{K} Z_k e^{z_k t}} = \sum_{k=1}^{K} z_k p_k$, where p_k is the share of the kth component.
If $z_{\overline{k}}$ is the dominant r.o.g. only in the limit there will be a country variable convergence. In fact, the result will be $z_{\overline{k}} \to 1, z_{k \neq \overline{k}} \to 0$ and so $\frac{\dot{Z}}{Z} \to z_{\overline{k}}$.

[16]Detailed tables for each countries available upon request.

[17]In Maggi et al. (2009), under a different context as explained before, such eigenvalue resulted close to zero and positive.

Table 3 Stability analysis

Eigenvalues	Real part	Modulus	Damping period
λ_1	−0.00014	0.00014	6945.978
λ_2	−0.00215	0.00215	465.978
λ_3	−0.00391	0.00391	255.606
λ_4	−0.0105	0.0105	95.238
λ_5	−0.0105	0.0105	95.238
λ_6	−0.0105	0.0105	95.238
λ_7	−0.0105	0.0105	95.238
λ_8	−0.0105	0.0105	95.238
λ_9	−0.0105	0.0105	95.238
λ_{10}	−0.0105	0.0105	95.238
λ_{11}	−0.0105	0.0105	95.238
λ_{12}	−0.0105	0.0105	95.238
λ_{13}	−0.0105	0.0105	95.238
λ_{14}	−0.01220	0.01225	81.664
Austria: $-\sum_{i=1}^{n+v} IC_{AU}^{i} = \lambda_{15}^{AU}$	−0.15888	0.15888	6.294
Germany: $-\sum_{i=1}^{n+v} IC_{GE}^{i} = \lambda_{15}^{GE}$	−0.49056	0.49056	2.038
Denmark: $-\sum_{i=1}^{n+v} IC_{DE}^{i} = \lambda_{15}^{DE}$	−0.16848	0.16848	5.935
Finland: $-\sum_{i=1}^{n+v} IC_{FI}^{i} = \lambda_{15}^{FI}$	−0.17299	0.17299	5.781
France: $-\sum_{i=1}^{n+v} IC_{FR}^{i} = \lambda_{15}^{FR}$	−0.15167	0.15167	6.593
UK: $-\sum_{i=1}^{n+v} IC_{UK}^{i} = \lambda_{15}^{UK}$	−0.15287	0.15287	6.541
Italy: $-\sum_{i=1}^{n+v} IC_{IT}^{i} = \lambda_{15}^{IT}$	−0.15477	0.15477	6.461
Japan: $-\sum_{i=1}^{n+v} IC_{JP}^{i} = \lambda_{15}^{JP}$	−0.31354	0.31354	3.189
Netherland: $-\sum_{i=1}^{n+v} IC_{NE}^{i} = \lambda_{15}^{NE}$	−0.15167	0.15167	6.593
Sweden: $-\sum_{i=1}^{n+v} IC_{SW}^{i} = \lambda_{15}^{SW}$	−0.12174	0.12174	8.215
US: $-\sum_{i=1}^{n+v} IC_{US}^{i} = \lambda_{15}^{US}$	−0.1943	0.1943	5.147

estimation of the linearized model would have been furnished different coefficients falsifying the result. Third, the full consideration of the diffusion process in terms of an explicit interaction among countries confers the speeds of adjustments of each country the nature of the eigenvalues, which therefore become crucial for the attainment to the equilibrium. Fourth and importantly, the technology eigenvalue has been found to be dominant, being the highest in absolute value, and therefore the most relevant for growth and stability. This is the confirmation of the same result obtained in the literature with other structural approaches [see for instance Eaton and Kortum (1999)]. From a pure conceptual point of view, here the rate of change of technology represents the fuel of the productive process assisted by business services and, for such a reason, is the main eigenvalue. The relevance for the associated index, afore mentioned, is in such an explanation. Its range is [0, 1] and is decreasing over time, by fixing theoretically that at the beginning of the observation period the change equals the stock. Such a property gives, in its simplicity, the possibility to make comparisons at parity conditions, between different countries, on the effort they are *currently* undertaking in the stability and convergence process, where the adjective currently is to emphasize the effect of nonlinearity which modifies the state-space matrix at any instant. Therefore, what really matters in the nonlinear dynamics is the capability of the current conditions to settle the bases for the future speed of convergence, which is, as time passes, what is represented by the dominant eigenvalue under consideration. At this purpose we observe that the fastest convergence process to the equilibrium is attributable to Germany followed by Japan and US after which are the other countries in a, more or less, homogeneous way with the exception of Sweden which figures as the last one. Actually, as it is shown in Maggi and Muro (2012), the path of this critical eigenvalue was in the past better for the US and for Sweden in Europe. From a technical point of view, this is an implication of that matrix $\mathbf{A}_j$ in formula (8) is time and space varying. Accordingly, for each country the last eigenvalue has been calculated as the time average of the contribution from all countries to the relative change in the stock of technology. Therefore, in this study, the economic counterpart of the nonlinearity is that each country may modify the eigenvalues at each time as happened for Sweden which undertook the highest investment in ideas at the beginning of the sample period, and consequently the highest eigenvalue at that time, but not so in the final part. It goes without saying that such arguments are important for the analysis of the convergence to and the stability of the steady state for which what is relevant are the coefficients of the endogenous variables in the homogeneous equations of which the eigenvalues are complex function. [18] Differently, in the analysis of the steady state what matters are the rates of growth which are clearly linked to the path of the endogenous and exogenous variables. In such an analysis the ranking of countries for the rates of growth of technology may well be different from that of Table 3, as found in Maggi and Muro (2012) where Sweden jumps at the first place. They have been found supported by the almost-

[18] As anticipated before, we consider λ_{15} as the "eigenvalue of technology" we have in mind that in the general complete solution of homogeneous system associated to (2) the dynamics of technology is characterized by very small eigenvectors elements associated to the first 14 eigenvalues and a significant one to the 15°.

highest rates of growth of business services, especially if imported, which on their turn are linked to a consistent rate of growth of ICT. Of course, the initial levels of endogenous variables account for all past investments in innovations.

The small speeds of adjustment are coherent with the high dumping period observed and confirm the difficulty for Europe to approach the stability even if the effect of the dominant technology eigenvalue tends to reduce this problem. This suggests to find, possibly, some other explanatory variables, concerning the functioning of the institutions or the social organization, in order to understand the present sluggishness.

As for the sensitivity, we evaluate the impact, on the convergence and stability, of a change in the structural parameters. This analysis moves from the basic relationship between eigenvalues and eigenvectors and exploit the following formulas to answer the now mentioned question:

$$\frac{\partial \lambda_{ji}}{\partial A_j} = \left[\frac{\partial \lambda_{ji}}{\partial a_{jik}} \right] = h_{ji}^{*} h_{jk}' \tag{11}$$

$$\frac{\partial \lambda_{ji}}{\partial \vartheta_{jl}} = \sum_i \sum_k \frac{\partial \lambda_{ji}}{\partial a_{jik}} \frac{\partial a_{jik}}{\partial \vartheta_{jl}}; \quad j = 1 \ldots n + v; \quad i, k : 1 \ldots 15. \tag{12}$$

Where $\mathbf{A}_j$ is the state-space matrix with generic element a_{jik}, ϑ_l is the lth *structural* parameter of an endogenous variable of system (2), λ_i is the ith eigenvalue, h_i* the ith transposed row vector of the inverse eigenvector matrix and h_k' the kth transposed column vector of the eigenvector matrix (a detailed proof is in Gandolfo (1981)). The implementation of formulae (11) and (12) brings to the elaboration of $n + v = 11$ sensitivity matrices, as many as the countries considered but, given the strong similarities of the outcoming figures we concentrate our results uniquely in Table 4.[19] Such similarities reside in the fact that, as said, our estimation is country specific thanks to the presence of bilateral variables and of some dummy constant variables but not for the characterizations of the coefficients in formula (12) apart those of the linearized equation. For the same argument in Table 4 the impact on the eigenvalues of $IC^i{}_j$ is the same as that of T^j, being the former an additional part of the latter. A straightforward, but nonetheless relevant, result is the 100 %—favourable—impact of the last element in the main diagonal of $\mathbf{A}_j$ on the same 15th eigenvalue, and of the speed of adjustment[20] of the innovations processes on the eigenvalues numbered from 4 to 13. However it is valuable noticing that all speeds of adjustment exert a generalized beneficial effect to the stability and convergence, meaning that the partial adjustment relationships are worthy to be encouraged in reaching the targets. This may be typically done by reducing the costs of bureaucracy, in terms of binding and protecting legislation in market (not primary) activities and, more in general, the cost of politics, as far as the political

[19]The whole set of tables is of course available upon request.

[20]Note the sign in the sensitivity matrix is the opposite coherently with formula (9).

Table 4 Sensitivity analysis

	Eigenvalues	λ_1	λ_2	λ_3	λ_4	λ_5	λ_6	λ_7	λ_8	λ_9	λ_{10}	λ_{11}	λ_{12}	λ_{13}	λ_{14}	λ_{15}
Eq. *Y*	Variables															
α_1	*T*	0.3975	0.0197	−0.1382	0	0	0	0	0	0	0	0	0	0	−0.3055	0.0265
α_2	*Sh*	0.361	−0.1685	−0.2056	0	0	0	0	0	0	0	0	0	0	0.0132	−0.0001
$\alpha^m{}_2$	*Sm*	0.4443	0.058	−0.5462	0	0	0	0	0	0	0	0	0	0	0.0442	−0.0003
α	*adj. speed-Y*	−0.4124	−0.0114	−0.5026	0	0	0	0	0	0	0	0	0	0	−0.074	0.0004
Eq. *Sh*																
γ_1	*Y*	0.1446	−0.056	−0.1077	0	0	0	0	0	0	0	0	0	0	0.0191	−0.0001
γ_2	*T*	0.1394	−0.0968	0.0296	0	0	0	0	0	0	0	0	0	0	−0.0788	0.0066
γ	*adj. speed-Sh*	−0.1266	−0.826	−0.044	0	0	0	0	0	0	0	0	0	0	−0.0034	0
Eq. *Sm*																
$\gamma^m{}_1$	*Y*	0.2857	0.0303	−0.4317	0	0	0	0	0	0	0	0	0	0	0.1162	−0.0005
$\gamma^m{}_2$	*T*	0.2753	0.0524	0.1187	0	0	0	0	0	0	0	0	0	0	−0.4799	0.0334
γ^m	*adj. speed-Sm*	−0.3078	−0.1539	−0.4692	0	0	0	0	0	0	0	0	0	0	−0.0694	0.0004
Eq. Pat_{AUj}																
β_1	*Sh*	0.1307	−0.0717	−0.0232	0	0	0	0	0	0	0	0	0	0	−0.0404	0.0046
β_2	*Sm*	0.1609	0.0247	−0.0616	0	0	0	0	0	0	0	0	0	0	−0.1355	0.0116
β_3	*Y*	0.1493	0.0049	0.0566	0	0	0	0	0	0	0	0	0	0	−0.2268	0.016
β	*adj. speed-*Pat_{ij}	−0.1438	−0.0083	0.0152	−1	−1	−1	−1	−1	−1	−1	−1	−1	−1	−0.864	0.0008
Eq. *T*																
IC_j^{AU}	Pat_j^{AU}	0.0094	0.0004	−0.0006	0	0	0	0	0	0	0	0	0	0	−0.0099	0.0008

(continued)

Table 4 (continued)

	Eigenvalues	λ_1	λ_2	λ_3	λ_4	λ_5	λ_6	λ_7	λ_8	λ_9	λ_{10}	λ_{11}	λ_{12}	λ_{13}	λ_{14}	λ_{15}
IC_j^{GE}	Pat_j^{GE}	0.0031	0.0001	−0.0002	0	0	0	0	0	0	0	0	0	0	−0.0031	0.0001
IC_j^{DE}	Pat_j^{DE}	0.0088	0.0004	−0.0006	0	0	0	0	0	0	0	0	0	0	−0.0093	0.0007
IC_j^{FI}	Pat_j^{FI}	0.0086	0.0004	−0.0006	0	0	0	0	0	0	0	0	0	0	−0.0091	0.0006
IC_j^{FR}	Pat_j^{FR}	0.0098	0.0005	−0.0007	0	0	0	0	0	0	0	0	0	0	−0.0104	0.0009
IC_j^{UK}	Pat_j^{UK}	0.0097	0.0005	−0.0007	0	0	0	0	0	0	0	0	0	0	−0.0104	0.0008
IC_j^{IT}	Pat_j^{IT}	0.0096	0.0004	−0.0006	0	0	0	0	0	0	0	0	0	0	−0.0102	0.0008
IC_j^{JP}	Pat_j^{JP}	0.0048	0.0002	−0.0003	0	0	0	0	0	0	0	0	0	0	−0.0049	0.0002
IC_j^{NE}	Pat_j^{NE}	0.0098	0.0005	−0.0007	0	0	0	0	0	0	0	0	0	0	−0.0105	0.0009
IC_j^{SW}	Pat_j^{SW}	0.0122	0.0006	−0.0008	0	0	0	0	0	0	0	0	0	0	−0.0133	0.0014
IC_j^{US}	Pat_j^{US}	0.0077	0.0004	−0.0005	0	0	0	0	0	0	0	0	0	0	−0.008	0.0005
$-\sum_{i=1}^{n+v} IC_{AU}^i$	T^{AU}	0.0094	0.0004	−0.0006	0	0	0	0	0	0	0	0	0	0	−0.0108	1.0016
$-\sum_{i=1}^{n+v} IC_{GE}^i$	T^{GE}	0.0031	0.0001	−0.0002	0	0	0	0	0	0	0	0	0	0	−0.0031	1.0002
$-\sum_{i=1}^{n+v} IC_{DE}^i$	T^{DE}	0.0088	0.0004	−0.0006	0	0	0	0	0	0	0	0	0	0	−0.0101	1.0014

(continued)

Table 4 (continued)

$-\sum_{i=1}^{n+v} IC_{FI}^{i}$	T^{FI}	0.0086	0.0004	−0.0006	0	0	0	0	0	0	0	0	0	0	−0.0098	1.0013
$-\sum_{i=1}^{n+v} IC_{FR}^{i}$	T^{FR}	0.0098	0.0005	−0.0007	0	0	0	0	0	0	0	0	0	0	−0.0114	1.0018
$-\sum_{i=1}^{n+v} IC_{UK}^{i}$	T^{UK}	0.0097	0.0005	−0.0007	0	0	0	0	0	0	0	0	0	0	−0.0113	1.0017
$-\sum_{i=1}^{n+v} IC_{IT}^{i}$	T^{IT}	0.0096	0.0005	−0.0007	0	0	0	0	0	0	0	0	0	0	−0.0111	1.0017
$-\sum_{i=1}^{n+v} IC_{JP}^{i}$	T^{JP}	0.0048	0.0002	−0.0003	0	0	0	0	0	0	0	0	0	0	−0.0051	1.0004
$-\sum_{i=1}^{n+v} IC_{NE}^{i}$	T^{NE}	0.0098	0.0005	−0.0007	0	0	0	0	0	0	0	0	0	0	−0.0114	1.0018
$-\sum_{i=1}^{n+v} IC_{SW}^{i}$	T^{SW}	0.0122	0.0006	−0.0008	0	0	0	0	0	0	0	0	0	0	−0.0148	1.0029
$-\sum_{i=1}^{n+v} IC_{US}^{i}$	T^{US}	0.0077	0.0004	−0.0005	0	0	0	0	0	0	0	0	0	0	−0.0086	1.0011

decisional levels are concerned. Also the coefficients of the other variables *Y*, *Sh*, *Sm* and *T* in the several equations have a strong impact but with a mixed effects, which is to be expected given the complexity of the interactions in the model. As to the comparisons among countries in terms of *innovative effort* index, a small though relevant evidence is that the sensitivity reveals a constantly stronger beneficial effect in the less performing countries, especially when referred to innovations and technology. This is, once again, in favour to invest in the research activity especially in the case of low performance.

We conclude this section by observing that from the analysis now developed we can only asses on the stability of the growth process towards the equilibrium. Another approach to study the dynamics, accounting also for the initial levels, is that of considering the evolution of the system under consideration.

5 Policy Implications: Controlling for the Growth-Path Evolution

The presence of the exogenous variables in system (2) may affect both the rates of growth and initial levels of the endogenous variables on the basis of an a priori known behavior or a control rule. Maggi and Muro (2012) devoted special attention to such an issue by studying, in particular, their functional form with respect to the parameters and the control variables, that gives the opportunity to evaluate the comparative dynamics of the model. In this section we study the dynamics of our model looking at its actual path and asking whether and how it is possible to match with a target value for the endogenous variables in the future. In pursuing such a target we might also be asked to answer about when the intervention to this aim is more appropriate to occur and, possibly the length of the period required to get the desired result, so that both the initial values and the time elapsing become policy instruments. These problems may find the answer in the implementation of the convolution integral associated to system (2).[21] The first step is to start from the complete general linearized solution of such a system, that is for the generic *j*th country at time *t*:

$$\mathbf{x}_j^o(t) = e^{\mathbf{A}_j(t-t_0)}\mathbf{x}_j^o(0) + \int_{t_0}^{t} e^{\mathbf{A}_j(t-\theta)}\mathbf{B}_j\mathbf{u}_j^o(\theta)\,d\theta \tag{13}$$

where the $\mathbf{A}_j$ matrix assumes the role of the Jacobian, the superscript *o* indicates the double integration because of the presence of stocks and flows coherently with formula (3), and the $\mathbf{B}_j$ matrix is country specific since it includes the distances of all countries with respect to the *j*th one, other than the estimates of the exogenous variables parameters. This is because, here, in order to compute the integral, we

[21] To this aim a Matlab code has been appositely written and tested.

group all the constants referred to the control—exogenous—variables in $\mathbf{B}_j$, which is therefore associated to a **B** matrix of order 165*209. The $\mathbf{u}_j(t)$ vector is composed of the following exogenous elements:

$$\begin{aligned} &ICT_j = ICT_j(0)e^{\rho_{ICTj}t};\ K_j = K_j(0)e^{\rho_{Kj}t};\ L_j = L_j(0)e^{\rho_{Lj}t};\ HKS_{ji} = HKS_{ji}(0)e^{\rho_{HKSji}t}\\ &HKR_j = HKR_j(0)e^{\rho_{HKRj}t};\ REG_j = REG_j(0)e^{\rho_{REGj}t};\ STR_j = STR_J(0)e^{\rho_{STRj}t}\ \ ; t; const \end{aligned} \tag{14}$$

where both the initial conditions and the rates of growth (ρ_j) for the variables have been calculated from the data coherently with the historical paths. The $\mathbf{B}_j$ matrix is of a shape like this:

$$\mathbf{B}_j =$$

$$\begin{bmatrix}
\alpha\alpha_0 & \alpha\alpha_3^K & \alpha\alpha_4^L & 0 & 0 & 0 & 0 & 0 & 0 & 0\\
\gamma_{sh}\gamma_0^{sh} & 0 & 0 & \gamma_{sh}\gamma_3^{STR} & \gamma_{sh}\gamma_4^{ICT} & \gamma_{sh}\gamma_5^{REG} & 0 & 0 & 0 & 0\\
\gamma_{sm}\gamma_0^{sm} & 0 & 0 & \gamma_{sm}\gamma_3^{STR} & \gamma_{sm}\gamma_4^{ICT} & \gamma_{sm}\gamma_5^{REG} & 0 & 0 & 0 & 0\\
\beta^{AU}\left(\beta_0^{AU} + \beta_1^{AU}a * dist_j^{AU}\right) & 0 & 0 & 0 & 0 & 0 & \beta^{AU}\beta_5^{AU,HKR} & \beta^{AU}\beta_1^{AU}b * dist_j^{AU} & \beta^{AU}\beta_2^{AU,HKS} & 0\\
\beta^{GE}\left(\beta_0^{GE} + \beta_1^{GE}a * dist_j^{GE}\right) & 0 & 0 & 0 & 0 & 0 & \beta^{GE}\beta_5^{GE,HKR} & \beta^{GE}\beta_1^{GE}b * dist_j^{GE} & 0 & \beta^{GE}\beta_2^{GE,HKS}\\
\beta^{DE}\left(\beta_0^{DE} + \beta_1^{DE}a * dist_j^{DE}\right) & 0 & 0 & 0 & 0 & 0 & \beta^{DE}\beta_5^{DE,HKR} & \beta^{DE}\beta_1^{DE}b * dist_j^{DE} & 0 & 0\\
\beta^{FI}\left(\beta_0^{FI} + \beta_1^{FI}a * dist_j^{FI}\right) & 0 & 0 & 0 & 0 & 0 & \beta^{FI}\beta_5^{FI,HKR} & \beta^{FI}\beta_1^{FI}b * dist_j^{FI} & 0 & 0\\
\beta^{FR}\left(\beta_0^{FR} + \beta_1^{FR}a * dist_j^{FR}\right) & 0 & 0 & 0 & 0 & 0 & \beta^{FR}\beta_5^{FR,HKR} & \beta^{FR}\beta_1^{FR}b * dist_j^{FR} & 0 & 0\\
\beta^{UK}\left(\beta_0^{UK} + \beta_1^{UK}a * dist_j^{UK}\right) & 0 & 0 & 0 & 0 & 0 & \beta^{UK}\beta_5^{UK,HKR} & \beta^{UK}\beta_1^{UK}b * dist_j^{UK} & 0 & 0\\
\beta^{IT}\left(\beta_0^{IT} + \beta_1^{IT}a * dist_j^{IT}\right) & 0 & 0 & 0 & 0 & 0 & \beta^{IT}\beta_5^{IT,HKR} & \beta^{IT}\beta_1^{IT}b * dist_j^{IT} & 0 & 0\\
\beta^{JP}\left(\beta_0^{JP} + \beta_1^{JP}a * dist_j^{JP}\right) & 0 & 0 & 0 & 0 & 0 & \beta^{JA}\beta_5^{JA,HKR} & \beta^{JA}\beta_1^{JA}b * dist_j^{JA} & 0 & 0\\
\beta^{NE}\left(\beta_0^{NE} + \beta_1^{NE}a * dist_j^{NE}\right) & 0 & 0 & 0 & 0 & 0 & \beta^{NE}\beta_5^{NE,HKR} & \beta^{NE}\beta_1^{NE}b * dist_j^{NE} & 0 & 0\\
\beta^{SW}\left(\beta_0^{SW} + \beta_1^{SW}a * dist_j^{SW}\right) & 0 & 0 & 0 & 0 & 0 & \beta^{SW}\beta_5^{SW,HKR} & \beta^{SW}\beta_1^{SW}b * dist_j^{SW} & 0 & 0\\
\beta^{US}\left(\beta_0^{US} + \beta_1^{US}a * dist_j^{US}\right) & 0 & 0 & 0 & 0 & 0 & \beta^{US}\beta_5^{US,HKR} & \beta^{US}\beta_1^{US}b * dist_j^{US} & 0 & 0\\
0 & 0 & 0 & 0 & 0 & 0 & 0 & 0 & 0 & 0
\end{bmatrix}$$

$$\times \begin{bmatrix}
0 & 0 & 0 & 0 & 0 & 0 & 0 & 0 & 0\\
0 & 0 & 0 & 0 & 0 & 0 & 0 & 0 & 0\\
0 & 0 & 0 & 0 & 0 & 0 & 0 & 0 & 0\\
0 & 0 & 0 & 0 & 0 & 0 & 0 & 0 & 0\\
0 & 0 & 0 & 0 & 0 & 0 & 0 & 0 & 0\\
\beta^{DE}\beta_2^{DE,HKS} & 0 & 0 & 0 & 0 & 0 & 0 & 0 & 0\\
0 & \beta^{FI}\beta_2^{FI,HKS} & 0 & 0 & 0 & 0 & 0 & 0 & 0\\
0 & 0 & \beta^{FR}\beta_2^{FR,HKS} & 0 & 0 & 0 & 0 & 0 & 0\\
0 & 0 & 0 & \beta^{UK}\beta_2^{UK,HKS} & 0 & 0 & 0 & 0 & 0\\
0 & 0 & 0 & 0 & \beta^{IT}\beta_2^{IT,HKS} & 0 & 0 & 0 & 0\\
0 & 0 & 0 & 0 & 0 & \beta^{JA}\beta_2^{JA,HKS} & 0 & 0 & 0\\
0 & 0 & 0 & 0 & 0 & 0 & \beta^{NE}\beta_2^{NE,HKS} & 0 & 0\\
0 & 0 & 0 & 0 & 0 & 0 & 0 & \beta^{SW}\beta_2^{SW,HKS} & 0\\
0 & 0 & 0 & 0 & 0 & 0 & 0 & 0 & \beta^{US}\beta_2^{US,HKS}\\
0 & 0 & 0 & 0 & 0 & 0 & 0 & 0 & 0
\end{bmatrix}$$

From formula (13), by imposing at the final time the target value $\mathbf{x}_j{}^o(t_{fin})$, it is possible to retrieve the initial condition at the beginning of the desired elapsing period $\mathbf{x}_j{}^o(t_{in})$:

$$\mathbf{x}_j^o\left(t_{in}\right)\left[e^{\mathbf{A}_j\left(t_{fin}-t_{in}\right)}\right]^{-1}\mathbf{x}_j^o\left(t_{fin}\right) - \int\limits_{t_{in}}^{t_{fin}} e^{\mathbf{A}_j\left(t_{fin}-\theta\right)}\mathbf{B}_j\mathbf{u}_j^o\left(\theta\right)d\theta. \tag{15}$$

The above formula has been implemented by remembering that $e^{\mathbf{A}_j} = \sum_{k=0}^{+\infty} \frac{\mathbf{A}_j^k}{k!}$ and using the trapezoidal rule with a reasonable small pace of integration (O.M = 110^{-1}). From this calculus we obtain that, given a final target value, it is possible to impose reasonable (i.e. compatible with the historical values) intermediate targets—initial values—of the endogenous variables in order to get for three consecutive years an increment for real output in the range (percentage values) of [1, 1.33], for business services (domestic and imported) [2, 2.5] and for patents and technology [3, 3.5]. Importantly, the same total increments would not have been viable in a different period of time or replicable by shifting the same time interval, moreover such increments may be different for the countries considered and, of course, there exists an interdependence among countries in such a respect.

We tried also several additional experiments, conducted separately, to better qualify the impact of a change in the exogenous variables on the results now commented. In particular, maintaining the same target values as before, we evaluated the results on the initial conditions coming from: (1) doubling specialized personnel (Human Capital) and (2) ICT, (3) halving Regulation. We reckon as beneficial the effects consisting in a reduction of the initial conditions of the endogenous variables within the same 3-year time-interval of the previous simulation, when improvements of policies (1)–(3) were not implemented. Unfortunately, but not surprisingly, we obtained confirmation of the slow—though potentially relevant-dynamics of the estimated system in the short run. We did obtain beneficial results but, as for policy (1) it requires a time interval of *at least* 5 years (i.e. almost the double of the previous experiment) for output to get a decrement in the initial condition significantly different from 0 as well as for domestic and foreign services, while technology performs, with a decrement—averaging through countries—of about 0.8 %, maintaining the interval of 3 years. As for policies (2) and (3) we got very similar results for output and a decrement of about 0.03 % and 0.05 % for domestic and foreign services respectively while, for policy (3), they amount to 0.04 % and 0.07 % in the 3-years interval. The effects on new inventions are again more consistent around 0.4 % for both policies in the short run. However, beyond the quantitative results recordable what emerged in qualitative terms is that the time interval of 5 years, i.e. the medium term, is the period required to start looking at any improvements deriving from the policies experimented, which is coherent with the sluggishness observed and pictured by the small speeds of adjustments and eigenvalues estimated. Technically, this means that the surface represented by integral (15) accelerates over time only from the medium-long run on and that, within the short run, the only ascertainable, although small, improvements occur in the non-manufacturing sectors i.e. business services and inventions. In the long run the improvements of output from the policies adopted are, as expected, remarkable and go from an—approximately—additional 1 % per year in the case of doubled human capital and slightly more for the other two policies because of the longer time required for new inventions to be accumulated across countries and embedded in the production function.

Summing up, we underline the following points. First, specific initial conditions in time are required for growth to be viable and, to this aim, it is necessary an appropriate dynamic model capable to pick frictions and lags in the countries considered. Second, the adjustment required in the manufacturing sector to the innovation process is a key aspect in promoting growth. Third, in accordance with what observed in Sect. 3, the reaction of foreign business services to the policies implemented is always higher than that of domestic ones thus revealing, again, a greater capacity of competing.

Other important studies, on the similar line, might be conducted in terms of the implications in the use of **B** and **u** with interest also in other strategic variables for the Union such as the ones representing the effect of inequality or social inclusion.

6 Conclusions and Further Research

This research provides an alternative method for the study of the structural models in economic dynamics. The main characteristic is that the continuous time model developed may be theoretically studied and statistically implemented by *exactly* matching its dynamics with the data. Among the several advantages, we do not impose a priori an equilibrium and the disequilibrium relations we use serve to study the transitional dynamics in a Schumpeterian evolutionary context. In the specific framework of growth, business services and technology, we have found their interaction significant and of important implications. Summing up, we underline: (I) the role of rate of growth of technology as a stabilizer of the economy given its intrinsic nature of eigenvalue; (II) the possibility to improve such a stabilizer over time and across countries, in terms of new initial conditions, according to the nonlinearity of the model; (III) the relevance of the business services in this process as a vehicle of technology towards the production and with a virtuous interaction together with technology itself; besides, such a process highlights the benefits of an offshoring activity. We characterized such results on a detailed geographical bases by estimating systems of continuous time panel data. To that aim we used explicative bilateral variables such as distance and researchers. A certainly promising research area in this field is to posing in continuous way also the space, like in Donaghy and Plotnikova (2004). Specifically, it would be possible to avoid to consider as homogeneous wide geographic areas or to test the similarities in regions inside different areas.

The small speeds of adjustment from our model confirm the difficulty for Europe to approach the stability even if preserved by the dominant eigenvalue of technology, and suggest to find some other explanatory variables, concerning the functioning of the institutions or the social organization, in order to understand the prolonged present sluggishness. To conclude, one interesting avenue for future research also relates to considering current data, in order to see how the consolidation of the EU integration process and the recent crisis may affect the dynamics of the model.

Acknowledgments This research is the follow up of a wide project, focused on growth, technology and services, started with the European Commission and then financed by Miur and University "La Sapienza". It has been presented at the 14th ISS Conference, Brisbane and at the UTS University, Sydney, Australia, during the visiting period of Bernardo Maggi in July 2012. We thank Carl Chiarella for his helpful assistance and kind hospitality at the UTS, Kieran Donaghy for his notable advices and an anonymous referee for his valuable comments. Finally, we are especially indebted to Clifford Wymer for precious suggestions and for having allowed the utilization of the most recent version of his programs for estimation of panel data systems in continuous time. Although the present research has been conducted with the joint contribution of both of the authors, Sects. 1, 2.1, 2.2, 3, 4.2 and 6 are attributed to B. Maggi while Sects. 4.1 and 5, to D. Muro. The usual disclaimer applies.

References

Coe DT, Helpman E (1995) International R&D spillovers". Eur Econ Rev 39:859–857

Coe DT, Helpman E, Hoffmaister AW (2008) International R&D Spillovers and institutions. IMF working paper, WP/08/104

Donaghy KP, Plotnikova M (2004) Econometric estimation of a spatial dynamic model in continuous space and continuous time: an empirical demonstration. In: Getis A, Mur J, Zoller G (eds) Spatial econometrics and spatial statistics. Palgrave Macmillan.

Eaton J, Kortum S (1996) Trade in ideas: patenting and productivity in the OECD. J Int Econ 40:251–278

Eaton J, Kortum S (1999) International technology diffusion: theory and measurement. Int Econ Rev 40:537–570

Englmann FC, Walz U (1995) Industrial centers and regional growth in the presence of local inputs. J Reg Sci 35:3–27

Evangelista R, Lucchese M, Meliciani V (2013) Business services, innovation and sectoral growth. Struct Change Econ Dynam 25:119–132

Gandolfo G (1981) Qualitative analysis and econometric estimation of continuous time dynamic models. North Holland, Amsterdam

Gandolfo G (1993) Continuous time econometrics: theory and applications. Chapman and Hall, London

Guerrieri P, Meliciani V (2005) Technology and international competitiveness: the interdependence between manufacturing and producer services. Struct Changes Econ Dynam 16:408–502

Hall BH, Jaffe AB, Trajtenberg M (2001) The NBER patent citations data file: lessons, insights and methodological tools. CEPR Discussion Papers n. 3094

Hamilton JD (1994) Time series analysis. Princeton University Press, New Jersey, NJ

Holden T (2010) Products, patents and productivity persistence: a DSGE model of endogenous growth, vol 512. Department of Economics, Discussion Paper Series: Oxford

Jones CI (1995) R&D based model of economic growth. J Polit Econ 103:759–784

Keller W (2002) Geographic localization of international technology diffusion. Am Econ Rev 92:120–142

Krugman P (1991a) Geography and trade. MIT Press, Cambridge, MA

Krugman P (1991b) Increasing returns and economic geography. J Polit Econ 99:483–499

Lichtenberg F, van Pottelsberghe de la Potterie B (1998) International R&D spillovers: a comment. Eur Econ Rev 42:1483–1491

Maggi B, Muro D (2013) A multi-country nonlinear dynamical model for the study of European growth based on technology and business services. Struct Change Econ Dynam 25:173–187

Maggi B, Padoan PC, Guerrieri P (2009) A continuous time model of european growth, integration and technology diffusion: the role of distance. Econ Model 26(3):631–640

Marrewijk C, Stiborab J, de Vaal' A, Viaene J-M (1997) Producer services, comparative advantage, and international trade patterns. J Int Econ 42:195–220
Muller E, Doloreux D (2009) What we should know about knowledge-intensive business services. Technol Soc 31(1):64–72
Nelson RR, Winter SG (1982) An evolutionary theory of economic change. The Belknap Press of Harvard University Press, Cambridge, MA
Nicoletti G, Scarpetta S, Boylaud O (2000) Summary indicators of product market regulation. OECD Economic Department Working Papers n. 226
Rubalcaba L, Kox H (2007) Business services in european economic growth. Palgrave-MacMillan, New Jersey, NJ
Schumpeter JA (1934) The theory of economic development. Harvard University Press, Cambridge
The Anh P (2007) Growth, volatility and stabilization policy in a DSGE model with nominal rigidities and learning-by-doing. DEPOCEN working paper series no. 2007/04
van Welsum D, Vickery G (2005) Potential offshoring of ICT-intensive using occupations. In: Enhancing the performance of the services sector. OECD, Paris, pp 179–204, report also available at: www.oecd.org/sti/offshoring
Venables A (1996) Equilibrium locations of vertically linked industries. Int Econ Rev 37:341–359
Walz U (1996) Transport costs, intermediate goods, and localized growth. Reg Sci Urban Econ 26:671–695
Wymer CR (1997) Structural nonlinear continuous time models in econometrics. Macroecon Dynam 1:518–548
Wymer CR (2005) WYSEA: systems estimation and analysis reference and user guide, mimeo

[illegible]

A History-Friendly Model of the Internet Access Market: The Case of Brazil

Marcelo de Carvalho Pereira and David Dequech

Abstract This paper presents a simulation model of the internet access services market. The model is based on neo-Schumpeterian evolutionary theory, as well as on the contemporary institutional theory. One key driver of the internet sector has been the significant technological opportunities. However, competition in the internet access services market has proved less intense than in other technology-driven industries in most countries, including other segments of the internet sector itself. Usual theoretical approaches do not adequately explain this empirical observation. Our hypothesis is that institutional mechanisms were determinant for the dynamics of competition. Institutions are broadly understood as socially shared, formal or informal, recurring rules of behaviour or thought. To test this hypothesis, a sectoral agent-based simulation model is proposed, modelling with some detail both demand and supply agents' behaviours. Model parameters and initial conditions were calibrated using empirical data from the Brazilian market. The competitive mechanisms unveiled by simulation were clearly dependent on institutional processes, particularly at user preferences setting and informal business rules adoption. Institutional phenomena were strong enough to produce results that are significantly different from other technologically dynamic industries.

1 Introduction

The internet sector has originated from the revolution of the information and communication technologies (ICT), starting in the 1960s.[1] The telecommunications industry, a key participant of the internet sector from its inception, has become an even stronger driver of the internet development since the 1990s, after the worldwide processes of privatisation, deregulation and stimulus to competition. In this scenario,

[1]Segments of the internet sector include: access services, equipment manufacturing, systems development, and content provision.

M. de Carvalho Pereira (✉) • D. Dequech
University of Campinas, Campinas, Brazil
e-mail: marcelocpereira@uol.com.br

A. Pyka, J. Foster (eds.), *The Evolution of Economic and Innovation Systems*,
Economic Complexity and Evolution, DOI 10.1007/978-3-319-13299-0_22

ex ante analysis would suggest that the resulting internet access services market[2] (IASM) would operate under strong competition, due to the promising association of usually low barriers to entry, significant technological opportunities, and rapidly growing demand. However, actual IASM seems better described by low-intensity competition in countries like Brazil and others. Indeed, market concentration has frequently increased to very high levels. The central question of this article is to explain some of the reasons for the apparent discrepancy between a potentially competitive market and the restricted competition verified in practice.

Most of the technological innovation in the IASM is embedded in capital equipment. In Pavitt's (1984) terms, the IASM is a typical *supplier dominated* industry, marked by the steady infusion of new generations of increasingly powerful (and more productive) network equipment. Few large transnational suppliers provide domestic internet access service providers (IASPs) with the required network infrastructure. However, the competitive configuration of each national IASM seems to be country specific, notwithstanding the unrestricted availability of the newer technologies and their relatively straightforward application.[3] This suggests that technological dynamics alone, although relevant, may have limited potential to explain the asymmetries among national IASMs.

Empirical research suggests that explanations for this scenario may require a deeper than usual analytical approach. Usual methods for investigating competition seem to provide only partial answers, at best. We propose here that institutional issues significantly influenced the IASM competitive scenario in Brazil—and possibly in other countries. Considering the apparent intertwining of technological and institutional phenomena, we advocate that a co-evolutionary approach may be more appropriate to explain the market dynamics. In order to complement an innovation-driven evolutionary perspective, our central analytical hypothesis is thus that country-specific differences in the IASMs are, to some extent, due to the heterogeneous development of some key institutions.[4]

We propose modelling the theoretical mechanisms supposed in action in the IASM through agent-based simulation techniques. The main task of the model is to test how well the institutional dominance hypothesis may hold. From a methodological standpoint, we embrace the History-friendly approach proposed by Malerba et al. (1999). On the empirical side, we selected data from Brazil to inform the analysis and set up the model. We believe Brazil is a compelling case to start with because of the reasonably complex institutional scenario and the availability of

[2]Internet access services provide bi-directional transport of information (data, sound and images) between the end-user location and the final destination service or person, within the worldwide internet.

[3]Internet access technology usually presents low cumulativeness and tacitness at the IASP level, given that network equipment suppliers lead most of the innovation. This is reinforced by the extensive technical support available from those suppliers to all IASPs.

[4]Following Dequech (2013), "institutions are broadly understood here as socially shared rules of behaviour or of thought. They include legal norms, which have a formal character, together with conventions and informal social norms, which do not".

detailed data. From there, it should be relatively straightforward to reconfigure the model to handle particular conditions applicable to other countries.

This paper presents initial results from a model designed to answer a variety of questions about the IASM. Here, we propose to focus on the dynamics of market competition, in which institutional factors may have played an important role. In particular, we emphasize the informal rules of behaviour related to quality assessment by consumers and to competition regulation by the state. Competition among IASPs is evaluated in terms of technological trajectories, services price/quality, firm entry/exit turbulence, and market share evolution. Effectively, the model replicated the general dynamics present in the real IASM. Results seem to confirm the relevance—and in some circumstances, the dominance—of the simulated institutional mechanisms. Among the main institutional features, the behavioural rules employed by users to form preferences and the licencing informal rules adopted by the regulatory agency were particularly important.

The remainder of the paper is organized as follows. The next section presents the theoretical framework employed in the model. Section 3 offers an empirical analysis of the IASM in Brazil, providing an overview of the stylized facts. Section 4 describes the specification of the simulation model (with further details in the Appendix). In Sect. 5, some relevant results are presented and analysed. The paper closes with a brief review of the main conclusions.

2 Theoretical Framework

There is some tradition of investigating competition in telecommunications markets by the application of mainstream industrial organization tools: barriers to entry, network externalities, game-theoretic strategic competition, incentives-based regulation, and so on (Laffont et al. 1998, 2003; Laffont and Tirole 2000; Shy 2001; Varian 2002; Viscusi et al. 2005). Other research strands point to the relevance of innovation processes and formal institutions to the development of markets for internet goods and services, in particular those approaches built around the useful concept of a sectoral system of innovation and production (Davies 1996; Kavassalis et al. 1996; Corrocher 2001; Edquist 2004). Newer research further advances the analysis of internet markets, often sharing the same analytical roots of the seminal authors, more frequently exploring the sectoral dynamics from a supply-side perspective (Funk 2008; Greenstein 2010; Pereira and Ribeiro 2011; Besen and Israel 2012).

Conversely, fewer authors have considered the relevance of demand-side factors on the industry organization. Although consumers/users of complex and sophisticated products and services are frequently recognized as an important part of the corresponding markets, most analysis and models simply treat them as a rather static and homogeneous group of atomized individuals (e.g., see Schmidt and Missler-Behr 2010). Along the lines of works like Jonard and Yildizoğlu (1998), Birke and

Swann (2006), and Tscherning and Damsgaard (2008), we propose investigating the influence of demand-side factors on internet access services market (IASM).

However, a more detailed investigation of the demand's effect on market performance should not prevent us from paying attention to the scenario behind supply and demand interaction. Due to this interactivity, we follow Nelson (1995) and suggest that the theoretical framework required for the investigation of the IASM be based on technological and institutional analytical vectors. So, we propose trailing the *co-evolutionary* approach proposed by authors from both the Schumpeterian and the institutional traditions (Hodgson 1988; Nelson and Sampat 2001; Fligstein and Dauter 2007; Scott 2008).

Neo-Schumpeterian evolutionary theory is an alternative that explains competition by means of out-of-equilibrium analysis (Fagerberg 2003). Evolutionary theory is particularly adequate to investigate sectors driven by the technological innovation dynamics and where the interaction of the agents beyond pure market transactions is relevant (Malerba 2006). Innovation relentlessly changes the competitive environment by dynamically redefining the relative advantages held by competing firms (Dosi and Nelson 2010). In an evolutionary perspective, static efficiency issues frequently do not drive competition directly, because of the idiosyncratic character of innovation and its diffusion among firms and users. Competing firms have different capabilities on the bases of which they try to continuously adapt to the competitive scenario by innovating (Teece et al. 1997). Accordingly, when *Schumpeterian competition* takes place, market organization becomes endogenous, presenting itself as an emergent property of the differential innovative and absorptive capabilities among firms (Metcalfe 1998). Such persistent heterogeneous capabilities represent contradictory forces leading, at the same time, to concentrated markets and to turbulent competitive dynamics. The sector-specific balance between these two features is determinant to industry organization (Dosi 1988).

Nevertheless, the coexistence of markets with highly distinct competitive profiles within the same sector, as in the case of the internet, is not straightforward to grasp from a pure evolutionary standpoint. Considering that components of a sector usually share a *technological regime*[5] (Malerba and Orsenigo 2000), as it seems to be the case, some broad similarities would be expected, as suggested by usual typologies (e.g., see Pavitt 1984; Klepper 1996). For example, in sectors where technological opportunities are high and appropriability is low, like the internet, the archetypical features expected are frequent technological innovation, fast innovation diffusion, high turbulence (intense entry and exit), and constant erosion of the incumbents' market shares (Breschi et al. 2000). Although this is an adequate description of most segments in the internet sector (e.g., equipment, software, content), it may be not fully applicable to the IASM, as discussed next.

[5]As defined by the relevant technological features, like the available opportunities, the appropriability conditions, the knowledge cumulativeness profile and the nature of the knowledge base (Dosi 1982).

To handle the seeming discrepancy of the IASM from the canonical *supplier dominated* profile, we propose a complementary institutional perspective. The application of concepts derived from institutional theory, in particular the approach offered by the contemporary organizational studies branch (DiMaggio and Powell 1983), seems adequate to clarify points not addressed by evolutionary or other customary industrial organization theories. In this approach, institutions have a role in the economy beyond the usual normative and regulatory functions; a *cultural-cognitive* dimension is also essential to fully understand the effects of institutions on economic behaviour (Tolbert and Zucker 1996). From this perspective, cognitive frames shared among actors are also considered as institutions because they generally condition—and sometimes strictly constrain—the behavioural alternatives available to agents (Scott 2008). In addition to the instrumental and formal institutions considered by new institutional economics authors (North 1990; Williamson 2000), the organizational studies approach emphasizes the roles of culture, cognition and social interaction in producing informal and *taken-for-granted* types of institutions (DiMaggio 1988; Beckert 1999).

Culture and mental models provide the cognitive elements required by agents to make sense of the actions of other individuals with whom they interact, as well to perceive the prevailing institutions and their changes (Denzau and North 1994). Ideas—mental schemes or premises—are powerful elements of institutionalization because they provide the actors with the cognitive frames that justify and legitimate action (Scott 2008). As a result, over time, agents adopt shared mental model as taken-for-granted institutions, which help structure their action and interaction. However, the appearance of such taken-for-granted institutions is not entirely disconnected from purposeful action (DiMaggio and Powell 1983). Agents still take into account their own particular interests. Purposeful agency remains a crucial driver of institutional dynamics, even at the cognitive level (Battilana et al. 2009). Consequently, conflicts, contradictions, and ambiguities are intrinsic to this process (Fligstein 2001).

A relevant institutional aspect of the IASM case is related to the choices of the users. Most market models, evolutionary or not, assume that users have well defined preferences and enough information to choose among the goods/services available in the market (Stigler and Becker 1977; Nelson 2005). However, quality uncertainty—frequently associated to new or complex products—stimulates users to develop alternative, non-price strategies for choosing, usually giving origin to new, taken-for-granted quality-setting institutions (Tordjman 2004). In such a scenario, preferences cannot be treated separately from exchange, as usual, because information about prices and quantities is no longer sufficient to fully orientate buyers' choices. Now, users have to resort to strategies like observing acquaintances' experiences—leading to what DiMaggio and Louch (1998) called *search embeddedness*—to assess their own preferences. Thus, a sort of backward-looking quality evaluation shall be derived, *ex post*, from the judgements of actual users interconnected by strong or weak ties (Granovetter 2005; Beckert 2009), creating a new type of reflexive interdependence between agents that can hardly be analysed under the usual premises of an atomistic, homogeneous, and well-behaved consumer (Orléan 2003).

Therefore, as users are required to associate subjective value to competing offers even when quality information is unavailable, preferences are likely going to be endogenously formed in the market. This is particularly critical in case of services, where usually quality is not fully defined *ex ante*.[6] It should be noted that this is not the traditional case of asymmetric information (Akerlof 1970), when quality is not known by just one of the parties transacting, but a more complex situation where quality is not knowable *ex ante* (as discussed in Sect. 4).

3 Empirical Analysis[7]

Our empirical investigation explores the interactions among agents (supply and demand-side), knowledge (including technologies) and institutions that constitute the IASM. The objective here is to list the key stylized facts relevant to the themes presented before and to associate alternative theoretic accounts to them.

Internet access service gradually became a very concentrated business in Brazil. The 4 incumbent IASPs, originated from the privatization of the telecommunications monopoly, dominated almost 80 % of the domestic IASM in 2011. If we exclude (technically obsolete) dial-up services, their joint market share goes over 90 %. The usual indicators ($HHI > 0.25$, $C4 > 0.85$) point to high market concentration at the national level, in a scenario of relative market participation stability and limited price competition among the incumbents, who have historically focused on different geographical regions to avoid direct competition for users. Figure 1 presents the evolution of these indicators. When analysed at the regional level,[8] concentration is even higher: each privatized incumbent IASP alone holds in average 60 % of market share in the region. Despite the open market and the 1,900+ small firms providing internet access services in Brazil (2011), only one new company successfully became a significant player in the IASM.[9]

The exponential rise in data volumes transported by the internet over time also made evident the pace of diffusion of new technological generations in the IASM. In most OECD countries (including several markets smaller than Brazil), each

[6]Uncertainty in services hiring is aggravated, among other issues, by the high human-asset specificity, considering the start-up costs usually associated with replacing service providers (DiMaggio and Louch 1998).

[7]For details on empirical data presented in this section, as well as the respective sources, see Pereira (2012).

[8]Brazil is subdivided into 26 states plus the federal capital district. The original telecom monopoly was split in 4 regional operators.

[9]GVT, an aggressive challenger firm, succeeded in entering the Brazilian IASM, acquiring more than 6 % national market share in less than 5 years. It was a unique case, as all other entrants remain with national market shares well below 1 %.

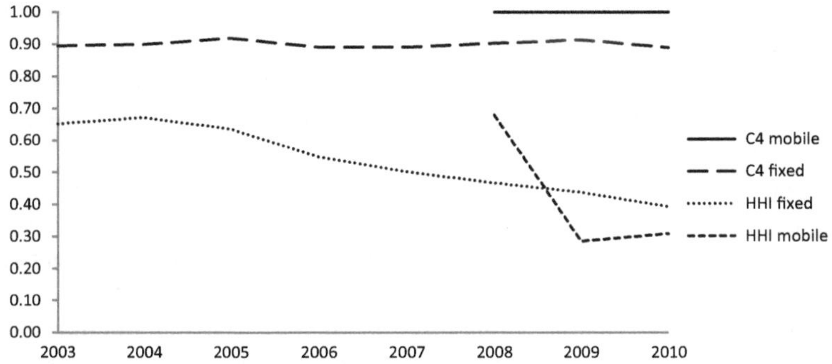

Fig. 1 Four-firm concentration (C4) and Herfindahl-Hirschman (HHI) indexes over time for the internet access service market in Brazil (fixed and mobile access)

consecutive "vintage" of network equipment has diffused in shorter timeframes. However, in Brazil the same process has taken the opposite direction. From 5 years for diffusion of dial-up access (the "1G" internet access technology) in 1996, it took 6 years for fixed broadband ("2G") and 8 years for 3G mobile broadband to get to the mainstream (no 4G in large scale yet). It should be noted that each access generation, embedded in new network equipment developed and sold by a few large transnational firms, was fully available during the entire period for deployment by all IASPs, in Brazil and abroad. However, new technology diffusion was frequently delayed because of the lack of essential complementary assets, as in the case of State-granted radio spectrum licenses and rights of access to existing infrastructure.

In summary, three stylized facts (SFs) seem to deserve special attention.[10] First, there is *persistent market concentration* (SF1), under the dominance of legacy incumbents originated from the privatized public monopoly. Second, empirical data shows a *low rate of successful entry* (SF2), although temporary or marginal entry of IASPs in the market is not difficult, as the intense entry/exit turbulence suggests. Third, *longer than expected technological diffusion cycles* (SF3) have characterized the introduction of new generations of technologies, in a pattern of longer diffusion cycles than in markets that are more competitive. The first two stylized facts are commonly understood as directly correlated. As will be shown next, SF3 is probably also correlated to SF1 and SF2. Thus, it may seem reasonable to suppose that the same causal mechanism may be generating all the three. Without denying the evident intertwining among the stylized facts above, we propose to investigate if particular mechanisms may be in operation in each specific case.[11]

[10]Research pointed to other interesting stylized facts (see Pereira 2012) but we have chosen to focus on the three most relevant here.

[11]The suspicion that multiple causal mechanisms may be in place comes from the analysis of data from different national IASMs. There seems to be no support to the case that a unique form of correlation between the three stylized facts exists among countries.

Several theoretical hypotheses have been proposed in the economics literature to justify the stylized facts observed in our case. The most frequent are: (1) static barriers to entry, usually associated to economies of scale or minimum efficient sizes (Varian 2001; McAfee et al. 2004); (2) strategic behaviour of incumbents, based on some sort of sunk costs, first mover advantages or price discrimination (Baumol et al. 1982; Laffont et al. 1998; Schmalensee 2004); (3) collusion among incumbents, either tacit or not, or institutional capture of government agents (Laffont and Tirole 2000; Fligstein 2001; Viscusi et al. 2005); (4) network externalities, increasing returns of adoption and lock-in (Arthur 1989; Shy 2001; Varian 2002); and (5) dynamic competitive advantages, due to particular innovative capabilities (technical or organizational) that are difficult to replicate (Klepper 1996; Dosi et al. 1997; Teece et al. 1997; Breschi et al. 2000). These hypotheses may be applied to one or two of the presented stylized fact in isolation, although no one seems to fit all of them.

In addition to these hypotheses, we suggest that a more specific one is also plausible in this case: the institutional influence of taken-for-granted shared rules on specific behaviours of the market agents, both on the supply and on the demand side (DiMaggio and Powell 1991; Scott 2008). For example, we propose that the technical governance model that prevailed for more than 100 years, during the monopoly period has survived informally, influencing the way agents understand and act in the IASM for several years after the state-owned operator privatization and the introduction of competition. Alternatively, as another example, we suggest that users develop socially-constructed quality evaluation rules to select among heterogeneous IASPs, because quality is unknowable *ex ante*—and is constantly changing *ex post*—so the price and the available data on services do not carry all the information required by users when comparing offers. In this case, institutions are established to partially solve a coordination failure (Bowles 2004).

In the particular case of shared mental models inherited from the monopoly period, we are especially interested in the consequences of informal rules regarding about the "most adequate" pace of replacement of network equipment, involving IASPs (entrants and incumbents alike) and the regulatory agency (ANATEL). The existence of any commonly accepted rule about "when is the right time to introduce a new network technology generation?" may prove critical. The answer each national IASM provides to this question may have significant impact on competition. If the answer is "as soon as an adequate new technology is available" then Schumpeterian-type dynamics may well be the outcome, as it seems to be the case in several countries. On the other hand, if the response is "when existing capital is adequately depreciated", as appears to be the case of Brazil, reduced technological opportunities to entrants and slower market dynamics may be the expected consequence. While pertinent during the period of slow technical change and limited resources of the state monopoly, from the perspective of the government (and the users) this last strategy does not seem reasonable in a sector where technology evolves fast and competing firms usually have access to significant capital financing, as will be shown in Sect. 5.

When evaluating the impact of an informal shared rule about depreciation strategy, one key condition for the acceptance of such a hypothesis is to make sure we are not dealing with a situation where ANATEL was directly captured by the incumbents' interests. Otherwise, we would be dealing with a purely strategic move by the incumbents to artificially create a hostile environment to entrants, using the regulatory agency as a spurious ally. It seems obvious that delaying the introduction of newer technologies, immediately after incumbents deploy their own networks, is beneficial to them and detrimental to entrants. Nevertheless, the potentially harmed parties—entrants and users (or their representatives)—would have contested such potentially anticompetitive action, at least through the media. However, research on anecdotal information, in general and specialized press vehicles, offers no indication that industry members, potential entrants, specialists or consumer associations have contested ANATEL's decisions about new technologies licensing timing. Quite the contrary, on several occasions non-incumbent agents publicly supported the "long depreciation, scarce resources optimizing" strategy adopted by ANATEL, at least until recently. Only in the last few years there was the emergence of discussions about the delay in the introduction of new network technologies. It seems that a migration to a new network depreciation paradigm is now under way, based on the collective—and gradual—acknowledgement of the problems associated to the old practices. ANATEL and the incumbents seem to be also taking part in this change process, toward a "technology-driven" depreciation arrangement, apparently in a non-conflictive manner. In principle, this is compatible with the proposed taken-for-granted character of the legacy strategy, now superseded by a shared new rule, at this moment not yet internalized—or taken-for-granted—by agents.

When the Brazilian IASM is analysed from a historical perspective, it becomes clear that elements pointed out in most of the above theoretical explanations may have contributed to the observed outcomes. The problem, then, is to evaluate which ones are the most relevant to explain the real IASM. While some of the explanations may be quickly discarded, others require some careful analysis to be adequately qualified. Our proposal for the simulation model is, precisely, to create an analytical tool that would make this task easier. The model shall therefore be configured to test the relative relevance of most of the hypotheses listed above: (1) static barriers to entry (economies of scale and minimum efficient size), (2) strategic behaviour (sunk costs and first mover advantages), (3) collusion, (4) differential dynamic capabilities, and (5) taken-for-granted, informal rules of behaviour (regarding network depreciation and quality valuation).

Two of the usual hypotheses were not selected for testing with the model—network externalities and government capture—according to evidence coming from the empirical analysis. The reason for not considering capture has already been presented above, at least in part. On top of that, it would be technically complicated to separate in a model the effects of traditional (i.e., illicit) capture from taken-for-granted mental rules influencing the actions of the regulator. Thus, the model assumes that only one form of governmental influence is in action in the IASM and we interpret this influence as the (licit) result of shared mental models inherited from the monopoly period.[12]

Discarding the importance of network externalities in the case of the internet may seem paradoxical. After all, telephony networks are perhaps the most typical example of this phenomenon (Shy 2001). However, internet networks have both similarities and differences in relation to the old-time telephony networks. In telephony networks, network externalities arise from the fact that "on-net" calls are intrinsically cheaper than "off-net" calls, due to the interconnection fees usually charged by incumbent operators. However, owing to the significant efforts on standardization and to the general open attitude to cooperation among internet community members, thanks to strong internet governance organizations (Funk 2008), interconnection amongst competing internet network operators is almost compulsory, universal and low-cost.[13] Consequently, the significant network externalities offered by the internet—as a whole—to the users (Varian 2002) are not directly reflected on the supply side. In the internet case, and differently from the case of telephony, larger user bases do not provide bigger IASPs with relevant *ex ante* advantages in most situations,[14] at least in terms of cost, quality or interconnection revenue. Thus, it is in principle possible for entrant IASPs to challenge incumbent operators successfully (Noam 1994), even if not always easily, as demonstrated by relevant examples in many countries. This is not usually the case in telephony.

4 Model Specification and Setup

The use of simulation models as analytical devices is a feature of evolutionary theory from its inception (Garavaglia 2010). However, simulation adoption is far less frequent in institutional studies, despite several recent advances (Arthur 2000). Complex economic systems, as the IASM, are adequately modelled by *agent-based* simulation, that allows for the inquiry of the "meso"-level phenomena that are critical to understanding real social interaction (Tesfatsion 2006), but where other

[12]ANATEL has a good record of transparency and adequate governance. In more than 15 years of existence, no legal case of bribery/corruption was open against any ANATEL officer/manager. Cases of "denunciation" in the press have been very rare and never proved. In this sense, ANATEL's track record is well above the average federal government administration in Brazil.

[13]At least among same tier IASPs (Faratin et al. 2009), but anecdotal evidence at the national level is that interconnection ("peering") costs may not be significant barriers for domestic competition in most countries, even for smaller players (Besen and Israel 2012). However, this may not be the case for international interconnection ("transit") in smaller countries, despite the steadily dropping costs (Internet Society 2010). For a discussion on internet interconnection models, see Dodd et al. (2009)

[14]Once all networks are directly or indirectly interconnected, it is irrelevant to the majority of users whether they access the internet from a large or small IASP, provided that both adopt the prescribed technical and quality standards for the access networks.

approaches are frequently inapplicable due to tractability issues (e.g., evolutionary games). Analysis at the aggregated level is essential to the modelling of economic phenomena—like markets—from an institutional perspective (Colander 2005; Tesfatsion 2011). From this foundation, we propose a *History-friendly* modelling approach, as a suitable methodology for the study of specific industrial sectors at a more limited level of generality (Malerba et al. 1999). The main objective of a History-friendly model is to test if (and to what extent) its theoretical hypotheses are logically compatible with the empirical stylized facts (Pyka and Fagiolo 2005; Windrum et al. 2007).

The model presented next was specified on the basis of the theoretical premises presented above, so in the next section we can test if they can reproduce the collected empirical stylized facts. The model is represented here as a set of difference equations defining discrete time series for the state variables of the model (a comprehensive list of variables is available in the Appendix). Each simulation run[15] is then defined by the set of times series for all state variables. The simulation is *time driven* and all contemporaneous events are supposed to take place simultaneously at each time step, $t = 1,2,3\ldots250$. One time step is equivalent to 3 months in real calendar time. To avoid ambiguities, the lag structure of each variable was defined to ensure contemporaneous time convergence independent from the valuation order of equations.

There are three types of agents in the model: users, IASP firms and a network equipment vendor. The model simulates the interactions among sets of those agents: multiple users (with heterogeneous attributes), several IASPs (both incumbents and entrants) and one equipment vendor. The agents handle other relevant entities in the model: technologies (generations of network equipment), capital equipment (forming the networks owned by IASPs), internet access service offers (set by IASPs and hired by users) and particular institutions (as pointed out in the empirical analysis). Interactions among agents drive the model along the time steps, in a logical order, as follows. A single network equipment vendor performs technology search, trying to increase the productivity of existing technological vintages and, eventually, launching new, more productive technology generations, subject to institutional constraints. Prospective entrant IASPs evaluate the convenience (profitability and opportunity) of entry and, if a positive assessment is made, select initial network capacity. IASPs define prices and network investments for the period, given the (myopic) expectations of increase (or decrease) in the number of users. Bankrupt or too small IASPs leave the market. Over time, new users come to the market and search for an IASP, considering both price and perceived quality, subject to their budgets and under the influence of current users. Periodically, existing users evaluate the convenience of replacing their IASP, considering switching costs.

The simulation starts with 4 IASPs and 1.8 million potential service users, conforming to empirical data. The growth of potential users is modelled as a

[15]Model was coded in C++ using the Laboratory for Simulation Development (LSD) version 6.1, created by Marco Valente (2002).

contagion process leading to a logistic curve, adjusted to the Brazilian data. Users growth reaches saturation around $t = 150$, so the analysis focuses on the period $1 \leq t \leq 175$ (43.75 years). New users have random individual budgets distributed according to real data. They also have heterogeneous preferences (as defined by the parameters presented below) defined randomly and uniformly. Most of the remaining model's parameters and lagged variables (requiring non-zero initial conditions) were calibrated using empirical data. The list of adopted values is in the Appendix. After initial calibration, sensitivity analysis of all parameters and initial conditions was performed, so as to identify critical parameters. Parameters and initial conditions were tested around calibration figures in ranges of values compatible with empirical magnitudes. Sensitivity analysis of parameters and initial conditions was performed using ANOVA tests at 1 % significance on relevant market indicators.[16] Only a relative small number of parameters (11) were critical to producing the main model qualitative results.[17]

The key transaction in the model is the selling (by IASPs) and the buying (by users) of internet access service. This sell-buy transaction is of a particular kind because the quality of the product is only defined *after* the transaction takes place. Quality is effectively unknowable *ex ante*, due to a technical reason. A typical internet user drives internet data—in and out of the hired access network—during a small fraction of the time the service is available. For each individual user, most of the time there is no data to be transported over the access network provided by the IASP to support the service. Given that all users of a single IASP usually share the same access network, it makes sense to determine the size of this network according to the expected joint data traffic coming from all users, in order to avoid idle capacity. This significantly reduces the required network resources to service each user, on average, because several users can share the same facilities at the same time. Shared facilities networks cut costs and prices by orders of magnitude when compared to old dedicated networks. Now, the problem is how to guarantee quality in such a shared network scenario. Since networks are planned and built long before users effectively contract services, real IASPs plan their networks according to the expected number of users and their usage profile. Of course, this is an adaptive learning process where "planning errors" are unavoidable. If they "overbuild" capacity, the quality perceived by the users tends to improve in comparison to the planned quality. On the other hand, if they "underbuild", quality will diminish—as traffic above the planned level will share the same network facilities.

In the model, as a simplification, we suppose that users have fixed usage profiles. We also assume that each IASP has only one type of service, meaning all its users

[16]Indicators used: concentration indexes (HHI, CR4), number of operating IASPs, market size, profitability, average age of competitors, and weighted averages and variances of market price and quality.

[17]Further details about parameter and initial conditions selection and sensibility analysis are available in Pereira (2012).

experience the same quality. Therefore, the quality of each IASP depends on how effective demand compares to the network capacity actually installed. We thus define the *ex post effective* quality level, M_t^i, offered by the IASP i to all its users in a given period t as[18]

$$M_t^i = \left(\frac{Q_t^{M,i}}{Q_t^i}\right)^q \tag{1}$$

M_t^i is inversely proportional to the current number of IASP i users, Q_t^i, and directly related to the installed capacity of the network in the same period, $Q_t^{M,i}$. q is a fixed parameter (set to 0.5) that accounts for any nonlinearity between capacity mismatch and quality. Each IASP plans its network to provide quality $M_t^i = 1$. Of course, this quality is achieved only if the real number of users equals the expected quantity. We are assuming, then, that the unit used for network capacity measurement is the number of "average users" it can support under a (notional) fixed level of target quality. The capital equipment vendor thus designs one unit of network physical capacity in order to exactly meet the demand from one user under such target quality level.

The network built by each IASP may consist of equipment of different technological generations (or "vintages"). When network expansion is required, the IASP acquires new equipment using the latest technology available. There is no substitution of capital already in place, except if equipment is fully depreciated (end of economic life). The total installed capacity in the network of IASP i, $Q_t^{M,i}$, depends on the productivity a_t^j and the stock $K_t^{i,j}$ of capital of each vintage j operating at the time. $N_t^{tech,i}$ represents the number of distinct vintages in operation in time t at IASP i.

$$Q_t^{M,i} = \sum_{j=1}^{N_t^{tech,i}} a_t^j K_t^{i,j} \tag{2}$$

IASPs assess the need for increasing installed capacity periodically (every 4 time steps or 1 year). To install new capacity, an investment I_t^i from IASP i is required in period t. New investment always incorporates the most recent technology available at t, j_t^C. Firms decide investment I_t^i based on the planned network capacity, $Q_t^{P,i}$, considering the existing capacity, $Q_t^{M,i}$, plus the running depreciation, D_t^i.

$$I_t^i = \begin{cases} \left(m_M^i Q_t^{P,i} - Q_{t-1}^{M,i} + D_t^i\right) P_t^{tech,C} & \text{if } m_M^i Q_t^{P,i} - Q_{t-1}^{M,i} + D_t^i \geq Q_{min}^j \\ Q_{min}^j P_t^{tech,j_c} & \text{if } m_M^i Q_t^{P,i} - Q_{t-1}^{M,i} + D_t^i < Q_{min}^j \end{cases}, \tag{3}$$

[18]Only some key equations are presented next. The full set of equations is reviewed in Pereira (2012). In what follows, the subscript t represents the t-th time step, the superscript i represents the i-th IASP, j, the j-th technology generation, and k, the k-th user.

$P_t^{tech,C}$ is the unit price of technology j_t^C. m_M^i is an adaptive parameter, adjusted according to the learning of IASP i along the simulation. The investment decision is subject to a technology-specific fixed minimum scale Q_{min}^j, even if the desired investment is below that threshold. As new technologies are launched, minimum scales increase with market size.

Firms plan network capacity, $Q_t^{P,i}$, prospectively for n periods (set to 4), by setting expectations about acquisition (or loss) of new users, that is, changes in relation to Q_t^i.

$$Q_t^{P,i} = \begin{cases} Q_t^i & \text{if } Q_t^i < Q_{t-n}^i \\ Q_t^i + \dfrac{m_Q^i \left(Q_t^i - Q_{t-n}^i\right)}{n} & \text{if } s_t^i \leq s^{inc} \\ Q_t^i + \dfrac{m_Q^i s_t^i \left(N_t^{user} - N_{t-n}^{user}\right)}{n} & \text{if } s_t^i > s^{inc} \end{cases} \tag{4}$$

The equation reflects a more aggressive behaviour of entrants. Smaller firms, with market share s_t^i below the fixed parameter s^{inc} (set to 0.2), project demand based on their own customer base evolution in previous planning period ($Q_t^i - Q_{t-n}^i$). On the other hand, larger firms ($s_t^i > s^{inc}$) evaluate future demand in terms of total market growth ($N_t^{user} - N_{t-n}^{user}$). N_t^{user} is the total number of effective users in the market (the sum of users of all IASPs). Parameter m_Q^i (set to 0.5) represents the qualitative expectations about the future, adjusting for how much of the past growth is expected to repeat itself in the future. When the IASP has an expectation of reduction in the number of customers ($Q_t^i < Q_{t-n}^i$), it keeps the existing installed capacity. This way, a reduction of capacity, if necessary, occurs only through equipment depreciation (D_t^i) without replacement, as described in (3), eliminating first the older vintages of network equipment.

IASPs may adjust their prices at every time step. Prices P_t^i are determined, in principle, based on the desired price $P_t^{d,i}$ that is compatible with a fixed target profitability margin on invested capital, m_L^i (set to 0.17).

$$P_t^{d,i} = \max\left[m_L^i \bar{k}_t^{e,i} + \bar{c}_t^{e,i}, \bar{P}_{t-1}\right], \quad \bar{k}_t^{e,i} = \frac{K_{t-1}^i}{Q_{t-1}^i}, \quad \bar{c}_t^{e,i} = \frac{C_{t-1}^i}{Q_{t-1}^i} \tag{5}$$

$\bar{k}_t^{e,i}$ is the expected average unit cost of capital of IASP i in t, K_{t-1}^i is the total capital employed in last period and Q_{t-1}^i is the number of users. $\bar{c}_t^{e,i}$ is the expected variable unit cost for the period and C_{t-1}^i is the total variable cost in last period. Therefore, the desired price is the one that produces the target profitability or the average weighted market price ($\bar{P}_{t-1}$), whichever is higher. $P_t^{d,i}$, $\bar{k}_t^{e,i}$, $\bar{c}_t^{e,i}$ and $\bar{P}_{t-1}$ are measured in monetary units (Brazilian Real).

The final price set by each IASP, P_t^i, depends also on its current market share change rate ($\dot{s}_t^i$) and the expected unit cost ($\bar{c}_t^{e,i}$). In a "*tâtonnement*" process, the IASP gradually increases P_t^i while it is below the desired price $P_t^{d,i}$ and market share is increasing ($\dot{s}_t^i > 0$). When losing market share ($\dot{s}_t^i > 0$), and its price is above unit cost ($\bar{c}_t^{e,i}$), the IASP gradually reduces price P_t^i. Otherwise, price is kept constant.

The entry of a new IASP may happen periodically (every 4 time steps). Entry is modelled as a decision event, whenever the average market profitability r_0 (set to 0.042) and the proportion of individuals without internet access over the total population s_e (set to 0.05) reach the thresholds.

$$Entry_t = \begin{cases} \text{no if } \frac{\pi_t^{aver}}{K_t^{aver}} \leq r_0 \quad \text{or } 1 - \frac{N_t^{aver}}{Pop_t} \leq s_e \\ \text{yes if } \frac{\pi_t^{aver}}{K_t^{aver}} > r_0 \quad \text{and } 1 - \frac{N_t^{aver}}{Pop_t} > s_e \end{cases} \tag{6}$$

π_t^{aver} are the market total profits, K_t^{aver} is the market total capital, N_t^{aver} is the total number of users, all measured as weighted moving average over 4 time steps, and Pop_t is the population size at time t. Once entry occurs, entrant installs a network that is, on average, a fraction of the total market capacity (set to 0.055) with fixed variance (equal to 0.03).

Exit of IASPs is driven by two factors: market share and profits. After a fixed number of time steps (set to 20) of negligible market share (<1 %) or negative profits, the IASP leaves the market.

Demand is modelled assuming that users are heterogeneous in two dimensions: budget and preferences. Each user k is interested in contracting internet access services for a given term (set to 1 year). After contracting with an IASP, user k pays a fixed price P_t^k each period, for the term of the contract, even if the IASP offers to new users a different access price in the future ($P_{t+k}^i, k = 1, 2, \ldots$). Quality M_t^i is the same for all users of IASP i in any time step t.

Every time a user is new or her contract expires, she ranks all IASPs according to a Cobb-Douglas expected utility function, $\widetilde{U}_t^{i,k}$, and selects the IASP with the highest expected utility considering her budget B_t^k (normally distributed with average 84).

$$\widetilde{U}_t^{i,k} = \left(\frac{\bar{P}_{t-1}}{P_t^i}\right)^{b_1^k} \left(\widetilde{M}_{t-1}^{i,k}\right)^{b_2^k} \left(s_{t-1}^i\right)^{b_3^k}, \quad b_1^k + b_2^k + b_3^k = 1 \tag{7}$$

Parameters b_1^k (random uniform in [0.3,0.6]), b_2^k (~[0.1,0.6]) and b_3^k (~[0.1,0.3]) represent the weights the user attributes to price, quality and market share when valuating IASPs. P_t^i is the IASP i current price, s_t^i is its market share and $\bar{P}_t$ is the weighted average market price.

$\widetilde{M}_t^{i,k}$ is the expected quality of IASP i as perceived by user k. Expected quality $\widetilde{M}_t^{i,k}$ will be usually different from M_t^i, the real quality experienced *after* the service is contracted. The expected quality $\widetilde{M}_t^{i,k}$ is derived from M_{t-1}^i plus some normal random noise ($\mu = 0, \sigma = e_d^k = \sim[0, 0.5]$), assuming the user can learn about quality only through inaccurate social interaction.

The $\left(s_{t-1}^i\right)^{b_3^k}$ term in (7) is a proxy to the relational influence of other users' choices on the individual preferences (a kind of "word of mouth" social effect) and represents an *expected* positive externality to larger IASPs. This bias might cause the user to choose an IASP with inferior objective attributes (in price or quality), but more "popular", even in the absence of tangible benefits. The mechanism was inserted to allow the testing the relevance of social interaction when defining users' preferences. Thus, the *ex ante* expected utility $\widetilde{U}_t^{i,k}$ is usually different from the *ex post* effective utility the user experiences. If network externalities are not present—at least for the user's benefit, as discussed in Sect. 3—the effective utility shall depend only on the price and the effective quality (M_t^i) and not on the IASP size (s_{t-1}^i) or the expected quality ($\widetilde{M}_{t-1}^{i,k}$).

The selection mechanism on Eq. (6) also represents an implicit *replicator equation* (Metcalfe 1998) because, as all individual users choose their IASPs, it defines the resulting market shares for each IASP, in each period. There is no automatic market clearing, once users with insufficient budget B_t^k remain out of a contract even if no IASP cheap enough exists (prices are sticky during the time-step).

To keep the model simple, no competition was assumed in the market for capital goods (network equipment). A single vendor performs all technical innovation and supplies network equipment to all IASPs under the same conditions. At any time, there is a single best technology generation, in terms of productivity, and all IASPs are aware of it.

There are two types of technological innovation drivers in the model: "incremental", associated to improvements of existing technology vintages, and "radical", when new equipment vintages are introduced. Accordingly, two types of search routines are configured, both modelled as two-stage stochastic, productivity-enhancer processes. Thus, stochastic components are not required in the technical search of IASPs, since the model assumes that they simply pick the most current equipment vintage available, when convenient.

There is at each time step a probability $0 \leq \Pr\left(d_t^j = 1\right) \leq 1$ of an incremental technological advance for every existing technology j. The creation of a new technology at time t has probability $0 \leq \Pr\left(d_t = 1\right) \leq 1$. These probabilities have Poisson distribution:

$$\Pr_{\text{incr}}\left(d_t^j = 1\right) \sim \text{Poisson}\left[\frac{\left(t - t_0^{incr,j}\right)}{p_{incr}}\right], \quad \Pr_{\text{rad}}\left(d_t = 1\right) \sim \text{Poisson}\left[\frac{(t - t_C)}{p_{rad}}\right] \tag{8}$$

The success parameters are p_{incr} (incremental innovation period of existing vintages, set to 8 or 2 years) and p_{rad} (period between new technology vintages, set to 28 or 7 years). $t_0^{incr,j}$ is the last period at which an incremental innovation was applied to technology j and t_C is the period at which the current top technology was introduced.

If the first stage, in (8), spawns a technical advance, a new potential for the technology productivity, $\hat{a}_t^j$ (incremental) or $\hat{a}_t^{jc+1}$ (radical), is generated from a normal distribution, with average based on current productivity a^j_{t-1} or $a^{j_c}_{t-1}$, respectively.

$$\hat{a}^j_t \sim \mathrm{N}\left(a^j_{t-1}, v^j_t a^j_{t-1}\right), \quad \hat{a}^{jc+1}_t \sim \mathrm{N}\left[\left(1+v_{rad}\right) a^{jc}_{t-1}, v_{rad} a^{jc}_{t-1}\right] \tag{9}$$

a^j_{t-1} is the current productivity of technology j and v^j_t is the standard deviation of incremental productivity improvements, decreasing as technology gets mature.

$$v^j_t = v_{incr} - \frac{v_{incr}}{1+\exp\left(v_0\left(1-\frac{t-t^j_0}{p_{rad}}\right)\right)} \tag{10}$$

v_{rad} (equal to 1.7), v_{incr} (equal to 0.049), and v_0 (equal to 5), are fixed parameters that define the range and the decay over time of expected innovation results.

Technical advance is adopted only if it improves productivity. This means if $\hat{a}^j_t > a^j_{t-1}$, for incremental innovation, or if $\hat{a}^{jc+1}_t > a^{jc}_{t-1}$, for radical innovation.

$$a^j_t = max\left(a^j_{t-1}, \hat{a}^j_t\right), \quad a^{jc+1}_t = \begin{cases} 0 & \text{if } \hat{a}^{jc+1}_t \le a^{jc}_{t-1} \\ \hat{a}^{jc+1}_t & \text{if } \hat{a}^{jc+1}_t > a^{jc}_{t-1} \end{cases} \tag{11}$$

Adoption of new vintage equipment by IASPs may yet depend on the requirement of a government license. It is configured in the model as a synchronization of radical innovations and incumbent's capital stock depreciation. This mechanism should allow us to test the institutional hypothesis, as described in the previous section.

5 Model Results and Analysis

In general, our model outcomes were qualitatively close to the empirical data and stylized facts. In principle, results seem compatible with the two institutional hypotheses proposed in Sect. 3, but this conclusion is not trivial, because the other mechanisms probably were also in action. We start this section with a brief overview of the results from the simulated IASM, then we move on to the analysis of the mechanisms reproducing the empirical stylized facts in the virtual IASM.

All model results were evaluated by statistical parameter estimation over samples of 100 simulation runs, due to the presence of stochastic elements in the model. Sample size was selected to ensure at least ±5 % precision of results, at 95 % confidence level. The statistical distributions of most variables were unimodal and reasonably symmetrical to justify the adoption of averages and variances as descriptive parameters of model results.

The total number of IASPs in the simulated market usually grew up to $t = 100$, from 4 to around 10 players, falling from there on and converging to about 5 firms at $t = 250$ (the end of simulation). Model data investigation shows that restless

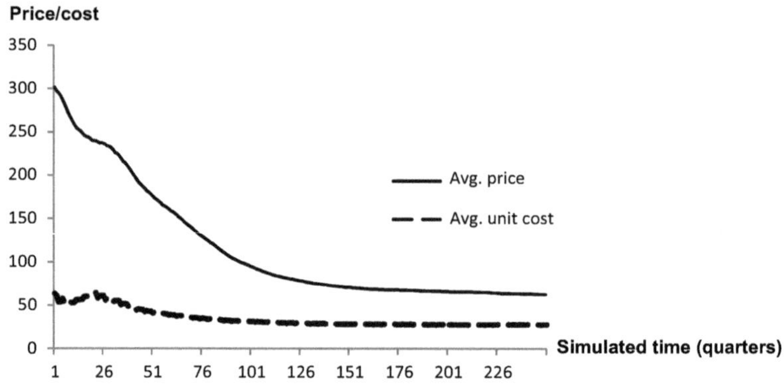

Fig. 2 Average market weighted price and unit cost (in BRL). (Empirical calibration scenario)

turbulence among entrants, associated to relative stability among incumbents, had an unequivocal outcome: the tendency of lasting concentration of the IASM in the hands of few incumbents. The overall market competition remained very limited in most simulation runs, with the Herfindahl-Hirschman index (HHI) for market shares relatively stable and above 0.6 for most of the simulated time. Calculation of the HHI for capital shares (network sizes) provided similar results. Concentration, in any case, was substantially above the levels that conventionally characterize a market as highly concentrated.

The weighted average price in the virtual market showed a continuous downward trend, also compatible with the real case. During the phase of fast market growth ($t < 100$) average prices fell more quickly, but stabilized afterwards, as shown in Fig. 2. Conversely, average profitability decreased during the fast growing phase and stagnated after all, as represented by the gap between the average price and unit cost in Fig. 2. Nonetheless, average mark-ups remained high and the rate of return on invested capital (RoIC) of incumbents were up to 10 times higher than that of entrants when market matures ($t > 100$). In-depth analysis of model runs shows that incumbents usually decreased prices less frequently, due to more stable market shares and better margins. During the market growth phase, entrants usually adopt price-based competition, by being more price-aggressive than incumbents are. Entrants more frequently adopted low prices, led by the need to acquire market share. However, as market matured, flimsy financial conditions frequently drove entrants out of the market. These general outcomes are also comparable with empirical data.

The market concentration results are consistent with stylized fact SF1 (*persistent market concentration*), as the HHI plots in Fig. 3, well above the usual concentration thresholds, illustrate. The "calibration" curve (or scenario 0) shows the model output under the "history-friendly" calibration values. It is interesting that this result is not a structural feature of the model. Configuring the model with adequate counterfactual parameter sets, one can generate remarkably distinct competitive results. Figure 3

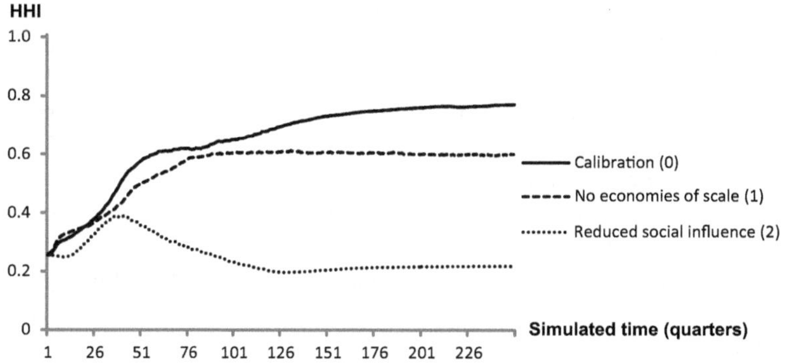

Fig. 3 Herfindahl-Hirschman index for market share. (Empirical calibration plus two counterfactual scenarios)

also presents model's results when employing two counterfactual parameter sets (scenarios 1 and 2), chosen because they test the relative influence of some of the theoretical hypotheses presented in Sect. 3.

The presence of economies of scale in a sector such as the internet is usually acknowledged as a concentration driver—and was therefore considered in the calibration scenario. Counterfactual scenario 1 tests the importance of economies of scale for the observed results, by removing its influence in the model. However, this does not change the general competitive outcomes, in spite of a reduction of about 0.20 in the HHI, as depicted in Fig. 3 ("no economies of scale" curve).

Other candidates for explaining the high market concentration were also tested. Of special interest is scenario 2 presented in Fig. 3 ("reduced social influence" curve), because concentration is strongly reduced. HHI is reduced from about 0.8 to 0.2 at the end of simulation. The key parameter changed to this effect was b_3^k (from the interval [0.1, 0.3] to [0.0, 0.2] in Eq. (7)), already described in Sect. 4. This represented a reduction, on average, of 50 % of the influence of other users' choices when defining individual preferences—and corresponding increases in the relevance of price and expected quality. Interestingly, the results produced in scenario 2 are much closer to the usually expected outcomes of a market operating under standard Schumpeterian, technology-driven competition.

Several other scenarios were tested: more or less non-linearity in quality perception (q in Eq. (1)), reduced uncertainty about past quality (e_d^k), increased aggressiveness in price and quality (network capacity) of IASP offers (m_Q^i, s_{inc} in Eq. (4)), lower minimum required technology scale (Q_{min}^j in Eq. (3)), reduced target profitability margins (m_L^i in Eq. (5)), greater average size and number of entrants (k_0, e^{max}), smaller entry threshold parameters (r_0, s_e in Eq. (6)), among the more relevant. In all cases, the counterfactual parameter sets produced changes in market concentration in the expected directions, but of modest magnitude. HHIs remained consistently above 0.4 at the end (and during most) of the simulated time, even when we combined some of the extreme parameter sets.

The results above seem to reject the dominant role of most of the theoretical hypotheses discussed before. Static barriers to entry, although relevant, were not decisive, at least in the form of economies of scale and minimum efficient size. Sunk costs and first mover advantages were not decisive to incumbent success and concentration level. In several simulation runs, incumbents failed and a few entrants became new incumbents over time. As will be shown next, reducing the importance of sunk costs (in installed networks) helps entrants, but not to a degree at which overall competition is improved. Collusion among incumbents also did not play a role, once the base history-friendly scenario already preclude this hypothesis—and its inclusion certainly would not have a positive influence on concentration—reducing it.

As the model is configured, the most relevant cause for concentration in the model is the positive feedback between the number of users of an IASP and its perceived utility, creating a positive externality to larger IASPs. Even when this feedback is reduced by a relatively modest amount—but not removed—the level of concentration can be significantly reduced, as depicted in Fig. 3. However, why not explain this outcome in terms of standard network externalities? Here we have to go back to the theoretical definition of the concept. In general, the concept of network externality is associated to increased returns to adoption by *users*. The idea behind it is that products or technologies "that by chance gains an early lead in adoption [...] often display increasing returns to adoption in that the more they are adopted, the more experience is gained with them, and the more they are improved" (Arthur 1989). In this situation, "the [effective] utility of each consumer increases with an increase in the total number of consumers purchasing the same [product]" (Shy 2001). However, the point in case is *why* utility increases when more consumers purchase the same product. In all the classical examples (telephony, hardware standards, etc.), the increase in the consumers' effective utility is clear. A phone network with more users to call to is definitely more useful than one with fewer correspondents. A computer that adopts a hardware specification that is compatible with a broader selection of software is certainly preferable to a non-standard one, for which few developers would be interested to develop applications. In summary, the usual network externalities concept implicitly assumes that some concrete product attribute is actually enhanced by its increased adoption, so rational users—or at least part of them—have a tangible increase in their utilities and are in a better situation if most select this product instead of others.

In our case, however, the recurrent selection of larger IASPs does not place users in a better situation, although under uncertainty the user may attach more value to bigger IASPs, increasing its expected utility. To be sure, the *expected* utility attributed to an IASP may increase with the number of other agents choosing that IASP, but users are not better off simply because more users adopt a specific IASP, i.e., their *effective* utility is not improved. Frequently, exactly the opposite happens. As users rush for the same few large IASPs, it is common that those firms' networks become the busiest and so provide low effective quality to its users—this is a common situation in practice. Typically, other things being equal, *ex post* the most utility-enhancing choice would have been picking a smaller IASP. In our case, the purchase decisions of users, if taken in a perfect foresight scenario, would be *unaffected* by any network effects associated to IASP network size.[19] However, as IASPs are unable to precisely forecast the demand or to freely adjust their networks capacity, there is nothing close to a "perfect foresight" scenario on the demand side. Similarly, because quality is only defined *ex post*, users' choices are also hardly optimizing and are all the more subject to the application of adaptive, experience-based rules. The empirical evidence seems to corroborate out-of-equilibrium outcomes, showing (1) cyclical behaviour of IASPs in terms of both network expansion and the ratio between installed capacity and the number of users, and (2) significant levels of constant user migration among (mostly large) providers (Pereira 2012).

Considering the above, we suggest that a better explanation for the inclination of users towards larger IASPs may be the adoption of institutional rules, usually taken-for-granted. Institutional-based, endogenous preferences are not a usual justification for market concentration, despite being highlighted by other authors, such as Jonard and Yildizoğlu (1998) and Birke and Swann (2006). In accordance with Beckert (2009), we propose that "uncertainty leads actors to resort to socially anchored scripts or 'conventions' that serve as a 'collective recognized reference', providing orientation for intentionally rational actors in situations where optimal responses cannot be foreseen". Among the uncertainties that agents face in the market, the one regarding how to assess the "fair" value of a product like internet access is probably one of the toughest, considering that even the sellers (IASPs) cannot reliably demonstrate the value of their service offers.

Nevertheless, acknowledging that the usual perspective of stable, well defined preferences may not be adequate in markets like the IASM is far from implying that choice is purely random, as sometimes suggested (e.g., Stigler and Becker 1977). To circumvent these polar alternatives, we suggest that users are frequently able to establish alternative forms of classification for heterogeneous products, and, among those, imitation may be a simple and effective choice. Without all information required to adequately assess the value of a product, relying on socially constructed judgements is a customary approach and the use of one's network ties to search for information may become an effective form of preference linking among users—or imitation (DiMaggio and Louch 1998; Orléan 2003).[20]

As mentioned before, weak financial performance was the immediate cause of SF2 (*low rate of successful entry*) in the simulation. The persistently low margins captured by the average entrant—79 % less than those of incumbents—made them financially fragile, particularly after the introduction of new technological generations, as the model data show. The comparatively low RoIC of entrants is somewhat intriguing, given the usual advantage of more up-to-date technology held

[19]Considering the full interconnection of the competing access networks, as it is generally the case as discussed before.

[20]Our argument here involves two of the several explanations for conformity with a shared rule of behavior or thought discussed in Dequech (2013): uncertainty; and the possibility that others have better information.

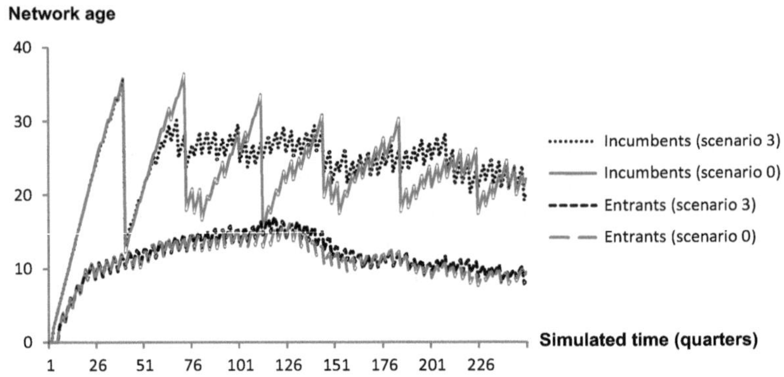

Fig. 4 Weighted average age of network equipment (in quarters). (Empirical calibration plus counterfactual scenario 3)

by entrants, who consequently operate under higher productivity and lower unit costs than incumbents. The simulation data on the average age of networks of incumbents and entrants in Fig. 4 shows the relevant advantage of entrants (see curves for the base scenario 0). On average, the incumbents' networks were about two times older than the entrants' (20.9 vs. 10.9 months).

The average capital productivity curves (shown in Pereira 2012) present a similar advantage of entrants in terms of unit costs. However, model data analysis shows that the incumbents' advantage continued essentially because of the persistently larger user bases. The relative ease of retaining old users and attracting new ones drove the incumbents' prices high and costs low, even when unit cost is not close to industry's benchmark. Elevated average prices are a consequence of the limited need to resort to price competition. Lower total costs are due to economies of scale and high network utilization compensating the higher unit costs. On the other hand, the entrants' relatively lower prices and higher costs squeeze their margins and cash flows. Again, the same root cause found above for SF1 seems to be at play here. The positive feedback of a larger user base increases the perceived value or utility of an IASP and creates a vicious circle to entrants, preventing their growth. This situation seems to be rarely avoided, both in the simulation and in the real IASM.

The stress on financial resources of entrants is critical in moments of radical innovation. When new vintages of equipment are introduced, the additional investment necessary to keep up with the competition may prove incompatible with the cash flows of entrants. This mismatch increases the probability of bankruptcy of entrants, due to excessive debt or higher costs. However, for entrants able to survive to new technology introduction, newer equipment generations enhance the competitive position of the entrant *vis-à-vis* the incumbents, because of lower unit costs. Therefore, there is a balance between risk and opportunity associated to the radical innovation adoption.

Figure 5 shows some counterfactuals on this last point. It presents the impact of different scenarios for the radical innovation cycle period (p_{rad} in Eq. (8)) over

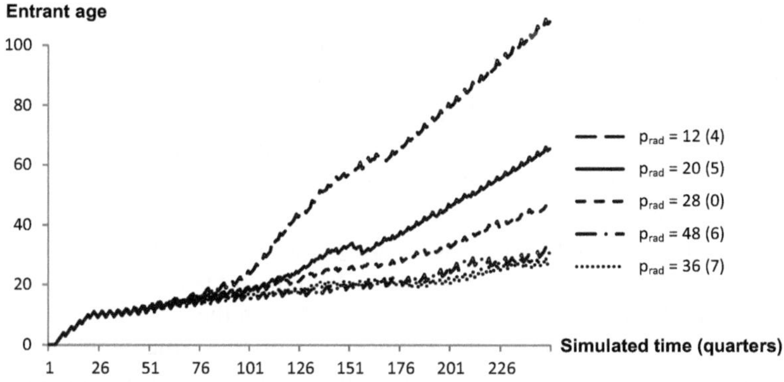

Fig. 5 Average lifetime of entrants (in quarters). (Empirical calibration plus 4 counterfactual scenarios for different average periods between radical innovations)

expected entrant lifetime. As before, scenario 0 ($p_{rad} = 28$ or 7 years) is the history-friendly base case. From Fig. 5, it is evident that short innovation cycles result, on average, in longer life for entrants. In the shortest case ($p_{rad} = 12$ or 3 years), entrant's life expectancy almost triples and the average survival rate reaches 44 %. On the opposite, in the case of $p_{rad} > 36$(9 years), lifetime is less than two times below the base case and the average survival rate is only 8 %. Notwithstanding the entrant's greater exposure to financial failures during new technology introduction, shorter innovation cycles also create more *windows of opportunity* for entrants with sound balance sheets. During these periods, fit entrants can aggressively undercut incumbents' prices and conquer enough market share to try to escape from the small-size vicious cycle. The larger investments required for network upgrade impose financial strain also on incumbents, momentarily reducing the space they have to compete in price while keeping enough quality (i.e., expanding the network). In simulation, the windows of opportunity were the main factor allowing entrants to cross the critical 20 % mark for market share long enough to become an established incumbent IASP. The (relatively small) probability of this migration was inversely proportional to p_{rad}.

The discussion about the importance of frequent introduction of new network generations (i.e., radical innovation) leads us to SF3 (*longer than expected technological diffusion cycles*). The simulation presented a system-level behaviour that seems similar to the real IASM. According to anecdotal evidence, incumbents have a competitive advantage over entrants when new technologies are introduced after their existing networks have been adequately depreciated. At this moment, they are usually at their peak cash position and fully ready to start a deep and fast network investment cycle. These massive technology upgrade cycles are easily identified in Fig. 4 (incumbents, scenario 0 curve), when incumbents quickly upgraded 47 % of their network facilities in average. Even so, incumbents were able to sustain an average RoIC above 20 % even in the harshest competitive situations. At the same moments, entrants frequently have presented negative RoIC.

As discussed in Sect. 3, we suspect that an informal institutional rule may have supported the operation of the Brazilian IASM in a "financially-driven" pace of new technological generation introduction. To test if this (possibly taken-for-granted) strategy of the regulatory agency would have a relevant impact on competition, another counterfactual scenario was created. Therefore, in scenario 3, the mechanism that had been included in the simulation model to adjust the pace of radical innovation to the financial depreciation of networks, according to the historical timing of regulatory licenses issuing, was disabled. The scenario 3 curves presume no correlation between investments from incumbents and new technology introduction, introducing a "technology-driven" rule in the model.

As can be noted in Fig. 4, the replacement of the "financially-driven" rule resulted in substantial changes in incumbent investment behaviour, despite the absence of impact on entrants. The well-marked cycles of incumbents' networks upgrade are mostly gone. This move considerably increased the cost advantage held by entrants during the critical periods of strong technical change. Incumbents could no longer cover the gap to the entrants' more productive networks fast enough, due to new financial constraints—the required cash flow to massively replace networks not yet fully depreciated. The average RoIC of incumbents under the "technology-driven" rule went as low as 12 % during competitive stress moments (40 % less than before), while the entrants' RoIC barely changed. Along the full simulation, the elimination of the "financially-driven" rule decreased the lifespan expectancy of incumbents by about 25 %, while increasing average entrant lifetime by 51 %. Consequently, the model shows the clear competitive edge provided to incumbents by a "financially-driven" rule.

It stands clear, though, that the policy promoted by the regulatory agency probably was deviated from its intended target of fostering competition in the Brazilian IASM. If we assume no (illicit) capture of ANATEL, for the reasons presented in Sect. 3, it is plausible that this situation may have taken place because of a particular taken-for-granted mental model, used for a long time to manage the uncertainty associated to the technological dynamics during the State monopoly time. Even if such a model had been clearly inadequate to provide good advice for the post-privatization period, it is reasonable to expect that such taken-for-granted mental schemes would take some time to vanish. Of course, this does not preclude the simultaneous coincidence of strategic behaviour of incumbents interested in the *status quo*. However, other than supposing that they are the only rational agents in this game, is seems unlikely that a purely utilitarian explanation provides an adequate account of the game.

6 Conclusion

Our empirical analysis suggests the description of the Brazilian internet access services market by at least three stylized facts: persistent market concentration, low rate of successful entry of new competitor firms, and longer than expected technological diffusion cycles. These characteristics are distinct from other markets in the internet sector. We propose that different cooperation-competition profiles among the various markets of the internet sector were established over time. In Schumpeterian terms, time trajectories of markets like equipment, systems and content tended to a more *creative destruction*-type dynamics, while others, like access services, apparently took a *creative accumulation* path in some countries. From our point of view, this was due, to some extent, to the persistence of certain institutional characteristics of the former telecommunications monopoly regime and to the attributes of the sector's product itself. Firstly, some inherited informal institutions facilitated the dominance of the internet access services sector by firms originated from the privatized State monopoly. Secondly, special characteristics of the internet access service, in particular quality uncertainty, fostered the adoption of institutional mechanisms by users when evaluating this product, favouring established service providers. Such features seem to fit adequately to the case of Brazil, as empirical research indicated.

The proposed History-friendly simulation model produced results that were quite close, in qualitative terms, to those observed in the actual internet access market. Some of the main reasons for market concentration and limited competition could be objectively identified with emergent institutional phenomena. Of interest are the effects of *downward causation* of collective choices in the setting of user preferences. The model also provided explanations for other mechanisms dampening competition, highlighting the sometimes crucial effects of established informal and taken-for-granted rules on governmental decisions. The role of technological dynamics for the organization of the IASM was clarified, including its potentially contradictory effects. The relevance of institutional processes does not mean that traditional elements of industrial analysis, such as those emphasized in industrial organization or evolutionary theory, have not played their expected role. However, as the model demonstrated, some of the results, usually explained by these traditional elements exclusively, may depend crucially on the presence of the noted institutional factors.

Acknowledgments We wish to thank José Maria Silveira, Marco Valente, Esther Dweck, Paulo Fracalanza, Mariano Laplane, Thadeu Silva, André Gimenez, and an anonymous referee for their helpful comments on earlier versions of this work or otherwise their invaluable support to it. We are responsible for all remaining errors. This work was done with the support of CNPq, Conselho Nacional de Desenvolvimento Científico e Tecnológico—Brasil.

A.1 Appendix: Model Configuration

State variables				
Internet access providers (i)				
Name	Description	Lags	Initial value	Source
M_t^i	Network quality of access service in t	0		
P_t^i	Price of access service offered in t	1	300	CETIC.BR
s_t^i	Market share in t	1	0.25	Arbitrary
Q_t^i	Total number of users in t	0		
$Q_t^{M,i}$	Total installed network capacity in t	1	$\mu = 25$, $\sigma = 25$	IASM BR
K_t^i	Total capital employed in t	0		
$K_t^{i,j}$	Total capital in technology j in t	0		
I_t^i	Investment in t	0		
D_t^i	Depreciation in t	0		
$N_t^{tech,i}$	Number of technologies used in t	0		
$\bar{k}_t^{e,i}$	Expected average unit capital cost in t	0		
$\bar{c}_t^{e,i}$	Expected average unit variable cost	0		
C_t^i	Operational costs in t	0		
π_t^i	Profits/losses in t	0		
AL_t^i	Accumulated profits/losses in t	0		
Network technologies (*j*)				
$P_t^{tech,j}$	Unit price of technology in t	0		
Q_{min}^j	Minimum required capacity	1	10	Arbitrary
a_t^j	Productivity in t	1	0.00093	IASM BR
cm_t^j	Unit maintenance cost in t	0		

Internet access providers (i)				
Name	Description	Lags	Initial value	Source
$\Pr\left(d_t^j = 1\right)$	Probability of incremental innovation	0		
$\Pr(d_t = 1)$	Probability of radical innovation in *t*	0		
Users (*k*)				
B_t^k	User budget in *t*	1	$\mu = 84,$ $\sigma = 180$	CETIC.BR
$\widetilde{M}_t^{i,k}$	Expected quality of IASP *i* in *t*	0		
$P_t^{user,k}$	Price to be paid by user in *t*	0		
$\tilde{u}_t^{i,k}$	Expected utility of IASP *i* in *t*	0		
$Prov_t^k$	Selected IASP in *t*	0		
Other				
$\bar{P}_t$	Average weighted market price in *t*	0		
N_t^{user}	Total number of users in market in *t*	0		
N_t^{prov}	Total number of IASPs in market in *t*	1	4	TELEBRASIL

Parameters			
Name	Description	Value	Source
g_{users}	Logistic growth rate of the number of potential users	0.048	CETIC.BR
pop_0	Initial population of potential users (×10,000)	180	CETIC.BR
pop_{max}	Final population of potential users (×10,000)	11,700	CETIC.BR
T^{avg}	Average user contract duration	4	IASM BR
T^{var}	Variance of user contract duration	2	IASM BR
b_1^k	Price sensitivity in expected utility	[0.3, 0.6]	Arbitrary
b_3^k	IASP size sensitivity in expected utility	[0.1, 0.3]	Arbitrary
e_d^k	Standard deviation of quality perception error	[0.0, 0.5]	Arbitrary

Name	Description	Value	Source
e_s^k	Minimum utility improvement before IASP change	[1.0, 1.5]	Arbitrary
cm_0	Maintenance to initial cost of technology ratio	0.0053	TELEBRASIL
c_f	Fixed cost per user per quarter	102	TELEBRASIL
c_s	Scale factor for operating costs	0.9	IASM BR
m_L^i	Target rate of return on invested capital	0.17	IASM BR
m_Q^i	Response profile on forecasting user base growth	0.5	Arbitrary
T^{plan}	Network planning period	4	IASM BR
g_s^{sens}	Minimum acuity for market share change rate	0.05	Arbitrary
p_{step}	Price change incremental step rate	0.05	Arbitrary
p_{incr}	Poisson probability of incremental innovation	8	IASM BR
p_{rad}	Poisson probability of radical innovation	28	TELEBRASIL, SEPIN
v_{incr}	Standard deviation of incremental innovation	0.049	IASM BR
v_{rad}	Standard deviation of incremental innovation	1.7	IASM BR
e^{max}	Maximum number of entrants per period	1	ANATEL
s_e	Minimum available market share to entry	0.05	Arbitrary
k_0	Average size of entrant to total market	0.055	TELEBRASIL
s^{min}	Minimum market share to stay in the market	0.01	Arbitrary
T_{min}^e	Minimum period between entries	4	ANATEL
n_{exit}	Number of bad periods (share and profits) before exit	20	Arbitrary
s^{inc}	Minimum market share of incumbentes	0.2	SEAE/SDE
T^{inc}	Minimum period in market to become incumbent	20	Arbitrary
q	Quality sensitivity non-linearity	0.5	Arbitrary
r_0	Interest rate base per period	0.042	BNDES

Information sources	
ANATEL	Agência Nacional de Telecomunicações
Arbitrary	Selected as justified in Pereira (2012)
BNDES	Banco Nacional de Desenvolvimento Econômico e Social
CETIC.BR	Centro de Estudos sobre as Tecnologias da Informação e da Comunicação
IASM BR	Common anecdotal practices of the IASM in Brazil in Dec 2011
SEAE/SDE	Secretaria de Acompanhamento Econômico/Secretaria de Direito Econômico
SEPIN	Secretaria de Política de Informática e Automação
TELEBRASIL	Associação Brasileira de Telecomunicações

References

Akerlof GA (1970) The market for "lemons": quality uncertainty and the market mechanism. Q J Econ 84:488–500

Arthur WB (1989) Competing technologies, increasing returns, and lock-in by historical events. Econ J 99:116–131

Arthur WB (2000) Cognition: the black box of economics. In: Colander D (ed) The complexity vision and the teaching of economics. Edward Elgar, Cheltenham

Battilana J, Leca B, Boxenbaum E (2009) How actors change institutions: towards a theory of institutional entrepreneurship. Acad Manag Ann 3:65–107

Baumol WJ, Panzar JC, Willig RD (1982) Contestable markets and the theory of industry structure. Harcourt Brace Jovanovich, San Diego

Beckert J (1999) Agency, entrepreneurs, and institutional change: the role of strategic choice and institutionalized practices in organizations. Organ Stud 20:777–799

Beckert J (2009) The social order of markets. Theory Soc 38:245–269. doi:10.1007/s11186-008-9082-0

Besen SM, Israel MA (2012) The evolution of internet interconnection from hierarchy to "Mesh": implications for government regulation. SSRN 30

Birke D, Swann P (2006) Network effects and the choice of mobile phone operator. J Evol Econ 16:65–84

Bowles S (2004) Microeconomics: behavior, institutions, and evolution. Princeton University Press, New York, p 584

Breschi S, Malerba F, Orsenigo L (2000) Technological regimes and Schumpeterian patterns of innovation. Econ J 110:388–410

Colander D (2005) The future of economics: the appropriately educated in pursuit of the knowable. Camb J Econ 29:927–941

Corrocher N (2001) The internet services industry: sectoral dynamics of innovation and production and country-specific trends in Italy and in the UK. www2.cespri.unibocconi.it/essy/wp/corroch.pdf. Accessed 28 Nov 2011

Davies A (1996) Innovation in large technical systems: the case of telecommunications. Ind Corp Chang 5:1143–1180

Denzau A, North DC (1994) Shared mental models: ideologies and institutions. Kyklos 47:3–31

Dequech D (2013) Economic institutions: explanations for conformity and room for deviation. J Inst Econ 8:28. doi:10.1017/S1744137412000197

DiMaggio PJ (1988) Interest and agency in institutional theory. In: Zucker LG (ed) Institutional patterns organization: culture and environment. Ballinger, Cambridge, MA, pp 3–21
DiMaggio PJ, Louch H (1998) Socially embedded consumer transactions: for what kinds of purchases do people most often use networks? Am Sociol Rev 63:619–637
DiMaggio PJ, Powell WW (1983) The iron cage revisited: institutional isomorphism and collective rationality in organizational fields. Am Sociol Rev 48:147–160
DiMaggio PJ, Powell WW (1991) Introduction. The New institutionalism in organizational analysis. University of Chicago Press, Chicago
Dodd M, Jung A, Mitchell B et al (2009) Bill-and-keep and the economics of interconnection in next-generation networks. Telecommun Policy 33:324–337
Dosi G (1988) Sources, procedures, and microeconomic effects of innovation. J Econ Lit 26:1120–1171
Dosi G (1982) Technological paradigms and technological trajectories: a suggested interpretation of the determinants and directions of technical change. Res Policy 11:147–162
Dosi G, Malerba F, Marsili O, Orsenigo L (1997) Industrial structures and dynamics: evidence, interpretations and puzzles. Ind Corp Chang 6:3–24
Dosi G, Nelson RR (2010) Technical change and industrial dynamics as evolutionary processes. In Hall BH, Rosenberg N (eds), Handbook of the economics of innovation, vol 1. North-Holland, Amsterdam, pp 51–128
Edquist C (2004) The fixed internet and mobile telecommunications sectoral system of innovation: equipment production, access provision and content provision. In: Malerba F (ed) Sectoral system of innovation: concepts, issues and analyses of six major sectors in Europe Cambridge Press, Cambridge, pp 155–192
Fagerberg J (2003) Schumpeter and the revival of evolutionary economics: an appraisal of the literature. J Evol Econ 13:125–159. doi:10.1007/s00191-003-0144-1
Faratin P, Clark DD, Bauer S et al (2009) The growing complexity of internet interconnection. Commun Strateg 72:51–71
Fligstein N (2001) The architecture of markets. An economic sociology of twenty-first-century capitalist societies. Princeton University Press, p 274.
Fligstein N, Dauter L (2007) The sociology of markets. Annu Rev Sociol 33:105–128
Funk JL (2008) The co-evolution of technology and methods of standard setting: the case of the mobile phone industry. J Evol Econ 19:73–93. doi:10.1007/s00191-008-0108-6
Garavaglia C (2010) Modelling industrial dynamics with "history-friendly" simulations. Struct Chang Econ Dyn 21:258–275. doi:10.1016/j.strueco.2010.07.001
Granovetter M (2005) The impact of social structure on economic outcomes. J Econ Lit 19:33–50
Greenstein S (2010) The emergence of the internet: collective invention and wild ducks. Ind Corp Chang 19:1521–1562. doi:10.1093/icc/dtq047
Hodgson GM (1988) Economics and institutions. University of Pennsylvania Press, Philadelphia
Internet Society (2010) An introduction to internet interconnection concepts and actors. Internet Society Brief Paper 8.
Jonard N, Yildizoğlu M (1998) Technological diversity in an evolutionary industry model with localized learning and network externalities. Struct Chang Econ Dyn 9:35–53
Kavassalis P, Solomon RJ, Benghozi P-J (1996) The internet: a paradigmatic rupture in cumulative telecom evolution. Ind Corp Chang 5:1097–1126
Klepper S (1996) Entry, exit, growth, and innovation over the product life cycle. Am Econ Rev 86:562–583
Laffont J, Rey P, Tirole J (1998) Network competition: II. Price discrimination. RAND J Econ 29:38–56
Laffont J-J, Marcus S, Rey P, Tirole J (2003) Internet interconnection and the off-net-cost pricing principle. RAND J Econ 34:370–390
Laffont J-J, Tirole J (2000) Competition in telecommunications. MIT Press, Cambridge, MA, p 331
Malerba F (2006) Innovation and the evolution of industries. J Evol Econ 16:3–23. doi:10.1007/s00191-005-0005-1

Malerba F, Nelson RR, Orsenigo L, Winter SG (1999) "History-friendly" models of industry evolution: the computer industry. Ind Corp Chang 8:3–40
Malerba F, Orsenigo L (2000) Knowledge, innovative activities and industrial evolution. Ind Corp Chang 9:289–314
McAfee RP, Mialon HM, Williams MA (2004) What is a barrier to entry? Am Econ Rev 94:461–465
Metcalfe JS (1998) Evolutionary economics and creative destruction. Routledge, New York
Nelson RR (1995) Recent evolutionary theorizing about economic change. J Econ Lit 33:48–90
Nelson RR (2005) Physical and social technologies, and their evolution. In: Nelson RR (ed) Technology, institutions and economic growth. Harvard Press, Cambridge, MA, pp 195–209
Nelson RR, Sampat B (2001) Making sense of institutions as a factor shaping economic performance. J Econ Behav Organ 44:31–54
Noam EM (1994) Beyond liberalisation: from the network of networks to the system of systems. Telecommun Policy 18:286–294
North DC (1990) Institutions, institutional change and economic performance. Cambridge Press, Cambridge
Orléan A (2003) Réflexion sur les fondements institutionnels de l'objectivité marchande. Cah d' Économie Polit 44:181–196
Pavitt K (1984) Sectoral patterns of technological change: towards a taxonomy and a theory. Res Policy 13:343–374
Pereira MC (2012) O setor de internet no Brasil: Uma análise da competição no mercado de acesso. Universidade Estadual de Campinas
Pereira P, Ribeiro T (2011) The impact on broadband access to the internet of the dual ownership of telephone and cable networks. Int J Ind Organ 29:283–293
Pyka A, Fagiolo G (2005) Agent-based modelling: a methodology for neo-Schumpeterian economics. Working Paper 27.
Schmalensee R (2004) Sunk costs and antitrust barriers to entry. Am Behav Sci 94:471–475
Schmidt S, Missler-Behr M (2010) Importance of consumer preferences on the diffusion of complex products and systems. In: Locarek-Junge H, Weihs C (eds) Classification as a tool for research studies in classification, data analysis, and knowledge organization. Springer, Berlin, pp 725–733
Scott WR (2008) Institutions and organizations: ideas and interests, 3rd edn. Sage, Los Angeles, p 280
Shy O (2001) The economics of network industries. Cambridge University Press, Cambridge, p 331
Stigler GJ, Becker GS (1977) De Gustibus Non Est Disputandum. Am Econ Rev 67:76–90
Teece DJ, Pisano G, Shuen A (1997) Dynamic capabilities and strategic management. Strateg Manag J 18:509–533
Tesfatsion L (2006) Agent-based computational economics: a constructive approach to economic theory. In Tesfatsion L, Judd KL (eds) Handbook of computational economics, volume 2: agent-based computational economics, handbooks in economics series. North-Holland, Amsterdam, pp 831–880
Tesfatsion L (2011) Agent-based modeling and institutional design. East Econ J 37:13–19. doi: 10.1057/eej.2010.34
Tolbert PS, Zucker LG (1996) The institutionalization of institutional theory. In: Clegg SR, Hardy C, Nord WR (eds) Handbook of organization studies. Sage, Thousand Oaks, pp 175–190
Tordjman H (2004) How to study markets? An institutionalist point of view. Rev d'Économie Ind 107:19–36
Tscherning H, Damsgaard J (2008) Understanding the diffusion and adoption of telecommunication innovations: what we know and what we don't know. In: León G, Bernardos A, Casar J et al (eds) Open IT-based innovation: moving towards cooperative it transfer and knowledge diffusion. Springer, Boston, pp 39–60
Valente M (2002) Simulation methodology: an example in modeling demand. Mimeo, p 35.

Varian HR (2002) Market structure in the network age. In: Brynjolfsson E, Kahin B (eds) Understanding the digital economy: data, tools and research. MIT Press, Cambridge, MA, pp 137–150

Varian HR (2001) High-technology industries and market structure. University of California, Berkeley, p 33

Viscusi WK, Vernon JM, Harrington JE Jr (2005) Economics of regulation and antitrust, 4th edn. MIT Press, Cambridge, MA, p 928

Williamson OE (2000) The new institutional economics: taking stock, looking ahead. J Econ Lit 38:595–613

Windrum P, Fagiolo G, Moneta A (2007) Empirical validation of agent-based models: alternatives and prospects. J Artif Soc Soc Simul 10:8–37

Micro, Macro, and Meso Determinants of Productivity Growth in Argentinian Firms

Verónica Robert, Mariano Pereira, Gabriel Yoguel, and Florencia Barletta

Abstract In this paper we analyze the impact of micro-, meso-, and macroeconomic determinants on firm productivity growth from an evolutionary and systemic perspective, in small and medium-sized Argentinean enterprises during 2006–2008. This period is characterized by strong employment and productivity growth. In this context, increases in productivity are explained better by innovation rather than falling employment. The microeconomic dimension is tackled by resorting to innovation results (product and process), which in turn are estimated through innovation efforts, following the well-known Crepon, Duguet, and Mairess (CDM) approach. The meso dimension is considered in terms of each firm's position in the competitive space; that is, whether each firm's productivity level is below or above the sector average. The macro determinant of changes in productivity considered here is the expansion of domestic demand, estimated by the sectoral apparent consumption. The results show that the micro and meso dimensions contribute to explaining firm-level productivity growth. Innovation results, estimated through innovation efforts and linkages, explain productivity growth. The firm's position in the competitive space shows a U-shaped relationship with productivity growth. Finally, sectoral demand does not seem to have any impact on our study.

This paper was presented at the 14th Joseph A. Schumpeter Conference in Brisbane, and we would like to thank those present for the comments they made on it. We also want to thank Prof. G. Dosi for his comments in Buenos Aires on a previous version of this paper, as well as Prof. Keun Lee and F. Malerba. The usual disclaimer applies.

V. Robert (✉)
CONICET-UNGS, J.M.Guierrez 1150, Los Polvorines, Buenos Aires Argentina
e-mail: vrobert@ungs.edu.ar

M. Pereira
UNGS, J.M.Guierrez 1150, Los Polvorines, Buenos Aires Argentina

G. Yoguel
UNGS, J.M.Guierrez 1150, Los Polvorines, Buenos Aires Argentina

F. Barletta
UNGS, J.M.Guierrez 1150, Los Polvorines, Buenos Aires Argentina

A. Pyka, J. Foster (eds.), *The Evolution of Economic and Innovation Systems*,
Economic Complexity and Evolution, DOI 10.1007/978-3-319-13299-0_23

1 Introduction

There are two major motivations behind this paper. The first is the absence of studies addressing the relationship between innovation and productivity for Argentinean firms during the post-convertibility period (2002 onwards). This period has been characterized by the simultaneous increase in employment and labor productivity since the devaluation of the Argentine peso in 2002. This performance contrasts with the previous period, when the increase in labor productivity was unstable and was accompanied by plummeting employment rates. As employment and productivity have been increasing together in the new context, evidence supporting the apparent connection between innovation activities and productivity growth has mounted. Nevertheless, in the new scenario, the performance of domestic demand has played a central role in explaining employment and sales. The macro determinants of firms' productivity growth therefore need to be evaluated.

The second motivation is the lack of papers analyzing the relationship between innovation and productivity growth from a Schumpeterian perspective. This means that there is less work studying this topic compared with the abundant literature on the determinants of innovations, assuming that innovation has a positive impact on firms' productive and economic performance. In this paper we explore the hypothesis that firms may have creative or adaptive reactions (Schumpeter 1947) according to their position in the competitive space. If firms' productivity level is far below the sectoral average, they probably have to implement creative reactions in order to enhance their productive performance and prevent being excluded by the selection process. In contrast, when firms' productivity level is far above the sectoral average, they enjoy extra profits, and managers have the opportunity to fund research and innovative activities with their own internal funds (Antonelli 2011).

This paper analyzes the impact of micro-, meso-, and macro-economic determinants on firms' innovation performance and productivity growth. We follow the evolutionary tradition (Nelson 1981; Nelson and Winter 1982)—and, to some extent, the Crepon et al. (1998) empirical approach—to test the relationship between innovation and productivity. Innovation results are estimated through a set of variables that account for the firm's innovative behavior. The meso dimension is considered through each firm's position in the competitive space, which means the firm's productivity level related to the sector productivity average. Finally, the macro dimension was included using the expansion of domestic demand, following Kaldor's and demand pull arguments on the probabilities of introducing changes in products and processes in response to expanding demand. Meso and macro dimensions help explain firm innovation results from a systemic perspective that includes not only innovation efforts by also the possibilities that market competition imposes on firms.

The first section contains a theoretical discussion about the relationship between productivity and innovation, the conceptual framework, and the hypothesis. The second section presents the evolution of productivity and employment in Argentina during the period under analysis. This section also discusses the main variables used and presents a descriptive analysis of the micro data, which highlights the heterogeneity of firms in terms of size, productivity levels, and rates of change. The third section presents the methodological approach, the econometric model, and the results. The fourth section presents the main conclusions of the paper.

2 Backgrounds in Innovation and Productivity Growth: A Long Theoretical Road

Most of the studies that examine the relationship between R&D expenditure, innovation, and productivity growth at the firm level follow a traditional approach begun by Griliches and perfected by the CDM estimation approach. In these cases, the theoretical framework generally begins by using a representative agent's knowledge production function to estimate innovation results, and a production function (frequently the Cobb-Douglas) to estimate productivity from innovation results (Griliches 1985; Griliches and Mairesse 1981; Mairesse and Sassenou 1991; Crepon et al. 1998; Bartelsman and Doms 2000; Duguet 2006).

The theoretical background to this approach is as follows. First, the papers usually refer to the work of Solow (1957), which is presented as the largest body of empirical evidence for the fact that the sources of productivity growth are greater than those associated with a greater use of production factors, resulting in the so-called Solow residual. Secondly, they mention the contribution of Abramovitz[1] (1956), who emphasizes that productivity growth not explained by the expansion of capital and labor is attributable to a wide set of factors that range from measurement problems to technological change, and to the presence of increasing returns.[2] Finally, these authors quote subsequent studies that seek to reduce the residual size by including R&D expenditures and intangible assets, and by characterizing the composition of the workforce and capital equipment (Jorgenson and Griliches 1967). The main goal of this tradition is improving the measure of production inputs.

One of the major criticisms of this tradition can be found in Nelson (1981),[3] who argued that Griliches and his followers have applied the neoclassical analytical framework to analyze changes in productivity at the firm level, incorporating R&D expenditures to take into account productivity growth, along with other dimensions

[1]Abramovitz points out that the size of the Solow residual is nothing more than a measurement of our ignorance, and the growth accountability approach called it "total factor productivity" and its growth was attributed to technological progress.

[2]They also include changes in production capacities, both those embodied in the machinery and those present in the workforce connected to improvements in managerial skill, training, and capacity which reflect other capital investment (Kuznets 1952).

[3]From the aggregate perspective, the other relevant critique is capital controversy, at the end of the 1960s.

of firms' learning processes and innovative behavior. However, these works did not consider the possible interactions between these factors and other production inputs. For example, changes in workers' skills may result from the acquisition of capital goods or from disembodied innovation efforts. The traditional approach assumes that firm behavior is determined by management choices between defined options stemming from the available technology (Nelson 1981). Consequently, there is no technological difference among firms belonging to the same technological space. In this context, the differences in productivity level observed in empirical works are attributed to: (1) the uneven intensity in the use of inputs associated with differences in endowment and prices, and (2) the differences in the available capital vintage (Nelson 1981). Finally, the methodological approach used relies on the idea of a representative agent, which underestimates: (1) the heterogeneity of firms in the market and the effect of this on the diffusion of technological change, and (2) the macro determinants of productivity change associated with the evolution of sectoral demand.

The neoclassical roots[4] of this tradition set aside other key theoretical questions in order to understand the increase in productivity in firms as a systemic phenomenon, such as: (1) the way the competition process is related to development and structural change (Metcalfe 2010), (2) the linkages between firms and their effect on capacity building and productivity (Freeman 1991), (3) the relationship between the composition of the productive structure, its dynamics, and firm's performance (Cimoli and Porcile 2009), (4) the role of increasing returns and technological complementarities within the firm and within the industry (Marshall 1920; Young 1928; Kaldor 1972), and (5) the Smithian relationship between market expansion, division of labor, and improvements in firms' performances.

To sum up, the way the traditional approach has treated productivity growth at the firm level relegates innovation and technological change to R&D as another input in the production function that is entered additively from a static perspective.[5] According to Nelson (1981), this prevents taking the way in which productive factors interact in the context of the competitive process into account. In turn, it reduces inter- and intra-organizational heterogeneity to an empirical regularity that is abstracted from the theoretical treatment when the representative agent is resorted to.

Despite these critiques, the traditional approach has opened up a large research agenda on the sources of productivity growth at firm level. These insights have proven to be extremely prolific regarding the empirical analysis of the relationship between innovation and productivity, and they have given rise to new methodologies. In general, it may be noted that research following this tradition has

[4]This can be found by resorting to the representative agent production function.

[5]Taking into consideration the measurement difficulties that this implies, and assuming that it is possible to determine the change in output caused by a marginal change in the state of technological knowledge.

been characterized by its breaking down of production inputs and its increasing consideration of the heterogeneity of these.

Notwithstanding the strong empirical focus of the traditional approach, it is not concerned with the evidence of heterogeneity in productivity levels, whether between sectors or within them. Several authors from the evolutionary perspective agree that this heterogeneity is more than a mere empirical regularity, since it feeds into the transformation of the productive structure via (1) learning-based interactions, (2) technology diffusion through imitation, (3) inter-sectoral competition, and (4) cross-fertilization resulting from technological complementarities (Cantner and Harnush 2005). Thus, the evolutionary path is influenced by positive feedbacks between intra and inter-firm populations within the competitive space (Metcalfe 2010).

In contrast to the traditional approach, the evolutionary tradition suggests that the relationship between innovation and productivity and the heterogeneity of firm-level productivity is marked by an evolving disequilibrium dynamic. Nelson (1981) could be regarded as one of the fundamental contributions to this stream. His paper recognizes an evolutionary vein in some classical (Smith, Marx, and Mill) and neoclassical authors (Marshall).[6] In this sense, Kuznets, Schumpeter, and Kaldor emphasized, at different moments, that economic growth is an essentially a disequilibrium process, in which changes in production and industrial developments inhibit the application of dynamic optimization methodologies. The evolutionary tradition has identified heterogeneity as a source of variation in productivity through evolutionary notions of variety, selection, and retention. In this context, heterogeneity is an ontological assumption and therefore goes far beyond the empirical regularity of a cross-section analysis. Heterogeneity in the firms' performances feeds uncertainty and forces us to analyze growth as a disequilibrium process. Based on the notion of organizational routines, several authors from this school have stressed the differentiation between information and knowledge, thus criticizing the neoclassical position that considers knowledge to be a public good. In this evolutionary stream, far from giving rise to a process of convergence (of behavior, performance, production, growth, etc.), the interactions between organizations (firms and institutions) are key causes and consequences of diversity and divergence. At a meso-economic level, competitive pressure operates as a mechanism that feeds back into diversity and selection (Dosi et al. 2010). The combination of these processes results in average productivity growth in different markets, due both to the exiting of firms with low productivity and to the greater weight of incumbent firms where creative responses prevail.

[6]Metcalfe (2010) recognizes this same evolutionary thread in these authors' conceptions of competition.

2.1 Innovation and Productivity. The New Wave of Research

In recent decades the wide diffusion of micro-databases derived from the increase in technological surveys has led to a new wave of studies on the relationship between productivity and innovation in both the evolutionary and traditional approaches.

From the traditional approach, the empirical literature on the relationship between innovation and productivity has been greatly driven by Crepon, Duguet, and Mairesse's method (Bartelsman 2010; Crespi, et al. 2007; Iacovone and Crespi 2010; Benavente 2006; Crespi and Zuniga 2012). In part, these works were nourished by the conceptual developments of the evolutionary approach, incorporating the ideas of technological learning and capacity building.

In this sense, the major contributions of this new wave of works are centered on methodological and empirical issues. CDM Models put forward the notion that the firm's innovative activity has an impact on total factor productivity, but indirectly, through the results of the innovation process. Thus they propose a recursive three-equation system. The first equation accounts for the determinants of R&D, the second for the relationship between R&D and the innovation result, and the final equation captures the impact of product or process innovation on productivity. In this regards, endogeneity between innovation and productivity is tackled by using innovation inputs as instruments of innovation results.[7]Other determinants of linkages and capacities observed by evolutionary literature are not taken into account by the approach. For example, Iacovone and Crespi (2010) and Crespi and Zuniga 2012 stressed the relevance of other innovation efforts besides R&D, especially in developing countries.

From the evolutionary perspective, empirical studies focused on identifying and explaining the strong heterogeneity of innovative behavior and the firms' processes of acquiring skills and learning (Metcalfe 1997; Los and Verspagen 2006; Castelacci and Zeng 2010; Antonelli and Scellato 2011; Antonelli 2011). In this context, it was assumed that firms with relatively higher capacities and those that performed innovation efforts would be the most competitive and would perform best in terms of sales and productivity growth. Therefore the evolutionary contributions emphasize that innovative activity and firms' ability to command processes of technological change and innovation must have some impact on economic performance. In this way, the competitive process is manifested in the generation of heterogeneity and organizational variety, which, in turn, are the basis for knowledge complementarities and interaction-based learning.

[7]Despite these differences, there are numerous cross-references and some intellectual recognition between the two traditions. An example of this is a special section of Issue 6, 2010, of Industrial Change and Corporate Change coordinated by Giovanni Dosi, which reveals the coexistence of approaches that are rooted in the two main lines of thought discussed in the theoretical framework.

2.2 Analytical Approach and Hypothesis

In this article we return to the evolutionary approach in order to tackle the systemic nature of the relationship between innovation and productivity.

Our analytical framework stresses the importance of micro heterogeneity in accounting for innovation processes and productivity growth. In this context, productivity and innovation are explained not only by firms' innovative behavior and connectivity, but also by the position of each firm in the competitive space, and by macro determinants captured by the evolution of sectoral demand. The analytical approach considers that the capabilities of each firm become an opportunity for meso and macro conditions.

The main relationships proposed in the analytical model are summarized in Fig. 1. They are the basis for the formulation of our hypothesis.

We consider the micro, meso, and macro dimensions that impact on innovation results.

Firstly, we consider the relationship between productivity and innovation. In line with the different approaches discussed in the theoretical framework, we assume that *innovation performance has a positive impact on the firm's rate of productivity growth* (H1). Following Iacovone and Crespi (2010) and Crespi and Zuniga (2012), the determinants of innovation results that we consider include not only R&D but a set of innovation efforts and access to external knowledge via the presence of linkages with different institutions that promote innovation activities in Argentina.

Second, we consider that the heterogeneity of productivity at the sectoral level affects firms' productivity levels. In this sense, we propose that the position in the competitive space is relevant. The gap between firm productivity and the average productivity of the sector in which the firm is competing generates creative or

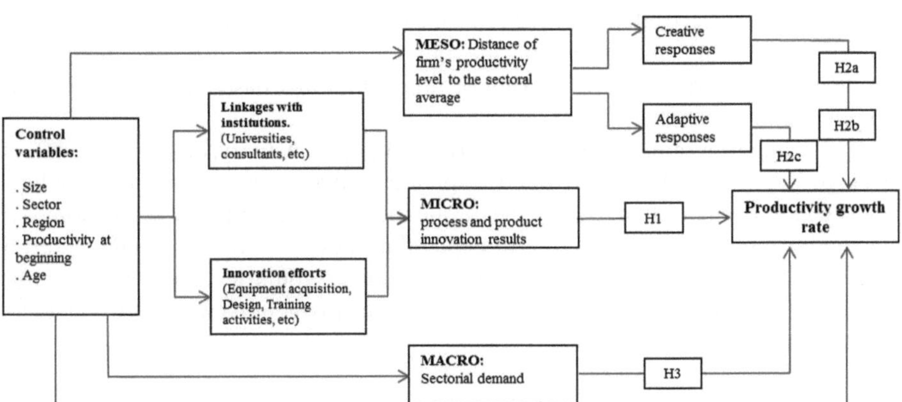

Fig. 1 Micro, meso, and macro determinants of firm-level productivity growth. *Source*: Own elaboration

adaptive behaviors that influence the rate of change in productivity. In this context, we propose three additional hypotheses:

(H2a) *Among firms that have productivity levels below the sector average, it is possible to identify a group that shows creative reactions, allowing them to improve their productivity. Firms that show creative reactions are those with greater capacities.*
(H2b) *Among firms with higher productivity levels, it is possible to identify a group that shows creative reactions, allowing them to improve their productivity.*
(H2c) *Firms with a productivity level similar to that of the sector they belong to show adaptive reactions and therefore lower rates of productivity change.*

This would show that there is a U-shaped relationship between heterogeneity measured as the difference between the productivity level and the sectoral average. As a result there are important changes in the intra- and inter-sectoral hierarchies.[8]

Last but not least, we suggest that the growth of domestic demand at the sectoral level, as estimated by the change in apparent consumption, would have a positive impact on productivity change. The growth of productivity in post-convertibility Argentina has been explained by the growth in demand (Azpiazu and Schorr 2010). In the model presented here, we propose to test this relationship at the firm level. *It is expected that in the context of domestic demand growth, firms which have benefited from relatively more dynamism in the markets in which they compete have been able to improve their productivity because of the exploitation of economies of scale* (H3).

3 The Data

The years under analysis are part of a positive industrial productivity dynamic, which is characterized by growth in levels of employment, production, and consumption. This allows us to rule out the possibility that the increase in productivity is part of a restructuring of production that has caused a decrease in employment.

According to Azpiazu and Schorr (2010), labor productivity, employee numbers, average wages, and the proportion of capital employed in productive activity have undergone a positive change since the devaluation of 2002. In this scheme, domestic demand has played a central role in explaining these dynamics in manufacturing activities. Moreover, while other Latin American countries underwent similar processes, the productivity growth of manufacture in Argentina was more than twice

---

[8] Antonelli and Scellato (2011) have also tested the hypothesis of a U-shaped relationship between levels of profitability and innovative activity, looking for evidence around the Schumpeterian hypothesis on innovation and competition (Aghion and Howitt 1992). They confirmed the U-shaped relationship for the Italian case.

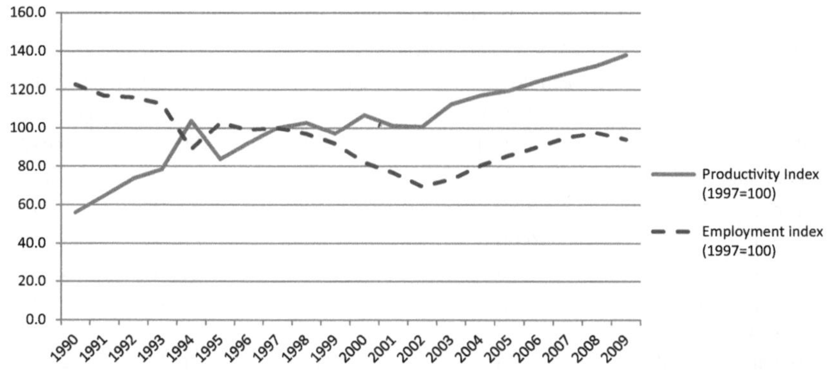

Graph 1 Evolution of labor productivity and employment in manufacturing. *Source*: Own elaboration based on INDEC

the average for Latin America. This performance contrasts with the previous period, when the increase in labor productivity was unstable and was accompanied by a sharp drop in employment.

These aggregate dynamics are the product of very different sectoral dynamics, which show a strong heterogeneity in the productivity growth rates for different branches of production.

Graph 1 and Table 1 show that the years under analysis (2006–2008) are part of a trend characterized by strong productivity growth, with employment growth going through a consolidation phase within this upward dynamic. In this context, it is worth making some comments regarding the contextualization and analysis of information.

Firstly, unlike the trend that prevailed during the model of openness and deregulation during the 1990s, and specifically during the nearly 10 years of the convertibility regime in Argentina, productivity growth is not due to a regressive restructuring of the manufacturing industry that pushes workers out, but is instead accompanied by an increase in industrial employment between 2003 and 2010.

Secondly, while it may be argued that Argentina's economic growth in the first years after the crisis was due to a rebound effect, it can also be argued that this effect should have been exhausted by 2006—indeed, probably by 2005. Therefore, the growth of the period under analysis must go beyond the starting up of installed capacity. In fact, there is abundant empirical evidence that stresses the importance of the investment process the country has undergone since 2005. In this context, it is interesting to study the impact of innovation activities that might accompany this investment process and its possible impact on productivity growth at firm level.

Thirdly, and in relation to the previous point, productivity growth must have been driven from the start by the expansion of domestic demand, which had been deeply depressed since the most recent crisis, which lasted for nearly 4 years, from late

Table 1 Employment and productivity growth in manufacturing industries (by industry during convertibility and post-convertibility growth phases)

Activity		Employment growth rate Annual average (%)		Productivity growth rate Annual average (%)	
		1998/1991	2008/2002	1998/1991	2008/2002
15	Food and beverages	−1.44	4.34	5.29	5.47
16	Tobacco	−7.87	1.39	11.18	2.19
17	Textiles	−6.66	5.86	3.26	5.34
18	Clothing	−6.26	6.02	5.46	5.90
19	Leather and leather products	−4.58	2.71	7.43	9.10
20	Wood and wood products	−1.76	4.22	6.32	2.19
21	Paper and paper products	−3.73	4.40	9.19	4.35
22	Publishing and printing	0.48	1.28	6.94	11.58
23	Gasoline and other petroleum distillation products	−13.06	2.13	15.49	0.78
24	Chemicals	−1.44	5.03	6.43	4.02
25	Rubber and plastics	0.86	5.49	6.32	2.64
26	Non-metallic minerals	−2.95	8.22	6.39	7.68
27	Basic metals	−5.45	4.39	12.39	4.19
28	Metal products	−0.32	8.54	1.26	5.77
29	Machinery and equipment	−2.87	9.86	5.86	5.36
31	Electrical appliances	−4.67	7.66	4.87	11.02
32	Radio and television equipment	−2.04	11.24	11.54	16.78
33	Medical and optical appliances. Precision machinery. Watches	−5.28	4.54	−1.93	14.09
34	Automobile	0.45	12.18	12.83	4.01
35	Other transport equipment	−4.05	7.33	4.64	1.67
36	Furniture	−1.25	6.00	9.69	8.00

Source: Own elaboration based on INDEC

1998 to mid-2002. In this context, demand played a key role as a factor of aggregate productivity growth especially in the early years after the crisis.

To carry out the econometric exercise, a microdata panel was built from the National Survey of Industrial and Service SMEs, carried out by the SME Map

Project.[9] Using a series of surveys conducted between 2007 and 2009, it was possible to build a balanced data panel[10] made up of 1,730 SMEs with information for 2006, 2007, and 2008.

The panel data includes information on most branches of industry.[11] At the same time, four branches of knowledge-intensive services (mail and communications, business services, software and computer services, and medical services) were included, due to the importance of innovation activities in these sectors. Micro-data was combined with information on: (1) evolution of domestic demand estimated by the variation of apparent consumption at three-digit ISIC level[12] and (2) price indexes at three-digit ISIC level that were used in order to deflate sales and intermediate consumptions.

The database used is one of the few that combines detailed information on a firm's economic development with its innovative behavior and linkages. This database has sectoral and regional representation for the universe of industrial and knowledge-intensive service SMEs. The database used allows us to estimate the level and variation of firm-level productivity and added value per worker. The advantage of this indicator is that it does not involve any special assumptions about the shape of the production function or the returns to scale as would be required in the case of total factor productivity. On the other hand, the availability of information on intermediate consumption will overcome the restrictions of the estimates of productivity as sales per employee, which show bias depending on the position of the firm in its value chain and its degree of vertical integration.

Although the balanced panel includes information to estimate productivity as value added per worker, questions about the variables relating to innovative behavior (linkages, innovation efforts, and innovation outputs) were asked only in 2008, and therefore they appear as time-invariant variables.[13] As such, we could not apply panel-data analysis to the relationship between innovation and productivity.

Within the database, small and non-innovative firms prevail, while innovative ones stand out in the segments containing relatively larger firms (see Tables 10 and 11 of the statistical annex). A similar situation can be seen in relation to

---

[9]Subsecretariat of SMEs at the Ministry of Production.

[10]This is revealed by the fact that observations have been made of each firm every year. Since we cannot be sure why firms did not stay in the database (firm mortality or rejection rate), we preferred to keep only the firms with observations for the three periods.

[11]As the aim of the SME Map is to survey the economic activity of SMEs in the trade, industry, and service sectors, we have excluded some industries where there is economic and productive concentration (e.g., tobacco). Graph 4 of statistical annex show the compare the productivity evolution of the sample with total manufacture industry.

[12]Source: Center for the Study of Production (CEP), Ministry of Production.

[13]The questionnaire asks, for example, if a set of innovation efforts were made during the last 2 years.

innovation efforts and the linkages that firms establish with various institutions within the national innovation system. In general those firms making various kinds of efforts are those that are most likely to innovate. In turn, the composition of firms by ownership sector reveals that the most likely to innovate are the rubber and plastic industry, machinery and equipment, vehicles and automotive parts, and software.

However, the most striking feature of the data is the high level of heterogeneity that can be observed in multiple dimensions. Regarding firm size, although only a sample of SMEs is included here, a power law distribution can be seen, with differential attributes within each sector (Graph 5 of the statistical annex). Something similar to what was described by Bottazzi et al. (2008) can be seen, whereby size distribution by sector takes on different forms, including bimodal and multimodal—and usually asymmetrical—distributions, but with different intensities. According to Dosi et al. (2010), the robustness of this fact goes against the idea of a classically U-shaped optimum firm size and average costs.

Another dimension to analyze heterogeneity is the rate of productivity change, which is evident, both within and between different groups defined by: (1) their relative size, (2) the sector they belong to, and (3) whether or not they have carried out innovation activities. The heterogeneity between these groups can be seen by comparing the distance between the group average and the panel average. For its part, the variability within each group can be seen from the standard deviation of the rates of change in productivity.

Table 2 shows significant differences in the average rates of productivity change and productivity level between different segments of firm sizes. In this context, the productivity levels of larger companies were up to 20 % higher than the panel average, while their productivity growth was between 1 and 3 percentage points above the average. On the other, the internal variability within each segment is very large.

These features are replicated in the case of sector heterogeneity, which showed sectors with productivity growth rates of up to 5 percentage points above the average and 10 below. At the same time, there is great heterogeneity within each group (Table 3).

Finally, when the differences in productivity rates between firms that reach innovation results (innovating firms) and those that do not (non-innovating firms) are taken into account, the productivity levels and rates of the innovating firms are above the panel average and above those of non-innovating firms. Again, the intra-group heterogeneity remains as high as in previous cases (Table 4).

These features are consistent with a number of empirical regularities discussed in the theoretical framework, particularly the high heterogeneity in productivity levels and growth rates even among firms within the same sector. This heterogeneity is persistent even in balanced panels. This reflects issues already raised by Dosi et al. (2010), such as the existence and persistence over time of differences in productivity levels within the same sector, taken as a proxy meso unit and a proxy for the competition processes. Second, the data shows that the heterogeneity of the variation

Table 2 Inter- and intra-group variability by firm size

	Heterogeneity on productivity level (2006)[a]		Heterogeneity on productivity growth rate[b]		
Size—number of employees	Inter-group variability—diff. %	Intra-group variability intra-groups—var. coeff.	Inter-group variability—diff. in % points	Intra-group variability—SD	N
Less than 10	−30	0.88	−0.03	0.25046336	236
Between 10 and 50	−8	0.94	−0.01	0.28632909	848
Between 50 and 150	20	0.75	0.00	0.27858567	430
More than 150	15	0.60	0.05	0.30858158	216
ANOVA	No sig. Inter-group variability represents 4.1 % of the total variability.		<1 % Inter-group variability represents 0.6 % of the total variability.		

[a]Average percentage difference of the group from the panel average standard deviation of variation within the group and the coefficient of variation within the group

[b]Difference between group and panel mean and standard deviation within the group in percentage points

Source: Own elaboration based on SME Map

Table 3 Inter- and intra-group variability by sector

Sector	Heterogeneity on productivity level (2006)[a]		Heterogeneity on productivity growth rate[b]		N
	Inter-group variability—diff. %	Intra-group variability intra-groups—var. coeff.	Inter-group variability—diff. in % points	Intra-group variability—SD	
Food products and beverages	−13	0.89	0.04508964	0.32593212	268
Textile products	11	0.78	−0.01679657	0.23912037	63
Manufacture of wearing apparel	−31	0.94	0.04953401	0.30665703	48
Leather and leather products	−11	0.61	0.02672406	0.28313343	51
Wood and furniture	−40	0.87	−0.01346067	0.28214408	100
Manufacture of paper and paper products	−5	0.50	0.02831605	0.30838649	56
Publishing, printing and reproduction of recorded media	10	0.73	−0.00870712	0.24236138	105
Manufacture of chemicals and chemical products	38	0.90	0.01892229	0.30995181	76
Rubber and plastics	20	0.82	−0.02141008	0.25101105	131
Non-metallic mineral products	2	0.92	−0.06584973	0.19909347	74
Basic metals and manufacture of fabricated metal products	−3	0.84	−0.00071198	0.28529254	195

(continued)

Table 3 (continued)

Machinery and equipment	23	0.69	0.01461125	0.3027247	146
Electronic and other electric equipment	13	0.64	−0.00378528	0.28703359	50
Automobiles and Parts	−3	0.65	−0.02551881	0.25861098	128
Telecommunications	3	–	−0.1033031	0.22532249	58
Software and information services	5	0.71	−0.01442719	0.26496171	46
Business consulting services	7	0.56	−0.00927197	0.3007058	56
Health services	−17	0.99	0.00991719	0.28442035	79
ANOVA	<1 % Inter-group variability represents 4.5 % of the total variability.		<10 % Inter-group variability represents 1.4 % of the total variability.		

a Average percentage difference of the group from the panel average standard deviation of variation and the coefficient of variation within the group
b Difference between group and panel mean and standard deviation within the group, in percentage points
Source: Own elaboration based on SME Map panel

Table 4 Inter- and intra-group variability by innovative behavior

Innovation	Heterogeneity on productivity level (2006)[a]		Heterogeneity on productivity growth rate[b]		N
	Inter-group variability—diff. %	Intra-group variability intra-groups—var. coeff.	Inter-group variability—diff. in % points	Intra-group variability—SD	
Non-innovating firms	−8	0.90	−0.7	0.27877888	1,199
Innovating firms	17	0.74	1.6	0.29278135	531
ANOVA	No sig		<10 % The variability among groups representing 0.2 % of the total variability.		

[a]Average percentage difference of the group from the panel average standard deviation of variation and the coefficient of variation within the group
[b]Difference between group and panel mean and standard deviation within the group, in percentage points
Source: Own elaboration based on SME Map panel

in productivity reflects the diversity of firms' innovative behavior and their different abilities to generate creative and adaptive reactions.

4 The Model

In this section we present the econometric model adopted to estimate the relationship between innovation results and productivity growth following, to some extent, the approach proposed by Crepon, Duguet, and Mairesse (1998) (hereafter, the CDM Model). We resorted to the use of instrumental variables in order to control the simultaneity bias that arises between innovation and productivity. To do so, we followed the methodology set out by Wooldridge (2002), because the endogenous regressor is a discrete variable. Wooldridge's method allows us to apply a maximum likelihood estimation for the endogenous variable during the first stage of the two-stage least squares (2SLS) procedure.

The model presented in this section shows some differences with the original CDM Model. Firstly, we propose a set of instrumental variables that are different to those used by the authors. From a theoretical perspective, as Nelson (1981) explains in his survey on the relationship between innovation and productivity, the notion of knowledge production function relating inputs to outputs of the innovative process does not recognize innovation as a systemic process. Additionally, from a methodological perspective, the set of instruments were limited to firms' R&D stock, not and innovations efforts and linkages that we consider key determinants from a systemic perspective were not taken into account.

Secondly, in line with our theoretical perspective, we propose a set of micro, meso, and macro determinants to estimate firms' productivity growth rate. The micro determinant was incorporated by including the innovations results in the model. The meso determinant considers a measure of an adjustment process of each firm's productivity level in relation to the industry to the population average. Using this procedure, we hope to identify firms' creative and adaptive responses in terms of competitive dynamics. In this way we account for the heterogeneity of behaviors as an essential component of the system. Finally, the macro determinant was included taking into account the evolution of each sector's domestic demand. This variable allows us to capture sector-specific dynamics of productivity growth associated with the expansion of the domestic market.

To this end, we suggest a recursive structural equation model[14] to test the effect of firms' innovation results on productivity growth:

$$\pi_i = \beta_0 + \beta_1 INNO_i + \beta_2 DELTA_{i,j} + \beta_3 DELTA_{i,j}^2 + \beta_4 DEM_j + \beta_5 Control\ Vbles_i \quad (1)$$

[14]Following Goldberger (1972), we define structural equation models as "stochastic models in which each equation represents a causal link, rather than a mere empirical association".

$$INNO_i = \delta_0 + \delta_1 INNO\_EFFO_i + \delta_2 LINK_i + \delta_3 Control\ Vbles_i \tag{2}$$

Where the annualized rate of labor productivity growth of firm *i*, π_i, is a function of:

1. $INNO_i$: the product or process innovation result reached during the period;
2. $DELTA_{i,j}$: the distance of the productivity of firm *i* relative to the sector average
3. $DELTA^2_{i,j}$: DELTA squared
4. DEM_j: the annual growth rate of apparent consumption of sectors *j*
5. Control $Vbles_i$: a set of control variables which include size, age, region and productivity level at 2006.

The second equation shows that innovation results of firm *i*, $INNO_i$, depend on:

6. $INNO\_EFFO_i$: firms' innovation efforts, which can be estimated including a set of variables such as quality assurance, equipment acquisition, license acquisition, design, training activities and marketing.
7. $LINK_i$: linkages that firms maintain with different institutions of the national innovation system, such as the National Secretariat of SMEs (SEPYME), National Institute of Industrial Technology (INTI), the Argentinian Technological Fund (FONTAR), and others related to regional or local innovation systems like consultancies, local agencies, and universities.
8. Control $Vbles_i$: a set of control variables which include sector, size, age, and region.

The estimated annualized rate of labor productivity was deflated using the Producer Price Index (PPI) to three digits calculated by the Argentinian National Institute of Statistics (INDEC).[15] This index is published only for industrial activities, so in the case of services we use the Services GDP deflator.

The model seeks to introduce intra-sectoral heterogeneity and location in the multidimensional space in terms of the distance between the firm's productive performance and the average for the industry to which it belongs. We propose to introduce a variable to measure the percentage difference of each firm's productivity over the average for the sector to which it belongs. Additionally, to capture the existence of a threshold at which the impact of heterogeneity on productivity within each sector changes sign, the DELTA squared variable is also introduced. In order to distinguish adaptive from creative reactions, we propose to compare the average values of different regions' continuous propensity to innovate, as determined by the productivity level for 2006 (related to the sectoral mean) and the productivity growth rate.

In order to introduce the interrelationships within this process into the macroeconomic dimension, the annualized rate of change of real apparent consumption was incorporated into the model. This regressor is expected to capture the impact of the growth in domestic demand on the development of productive performance in the period under study.

[15]This index measures the average change in prices received by producers for their output, and so excludes the supply of imported goods and includes exports.

5 Results

The main results are shown in Tables 5 and 6. Table 5 shows that the proposed instruments were not correlated with the rate of productivity growth *ceteris paribus* product and process innovation, nor with the first stage of the 2SLS method, which shows that the proposed instruments were partially correlated with innovation results.

The first hypothesis (H1) referred to the micro determinants of productivity growth. The first row of Table 6 shows that innovation performance has a positive effect on productivity dynamics. This result is observed in both the OLS models and in the one that applies IV. They show the robustness of these results.

Secondly, in relation to meso determinants, the model confirms the existence of a causal relationship between the heterogeneity of intra-level productivity and the productive performance of each firm (H2). The second and third rows of Table 6 show that both the variable that captures the productivity gap with the average of each sector (DELTA) and its square are statistically significant. The sign of each estimated parameter suggests that the relationship between the development of the firm's productive performance and its location relative to the sector average is U-shaped. Nevertheless, this finding does not show that firms with low and high productivity level *vis á vis* their sectoral average have performed creative reactions. Graph 2 sheds light on this issue. It shows the distribution of firms in two dimensions: on the X axis is the gap between the firm's productivity level and the sector productivity average at the start of the period (DELTA); while the Y axis shows the productivity growth rate.

To test differences in the strength of firms' innovative behavior according to their location in the competitive space we follow two steps.

Firstly we identified six regions in Graph 2. To build the regions we considered: (1) the median productivity growth (Y axis), and (2) the first and third quartiles of the DELTA variable (X axis) as limits between regions. The region A and B is made up of a set of firms that experienced well-below-average productivity levels compared with the sector mean, but then had low/high rates of productivity growth, respectively. The region C and E captures a set of firms with productivity levels that are near the sector average and then experience a productivity growth rate below/above the median. Finally, the region E and F is made up of firms that show productivity level well-above sector average at the initial period, but then had low/high productivity growth rate.

Secondly we use the measurement of the propensity to innovate (predicted value of innovation results from the first step) to test the difference in means between regions A and B, between C and D, and between E and F. In line with what was stated in hypothesis 2a, for this set of firms the continuous measurement of the propensity to innovate was significantly higher in firms in quadrant B, as is shown in Table 8. We consider that this proves the existence of a set of firms that show creative reactions to an unfavorable situation in the competitive context. In this case, firms which increased their productivity above the median showed an average continuing propensity to innovate of 27 %, while among firms in quadrant B, the

Table 5 Validity of instruments and first stage

	OLS	PROBIT
Dependent variable	Annualized rate of productivity growth	Product and process innovation (INNO)
Independent variables	*beta/t*	*beta/t*
INNO	−0.007	−0.30
Quality	−0.017	0.187
	−0.88	1.70
Equipment	0.012	2.055***
	0.54	20.63
Licenses	0.039	0.523*
	0.98	2.10
Design	0.042	0.821***
	1.90	6.99
Training	−0.021	1.003***
	−0.86	7.28
Marketing	0.036	0.783***
	1.25	4.60
Sepyme (Secretariat of SMEs)	0.004	−0.042
	0.15	−0.29
Consultancies	−0.025	−0.305*
	−1.01	−2.04
Universities	0.040	0.219
	1.57	1.49
INTI	0.026	0.302*
	1.04	2.08
Fontar	0.047	0.044
	1.64	0.25
Local institutions	0.000	0.506
	0.01	1.83
Control variables		
Size	***	***
Sector	***	***
Region	***	***
Productivity at start	***	***
Age	***	***
N	1,734	1,734

Source: Own elaboration based on SME Map Panel
* sig. >10% ** sig.>5% and *** sig.>1%

same average stood at 15 %. This quadrant brings together firms with poor relative performances in 2006 which later show a rate of productivity change below the median (see Table 7).

In disagreement with hypothesis 2c, among firms with initial productivity levels that were near the sector average, significant differences were noted between regions C and D. These differences show that those firms that succeeded in surpassing

Table 6 Determinants of annualized rate of productivity growth

Dependent variable: Annualized	OLS	IV
Rate of productivity growth	beta/t	beta/t
INNO	0.028**	0.055***
	2.01	3.09
DELTA	−0.088***	−0.085**
	−2.58	−2.48
$DELTA^2$	0.051***	0.052***
	6.58	6.53
DEM	−0.033	−0.049
	−0.19	−0.28
Control variables		
Size	***	***
Sector	***	***
Region	***	***
Productivity at start	***	***
Age	***	***
Model statistics		
Prob > F	0.000	0.000
N	1,734	1,734

Source: Own elaboration based on SME Map Panel
* sig. >10% ** sig.>5% and *** sig.>1%

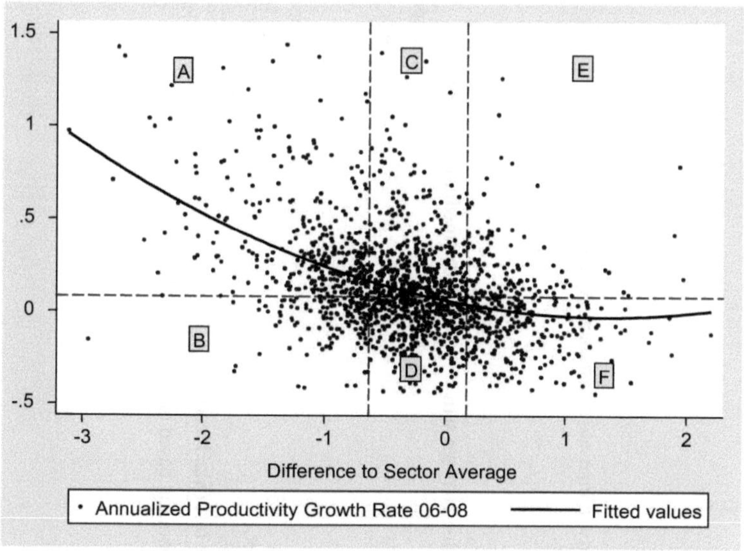

Graph 2 Firms' innovation propensity distribution according to productivity change and distance to sectoral average (2006–2008). *Source*: Own elaboration based on SME Map Panel

Table 7 Propensity to innovate by productivity level and growth

			Difference of productivity level to the sector average		
			1st quartile	**2nd and 3rd quartile**	**4th quartile**
			H2a	**H2c**	**H2b**
Annualized productivity growth	**> = 0.08 (median)**	**Region**	**A**	**C**	**E**
		Mean propensity to innovate	27	32	42
		N	308	426	131
	<0.08	**Region**	**B**	**D**	**F**
		Mean propensity to innovate	15	25	39
		N	122	437	306
Mean difference test (Sig. level)			<0.001	<0.001	No sig

Source: Own elaboration based on SME Map Panel

Table 8 Heterogeneity in firms' productivity growth trajectories

	Change in relative position: 2008–2006			
	Worse	Unchanged	Better	Total
% of firms in each group	23.2	54.3	22.6	100.0
SD (standard deviation)		0.17		

Source: Own elaboration based on SME Map Panel

the median productivity growth rate experienced significantly higher innovative intensity. In these terms, the activities and innovation performance achieved in this segment of the competition area have a strong impact on productivity.

Finally, regions E and F contain empirical evidence refuting hypothesis 2b. Firms with recorded productivity levels in 2006 that were well above the sector average did not later show innovative behavior that differed in a statistically meaningful way. However, regardless of the productivity growth rates achieved, these firms had the highest continuous levels of innovative strength. This result suggests that in this set of firms with high performance and high levels of innovation, "path dependence" behavior predominated which tended to reinforce the technological leadership. This process was encouraged by the competitive dynamics between firms that share a set of similar attributes in terms of capabilities, linkages, and innovation performance. The absence of significant differences would seem to suggest that the innovation efforts among these firms have less impact on initially high productivity growth rates, but the presence of innovation activities highlights the need to develop skills and behaviors if firms are to compete in this innovative segment.

It is interesting that the process of changes in firms' productive performance arising from the mesosphere did not result in a scenario of convergence in the rates of change in firms' productivity (Table 8). In contrast, highly diverse behaviors are the main feature presented by the population of firms. The persistence of micro-heterogeneity and variability in a context of stability of the global population features is addressed by the theory of complexity. It therefore allows us to recognize the emergence of a macro structure from interaction in a context of strong micro-diversity.

Our analysis of firms' trajectories shows changes in position between 2006 and 2008. In this way high level of mobility can be seen for firms moving from low productivity segments (region A and B) to those with higher levels (regions C to F). This situation is better than the reverse, which can also be observed: firms moving from high productivity positions (regions E and F) to segments with lower levels. Although about half of the panel did not alter their relative position, huge variance can be observed within this group (that is, among those that did not unchanged segment). This shows that high productive performance heterogeneity persists even among firms that failed to reach the critical change threshold.

Of the total sample, 23 % of firms transitioned to a worse relative position than held at the start of the period under study, while 22 % showed improvement, and the remaining 54 % remained unchanged. As we said, even in this latter group, the variance in productive performance marks significant volatility. When this analysis is repeated controlling membership by sector, size, and age of the firm, the results do not alter. Ultimately, this emphasizes the idea of diversity as central to the explanation of changes in firms' productivity: in particular, how the evolution of productive performance can be explained in a world of heterogeneous but coordinated behaviors.

Finally, in regard to the development of firms' productive performance derived from the macro field, it can be said that the annualized rate of change in apparent consumption—as a variable that captures the growth in domestic demand—has no statistically significant impact on productivity developments. This result could be explained by the absence of large firms from the sample, where growth in domestic consumption could be significantly impacted. On the other hand, due to the heterogeneity of firms that make up the panel, it is important to note that the causal impact of this macro-determinant has led to reactions of varying intensity and direction, making it difficult to capture statistically significant average behavior. However, these caveats aside, the graph shows that the two variables are statistically independent, which allows us to reject the third hypothesis. The following chart shows the distribution of firms and the estimated line for the relationship between rates of productivity change and apparent consumption, revealing that heterogeneous responses dominate the causal relationship between the two variables.

In this regard, when the focus is on individual firms' responses to changes in the evolution of domestic demand, what is expressed is the absence of an unequivocal response to the stimulation of market growth. This does not refute the fact that different firms were able to take advantage of favorable conditions for economic growth, but heterogeneity remains the dominant trait, at least in a relatively narrow timeframe like 2006–2008 (Graph 3).

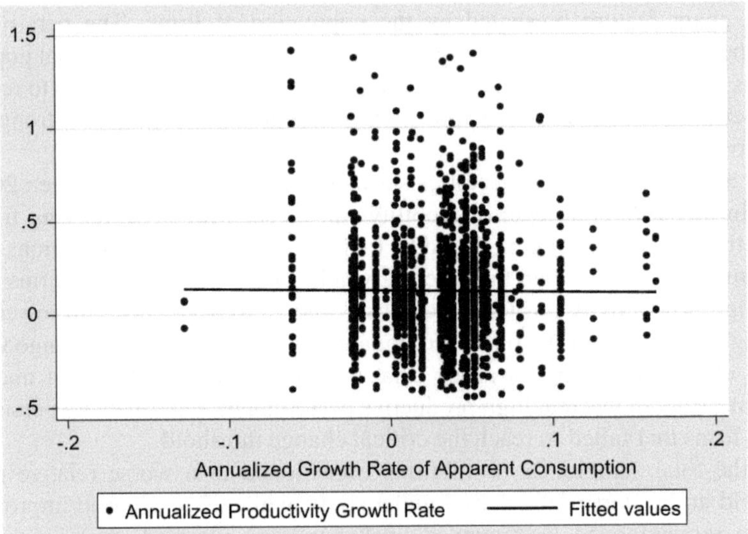

Graph 3 Firms' productivity versus apparent consumption (2006–2008). *Source*: Own elaboration based on SME Map Panel

At the same time, as discussed in the previous section, the period under analysis corresponds to a phase of consolidation of the economic model in which economic growth is a consequence of investment processes rather than of expanding production on the basis of existing installed capacity. In this context, it is possible that the decisive effect of domestic demand on productivity growth via scale economies occurred in the previous period (2003–2006).

6 Conclusions

The changes in international conditions and Argentina's macroeconomic regime during the last decade, together with an incipient set of industrial and technological policies, have helped to reverse a downward trend in the added value of Argentina's industrial and service enterprises, favoring the expansion of production. In this context there were simultaneous increases in productivity, output, and employment. This growth scenario is ideal for studying the impact of innovative processes, competition dynamics, and the expansion of domestic demand on changes in productivity at the firm level.

While macroeconomic trends have played a central role in the recovery of production, other factors also contributed to productivity growth at the firm level, namely firms' innovative behavior, the building up of their technological and organizational capacities, intra-industry heterogeneity, and the location of the firm in the competitive space, as a meso unit.

This paper thus presents a long-standing theoretical debate which has been contributed to by both the traditional and the evolutionary approaches. In this context, although the traditional approach has provided a set of empirical and methodological contributions that has allowed the relationship between productivity and innovation to be understood, the theoretical and methodological framework limits the possibility of analyzing this relationship as an unbalanced dynamic process with feedback.

In this article, we proposed that the evolutionary approach must include the contributions of Smith, Marshall, Schumpeter, Young, and Kaldor, who argue that productivity growth follows an unbalanced path driven by the expansion of demand and its impact on productivity, through processes of increasing division of labor, innovation, the generation of externalities, technological complementarities, and the presence of increasing returns. Nelson (1981) has highlighted the limitations of the traditional approach rooted in neoclassical economics. He has also emphasized the relevance of the problems of interaction between the independent variables of the production function used in neoclassical models. In this context, it has been proposed that heterogeneity and disequilibrium are key elements for explaining productivity dynamics. Dosi et al. (2010) have demonstrated the importance of these factors, as have other authors from the evolutionary tradition.

From an empirical perspective, we focused on a number of stylized facts that seem to go in the direction suggested by evolutionary theory. These include heterogeneity of both firm sizes and firm behavior, and productivity changes. The descriptive statistics show that the database used does not deviate from this stylized fact: that is, there is strong inter-organizational heterogeneity.

In this context, we propose that the strong heterogeneity revealed by the large distances between firm productivity and the average for the sector in which they compete is manifested in creative and adaptive responses that influence subsequent changes in productivity.

Following the evolutionary approach, the estimated econometric model takes into account micro, meso, and macro dimensions as determinants of productivity change. In this sense, the model suggests that beyond the effect of sectoral dynamics on competition processes, there is also relevant heterogeneity among firms, thus highlighting the importance of a variety of growth rates at the micro level, and the relationship between these and sectoral dynamics.

At the micro level, the model shows that productivity changes are related to the outputs of innovation. At the meso level, the model shows that the firm's position in its competitive space has a non-linear impact on productivity change. The data reveals that firms that have levels well above or well below the average productivity for the industry show strong increases in productivity, although for different reasons. Among low-productivity firms, we have detected a set of firms with creative responses which are manifested in a high propensity to innovate. At the other end of the spectrum, high-productivity firms are characterized by a high propensity to innovate as a result of their path dependence. This shows the presence of creative and adaptive reactions by firms along their path dependence. In turn, the macro factor under consideration, the evolution of domestic demand, does not seem to have played a key role in the dynamics of firm-level productivity. In this sense the results show that heterogeneous reactions to changes in demand have prevailed over homogeneous behavior.

The study also reveals a set of issues that should be considered in future research. First, the need to introduce the different dimensions in which heterogeneity is manifested in order to analyze the variation in productivity at both aggregate and firm levels. Within this scheme, the population perspective, rather than the representative agent perspective, redefined firms' interaction in the competitive process. To this end, we have highlighted both the coexistence of firms with different levels and rates of productivity growth in one sector, and the persistence of this heterogeneity over time. Second, this paper has highlighted the need to identify meso units that account for competitive spaces in a better way that industrial branches do. The centrality of the meso scale lies in that this is where positive feedback processes, disequilibrium dynamics, and heterogeneity are manifested.

A.1 Statistical Annex

Table 9 List of variables

Variables	Description	Empirical measurement
INNO	Innovation results (product and process)	0: Non-innovating firm
		1: Innovating firm
PROD	Annualized rate of firms' labor productivity growth	Continuous variable
DELTA	Distance of firms' productivity level from sector average	Continuous variable
$DELTA^2$	DELTA squared	Continuous variable
DEM	Annualized rate of apparent consumption growth	Continuous variable
Quality	Innovation efforts focused on quality assurance	0: no
		1: yes
Equipment	Innovation efforts focused on machinery and equipment acquisition	0: no
		1: yes
Licenses	Innovation efforts focused on license acquisition	0: no
		1: yes
Training	Innovation efforts focused on training activities	0: no
		1: yes
Design	Innovation efforts focused on design	0: no
		1: yes
Marketing	Innovation efforts focused on marketing activities	0: no
		1: yes
SEPYME	Linkages with SEPyME (National Secretariat of SMEs)	0: no linkage
		1: linkage
Universities	Linkages with universities	0: no linkage
		1: linkage
INTI	Linkages with INTI (National Institute of Industrial Technology)	0: no linkage
		1: linkage
FONTAR	Linkages with FONTAR (Argentinian Technological Fund)	0: no linkage
		1: linkage
Local institutions	Linkages with Local Institutions	0: no linkage
		1: linkage
Consultants	Linkages with Consultancies	0: no linkage
		1: linkage
Control variables		
Sector	Dummy variables for industrial sectors classified according to ISIC 3	0/1
Region	Dummy variables for each of the 5 regions of Argentina	0/1

(continued)

Table 9 (continued)

Variables	Description	Empirical measurement
Age	Firm age	Year firm was founded
Size	Firm size according to number of employees	Firm size in log
Size square		Square firm size in log

Table 10 Innovation efforts and results

	Product and process innovation			
	Innovative firms (%)	Non-innovative firms (%)	Total (%)	Pearson chi²
Quality	38.97	1.93	12.22	Pearson chi²(1) = 698.8316 Pr = 0.000
Equipment	71.80	4.90	25.50	Pearson chi²(1) = 865.3829 Pr = 0.000
License	8.50	0.80	3.20	Pearson chi²(1) = 69.6569 Pr = 0.000
Design	45.40	5.80	18.00	Pearson chi²(1) = 389.6135 Pr = 0.000
Training	39.90	2.60	14.10	Pearson chi²(1) = 424.2568 Pr = 0.000
Marketing	20.00	1.90	7.50	Pearson chi²(1) = 173.3041 Pr = 0.000

Source: Own elaboration based on SME Map Panel

Table 11 Innovation results by activity

Sectors grouped at two-digit level	Product and process innovation		
	Innovative firms (%)	Non-innovative firms (%)	Total (%)
Food and beverages	16.50	13.00	15.50
Textile products	4.20	2.40	3.60
Confections	3.30	1.70	2.80
Leather and leather products	2.90	3.00	3.00
Wood and furniture	6.50	4.10	5.80
Paper and allied products	3.40	2.80	3.20
Printing and publishing	6.20	5.80	6.10

(continued)

Table 11 (continued)

Sectors grouped at two-digit level	Product and process innovation		
	Innovative firms (%)	Non-innovative firms (%)	Total (%)
Substances and chemical products	4.30	4.70	4.40
Rubber and plastics	6.30	10.40	7.60
Nonmetallic minerals	4.20	4.50	4.30
Primary and fabricated metal products	12.70	8.10	11.30
Industrial machinery and equipment	5.80	14.10	8.40
Electronic and other electric equipment	2.30	4.30	2.90
Automobiles and parts	6.20	10.20	7.40
Mail and communications	4.50	0.80	3.40
Software and information services	2.00	4.10	2.70
Business consulting services	3.30	3.00	3.20
Health services	5.30	2.80	4.60
Total	100.00	100.00	100.00

Source: Own elaboration based on SME Map Panel

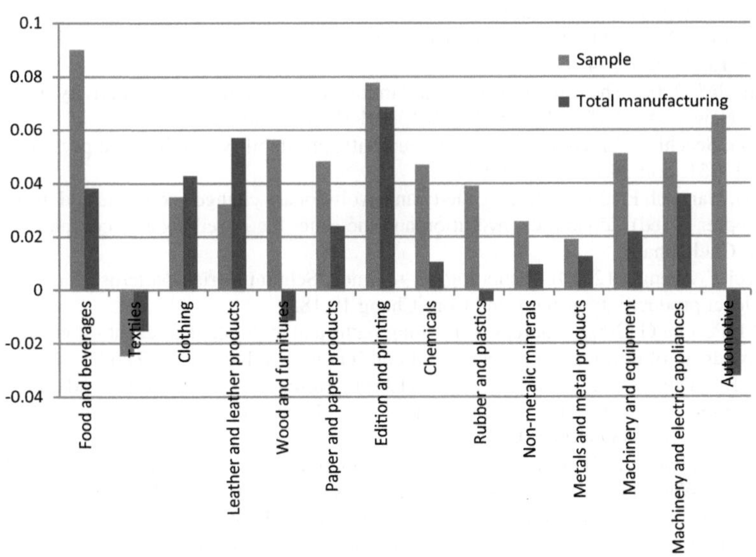

Graph 4 Productivity growth (2006–2008) in sample and total manufacturing industry

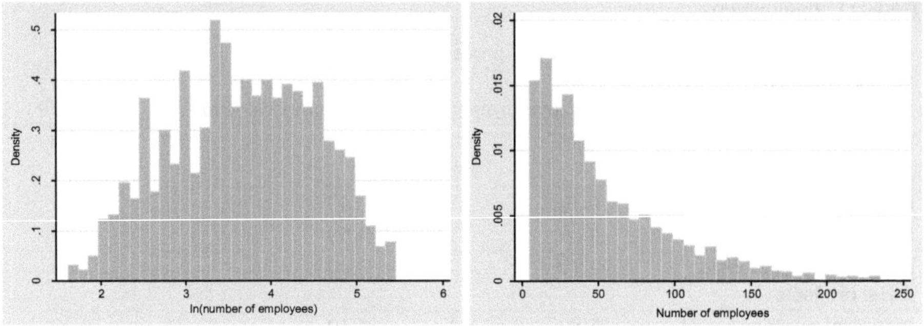

Graph 5 Firms size distribution (in logs and number of employees)

References

Abramovitz M (1956) Resource and Output Trends in the United States Since 1870. NBER, New York

Aghion P, Howitt P (1992) A Model of Growth Through Creative Destruction. Econometrica 60:323–351

Antonelli C (2011) Handbook on the economic complexity of technological change. Edward Elgar, Cheltenham

Antonelli C, Scellato G (2011) Out-of-equilibrium profit and innovation. Econ Innov New Technol 20:405–421. doi:10.1080/10438599.2011.562350

Azpiazu D, Schorr M (2010) La Industria Argentina en la Posconvertibilidad: Reactivación y Legados del Neoliberalismo. Problemas del Desarrollo. Revista Latinoamericana de Economía 41(161)

Bartelsman EJ (2010) Searching for the sources of productivity from macro to micro and back. Ind Corp Chang 19:1891–1917. doi:10.1093/icc/dtq059

Bartelsman EJ, Doms M (2000) Understanding productivity: lessons from longitudinal microdata. J Econ Lit 38:569–594

Benavente JM (2006) The role of research and innovation in promoting productivity in chile. Econ Innov New Technol 15:301–315. doi:10.1080/10438590500512794

Bottazzi G, Secchi A, Tamagni F (2008) Productivity, profitability and financial performance. ICC 17:711–751. doi: 10.1093/icc/dtn027

Cantner U, Hanusch H (2005) Heterogeneity and evolutionary change - concepts and measurement. In: Dopfer K (ed) Economics, evolution and the state: the governance of complexity. Edward Elgar, Cheltenham

Castellacci F, Zheng J (2010) Technological regimes, Schumpeterian patterns of innovation and firm-level productivity growth. Ind Corp Chang 19:1829

Cimoli M, Porcile G (2009) Sources of learning paths and technological capabilities: an introductory roadmap of development processes. Econ Innov New Technol 18(7):675–694

Crepon B, Duguet E, Mairessec J (1998) Research, innovation and productivity: an econometric analysis at the firm level. Econ Innov New Technol 7:115–158. doi:10.1080/10438599800000031

Crespi G, Zuniga P (2012) Innovation and productivity: evidence from six Latin American countries. World Dev 40:273–290. doi:10.1016/j.worlddev.2011.07.010

Crespi G, Criscuolo C, Haskel J (2007) Information technology, organisational change and productivity growth: evidence from UK firms. http://cep.lse.ac.uk. Accessed 18 Feb 2014

Dosi G, Lechevalier S, Secchi A (2010) Introduction: interfirm heterogeneity-nature, sources and consequences for industrial dynamics. Ind Corp Chang 19:1867–1890. doi:10.1093/icc/dtq062

Duguet E (2006) Innovation height, spillovers and tfp growth at the firm level: evidence from French manufacturing. Econ Innov New Technol 15:415–442. doi:10.1080/10438590500512968

Freeman C (1991) Networks of innovators: a synthesis of research issue. Res Policy 20(5):499–514

Goldberger AS (1972) Structural equation methods in the social sciences. Econometrica 40:979–1001. doi:10.2307/1913851

Griliches Z, Mairesse J (1981) Productivity and R and D at the firm level. National Bureau of Economic Research, Cambridge

Griliches Z (1985) Productivity, R&D, and basic research at the firm level in the 1970s. National Bureau of Economic Research, Boston

Iacovone L, Crespi G (2010) Catching up with the technological frontier. Micro-level evidence on growth and convergence. Ind Corp Change 19(6):2073–2096

Jorgenson DW, Griliches Z (1967) The explanation of productivity change. Rev Econ Stud 34:249–283. doi:10.2307/2296675

Kaldor N (1972) The irrelevance of equilibrium economics. Econ J 82(328):1237–1255

Kuznets S (1952) Long-term changes in the national income of the United States of America since 1870. Rev Income Wealth 2:29–241. doi:10.1111/j.1475-4991.1952.tb01048.x

Los B, Verspagen B (2006) The evolution of productivity gaps and specialization patterns. Metroeconomica 57:464–493.

Mairesse J, Sassenou M (1991) R&D productivity: a survey of econometric studies at the firm level. National Bureau of Economic Research, Cambridge

Marshall A (1920) Principios de economía. Fundación ICO: Síntesis, Madrid

Metcalfe JS (1997) The evolutionary explanation of total factor productivity growth: macro measurement and micro process. Revue d'économie industrielle 80:93–114. doi:10.3406/rei.1997.1670

Metcalfe JS (2010) Dancing in the dark: la disputa sobre el concepto de competencia. Desarrollo Económico Revista de Ciencias Sociales 50:59–79

Nelson R (1981) Research on productivity growth and productivity differences: dead ends and new departures. J Econ Lit 19(3):1029–1064

Nelson R, Winter S (1982) An evolutionary theory of economic change. Harvard University Press, Cambridge

Schumpeter J (1947) The creative response in economic history. J Econ Hist 7(2):149–159

Solow RM (1957) Technical change and the aggregate production function. Rev Econ Stat 39:312. doi:10.2307/1926047

Wooldridge JM (2002) Econometric analysis of cross section and panel data. MIT Press, Cambridge

Young AA (1928) Increasing returns and economic progress. Econ J 38(152):527–542

MIX
Papier aus verantwortungsvollen Quellen
Paper from responsible sources
FSC® C105338

If you have any concerns about our products,
you can contact us on
ProductSafety@springernature.com

In case Publisher is established outside the EU,
the EU authorized representative is:
Springer Nature Customer Service Center GmbH
Europaplatz 3, 69115 Heidelberg, Germany

Printed by Libri Plureos GmbH
in Hamburg, Germany